PSYCHOLOGY IN
INDUSTRIAL
ORGANIZATIONS

PSYCHOLOGY IN INDUSTRIAL ORGANIZATIONS
fourth edition

Norman R. F. Maier
University of Michigan

Houghton Mifflin Company · Boston

Atlanta
Dallas
Geneva, Illinois
Hopewell, New Jersey
Palo Alto

To
Ayesha

Preface

Psychology in Industrial Organizations is a textbook for courses in industrial and organizational psychology. It emphasizes preparing students for advanced work in these specialized fields and for management positions in organizations. Since the scope of the book is rather broad, it can also be a sourcebook of principles and methods for personnel managers, training directors, and students in related fields. By selecting chapters a teacher can adapt the book to briefer courses in interpersonal relations, personnel, management leadership, communications, and applied psychology. It can also be adapted as a text for management training programs in industry by using appropriate chapters for home study and the Laboratory Exercises for classroom activities.

The major revisions in this edition reflect recent research and innovation in organizational psychology. Because of the shifting emphasis that has accompanied such developments, I have changed the title of the book from *Psychology in Industry* to *Psychology in Industrial Organizations*. Although this new title may appear to restrict the applications of the behavioral sciences to industrial organizations, all organizations, whether school systems, churches, hospitals, or government, have similar problems and related solutions. It seems appropriate to build a systematic treatment around industrial organizations, however, because they have been studied most intensively and have served as the testing ground for such organization concepts as participation in management, executive training, creativity in group decision making, organizational climate and effectiveness, job satisfaction, nonfinancial motivators, and management roles.

A second new development in organizational spheres has been the increased recognition of the need for managerial skills. The gap between knowing and doing is wide, and past literature has not sufficiently emphasized the importance and the nature of skill training. Teachers and researchers have stressed the cognitive content of management development and neglected the contribution of skill. Recent feedback, however, has revealed an increasing interest in laboratory exercises designed to develop such skills through personal experience. People may be taught that they should withhold judgments until they have considered all relevant information, yet most people continue to make premature judgments. Students can learn that arguing with a frustrated person will not improve a hostile attitude, yet they continue to argue under such circumstances. Interpersonal skill, like all skill, requires practice. The Laboratory Exercises which follow each chapter can serve this function.

Another recent trend is appreciation of the role played by leadership skills insofar as they relate to problem solving and decision making. The skill of the leader of a group and the type of discussion he introduces can constructively influence the resulting decision, thereby increasing the quality of the end product, its general acceptibility to those involved, and the understanding and appreciation of its implications. The effective leader can capitalize on the assets and avoid the liabilities involved in various approaches to group thinking. Disagreement can divide people in unconstructive dissent or stimulate them to discover innovative solutions. The leader becomes the nervous system for the group so that it can efficiently function as an integrated organism.

All chapters have been carefully revised and reorganized to include recent developments in various fields, some resulting from changes in modern psychological theory, others from different social values and trends. Two additional chapters, Organizational Psychology and Problem Solving for Organizations, deal with special problems of an organizational nature. The early chapters, in general, are concerned with the problems of managing people and jobs, whereas Chapters 12, 18, 19, 21, and 22 concern problems related to the organization as a whole.

As in previous editions, the content of the behavioral sciences is described in sufficient detail to provide an understanding of individual and group processes. There is no one way to motivate people, build morale, introduce change, train personnel, develop constructive attitudes, prevent accidents, or make jobs more interesting. To apply psychology one must first understand the discipline and realize that broad generalizations can do harm as well as good. A knowledge of human beings and groups can then be translated into organizational behavior. As a matter of fact, this understanding, once reached, becomes applicable to all situations in which human beings interact. However, before making general applications, one must be able to make specific ones. Having once solved a specific problem, one may apply the solution to similar problems, be they problems of a manager working with subordinates or a teacher working with students.

I am indebted to my students for their insights, to executives who have increased my awareness of problems they face, and to other teachers for their suggestions for improvements in this book. The comments of Dr. Jack Bernard of Queens College were especially helpful. A number of people have aided me in the preparation of several chapters: Professor Marshall Sashkin of Wayne State University permitted me to read his manuscript on organizational psychology; Professor Robert J. House of the City University of New York offered valuable suggestions for Chapters 21 and 22; Trudy Casselman Verser of B. F. Goodrich, Co., supplied many suggestions, particularly related to motivation and personality. Special thanks are extended to Ellen Panza McRay who shared responsibility from the beginning to the end of the revision, acting as a severe critic and a constructive contributor, and showing unlimited patience for this task. Gratitude is also extended to my wife, Ayesha, to whom this book is dedicated, who carefully read and critiqued several drafts of the whole manuscript, played a major role in reading galley and page proof, and consistently detected errors that eluded others.

Norman R. F. Maier

Contents

PSYCHOLOGY IN INDUSTRIAL ORGANIZATIONS

The Application of Psychology to Industrial Organizations

1

Historical Perspective

Man's Place in the Organization

Industries, as well as most other organizations, are concerned with the production of goods and services. They require materials, machines, and people, and insofar as people are involved, psychology becomes relevant to industrial operations. Before the advent of psychology, instinct and common sense were man's only resources for dealing with each other. The first adequately insured the survival of the species; common sense provided the entrepreneurs with devices of control, the most primitive method being fear, a natural outgrowth of the principle of the survival of the fittest. As man developed, this method of motivation through fear became more sophisticated. Industrial leaders administered punishment or threat of discharge without recourse, thinking only in terms of how *man can best serve the organization.* Gradually, however, more humane methods of motivation came into use; positive reinforcements were introduced to gain good will, but the organization leaders still held power by determining what the rewards would be.

Later, scientists and engineers such as Taylor[1] conceived of workers in terms analogous to machines and attempted to analyze the job in order to increase its efficiency and, therefore, productivity. They were followed by others, like Gilbreth,[2] who divided jobs into a series of separate motions, timed each part, and then attemped to devise the one most efficient method of performing each job.

During these years, while engineers were studying workers in an attempt to increase work efficiency, administrators reviewed their experiences with subordinates and derived from them sets of principles for "proper" management. This approach is often called "classical management theory." The use of written rules was an outgrowth of the bureaucratization of industry which occurred as the complexity and size of corporations increased. The entrepreneurial firm became outdated—no one

[1] Taylor, F. W. *The principles of scientific management.* New York: Harper & Row, 1911.
[2] Gilbreth, F. B. *Primer of scientific management.* New York: Harper & Row, 1912.

man could oversee all of his employees, so professional managers utilizing written policy became the means of dealing with problems. The conception of the organization, however, was still in nonhuman terms; while some saw the corporation as a giant machine, others, such as Davis,[3] viewed it as an abstract legal entity, created and administered by a rational system of rules and authority.

Managers were advised by writers of the classical school (such as Gulick and Urwick,[4] and Fayol[5]) about what they should do in any given circumstance. Management was normative, that is, based on the prevailing social norms, rather than upon scientific evidence. Those theories were often based on erroneous or limited assumptions implicit in the "universal principles" enumerated.

However, in 1927 Elton Mayo[6] began investigations at Western Electric's Chicago Hawthorne works (see p. 39) which revealed the importance of considering a worker as a man with feelings and the work situation as a society. Psychology and sociology thus became as relevant as engineering and economics in the running of a business. Supervisory training programs began to place emphasis on developing good interpersonal relations. The legalistic handling of grievances gave ground to considerations of human values.

More recent developments have made many older methods obsolete. Government regulations restrict monopolistic practices and hold companies accountable for pollution; laws prevent the use of corporal punishment, discriminatory practices, dishonest packaging, and inadequate wages; unions greatly influence wages, hours, and fringe benefits; and changing social values influence job expectations, attitudes regarding personal freedom and individual values. Under these changing circumstances, man cannot be controlled by the basic needs such as hunger, thirst, security, and health, and higher needs, such as self-esteem and self-actualization are indeed determining the motivations of increasing numbers of people.[7] The production methods that generate current affluence have changed the motivation and values in a short time and have complicated as well as enriched man's physical well-being. New approaches to management must take into account advances in technology, increases in the size of organizations, economic trends, the goal of full employment, and the acquisition of new values. With increasing frequency talk centers on how *the organization can best serve man.*

Other changes, such as nondiscrimination based on race or sex, while moving mankind toward a more just and humane world, further restrict an organization's freedom. The changes must be integrated into organizational practices, which often requires reformulating company policy as well as reeducating employees. The sheer physical size of many organizations creates new problems in implementing these changes as swiftly as the law requires, particularly when several readjustments are required at once. How rapidly and thoroughly industry is to change with the times

---

[3] Davis, R. C. *The fundamentals of top management.* New York: Harper & Row, 1951.

[4] Gulick, L., and Urwick, L. (Eds.). *Papers on the science of administration.* New York: Columbia University Press, 1937.

[5] Fayol, H. *Industrial and general administration* (1916). London: Pitman, 1930.

[6] Mayo, E. *The human problems of industrial civilization.* New York: Macmillan, 1933.

[7] Maslow, A. H. *Motivation and personality.* New York: Harper, 1954.

depends in part on the innovative and rapid solutions prepared by its management.

Drucker[8] analyzes some of the social changes in values in terms of the changing size of various age groups in the population. During the post–World War II baby boom (1948–1953) births increased by nearly 50 per cent. For the period 1964–1971 the 17-year-old group showed an annual increase in proportion of the total population. Because of the size of this idealistic and rebellious group its social influence is great. However, this large age group, spanning nearly eight years, is maturing, marrying, working, buying homes, and paying taxes. These factors foster material values which may alter the direction of the influence exerted on social, economic, and political trends.

Fields of Application

The applications of psychology involve practically all areas of psychology and all phases of industry.[9] Table 1.1 shows the fields of industry in which psychology has played and is playing an active role. The first column represents the earlier developments. Some of these fields utilize both psychology and engineering knowledge; others simply entail economics, business, or physiology. Only in the development of employment tests was psychology the primary discipline.[10]

The second column represents the fields in which psychological research played the major role and in which psychology largely replaced common sense. This period roughly spans the years 1935–1960.

The third column includes fields that depend largely on the acceptance of psychology as a mature discipline. Executives are turning to psychology and the behavioral sciences for answers, and as they do, the role of common sense diminishes. Most of the fields in this column are relatively new research areas.

Table 1.1 / Fields of Application

Earliest Fields of Application (before 1935)	Human Relations Era (1935–1960)	Most Recent Fields (1960–present)
Financial incentives	Nonfinancial incentives	Higher need satisfaction
Job training	Supervisory leadership	Executive training
Fatigue and boredom	Interpersonal relations	Job satisfaction
Lighting and ventilation	Employee attitudes	Organizational climate
Employment tests	Morale surveys	Problem solving
Labor turnover	Executive appraisal	Decision making
Motion and time study	Interviewing	Effecting organizational change
Safety	Counseling	Organizational stress
Discipline	Engineering psychology	

8 Drucker, P. F. The surprising seventies: Why the young will soon find themselves concerned with issues that they don't expect. *Harper's Mag.,* 1971, 243, 35–39.

9 Munsterberg, H. *Psychology and industrial efficiency.* Boston: Houghton Mifflin, 1913.

10 Viteles, M. S. *Industrial psychology.* New York: Norton, 1932.

Not included in the table are the fields of marketing, labor-management relations, industrial medicine, and psychiatry. Although each of these fields has psychological implications, they are specialized topics which fall outside the primary concern of this book.

All of the fields shown in Table 1.1 represent areas in which advances can be made in the future. The third column represents new areas that have developed in response to a growing respect for the dignity of man. This change is reflected in our social values as society has assumed more responsibility for the health and welfare of all people. Industry should assume responsibility for a man's mental health and job satisfaction not merely because they make him more efficient, but because society reasonably expects industry to do it. Thus industrial applications not only change with increasing scientific knowledge but with changing social values as well.

As concern for employee welfare increases, work efficiency will sometimes conflict with social considerations. In shift work, for example, workers must make physiological adjustments each time they rotate shifts. From the point of view of health and productivity, rotation should be abolished, but this alternative is not acceptable to workers. If the four-day, 40-hour week becomes more popular, fatigue effects may lower efficiency per hour, and the long weekend may generate more off-the-job activities and decrease job interest. The initial benefits in productivity claimed[11] may be due to a temporary boost in morale. If such schedules become widespread the reason will be worker demands rather than efficient use of energy. More and more, industry will have to take into account the workers' values, which will increasingly center around home and recreation rather than job satisfaction. This shift in focus may necessitate the sacrifice of traditional concepts of what is best and for whom.

There are limitations, however, to the ability of industry to satisfy values that conflict with efficiency. Efficiency creates both leisure and wealth. A society that underestimates the values of efficient work methods to gain costly social values ultimately may not be able to afford them.

The student who has worked in industry will find that actual management practices may seem quite different from those discussed here, for reality is seldom what it might be. Research frontiers are always ahead of the times, but teaching the best available practices will prepare the student for the future.

Science and Life

Two Kinds of Interest in Knowledge: Curiosity and Utility

In one sense, scientific knowledge seems to satisfy curiosity. Scientific investigators, like explorers, want to discover something. They ask "why" and "how" an event occurs in nature, and they obtain answers by making investigations. A man might ask a series of questions about what occurs in nature, and his only concern might be to satisfy his curiosity. He may ask: "How do geese know when to migrate?" and

---

[11] Poor, R. *4 days, 40 hours.* Cambridge, Mass.: Bursk & Poor, 1969.

"How do bees find nectar and return to their hives?" A scientist designs tests and experiments to acquire answers. Each tedious experiment might narrow the field of possible answers and lead to a satisfactory conclusion, which in turn might raise other questions. An investigator need not be concerned with the value of such information. The objective may be to fit the information into a coherent pattern, which then becomes a theory.

A second way to look at scientific knowledge is to ask how it can be used or put to work. Suppose one knows how bees find a source of honey. What use can be made of that information? First thoughts might suggest ways to improve the production of honey. However, a highly creative person might think of rather ingenious ways to apply this knowledge, as in the development of a new kind of guidance control for missiles, using cues overlooked by man but used by bees. Often unusual bits of information find unexpected uses. For example, the solar battery suddenly became practical when exploration of outer space became a reality. Thus, knowledge in itself may not be useful; it is necessary to find a way to use it. Discovering knowledge and finding a use for it represent different operations and different interests.

Since a piece of knowledge, as well as a theory, in some way describes the nature of reality, it is potentially useful if applied in a life situation. For this reason, pure research (the quest of knowledge for its own sake) represents a good practical investment. Purely theoretical research today enjoys a degree of acceptance that it never enjoyed before.

This analysis of applied science is somewhat oversimplified, however. Often when attempting to put knowledge to work, new problems arise. This forces the practical person to become curious, and to ask "Why?" Soon the practical man finds himself raising the same kinds of questions as the scientist.

The Divergent Approach to Application

One approach to the application of knowledge is to take some information or a theory and think of the ways it can be used. For example, take the learning principle that retention of material to be memorized is better if a rest period follows each repetition than if repetitions follow one another. This knowledge could be applied to memorization of poems, speeches, plays, skills, and jobs. Little ingenuity is needed to make this application, and no new relationships are required. If, however, this information were put to use in an unusual way and some new relationship emerged, one might more rightly call it an invention. (In using the knowledge of electricity to make an electric light, Edison went beyond the obvious application of knowledge, and so he is credited with an invention.)

One company employed a large number of women who had just graduated from high school. After being hired, the women participated in a three-month training program. It was suggested that the company try employing high school students during their senior year on a part-time basis. They found that these women who worked two hours per day for one school year were better qualified than those who worked for three months for an eight-hour day. This application of the learning principle approaches innovation because it requires some rethinking of the training program and changes in company practices.

Figure 1.1 illustrates the separation between knowledge and its application. The body of scientific knowledge (knowledge for its own sake) is shown as the rectangular area on the left, while life situations are represented by the rectangular area on the right. In order to put knowledge to work it is necessary to bridge the gap between knowledge and life.

The Convergent Approach

Another approach to applying knowledge is to begin with a practical problem. For example, a manager might ask whether psychology has any information that will increase job satisfaction. Immediately some areas come to mind. What about the psychology of individual differences, boredom, and intelligence? Each may impinge on the problem in a different way. This type of application is characterized by the convergence of separate areas of knowledge which might suggest a new kind of work pattern, one which not only enlarged the job to increase interest, but also permitted goal setting and individual initiative. Often the manager finds the psychologist has knowledge that suggests certain changes be made and that certain

Figure 1.1 / The Divergent Method. Scientific knowledge and life problems are depicted as two separate rectangles, with a space representing the gap between science and life. This gap must be bridged if the knowledge of science is to be applied to the problems of life.

The divergent method is depicted as a funnel in which a segment of knowledge, "x," is useful to various life situations, "a," "b," and "c." A given segment of scientific knowledge or a particular theory is the focal point or starting place; the process of application is one of seeking ways in which this knowledge might solve life problems. The arrows indicate various life problems in which this segment of knowledge might be applied. Thus a number of applications might result if one focused on a given piece of knowledge and speculated about how to put it to work. Some applications are more remote than others and are shown as "d" and "e." This difference in the extent to which ingenuity must be used for various applications is indicated by the relative distance of various applications from the gap. Applications lying in the far right portion of the life area may be regarded as inventions.

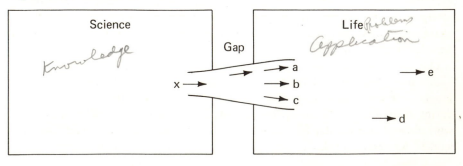

things that seemed a matter of common sense were actually psychologically unsound.

Figure 1.2 illustrates the convergent approach. In this instance the funnel is reversed, indicating how separated knowledges and theories might be brought to bear on a single problem. Attention is focused on the problem faced in reaching a desired objective, which serves as the stimulant for recalling and searching for relevant facts and theories that might aid in solving it. In this type of application the problem becomes the organizing principle.

Exploring the Gap between Science and Life

In following the convergent approach, gaps in our knowledge soon appear. The method raises many problems in life that do not occur to the theoretical investigator. Industry is concerned with problems associated with boredom, delegation of authority, promotion, seniority rights, and so on. Although these are psychological problems they are not likely to be discussed in a text on pure psychology. Often laboratory knowledge may suggest practices that backfire. For example, laboratory studies indicate that competition increases motivation, but attempts to promote competition in industry are likely to cause superior workers to slow down, to protect their less fortunate fellows.

Although laboratory studies may suggest leads, life problems place such knowledge in a different setting. Thus the process of trying to solve life problems again raises the question "why." What is boredom and why does it occur? Why is it so difficult to delegate responsibility and why is delegation desirable? Why should there be so much disagreement over the question of whom to promote? Why do people want to change one another and why do people resist correction? What is all the fuss over seniority and why should people feel they deserve more rights when they have seniority?

Figure 1.2 / The Convergent Method. Applications of scientific knowledge may be made if one begins with a life problem and then goes to science for useful knowledge. The "p" represents a problem in life which is the starting point. The process of application is one of finding items of scientific information, "w," "x," "y," and "z," that may bear on the problem. These items are suggested by the problems and are depicted as arrows converging on the problem area. Here, science funnels selected knowledge across the gap to a specific problem in the life area.

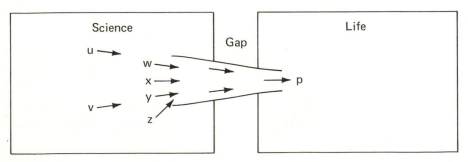

These questions can be raised out of pure curiosity, without any concern about how to deal with them. Although an understanding of the "why" may lead to direct application, the application is not a prerequisite for raising the question.

An example of how application raises new problems comes from studies of learning, a subject that has been explored more thoroughly than any other. It is central to many theories of psychology and has been explored by experimenting with the mastery of a great variety of tasks, comparing the abilities of animals at different levels of the evolutionary scale, studying the changes occurring with growth, noting the effects of injuries to the brain, studying the effects of diet and drugs, and setting up a great variety of experimental conditions. Questions posed by conflicting theories and by the effects of experimental variations largely determine the research in the laboratory.

Training computer programmers, radar technicians, and troubleshooters for locating malfunctions in equipment are life problems. It is reasonable to suppose that application of learning principles should facilitate such training. Nevertheless, Gagné[12] found the many data from the psychology of learning of little value in training men in such skills. In many instances they led him astray. Training was more effective when the specific task to be learned was analyzed. Making a detailed study of the task, breaking it into meaningful component parts, and arranging a proper sequence are examples of guiding principles that were more helpful than a knowledge of learning principles. This experience does not mean that learning principles are incorrect; rather, it demonstrates that training involves more than is apparent from a study of learning. As a consequence, these training problems must be taken into the laboratory and investigated with the same interest and techniques as pure science. This is what is meant by exploring the gap between pure science and life.

Figure 1.3 diagrammatically describes this third type of application. Here the connection between science and life becomes a new area rather than a bridge across

Figure 1.3 / Exploring the Gap. The new area of investigation is represented as a circle, and its area not only includes the gap between science and life areas but also overlaps and enlarges them.

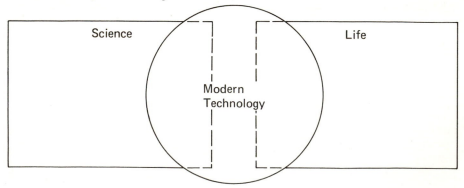

[12] Gagné, R. M. Military training and principles of learning. *Amer. Psychologist*, 1962, *17*, 83–91.

a gap. The circle represents this new area of scientific exploration brought into focus by attempts to apply scientific knowledge to life's problems. This new area not only includes the space between science and life, but also overlaps them, showing that applied science invades or modifies some of our life problems and also influences scientific thinking.

There are two possible approaches to such an exploration. One is for the research worker to leave the laboratory and explore the problems in the life setting. This is the field approach, and its effectiveness depends on comparisons of differing conditions and populations already existing. It requires effective selection of sites, conditions of work, and populations so that differences in results can be related to the factor investigated. Studies of the relationship between productivity and morale, effects of organizational changes on communication, behavior of small and large work groups, and so on, are examples of research that can be carried out through the field approach. Survey methods (that use interviews and questionnaires to determine opinions, attitudes, and motivations), case studies, and feedback procedures are common techniques.

The second approach is to take the life problems to a laboratory in which lifelike conditions are simulated. This method allows more rigid controls and permits repetition of a single experimental condition so that individual variations can be explored. This is the experimental approach to life problems, but in taking the problem into the laboratory some of the realities of life are lost. Each approach, therefore, has certain limitations and certain merits so that one tends to complement the other.

Interpersonal Relations

The subject matter of interpersonal relations includes practically all aspects of pure psychology: attitudes, frustration, motivation, learning, problem solving, and individual differences; but in the context of interpersonal relations, they occupy a unique relationship to one another, and raise new questions. Thus the field of interpersonal relations is a discipline that selects from and integrates a good many psychological findings and concepts; it includes phases of sociology, such as notions of status and membership; and even borrows from anthropology, which has contributed to our understanding of cultural influences.

Examples of new questions raised by the study of interpersonal relations are:

How can a supervisor be liked by subordinates and still keep production up?
How can one be fair to subordinates when each has a different notion of what is fair?
How should a supervisor deal with an old friend who resents this promotion over him?
How can one improve relations between inspectors and assembly workers when assembly workers consider themselves superior to inspectors (and often receive more pay), yet must be corrected by them?
How does one bridge the communication barrier that is created by differences in rank in an organization?
How can a superior correct a subordinate without creating resentment?

How can management convince workers to change to more efficient work methods?
How can one increase the initiative of subordinates?
How can the knowledge of several engineers be integrated by the executive who must make the final decision?
What is the best way to resolve conflicts regarding priorities?
How can competition and cooperation between supervisors be reconciled?

Supervisors raise such problems in interpersonal relations training programs. Note that they refer to specific, concrete situations, while psychological explanations are likely to be conceptual generalizations and principles. Adapting principles to specific situations requires careful study so that appropriate principles are used.

For example, "resistance to change" might indicate lack of motivation, fear of change, failure to understand the change, or distrust of the person initiating the change. The remedy would be different in each instance, so that the scientist could not supply the solution even if he knew all the remedies. Diagnosing the situation thus becomes a prerequisite to solving the problems in life situations. It is quite possible that research will indicate that some of the possible causes of resistance to change are more common than others. If distrust of the person who initiated the change were found to be the most usual cause of resistance to change, a whole new series of research questions would be raised.[13]

Researching Psychological Problems in Life

There was a time when the psychological laboratory was purposely isolated from life so that the data would not be contaminated by variables in real-life situations. Responses were measured by instruments in order to reduce the need for language; the experimenter often was unseen to exclude any influence his presence might have; tests were run under controlled environmental conditions (specific temperature, noise, lightning); and subjects were tested in separate cubicles to prevent social effects. Only the experimental condition studied was subjected to variation. These controls were regarded as merits of scientific experimentation because the aspect of behavior studied was isolated.

Gestalt psychology[14] emphasized the dangers of isolating psychological processes since the organism functioned as a whole in real life. It is not surprising, therefore, that Lewin,[15] a follower of this school of thought, was considered a pioneer when he experimented with real-life–type situations in order to study behavior.

Many laboratories now simulate life situations. Various kinds of social situations are created in which power or prestige factors, personality conflicts, leadership styles, and prejudices are introduced into the experimental design to reproduce some of life's problems.[16] Research on solving industrial problems is being done

---

[13] Lippitt, R., Watson, J., and Westley, B. *The dynamics of planned change.* New York: Harcourt Brace, 1958.
[14] Köhler, W. *Gestalt psychology.* New York: Liveright, 1929.
[15] Lewin, K. *Resolving social conflicts.* New York: Harper, 1948.
[16] Cartwright, D., and Zander, A. (Eds.). *Group dynamics* (3rd ed.). Evanston, Ill.: Row, Peterson, 1967.

by having subjects play the roles of company executives and employees.[17] It be-comes clear that solving problems involves more than facts and logic when dealing with life situations. Recently interest has increased in "Business Games,"[18] in which groups of individuals compete in running businesses. They are required to make a series of decisions dealing with investments, budgets, and the like and learn the consequences of each decision they acted upon. Some of these "games" last several days and simulate the operation of a business over a year or more.

These trends clearly reveal that the "ivory tower" laboratory is no longer the *only* laboratory. New ways of simulating life problems and translating them into situations that can be tested and retested are increasing. Simulation of life conditions is needed because life conditions at one instant cannot be replicated to determine the important variable. Each life situation happens only once and one cannot learn very much from a single run through. However, by creating the situation in the laboratory a given circumstance can be repeated with many groups. Because a par-ticular kind of conference problem can be repeated many times in a simulated situa-tion the effect of conference methods and conference skills can be studied and com-pared. The more closely the laboratory situation simulates the life situation the more accurate and dependable are the results and conclusions. The findings may still need to be verified under real-life conditions; if they fail to meet the test, researchers have overlooked some important factor. A new research problem is then created—that of finding the discrepancy between the laboratory and the real-life test conditions.

Changes in the Concept of Leadership

The leadership of industry has changed radically within our life span, not merely as the result of technical development and expansion; it was due also to the growth of new social values. At the beginning of this century the industrialist acted as a *dictator.* He was strong and often ruthless; the philosophy of "might makes right," which characterized the thinking of aggressive and successful warriors, determined his values. The industrial leaders of this period have been described as "robber barons,"[19] because of their self-centered and ultraindividualistic attitudes. Pleas for generosity and kindness directed toward them by socially-minded people were met with the cold response, "Business is business." The employee was of little concern to these leaders, whose foremost problem was to destroy their competitors.

Gradually it became apparent that competitors did not necessarily have to be defeated, and a new kind of leader emerged. This new type may be described as the *paternalist.* He was kindly, and because he had the interests of his employees at heart he functioned much like a parent toward his children. He expected loyalty,

---

[17] Maier, N. R. F. *Problem solving discussions and conferences.* New York: McGraw-Hill, 1963.

[18] Ricciardi, F. M., *et al. Top management decision simulation.* New York: American Management Assn., 1958; Biel, W. C. Training programs and devices. In R. M. Gagné (Ed.), *Psychological principles in systems development.* New York: Holt, 1962.

[19] Josephson, M. *The robber barons.* New York: Harcourt, 1934; Saveth, E. N. Exit "rob-ber baron and co." *New York Times Book Review,* July 4, 1954, 6–7.

demanded respect, and gave his employees what he thought was good for them. The underlying philosophy seemed to be "fair but firm." Employees responded to this kind of leadership, and companies developed the reputation for being good places to work. As a result, paternalistic leaders were successful in their ventures and effectively competed with ruthless industrialists.

The third type of leader to emerge was the *sales executive,* who recognized that the support of employees was needed for the success of a business and that the use of force to control employees only met with counterforce. Since business sales departments had learned ways of gaining the approval of customers, it was only natural that some sales officials should be promoted to top positions, where they brought the techniques of selling to the company's relationship with its employees. Some such leaders were insincere and made promises they never intended to keep in order to win support; others, by nature, were considerate of the feelings of employees and as a result were able to see different sides to a question. In both cases, the approach was to control through diplomacy rather than force.

The appearance of the persuasive executive as an industrial leader was not entirely due to his success in running the business. Two other circumstances contributed. First, the enormity of business made one-man operation impossible; as a result, the leader was dependent upon others for formulating and executing decisions. This meant working with a group, and management-by-conference, a technique to which the persuasive talents of sales executives were well adapted, emerged. The second circumstance was that the man at the top no longer was the founder of the business or necessarily his heir. The new leader was chosen by the board of directors, and the qualifications that make directors view a man favorably differ from those possessed by a founder. Ownership and management became separate functions—administered by different individuals. As a result, the prerogatives of management, the rights of employees to their jobs, and the social responsibility of business took on new meaning.

With the growth of the union the employee learned that he had rights and began to make demands rather than rely on management's generosity. This change in values was so rapid that many industrial leaders could not adapt to it. Over a period of only 19 years, for example, the UAW (United Automobile Workers) grew from a group of workers who met in a basement to the largest union in America.[20] The change in employee status made it difficult for the authoritarian type of leader to function, whereas the persuasive executive enjoyed a considerable degree of success.

More recent concepts of leadership have emerged, all of which utilize the principle of participation. Such concepts as multiple management, consultative management, and group dynamics are being evaluated because it is apparent that employees at all levels are no longer content simply to do as they are told; they want to use their knowledge, and they want some control over their jobs. New concepts in

---

[20] Vorse, M. H. The union that grew up: An informal portrait of the UAW. *Harper's Mag.,* 1954, *209,* 83–88.

leadership involving social responsibility for the environment and equal employment opportunities are beginning to emerge. Thus not only employees, but society in general is influencing the nature of organizational leadership. These developments will be discussed in later chapters.

Three Locations of Problems

The Situation

The leader of any group ordinarily is in charge of a situation. In industry this is a work situation which includes the machinery and equipment as well as the work area. It is within a supervisor's control to alter some aspects of this situation and to recommend other changes. Many problems can be solved by making changes in the work environment, the machinery, the work tools and equipment, or the spatial relationships of the subordinates. Thus the situation in which people work and interact represents one direction in which a leader may look in order to improve performance. Working with the overall situation is a way in which a leader can attempt objective problem solving. The potentialities of problem solving in the objective situation will be discussed in detail in Chapters 2, 18, and 21.

The Individual

Leaders interact with individuals when they give instructions, make assignments, conduct interviews, meet them informally in the elevator or coffee shop, or are faced with an emotionally disturbed employee. This is the area of interpersonal relations, where problem-solving activity may center around feelings and attitudes. A leader's knowledge and skills in dealing with these human relationships can influence each individual's performance and job satisfaction. Essential principles in these areas will be discussed in Chapters 3, 4, 7, 13, 14, 20, and 22.

The Group

Most supervisors have more than one subordinate reporting to them. Insofar as coordination of the activities of these individuals is involved they constitute a group. Thus the leader must not only relate to each individual, but to the combination of individuals.

Whenever a leader has more than one subordinate, an additional location for problem solving is introduced, the problem of being fair. A supervisor cannot grant one individual's request without influencing the expectations and judgments of others. Fair treatment greatly depends on each person's opinion. Since these opinions conflict, misunderstanding can result.

Group problems, viewed from the position of the supervisor, are primarily leadership problems. These will be dealt with in detail in Chapters 5, 6, 21, and 22.

Diagnosing the Location

Some problems may be solved by changes made in any of the three locations. A problem involving two persons who do not get along with each other may be handled by separating them, by effectively correcting one of them, or by improving communications between them. Other problems might be solved more effectively by one route than another. The person who can diagnose and pinpoint the difficulty is in the best position to select the most fruitful approach. For this reason factors in behavior should be more fully explored.

Three Kinds of Learning

Management training should produce three kinds of learning. The most obvious is acquiring information, which includes general knowledge, job knowledge, technical know-how, and facts and principles in the behavioral sciences. This is the intellectual aspect of any learning and is gained through lectures, textbooks, and movies.

Less obvious in most management-training situations is the development of skills in leadership and group problem solving. A mechanic must be trained in the use of certain skills, but managers are seldom given equivalent practice training. Essential skills for managers include sensitivity to feelings, ability to state problems so as not to offend, ability to teach, skill in interviewing, and conference skills. The role-playing exercises at the end of some chapters are designed to give practice in bridging the gap between "knowing" and "doing."

"Discussion 66" in progress (see pp. 15–16). Here about 150 management personnel have been divided into small groups and given an assignment. Later the group leaders will report conclusions.

The third kind of learning is the acquisition of constructive attitudes. A manager who dislikes working through others will have difficulties even after he thoroughly learns the basic principles and has practiced them in a training problem. If training can develop an interest in organizing work rather than doing it, seeing problems as challenges rather than headaches, and reacting to subordinates as people to understand, rather than to evaluate, he will behave differently. Class discussion and group problem solving as well as role playing provide this learning opportunity. The exercises are designed to aid the development of such constructive attitudes.

Laboratory Exercise

Small Group Discussions

A. Preparing for discussion.

The instructor will:

1. Divide the class into groups of five or six persons.
2. Ask each group to select a discussion leader.
3. Instruct leaders to conduct a discussion on a current controversial topic such as:
    "How does full employment in industry make the need for a knowledge of psychology more important?"
    "What is the compelling argument for and against equal treatment for men and women in industry?"

B. Discussion procedure.

1. Each leader should develop a final list of no more than three factors from his group's discussion. The discussion should require nearly half an hour.
2. It is suggested that leaders first develop a relatively complete list, encouraging participants to be uncritical of each other.
3. Each factor should be briefly recorded.
4. When the group ceases to produce new ideas, the discussion should turn to an evaluation of the items. The objective is to reduce the list to the best three.

C. Reports to class.

1. Each group leader should report his group's contributions to the class instructor, who writes them on the board, abbreviating lengthy statements.
2. It is best to have each group make one contribution at a time, in turn, so as to keep all groups actively interested.
3. Duplicate entries should be starred.

D. Method used.

The discussion method experienced in this laboratory period is known as "Phillips 66,"[21] "discussion 66," or just "buzz session." (The photograph at the bottom of

---

[21] Phillips, J. D. Report on discussion 66. *Adult Educ. J.*, 1948, 7, 181–182.

page 14 shows the method in action.) Audiences of 20 to 100 can be divided so that everyone can participate in the discussion. The discussion topic should be clearly stated and should be one that the group feels competent to handle. Experience has shown that the time allowed should depend on the complexity of the topic and on the size of the group. In all cases the time should be long enough to allow interaction and a jelling of ideas. Although the original idea ("66") was for groups of *six* to discuss for *six* minutes, the writer has found that only superficial problems can be handled in so short a time. Attempts to use groups of more than eight persons are unsatisfactory; groups of three to six are most successful.

The number of ideas to be reported by each group should be fewer than the number of persons in a group. This prevents the group product from being a list of the contributions made by each member. Good discussions require resolution of differences in opinion, and one way to introduce such differences is to require the group to be selective and integrative rather than additive.

Suggested Readings

Dembo, T., Leviton, G. L., and Wright, B. A. Adjustment to misfortune—a problem of social psychological rehabilitation. *Artificial Limbs,* 1956, 3, 4–62.

Filley, A. C., and House, R. J. *Managerial process and organizational behavior.* Glenview, Ill.: Scott, Foresman, 1969.

Gellerman, S. W. *People, problems and profits.* New York: McGraw-Hill, 1960, Ch. 1.

Maslow, A. H. *Motivation and personality.* New York: Harper, 1954, Chs. 1 and 2.

McGehee, W., and Thayer, P. W. *Training in business and industry.* New York: Wiley, 1961, Ch. 1.

Meltzer, H. Review of reviews in industrial psychology, 1950–1959. *Personnel Psychol.,* 1960, *13,* 31–58.

Nunn, H. L. *Partners in production.* Englewood Cliffs, N.J.: Prentice-Hall, 1961.

2

Causation in Behavior

The Psychological Approach

Understanding versus Evaluating Behavior

We *understand* behavior when we know what caused it or what made the person do it. We *evaluate* behavior when we approve or disapprove of it. Both understanding and evaluation are common human reactions. Our systems of values, be they religious, cultural, or philosophic, furnish frames of reference which we use to appraise ourselves and others. Our laws reflect these values, and persons who break these laws are subject to punishment.

The activity of science should lead to an understanding of nature. Psychology as a science, therefore, must devote itself to exploration of behavior with understanding as its goal. It is possible to understand why a worker steals from a company without approving or disapproving of him or his actions. When we discover that a man killed his wife because he hoped to collect her insurance we understand him better, but this does not mean we approve or support his action. Thus the first step in a scientific approach to behavior is to divorce value judgments from behavior analysis.

The psychological approach to correction is more effective than the legalistic approach. The former tends to bring into focus the objective to be achieved, hence has a future reference, while the latter focuses on behavior which has already occurred and has a past reference. Both approaches have a place in our culture and the desired objective should determine the approach we use. Since our major concern is influencing future behavior, this book emphasizes the psychological approach.

Factors Influencing Behavior

Behavior is always the product of two factors, the nature of the organism that behaves and the nature of the situation in which the organism finds itself. The situation is a source of stimulation, and behavior is always the organism's response to stimulation from the environment. Often we are not aware that we have been stimulated and assume that the behavior is spontaneous, yet spontaneous responses are more likely to be the exception than the rule. For example, a person may suddenly look at his watch to see if it is time for lunch. What was the stimulus for this behavior? It might have been a minor stomach contraction, the sound of someone eating an apple, or the chiming of a clock. One aspect of the psychologist's job is to locate the stimulus or the pattern of stimuli if he is to understand the behavior under investigation.

The individual or the particular organism behaves by responding to the stimulation he receives from the environment. The makeup of a particular individual, therefore, will contribute to the behavior. The nature of an individual depends on heredity, physical and emotional environment, culture, and learning. Individuals differ not only in their appearances but also in their sensitivities, response repertoires, intelligence, interests, motivations, and personalities. Any aspect of man that can be measured thus reveals certain differences, and the psychologist must take these variations into account.

Individuals not only show differences, they also show similarities in behavior. These similarities may be biological or cultural in nature, or they may be the result of common experiences. People are alike, for example, in that they all can see better under good illumination, yet they differ in their visual acuity. Various children might respond differently to punishment yet one method of discipline may be universally more effective than another. The psychologist is concerned with the contribution of the organism to behavior and also with the determination of the similarities and differences that exist within species, races, and groups.

Interaction between Person and Situation

In simple reflex behaviors the stimulus acts on the organism and elicits the response; the organism plays no active part in selecting or interpreting behavior. However, for the behaviors with which we are concerned, the organism does *interact* with the environment.

We speak of the *interaction* between stimulus and organism because the condition or nature of the organism may influence the stimulus as well as being influenced by it. A hungry person sees food differently than a sick one, because the supplementary stimulations in the body alter the properties (for the person) of the external stimulus. We must distinguish between the physical properties of a stimulus and the properties it has for the organism. If a person experiences a stick of wood as a snake, we can best understand that person's behavior if we consider a snake, not a piece of wood, as the stimulus. Since the organism contributes to the determination of the nature of a stimulus, behavior is the product of an interaction between the stimulus and the organism rather than a reaction of the organism to the stimulus. The product of this interaction in psychology is called *perception.*

One example of how the same pattern can be viewed in quite different ways is illustrated by Figure 2.1. This figure may be seen as a pair of Xs or as an upright and an inverted *V*. To argue about which is right is futile: both interpretations are consistent with the nature of the figure. If one person expected to see the Xs, he would be more likely to see them than another who expected to see the *V*s.

analogous to different employees seeing their supervisor in different ways.

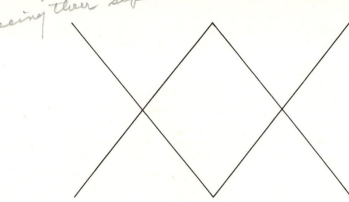

Figure 2.1 / Variations in the Perception of Objects. This figure may be seen as two Xs or as an upright V superimposed on an inverted V. If it is suggested that a W rests on top of an M, these will appear. Mention of a diamond will again change the perception. What is really pictured depends on a perceiver's point of view.

Suppose seeing an *X* makes you angry. If I innocently place the figure before you, am I responsible for your anger, or is your interpretation responsible? There are even more ways of seeing this figure. To aid you in finding them it is necessary only to give you some added experience. I suggest that the figure represents a *W* on top of an *M,* and now you too can see these letters. You will even see a diamond with whiskers on its sides as soon as it is suggested. With a stimulus like this, most people can be open-minded and see other people's points of view when these are suggested.

The importance of this interaction is evident if we consider how different employees react to a particular supervisor. Some may resent his presence because they see him as a slave driver; others may be callous and overlook his remarks because they see him as a nervous, hot-tempered person; still others may be glad to have him around to help them and regard him simply as a person doing his job. The supervisor may consider himself a good-hearted fellow who is taking the interests of his workers too seriously, and believe that he really should have a little more respect and cooperation for his efforts.

An understanding of behavior, therefore, not only requires that we determine the stimulus to which an individual reacts but also that we discover how the stimuli are organized. It is perceptions that give stimuli their meanings, and individuals' responses are determined by these meanings. For example, quick movements are often seen as threatening, slow movements as friendly.[1] Animals and small children show this different interpretation of movements regardless of the intent of the individual making the gesture. Thus slow-moving people are regarded as more gentle and kind

[1] Schneirla, T. C. An evolutionary and developmental theory of biphasic processes underlying approach and withdrawal. In M. R. Jones (Ed.), *Nebraska symposium on motivation.* Lincoln, Nebr.: University of Nebraska Press, 1959.

than fast-moving people, and people in a hurry are sometimes thought to be angry. That angry movements are quick supports these simple interpretations.

Behavior and Accomplishment

The behavior of an organism leads to a consequence which may be called an accomplishment. Migration behavior in birds takes them to a different climate, the eye wink in man protects his eyes, dropping a heavy tool may injure the foot, driving through a red light may result in a traffic ticket. Accomplishments may be desirable or undesirable but are always the products of behavior and should not be confused with the causes of behavior. Causes precede the results of an action.

The reason accomplishments frequently become a source of confusion is that they are the aspects of behavior that often are disturbing to others. When a traffic violation results in an accident, it is taken more seriously than one resulting in a near miss. The man who shoots and kills is guilty of murder, but the man who shoots and misses is guilty only of intent. Thus the accomplishment of behavior causes us to evaluate it and to focus on the organism. Revenge rather than prevention of a repetition of the behavior becomes the focus of attention. It is difficult for us to analyze behavior dispassionately when it has been harmful to us.

Often we falsely attribute motives to another on the basis of his accomplishments. A man drops a wrench while working aloft. If it drops near me I may accuse him of trying to kill me. An employee leaves a lighted cigarette on the edge of a desk and is accused of disrespect for company property. A neighbor crosses a property line in mowing his lawn and is accused of trying to steal the land from the owner. A nation builds up its armed strength to defend its borders, and a hostile nation accuses it of planning an invasion. Misunderstandings arise when we falsely attribute intent to an action. Behavior and its accomplishments are only part of the story. We must seek out the stimulus conditions and relate them to the behavior.

Accomplishment enters into the causation sequence only when it plays a part in the organism's planning. In such cases the accomplishment is something that is anticipated; it is part of the organism's makeup, hence precedes the behavior. This is the meaning of purpose. Birds do not plan their flights, they react to the shorter periods of daylight, a decrease in available food, and temperature gradients.

The man who drops a tool might do so because of distraction, lack of training, or any other combination of stimulus and organismic characteristics. The man who drives through a red light may not see the light or he may be in a hurry, anticipating that he will get to work on time, rather than receive a traffic ticket. Whatever the accomplishment, it serves as an opportunity for learning, which alters the organism and thereby may influence future behaviors by building up anticipations.

The Causal Sequence in Behavior

The psychological approach to behavior follows the formulation shown in Figure 2.2. S represents the situation which supplies the stimulation to the individual or organism, O. The double-headed arrow indicates that O interacts with S, giving rise to the organism's perception or interpretation of the S. The response of the organism is shown by the single-headed arrow leading to B, which represents be-

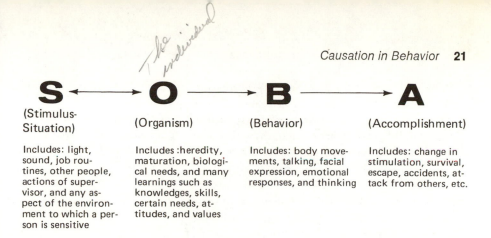

S ←——→	**O** ——→	**B** ——→	**A**
(Stimulus-Situation)	(Organism)	(Behavior)	(Accomplishment)
Includes: light, sound, job routines, other people, actions of supervisor, and any aspect of the environment to which a person is sensitive	Includes :heredity, maturation, biological needs, and many learnings such as knowledges, skills, certain needs, attitudes, and values	Includes: body movements, talking, facial expression, emotional responses, and thinking	Includes: change in stimulation, survival, escape, accidents, attack from others, etc.

Figure 2.2 / The Causal Sequence. To explain behavior, one must include a description of the *S* as well as of the *O*. The interaction between them must precede the behavior which results from the interaction. The behavior (B) causes the changes which alter the relationship between the organism (O) and its world. The change produced by behavior is an accomplishment (A) which may be desirable or undesirable. In either case it may alter the stimulus situation for the organism, or it may serve as the stimulus for other organisms.

havior. The interaction between *S* and *O,* therefore, precedes the behavior.

The behavior in turn acts on the outside world and this leads to an accomplishment, *A.* The accomplishment may alter the stimulating conditions and thereby influence the subsequent behavior, or it may initiate new behaviors by creating new situations for the organism. The man who runs a red light may save time, receive a traffic ticket, or suffer an injury. In any event, he moves into a new situation which in turn initiates another unit of behavior. Although the accomplishment is a product of the behavior which precedes it, the nature of the accomplishment can play a part in subsequent behavior, providing the organism learns. This learning may be profitable or detrimental. The man who runs the red light may be rewarded by saving time and as a consequence may run a red light on a future occasion, when he may receive a traffic ticket.

Since chance factors influence accomplishment, in the sense that the same behavior can have a number of different results, it is difficult to control accomplishment. More can be gained by emphasizing behavior and attempting to control it.

The relation between the S-O-B-A sequence can be illustrated by a simple situation. A person is pricked with a pin, jumps, and escapes the pinprick. Here the pinprick is the *S,* the person is the *O,* the jump is the *B,* and escape is the *A.* A satisfactory explanation should identify each factor. An explanation of behavior that does not identify the stimulus is incomplete, yet this is most often overlooked. The person is likely to say he jumped to get away from the pin, or because he was hurt, or because he wanted to. The first explanation makes accomplishment the cause, the other two mention only the organism.

Purpose in the Behavior of Man

Let us take a complex situation and see how effectively we can explain behavior in terms of an interaction between stimulus and organism.

A man is running down the street. We stop him and ask him why he is running and he replies, "I'm running to catch the 4:15 train to Chicago."

Should we accept this answer as an explanation? Catching the train would be the accomplishment of his running; how then could it be the cause? Moreover, if the train turned out to be an hour late, it would not be necessary for him to run, yet this fact would not have prevented the running. The reason given by the man is not accurate.

Now let us explore the antecedent conditions. First, we must find a stimulus. A little reflection reveals that the man must have looked at a watch or a clock. If a clock is the stimulus, it follows that the behavior of a given organism will change if the stimulus is altered. By setting his clock ahead, the man can be made to run when he need not for the sake of accomplishment; and he can also be made not to run, when for the sake of accomplishment he should, by setting his clock back. Because altering the clock will influence the running behavior of a given man, we must accept it as a stimulus.

Now we must explore the contribution of the organism (in this instance the man who runs) to the behavior in question. All men do not run when they see a clock; we have a special kind of man. All things we say about him, however, must be reducible to antecedent events. It is reasonable to suppose the man (1) has a need for this train (motivation); (2) knows the train schedule, the distance to the station, and that running saves time (knowledge); and (3) has the ability to run (aptitude and physical makeup). All these conditions existed before the running took place and so are antecedent events. Altering any one of them will modify the man's responses to the clock. A telegram stating that he is not needed in Chicago will alter his behavior so that he will no longer run when he sees the clock. He will also respond differently if misinformed about the train time or about his distance from the station. Finally, it must be granted that a man with a bad heart or paralyzed legs will not run even if the need for catching the train is urgent.

An explanation of behavior in terms of antecedent events is fairly complex, but once the details are filled in, a variety of ways to influence behavior one way or another are suggested immediately.

If the above type of explanation is satisfactory, why does the man explain his behavior in terms of consequences or purpose? This behavior too must be explained. Purpose refers to anticipations or expectations. Anticipations are a product of many past learnings and are a part of the man's makeup, as are all his memories. This man anticipates that the train will leave at 4:15 because it has left at this time on previous occasions. He expects certain things to happen today because they have happened on previous days. Relying on expectations is quite effective because many of today's events are duplicates of yesterday's. When the man refers to catching "today's" train, he is actually describing his memory of past trains.

But we must not confuse an anticipation with a cause. Present events are not always duplicates of the past. Take the example of an employee who stops being tardy for a week after being reprimanded. Will the reprimand method work a second time? Will it work for all tardy employees? Are there different causes for tardiness? If so, might it be better to explore the *S* and the *O* before accepting anticipated events as dependable explanations? As a matter of fact, most common-sense explanations omit reference to the contribution of the *S,* which we shall see later is important to correcting behavior.

Basic Causes of Behavior Often Unknown to the Individual

Although the expressed explanation of behavior may reveal a man's anticipations and desires, his *account* of his responses may be quite incidental or even inaccurate. The important causes of behavior are often unknown to the individual, since they do not reach the level of consciousness. A person who fears snakes seldom knows why. The fear may have originated in an incident in early childhood. The incident is repressed and apparently forgotten, but the fear of the snake which the incident generated remains. Or, we may take the case of a worker who attributes a decline in productive ability to fatigue, while the more basic cause may be worry over personal problems.

In other cases, people may think they know the *why* of an action and be entirely mistaken. For instance, a group of workers may say they are out on strike to get higher pay, but it is possible that low pay is not the true cause of their striking. Under other conditions of work, the same group may not go out on strike. Clean toilets, sanitary drinking fountains, security in their jobs, and sympathetic consideration of their problems may prevent workers from striking for higher pay. On the other hand, unsatisfactory working conditions may make employees so dislike a job that they demand higher wages if they are to continue to work. It is not always the most poorly paid group which strikes for higher wages, a fact which sometimes puzzles the employer. One cannot find the cause of such behavior merely by analyzing demands or expressed purposes. These demands are responses to some kind of stimulation, and the effective stimuli may not even be known to the individuals who make the demands.

When people do not get along, they quarrel about almost anything, and what they quarrel about is not necessarily the basic cause of the trouble. The important thing is to get at the cause of the lack of congeniality; the bickering will then take care of itself. Investigations of this sort of problem clearly show that actual causes may be unknown to the individuals and that these causes frequently go back to situations entirely unrelated to the present difficulty. A supervisor will readily recognize among his employees a few individuals who always have something to complain about. These are poorly adjusted individuals, whose complaints are symptoms of disorder rather than descriptions of grievances.

Excuses Are Not Causes

Many so-called reasons for behavior are excuses rather than causes. A man may give many logical reasons for why he evaded his income taxes, why he is against certain laws, why he voted for a particular candidate, why he considers his employer unfair, or why his employees are overpaid; but none of these may actually be a cause of his point of view or of his behavior. Sometimes he knows the expressed reasons are false, but often he is so intrigued by his reasons that he believes they must have been basic causes. The psychologist cannot risk using such material as a basis for an analysis of behavior. For this reason he prefers to analyze situation and behavior data rather than rely on verbal reports when he wishes to understand the real reasons behind behavior.

How Behavior Varies with the Nature of the Stimulus

That people do widely different things in different situations is quite obvious. Sometimes we may forget the obvious and blame the individual for the changed behavior. We know, for example, that honesty depends upon the situation (a complex stimulus) in which people find themselves, yet we sometimes classify people as honest or dishonest.[2] If the situation determines whether or not the behavior is honest, then people will differ only in the number of situations in which honest behavior appears. Consequently, most people will be honest in some situations and dishonest in others, and only in a few extreme cases will be consistently honest or consistently dishonest.

The frequency of honest behavior can be increased with training, but it can also be increased by changing the situation. Locked cars, business credit records, well-lighted and busy streets, and the like reduce the amount of dishonest behavior. Jacobs points out how the crime rate in modern housing areas can be reduced by arranging construction so that there are many eyes in the close vicinity, particularly the eyes of persons who belong in the neighborhood.[3] Expanses of halls and dim stairways in apartment buildings encourage crime. Even social pressure, such as that furnished by honor examinations, may serve as a stimulus for honesty. A student refrains from cheating because he has learned that his associates disapprove of such behavior.

The amount of labor trouble, turnover, and breakage varies with the situation. Foremen who create a work climate by showing consideration for the workers' needs have fewer grievances and less turnover.[4] Man's nature changes little from one era to another, but his behavior varies greatly with the times. When we say that people are getting worse or that the younger generation is different from ours, we fail to take complete account of the part the stimulus situation plays in behavior.

In industry, we find that in many plants there is resentment at punching the time clock. Because 15 minutes are deducted if a man is two minutes late, we find men waiting until the full 15 minutes are up before they "check in." This condition actually makes some employees later than they would be otherwise. Other workers begin packing their tools 10 or 15 minutes before the end of the work period, or refuse to work a few minutes overtime to finish a job. Like the time-keeper, they also exaggerate the importance of a few minutes' time. This behavior may be called "small" and be a source of irritation, yet it is directly related to the

---

[2] Hartshorne, H., and May, M. A. *Studies in deceit* (Vol. 1). New York: Macmillan, 1928.
[3] Jacobs, J. *The death and life of great American cities.* New York: Harper, 1961.
[4] Fleishman, E. A., and Harris, E. F. Patterns of leadership related to employee grievances and turnover. *Personnel Psychol.,* 1962, *15,* 43–56.

stimulus situation. In plants where a responsible individual passes judgment on tardiness, and arbitrary methods are not used, such behavior symptoms occur less frequently.

How the Nature of Man Determines Behavior

An individual's nature depends upon the way he grew and was modified by experience. How he grew depends upon the quality of the chemical substance in the fertilized egg which his parents produced, as well as upon the environmental conditions under which this egg developed into a living person. Since an egg does not grow unless conditions are favorable, the early environmental factor is very similar for the majority of people. Such differences in growth as do appear therefore are largely influenced by the chemical constitution of the egg. We speak of this influence as "heredity." These differences, in turn, may be transmitted to the next generation. Clearly, heredity is an important factor in determining the nature of the individual. Its importance can be seen when we compare the physical likenesses of parents and offspring. The potential abilities of offspring also tend to show similarities with those of their parents. If one member of the family is a good worker on a given kind of job, there is some probability that his siblings will be equally satisfactory both in temperament and in potential ability. This relationship is perhaps as good a recommendation as any that can be given without resorting to psychological tests. To a lesser degree, cousins show similar abilities. It is partly because of this hereditary factor that we may expect musicians, football players, expert machinists, and the like to appear in certain families.

As a child grows, his ability to learn increases; as a consequence, his behavior is further modified. We speak of such changes in behavior as "acquired." Knowledge, skill, and language are obviously acquired and represent important modifications of behavior. Learned modifications in behavior are not passed on to children, but must be acquired by them through their own personal experience. Such aspects of behavior are culturally determined.

Because man's characteristics are both inborn and acquired, we must always distinguish between these two types of influence. We cannot expect skill from an untrained individual, nor can we expect two individuals with the same training to be similar in their skills or in their ability to produce. Blaming a man for not doing a job which requires a skill that he has little inborn capacity to acquire is as pointless as blaming one chemical substance for not being another. It is as unjust as censuring a man for not having a skill before he has been trained in that skill.

Applications of the Causation Formula to the Job[5]

Increasing Opportunities for Influencing Others

Once one accepts the view that all behavior is dependent on both the S and O, many new opportunities for influencing behavior appear. Since all behavior is in-

[5] Refer again to Figure 2.2.

fluenced by these two independent factors, a basic change in either will alter the behavior. One must analyze conditions carefully so that the resulting changes are in the right direction, do not introduce worse problems, and are not uneconomical.

Changing the S *[stimulus situation]*

Imagine a situation where many errors are made on a job. What are some changes in the S that might be made? Immediately we think of such improvements as better lighting, reduced noise, a change in work procedure, eliminating interruptions. By making further checks, some of these can be ruled out and others clarified. If the lighting conditions are different in two parts of the room, a comparison of errors occurring in the two sections will increase knowledge of the influence of the lighting factor. By exploring and making a variety of comparisons, practical changes in the S can be suggested. One should not overlook the fact that the supervisor and other employees are also stimuli.

If errors are greater in one unit than in another, one should locate the S factors which are different in the two units and see if any of the differences will yield a clue. Exploratory analysis of this kind should precede any contemplated changes.

Examples of accomplishments due to improved behavior resulting from changes in the S include:

1. Reduction in highway accidents, by painting a white line on the center of the road.
2. Reduction in industrial accidents by introduction of safety devices.
3. Better inspection resulting from increased lighting.
4. Better production through less close supervision.
5. More prompt return from coffee break as a result of improved elevator service.
6. Improved care of trucks by giving each man the same truck every day.

Changing the O *[organism (the individual)]*

Opportunities for changing the O are less numerous, but they also require analysis. Some employees make many errors while others make few. If employees working under similar conditions consistently perform differently, it is reasonable to explore ways for changing the O.

One way to change the O in a given job is to exchange one worker for another. This is a problem of placement which will be developed more thoroughly in subsequent chapters. Suffice it to say here that many differences among individuals should be taken for granted before this factor is explored too seriously. Furthermore, it is better to place people properly at the outset than to make many changes in placement after employment.

A more common way to change the O is through education and development of skill. If experienced employees perform better, training should be considered. Training is also suggested if employees who do the best work use certain methods which the less effective employees do not follow.

Modifying a person's attitudes or his needs also represent changes in the *O*. If certain employees are social misfits or unusually lacking in job interest, the problem may be emotional or social adjustment. Insofar as such adjustments can be improved and needs can be altered, changes in the *O* will occur.

Examples of accomplishments due to improved behavior by working with the *O* include:

1. Increased job satisfaction and work performance by the use of aptitude tests. (When one places employees on the basis of test results, he is manipulating the *O*. Behavior in a given work situation is improved by placing the proper *O*s in it.)
2. Decreased accidents and increased production resulting from job training.
3. Increased production resulting from reduced emotional conflict.
4. Improved morale through use of gripe sessions.

When to Change the S and When to Change the O

Since both the *S* and the *O* influence behavior, only one may need to be changed in any given instance. It is natural to determine, for example, what each type of change will cost and which can be accomplished most easily.

Opportunities for changing the *S* are often overlooked, and attempts are sometimes made to change the *O* in the wrong way. This is partly because one becomes emotionally involved when things go wrong. Under such conditions, one sees only the *O* and blames it. Thus possibilities for preventing future trouble are overlooked in the process of being angry. Becoming angry with an employee does not increase his judgment or his skill. If these were contributing factors in causing the trouble initially, it is apparent that preventive measures have not been taken.

As in dealing with mechanical problems, there are certain general guides which help one locate a problem. One is to determine how widespread a problem is. If the average tardiness is excessive, one should determine whether this figure is due to a few persons or if it involves all employees. If a problem exists because of 5 per cent of the employees, it is reasonable to approach the problem by making a study of the *O*. If 90 per cent of the employees are involved or contribute to a condition, it is wise to spend a good deal of effort exploring the *S*.

Analyzing the Problem of Grievances

In a certain company the number of grievances[6] to be processed was excessive. Analysis of the outcomes revealed that the number of cases won by the company compared favorably with other companies. This suggested that the company was not particularly stubborn or backward as far as general policy was concerned.

---

[6] A grievance is a complaint against the company that has been formalized and is handled through the systematized procedure established by collective bargaining. For example, an aggrieved employee takes his trouble to his union steward, who thereafter represents him to the company. The steward attempts to reach a solution in conference with the foreman. If this fails, the case is appealed and higher levels of management become involved. Filing a grievance is similar to taking a case into court in that the procedure is formalized and the goal of winning the case often clouds the issue.

Two approaches to safety: (a) training men to work safely and (b) use of safety guard.

Frank Siteman, with cooperation of U S M Corporation

Classifying grievances on a departmental basis revealed no pattern that indicated that type of work was a factor.

The grievances were then analyzed according to subject. This analysis revealed no basic common factor such as overtime, disciplinary problems, or disputes over seniority. There seemed to be no one practice of work relationship to correct.

The next breakdown was in terms of stewards. This indicated some relationships in that some stewards were involved in more grievances than others. There were inconsistencies, however. This led to a breakdown of the grievances in terms of foremen involved, which revealed that 10 per cent of the foremen had 46 per cent of the grievances.

From this analysis it became apparent that the best way to reduce grievances was to train or remove certain foremen. Previously, the company had felt it was doing well in labor relations when it won a high percentage of decisions, and foremen were often blamed when a case was lost. The analysis indicated that the poorest foremen had the best record as far as victories were concerned, because workers reporting to these foremen were ready to make trouble even if they had a weak case.

The Same Behavior May Have Different Causes

On one occasion a truck driver's skill was increased greatly by giving him a truck with less leg room than the one he had previously used. Having rather short legs, he had difficulty in operating the brake pedal. The reduction in the man's collision record by this change in trucks so impressed the department head that he became biased in favor of what he called the "safe" model. Such generalization of solutions is erroneous and defeats the purpose of analysis.

Any given kind of behavior may have many causes. A man working at a drawing board leans back in his chair and gazes out the window. Why does he do this? Immediately explanations come to mind:

a) His eyes are tired.
b) He's thinking.
c) He's worried about something.
d) He's out of work.
e) He's waiting for the supervisor.
f) He's bored.
g) He's loafing.

In order to deal adequately with the behavior, it is necessary to determine which explanation is involved in a particular instance. The first two items suggest no need for changing the behavior; the third, that the man may require help; the fourth, that he is completing more work than is expected of him; the fifth suggests the need to improve supervisory coverage or training; the sixth and seventh indicate the exigency of improving motivation or job placement. The kind of treatment of the *S* or the *O* that will work in one case may not work in another, or even with the same case on a different occasion.

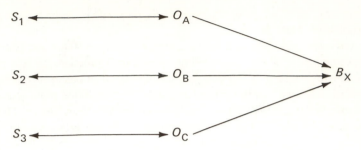

Figure 2.3 / The Same Behavior May Have Several Causes. There is no one solution to problems such as tardiness, inspection errors, and daydreaming because various persons might engage in any of these behaviors for entirely different reasons. S_1, S_2, and S_3 indicate three different situations in which individuals O_A, O_B, and O_C find themselves. The resulting behavior, B_X, can be the same for all three persons, but the best way to change B_X might be quite different in each instance.

There is no one solution to problems of tardiness, overstaying rest pauses, quitting early, clerical errors, and poor service, thus there is no escape from the necessity of analysis. Figure 2.3 diagramatically describes why the same behavior might require different remedies for various individuals.

The Same Cause May Have Many Behaviors

Let us choose a single factor such as worry. How might a home problem affect an employee's behavior on the job? The following behaviors are possible:

a) daydreaming
b) neglecting to follow safe practices
c) poorer attention to quality of work
d) increased work-pace
e) hypersensitivity to supervisor's remarks, and consequent uncooperative behavior
f) disagreeableness to other employees
g) failure to report for work.

Persons in the same home condition would behave quite differently and their conduct on the job would reflect this condition in various ways. Since an employee's behavior gives no clue to the causes, one cannot deduce the nature of the remedy from the behavior. Unexpected benefits may appear, however, when one makes certain corrections on the job, because a great number of behaviors may thereby be improved. If a company offered a counseling service to help employees with difficult emotional adjustments to home problems, the benefits would be numerous though often difficult to locate or measure. Figure 2.4 shows how behavior varies for different individuals in the same situation and why a correction in the S could result in several behavior changes.

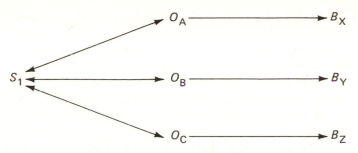

Figure 2.4 / The Same Situation May Cause a Variety of Behaviors. Several people, O_A, O_B, and O_C, in the same situations, S_1, may respond quite differently by showing behaviors B_X, B_Y, and B_Z.

Differences to be Expected Between Management and Labor

Since actions and thoughts depend upon the organism and the situation, labor and management will not agree with each other on a good many questions. From the economic viewpoint alone, they are in different situations and have different backgrounds of experience. Labor is interested in high wages; management is interested in good profits. These goals necessarily conflict. The solution to the problem involved in the conflict hinges on the question of what constitutes a fair division of the return from goods produced. Any satisfactory adjustment requires an appreciation of the fact that this conflict originates in differences in points of view and is not a question of right or wrong. In order to preserve an economic system which permits development of such opposed interest, both parties must recognize the basis of the difference. To condemn one for not agreeing with the other is to demand that people with different past experiences and in different situations show the same behavior. This amounts to demanding an adjustment which does not naturally occur in human nature.

Other basic differences between management and labor may be caused by variances in social and economic security, pleasantness or unpleasantness of the work performed, kind of opportunities for travel and relaxation, educational backgrounds, and opportunities for satisfying the ego. A general difference in intelligence will affect ambitions, interests, and aptitudes and make one group more dependent upon leadership than the other. These and many other factors will inevitably lead to conflict between labor and management or between employer and employee. Differences between groups of people (or even between individuals) are sometimes assets, which, if properly utilized, may effect a better division of effort or a more satisfying social order.

As soon as groups with opposing interests recognize that both points of view must be acknowledged and understood, they can approach the differences as problems to be solved rather than as signs of perversity and wickedness in their opponents. Labor and management can accomplish much at a conference table with mutual respect. Failure to respect different points of view is actually a refusal to recognize the fact that experience and heredity determine the way men see things and the manner in which they react to them.

Actually, labor and management can agree on many issues despite differences in experience. Increased production can benefit both. In plants where understanding and good relations exist, labor, as well as management, has frequently contributed to the establishment of improved methods of production. Points of agreement cannot be found, however, as long as each is ready to gain its ends at the expense of the other.

We have seen that, because of different backgrounds and experience, labor and management are likely to differ in economic and social outlooks, as well as in their general points of view. Because of these differences, problems necessarily arise. The solution to these problems lies in accepting the differences and in dealing with them on a basis of mutual understanding and respect, or, when desirable, in modifying them by modifying the situations which cause them. The importance of finding the solution may be emphasized by an understanding of social responsibility.

Security against unemployment is one of the major responsibilities of industry. Unemployment is a great economic loss to society, but this loss is dwarfed when compared with the damage it does to human beings. In general, the spirit of an unemployed person is broken, and he becomes an unemployable man.[7]

A history of insecurity in work is the background for many of the differences between management and labor. It has caused labor unions to demand seniority rights and to oppose methods designed to increase efficiency in production. With proper understanding between labor and management, labor can benefit from increased production and will thereafter tend to favor improvements and may even suggest them. Many industries are learning that such cooperation makes it possible not only to survive in competitive markets but also to grow. To make adjustments too slowly, however, will draw the lines of difference more sharply and exclude innovative solutions.

Laboratory Exercise

Group Problem Solving: The Case of the Sewing-Machine Operators

Preface to Group Problem Solving

Life situations do not describe a problem, but merely indicate when something is wrong. It is up to the problem solver to locate obstacles in the life situation and then find ways to remove them. Thus life problems differ from textbook problems, because the solver must locate the problem having only the facts that are given. Much of the ability in solving life's problems depends upon the skill in locating

[7] A summary of many studies is given in a review of the literature by P. Eisenberg, and P. F. Lazarsfeld, The psychological effects of unemployment. *Psychol. Bull.*, 1938, 35, 358–390.

the basic obstacles. Some life situations permit the solver to find ways of obtaining additional information, but in the present life situation no additional information is available. In the case presented below the problem solvers will be outsiders. Outsiders do not have to live with the solution and therefore can be more objective. Nevertheless various groups may come to quite different conclusions even though the members within each group will reach agreement.

A. Reading of script.

serving room supervisor

1. Two persons will be chosen by the instructor to read the parts of Bill Wilson and Martha Johnson.— Dept Head
2. The instructor will read aloud the background of the case (Section G. 1).
3. Arrange office setting for Johnson (desk or table, and chairs) in front of class and place at angle so that both chairs half face the class.
4. Johnson takes seat behind the desk; Wilson takes the other chair. They begin reading the script:

B. Solving Wilson's problem.

1. When the reading is completed, the participants will rejoin the class.
2. The instructor will now take over and will:
   a. Divide the class into groups of four to six persons so that there will be four to six groups. Each group will serve as a consulting firm to solve the problem for the company.
   b. Request each firm to recommend no more than three specific corrective actions. No additional information can be obtained (e.g., interviewing the women). Vague solutions cannot be implemented (e.g., improve working conditions) and should be rejected; and the 30-day warning given Bill by Mrs. Johnson can be rescinded.
3. A copy of the materials (G. 1, 2, and 3) should be available to each group for reference in discussing all aspects of the problem.
4. The groups are now to discuss Wilson's problem and to agree on the three recommendations they feel most confident will produce results.
5. When about half the groups have finished, the instructor should ask the remaining groups to try to finish in the next three minutes. (About 40 minutes should be adequate.)

C. Collecting contributions from groups.

1. Each group in turn will report its first suggestion to the instructor, who will briefly record these on blackboard.
2. Continue until all groups have reported their three items.

D. Classifying solutions submitted.

1. Discuss each solution to determine whether it represents a change in the S or the O. (Training or discharging Bill is a change in the S because he is part of the situation for the operators.) Altering needs is a change in the O, but

using incentives is a change in the *S*. In case of doubt record both *S* and *O*. When the type of change is determined the instructor should place an *S* or *O* in front of the item.

2. When all solutions have been classified the instructor should count the number of *S* and *O* type changes. Invariably there are more *S*s than *O*s so the groups can be described as S-minded.

E. Classifying solutions of Wilson and Johnson.

1. List the solutions discussed by Wilson and Johnson in the interview. (The script may be reexamined).

2. Place an *S* or an *O* in front of each item. Invariably there are more *O*s than *S*s, so Wilson and Johnson are described as O-minded.

F. Solutions of outsiders vs. insiders.

1. Make a list of the causes for the differences between the group solutions and those of Wilson and Johnson.

2. In what ways do outsiders (consultants) have an advantage over insiders (Wilson and Johnson)?

3. S-type solutions are not necessarily better than O-type solutions, but a failure to consider them indicates emotional involvement.

4. If the consulting groups engaged in problem solving, what were Wilson and Johnson doing?

G. Materials for the case. *Instructor Read*

1. BACKGROUND

For the past six months Bill Wilson has been the supervisor of a sewing room of 25 women in a garment factory. The women are all union members. Until recently, his main problem was getting out enough production. Three months ago, however, all sewing machine operations were changed over from an hourly to a team piece-rate system so that production now is fairly satisfactory. Quality is now the big problem; not only are there too many rejects, but serious complaints are coming in from salesmen in the field. Since the women are not paid for rejected items, it is difficult to understand why they are not more careful.

Bill has been called in by his department head, Martha Johnson, to discuss the matter.

2. SCRIPT

MRS. J: Bill, I want to talk to you again about the kind of work your unit is turning out. What's the matter down there anyway?

BILL: Darn it, I don't know. On the old hourly rate the operators weren't turning out anything, and now on this new group piece-rate a lot of the work they do isn't any good. When I make them do it over they say I'm picking on them.

MRS. J: Steve and Jane aren't having the trouble with their operators that you do with yours.

BILL: Well, I'm not having trouble with all of mine. There is just this small group of five or six who are the real troublemakers. They all want to be finishers or anything but what they are. I've got them spotted next to my desk where I can keep an eye on them, and I tell them that I won't move them until they learn to cooperate. Even so, I'd like to see Steve or Jane or anybody else get any work out of them.

MRS. J: You're not trying to tell me that just a few women out of more than two dozen make your crew look that bad.

BILL: No, but they are the worst ones. I called all the women in the "C" and "D" teams together last week and gave them a good talking to and now they're worse than ever. Production and quality are both down.

MRS. J: I'm beginning to think that you don't have *any* that are any good.

BILL: No, that's not right. I'll take the women in my "A" team and put 'em up against any we've got. As a matter of fact, all my finishers are a pretty decent bunch. The "B" team has a couple of good workers in it and there's nothing wrong with the "E" team.

MRS. J: Yes, but their rejects are too high.

BILL: Well, that might be true, but those women certainly produce. Maybe if I can get them to slow down a little the quality will go up. It's going to make them sore, though.

MRS. J: That's *your* problem. You're not afraid of them, are you?

BILL: No, but they didn't even like it the other day when I got after them for talking on the job. Come to think of it, all that gabbing may be the reason they don't pay any attention to quality.

MRS. J: Well, tell them that if they don't stop talking you'll break up their little club. You're the boss down there, aren't you?

BILL: Well, you've kind of got me there. I hired everybody in Team "E" in one batch with the understanding that they could work together, and I hate to go back on my word.

MRS. J: Well, give them a good lecture and threaten to do it.

BILL: I know, but it's a headache and those women stick together and you can't locate the troublemaker. For example, I gave these girls in Team "C" a safety lecture the other day after one of them got her hands caught and all they did was to gripe and pick on me about everything under the sun. I never saw such a bunch of sour people before in my life.

MRS. J: What's eating them anyway? Certainly there must have been some one thing they picked on.

BILL: Oh, it was just the same old complaining about all of them wanting to be finishers. After they've been on the job a few weeks they think they know everything.

MRS. J: Sounds like you've been giving some of those new women a lot of half-baked ideas about the jobs around here. What's there to being a finisher anyway? The pay is the same.

BILL: I don't know. I think it's just a dumb idea they've got in their heads. I know the end job's no easier.

MRS. J: Was that all they griped about, or do they want us to give 'em the factory too?

BILL: No. Quite a few of them were sore because they said they couldn't make standard. Most of the women think the bogey is too hard to hit anyway.

MRS. J: I haven't heard any other complaints about it. After all, 80 isn't so high. Why should your women complain when none of the rest of them do?

Figure 2.5 / Sewing Room Layout. The five teams of women do the same kind of work, and the product moves from starters (women on extreme right of each team) to finishers (women on extreme left of each team). Each team's production and percentage of rejects is shown. The Production Standard is 80 per team and the Quality Standard is 8 per cent rejects. The problem employees are Pat, Nora, Fran, Bea, Marg, and Alma.

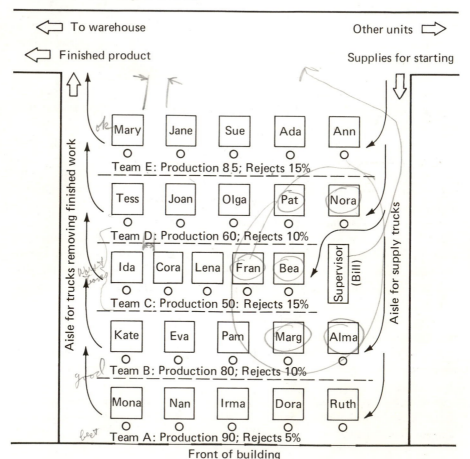

BILL: All I know is that they do. Except for Team "A" and a few others who really turn the stuff out, they're just about the worst bunch I ever saw. I don't know why I have to have all of them.

MRS. J: Bill, we've been over all this before and I'm tired of listening to you feel sorry for yourself. Either get those operators working, or we'll have to put somebody down there who knows how to run things. I don't want to be rough about it, but that's the way it is. I'll give you 30 days to get that mess straightened out, and I'll back you up on anything that seems reasonable. If you can show me some results by the end of that time you can stay; if you don't, we'll have to find something else for you. Is that clear?

BILL: I guess so. But after racking my brains like I have for the past six months I don't know what you or I or anybody else can do with those women. I've tried everything.

(End of Script)

Suggested Readings

Heider, F. *The psychology of interpersonal relations.* New York: Wiley, 1958.

Heyns, R. W. *The psychology of personal adjustment.* New York: Dryden, 1958, Ch. 1.

Krech, D., Crutchfield, R. S., and Livson, N. *Elements of psychology* (5th ed.). New York: Knopf, 1969, Part One.

Maier, R. A., and Maier, B. M. *Comparative animal behavior.* Belmont, Calif.: Brooks/Cole, 1970.

Munn, N. L. *Psychology* (4th ed.). Boston: Houghton Mifflin, 1961, Chs. 1 and 2.

Scott, W. J. *Human relations in management.* Homewood, Ill.: Richard D. Irwin, 1962.

Simon, H. A. *Models of man.* New York: Wiley, 1962.

Stagner, R. *Psychology of industrial conflict.* New York: Wiley, 1956, Chs. 1–3.

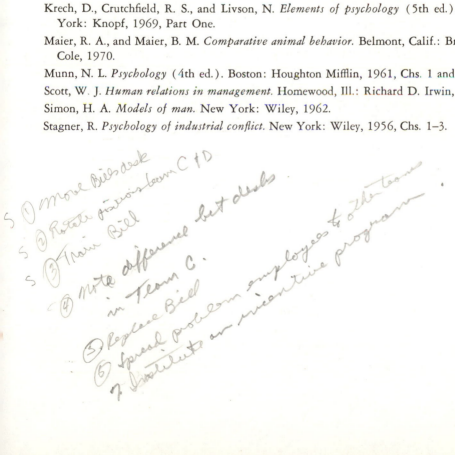

3

The Psychology
of Attitudes

Introduction

The preceding chapter considered how the behavior of an individual depends upon the manner in which he experiences the stimulus. The reactions of a factory owner may be quite different from those of a workman employed in the factory, because each experiences the factory situation in a different way; that is, the factory situation may be a different stimulus for the owner than for the worker. As a matter of fact, we cannot even suppose that all employees will agree on the nature of such a complex stimulus. Although taking all the individual variations into account is quite impossible, it is of interest to determine whether or not there are common trends and basic principles, so that some guide to an understanding of people in general may be obtained. Psychologists are aware that the attitude of the individual is an important factor in determining the way in which he will experience a stimulus situation. Therefore a knowledge of attitudes greatly contributes to an understanding of the reactions of people.

Before dealing with the general question of attitude, it is desirable to know to what extent the employee's attitude toward the factory, the owner, the supervisor, or the other employees influences his behavior on the job. The managers who are interested in obtaining a good day's work from each employee may feel that what the employees think about them or the factory is quite irrelevant. Even if a few socially minded employers or plant managers are concerned with the pleasantness of the employees' reactions, this interest is too elusive to influence employers in general. If the subject of attitude is to be a major concern of industry, it must have a direct bearing on efficiency. That it may also have a bearing on other problems we shall see when we consider its effect on labor relations, labor-union activities, social legislation, and the quality of job applicants.

A Practical Demonstration of the Effect of Attitudes on Production

The Hawthorne Study

The pioneering research program undertaken by the Western Electric Company, Hawthorne Works, Chicago, clearly demonstrated the effect of employee attitude on production.[1] The experiments were begun as an attempt to investigate the effects on production of such factors as temperature, humidity, lighting, rest pauses, and length of workday. An experimental room was designed in which a standard operation could be performed under varying conditions without disrupting the work of the remainder of the plant. The results of the preliminary studies revealed that the factors under investigation could not explain many of the results. Although the introduction of rest periods of varying lengths, rest periods with lunches, and different lengths of work periods showed trends in production which indicated their beneficial effects, a general upward trend in production also was evident. The general trend became very clear when removal of the favorable conditions did not return production to its previous level.

Analysis of the data revealed that a more favorable work attitude had gradually developed. Since the experimental room was in the charge of an observer rather than a supervisor, the employees felt more free. They talked freely with him, and they developed confidence in the company. As a consequence, conversation between employees became more frequent, their social relations more friendly, social activities were carried on outside the work situation, absenteeism declined sharply (in one case to nearly one-fourth of that shown outside the experimental room), and production rose.

Increased cooperation between employees was apparent from the fact that workers helped each other out; when one had an off-day, another made up for it. Employees set their own pace and felt free to slow down or speed up as they wished. Although part of the cooperative effort was due to the fact that pay was based upon the production of the group, this factor did not account for all the changes.

In another experiment a fall in production was associated with a rumor that a job was to be moved from the Chicago plant to New Jersey. The feeling of insecurity caused by this rumor immediately had an effect on attitudes, and production was affected even though there was no conscious intent to limit production and employees reduced their pay by doing so.

New Insights

The importance of attitude revealed in the initial experiments caused the investigation to take an entirely different turn. Emphasis was placed on improving supervision to obtain more favorable work attitudes, and an extensive program of employee interviewing was begun. Interviewers were trained to listen and to encourage free expression. They were careful not to take a stand on any issue and avoided any attempt to change an employee's point of view.

[1] Roethlisberger, F. J., and Dickson, W. J. *Management and the worker.* Cambridge, Mass.: Harvard University Press, 1939.

The interview material clearly showed that opinions about the company were influenced by home conditions (for example, indebtedness encouraged the opinion that pay was inadequate), by the employee's social position in the group in which he worked (what privileges and opportunities he had in comparison with those of others), as well as by the visible working conditions. The investigators began to realize that the factory was a social as well as a work environment and that these background conditions could not be ignored in the study of employee satisfactions and productivity.

The actual interviewing program had some immediately beneficial effects, in addition to furnishing insight and material for future investigation. Three of the important benefits are given below.

1. It allowed for correction of unfavorable work conditions. Although actual working conditions are known to management, it does not know how employees feel about these conditions. This feeling is an important factor in efficiency.

2. It caused supervisors to realize that their methods were being studied, thus stimulating them to greater effort and interest in their work. The results of the study also aided in the selection and training of interviewers and furnished valuable case material to be used as a basis for the training of supervisors.

3. The employees benefited by the "lift" they experienced. There was no question about the desirable effect of expressing their feelings and emotions freely. They saw improvements in working conditions where none had been made (e.g., improved lighting); they also saw their boss as a changed person.

To gain a further understanding of some of the social factors, a final experiment was conducted. The experimental group of workers was again segregated in the experimental room, but the departmental foreman was kept in charge. This time the segregated group did not improve its proficiency. Although it developed a social structure, its informal organization resisted change. Incentive group pay in this case elicited quite different attitudes from those found in the previous experimental group. Such values as the following became apparent.

1. You should not turn out too much work or you will be a "ratebuster."
2. You should not turn out too little work or you will be a "chiseler."
3. You mustn't tell a supervisor anything which will cause a reaction against an associate or you will be a "squealer."
4. You must not act officious or you are "for the company." According to this "code," an inspector must not act like an inspector. If one does, there are many ways in which the worker can interfere with production.

The Factory as a Society

Another interesting development was the appearance of informal organizations and social hierarchies within the experimental room. Each kind of work acquired a social level or status. Sometimes the mere location of the work (front or back of room) became a distinguishing feature, even if the work was the same. Other factors influencing the social status of the job were type of work, wages, vacations with or without pay, the kind of desk or work space, and any other feature which tended to go with one kind of work and not with another. Social meanings became attached to these distinguishing features, their meanings being derived from attitudes toward social status. The same words spoken by persons having different status had altogether different meanings. An office manager's mild criticism might be called a "bawling-out," whereas a unit supervisor's violent criticism might be passed off almost unnoticed.

The workers also formed subgroups, and the social relationships of each individual in the room were almost entirely limited to the subgroup of which he was a part. As all members of a social group tend to have a common interest, the key integrating object in this case seemed to be the inspector. Workers having the same inspector tended to become a closed group. Since the grouping was not on the basis of social status, men of varied social status appeared within each group. Although these groups developed different interests and different loyalties, the workers occupied social positions within the group according to their status. Those low in status accepted the role of errand boy and ran out for hamburgers for high-status members.

Observations of this sort demonstrated the intricate informal structure which appears in any group of workers. Whether this informal organization resists change or cooperates depends upon its nature, which, in turn, depends upon the way the situation is handled. When actions are taken by management in such a way that they conform to the wishes of the persons involved, and when situations are made more free, carry responsibilities and privileges, and increase social status, cooperative behavior is most likely to appear. In a strict atmosphere, workers have many ways in which they can curtail productivity, the most common method being limitation of each individual's production to a specified number of units per day.

Some Implications

Recognizing the importance of these complex attitudes and the social factors in the work situation, the Hawthorne plant embarked on a counseling program. The counselor had no jurisdiction over workers. The counselor could hear complaints, draw people out, help them understand themselves, and help supervisors understand many problem cases by drawing attention to certain factors in their lives or in the work situation. If this job is handled by individuals outside the department who will not betray confidences, a company can obtain a realistic picture of the state of morale in the plant, as well as reduce formation of attitudes disruptive to cooperation and understanding.

However, industrial counseling programs have not survived. Companies within the American Telephone and Telegraph system, which pioneered this approach, abandoned it after trial periods of 12 to 15 years. A variety of factors led to dissatisfaction with the program. Many supervisors did not understand its purpose and saw the counselors as a threat to their positions; top management wanted proof that the program was a paying proposition and the counselors felt this was an infringement on their right to keep professional secrets; and initiators and supporters of the program either retired or died. None of these reasons in any way refutes the values gained from the Hawthorne study; rather, the applications of these research findings must be such that they are acceptable to company management. Present trends are three: (1) to train supervisors to be more considerate and understanding; (2) to route complaints to the personnel department where some individuals are trained to counseling procedures; and (3) to expand the medical department to include psychiatric help. There continues to be a committee on Industrial Psychiatry in the American Psychiatric Association, but to date its influence has been exceedingly limited. The approach that seems to have gained most acceptance by higher management is that of improving supervision. The content of supervisory training programs includes an increasing amount of human relations material and less business content.

A Closer Examination of the Nature of Attitudes

Attitudes as a Frame of Reference

Psychologically, an attitude is a mental set. It represents a predisposition to form certain opinions. An employee is asked what he thinks about the rate of pay. What he gives for an answer is an opinion. The attitude is more general and influences the opinion. An unfavorable attitude toward the company will cause a worker to express a series of unfavorable opinions. Opinions on matters not covered by direct questions can be predicted, once a knowledge of an attitude has been gained. If something happens to change the attitude, opinions on certain topics will show a marked modification.

In a sense, an attitude is a frame of reference. How a frame of reference influences our specific views can readily be illustrated by the diagrams in Figure 3.1. In these diagrams the interpretation of the inner figure depends upon the outer frame. In *a* and *b,* the inner figures are the same, yet one appears as a diamond and the other as a square. The same geometrical figure can be either a square or diamond, depending on how it is framed. If we think of the inner figure as a given objective fact (the rate of pay, for example), the diamond as a favorable opinion (pay is good), and the square as an unfavorable opinion (pay is too low), then it follows that our opinion of the objective fact depends upon the frame of reference. This outer frame corresponds to one's attitude, which may be *liking* or *disliking* the company. The attitude toward the company as well as the rate of pay influences the opinion expressed about pay.

Attitudes, Facts, and Opinions

When attitudes are treated as a frame of reference, they become a general background of feeling against which factual events can be viewed. Thus attitudes form frames of reference which supply the unique loading of feeling and emotion to our perceptions of things and events. Usually we classify attitudes as favorable or unfavorable and relate them to groups of people. There are favorable or unfavorable attitudes toward races, political parties, social groupings, religious denominations,

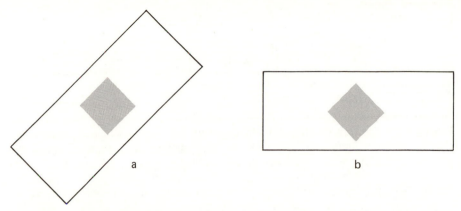

Figure 3.1 / The Influence of a Frame of Reference. Just as the frame gives specific meaning to the inner figure, so an attitude determines an opinion. A change in attitude may radically change opinions. When a person's attitude toward his company changes from an unfavorable to a favorable one, his opinions about the company's pay, training methods, and promotion opportunities tend to improve. (After K. Koffka, *Principles of Gestalt Psychology.* New York: Harcourt, Brace & World, 1935, p. 185.)

labor unions, and work groups. This means that we view members of such groups with either friendly or unfriendly eyes. Other examples of attitudes are conservatism or liberalism in economic issues, trust or suspicion of employees in general, and a feeling of superiority or inferiority to other groups of people.

Opinions, however, are specific in that they refer to an interpretation of some particular event, behavior, or object. To say that a rate of pay is unfair, that a law puts labor or management at a disadvantage, that corporation taxes are too high, that employees don't do a good day's work, that women should receive lower pay than men for a job, or that behavior on the picket line was disorderly, is to express an opinion.

Opinions represent an evaluation, not a description, of the factual evidence. They are always interpretations and in this sense the organism adds something to the objective events in question. When these interpretations have an emotional loading the framework is largely one of attitude, whereas when the interpretations lack emotional content the framework is largely intellectual. Since behavior is a response to the organism's interpretations, opinions determine behavior regardless of whether or not the opinion is justified.

Figure 3.2 diagrams the functional relationships between facts, attitudes, and opinions. It is important to note that an opinion is preceded and influenced by facts, attitudes, or both, and that although an attitude is like a generalization, it is not to be confused with a generalized conclusion. In other words, opinions do not lead to attitudes; opinions reflect attitudes and attitudes can be detected from expressed opinions.

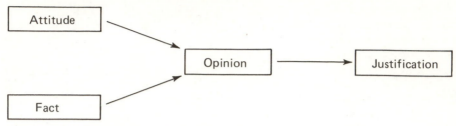

Figure 3.2 / Factors Contributing to Opinions. A given opinion represents an interpretation of facts, but the nature of this interpretation depends upon the attitude of the individual. However, when a person is asked why he has a particular opinion, he is likely to give a justification. Note that the opinion causes the justification and that the justification does not describe the cause of the opinion.

It should also be noted that justifications are the product of opinions, and should not be confused with their cause. A justification is an individual's defense of an opinion and the nature of the defense depends on the opinion to be defended. When the opinion changes, the defense changes, but a destruction of the defense does not destroy the opinion.

The relative influence of facts and attitudes in shaping opinions may vary from one extreme to another. A supervisor who has an attitude of suspicion toward employees in general interprets a workman's inactivity as *loafing.* Such an opinion could be based almost entirely on attitude and there need be little or no factual support of this interpretation. At the other extreme an opinion such as, *increased lighting will cut down our errors,* may represent an opinion influenced almost entirely by facts.

Opinions based largely on facts offer no problem. Such opinions change readily when conditions or facts are altered. Insofar as opinions are based upon attitudes, they constitute a particular problem because unfavorable attitudes can continue even after the facts have been corrected. The suspicious supervisor who accuses a worker of loafing will not change his opinion even if he finds the worker has completed his work. Instead he will watch for a new instance of loafing.

What Attitudes Do

Attitudes Determine Meanings

Disagreements over the nature of a given set of facts are possible because attitude influences the way the facts are experienced. Our various prejudices offer many illustrations of attitudes that determine the meanings which facts may assume. The actual facts which conflict with the prejudice are rationalized to fit with the general attitude, this rationalization protecting the attitude from change. The following excerpt describes how people and racial prejudices react to factual information about Mr. Miller, who is Jewish:

If Mr. Miller succeeds in business, that "proves" that "Jews" are "smart"; if Mr. Johansen succeeds in business, it only proves that Mr. Johansen is smart. If Mr. Miller fails in business, it is alleged that he nevertheless has "money salted away somewhere." If Mr. Miller is strange or foreign in his habits, that "proves" that "Jews don't assimilate." If he is thoroughly American—that is, indistinguishable from other natives—he is "trying to pass himself off as one of us." If Mr. Miller fails to give to charity, that is because "Jews are tight"; if he gives generously, he is "trying to buy his way into society." If Mr. Miller lives in the Jewish section of town, that is because "Jews are so clannish"; if he moves to a locality where there are no other Jews, that is because "they try to horn in everywhere." In short, Mr. Miller is automatically condemned, no matter who he is or what he does.[2]

In this instance the meaning of the behavior is largely determined by the attitude, since opposite behaviors (facts) were given similar (bad) meanings. The degree to which meanings are determined by attitudes varies, but the meanings and importance of things are always influenced by attitudes. We should not dismiss the above distortions of meaning by calling the person prejudiced or ignorant. Prejudice is another fellow's unfavorable attitude. To have attitudes is human. Criticizing people for having prejudice causes defensive behavior and increases their rationalizations.

How do attitudes influence behaviors on the job? A particular manager, Mr. Brown, believes that business gives jobs to people and that people ought to be appreciative and give a full day's work in return for a full day's pay. Another manager, Ms. White, believes that business needs employees to get its job done and that it is her job to build up a good team. Now we present Mr. Brown and Ms. White with the following set of facts:

Labor turnover has increased 30 per cent in the last two years.
Tardiness and absenteeism are greater for women under 20 than for those 30 or over.
Employees resent being told that they cannot use company phones for personal calls.
Nearly 50 per cent of the employees are from one to five minutes late when returning from their rest pauses.

The reader need only imagine himself to be Mr. Brown and Ms. White in turn to realize the difference in meaning these facts have for them. It also goes without saying that their subsequent behaviors would be influenced by these meanings.

Attitudes Reconcile Contradictions

Many people hold what appear to be conflicting opinions. Such apparent contradictions in thinking are not always due to lack of intelligence, as is frequently supposed. Rather, they are made possible by the development of certain attitudes. With the proper attitude as a background, intelligent people can reconcile what to others are obvious contradictions. It is possible, for example, for one person to

[2] Hayakawa, S. I. *Language in thought and action.* New York: Harcourt, 1939, pp. 142–143.

hold any of the following pairs of opinions, while another person will see them as contradictions:

1*a*. "I'm saving enough money so that I'll have a good income when I retire."
 b. "I'm underpaid and can't live the way someone in my position should."
2*a*. "A person ought to be put in his place if he does the wrong thing."
 b. "My boss had no business making a fuss over the small oversight I made."
3*a*. "I started smoking when I was sixteen."
 b. "My boy is only a junior in high school and he's too young to smoke."
4*a*. "Responsibility helps a person grow up."
 b. "The trouble with employees today is that they won't take orders."

It is possible for people to hate religion and yet give money to the church. They may feel no conflict, but others might accuse them of inconsistency.[3] So often contradictions are in the eyes of the beholder.

When we recognize that many of our beliefs are based on attitude, we are likely to react more reasonably because we do not suffer from righteous indignation. I can be tolerant of the worker's point of view if I know that we are both prejudiced. If each of us insists he is right, we merely become more prejudiced.

When a supervisor characterizes a work stoppage as loafing, while the worker considers it resting, the difference in meaning is one based on difference in position. When a manager thinks a certain employee is the logical one to be transferred, will that employee accept the reasons? These are important everyday problems in industry, and the one cannot logically prove to the other that his interpretation is the right one. Rather, the cause of the difference (that is, the attitude) must be altered if a meeting of minds is to occur.

Similar to attitudes which give rise to opinions of superiority are the attitudes which differentiate opinions concerning in- and out-groups. Persons who belong to one social group (union, church, or even race) are judged differently from those outside that group. The differential attitude toward the out-group is not so unfavorable as it would be toward an inferior group; nevertheless, sympathy and tolerance tend to be denied to the outsider. It takes less evidence to prove that a person outside the group is incapable of performing his duties or unworthy of help and protection than it does to prove the same things about members of the group. Loyalties and prejudices are frequently in-group and out-group attitudes, respectively, and although they are prevalent and normal, they must be listed as sources of error in arriving at objectively sound conclusions.[4]

Attitudes Organize Facts

It is difficult to view a set of facts without grouping or organizing them in a certain way. A list of words, such as *bottle, glassware, noise, alcohol,* tends to become

---

[3] Festinger, L. *Conflict, decision, and dissonance.* Stanford, Calif.: Stanford University Press, 1964.
[4] Kiesler, C., Collins, B., and Miller, N. *Attitude change: A critical analysis of theoretical approaches.* New York: Wiley, 1969.

organized to suggest a party. The party scene thus becomes a frame of reference into which the above elements are fitted and the words derive meaning from the relationships. The bottle then receives a shape and a content which go beyond the facts given. This is Stage 1 of Fig. 3.3. If we next add *men in white coats* and *blondes* to the list, waiters and party girls are perceived. These items serve to

Figure 3.3 / Attitudes Organize Facts. The same words experienced as elements of a party have a different meaning when experienced as elements of a laboratory. Stages 1 and 3 represent minor changes in meanings caused by additional items, but the addition of incongruous words in Stage 4 requires a reorganization with a resultant change in meanings of the initial items. Shifts in attitude are equivalent to reorganizations.

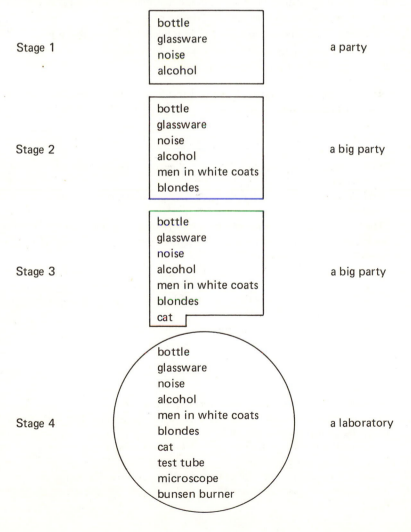

reinforce the party and make it larger as in Stage 2. The addition of the word *cat* to the list might cause a bit of difficulty at first, but by some adjustments in the meaning of cat or the frame of reference, the cat can be reconciled as belonging to the group of items. In Stage 3 the frame is modified to include the cat, but the change is not elegant—more of a patch job. Once the adjustment is made the party scene suffers no dissonance. However, if we add such items as *test tube, microscope,* and *bunsen burner* to the list it is possible that a sudden reorganization might occur, in that the party scene might change into a laboratory. With the laboratory frame of reference all of the meanings change. The shape and content of the bottle change, the glassware is different, the noise is different in volume and kind, the men change from waiters to scientists, the blondes become scientists and technicians, and the alcohol which livened the party now has a dead cat preserved in it. This shift in meaning came suddenly and the conflict in meanings caused by the last entries became reconciled by the new frame of reference.

A female employee who for some time has been receiving the top rate of pay for her job classification goes to her supervisor to complain about her wages. During the interview she makes the following statements:

1. "The only pay increases that I have had in ten years are those where the top rate has been raised. Everyone gets those increases. I think that I should get an increase once in a while that isn't due to the top being raised."
2. "A woman with a good attendance record should be given an increase for that reason alone."
3. "New women come into the office and they get increases whether they are any good or not."
4. "Lots of women working for the company get more money than I do and I'm just as good as they are."
5. "There is a woman who works for another company who gets 170 dollars a week and this company is making lots of money now and if others can pay those salaries so can this company."
6. "I have had to fight for every raise I ever got and that's what I'm doing now."
7. "You brought a new woman into our unit the other day. If you had given us women in the unit a raise then we would work harder and you wouldn't need to hire the new one."
8. "If there's no more money for me here why don't you transfer me? They have lots of good jobs in other departments and they don't work as hard as I do."
9. "If I were a pretty woman you'd give me an increase."
10. "You don't want me here. You just want young women. I'm getting old so I guess that I should get out."
11. (Crying:) "No one pays any attention to me any more."
12. "All my troubles seem to have started since my father died last year. Since then things haven't gone good for me."
13. "If I could find another woman to live with me maybe things would be better, but I can't find anyone I like."
14. "I won't be working very long anyway. I'm buying a 50 dollar savings bond every week and that has mounted up and with my pension I can get along all right."

At the outset these statements appear both unreasonable and unrelated. However, toward the end of the interview, the reader may have concluded that this woman is lonesome. Notice how this new frame of reference (looking at the employee as a lonesome individual rather than as a grouchy old woman) causes all the statements to make a new kind of sense. The talk about a pay raise that others don't get now communicates a need for personal attention and no longer is at odds with the problem of giving this woman an individual pay raise when she is receiving the ceiling rate.

In industry, such terms as equal production and "less friendly" when applied to a disliked group of older female employees might mean "less satisfactory" because despite all their experience they are no better than the younger ones, and in addition they are hard to get along with. With a friendly attitude the words might mean "highly satisfactory" because the older females do just as well as the younger ones despite their age and, in addition, they are more businesslike and less prone to socializing on the job. The frame of reference will determine the meaning the terms are given. Conflicting interpretations of the same facts are common in arguments.

Attitudes Select Facts

In addition to organizing facts, an attitude also selects them. From a mass of objective information, a person tends to select the facts that favor or are more consistent with his attitude, and to ignore or discount those opposed. An attitude is analogous to a filter or a screen: certain materials can pass through it while others are rejected. For example, persons with a friendly attitude toward a race, a religion, a political party, or a company will select from the known facts only those which are congruent with their attitude and will ignore those which are not. They then use these selected facts to prove the correctness of their attitudes. In turn, persons with an unfriendly attitude may select from the same body of information but tend to utilize only the facts that support their point of view.

An experiment involving simulated conflicts in attitude showed that people select the facts that support their artificially imposed attitude[5] and use those facts as reasons for the attitude. Even when one of the persons is cued to be a good listener and to be understanding rather than persuasive, selection still occurs. Because biased persons are often unreasonable and tend to mention only the facts that support their position, it is difficult for others to remain neutral. As a result, in a short time they interpose the neglected facts. Thus they select the facts supporting the opposite position and behave like biased individuals. In this way a prejudiced person traps a reasonable one into behaving at his level.

Disagreements and failures to communicate in organizations are frequently not merely due to conflicting information but to conflicting meanings resulting from

---

[5] Maier, N. R. F., and Lansky, L. Effect of attitude on selection of facts. *Personnel Psychol.* 1957, *10*, 293–303; Mills, J., Aromon, E., and Robinson, H. Selectivity in exposure to information. *J. abnorm. soc. Psychol.*, 1959, *59*, 250–253.

differing points of view or conflicting goals. It is important to realize that another person's attitude is not effectively changed by an opponent's selection of facts.

The Measurement of Attitudes

In order to analyze scientifically the factors that influence attitudes, it is necessary to obtain some objective measurement of attitudes. Some discussion of techniques will further clarify the nature of attitudes, as well as exemplify methods which have been used in industry.

The simplest method of measuring attitudes is merely to count the number of people who are for or against something. This approach does not measure the degree of feeling in any individual but registers only the direction of the attitude. When groups of people are studied, however, the number of people having a given attitude is some index of its strength. This is essentially what the Gallup Poll accomplishes in its "America Speaks" analysis. It is possible, however, that, a large number of people might be mildly opposed to something but would not be greatly disturbed if they had to accept it; or a smaller group might be strongly opposed to it and its adoption might cause a violent minority reaction. In such cases the number of people holding an opinion would not accurately indicate its actual social significance. To make possible a study of the strength of attitudes in the individual, more refined instruments of measurement are needed. We have one such instrument in the *attitude scale,* devised by Thurstone.[6]

In making up such a scale, a large number of statements bearing on any topic on which attitude is to be measured are collected. These statements are then experimentally analyzed to see that they are not ambiguous and that they are diagnostic in representing a position for or against the issue involved. Only the diagnostic items are retained, each of which is assigned a scale value between zero and 12. Those statements which strongly favor the issue receive a high (or low) value, those strongly opposed receive a low (or high) value, and those in between are given intermediate values. All these scale values are based upon previous experimentation and are arrived at objectively. The actual scale may consist of 40 or even fewer statements. An example of a scale used to measure attitudes of employees is shown in Table 3.1. Note that the degree of favorableness of each statement declines as one goes down the list.

To measure the attitudes of a group of people, one has each person place a plus sign in front of all items which express his sentiments, and a minus sign in front of all others. A person's score is the average of the scale value of all items checked with a plus sign. If a person's score is five, he has a more favorable attitude on the subject tested than a person who has a score of three. Low and high scores indicate the two extremes in attitude.

[6] Thurstone, L. L., and Chave, E. J. *The measurement of attitude.* Chicago: University of Chicago Press, 1929; Selltiz, C., Jahoda, M., Deutsch, M., and Cook, S. W. *Research methods in social relations.* New York: Holt, 1959, pp. 357–383; Clarke, A. V., and Grant, D. L. Application of a factorial method in selecting questions for an employee attitude survey. *Personnel Psychol.,* 1961, *14,* 131–139.

Statement	Scale Value
I think this company treats its employees better than any other company does	10.4
If I had to do it over again, I'd still work for this company	9.5
They don't play favorites in this company	9.3
A person can get ahead in this company if he tries	8.9
I have as much confidence in the company physician as I do in my own doctor	8.7
The company is sincere in wanting to know what its employees think about it	8.5
A wage-incentive plan offers a just reward for the faster worker	7.9
On the whole, the company treats us about as well as we deserve	7.4
I think a person should go to the hospital for even a scratch as it may stop blood poisoning	6.3
I believe accidents will happen, no matter what you do about them	5.4
The workers put as much over on the company as the company puts over on them	5.1
The company does too much welfare work	4.4
Soldiering on the job is increasing	4.1
I do not think applicants for employment are treated courteously	3.6
I believe many good suggestions are killed by the bosses	3.2
My boss gives all the breaks to his lodge and church friends	2.9
I think the company goes outside to fill good jobs instead of promoting people who are here	2.5
You've got to have "pull" with certain people around here to get ahead	2.1
In the long run this company will "put it over" on you	1.5
The pay in this company is terrible	1.0
An honest person fails in this company	0.8

From R. S. Uhrbrock, Attitudes of 4430 employees. *J. soc. Psychol.*, 1934, *5*, 365–377.

Table 3.1 / Statements Used in Uhrbrock's Scale for Measuring Attitude of Employees toward Their Company

Likert later developed a more simplified method.[7] He asked people to place a check on a five-point scale below a number of statements concerning a certain topic. One end of the scale was labeled "strongly against," the other "strongly for," and the middle is labeled "undecided." Each statement required only one judgment, and ambiguity in expression was carefully avoided. In this type of scale, the person rates or judges the intensity or strength of his own attitudes. By using a number of statements on the same subject and giving an intensity value for each, Likert obtained varying scores. The total score, then, represented strength of attitude. The virtue of this rating method is its simplicity.

In measuring attitudes one actually explores a set of opinions; when such a set leans in a particular direction (favorable or unfavorable) they indicate the influence of the attitude. Thus the attitude score is derived from measures of opinions on a limited feeling area.

Projective approaches to attitude measurement are sometimes used when the

[7] Likert, R. A technique for the measurement of attitudes. *Arch. Psychol.*, 1932, *22*, 55.

respondents are unable to describe their feelings accurately, when they are hesitant about expressing themselves, or when they may withhold cooperation if the topic under consideration is made explicit. Such approaches encourage spontaneity and freedom of expression since they do not require people to talk about themselves or state their feelings and views directly.[8] Among the projective methods most frequently used are techniques in which the respondent is asked to complete sentences,[9] arguments, or descriptions of people who would behave in specified ways. Further refinement of these approaches to attitude measurement is necessary, as are precautions in the use of such data. However, they appear to show considerable promise and have been successfully employed in market research.[10]

Industry cannot afford to make radical changes which backfire. Since attitude scales can furnish sufficiently delicate indices of changes in attitude, their use will indicate unfavorable trends, and thus make possible the prevention of open violence or mass work stoppages.

Experimental Findings

Typical Results

Attitude measurement has revealed that a single experience such as a movie can sometimes alter attitudes on racial,[11] social, and economic questions.[12] Other findings have shown that (1) unemployment disturbs former religious and economic values;[13] (2) radical students are more inclined to be highly intelligent than nonradical ones, despite the fact that children of professional classes tend to be conservatives;[14] (3) a speech given in person is more effective in influencing attitudes than the same speech given by radio, although the latter is more effective than reading the same speech;[15] (4) judgments made by individuals in two-person groups were more strongly influenced by the other member when he was a stranger than when he was a friend or acquaintance;[16] (5) support for civil liberties is significantly associated with the increase of years of higher education;[17] (6) beliefs can be changed as a result of posthypnotic suggestion;[18] (7) shifts in attitude,

[8] Selltiz, Jahoda, Deutsch, and Cook, *op. cit.*

[9] Greene, J. E., Sr., and Greene, J. E., Jr. Illustration uses of the "incomplete" sentences technique in investigating certain attitudes of middle management personnel. *Personnel Psychol.,* 1961, *14,* 305–316.

[10] M. Haire. Projective techniques in marketing research. *J. Marketing,* 1950, *14,* 649–656.

[11] Thurstone, L. L. The measurement of social attitudes. *J. abnorm. soc. Psychol.,* 1931, *26,* 249–264.

[12] Rosenthal, S. P. Changes in socio-economic attitudes under radical motion picture propaganda. *Arch. Psychol.,* 1934, *25* (166), 46.

[13] *Ibid.*

[14] Hall, O. M. Attitudes and unemployment. *Arch. Psychol.,* 1934, *25* (165), 65.

[15] Wilke, W. H. An experimental comparison of the speech, the radio, and the printed page as propaganda devices. *Arch. Psychol.,* 1934, *25* (169), 1–32.

[16] Ex, J. The nature of the relation between two persons and the degree of their influence on each other. *Acta Psychol.,* 1960, *17,* 39–54.

[17] Selvin, H. C., and Hagstrom, W. O. Determinants of support for civil liberties. *Brit. J. Sociol.,* 1960, *11,* 51–73.

[18] Rosenberg, M. J. Cognitive reorganization in response to the hypnotic reversal of attitudinal affect. *J. Pers.,* 1960, *28,* 39–63.

when they occur, often go from negative to positive agreement without an intermediate stand in the neutral position;[19] (8) radical attitudes are more difficult to modify than conservative attitudes.

Social psychologists are devoting considerable study to the means by which attitudes are developed and by which they can be changed.[20] Among the more interesting current formulations is Festinger's theory of cognitive dissonance. This approach holds that a person who knows various items of information which do not fit together psychologically (for him) will attempt to render these dissonant items more consistent in a variety of ways.[21] In other words, when our experiences do not agree with expectations we have accumulated throughout a lifetime, we try to reduce the inconsistency. We may change our attitudes or opinions; in fact, we may even go so far as to distort our perceptions or the information we receive regarding the world about us.

One phenomenon, illustrated in a variety of experiments, shows how attitudes may change once an irrevocable choice has been made between two attractive alternatives. In this instance, we tend to experience an increase in the desirability of the chosen alternative, a decrease in the attractiveness of the rejected alternative, or both. In this fashion we make our attitudes toward the alternatives more consistent or less dissonant with our choice than would be the case if the alternatives continued to be viewed as equally attractive.

Attitudes Based upon Information

Much of the research on attitude and opinion change utilizes topics of an unemotional nature. A topic such as "Should Puerto Rico be admitted to the union?" would elicit little emotional response from most people. Thus propaganda and logic presented for or against such an opinion might generate opinions having no deep-seated emotional investment. Attitudes developed by rational appeals might successfully be reversed by additional facts or logic.[22]

Generally speaking, attempts to change attitudes (measured before and after exposure to propaganda) are temporary and dependent upon the credibility of the propaganda.[23] Attitudes already held are more easily strengthened than changed by supplying more information.[24]

When participants are required to write their own argument on an issue (e.g., Puerto Rico should be the fifty-first state) rather than reading a supplied argument,

[19] Hall, *op. cit.*

[20] Katz, D. (Ed.). Attitude change. *Pub. Opin. Quart.*, 1960, *24* (2), 380.

[21] Festinger, L. *A theory of cognitive dissonance.* Evanston, Ill.: Row, Peterson, 1957; and Cognitive dissonance. *Scientific Amer.*, 1962, *207,* 93–98, 100, 102.

[22] Greenwald, A. G., Brock, T. C., and Ostrom, T. M. (Eds.). *Psychological foundations of attitudes.* New York: Academic Press, 1968; Greenwald, A. G. When does role playing produce attitude change? Toward an answer. *J. Person. soc. Psychol.*, 1970, *16,* 214–219; Rhine, R. J., and Severance, L. J. Ego-involvement discrepancy, source of credibility, and attitude change. *J. Person. soc. Psychol.*, 1970, *16,* 175–190.

[23] Whittaker, J., and Meade, R. Retention of opinion change as a function of the differential source credibility: A cross-cultural study. *Internatl. J. Psychol.*, 1968, *3,* 103–108.

[24] Haskins, J. B. Factual recall as a measure of advertising effectiveness. *J. Advertising Research*, 1966, *6,* 2–8; Klapper, J. T. *The effects of mass communication.* New York: Free Press, 1960.

opinion change is greater and more persistent, thus demonstrating the value of participation.[25] Another study showed that expressed opinions are more resistant to change than those privately held.[26] Thus, committing oneself tends to make opinions more rigid.

Inducing fear is more effective in influencing behavior change than attitude change, but whether mild or strong fear induction is more effective depends upon a number of variables.[27] Attitudes toward dental hygiene are influenced more by mild than intense fear appeals whereas information regarding the loss of eyesight, which induced relatively high fear levels, was effective in influencing behavior.[28] In the light of the present evidence, no general conclusions can be formulated.

Attitudes Based upon Group Affiliation

It is impossible to determine all the factors that influence formation of attitudes. Data collected from public opinion polls indicate that opinions vary with a number of factors. A striking difference in political and economic opinions can be obtained when respondents are grouped according to income, age, geographical location, size of community, amount of education, party affiliation, and religious denomination. The influence of family is apparent when one observes that most of us belong to the church of our parents and more of us hold political affiliations similar to those of our parents than different from them.

If Mr. Jones were accurately to describe why he is a Republican, he may include among his reasons that it is because he has a good income, lives in a prosperous section of the country, is beyond middle age, comes from a Republican home, wishes to identify himself with the Republican status group, and so on. But such reasons are seldom given. Mr. Jones is more likely to say that he votes Republican because that party has the best candidates, the best program for developing the country, the best foreign policy, and the like. When a person is asked about his opinions, he does not mention an attitude as a factor, but instead presents a set of justifications. This confusion between cause and justification was illustrated in the diagram shown in Figure 3.2.

Because people frequently give justifications for their opinions, arguing (introducing new facts and appealing to logic) has little effect on opinions and attitudes. If our mythical Mr. Jones were to suffer a great financial loss or move to another section of the country, these factors could do more to alter his frame of reference than a change in his party's foreign or domestic policy. For this same reason it is wiser to analyze the causes of communism rather than spend time developing argu-

---

[25] Watts, W. Relative persistence of opinion change induced by active compared to passive participation. *J. Person. soc. Psychol.,* 1967, *5,* 4–15.

[26] Gerard, H. B. Conformity and commitment to the group. *J. abnorm. soc. Psychol.,* 1964; *68,* 209–211.

[27] Karlins, M., and Abelson, H. I. *Persuasion: How opinions and attitudes are changed.* New York: Springer, 1970; Triandis, H. C. *Attitude and attitude change.* New York: Wiley, 1971.

[28] Kraus, S., El-Assal, E., and De Fleur, M. Fear-threat appeals in mass communication: An apparent contradiction. *Speech Mono.,* 1966, *33,* 23–29.

ments against it in an attempt to foster healthy attitudes toward our own form of government.

It is clear that the various factors given above as causes of attitudes indicate some kind of experience. Furthermore, they all suggest some kind of group membership,[29] be this membership a loose one, such as community, or a close one, such as family. All begin to fit together if it is assumed that attitudes are acquired from the group with which an individual identifies himself. Since this identification occurs early in life, it follows that children will have opinions on religious problems, on the relative capabilities of a party's political candidates, and on racial injustices long before they learn the facts. Asch[30] points out that one reason why group values and attitudes are adopted is because members feel that the group protects and promotes their interests.

Various experiments have demonstrated how people are influenced by the attitudes or opinions of others. Kelley and Woodruff found that students were more influenced in the direction of a speech heard from outside the lecture room when told that the applause stemmed from their own faculty, than when told that the applause emanated from an unknown group.[31] Moore[32] found that 50 per cent of a group of students changed their judgments about ethical matters when told (correctly or incorrectly) that the majority opinion was opposed to theirs. Information about the opinion of experts had a like effect. Similar research by Sherif[33] demonstrated that the prestige of an author influenced people's judgment of his literary contributions. Attitudes toward food purchases[34] and even confidence in the stability of business is influenced by what others think, so that we have come to realize that economic laws must be modified to incorporate psychological components.[35]

While group membership is not the sole factor in attitude formation, it is one of the more important forces, suggesting ways of influencing attitudes. It is common to find that workers' attitudes toward the company change when they are promoted from worker to union steward or supervisor.[36] It also follows that if all employees and first-line supervisors are called "hourly rated" employees, whereas higher management personnel are called "salaried," first-line supervisors develop attitudes different from those of other members of management. Classifying or grouping people is important, and often necessary, but one should recognize that in doing this, one is manipulating attitudes.

[29] Brown, J. F. *Psychology and the social order.* New York: McGraw-Hill, 1936, contains an interesting treatment of in-group and out-group attitudes.

[30] Asch, S. E. *Social psychology.* Englewood Cliffs, N.J.: Prentice-Hall, 1952, pp. 414–416.

[31] Kelley, H. H., and Woodruff, C. Member's reactions to apparent group approval of a counternorm communication. *J. abnorm. soc. Psychol.,* 1956, *52,* 67–74.

[32] Moore, H. T. The comparative influence of majority and expert opinion. *Amer. J. Psychol.,* 1921, *32,* 16–20.

[33] Sherif, M. *The psychology of social norms.* New York: Harper, 1936.

[34] Trier, H., Smith, H. C., and Shaffer, J. Differences in food buying attitudes of housewives, *J. Marketing,* 1960, *25,* 66–69.

[35] Katona, G. *Psychological analysis of economic behavior.* New York: McGraw-Hill, 1959; and Katona, G. *The powerful consumer.* New York: McGraw-Hill, 1960.

[36] Lieberman, J. The effect of changes in roles on the attitudes of role occupants. *Hum. Relat.,* 1956, *9,* 385–402.

Attitudes developed by membership in a group might be most effectively altered by a change in group membership. Thus college attendance is a crucial factor in changing attitudes.[37] Persons who conform most to group norms are least likely to be persuaded by appeals against group norms.[38]

Attitudes with Strong Emotional Investment

Attitudes against war are more resistant to change through propaganda than attitudes toward margarine as a substitute for butter. The former is likely to require an emotional investment and the latter is not.[39] Emotionally loaded attitudes resist rational and persuasive approaches and it is not uncommon for them to be strengthened rather than weakened.

Unfavorable attitudes often are developed by unhappy experiences and frustration. A single experience, such as being beaten and robbed, can develop a strong negative attitude toward crime which would resist logic. Information and social factors tend not to alter these attitudes unless they remove the source. Changes in attitudes having such origins may benefit from therapy.[40]

Individual Differences

Disregarding the cause and nature of attitudes and opinions, one might reasonably expect considerable individual variation. Women as a group have been found to be more persuasible than men,[41] but within each group differences are considerable. Authoritarian personalities are more influenced by remarks of authoritarian figures than by information booklets; for nonauthoritarian personalities, the reverse is true.[42] Persons who can be classified as creative or abstract thinkers are more inclined to seek information and are less vulnerable to persuasive appeals than concrete thinkers.[43] All things being equal, a person is most influenced when the communicator is a person like himself. Thus the type of appeal as well as the nature of the communicator determine the effectiveness of propaganda and advertising.

Summary

Since some opinions are primarily interpretations of facts, it is not surprising that such opinions will be altered by information. Attitudes developed by culture and group membership form emotional ties (e.g., security, affiliation, and loyalty) and

[37] Newcomb, T. M. *Personality and social change.* New York: Dryden, 1939.

[38] Nahemow, L., and Bennett, R. Conformity, persuasibility, and counter-normative persuasion. *Sociometry,* 1967, *30,* 14–25.

[39] Eagly, A., and Manis, M. Evaluation of message and communication as a function of involvement. *J. Person. soc. Psychol.,* 1966, *3,* 483–485.

[40] Katz, D., McClintock, C., and Sarnoff, I. The measurement of ego-defense as related to attitude change. *J. Pers.,* 1957, *25,* 465–474.

[41] Scheidel, T. Sex and persuasibility. *Speech Mono.,* 1963, *30,* 353–358.

[42] Rohrer, J., and Sherif, M. (Eds.). *Social psychology at the crossroads.* New York: Harper, 1951.

[43] Suedfeld, P., and Vernon, J. Attitude manipulation in restricted environments: Conceptual structure and the internalization of propaganda received as a reward for compliance. *J. Person. soc. Psychol.,* 1966, *3,* 586–589.

are influenced little by persuasion methods, regardless of whether the logic and facts used are accurate or misleading. The logic of feeling is different from the logic of the mind and for this reason the intellectual approach has little effect. Attitudes developed through frustration have strong emotional loadings and can influence opinions that may have no basis in fact. The way frustration develops rigid attitudes will be considered in the next chapter.

Ways to Improve Employee Opinions and Attitudes

Industrial Practices

Attitude surveys are now an accepted practice; trade magazines as well as the more technical journals frequently contain reports of significant findings. Although surveys made in different companies often yield similar results, each company must make its own survey to be convinced of the need for improvement. Survey findings can open the door to correcting unpopular practices, but they must be properly reported and interpreted to management. One approach involves management personnel in analysis of survey data to facilitate both communication and adequate use of findings at all levels within the organization.[44] A finding suggesting that employees want to know where they stand with their bosses should not be implemented with an order to supervisors informing them that each employee is to be told "where he stands."[45]

Attitude surveys measure symptoms, not causes. Unless properly interpreted, attitude and opinion polls can be misleading. Recently a large corporation investigated some of their experiences with attitude surveys and the meaning behind the resulting data.[46] In one work group studied, employees registered unfavorable opinions about their pay schedule. From the findings, one logical conclusion might be that they were dissatisfied with their pay rates. After some carefully planned group discussions aimed at identifying and resolving problems evidenced by the survey, the manager learned that employees were not dissatisfied with their pay. Rather, they were critical of the way in which a related procedure was handled. In this group, merit interviews and salary changes were annual, but not for all employees at the same time. Some were scheduled for the first of the year, the rest at midyear. Employees not interviewed at a given period felt conspicuous by their exclusion from the interview routine, and were distressed that others in the office might make baseless inferences about their competence and merit. The group wanted the routine changed to provide for interviewing all employees during each period, despite the fact that only part of the group would be scheduled for increases. This change was made, and the problem disappeared. The effectiveness of this problem-solving was confirmed one year later when another attitude survey reflected no criticism of pay matters in this group.

[44] Mann, F., and Likert, R. The need for research on the communication of research results. In R. N. Adams and J. J. Preiss (Eds.), *Human organization research*. Homewood, Ill.: Dorsey, 1960, pp. 57–66.

[45] Maier, N. R. F. *The appraisal interview.* New York: Wiley, 1958.

[46] Private communication from John J. Hayes.

In another example, a work group was critical of their supervisor on a survey question about his "interest in his employees." Confronted with such data, a supervisor may become defensive and rationalize the criticism. Even if he accepts the data, he can usually think of a host of possible explanations: perhaps he doesn't always say good morning, or smile enough, or listen well, or dispense enough compliments. The evidence suggests that such guessing is futile. In this case, the supervisor was using group methods of identifying and solving problems reflected by the survey. The real problem identified by the group was a unique form of insecurity. The group's work was in the nature of a service to others, somewhat intangible, and difficult to assess in terms of measurable results. The employees generally worked alone and on their own, so they had little way of knowing how they were doing. They felt unsure about their performance and competence. They wanted more personal attention from the supervisor in observing performance, coaching, and counseling on job techniques. The final decision also included provisions for mutual assistance among the group members, with emphasis on having senior employees help newer ones become more proficient.

In contrast to these cases, managers usually react to attitude surveys by taking the results too literally, or by acting on guesses about their meaning. Countless water coolers have been installed, parking lots assigned, procedures adopted, procedures revised, decisions made, decisions rescinded, dollars spent, facilities shuffled, and jobs reorganized on the basis of *assumptions* drawn from survey results that had little or nothing to do with the real problems. Attitude surveys reveal only that something is wrong in the work place; they don't reveal what it is.

Surveys reveal the importance of the immediate supervisor as well as higher levels of management in influencing employee attitudes.[47] Regardless of whether or not the attitudes are justified, they influence the behavior of those holding them. That attitudes about the supervisor are influenced by his behavior is indicated by the considerable similarity of attitudes among persons working for the same supervisor on different jobs, but the little similarity between those of persons working for different supervisors on the same job.[48] The objective of supervisory training programs is to develop management skills that promote employee satisfaction as well as productivity. These objectives will be treated in detail in Chapters 5 and 6.

The interview method, when properly handled, is highly effective in detecting the general attitude of specific employees, even though it is not reliable for obtaining factual information. In order that the interview may yield an accurate expression of attitude, the interviewer must shape his inquiry to harmonize with the interests of the person he is examining. The sharing of attitudes in an industrial interview presupposes the presence of a common goal. Obviously, the employee will not

[47] Likert, R. *New patterns of management.* New York: McGraw-Hill, 1961; Campbell, J. P., Dunnette, M. D., Lawler, E. E., III, and Weick, K. E., Jr. *Managerial behavior, performance, and effectiveness.* New York: McGraw-Hill, 1970.

[48] Campbell, D. B. Relative influence of job and supervision on shared worker attitudes. *J. appl. Psychol.,* 1971, *55,* 521–525.

express honest opinions if he runs the risk of putting himself at a disadvantage by volunteering certain attitudes, or if he feels he is being cross-examined. The interview is particularly valuable in that it takes the whole individual into account and gives a general picture of his state of mind.[49]

Changing Facts to Improve Opinions

In one company we examined the records of 13 employees who were regarded as qualified for supervisory positions but had been rejected because of their hostile attitudes toward the company. All had been told by their supervisors that if they improved their attitudes they could be promoted. However, none showed an improvement. In eight cases, the attitudes seemed to stem from the experience of having been bypassed for promotion some years before and in five instances the source of the attitude could not be traced. Since the goal of promotion did not change attitudes, we decided that changing the facts might. The eight whose attitude seemed to be related to lack of promotion were promoted. All became above average supervisors with improved attitudes.

In another company a bell was the signal for a rest pause; it was a source of disturbance because employees, many of whom were just out of high school where class bells had been used, saw it as regimentation. Exchanging the bell for chimes reduced this unfavorable reaction. If employees grumble about food in the company restaurant, complain of the heat, or call their jobs boring, it is possible to effect changes in the situation which will cause such opinions to become more favorable. However, employees with unfavorable attitudes can always find something to criticize, and one must carefully study the opinions expressed by employees in interviews, polls, or suggestion boxes before introducing reforms. Since the boss is an important factor in shaping employee attitudes, any changes in supervisory behavior or management procedures represent ways of influencing attitudes by changing the facts.

Influencing the Experience of Group Membership

Since attitudes are greatly influenced by an experience of belonging to a group, anything a company does to make employees feel they are a vital part of the organization should improve attitudes toward the company. The following are a few of many possibilities:

1. Stock purchase or profit-sharing plans properly administered.
2. Concern for the welfare of employees as evidenced by clean rest rooms, medical aid, concern for job satisfaction, and so on.
3. Setting up regulations and benefits that apply similarly to all employees.
4. Making employees feel they are group members.
   These possibilities are treated in detail in Chapters 5 and 6.

[49] Bingham, W. V., Moore, B. V., and Gustad, J. W. *How to interview* (4th rev. ed.). New York: Harper, 1957; Kahn, R. L., and Cannell, C. F. *The dynamics of interviewing.* New York: Wiley, 1952.

Use of Role Playing

In one company an employee was suspended by his immediate supervisor (on the advice of the superintendent) pending the return of the manager from an executive training program. The employee had an unusually long list of demerits, ranging from excessive tardiness to frequent violations of regulations, including safety. He had received three written warnings but the supervisor was reluctant to dismiss him because the union usually came to his rescue.

The custom in case of a dismissal is to have a meeting in which union and management representatives hear the company's case, then hear the employee's version or defense. On this occasion the manager on his return handled the meeting somewhat differently. He asked the three supervisors involved to take the role of union members while the three union representatives were asked to take the role of management. The case was then heard. Each group of three persons then held private discussions and each returned with a unanimous recommendation. The union representatives, in the role of management, recommended dismissal; the supervisors, in the role of union representatives, recommended full pay for the suspension period and one more chance.

The manager then asked the six participants to return to their real-life roles and try to agree on an action. With little difficulty the group agreed the employee should be clearly informed that he had one more chance and that he would be discharged after the next infraction. He was to receive his pay for the suspension period.

When the employee learned of the action he resigned. It appears that when he found the union no longer was willing to get him out of trouble he lost interest in pursuing his trouble-making activities. The manager felt the role playing laid the groundwork for improved communication between the union representative and the supervisors.

Role playing is used in various kinds of training situations, one of its functions being that of developing attitudes[50] consistent with the training objectives. In these instances individuals simulate real-life situations[51] and trainees are placed in either superior or subordinate positions to give them the experience of approaching and viewing problems from different positions.

Use of Listening Skills

In the case of the employee who expressed dissatisfaction with her wages (page 48), the real problem was loneliness. The supervisor discovered this state of mind because he was understanding and listened to the various ideas and feelings the employee expressed. Because he did not challenge any of her statements, she was able to move from one feeling to another until she finally realized her prob-

---

[50] King, B. T., and Janis, I. L. Comparison of the effectiveness of improvised versus non-improvised role-playing in producing opinion changes. *Hum. Relat.*, 1956, *9*, 177–186.

[51] Lawshe, C. H., Bolda, R. A., and Brune, R. L. Studies in management training evaluation: II. The effects of exposure in role playing. *J. appl. Psychol.*, 1959, *43*, 287–293.

lem. Arguing has just the opposite effect; progress in the expression of different things is blocked because each point is challenged. Then one begins to express only points that are safe, instead of points that are important.

The fact that the employee felt free to express her feelings led her to clarify them, and with this clarification there was a change in her feelings and in the attitudes associated with the feelings. The understanding attitude of the supervisor also made the employee feel she was being accepted and was consequently less alone in the world.

Evidence of an attitude change on her part was revealed by the fact that she thanked the supervisor for the visit and left in a positive frame of mind. Furthermore, she took steps to correct her situation: she changed her residence in order to live with 14 other women; she started attending company parties; she became friendly with the younger women and was soon accepted by them. All these improvements were not due to the interview itself, but depended upon the subsequent behavior of the supervisor, for he also altered his attitude as a result of the interview. Seeing the employee as a lonesome person caused him to pay more attention to her. He made it a point to visit her desk once a day, insisted that she go to company parties, and gave her jobs to do as a special favor to him. His altered behavior represented a change in facts.

Reference to listening as a means of changing attitudes has already been mentioned in connection with the Hawthorne study.[52] More and more this skill is being recognized as a first step in improving adjustment[53] and an essential technique in interviewing.[54] These topics will be discussed more fully in Chapters 4 and 20.

The group setting may offer even better opportunities to listen, particularly when members agree and support one another. The gripe session is an example. A supervisor will find that if he holds a group meeting for the sole purpose of hearing complaints the members will become less hostile and a solvable problem may be discovered.

Use of Discussion Skills

Closely related to the use of listening is employment of the discussion method. Properly conducted discussions create an opportunity for members of a group to bring their feelings out into the open. In this way attitudes toward fair distribution of overtime, favoritism, seniority privileges, introduction of changes, the abuse of coffee privileges, and so on, can be expressed. In addition to clarifying attitudes and correcting some misunderstandings discussions also introduce group membership forces. An employee who feels he is not getting a fair deal on overtime may find his needs for extra pay less justified than the needs of others in his group. He may also learn more about the problems faced by the supervisor, dis-

[52] Dickson, W. J. The Hawthorne plan of personnel counseling. *Amer. J. Orthopsychiat.*, 1945, *15*, 343–347.

[53] Rogers, C. *Counseling and psychotherapy.* Boston: Houghton Mifflin, 1942.

[54] Bingham, Moore, and Gustad, *op. cit.;* Kahn and Cannell, *op. cit.;* Sidney, E., and Brown, M. *The skills of interviewing.* London: Tavistock, 1961.

cover that there are viewpoints other than his own, and find he has responsibilities toward others.

Group discussion also utilizes the principle of involvement. Marrow and French[55] describe how management personnel changed their strongly entrenched hostile attitude toward older women employees when the supervisors participated in planning and executing relevant research. Similarly, labor unions take a constructive attitude toward improving production when they participate in solving the problem.[56] Another study[57] compared the lecture (persuasion) with the group discussion method in reducing bias in the way supervisors appraised the work of their subordinates. The lecture failed to accomplish change while the discussion method reduced bias significantly.

In assessing the possibilities of discussion as a method of improving attitudes, it should be recognized that attitudes of management personnel as well as those of subordinates are involved. One supervisor was critical of his drivers because they returned to the garage before five o'clock. He feared that the men would eventually be pulling in before mid-afternoon. Discussion revealed that the men were competing for parking spots in the garage. As a matter of fact, the last drivers in had to park outside. When the supervisor learned this he felt better about the men and several solutions became obvious. How would you solve this problem?

Supervisors can also profit from others if they meet to discuss common problems and have a skilled discussion leader. Discovering that no one answer is right and that misunderstandings rather than the perversity of human nature cause most problems, airing one's feelings in a constructive situation, and experiencing security in a group, all operate to foster improved attitudes, that is, attitudes which provide a more favorable climate for the solution of problems.

The fact that members of a group have similar attitudes should not mislead us into assuming that this similarity is caused by group membership. Newcomb[58] demonstrated that persons with similar attitudes are attracted to one another. Perhaps the most accurate statement of the influence of group membership is that people receive greatest satisfaction through affiliating with those who hold similar attitudes and that such persons have the most influence on their subsequent attitudes. Thus changes in group attitudes become an interaction process.

Persuasion

The most common procedures used in attempts to change attitudes are argument, debates, and selling approaches. They have one thing in common: they make one point of view appear in a favorable light while the opposing points of view are made to appear unfavorable. The tendency is to exaggerate the two extremes and

[55] Marrow, A. J., and French, J. R. P., Jr. Changing a stereotype in industry. *J. soc. Issues,* 1945, *1,* 33–37.

[56] Barkin, S. Trade-union attitudes and their effect on productivity. *Industr. Productivity,* Industrial Relations Research Assn., 1951, 110–129.

[57] Levine, J., and Butler, J. Lecture versus group decision in changing behavior. In E. A. Fleishman (Ed.), *Studies in personnel and industrial psychology.* Homewood, Ill.: Dorsey, 1961, Ch. 17.

[58] Newcomb, T. M. *The acquaintance process.* New York: Holt, 1961.

to make it appear that no middle ground exists. Too frequently the middle ground is excluded because the choice offered is one between two alternative positions or candidates.

Persuasion techniques are used in political campaigns. Despite the money and effort spent the number of persons who change their votes during a political campaign is small. Most of the surprises in election results come from a larger turnout than expected.[59]

Attitude Change Through Behavior Change

The objective of attitude change is to alter behavior. Since advertising and propaganda are largely concerned with the control of behavior, evidence of behavior change is often regarded as opinion change. Likewise management training programs are usually designed to change attitudes in order to achieve a behavior change. Generally speaking a good deal of material has been developed for management programs with little improvement in management behavior. Wohlking[60] suggests the use of behavior change to produce attitude change and thereby assure persistance of the altered behavior. Attitudes of resisting travel by air decline rapidly once the traveler experiences a pleasant trip. Participating in interpersonal relations exercises in which a person may be asked to try out a procedure he would not himself elect to use might develop a favorable attitude or remove an unfavorable one. Thus the question of which should come first (attitude change or behavior change) is a good one, and both approaches have their merits.

Forced integration would represent an approach to alter attitudes by altering behavior. The success of such a program for attitude change would obviously depend upon the experiences such forced behavior produced. The same problem arises when industry is forced to hire employees regardless of sex or race. If success depends upon the development of pleasant rather than unpleasant experiences, everything should be done to associate pleasant experiences with the program. Unfortunately, this important factor tends to be overlooked, yet all parties involved need to assume this responsibility.

Questionable Methods

Brainwashing is a method of behavior change that combines interrogation, forced confession, self-criticism, repetitious propaganda, and reward and punishment in group discussion patterns. It falls far short of the claims made by its proponents. Of the many thousand prisoners of war in Korea exposed to communism, only 21 refused repatriation when it was offered.[61] Insofar as it changes behavior, brainwashing has been a failure.

Subliminal advertising was used to sell products by flashing a suggestion (e.g., EAT POPCORN) periodically on the screen during a movie at a rate faster than is

[59] Campbell, A., Converse, P. E., Miller, W. E., and Stokes, D. E. *The American voter.* New York: Wiley, 1960.

[60] Wohlking, W. Attitude change, behavior change: The role of the training department. *Calif. Mgt. Rev.*, 1970, *13*, 45–50.

[61] Schein, E. The Chinese indoctrination program for prisoners of war. *Psychiatry*, 1956; *19*, 149–172; Brown, J. A. *Techniques of persuasion.* Baltimore: Penguin, 1963.

normally required to perceive the stimulus. The suggestion was barely bright enough to be seen, and the combination of low intensity and short exposure supposedly prevented the audience from being consciously aware of the message. The fear that such procedures could manipulate people by bypassing their consciousness was unfounded. Subsequent studies found the claim initially made by James Vicary in 1950 to be falacious.[62]

Truth serums (e.g., sodium pentothal), hypnosis, and electrical stimulation of the brain likewise fail to live up to their reputations as persuasive techniques. Illustrations of such methods are impressive to the layman, but these are selected and often exaggerated, rather than representative findings.

Mind control seems not to be a serious danger at this time and with these methods. As better methods for influencing behavior are developed, susceptibility to the methods declines. Thus advertisers claim they must improve their methods just to keep up with audience sophistication. The most wanted audience is usually least likely to listen.

A Word of Caution

In measuring attitude changes, can one always be sure that there has been a true or basic change? Kelman[63] distinguished among three conditions of influence: (1) compliance, where the person hopes to achieve a favorable reaction from the persuader; (2) identification, where the person wishes to establish a favorable relationship with the persuader; and (3) internalization, where the influence fits into the person's own value system. In the first two conditions, the influences revealed are superficial and represent expressions of change because of external pressures. The third is a valid acceptance of influence in that it incorporates new material into the person's system of values. By the same token, conflicting material would be rejected. In order to achieve an intrinsic attitude change, an influence would have to alter or reorganize an existing system of values and meanings.

For example, let us examine some values in a job situation. The meanings of the terms "high production," "no smoking," "strict inspection," and "must attend company parties" could be so organized that they would fall into a frame of reference that might be called an unpleasant and autocratic work climate. However, if one found a new boss to be understanding, friendly, and helpful, the meanings of the above terms could change to "efficiency," "fire hazards," "good product," and "expected to be with the group because they want me," respectively. An intrinsic change in attitude must introduce a new frame of reference to alter the interpretation of facts in the same way that the meaning of "high production" can change from unpleasant slave-driving to pride in efficiency. Thus changes in basic attitudes are accompanied by a series of new insights and discoveries of new meanings and values.

[62] Goldiamond, I. Statement on subliminal advertising. In R. Ulrich, T. Stachnik, and J. Mabry, (Eds.), *Control of human behavior.* Glenview, Ill.: Scott, Foresman, 1966.

[63] Kelman, H. C. Compliance, identification and internalization: Three processes of attitude change. *J. Confl. Resol.,* 1958, *2,* 51–60.

Laboratory Exercise

Multiple Role Playing: The Case of the "Old Girls"

Preface to Role Playing

Role playing is a procedure whereby various real-life situations are created and participants have an opportunity to practice specific human relations skills in a safe laboratory environment. Best results are obtained if the participants imagine themselves to be in the situations created for them and if they adopt the feelings and attitudes described to them as their own. Role playing differs from acting because the actor plays the part of someone else and must speak the lines supplied for this person, whereas the role player remains himself but is given a new name, a particular job, and certain past experiences. The interaction between the role players should represent their own personalities as supplemented or changed by the instructions, the situation, and the feeling engendered by the interaction. In the interest of spontaneous interaction, students are asked not to read the case materials before participating in role-playing exercises.

A. Preparation for role playing.
1. In this exercise members of the class will be asked to play the parts of persons in an actual case, the circumstances of which are given below.
2. Background material (F. 1) is read aloud to all.
3. The class is divided into groups of three. (One or two groups may contain two persons in order to handle groups not divisible by three.)
4. One of the three persons in each group takes the role of Ms. Jones; one takes the role of Mr. Smith; and the third acts as observer. (In groups of two, the observer is omitted.) The sex of the role player need not correspond to that of the role played.
5. When all have completed reading their instructions (F. 2, 3, or 4), the role players will set them aside and prepare to act out their parts as they feel them.
6. Observers should be ignored by the role players and should make themselves as unobtrusive as possible.

B. The role-playing process.
1. The instructor will ask the Mr. Smiths to leave their groups. At a signal they will return, indicating their arrival in the offices of the Ms. Joneses. From this point on, participants will act in their roles.
2. Role playing ensues for about 10 minutes of interaction between the Smiths and the Joneses.
3. Each Smith and each Jones will indicate on a slip of paper whether or not the other changed his attitude.
4. Observers prepare to report.

C. Reports from observers.

1. Brief report from each observer concerning procedure in his group.
2. Observer's opinion of good and bad practices.

D. Tabulation of facts mentioned.

1. List on the blackboard the facts given in the roles of Smith and Jones.
2. With the help of the observers indicate which of the facts were mentioned by the Smiths and which by the Joneses.

E. Discussion.

1. Analysis of tabulated data should permit the conclusion that the attitude selected the facts used in the discussion. (Smith would state a derogatory fact, and Jones would counter with "Yes, that may be true, but . . ." and go on to mention a favorable fact.)
2. Do the reports justify the conclusion that the Joneses who listened made more progress than those who argued?
3. The observers' opinions of attitude change should be checked against those of the role players to evaluate observers' sensitivity.
4. Any conclusion about how the case should be handled is premature. The important experience is developing an awareness of the numerous problems in human relations arising in an everyday situation.

F. Materials for the case. *Read aloud*

1. BACKGROUND

In a commercial office employing a large number of women there was a period when business was slack and very few new employees were hired. Following this period, business improved and there was a good deal of expansion. For the past five years many new employees have been hired. As a consequence of this development there are 90 women who have worked for the company ten or more years; 15 who have been with the company from five to nine years and who were hired during the slack period; and 450 young women who have less than five years of service. This hiring pattern has created an unusual situation in the office: there is a fair-sized group of old-timers and a large group of newcomers, with an age difference of at least five years between them. With this age difference, the members of these two large groups can be differentiated and hence discrimination can easily be practiced. These two groups do not get on very well with each other. The office force has recognized the problem and is accustomed to thinking and speaking of the women as the "old girls" and the "young girls."

Ms. Jones is in charge of the personnel office and for the past 10 years has done all the hiring and placing of employees. All transfers, changes in pay rates, etc., must be cleared through her. She is in a staff position and her office was set up as a service to the line organization.

Mr. Smith is the manager of one of five large offices. There are four supervisors who report to him and his position in the organization is comparable in rank to that of Ms. Jones. Since each of them report to a different vice president, neither one has authority over the other.

Ms. Jones has asked Smith to come and see her to discuss a problem in connection with "older women." Smith is about to enter Jones' office.

2. ROLE FOR MS. JONES OF THE PERSONNEL OFFICE (AGE 35 YEARS)

You have had a persistent problem with Mr. Smith, the manager of a large office group in the company. He objects to older employees and refuses to accept transfers. He also gives poor ratings to older women and tries to get you to find other places for them. As far as you can tell, he is prejudiced. You believe that the older women make good, stable employees. You find them more conscientious, more dependable, more businesslike, and generally more capable. You can't understand Smith's position and therefore have decided to talk to him to see if you can't convince him to take his share of older women and to give them a better deal. It's just about time for Smith to arrive. Stand up to receive him and thank him for taking time out. You've asked Smith to come to your office because you have private rooms for interviewing. If you went to Smith's office your presence would be observed and it might start an ugly rumor about someone getting fired.

Here are some things you know about the behavior of older women compared to younger ones:

Absenteeism lower
More time in rest rooms
Less tardiness
Less willing to do unpleasant jobs
Same production
Less sociable
Object more to changes
Can do a greater variety of jobs in company
Know company set-up better
Adapt more slowly to new jobs

3. ROLE FOR MR. SMITH, MANAGER OF THE OFFICE FORCE

You have had considerable trouble with Ms. Jones in the Personnel Office. She isn't cooperative with you regarding the kind of employees you want and doesn't help you in obtaining new jobs for those you want to transfer. Mostly, the issue centers on problems concerning older women. You refuse to accept women over 30 years of age, and you try to transfer your older women whenever you can. You like a young force. You have had dealings with all types of employees and you and the four supervisors who report to you all agree that older women are no good. You don't like to deal with them and see no reason why the company should put up with them. However, if the company wants to keep them, let those who like them take them into their units. As far as you are concerned they aren't worth the pay they get. They are inefficient, undependable, and slow. (Assume the attitude that you dislike them.)

You have an appointment with Ms. Jones of the Personnel Office. She asked to see you to discuss your views concerning older employees. You are a busy man and haven't the time to help Jones solve her problems, but you will be polite enough to see what she wants. Personnel people get paid for interviews, but you have to make up the time because your work piles up when you're out.

Here are some things you know about the behavior of older group compared to younger group of women.

Absenteeism lower
More time in rest rooms
Less tardiness
Less willing to do unpleasant jobs
Same production
Less sociable
Object more to change
Can do a greater variety of jobs in company
Know company set-up better
Adapt more slowly to new jobs

4. INSTRUCTIONS FOR THE OBSERVER

You are overhearing a discussion between Mr. Jones and Ms. Smith. Make special note of the following:

a. The manner in which Jones leads up to the discussion of older women.
b. The relative amount each talks.
c. The arguments each uses.
d. Evidences of any change in attitude.

Do not enter into the discussion in any way. Learn what you can by "listening in," since your opinions will be asked later.

Suggested Readings

Hanley, C. Attitudes and social issues. In A. D. Calvin, *et al.* (Eds.), *Psychology*. Boston: Allyn & Bacon, 1961, Ch. 22.

Jones, E. E., and Gerard, H. B. *Foundations of social psychology.* New York: Wiley, 1967, Ch. 12.

Karlins, M., and Abelson, H. I. *Persuasion: How opinions and attitudes are changed.* New York: Springer, 1970.

Katz, D. (Ed.) Attitude change. *Pub. Opin. Quart.,* 1960, *24*(2), 380.

Marrow, A. J. *Changing patterns of prejudice.* Philadelphia: Chilton, 1962.

Newcomb, T. M., Koenig, K. E., Flacks, R., and Warwick, D. P. *Persistence and change.* New York: Wiley, 1967.

Shaw, M. E., Wright, J. M. *Scales for the measurement of attitudes.* New York: McGraw-Hill, 1967.

Triandis, H. C. *Attitude and change.* New York: Wiley, 1971.

4

Frustration as a Factor in Behavior

The Nature of a Problem Situation

A good deal of activity is a matter of following learned procedures and routines. Many jobs can be performed almost entirely without making decisions or discovering new procedures. As long as life's situations remain much the same from one day to the next, a person can obtain satisfaction by merely practicing the behaviors he has learned. Under such circumstances there are no problems.

A problem arises for a given individual when his behavior toward a goal or objective is blocked, and he has no learned techniques to meet the new situation. This occurs when a person suddenly comes to a parting of the ways and must choose one of several alternatives, and it occurs whenever a barrier in his path blocks current activity.

Problem-Solving Behavior

The healthy and mature reaction to a problem situation is problem-solving behavior which is characterized by *variability* in thought and action. Variability in behavior may be relatively simple, such as shaking a vacuum cleaner when it doesn't start, or it may be creative, such as reorganizing a job to remove a bottleneck.

Regardless of the complexity, variability is the basic characteristic of problem-solving behavior. Even when variability in behavior is simple, it has a chance of solving a problem, because it frees a person from the old ineffective way of doing something.[1]

Figure 4.1 shows how variability in behavior may lead the person around an obstacle and to his goal. It is clear that an obstacle which can be overcome by one

---

[1] Maier, N. R. F. The behavior mechanisms concerned with problem solving. *Psychol. Rev.,* 1940, *47,* 43–58; Maier, N. R. F. The integrative function in group problem solving. In Aronson, L. R., Tobath, E., Lehrman, D. S., and Rosenblatt, J. S., *Development and evolution of behavior: Essays in memory of T. C. Schneirla.* San Francisco: W. H. Freeman, 1970.

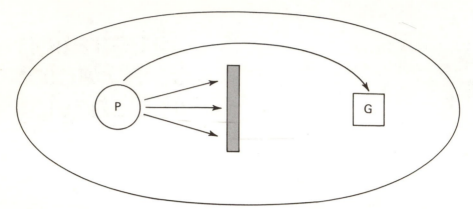

Figure 4.1 / Variable Behavior May Lead to a Solution of a Problem. The person (P) is blocked from his goal (G) by some obstacle. After trying several behaviors (arrows), he finds one which takes him to his goal. (Modified from N. R. F. Maier, *Frustration.* Ann Arbor, Mich.: University of Michigan Press, 1961. Copyright © 1961 by The University of Michigan.)

individual may continue to block another, and also that some obstacles cannot be overcome. What happens when the variable behavior at a given individual's disposal is inadequate?

Figure 4.2 demonstrates how the individual may abandon an objective which cannot be reached and settle for a lesser goal that was previously unnoticed. A young man might be content with a lower-paying job when he finds he must take a series of courses to qualify for a job in the drafting department.

Figure 4.2 / Insurmountable Obstacles May Cause a Change in Goals. If an obstacle blocks access to Goal A, the person (P) may solve his problem by switching to Goal B, which may initially have been outside the situation.

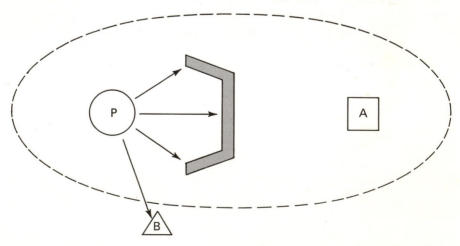

Frustration as a Reaction to Problems

When substitutes are not available or when pressures for solving the problem are present and escape is blocked, failure may introduce tension and the person may become frustrated rather than employ problem-solving behavior. Figure 4.3 illustrates how persistent failure in overcoming an obstacle causes it to be avoided, pressures created by deadlines or threats drive the person into the obstacle and the confining walls of the situation prevent escape. Under these conditions tensions build up inside the person, and these rather than the goal determine behavior. Expressions such as "He blew his top," or "He went to pieces" indicate that there has been a qualitative change in behavior. Such terms are used to describe the behavior because it no longer appears goal oriented. Sensible behavior is adaptive, which means that the behavior leads to goals or solves a problem.

Frustration as a Factor in Behavior

Whether or not an interference will produce symptoms of frustration depends upon the individual's tolerance, his previous history of frustration, the pressure under which he is functioning, and his interpretation of the situation. We are more apt to be frustrated by an interference caused by another person than by one caused by a physical object, because we are more likely to experience people as interferences than as problems. Since a child does not make this distinction as readily as an adult, he is about as likely to be frustrated by his blocks as by his mother. This does not mean that frustration in adults is always dependent upon human interference. Un-

Figure 4.3 / A Problem Situation May Produce Frustration. Pressures, failure, and inability to escape from a situation produce frustration. A frustrated person is under emotional tension and this, rather than the nature of the situation, determines his behavior. (Modified from N. R. F. Maier, *Frustration.* Ann Arbor, Mich.: University of Michigan Press, 1961. Copyright © 1961 by The University of Michigan.)

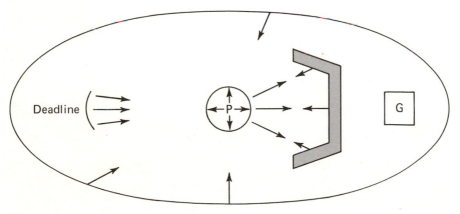

employment, a fire, or a stalled car can serve the purpose when tolerance is not very high or when pressure in the situation demands that the problem be solved. The absolute necessity of finding a solution to a problem, or the anticipation of punishment if the problem is not solved, tends to make problems frustrating situations.

When a situation becomes frustrating to the individual his behavior undergoes a distinct change. What previously was healthy, unemotional activity now shows a degree of emotionality and unreasonableness. Variable and constructive behavior is replaced by stereotyped and destructive behavior. In extreme cases, the behavior becomes quite pointless in the sense that nothing positive is gained. However, such activity sometimes obtains a valuable end in that it overcomes the source of frustration. In such cases the behavior is adaptive. We recognize therefore, that the symptoms of frustration are not necessarily undesirable and that a distinction must be made between adaptive and unadaptive expressions of frustration.

Some writers do not make a qualitative distinction between goal-oriented behavior and behavior arising out of frustration. The following discussion is guided by the theory that frustration and motivation represent two distinct sources of action in the individual.[2] At certain times, one of these mechanisms dominates and controls the behavior; at different times, the other takes over. Which psychological process is brought into function will depend on the individual's makeup (his frustration threshold) as well as on the situation. To understand the behavior at any particular time we must know which mechanism is dominating. We understand a man's behavior when he commits a crime, provided we can discover his motive. Similarly, we can better understand a man's actions when he attacks an innocent bystander if we are aware of his state of frustration. Since such an attack does not achieve a goal, the behavior is senseless when we approach it from the point of view of motivation. Even an attack on a guilty person may be considered irrelevant in that it may not solve a problem.[3]

---

[2] Maier, N. R. F. *Frustration*. New York: McGraw-Hill, 1949. Reissued Ann Arbor, Mich.: University of Michigan Press, 1961; Yates, A. J. *Frustration and conflict*. New York: Wiley, 1962.

[3] For a summary of technical studies which deal with the basic distinction between motivation and frustration, see: Eglash, A. Perception, association and reasoning in animal fixations. *Psychol. Rev.*, 1951, *58*, 424–434; The dilemma of fear as a motivating force. *Psychol. Rev.*, 1952, *59*, 376–379; Fixation and inhibition. *J. abnorm. soc. Psychol.*, 1954, *49*, 241–245; Feldman, R. S. The role of primary reduction in fixations. *Psychol. Rev.*, 1957, *64*, 85–90; Feldman, R. S. The prevention of fixations with chlordiazepoxide. *J. Neuropsychiat.*, 1962, *3*, 254–259; Jenkins, R. L. Adaptive and maladaptive delinquency. *Nerv. Child.* 1955, *11*, 9–11; Klee, J. B. The relation of frustration and motivation to the production of abnormal fixations in the rat. *Psychol. Monogr.*, 1944, *56*, 1–45; Maier, N. R. F. Frustration theory: restatement and extension. *Psychol. Rev.*, 1956, *63*, 370–388; Maier, N. R. F., and Ellen, P. Can the anxiety-reduction theory explain abnormal fixations? *Psychol. Rev.*, 1951, *58*, 435–445; Maier, N. R. F., and Ellen, P. The integrative value of concepts in frustration theory. *J. consult. Psychol.*, 1959, *23*, 195–206; Salter, A. *Conditioned reflex therapy*. New York: Capricorn, 1961; Shimoyama, T. Studies of abnormal fixation in the rat. I. Effects of frequency of punishment in the insoluble situation. *Jap. J. Psychol.*, 1957, *28*, 203–209.

The Symptoms of Frustration

The major characteristics of frustrated behavior are *aggression, regression,* and *fixation.* Each of these has been experimentally produced in the laboratory. Another symptom, which may be called *resignation,* is frequently found in case-history studies. The different symptoms of frustration frequently occur in mixed form; hence they are sometimes difficult to recognize unless one knows what to expect. They are here presented separately for clarity, not because they represent different stages through which the individual passes.

Aggression

Aggression in behavior represents some kind of attack. The attack may be one of physical violence against a person, such as striking the person who steps ahead in line; it may be directed toward an object, such as kicking a door when the lock doesn't work; it may be verbal abuse, directed at one's spouse for buying an unnecessary item. As used in relating the term to frustration, aggression in behavior means a hostile act and is associated with the emotion of anger. A boxer who is aggressive in carrying the fight to his opponent would not be showing aggression (as the term is here used) unless his actions were determined by anger rather than strategy.

The relationship between frustration and aggression has been experimentally established[4] and is now generally accepted. This relationship is perhaps most obvious in children because they show their aggression in less circuitous ways and are more likely to attack physically than are adults.[5]

When aggression against the frustrating agent is prevented, the energy may be directed at substitute objects. A foreman may "bawl out" a workman; the frustration evoked in the workman may cause him to go home and abuse his wife. It has been shown statistically that parents who are unhappily married are 2½ times as likely to be strict and abusive in bringing up their children as are parents who are happily married.[6] Frustrated parents take their frustrations out on their children, who in turn take theirs out on school or society.[7]

The attack on substitute objects often takes the form of *scapegoating,* in which certain individuals or groups are blamed for social evils. In such cases propaganda or leadership singles out the substitute object of attack, and the aggression tends to be confined to this object rather than to be distributed indiscriminately. The relationship between scapegoating and frustration is suggested by the fact that

[4] Dollard, J., *et al. Frustration and aggression.* New Haven, Conn.: Yale University Press, 1939, reissued in paperback, 1961; McNeil, E. B. Psychology and aggression. *J. Confl. Resol.,* 1959, *3,* 195–293; Scott, J. P. *Aggression.* Chicago: University of Chicago Press, 1958.

[5] Sears, P. S. Doll play aggression in young children. *Psychol. Monogr.,* 1951, *65;* McNeil, E. B. Psychology and aggression. *J. Confl. Resol.,* 1959, *3,* 195–293; Feshbach, S. Dynamics and morality of violence and aggression: Some psychological considerations. *Amer. Psychologist,* 1971, *26,* 281–292.

[6] Watson, G. A comparison of the effects of lax versus strict home training. *J. soc. Psychol.,* 1934, *5,* 102–105.

[7] Merrill, M. A. *Problems of child delinquency.* Boston: Houghton Mifflin, 1947.

scapegoating becomes more prevalent during periods of widespread unrest, dissatisfaction, and worry.

Depressed areas, where the opportunities for frustration are greatest, have the highest degree of violence and vandalism. The cost of replacement of glass in public telephone booths was found to be characteristically high in all those sections of an industrial community where housing and living problems were greatest.

It should not be assumed that aggression is necessarily undesirable or unadaptive. An attack on an obstruction, be it an enemy or an object, may remove it and permit the individual to resume progress toward his goal. Such behavior has aided lower animals to survive in the struggle for existence. In man, this primitive and individualistic behavior is of less value because, in his case, survival depends to a greater degree upon reason and cooperation.

When aggression is directed toward obstacles which cannot be overcome, the aggression results in further frustration rather than relief. This happens when the obstacle strikes back. Thus, frustration is piled on frustration, and the behavior must be regarded as unadaptive.

Substitute objects are frequently attacked under these conditions, but this behavior is also unadaptive in not being directed at the source of the frustration. The substitute objects, when they happen to be other people, also strike back. Since they are frustrated by the attacking individual, they may direct their aggression against him. Thus the attacking individual soon becomes regarded as an antisocial person; he is socially undesirable. This position in society is a further source of frustration, and instead of having solved his original problem, he has acquired more problems.

The attitudes of frustrated people also reflect aggressiveness, in that such people tend to be on the defensive. They interpret compliments as insults, are overly suspicious, and want to get even with someone. These attitudes may prevail only in the frustrating situation and influence opinions about a few people, or, like other behavior traits, they may become quite general and apply to innocent bystanders.

Symptoms of aggression commonly met in industrial employees are excessive criticism of management, constant voicing of grievances, damage to equipment, inability to get along with others, and absenteeism. Whether or not the aggression expressed justifies the frustration is quite beside the point, since justice for the frustrated individual is what he sees it to be. A man can readily prove to his own satisfaction that he is underpaid, but the cause of the dissatisfaction may be the frustration arising from unpaid hospital bills, an invalid wife, or losses in gambling. In correcting the situation, however, it is desirable to know whether the aggression is directed toward the source of frustration or toward scapegoats. Sometimes management is labor's scapegoat and sometimes labor is management's scapegoat.

Regression

Regression is a breakdown of constructive behavior and a return to childish action. In extreme cases, adults regress to the infantile stage and must be treated as babies. Even their speech and habits of cleanliness are those of infants.

That regression may be produced experimentally by frustration was demonstrated at the Iowa Child Welfare Station.[8] When children were deprived of certain toys to which they previously had access, their play with the remaining toys became more primitive than when such frustration was not present. This mild frustration caused the average child's play to become like that of a child 1½ years younger. For example, a toy truck, which before frustration was used to haul a doll about in complex play activity, was now pushed around in a simple and unimaginative way.

These experiments correlate with clinical studies[9] and with many of our own personal experiences. Most of us know of children who begin wetting the bed when a new baby arrives, of children who become thumb-suckers when their fathers leave home, of children who whine and hang onto their mother's apron strings when their parents fight, and of youngsters who build a world of make-believe when they are not wanted. When children or adults are unable to act their age in situations which make demands on them, they are exhibiting the symptoms of regression. Although one symptom does not prove the presence of frustration, it must be accepted as one of the signs.

Another regressive trait is suggestibility. One can easily suggest ideas for action to a child because he is uncritical. A critical attitude comes with reason. If we regress to a more primitive state, we tend to lose our critical ability and become suggestible, though only to the extent that the suggested behavior is not contrary to other primitive tendencies.

It will be seen that regression serves no useful purpose. In the development of children, the desire to grow up, to want to be older than they are, is recognized as a healthy sign. Adequate adjustments in childhood are a safeguard against regression in later life.

Signs of regression in industrial employees are loss of emotional control, "following the leader," primitive social organization, lack of responsibility, "horse play," unreasoned fear, and responsiveness to rumors. Likewise, men who pout, women who cry easily, and workers who form childish cliques or gangs within the plant are displaying regressive behavior.

The supervisors, too, may show signs of regression. Managers who refuse to delegate responsibility, who have difficulty in making simple decisions, who are hypersensitive, who cannot distinguish between reasonable and unreasonable requests, who engage in broad and unreasonable generalizations on the subject of labor, and who form blind loyalties for particular persons or organizations, show symptoms of regression. When intelligent people lose their perspective and fail to make obvious distinctions, they have regressed, since inability to make fine distinctions is a

---

[8] Barker, R., Dembo, T., and Lewin, K. *Frustration and regression.* Iowa City, Iowa: University of Iowa Press, 1942; Kleemeier, R. W. Fixation and regression in the rat. *Psychol. Monogr.,* 1942, *54,* No. 4 (whole No. 246), 34.

[9] Bostock, J., and Shackleton, M. The enuresis dyad. *Med. J. Australia,* 1952, *3,* 357–360; Baruch, D. W. Therapeutic procedures as part of the educational process. *J. consult. Psychol.,* 1940, *4,* 165–172; Axline, V. M. *Play therapy.* Boston: Houghton Mifflin, 1947.

sign of mental immaturity. It is on emotionally loaded topics that distinctions most often fail to be made. A manager may pass unfavorable judgment on a worker simply because the worker belongs to a union, and the employee may pass unfair judgment on a supervisor because he generalizes that all supervisors are stooges.

Abnormal Fixations

The term *fixation* is here used to designate a compulsion to continue a kind of activity which has no adaptive value. A fixated action is repeated, despite the fact that the person knows it will accomplish nothing. Because of the compulsive character of such behavior, its replacement by more adaptive responses is prevented. Lady Macbeth's persistent hand-washing is a classic example of the abnormal fixation.

The relation between such persistent responses and frustration has been experimentally demonstrated in a number of studies.[10] These studies also show that continually forcing an animal to attempt to solve a problem that cannot be solved is an effective method for building up a state of frustration. Punishment, when severe or when continued for a sufficiently long period, may also serve as a source of frustration and produce similar symptoms. A rat can be made to bang its head against a locked door hundreds of times without ever trying the unlocked door next to it. This behavior completely prevents the animal from ever learning a new adjustment which it would readily have learned prior to the frustration. Even if the animal is taught that it can avoid punishment by choosing the other door, it still cannot make that choice. The compulsion to perform the old response makes the animal unable to practice a new alternative that it knows is better.

Similar experiments have been performed with college students. After a period of mild frustration, their ability to learn a new problem can be reduced by one-half because one of the effects of frustration is to freeze old behavior and prevent the practice of new responses.[11]

Although a fixation may have the outward appearance of a normal habit, the difference appears when attempts are made to alter the fixation. A habit is normally broken when it fails to bring satisfaction or leads to punishment, whereas a fixation actually becomes stronger under these conditions.

[10] Hamilton, G. V. A study of perseverance reactions in primates and rodents. *Behav. Monogr.*, 1916, *3*, 1–65; Hamilton, J. A., and Krechevsky, I. Studies in the effect of shock upon behavior plasticity in the rat. *J. comp. Psychol.*, 1933, *16*, 237–253; Patrick, J. R. Studies in rational behavior and emotional excitement: II. The effect of emotional excitement on the rational behavior in human subjects. *J. comp. Psychol.*, 1934, *18*, 153–195; Maier, N. R. F., Glaser, N. M., and Klee, J. B. Studies of abnormal behavior in the rat: III. The development of behavior fixations through frustration. *J. exp. Psychol.*, 1940, *26*, 521–546; Kleemeier, R. W. op. cit.; Maier, N. R. F., *Frustration, op. cit.*; Maier, N. R. F., and Ellen, P. Studies of abnormal behavior in the rat: XXIV. Position habits, position stereotypes and abortive behavior. *J. genet. Psychol.*, 1956, *89*, 35–49; Ellen, P. The compulsive nature of abnormal fixations. *J. comp. physiol. Psychol.*, 1956, *49*, 309–317; Solomon, R. L., and Wynne, L. C. Traumatic avoidance learning: The principles of anxiety conservation and partial irreversibility. *Psychol. Rev.* 1954, *61*, 353–385.

[11] Marquart, D. I. The pattern of punishment and its relation to abnormal fixation. *J. Psychol.*, 1944, *19*, 133–163; and Marquart, D. I., and Arnold, P. A study in the frustration of human adults. *J. gen. Psychol.*, 1952, *47*, 43–63.

Punishment, therefore, may have two quite different effects on the organism. On the one hand, it may discourage the repetition of an act. On the other hand, it may function as a frustrating agent, and produce the fixations as well as the other symptoms associated with frustration. Because of this dual function, punishment is a rather dangerous tool, since it may produce effects which are the opposite of those desired.

Common illustrations of fixations occur in panic. In a burning building people persist in pushing at exits, even though the exits are barred. The more they push, the less opportunity for escape; nevertheless, this useless behavior continues.

Because persistent attitudes are associated with situations in which frustration has occurred, they serve as evidence to support the view that attitude fixation and frustration are related. This explains why unfavorable attitudes are so difficult to change. Instead of recognizing that the person with the rigid attitude is insecure, afraid, or feels rejected, we try to reason with him. If we approach rigid and persisting attitudes as problems in frustration, we may discover that such attitudes can be changed.

We often hear in industry that old people are set in their thinking and that they block progress. It seems now that it is not simply their age that creates the problem but also that older people are often made to feel less wanted than younger people. They no longer get merit pay increases and have reached the top rate of their job classification; on some jobs they can't keep up the pace; they can't find employment in other companies easily and feel they must stay on; they have been bypassed more often than younger employees; and they get less attention than new employees because they are supposed to know their way around.

Examples of fixations commonly met in industry are to be found in individuals who are unable to accept change. Old ways seem best, whether they concern the method of work or the nature of industrial relations and economic outlook. Frustrated individuals are blindly stubborn and unreasonable, although they may consider themselves merely persistent or cautious. They defend their refusal to change by building up logical defenses for their actions.[12] Logic thus follows their decisions, rather than precedes them. Industrial firms which are relatively free from frustrating situations and have high employee morale are made up of individuals who *seek* new ways, rather than *fear* them. To them something *new* suggests something *better*.

Resignation

Studies of unemployed people[13] and refugees,[14] in addition to revealing the traits already described, frequently contain evidences of a state of mind which we may describe as one of "giving-up." All forms of activity seem to be closed to the in-

[12] McNeil, E. B. Personal hostility and internal aggression. *J. Confl. Resol.,* 1961, *5,* 279–290; Miller, D. R., and Swanson, G. E. *Inner conflict and defense.* New York: Holt, 1960.

[13] Eisenberg, P., and Lazarsfeld, P. F. The psychological effects of unemployment. *Psychol. Bull.,* 1938, *35,* 358–390; Zawadski, B., and Lazarsfeld, P. The psychological consequences of unemployment. *J. soc. Psychol.* 1936, *6,* 224–251.

[14] Allport, G. W., Bruner, J. S., and Jandorf, E. M. Personality under social catastrophe: ninety life-histories of the Nazi revolution. *Charact. and Person.,* 1941, *10,* 1–22.

dividual, so he surrenders. This is a frame of mind which oppressive rulers may desire to create. That inactivity and an attitude of resignation will continue when an avenue for action is made available to the individual is highly questionable. Resignation is probably a dormant condition, in which all aggression has been temporarily blocked. People in this state obviously have low morale and will remain socially neutral unless their mental condition changes.

In industry, the resigned individual is one who has lost hope of bettering his conditions. "There's no use to try to do anything around here," "I've stood it this long and can wait until I retire," "I've learned to put up with conditions," and "It's always been this way and it will always be this way," are characteristic statements of hopeless and apathetic employees. Such persons depress others and make no contribution to reform.

Evaluating Frustrated Behavior

Recognizing Instances of Frustration

The symptoms of frustration should be used primarily to determine whether or not an individual's behavior is a reaction to frustration or an attempt to solve a problem. Before a counselor can deal with behavior properly, he must make a diagnosis. To correct behavior it is important to attack causes rather than symptoms. A man who violates a safety practice in order to save time and get better production is problem solving in that his behavior has something to do with overcoming a difficulty on the job, but a man who smokes in a restricted area in defiance of regimentation is expressing hostility. Because such behaviors are intrinsically different, the remedies also must differ.

In the first instance, if the employee were reprimanded for violating the rule, he might be more inclined to obey it in the future. Better, the foreman might explain to him why safety is more important than production. The frustrated employee, however, would not respond to an explanation of the reason for the no-smoking rule, and reprimand would only make him feel more regimented.

The distinction between problem-solving or goal-motivated behavior and frustration-instigated behavior is not too difficult to make, for in many ways the characteristics of these behaviors are direct opposites. However, one must not attempt to classify certain behaviors on this basis. Safety violations, tardiness, low productivity, discontent, filing of grievances, and holding office in a union can be caused by either frustration or motivation. In order to differentiate, one must have a large enough sample of behavior so that the essential distinctions can be made.

Table 4.1 describes some of the differences which are useful in making a diagnosis of frustrated versus motivated behavior. Note that the symptoms of aggression, regression, and fixation can be recognized in these behavior descriptions and that certain additional differentiations are possible because of the comparison with motivated or goal-oriented behavior.

Since frustrated behavior is unrelated to clear-cut objectives, such behavior gives no clues about a remedy. Whether a person shows aggression, regression, or fixa-

Motivation — Induced	Frustration — Instigated
Goal-oriented	Not directed toward a goal
Tension reduced when goal is reached	Tensions reduced when behavior is expressed, but increased if behavior leads to more frustration
Punishment deters action	Punishment aggravates state of frustration
Behavior shows variability and resourcefulness in a problem situation	Behavior is stereotyped and rigid
Behavior is constructive	Behavior is nonconstructive or destructive
Behavior reflects choices influenced by consequences	Behavior is compulsive
Learning proceeds and makes for development and maturity	Learning is blocked and behavior regresses

From N.R.F. Maier, Experimentally induced abnormal behavior. *Sci. Mon.*, September 1948, *67,* 210–216.

Table 4.1 / Characteristics of Motivated and Frustrated Behavior

tion is beside the point, because all have the same cause—frustration. These symptoms might be present in a single sample of behavior. A person who gossips shows the traits of regression (tattle-tale behavior common in children) and aggression (injury to another's reputation) by a single act. If such an individual persists in believing a rumor when evidence to the contrary exists, the trait of fixation is also present.

The Principle of Availability

Since the symptoms of frustration form no logical connection with the situation in which they occur, what determines the behavior that will be expressed? Not too much is known at present, but clearly convenience or availability is an important condition. Objects attacked must be within reach. The obstacle that frustrates is often physically close at hand, hence it is sometimes attacked. This is the only form of attack that makes sense. Family, work companions, and others encountered in the daily round are frequently attacked just because they are so accessible.

Availability, however, does not mean mere physical nearness. Training also makes other objects accessible, even though they are not physically associated with the frustrating situation. That is, because of what we hear from others and because of the habits we have established in the past, certain objects are made available for blame and persecution in our culture, regardless of their relevance to the given situation. Thus the military, public schools, and other groups and institutions have been made "available" for attack through various cultural pressures.

Availability is not only influenced by training and physical nearness but also by the simplicity of an act. Regressive behavior is immature and generally simple. Thumb-sucking may be practiced in infancy and a five year old may revert to thumb-sucking because it was previously practiced and is physically handy. Strict toilet-training tends to cause children who are later frustrated to become bedwetters, because the attention placed on toilet habits makes this behavior more available to the strictly trained children than to others.[15]

Availability also operates in fixation. The most simple responses and those practiced at the time of frustration are likely to become fixated. If an animal is punished severely for a particular act, this very act is the one that the animal is compelled (by his fixation) to practice in the future. This suggests that if a person were severely punished for stealing, he might become a compulsive stealer, a condition known as kleptomania. Punishment does not help the alcoholic, and there is good reason to believe it makes him worse.

Individual Differences

In discussing the symptoms of frustration, basic trends have been emphasized and differences between individuals have been neglected. All people do not do the same things when they are frustrated, any more than they behave identically when they are motivated. The variations in behavior which may appear in frustrating situations have at least three basic causes. One cause of variation lies in the fact that different people may express any one of the four types of symptoms in different ways. Another is that certain people show a predisposition to display one symptom rather than some of the others. The final and most important cause is individual difference in susceptibility to frustration. Some individuals are less inclined than others to become frustrated, either because they view the situation differently or because they have a higher level of tolerance. As situations become more stressful, a greater number of people shift from goal-motivated to frustration-instigated behavior.

The causes of the differences in behavior undoubtedly depend upon personality differences,[16] cultural differences,[17] and to some extent, upon differences in intelligence. Many of these differences must be attributed to heredity. Acquired differences will depend upon previous experiences (1) in developing emotional adjustments, (2) in learning to cooperate, and (3) in handling feelings of insecurity and social status in a group.

The presence of individual differences complicates prediction in behavior; nevertheless, the general effect of frustration is to cause certain changes in behavior. A knowledge of these changes increases our understanding of individuals as well as of groups because it furnishes us with certain principles. These principles aid in recognition of the symptoms and indicate the kind of behavior we may expect. Although we cannot hope that they will allow us to predict with certainty, they do permit us to work with probabilities.

[15] Bostok and Shackleton, *op. cit.*

[16] Socially dependent persons are more inclined to develop fixations than others; and extroverts are more inclined to show aggression than introverts, according to the work of Marquart, *op. cit.*

[17] Miller and Swanson, *op. cit.*

The Relation Between Frustration and Social Movements

Goal Oriented Groups

Most social organizations or social groups with which we are familiar are small and overlap in their membership. The various influences they exert on customs and on manner of living tend to neutralize each other. A heterogeneous assortment of social groups within a country may influence the lives of individuals but will be unlikely to make history. It is only when a large mass of people join in a single movement that they become a social force to be reckoned with.

Any important social movement can transform the social, political, and economic structure of a country. It is to the interest of the industrial leader, therefore, not to ignore these social trends.

Under normal conditions, social groups may be characterized as organizations of individuals having common interests or goals. These groups may be characterized as goal-motivated. People who wish to attain certain ends work together for a common purpose. They have leaders who represent them in their interests and whose duty it is to coordinate the activities. Athletic clubs, bridge clubs, university clubs, political clubs, religious organizations, ecology groups, and the like are common examples of social groups.

Frustration-Instigated Social Movements

It is also possible for a frustrated group of people to become organized.[18] Since aggressive behavior tendencies are present in such people, they are susceptible to being organized or united around a pattern of aggression. We have already seen that no specific aggression is demanded by the frustrated individual, thus any form of aggression will appeal to him.

The study of riots and mob behavior reveals the attractiveness of destructive behavior to certain groups of people, once an avenue for such activity is opened for them or merely made apparent to them. It is impossible to explain mob behavior just by referring to the incident which released it. Frustrations and tensions on a wide scale precede these outbursts and are the underlying causes.[19] Incidents and suggestions precipitate, coordinate, and direct the course of aggressive action as well as furnish the security of group action.

The nonspecific nature of feelings of aggression makes it relatively easy to organize large numbers of frustrated people. Social movements of this type are potentially large and the program of action is destructive. Such a movement can be very strong because the action of a large mass of people is channeled and synchronized.[20] Thus an organized minority can defy the unorganized majority.

[18] Maier, N. R. F. The role of frustration in social movements. *Psychol. Rev.*, 1942, *49*, 586–599; Cohen, N. (Ed.). *The Los Angeles riots: A sociopsychological study.* New York: Praeger, 1970.

[19] Lee, A. M. and Humphrey, N. D. *Race riot.* New York: Dryden, 1943.

[20] White, R. K. Hitler, Roosevelt and the nature of war propaganda. *J. abnorm. soc. Psychol.,* 1949, *44*, 157–174.

The leader of a movement organized around a pattern of aggression is in a very powerful position. He determines the form the aggression will take. He times the action. The large supply of destructive energy generated by frustration is ready to be harnessed, and the leader may not only do the harnessing, but he may also do the driving. In this capacity he becomes a determiner of history if his movement comes to power.

The other types of behavior which are characteristic of frustration lend support to an organization built around aggression. Regressive tendencies make people suggestible and easily led; they become uncritical and are not likely to recognize inconsistencies. The tendency to fixate makes their behavior stereotyped, so that they can be made to persist in any activity in which they get started. Taken together, the effects of frustration make possible a fanatical type of social movement in which the individuals are relatively homogeneous and are dominated by hatred and destruction. They are persistent, irrational, and ready to follow a leader. Whether or not they will sweep away those things which are good or evil in society depends largely on circumstances outside themselves. If the activity is directed at innocent bystanders, social progress is impeded. If it is directed at groups of individuals interested in reform, social regression may occur. Frustration-instigated social movements thus constitute a social risk, since they are not oriented to a future goal. Insofar as goals are mentioned in the propaganda of such movements, they are accessory factors which may influence sympathetic individuals.

Frustration-instigated movements may form the nucleus of a force from which violent revolution develops. A frustration-instigated movement brought about the Second World War. To suppose that leaders create unrest is to miss an important point. Unrest may be utilized by a potential leader, but the causes of unrest lie in the frustrations already there. No leader can organize a mass of well-adjusted people into a destructive movement.

The manner in which frustration influences the character of a social organization is well illustrated by a comparison of the communist and socialist movements. The economic beliefs of communism and socialism are similar, but the character of the two movements is quite different. Communism is militant in nature, placing a great deal of emphasis on the overthrow of capitalism. The words "down with," so frequently used in communist slogans, are aggressive. Socialism, on the other hand, emphasizes the better life, and offers a means of dealing with problems arising when private capital is not available. Its slogans tend to describe goals. This distinction explains why communism has been the more vigorous movement. It gives frustrated people an aggressive pattern of action rather than a promise of better things. In countries where economic frustration has been widespread, communism has played the more dominant part.

The absolute standard of living, however, does not determine the extent of frustration. Rather, the relative standard of living determines the extent of dissatisfaction. Since frustration is always a reaction on the part of the individual, not a description of the situation to which he reacts, it is essential, in considering economic frustration, to determine how a man views his standard of living when he compares his status with that of others, rather than to determine what his standard of living actually is.

Unions must adapt their efforts to changing conditions if they are to retain their influence. Past union pressure has caused modern management to give workers a high standard of living and improved relations. Unless the unions can find new ways to serve their membership the need for their existence becomes less evident. Today's union leaders complain about the lack of interest of their membership; and the intellectuals, so important to the development of these unions, are leaving the movement.[21] If the goals of union leaders are confined to economic gains the ability of U. S. industries to compete with foreign industries will be lost.

Reversing the Process

We have seen that a problem situation normally sets problem-solving behavior in motion. But if the individual becomes frustrated by the problem or enters the problem situation with a lowered tolerance (low frustration threshold), his variable constructive behaviors, so characteristic of problem-solving activity, are replaced by hostile, childish, and rigid behaviors. Actually lower brain centers which control the autonomic nervous system play a dominating role in determining behavior

Figure 4.4 / Problems Embedded in Frustrated Feelings. The state of frustration is accompanied by varied and mixed feelings which hide or distort the real problem from the frustrated individual as well as from others. These feelings must be removed before the problem can be brought into focus and solved. Therapy is a process of releasing frustrated feelings under conditions that permit relief, discovering and clarifying the problem, and finding an acceptable solution.

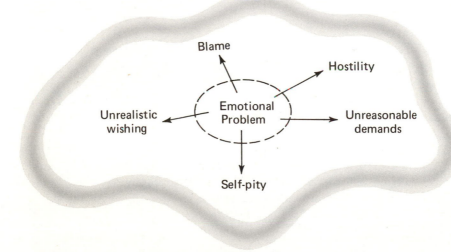

---

[21] Harris, H. Why labor lost the intellectuals. *Harper's Mag.*, 1964, *228*, 1369, 79–86.

so that rational cortical activity is to some extent shunted out.[22] In order to restore the problem-solving activity this process must be reversed; the pent-up emotions must be released, and the real problem located in order to restore the problem-solving state of mind.

Although the problem itself may generate the feelings, these feelings do not describe the problem and are likely to be misleading. Figure 4.4 illustrates how a problem condition may be buried in a mass of emotional reactions. Problem-solving behavior begins when the person wishes to explore what *he* can do about a problem. The amputee must reach the state of mind of seeking what he can do to have as rich a life as possible with his handicap; the man who can't live on his income must face the problem of finding additional income or ways to reduce expenses; the unhappy woman who cannot see divorce as a solution must think in terms of what she can do to salvage as much of the marriage as possible. Some problems are difficult and solutions may not be readily forthcoming. Thus a disturbed person may require aid in finding a solution as well as in getting release from the pent-up feelings.

Dealing with Frustration

Although some methods for dealing with frustration in individuals and in groups will be discussed at length in later chapters, it is desirable at this point to indicate the variety of approaches that exist, some of which need no elaboration. One should never depend on a single simple remedy, for circumstances often exclude one remedy but permit another. If a variety of approaches to each problem can be considered, it is often possible to select a method that is best adapted to the individual's needs as well as see to it that the practical aspects of the situation have been properly evaluated. Naturally, the prevention of frustration is more desirable than the best cure.

The Constructive Viewpoint

When an employee slams a door after being reprimanded, this behavior can be a sign of disrespect—a hostile act directed toward the reprimander—or a symptom of frustration. If the reaction to the hostile behavior is striking back, a bad situation can be made worse. If the action is allowed to pass and the act accepted as natural for a frustrated person, an unhappy situation does not deteriorate into a worse one.

Often people feel that they must defend themselves from attack so that they will not appear weak. This interpretation assumes that the other person is doing some problem solving, which is not indicated in the above illustration. An employee's criticism of a supervisor's action does not mean that the supervisor must defend himself. A well-adjusted person must expect to be a scapegoat at times, both at

---

[22] Gardner, E. *Fundamentals of neurology* (3rd ed.). Philadelphia: Saunders, 1958; Jost, H., Ruilmann, C. J., Hill, T. S., and Gulo, M. J. Studies in hypertension: I. Techniques and control data; II. Central and autonomic nervous system reactions of hypersensitive individuals to simple physical and psychological stress. *Jour. Nerv. ment. Dis.,* 1952, *33,* 183–198; Cofer, G. N., and Appley, M. H. *Motivation theory and research.* New York: Wiley, 1967, Ch. 9.

home and on the job. This does not mean that one person has the right to push another around. Rather it means that there may be better ways for dealing with such attacks than striking back. Before seriously considering them, however, one must learn how to avoid becoming angry. An important attitude in avoiding anger is to be able to see frustrated behavior as a condition that creates problems and to see a frustrated person as one in need of help. This attitude is not an act of generosity; it can be self-centered because it can prevent us from becoming angry and can instead encourage a problem-solving state of mind.

This problem-solving attitude applies to the ability to deal with disgruntled individuals, and to finding ways to handle mass violence, such as is often created during long and punishing strikes. Sometimes prolonged strikes create face-saving problems because management wishes to discharge certain individuals for irresponsible behavior during the strike, and the union refuses to settle unless such individuals are protected. Past punishment and the threat of punishment do not deter destructive behavior caused by frustration; they increase it. Punishment is only a deterrent to motivated behavior.

Regressive and fixated behaviors are less likely to elicit hostility in us than are acts of aggression. However, we are likely to misjudge persons showing these behaviors and treat them as incompetent and stubborn people. These behavior characteristics should be used as clues to detect instances of frustration.

Correcting the Situation

Perhaps the most desirable procedure for dealing with frustration is to correct the situation which produced the behavior. School bullies have been cured by giving them special instructions in reading to bring their reading performance up to that of other children in class; delinquency has been cured by operations which correct an abnormality; antisocial children have been cured by creating situations that give them the experience of being accepted as members of a club; and vandalism has been reduced by recreation programs. Parental rejection is a common source of childhood frustration, and counseling parents is often the best way to cure their children. Similarly supervisory training in human relations can reduce the number of frustrated employees.

Unfortunately these remedies are often not easy to put into practice, even when the situation allows. A frustrated person is obnoxious, and it is more natural to want to punish him than to accept him. The importance of creating a situation in which a person feels accepted is strikingly demonstrated by the fact that even in the ultimate frustration of a prison setting, work situations can be created that will call forth cooperative and loyal behavior from hardened criminals.[23]

Catharsis

The term *catharsis* refers to the relief that is created by the mere expression of frustration. In the Hawthorne study[24] interviewers were encouraged to make it easy for

[23] Wilson, D. P. *My six convicts.* New York: Rinehart, 1951.
[24] Roethlisberger, F. J., and Dickson, W. J. *Management and the worker.* Cambridge, Mass.: Harvard University Press, 1939.

employees to express their hostility. One of the functions of therapy[25] is to create a situation in which the patient is free to release his pent-up feelings. Because frustration builds up emotional tensions and creates a state which replaces rational behavior, it is necessary to reverse this process before an individual can return to his rational self.

An appreciation of the feeling of relief that catharsis gives may be obtained if the reader will recall how much better he has felt after writing a hostile letter to someone who has treated him unfairly. In order to get this relief, it was not necessary to mail the letter. The expression of emotion, not what the behavior does to the other person, was the important value. But because the expression of frustration frequently injures or annoys another person, the benefits of expression often are lost. Thus it is desirable to write hostile letters, but not to mail them. In fact, if one holds such a letter overnight, the very desire to mail it may be gone by morning.

The laboratory exercise at the end of this chapter is designed to show how expression of feeling can reduce frustration. Accepting feelings and trying to understand them rather than judging or criticizing them is most likely to clarify the problem and reduce the tendency to find fault.[26] Since a superior is inclined to give advice and to pass judgment, the situation presented requires him to suppress the inclination.

The procedure of catharsis can be used with groups also, particularly when the members have a common problem. Understanding supervisors often hold gripe sessions in which employees are encouraged to say what they think and the supervisor accepts the statements without arguing, without explaining the company's side, and without holding anything that is said against any member.

The following case illustrates such a gripe session. A department head found that someone had left a lighted cigarette on a toilet seat in the women's washroom, which made a nasty black burn. He became angry because to him this meant a complete disrespect for company property. Since he had the power to act he executed an order prohibiting smoking in the washroom.

The response of the women affected by this rule was one of hostility, reflected in their manners, job performance, attendance, and service. Supervisory personnel believed that the order was unfortunate, but felt they could do nothing about it. One of their number was encouraged to hold a gripe session with his group of 24 women.

He opened the meeting by indicating that he would like to talk about the matter. The women responded by showing little interest since there was really nothing to discuss. The order was silly and should be changed. He indicated a desire to learn what it was about the rule that upset them.

The discussion revealed the following four areas of feeling:

1. The ruling was unfair—all employees were punished because one woman had done some damage. Some doubted that it was even done by one in their midst.

[25] Rogers, C. R. *Counseling and psychotherapy.* Boston: Houghton Mifflin, 1942.
[26] Ginott, H. *Between parent and teenager.* New York: Macmillan, 1969.

2. They wanted to know who had complained. It appeared that no one in the group knew, and none objected to the damaged seat. Since they had to use the washroom and the department head did not, they wanted to know why he complained.

3. The ruling indicated that the company was getting awfully cheap. Prices of toilet seats were bandied about. If the company had so little money why were not economies made in important areas? One woman suggested that they chip in and buy a toilet seat. Another suggested the purchase of two. A third woman suggested that the second be given to the department head.

4. They wanted to know what the department head was doing in the women's washroom.

Each of these areas released a good deal of hostility and as the meeting progressed the participation increased. After the feelings had been exhausted the supervisor said he understood their feelings on the matter but he wasn't too sure he understood why smoking in the washroom was so important since they could still smoke in the lounge.

He was told that they smoked while they did their hair, and they did their hair in the washroom. He then asked why they didn't do their hair in the lounge where smoking was permitted. The response was, "Because there is no mirror in the lounge." He then asked, "If there were a mirror in the lounge, would that help?" To this they readily gave an affirmative response. He then asked, "Would you like me to buy a mirror for the lounge?" This suggestion was greeted favorably. He was able to do something about getting a mirror and it was generally agreed that the problem was solved.

This example shows how soluble problems often lie beneath a mixture of feelings and demands. Managers often fear that these will be so unreasonable that they cannot be discussed. They often avoid discussing such touchy topics and overlook the fact that the opportunity to express unreasonable feelings in a non-critical situation makes people more reasonable and permits the discovery of a soluble problem.

Creating Outlets for Temporary Frustration

A thoughtful supervisor may let an employee blow off steam in an interview or gripe session, but what about the frustrated employee who has no one to go to? Can a company furnish outlets for the frequent temporary frustrations on the job?

In exploring the switchboard panels in some telephone offices a consultant found marks made by shoes. They were not mere scratches but kicks. It is not uncommon for telephone operators to be insulted, and they are not permitted to talk back. In interviews the women indicated that they kick the panel as a result of their frustration; but this action hurts and with some shoes it could cause injury.

In order to make aggression less painful the consultant suggested to managers that the panel be padded. Despite the appropriateness of the suggestion it was not taken seriously. Nevertheless the company medical department did concede that there were a number of toe injuries in their records, but the causes of many of them were unknown.

On another occasion this author suggested that department stores should have rubber dummy placed below the counter with a convenient mallet hanging next to it. This would permit the sales personnel to excuse themselves from a disagreeable customer to bend over and hit the doll. This suggestion also has been unheeded.

It has come to our attention that the giant Matsushita Electric Industrial Company of Osaka, Japan, has set up a "Human Control Room," illustrated in Figure 4.5. The room was designed to promote employee harmony. The photographs on page 89 show employees giving vent to their feelings.[27] With a portrait of the big boss smiling benignly down from the wall, employees may smack a dummy, slug a punching bag, or select bamboo sticks from a handy rack and belabor a stuffed figure. A sign on the wall says: "To your heart's content, if you please." Executive Kuninari Azuma, who dreamed up the plan, claims that workers return to their jobs calmer and happier after working off their anger.

The value of this method seems worth further study. It would be difficult to investigate in a laboratory setting. The best test situation would require a real-life setting and the willingness of management to take such a device seriously. The alternative is to have counselors or good listeners readily available to give immediate relief.

Counseling

Many instances of frustration occur in daily life. In most of these day-to-day problems time dissipates the emotions aroused, and no serious damage is done. Although

Figure 4.5 / Diagram of Human Engineering Room in Japanese Plant. The room contains items for relieving frustration. See Objects E, F, and G. Bamboo sticks for striking figures are available in racks. (Diagram supplied through courtesy of Mr. Kuninari Azuma.)

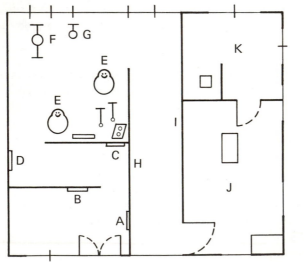

A. Plane mirror
B. Plane mirror
C. Concave and convex
   mirrors
D. Concave and convex
   mirrors
E. Man-size doll
F. Punching ball
G. Upper punching ball
H. Short history of
   Matsushita Electric
I. Pictures indicating
   contrasting scene
J. At home room
K. Consultation room

[27] Jampel, D. Hate your boss? Slug him. *Mechanics Illustrated*, 1962, *58*, 86–87.

Disgruntled Japanese workers letting off steam by going to work on a dummy of their boss with bamboo staves and fists.

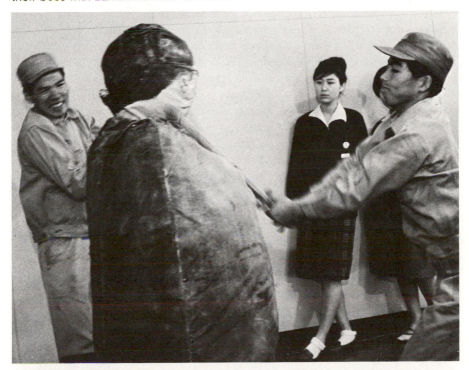

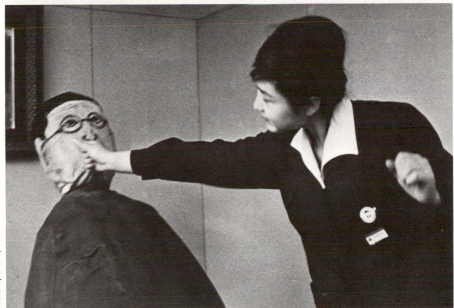

Photoreporters, Inc.

it would be desirable to avoid these difficulties, we may consider them routine; one would speak of the behaviors as frustrated acts rather than describe the persons involved as frustrated individuals.

When unresolved frustrations go far back in an individual's life, however, the feelings engendered by them continue to function and are reflected in practically all of a person's dealings with other people. Childhood experiences, such as the insecurity created by quarreling parents, a broken home, or a parent's rejection, are common sources of frustration which may mar a personality. Conditions or situations of this nature are too long-standing to correct in the case of employees, and it is therefore more important to develop an adjustment in the individual. We cannot expect time alone to heal the frustrations arising from childhood insecurity, shock experiences, and physical handicaps. The causal condition may actually become worse because the individual has difficulty in his relations with others. Such conditions may be relieved by expression, but the counseling process must be carried further in order to have a lasting value. In some instances psychiatric treatment is in order, but supervisors and lay counselors can do much, if not to help such persons reach a better adjustment, at least to cause disturbed persons to seek skilled help. The supervisor's role in cases of this kind will be discussed in Chapter 20.

For our present purposes the difference between a temporary state of frustration and a personality disorder is important. The latter has a history and requires professional treatment. It is also important to recognize that continued stress either off the job or on the job may result in a change. Excessive absenteeism, alcoholism, excessive accidents, interpersonal difficulties, frequent medical visits, and sudden changes in behavior patterns are cues (symptoms) the psychiatrist uses to indicate the existence of stress situations.[28] Work as such does not produce mental breakdowns, but work conditions may uncover and aggravate underlying tensions, conflicts, and emotional complexes already present.[29] An understanding listener can do much to help disturbed individuals overcome their resistances to seeing a psychiatrist.

[28] Howe, H. F., and Wolman, W. Guide for evaluating employability after psychiatric illness. *J. Amer. Med. Assn.,* 1962, *181,* 146, 1086–1089.

[29] Himler, L. E. *Dealing with difficult personality problems in an organization.* Ann Arbor, Mich.: University of Michigan Bureau of Industrial Relations, 1955; Kahn, R. L., Wolfe, D. M., Quinn, R. P., Snoek, J. P. and Rosenthal, R. A. *Organizational stress: Studies in role conflict and ambiguity.* New York: Wiley, 1964; Rogers, C. R. *On becoming a person.* Boston, Houghton Mifflin, 1968.

Laboratory Exercise

Role Playing: The Case of the Frustrated Supervisor

(*Students are asked not to read the case materials before participating in the laboratory exercise.*)

A. Preparation for role playing.
1. Class is to be divided into pairs seated side by side.
2. One member of pair is to take the role of Jim Wells; other member, the role of Bill Jackson. Each reads only the instructions for his own role.
3. Bill Jacksons leave seats; at a given signal they return and role playing begins:

B. Role playing.
1. Pairs play simultaneously. They should finish after about 15 minutes of interaction.
2. When half of the pairs have finished, the instructor can give the others a two-minute warning.

C. Discussion.
1. Determine how each of the Bill Jacksons feels toward Jim Wells.
2. Determine how each of the Bills feels toward Joe.
3. Determine what was done in each case with Joe.
4. Discuss what Wells could have done to make Bill feel better about Joe.
5. Other points should be discussed as the class wishes. No specific conclusions need be attempted by the class or contributed by the instructor. The objectives are to increase sensitivity to feeling, stimulate a permissive attitude, and develop listening skills.

D. Follow-up (use only if time permits).
1. Assign role of Joe Blake (E.3) to a class member.
2. After he has read the role he should be seated at a desk, supposedly having returned to the job.
3. Various Jacksons will have been willing to take Joe back, but they will disagree as to how he should be treated or talked to. Several viewpoints for the proper treatment should be posted.
4. Jacksons having differing opinions should then be assigned to go to Joe's desk and demonstrate how they think Joe should be handled. These demonstrations should be terminated as soon as Joe has had a chance to respond, thus indicating how he feels about the approach. After several demonstrations this aspect of the case may be opened for general discussion.

E. Materials for the case.

1. ROLE FOR JIM WELLS, DIVISION SUPERVISOR

You are the supervisor of a division employing about 75 men and women and six first-line supervisors. You like your job and the supervisors and employees who work for you, and you feel that they cooperate with you in every way.

This morning you noticed that one of your first-line supervisors, Bill Jackson, was rather late in getting to work. Since Bill is very conscientious and was working on a rush job, you wondered what had happened. Bill is thoroughly dependable, and when something delays him he always tries to phone you. For this reason you were somewhat concerned and were about to call his home when one of Bill's men, a young fellow named Joe Blake, came in. Joe is a good-natured kid, just out of high school, but this time he was obviously angry, and said that he was not going to work for Bill another minute and was going to quit unless you got him another job. Evidently Bill had come in, started to work, and then lost his temper completely when young Joe didn't do something quite right.

Although Bill occasionally has his bad moods, it is unlike him to lose his temper this way. This latest rush job may have put him under too much pressure but even so his outburst this morning seems difficult to explain on any reasonable grounds. You feel, therefore, that something must be seriously wrong and if you can get Bill to talk about whatever it is that is bothering him, you may get the situation straightened out. In any case you are determined not to get into an argument with Bill or criticize him in any way. Instead you are going to try to get him to talk about his troubles; you will listen to what he has to say, and indicate that you understand how he feels about things. If Bill seems more angry than Joe's mistake would reasonably justify, you might suppose that there is something more behind all this and Bill would probably feel a lot better if he got it off his chest. If Bill is thoroughly angry with Joe, you may suggest that Joe be fired in order to demonstrate that you have not taken Joe's side in the matter.

You talked with Joe for several minutes and, after he had told his side of the story, he felt better and was ready to go back on the job. You just phoned Bill and asked him to drop around when he had a chance. Bill said he'd come right over and is walking toward your office now.

2. ROLE FOR BILL JACKSON, FIRST-LINE SUPERVISOR

You have just come to work after a series of the most humiliating and irritating experiences you have ever had. Last night your next-door neighbor, Sam Jones, had a wild, drunken party at his house that kept you awake most of the night. Jones is a blustering, disagreeable man who has no consideration whatever for others. When you called him at about 3:00 A.M. and told him to be less noisy, he was abusive and insulting. Things quieted down later on, but when you finally got some rest, you overslept.

Since you were in the midst of a rush job at the company, you skipped breakfast to hurry to work. As you were leaving the house, you noticed that someone had driven a car across one corner of your lawn and torn out several feet of your new hedge. You were certain that Jones or one of the drunks at his party had done it, so you ran right over to Jones's house, determined to have it out with him. He not only denied everything, but practically threw you out and threatened to knock your teeth out if you didn't shut up and behave yourself; and you knew that he was big enough to do it.

When you came to work, more than an hour late, your nerves were so ragged that you were actually shaking. Everything conceivable had gone wrong. The last straw was when you discovered that Joe Blake, a young high school recruit, had made a mistake that delayed you several hours on your rush job, or at least it would have if you hadn't caught him in time. Naturally you gave him a good going over for his carelessness. Blake said he wouldn't take that kind of abuse from anyone and walked out on you. You noticed that he went in to see your supervisor, Jim Wells. Obviously he is in there accusing you of being rough on him. Well, you don't like that kind of attitude in a trainee either, and if he has gone in there complaining you'll make him wish he'd never been born. You have had all you can stand, and the big boss had better not get tough with you because he'll have one hell of a time getting the job done without you. Jim had that complainer in there and talked to him for quite a while before he phoned you to come in. Gabbing when there's work to be done—that's certainly a hell of a way to run things. You are on your way to Jim's office now and have no intention of wasting time on words.

3. ROLE FOR JOE BLAKE
(To be used only if Section D is incorporated)

This morning when you came to work, Jackson wasn't there to get you started. Since you are just out of high school and are learning the job, Mr. Jackson always was on hand to outline the program you are to follow on a given day.

You know that your unit is in the middle of a rush job and so you became anxious about getting started. After waiting half an hour you decided to see what you could do about setting up the operation by yourself. You had a good idea about what was wanted and after looking over the job and doing some figuring on it you felt you had it ready to go. Just as you'd finished your preparations, Jackson showed up. Instead of praising you for your initiative he lit into you for a small technical oversight you'd made. At first you couldn't believe your ears but he went on abusing you and talking about the damage you would have done, if he hadn't caught the mistake in time. You decided you wouldn't work for a boss like that and told him you weren't used to that kind of treatment. You went to Mr. Wells' office and told him you wanted a transfer. Mr. Wells listened to your side of the story and suggested you wait a while until things simmered down. Mr. Wells is a very nice man so you decided to go along with his suggestions and have returned to the job to await further developments.

Suggested Readings

Berkowitz, L. *Aggression: A social psychological analysis.* New York: McGraw-Hill, 1962.

Carkhuff, R. R. Differential functioning of lay and professional helpers. *J. consult. Psychol.,* 1968, 15, 117–126.

Gregory, I. *Fundamentals of psychiatry.* Philadelphia: Saunders, 1968.

Kahn, R. L., Wolfe, D. M., Quinn, R. P., Snoek, J. P., and Rosenthal, R. A. *Organizational stress: Studies in role conflict and ambiguity.* New York: Wiley, 1964.

Maier, N. R. F. *Frustration.* New York: McGraw-Hill, 1949. Reissued Ann Arbor, Mich.: University of Michigan Press, 1961.

Rogers, C. R. *On becoming a person.* Boston: Houghton Mifflin, 1968.

Yates, A. J. *Frustration and conflict: Selected readings.* Princeton, N.J.: Van Nostrand, 1965.

5

Morale and Group Processes

General Considerations

G. W. Allport defined national morale as an individual attitude in a group endeavor.[1] This statement implies that both personal and social features are involved in the mental condition we call morale. To have high morale, he believed (1) that the individual must possess firm convictions and values which make life worthwhile for him so that he has the energy and confidence to face the future; (2) that he must be aware of a job to be done to defend or extend his store of values; and (3) that his values must be in essential agreement with those of his group, and there must be a coordination of effort in attaining objectives. Another authority on this subject points out that morale involves two factors: the presence of a common goal among the group members and the acceptance of socially recognized pathways toward that goal.[2]

The term morale is a group concept referring to the relationships existing in a group of individuals.[3] We will follow the same usage and not refer to the morale of individuals. Without groups there is no need for the term.

Group Conditions Affecting Morale

The group conditions affecting morale are at least three in number: (a) the extent to which the members of a group have a common goal; (b) the extent to which the goal is regarded as worthwhile; (c) the extent to which members feel the goal can be achieved.

[1] Allport, G. W. The nature of democratic morale. In G. Watson (Ed.), *Civilian morale.* Boston: Houghton Mifflin, 1942, Ch. 1.

[2] Katz, D. Group morale and individual motivation. In J. E. Hulett, Jr., and R. Stagner (Eds.), *Problems in social psychology.* Urbana, Ill.: Allerton Conference on Social Psychology, University of Illinois, 1952, Ch. 14.

[3] Stouffer, S. A., *et al. The American soldier: adjustment during Army life* (Vol. 1). Princeton, N.J.: Princeton University Press, 1949.

A baseball team can have poor morale even though each individual player is highly motivated and has a healthy attitude. This occurs when one player is motivated to achieve a home-run record, another to get the lead on stolen bases, another to increase his batting average, still another to hold the lead in runs batted in, and so on. Such a team does not have team spirit or high morale because the first essential condition is lacking—a common goal. Similarly, when employees strive for individual recognition or to protect themselves from criticism, there is no tendency to help one another or to cooperate in a team score.

Even if the team members had no personal goals and had a common objective, this would not be enough. If a major league baseball team sets its goal for fourth place, the players may question whether or not the effort is worth the victory, since they will not share in any World Series bonus. If a group is to cooperate willingly in expending energy, the common goal must satisfy needs recognized as important to the membership.

To have high team spirit, goals which are common and worthwhile must also be realistic. For a ball club to aspire to first place in the league might be a natural and worthwhile goal, but if the team finished the previous year in last place, there would be no strong belief that the goal could be achieved. The first bit of misfortune would break the team spirit. Similarly, an industrial inspection goal of no rejects, or an accident record goal of a 50 per cent decrease from the year before, may be viewed by workers as unattainable, hence may cause them to become irritated with management rather than to work as a team.

Generally speaking, success raises a group's morale while failure lowers it.[4] Thus high morale and group effectiveness interact and influence each other. One of the values of group success is that the achievement is shared and the person who contributes the most becomes a helpful member rather than a threat.

Characteristics of High Morale

Words commonly used to describe high morale are: (*a*) team spirit; (*b*) staying quality; (*c*) zest or enthusiasm; and (*d*) resistance to frustration. Groups with high morale also accomplish things with a minimum of bickering, and do things because they want to rather than because they are afraid not to. In describing groups with low morale, such terms as (*a*) apathy, (*b*) bickering, (*c*) jealousies, (*d*) disjointed effort, and (*e*) pessimism, are relevant. Despite the fact that these two sets of words are not all antonyms, the general picture portrayed is one of opposites.

Measuring Morale and Related Phenomena

Some Definitions

The possibility that morale and productivity are related made social conditions in a factory an important field for investigation. A review of the literature,[5] however,

---

[4] Zander, A. *Motives and goals in groups.* New York: Academic Press, 1971.

[5] Brayfield, A. H., and Crockett, W. H. Employee attitudes and employee performance. *Psychol. Bull.,* 1955, *52*, 396–424.

revealed that the problem was far more complex than initially supposed. Morale and productivity seemed related up to a point but it was also possible to raise production while lowering morale.[6] Thus it seems that poor morale is related to low production but high production depends upon a variety of motivating conditions.

Investigators used a variety of techniques for measuring morale which may account for some of the inconsistencies in results pertaining to the relationship between morale and productivity. It soon became clear that more specific concepts were needed. Therefore, concepts such as group cohesiveness, supportive behavior, attraction to the group, job attitudes, and job satisfaction were used and, although somewhat more restrictive in meaning, we will find that they too have more than one dimension. In general it is now believed that descriptions of group organization must be multidimensional.

Group Cohesiveness. Likert[7] refers to cohesiveness as a condition of a group which causes members to (1) work toward common goals, (2) think in terms of "we," (3) manifest friendliness toward one another, (4) stick together, and (5) function as a unit. These qualities or dimensions are strikingly similar to those discussed under morale, but there is a difference. Cohesiveness stresses the desire to belong to a group, whereas morale stresses more the unified goal orientation.[8]

Seashore,[9] for example, found that high-cohesive groups could either show high production through cooperating with management, or effectively curtail production by their united opposition. Thus, production was related to high cohesiveness only when group and company goals were in harmony. The concept of high morale, if differentiated from high cohesiveness, would only incorporate groups which had goals in harmony with the leadership goals. This type of difference in meanings perhaps also accounts for some of the discrepancies in the relationship between productivity and various morale measures.

Supportive Behavior. Likert[10] uses the term *supportive* to describe the behavior of both leaders and group members. It refers to acts which make an individual feel he is accepted and belongs in a group. This concept incorporates the leader as part of the group and is suggestive of a family unit.

Attraction to the Group. The degree to which individuals like their membership in a group is obviously related to cohesiveness of the membership. However, it represents a description of individual attitudes toward membership and thus is less

---

6 Likert, R. *Developing patterns of management.* New York: American Management Assn., 1955, General Management Series, No. 178.

7 Muldoon, J. F. The concentration of liked and disliked members in groups and the relationship of the concentration to group cohesiveness. *Sociometry,* 1955, *18,* 73–81.

8 Albert, R. S. Comments on the scientific function of the concepts of cohesiveness. *Amer. J. Sociol.,* 1953, *59,* 231–234.

9 Seashore, S. E. *Group cohesiveness in the industrial work group.* Ann Arbor, Mich.: Survey Research Center, University of Michigan, 1954.

10 Likert, R. *New patterns of management.* New York: McGraw-Hill, 1961.

a description of a group phenomenon. In order to obtain a group value one would have to average individual reactions. The merit of the term lies in the fact that it is specific and easy to measure.

Job Satisfaction. Like attraction to the group, job satisfaction represents an individual's reaction. Its relationship to morale resides in the fact that job satisfaction is influenced by one's associates or teammates and by the leadership. However, job satisfaction is also influenced by individual adjustments to the job, and thus represents a complex of satisfactions.

Measuring Instruments

The Questionnaire. The survey type of approach to measuring group conditions uses either standardized interviews or questionnaires. From a general survey, questions relevant to the group condition are used to develop a morale index by assigning values to alternative answers. Table 5.1 reproduces the items used by Seashore[11] to measure group cohesiveness. The individual's score is obtained by adding the values assigned to each of his responses, while the group score is obtained by averaging the individual scores of the various work groups. Seashore used the group scores for classifying 228 work groups into seven levels of cohesiveness. The fact that groups with high cohesive scores were happier and better adjusted suggests that high cohesive scores did measure a group climate, but the fact remains that the group measure is the average member's report of the way he feels about the group, and his opinion of how the members relate with one another. Two groups with the same average could have quite different interpersonal relations, but the group scores nevertheless serve as approximations.

In-group versus Out-group Choices. Another way of measuring group solidarity is to determine the number of friendship ties existing among members of a group. Cohesiveness or attraction to the group would be indicated by the ratio of in-group choices to out-group choices or in terms of the percentage of in-group choices to choices available.[12] The group score would be based on some method for combining the individual scores. This type of group analysis, known as sociometry, will be discussed later in this chapter.

Ratings. Finally, members may reveal their feelings toward one another by having each person rate how much he liked each of the other members. The average rating an individual assigned to other members would become that individual's attraction to the group.

That the three measures of group organization are inconsistent causes one to question the objective value of some of the research.[13] Are some measures more

[11] Seashore, *op. cit.*

[12] Torrance, P. E. Sociometric techniques for diagnosing group ills. *Sociometry*, 1956, *18*, 597–612.

[13] Hoffman, L. R. A note on ratings versus choices as measures of group attraction. *Sociometry*, 1962, *25*, 313–320.

Value Assigned	

Q. 51. Do you feel that you are really a part of your work group? (Check one)

5	_____	Really a part of my work group
4	_____	Included in most ways
3	_____	Included in some ways, but not in others
2	_____	Don't feel I really belong
1	_____	Don't work with any one group

Q. 52. If you had a chance to do the same kind of work for the same pay, in another work group, how would you feel about moving?

1	_____	Would want very much to move
2	_____	Would rather move than stay where I am
3	_____	Would make no difference to me
4	_____	Would rather stay where I am than move
5	_____	Would want very much to stay where I am

Q. 50. How does your work group compare with other work groups at Midwest on each of the following points:

a. The way men get along together

3	_____	Better than most
2	_____	About the same as most
1	_____	Not as good as most

b. The way the men stick together

3	_____	Better than most
2	_____	About the same as most
1	_____	Not as good as most

c. The way the men help each other on the job

3	_____	Better than most
2	_____	About the same as most
1	_____	Not as good as most

5 represents the lowest cohesiveness score possible.
19 represents the highest cohesiveness score possible.
Group indexes were obtained by taking the average score in the group.

After S. E. Seashore, *Group cohesiveness in the industrial work group*. Ann Arbor, Mich.: Survey Research Center, University of Michigan, 1954.

Table 5.1 / Questionnaire Items Used to Measure Cohesiveness

accurate than others, or does each measure pick up a somewhat different aspect of group phenomenon? It appears that in the haste to obtain quantitative scores, qualitative distinctions have been overlooked. It is the qualitative distinctions that give us the various dimensions of a phenomenon.

Lack of Group Index. Although morale has been defined as a group phenomenon, all approaches to its measurement have been based upon the opinions of group members rather than on group behavior. Perhaps staying quality, group enthusiasm, and resistance to frustration can be inferred from members' attraction toward one another, but the structure of the group, as an organization, has not been determined by the studies of individual opinions. It would seem that the ratings of observers of group behavior would be more relevant for the analysis of group phenomena. The roles a person plays in one group may be quite different from his roles in another group. Similarly, communication and cooperation would take on different forms. The change in group activity when the group process changes from conflict to problem solving is very striking. The same group may carry out a variety of group processes from one day to the next, yet members might not change their responses on a morale questionnaire. We will return to the topic of group process later in this chapter.

Even though surveys have failed to measure group behavior as such, the investigations do not necessarily lack value. The feelings an individual experiences in being an accepted member of his work group, in having a job the company thinks is important, and in being respected by his supervisor are important and can reveal information of value to the company. Even if investigators have used different items to make up a morale index, the results obtained with one index are useful in evaluating departments and companies. The error lies in combining data obtained from different instruments and assuming that each instrument is valid.

Cohesiveness scores based on individual measures do reflect aspects of group behavior. Highly cohesive groups are less prone to be disrupted and divided by failure.[14] Actually, threat from the outside increases a group's cohesiveness score.[15]

Results of Surveys

Satisfaction with the Company

Some work situations are more conducive to job satisfaction than others. Such factors as company attitude toward employees and toward society in general, the type of foreman, the sanitary facilities, the lighting, ventilation, and attractiveness of the shop, all give the factory an atmosphere which influences the attitudes of the workers. Finally, past experiences, such as discouragements at home and at work, former insecurities, and status in society, determine the goals for which a person will work.

Many of these factors are controlled or influenced by top management personnel, who are therefore in a position to raise or lower the morale of their employees. A single decision of the president of a company may alter the morale of the whole company more than a big program of activity administered at a lower level.

Investigations show that general employee morale varies greatly from one company to another. In one study, data were obtained from 49,962 rank-and-file employees in 141 different groups from all sections of the country.[16] The average

[14] Lippitt, R. The morale of youth groups. In G. Watson (Ed.), *Civilian morale.* Boston: Houghton Mifflin, 1942, Ch. 7.

[15] Pepitone, A., and Kleiner, R. The effects of threat and frustration on group cohesiveness. *J. abnorm. soc. Psychol.*, 1957, 54, 192–199; Schachter, S. *The psychology of affiliation.* Stanford, Calif.: Stanford University Press, 1959.

[16] Hull, R. L., and Kolstad, A. Morale on the job. In G. Watson (Ed.), *Civilian morale, op. cit.*, pp. 349–364.

morale score for the different companies showed significant variations and indicated that the employers could influence the score to an important degree. Such factors as type of work performed and wage level were relatively insignificant, while the type of boss and various forms of job satisfaction were very important. The importance to morale of an employee's immediate superior was apparent from the fact that departmental variation within a company was more marked than the differences between companies. Even when pay and hours of work were matched, wide departmental variation was apparent, and analysis revealed that the conduct of the immediate superiors was the important factor. The importance of type of work and wages becomes evident, however, when other factors are equated. When jobs are classified according to ego involvement, job satisfaction is related to the type of work.[17]

Job satisfaction was shown to be important by demonstrating that the morale index was definitely higher among employees who were satisfied than among those who were dissatisfied on the following specific items:

1. A fair hearing and square deal on grievances
2. The prospects of a satisfactory future
3. The company's knowledge of the employee's qualifications and progress
4. Recognition of and credit for constructive suggestions offered
5. Friendly and helpful criticism of work or correction of errors
6. Pay increases when deserved
7. Recognition and praise for unusually good work
8. Selection of best-qualified employees for promotion when vacancies arise
9. Amount of work required not unreasonable
10. Pay at least as high as the going rate for the same type of work elsewhere
11. Freedom to seek help when difficult problems arise in work
12. Freedom from unjust reprimand
13. Satisfactory daily working hours
14. The company's vacation policy

The importance of these items in their influence on morale is in the order listed. Many of the psychological satisfactions tend to be higher in the list than the purely material ones. However, the relative importance of various factors changes with the times. Under certain economic conditions, such as the upswing in the economic cycle in 1940, concern over pay is the most important factor in satisfaction.[18] Interest in pay also depends upon the job. High-skill jobs make pay and working conditions less important than do low-skill jobs.[19]

Although relationships between high morale and productivity are frequently obtained, they are not different measures of the same thing and they are not invari-

---

[17] Gurin, G., Veroff, J., and Feld, S. *Americans view mental health.* New York: Basic Books, 1960.

[18] Stagner, R. Psychological aspects of industrial conflict: II. Motivation. *Personnel Psychol.,* 1950, *3*, 1–15.

[19] Fairchild, M. Skill and specialization. *Personnel J.* 1930, *9,* 28–71, 128–175.

ably related.[20] A survey of railroad workers[21] revealed that high- and low-producing sections did not differ in the degree to which they were satisfied with the work situation, the company, job status, and wages. Productivity and morale both depend upon many factors, and it is not surprising that they are related only under some conditions.

A review of studies of the relationship between job satisfaction and productivity also show mixed results, ranging from high positive relationships ($r = .86$) to low negative relationships ($r = -.31$).[22] It is evident that the sources of satisfaction are only in part related to those inducing motivation. Since satisfaction can come from the job, one's boss, company policy, work companions, and the challenge of the work, these mixed relationships obtained are not surprising.

Position in the Group

One study demonstrated a striking relationship between popularity and job satisfaction.[23] The most popular workers, when compared with the least popular ones, not only felt more satisfied with their jobs but they also (*a*) felt more secure, (*b*) considered their working conditions better, (*c*) felt their coworkers to be more friendly, (*d*) were more satisfied with their opportunities to communicate with management, (*e*) had more confidence in the ability of their supervisors, (*f*) were more inclined to believe that the company was interested in their welfare, and (*g*) had more confidence in the good intentions and good sense of the management. Employees' views of their jobs or their company depend not only upon the nature of their work and the kind of treatment the company gives them, but also upon their status with other employees. This means that management must concern itself with creating conditions for employees which make for mutual feelings of being wanted and liked in a group.

The dependence of morale on the experience of group membership is also borne out in survey data,[24] which show that problems of morale vary with large and small groups. Generally speaking, the problem of maintaining morale is easier if employees are divided into small work groups. In some organizational structures where work groups are large, employees actually have difficulty in identifying both their units and their bosses. Research with discussion groups shows that satisfaction declines if groups are increased from five to 12; when groups exceed 12 the skill of the leader becomes an essential feature in successful group discussions.[25] These find-

[20] Kahn, R. L., and Morse, N. C. The relationship of productivity to morale. *J. soc. Issues,* 1951, 7, 8–17; Wechsler, I. R., Kahane, M., and Tannenbaum, R. Job satisfaction, productivity and morale: a case study. *Occup. Psychol.,* London, 1952, 26, 1–14.

[21] Katz, D., *et al. Productivity, supervision and morale among railroad workers.* Ann Arbor, Mich.: Institute for Social Research, University of Michigan, 1951.

[22] Vroom, V. *Work and motivation.* New York: Wiley, 1964.

[23] Van Zelst, R. H. Worker popularity and job satisfaction. *Personnel Psychol.,* 1951, 4, 405–412.

[24] Pelz, D. C. Leadership within a hierarchical organization. *J. soc. Issues,* 1951, 7, 49–55; Pelz, D. C. Influence: A key to effective leadership in the first-line supervisor. *Personnel,* 1952, 29, 209–217.

[25] Hare, A. P. Interaction and consensus in different sized groups. *Amer. soc. Rev.,* 1952, 17, 261–267.

ings suggest that large work groups should be subdivided so that the number of persons reporting to a given supervisor does not greatly exceed 12. However, a possible source of error in survey data must be checked: large groups are more likely to report dissatisfactions on a questionnaire than small groups because identification is more remote.

The Immediate Supervisor

The immediate supervisor has more influence on the attitudes of his subordinates than does the job.[26] He is generally regarded as an important determiner of morale[27] and surveys repeatedly show the dependence of productivity on supervisory behavior. A survey of office workers[28] revealed that most of the differences between the high- and low-producing work groups were related to some aspect of supervision. Some of the more important conclusions are:

1. Supervisors in high-producing groups have been given more freedom and more general supervision from their superiors than those in low-producing groups, who tended to receive close supervision.

2. Supervisors of high-producing groups tend to be satisfied with the amount of authority and responsibility they have in running their jobs, whereas supervisors of low-producing groups tend to be dissatisfied on these points.

3. Supervisors of high-producing groups are more aware of their leadership function and spend more time in planning and organizing the work than do supervisors of low-producing groups, who are more inclined to help out by doing some of the actual work themselves.

4. Supervisors of high-producing groups tend to give general supervision and leave details to employees, while supervisors of low-producing groups tend to give close supervision.

Employees quickly develop attitudes toward their supervisors. In a study of telephone repairmen and installers, a variety of attitudes toward foremen was measured.[29] Pairs of foremen were then exchanged so that the change for a crew always involved a switch between an above-average and a below-average foreman. Four months after the switch, attitudes were again measured. It was found that within this time the foremen had developed the same kind of attitudes within their new crews as they had within their old crews.

One of the most striking relationships reported thus far is that between attitude

---

[26] Campbell, D. B. Relative influence of job and supervision on shared work attitudes. *J. appl. Psychol.*, 1971, *35*, 521–525.

[27] Baruch, D. W. Why they terminate. *J. consult. Psychol.*, 1944, 8, 35–46.

[28] Katz, D., Maccoby, N., and Morse, N. C. *Productivity, supervision and morale in an office situation.* Ann Arbor, Mich.: Institute for Social Research, University of Michigan, 1950; Katz, D., Maccoby, N., Gurin, G., and Floor, L. G. *Productivity, supervision, and morale among railroad workers.* Ann Arbor, Mich.: Institute for Social Research, University of Michigan, 1951. Kahn, R. L., and Katz, D. Leadership practices in relation to productivity and morale. In D. Cartwright and A. Zander (Eds.), *Group dynamics.* Evanston, Ill.: Row, Peterson, 1953, Ch. 41.

[29] Jackson, J. M. The effect of changing the leadership of small work groups. *Hum. Relat.*, 1953, 6, 25–44.

toward a superior (score on questionnaire) and productivity (based on ratings).[30] A careful study showed these two measures to yield a correlation coefficient of .86, which is exceptionally high.

Although there is a great deal of evidence on the importance of the supervisor in determining the effectiveness of a group, Kahn, after reviewing the Michigan Survey Research Center studies, concluded that the supervisor's behavior is not the only determiner of a group's motivation to produce.[31] He is just one of the important variables. The effectiveness of groups is also influenced by the size of the company unit (comparisons of eleven airline locations indicate that involvement and personal satisfaction decline with increasing size), locality, and type of work.[32]

Different work groups also require quite different forms of leadership. In technical and research groups the supervisor must steer between a policy of complete hands-off and one of overdirection, depending in part upon the length of service. One study[33] revealed that stimulation and job satisfaction of scientific personnel depends greatly on professional colleagues and periodic regrouping. Danielson[34] pointed out that engineers and scientists encounter frustration and need the supervisor as a safety valve. Certainly these groups are more varied in their ambitions and must be given individual consideration.

The early research in leadership focused on personality traits (e.g., intelligence, stability, decisiveness) that made a person a leader. It soon became evident that the requirements of leaders in government, education, science, supervision, and administration are different. Fiedler's studies relate leadership traits to types of groups and to the nature of the situation, but even with those considerations his findings reveal questionable trends.[35] It might also be expected that requirements for gaining leadership positions by force, by appointment, and by election would differ, and that obtaining a given leadership position might require different abilities than performing effectively once it was obtained. Other important variables are the changing concepts of leadership which depend on increased knowledge and new social values so that leadership requirements may differ from one generation to another. Because of these varied influences and because there is perhaps no one best way to lead, the trait approach has failed to be fruitful.[36]

A breakthrough in the study of leadership came from concepts of Kurt Lewin

[30] Lawshe, C. H., and Nagle, B. F. Productivity and attitude toward supervisor. *J. appl. Psychol.*, 1953, *37,* 159–162.

[31] Kahn, R. L. The prediction of productivity. *J. soc. Issues,* 1956, *12,* 41–49.

[32] Baumgartel, H., and Sobel, R. Background and organizational factors in absenteeism. *Personnel Psychol.,* 1959, *12,* 431–433.

[33] Pelz, D. C. Social factors in the motivation of engineers and scientists. *School Sci. & Math.,* 1958, June, 417–429.

[34] Danielson, L. E. *Characteristics of engineers and scientists.* Rep. 11. Ann Arbor, Mich.: Bureau of Industrial Relations, University of Michigan, 1960.

[35] Fiedler, F. E. *A Theory of leadership effectiveness.* New York: McGraw-Hill, 1967; Graen, G., Alvares, K., and Orris, J. B. Contingency model of leadership effectiveness: Antecedent and evidential results. *Psychol. Bull.,* 1970, 74, 285–296.

[36] Hollander, E. P., and Julian, J. W. Contemporary trends in the analysis of leadership processes. *Psychol. Bull.,* 1969, *71,* 387–397.

and his coworkers.[37] In laboratory experiments the effects of different locations of responsibility rather than personality differences were varied. Three locations were tested: the leader, the group, and the individual. These became arbitrary definitions of autocracy, democracy, and laissez-faire (anarchy), respectively, and sparked the emphasis on participatory leadership in surveys.[38] Since none of these styles exists in a pure state in real life situations unless training is given, most industrial surveys do not lend themselves to this classification of leadership. The implications of this research will therefore be treated in Chapter 6.

Leadership Styles Derived from Surveys

The Employee-Centered Supervisor

The Survey Research Center at the University of Michigan classifies supervisors as ranging between *employee-centered* and *job-centered* in their attitudes toward supervision.[39] This classification is based upon questionnaire responses relating to supervisory behaviors. A number of studies indicate that groups with employee-centered supervisors are more likely to be among the high-producing groups, while groups with job-centered supervisors are more likely to be among the low-producing groups. Figure 5.1 illustrates the type of evidence used to support this conclusion.

The employee-centered supervisor takes employees' needs into account, offers employees more freedom, and gives subordinates a sense of personal worth, (that is, is supportive). The *supportive* supervisor achieves both morale and productivity, providing he has high standards of performance and communicates his enthusiasm to his group.[40]

This conceptualization tends to make employee-centered and job-centered styles opposites on a continuum and indicates that both cannot be achieved simultaneously. Employee-centered is frequently regarded as participative and job-centered as autocratic, while supportive behavior seems to be a good definition of paternalism.

Consideration and Initiating Structure

Another classification of supervisory behavior widely used in research is based on measures of *initiating structure* and *consideration*.[41] Each is treated as a dimension. The dimension of *consideration* reflects the extent to which the leader establishes two-way communication, mutual respect, and a consideration of feelings for his

[37] Lewin, K., Lippitt, R., and White, R. K. Patterns of aggressive behavior in experimentally-created social climates. *J. soc. Psychol.*, 1939, *10*, 271–301.

[38] Vroom, V. H. *Some personality determinants of the effects of participation.* Englewood Cliffs, N.J.: Prentice-Hall, 1960; Marrow, A. J., Bowers, D. G., and Seashore, S. E. *Management by participation.* New York: Harper & Row, 1967; Likert, *op. cit.*

[39] Likert, *op. cit.*

[40] Kahn, *op. cit.;* Likert, R., and Seashore, S. E. Motivation and morale in public service. *Publ. Personnel Rev.*, 1956, *17*, 268–274.

[41] Stogdill, R. M., and Coons, A. E. *Leader behavior: Its description and measurement.* Research Monograph, No. 88, Bureau of Business Research, Ohio State University, 1957.

	Groups with job-centered supervisors	Groups with employee-centered supervisors
High-producing sections	1	6
Low-producing sections	7	3

Figure 5.1 / Relation between Productivity and Leadership. When supervisors are classified as either job-centered or employee-centered and their work sections are classified as either high- or low-producing, job-centered supervisors are most likely to have low-producing sections while employee-centered supervisors are most likely to have high-producing units. (After R. Likert, *New patterns of management.* New York: McGraw-Hill, 1961.)

subordinates. It represents the human relations aspect of leadership. *Initiating structure* reflects the extent to which the leader facilitates group interaction toward goal attainment. This involves planning, scheduling, criticizing, initiating ideas, and so on. Analysis of data based upon these measures shows these two dimensions to be quite independent. Both are measured by questionnaire responses that subordinates give to describe their supervisors. Table 5.2 shows some representative items from questionnaires used.

These two dimensions of leadership have been found to be related to absenteeism, accidents, grievances, and turnover. In general, these undesirable behaviors are associated with high initiating structure scores and low consideration scores.[42] High consideration thus seems to be more related to morale and job satisfaction factors and is similar to employee-centered supervision. High consideration was associated with production measures only when the work had no deadline. In situations where deadlines and production measures were important, high initiating structure was related to production.[43]

Supervisors, when evaluating subordinates, assign greater value to task-oriented

[42] Fleishman, E. A., and Harris, E. F. Patterns of leadership related to employee grievances and turnover. *Personnel Psychol.*, 1962, *15*, 43–56.

[43] Fleishman, F. A., Harris, E. F., and Burtt, H. E. *Leadership and supervision in industry.* Research Monograph, No. 33. Columbus, Ohio: Bureau of Education, 1955.

Consideration

_____ He sees that a person is rewarded for a job well done.
_____ He makes those in the group feel at ease when talking with him.
_____ He refuses to give in when people disagree with him. (scored negatively)
_____ He changes the duties of people without first talking it over with them. (scored negatively)
_____ He backs up his men in their actions.

Initiating Structure

_____ He offers new approaches to problems.
_____ He asks for sacrifices for the good of the entire department.
_____ He assigns people to particular tasks.
_____ He criticizes poor work.
_____ He encourages slow-working people to greater effort.

From E. A. Fleishman, The description of supervisory behavior. *J. appl. Psychol.,* 1953, *37*, 1–6. Copyright 1953 by the American Psychological Association, and reproduced by permission.

Table 5.2 / Items Illustrating Leader Behavior Patterns

behaviors than do subordinates, who in turn appreciate consideration and permissiveness.[44] Thus conflicts between the goals of higher management and of workers appear. If the subordinates perceive the supervisor as a helper rather than a critic when he tries to improve performance, some of the conflict between efficiency and permissiveness may be reduced. But for most supervisors the reconciliation would be difficult.

Conflict in Leadership Goals

Groups satisfied with their leadership and their interpersonal relations are superior from an organizational point of view in that cooperation and communication are enhanced. Production and work efficiency, however, depend on more than organization, and it is possible to raise production while sacrificing organization. Some companies use surveys to develop a morale index, and evaluate their supervisors on the basis of these indices as well as on production and service measures. The goals of efficiency and morale are not necessarily related. A supervisor can conceivably increase morale by relaxing standards. Certainly it would be easier for a supervisor with low standards to be supportive and considerate than one with high standards. Also, it would be possible to upgrade job performance by concentrating on immediate objectives and sacrificing morale for the time being. Economy drives frequently cut costs at the expense of organization.

How Employees Cause Leader's Behavior

The behavior of subordinates may also influence the superior's attitude. In a simulated study,[45] some foremen were told their subordinates were a superior perform-

[44] Filley, A. C., and House, R. J., *Managerial process and organizational behavior.* New York: Scott, Foresman, 1969.
[45] Farris, G. F., and Lim, F. G. Effects of performance on leadership, cohesiveness, influence, satisfaction, and subsequent performance. *J. appl. Psychol.,* 1969, *53,* 490–497.

ing group whereas other foremen were told that their subordinates were one of the worst groups. All foremen had the task of conducting a discussion with three subordinates in which the objective was to get the men to adopt a change in work procedure.

After the meeting the subordinates were asked to fill out a questionnaire revealing their attitude toward the foreman. The foremen of the low-producing groups compared to the high-producing groups were found to be significantly different with regard to:

Having more punitive attitudes
Exerting unreasonable pressure more often
Having less trust in his men
Being less sensitive to needs and feelings of workers
Being less inclined to give recognition for job well done
Having lower performance standards
Having less pride in the group
Giving less freedom
Being a poorer listener
Being a poorer communicator
Placing less emphasis on teamwork

Thus the very leadership characteristics that are related to low-producing groups were described, but in this instance the group's poor productivity caused the leader's behavior. Thus a leader is more inclined to supervise less closely, be more permissive, and be more supportive if he has a superior group of subordinates. The fact that superior and subordinate attitudes are the product of an interaction, not one the cause and the other the effect, must be kept in mind when examining relationships betwen leader behavior and worker productivity.

The Varied Duties of the Supervisor

Employees react to supervisors not only in terms of the personal face-to-face experience they have, but also in terms of the way they run the job and conduct themselves as group leaders. Roughly, a supervisor's duties place him in charge of (*a*) the job environment, (*b*) individual persons, and (*c*) a group of people. The essential aptitudes and skills in these three areas may be quite different and this may explain why there is so little agreement on the essential leadership traits. There is agreement on only 5 per cent of the "discovered" traits, and many studies are in actual disagreement.[46]

In dealing with situations or the job environment, objective problem-solving ability may be important, and technical knowledge as well as psychological information may be needed. For some administrative jobs, skills in this area might be more essential than in others.

Other administrative jobs require that a person perform leadership functions ranging from conducting discussions to making speeches. The relative importance

---

[46] Cartwright and Zander, *Group dynamics, op. cit.,* Ch. 36.

of these duties would vary greatly from one supervisory job to another and might increase as a person rose through the ranks.

Finally, a supervisor's ability in individual relationships, although always important in dealing with superiors, would vary in importance from one supervisory position to another.

Values and Limitations of Surveys

Surveys may give an overall measure of employee morale and obtain information that reveals the cause of specific dissatisfactions.[47] Questionnaires also may reveal the need for training, the effects of various working conditions on attitudes, the nature of employee needs, and many other relationships described in the preceding pages. If the data are to be useful, however, the questionnaire must be properly constructed and the results skillfully analyzed. This means that surveys must be conducted by qualified personnel if their full value is to be realized.

Even when these precautions are taken, one should recognize the primary limitations of the survey technique: it measures symptoms, not causes. When attitudes are unfavorable, employees are hypercritical, and as we have seen in Chapter 4, the object or condition criticized may not indicate the underlying cause of dissatisfaction. Employees may criticize the company restaurant or the rate of pay when a more basic factor may be a feeling that the work done in other departments is more important than their own. This feeling of being in an insignificant department may in turn be caused by the fact that the department has few high classification jobs, and as a consequence promotions are rare. Dissatisfied employees will find things to criticize; it is important to discover the causes of dissatisfaction before acting on complaints.

For a similar reason, discovering the most effective practices is impossible using the survey method. One can determine which of several procedures employees like best or which work groups yield the highest production, but one is limited to an evaluation of things already known and practiced. The best of all methods of supervision may not be practiced by anyone, hence could not be discovered by a survey.

In order to get a large proportion of a company's management interested in improving morale, they must be involved in the problem. The important requisite to this involvement is the use of data obtained in their own company. Company representatives should also be involved in collection of the data.[48] The Survey Research Center at the University of Michigan also advocates involving a company in analysis of the data and in discussions of corrective procedures.[49] The plan followed is to have a supervisor from each level present data obtained from his unit, section, or department to the supervisors reporting to him. The best results are gained when the data are treated as "information which may be helpful to us in

---

[47] Dunlap, J. The management of morale. *Personnel Psychol.*, 1950, *3*, 353–359.
[48] Jacobson, E., *et al.* Research in functioning organizations. *J. soc. Issues*, 1951, *7*, 64–71.
[49] Mann, F. C. Changing superior-subordinate relationships. *J. soc. Issues*, 1951, *7*, 56–63.

suggesting ways for improving conditions." Survey data, when used to show up weak groups, are soon self-defeating.

General Principles for Managers

Five fundamental concepts emerge from the review of literature on studies relating to morale and may serve as guiding principles for the supervisor. These are intended to indicate the important problem areas over which he has control.

Mutual Sacrifice and Fairness

People will tolerate deprivation and hardship if all in a group are subjected to the same conditions. However, when some are given special privileges or are shown favoritism, the others are demoralized. Hardships or benefits as such do not make or break morale, but the manner in which they are distributed does. The problem of being fair is a difficult one since each person usually applies his own standard of fairness rather than that of the group.[50]

The level of morale is raised if the group knows why certain practices are employed. Employers should also have definite rules and standards to guide them in the selection of individuals for special treatment or promotion, so that supervisors will not be suspected of showing favoritism.

Participation

When groups of people work together, morale is highest if each one is not merely allowed but actively encouraged to participate in achieving a common goal. Every person should be made to feel that his efforts are important; when a person feels indispensible, he is most likely to cooperate.

When men work together in relatively small groups or gangs, they should be matched as well as possible in ability. If certain persons feel inferior because of lesser ability or because of the others' criticism, they feel in the way, and absenteeism and dissatisfaction are likely to result. When employees work in close quarters, those who are congenial should be placed side by side. There are many kinds of work in which conversation does not interfere with efficiency. Arbitrary rules serve only as irritants and often appear to lower the worker's dignity.

Experience of progress

Group spirit remains high if joint efforts result in progress. Advancements or promotions always have a stimulating effect, but these are not the only ways to highlight the experience of progress. An improvement in skills, a better departmental safety record, better coordination of effort, better communication, and increased responsibility are all acceptable evidences of progress.

The experience of progress depends on developing both acceptable ways to

[50] Patchen, M. Absence and employee feelings about fair treatment. *Personnel Psychol.,* 1960, *13,* 349–360.

measure progress and skill in graphically describing improvement. Chapter 14 considers methods for accomplishing this objective. Important gains must also be recognized as important by management for workers to experience progress.

Tolerance and Freedom

Tolerance and freedom are essential for the development of cooperation and group spirit. The work atmosphere plays an important part in fostering these conditions. When everyone is under pressure and the atmosphere is authoritarian, tolerance and cooperation usually disappear. Frustration does not generate tolerance. The Hawthorne study described in Chapter 3 showed how production rose as employees felt more free to talk and move about without having to obtain permission. This study as well as others suggests that every effort should be made to remove unnecessary restrictions. Restrictions and rules make for a feeling of regimentation and depress spontaneous effort that might be diverted into productive channels. At the present time most companies have more rules and penalties for violations than foremen will enforce.

Type of Leader

In industry the supervisors are the leaders. Some individuals have a knack for handling workers, which is perhaps partly a matter of attitude and personality.[51] But the modern supervisor needs essential methods and skills, which require training.

Measuring Group Structure

Harmony exists in groups in which the individuals are homogeneous in the sense that each has similar standing in the group, or willingly accepts status differences of certain members.[52] When the group is subdivided into cliques, conflicts arise and certain individuals become scapegoats. Such dissensions disrupt harmony and create a condition of low morale.

Sociometry

Moreno developed an ingenious method of analyzing group status.[53] His technique is relatively simple, but diagnostic. Members of a group vote on their preferences

[51] Meyer, H. H. Factors related to success in the human relations aspect of work-group leadership. *Psychol. Monogr.*, 1951, 65; Weschler, I. R., *et. al.* Job satisfaction, productivity and morale: A case study. *Occup. Psychol., London*, 1952, 26, 1–14; Stogdill, R. M. Personal factors associated with leadership: A survey of the literature. *J. Psychol.*, 1948, 25, 35–71; Fiedler, F. E. *A theory of leadership effectiveness.* New York: McGraw-Hill, 1967; Campbell, J. P., Dunnette, M. D., Lawler, E. E., and Weick, K. E. *Managerial behavior, performance, and effectiveness.* New York: McGraw-Hill, 1970.

[52] Zaleznik, A., Christensen, C. R., and Roethlisberger, F. J. *The motivation, productivity and satisfaction of workers.* Cambridge, Mass.: Harvard University Press, 1958.

[53] Moreno, J. L. *Who shall survive?* Beacon, N.Y.: Beacon House, 1953. See also Murphy, G., Murphy, L. B., and Newcomb, T. M. *Experimental social psychology.* New York: Harper, 1939, pp. 306–320.

for one another. The voting is based on preferences in specific situations. For example, members of a work unit or office might be asked to vote on the following questions:

1. With whom would you prefer to work?
2. With whom would you like most to lunch?
3. Who would make a good supervisor?

Each person is usually asked to list three preferences in answer to each of the questions.

Analysis of results from such questions reveals that certain individuals receive a large number of votes. Such individuals are designated as *stars*. Others receive few or no votes and are designated as *isolates*. There are also those who invariably vote for each other. These are known as *mutual pairs*. Sometimes the voting takes the form of a *triangle*, in which three persons all vote for one another. This method readily reveals the existence of small cliques in which the votes are confined to close friends, thus producing a frequent number of mutual choices and triangles.

The existence of any subgroupings immediately becomes apparent on examination of the results. More can often be learned from a single test than from careful observation over a long period of time. The results check with general observations, and also reveal details and relationships which greatly augment those that may be discovered by an observer in constant contact with the group. The existence of isolates is of particular interest, as they are likely to be the unhappy and poorly adjusted individuals in the group. In school situations, they can be given special attention by the teacher who can involve them in activity and thus help improve their status in the group. Unfortunately, the teacher is usually inclined to turn against the isolate and for this reason special training is required.[54] In a factory, the foreman is likely to side against the isolates instead of trying to single them out for special attention and to help them make better adjustments to the group. Common practice thus has to be altered through better understanding.

Stars usually take care of themselves. A knowledge of their existence, however, would serve as one of the bases for choosing men for foremanship training. They are the individuals who very probably possess acceptable personality traits for leadership, since there is good assurance that they will not antagonize people.

Data obtained by the Moreno technique may be graphically represented by a *sociogram*. Each member of a group is represented by a circle, and choices are indicated by lines drawn between the circles. Arrows can indicate the direction of a choice. By using solid lines to indicate mutual choices and broken lines to designate one-way choices, we can differentiate between these two forms of preference. The number of votes received can be given in the center of each circle, together with the name or letter of the person. The sociogram in Figure 5.2 shows E to be

---

[54] Lippitt, R., and Gold, M. Classroom social structure as a mental health problem. *J. soc. Issues*, 1959, *15*, 40–49.

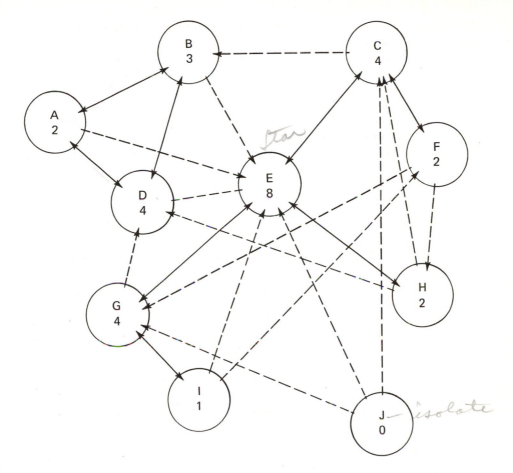

Figure 5.2 / Sociogram of a Group of 10 Employees. Each employee is represented as a circle, the letters of the alphabet substituted for names. Each member of the group was asked to vote for the three persons he most desired as working companions. The numerals in the circles show the number of votes each received. The arrows indicate the direction of the choices; solid and broken lines designate mutual choices and one-way preferences, respectively. Individuals A, B, and D form a triangle, E is a star, and J is an isolate.

a star, with eight votes, and J to be an isolate, with no votes. A, B, and D show definite preferences for one another, and, with the exception of one another, vote only for E. These three persons constitute a subgroup. If repeated sociograms revealed the same grouping, evidence of the permanence and strength of the clique would be apparent. Supplementary observation would reveal whether the subgroup was disruptive or was merely based upon external conditions, such as belonging to the same lodge. To simplify the picture, one would merely diagram the mutual choices and indicate in each circle the total number of choices received. Omission of the dotted lines in the graph would show more clearly the presence of clusters and isolates. The standing of each person in the group would be shown by the total number of votes he received.

Sociometry and Industry

Although sociometry has been used primarily as a research tool and its applications have been confined to schoolroom and sociological situations, its potential applications to industry seem great. It is now clear that a work situation is also a social situation, thus any procedure that increases the understanding of group behavior is of interest. It is around this topic that a new field of investigation, industrial sociology, is developing.[55]

The second type of application centers on the problem of leadership.[56] Sociometric methods supply a measure of leadership from the point of view of followers. Since a leader influences the morale and productivity of a group, the inclusion of this point of view may add essential data in the selection of leaders as well as accentuate the needs in their training. If the kinds of group relationship that are most satisfying to its members can be discovered, it will become possible to develop leaders who are able to facilitate these relationships.[57]

Following the conclusion of sociometrists[58] that attractions among group members heighten cooperation and that repulsions among them cause friction, productivity and morale was increased in a steam laundry.[59] The sociogram revealed various pairs of individuals in a team of seven women who rejected one another. By reassigning two members and replacing them with two others, it was possible to replace rejections with attractions for the benefit of all. Similarly, morale was benefited in the armed services when sociometric choices were used to select flying partners.[60]

In a large housing project separated by a highway, two procedures determined the assignment of carpenters and bricklayers to crews.[61] On one side of the road the foreman arbitrarily assigned the men to groups while for the crew on the other side of the road he followed sociometric choices. In the latter case each carpenter and bricklayer indicated three preferences for teammates and these were respected as far as possible in covering the various assignments. Where the sociometric procedure was used both labor and material costs were reduced to such an extent that every twenty-ninth building could be constructed from the savings.

Sometimes the values of work groups and management conflict. Automation is frequently rejected not because workers oppose efficiency but because some of their

[55] Miller, D. C., and Form, W. H. *Industrial sociology,* New York: Harper, 1951.

[56] Jennings, H. H. *Leadership and isolation* (2nd ed.). New York: Longmans, Green, 1950.

[57] Jacobs, J. H. The application of sociometry to industry. *Sociometry,* 1945, *8,* 181–198.

[58] Moreno, *op. cit.*

[59] Rogers, M. Problems of human relations within industry. *Sociometry,* 1946, *9,* 350–371.

[60] Zeleny, L. D. Selection of compatible flying partners. *Amer. J. Sociol.,* 1947, *5,* 424–431.

[61] Van Zelst, R. H. Validation of a sociometric regrouping procedure. Supplement to *J. abnorm. soc. Psychol.,* April, 1952.

members will be "bumped" out of their jobs.[62] On other occasions, the transfer of a particular worker might be welcomed. The type of reaction will be influenced by the group structure.

Group structure also influences the values within a group. The appearance of cliques creates values of status which may divide an office. Secretaries may feel superior to file clerks, and office boys may develop a kinship through matching pennies in the stock room.[63]

In one study an office staff was found to have divided into friendship groups, each group having its own set of values.[64] With regard to work, the values ranged from "work hard" to "take it easy," and with regard to supervision, the attitudes ranged from friendly to hostile. In general, productivity and popularity were inversely related (correlation coefficient equal to $-.67$). This became particularly pronounced when transfers required shifts in groups and in seating. High-producing employees were rejected by low-producing groups, whereas low-producing employees were acceptable to practically all groups.

An unhappy relationship, such as that between low productivity and popularity, is one that the leader can influence. If he stresses productivity above all things, if he degrades or threatens low producers, or if he makes "pets" out of high producers, he is promoting this inverse relationship. In order to prevent such a relationship or to create the opposite one, a leader would have to make individuals in the group feel secure; he would have to be aware and respectful of group values; and he would have to make the high-producing individuals an asset to their groups.

Generally speaking, the objectives of group members and of leaders are not opposed. Distrust and misunderstanding account for most of the conflicts. For naval recruits, sociometric tests of status showed that men who received demerits and men who received few sociometric choices tended to be the same individuals.[65] The relationship between adjustment and sociometric choice is a positive one, and when it is not found, the answer may be discovered in the leadership.

The use of sociometric methods in selection of supervisory personnel meets with a certain amount of resistance in industry because of the fear that popularity and the good of the company may not coincide. This makes applied research on this question difficult. Only five isolated instances of its use have been made in companies with which this author has been associated. In each case the supervisor who had the responsibility of making the decision had three preferences himself. After evaluating the men, each of the five supervisors consulted with his group. Each informed his group that a promotion was to be made and that he wanted their

[62] Walker, C. R. *Toward the automatic factory: A case study of men and machines.* New Haven, Conn.: Yale University Press, 1957.

[63] Odiorne, G. S. The clique—a frontier in personnel management. *Personnel,* Sept.–Oct. 1957, 38–44.

[64] French, J. R. P., Jr., and Zander, A. The group dynamics approach. In A. Kornhauser (Ed.), *Psychology of labor-management relations.* Champaign, Ill.: Industrial Relations Research Assn., 1949, pp. 71–78.

[65] French, R. L. Sociometric status and individual adjustment among naval recruits. In Cartwright and Zander (Eds.), *Group dynamics, op. cit.,* Ch. 35.

help in choosing wisely. He asked them to indicate on a questionnaire the names of the three persons they considered would make the most satisfactory supervisors. The questionnaires were not to be signed.

In all instances the persons with the highest number of choices included at least one name that was on the supervisor's own list. The fear that the supervisor would have to ignore the group preferences was not supported in any instance. Twice the person with the greatest number of sociometric choices had limited seniority. Both cases involved individuals that the supervisors considered the most capable, but whom they would not have promoted because the persons with greatest seniority were satisfactory and able to do the job. The fact that the most capable individuals had group support enabled the supervisors to promote on a basis of merit.

It should be noted, however, that isolated instances of this kind are select cases and may be atypical. Only supervisors who already enjoy good relations with their groups would attempt such tests. Experimentation on a broader scale is needed to explore the matter further, but the approach is sound insofar as it makes effective use of the principles of participation. It is hoped that this limited experience will encourage others to try it.

One final example of the use of sociometry in industry is of interest. A group of 10 women were being trained for responsible office positions involving contacts with the public. During the training period each woman had a chat with each of the eight managers who would eventually receive the women in their sections. At the end of the training period each manager was asked to list the names of the three trainees he would prefer to have placed in his section, and each trainee was asked to list the three managers for whom she would most like to work. The fear that all the women might prefer the same manager or vice versa was unwarranted. The results showed that it was possible to give every person one of his or her first three choices and in only two instances was it necessary to resort to third choices. The person making the test considered it a success and received satisfactory reports from the managers. His motivation for trying the method was the fact that managers had previously complained about the unfairness of his assignments.

This approach is of particular interest because it holds the possibility of making an asset out of the human tendency to rely on first impressions. Since favorable impressions encourage generosity while unfavorable ones generate hypercritical judgments, biased attitudes are used to improve interpersonal relations.

Factors Influencing Group Processes

Groups as Structures

Status, interpersonal influence, unofficial leaders, prestige, and security in the group have meaning only in the context of a group's structure. Each group has its own particular structure so that the behavior is influenced by the type of relationship experienced rather than the mere fact of group membership. Individuals may play quite different roles in a group, and members may have different needs satisfied by this membership. It is impossible for a supervisor to know all the interrelationships that emerge from such structures, and fortunately this knowledge is not necessary.

The group is capable of communicating, and if willing to listen the supervisor can learn much about his groups.

Size of the Group

The size of a group is one variable that influences a group's unity.[66] Leaders of large groups therefore have a more difficult task in maintaining morale than leaders of small groups. If a group is subdivided into smaller working groups it is desirable to introduce added levels of supervision, rather than to give the large-group leader assistants without authority.[67]

Competition

Whether or not the group is functioning in a competitive or cooperative capacity also influences its unity.[68] Competition tends to reduce a group's cohesiveness, and this factor becomes relevant to incentive pay programs. Group incentives can be expected to yield group structures different from individual incentives. Intragroup competition tends to decrease cohesiveness while intergroup competition increases it.[69]

Personal Attraction

The sociometric studies indicate that groups derive more satisfaction and work together more cooperatively when the members are attracted to one another. The attraction may be of different kinds, depending in part upon the goals and objectives of the group. A person who is preferred as a friend (social group) may not be chosen as a teammate (work group). However, individuals differ regarding whether they want friends or competent individuals on their teams, depending on whether they have strong needs to *achieve* or to *be liked*.[70] Furthermore, individuals tend to choose partners where the relationship is reciprocal.[71] Thus the most stable relationships occur when the feelings toward each other are mutual.

Similarity of Members

Various studies have shown that cohesive groups have more influence on one another than less strongly unified groups. However, persons with similar attitudes are attracted so that the influence between attitudes and attraction seems to be recip-

[66] Seashore, *op. cit.;* Hare, *op. cit.;* Indik, B. P. Organization size and member participation. Doctoral dissertation, University of Michigan, 1961.

[67] Pelz, D. C. The influence of the supervisor within his department as a conditioner of the way supervisory practices affect employee attitudes. Doctoral dissertation, University of Michigan, 1951.

[68] Deutsch, M. A theory of cooperation and competition. *Hum. Relat.,* 1949, *2,* 129–152; Deutsch, M. Some factors affecting membership motivation and achievement motivation in a group. *Hum. Relat.,* 1959, *12,* 81–95.

[69] Blake, R. R., and Mouton, J. S. Competition, communication, and conformity. In I. A. Berg and B. M. Bass (Eds.), *Conformity and deviation.* New York: Harper, 1961, Ch. 6.

[70] French, E. G. Motivation as a variable in work-partner selection. *J. abnorm. soc. Psychol.,* 1956, *53,* 96–99.

[71] Shaw, M. E., and Gilchrist, J. C. Repetitive task failure and sociometric choice. *J. abnorm. soc. Psychol.,* 1955, *50,* 29–32.

rocal. Newcomb[72] emphasizes similarity in values. Undoubtedly this similarity is a factor, especially when other factors for group organization are not operating. However, this condition could also lead to lack of challenge and boredom, the achievement being merely a lack of strife.[73]

Propinquity

Physical nearness and frequency of contact are important factors determining social groupings.[74] Since people in work groups have little opportunity to choose their companions it is natural that the work space and the relatedness of the work will influence friendships.

The extent to which the mere fact of having meetings develops groups and leads to group loyalties was shown in an experiment.[75] Students in four-person groups who had worked together for a semester were given a reward for their cooperation. The reward consisted of 19 points for each group, which they could divide among the members in any way the group decided. The points allotted would then be added to each individual's examination score and would influence his final grade in the course. In the event that the group failed to agree unanimously, each member would automatically receive four points, giving such groups only 16 points. However, this meant that no individual would have to settle for less than four points.

Out of 30 groups, not one failed to reach a unanimous decision. Each group remained united in order to get the maximum number of points. The grade points received ranged from zero to 19, and in only 27 per cent of the groups was the division fairly equal. The factor which most influenced the distribution of points was need. Students who were doing well in the course willingly gave up points to help keep a member from failing. This behavior represents a strong kind of unity, and the example covers merely a series of 14 two-hour laboratory sessions in a college course.

Considering the strong desire of group members to help one another, it is not surprising that groups of workers will protect a member if he is threatened by management. The mere fact of working together on a job tends to build friends. Members who "don't fit in" either learn to conform or seek work elsewhere. Studies show that the pressures to conform are very strong, and that if changes are to be introduced in a work situation it is better to work through a group method than with individuals.[76]

---

[72] Newcomb, T. M. The prediction of interpersonal attraction. *Amer. Psychologist,* 1956, *11,* 575–586.

[73] Hoffmann, L. R. Homogeneity and member personality and its effect on group problem solving. *J. abnorm. soc. Psychol.,* 1959, *58,* 27–32; Hoffman, L. R. Similarity of personality: A basis for interpersonal attraction? *Sociometry,* 1958, *21,* 300–308.

[74] Festinger, L., Schachter, S., and Back, K. *Social pressures in informal groups.* New York: Harper, 1950.

[75] Hoffman, L. R., and Maier, N. R. F. The use of group decision to resolve a problem of fairness. *Personnel J.,* 1959, *12,* 545–559.

[76] Festinger, L., *et al.* The influence process in the presence of extreme deviates. *Hum. Relat.,* 1952, *5,* 327–346; Jackson, J. M., and Salzstein, H. D. The effect of person-group relationships on conformity processes. *J. abnorm. soc. Psychol.,* 1958, *57,* 17–24.

Leader's Role in Resolving Conflicts

On some occasions the individuals are placed in a situation that sets members in conflict with one another, but the leader is not a part of the conflict. This type of relationship is shown in Figure 5.3. Situation A would arise if the supervisor had to assign office space in a new building and if one office were more desirable than the others. How should this conflict in interests be resolved? A case in point is given at the end of Chapter 6.

Situation B shows the group in conflict with the leader. Such a conflict occurs when the leader wishes to introduce a change in work methods or standards, or to remove some privilege. The conflict tends to unify the members so as to strengthen their opposition. This type of conflict appears in the exercise at the end of Chapter 11.

Situation C represents a split in the group. The more the subgroups are in conflict with one another, the more they are unified within themselves. Divided job interests, differences in status, and differences in privileges can produce these subgroupings.

Techniques for resolving conflict and using the differences for constructive ends are primarily dependent upon the leadership. Leadership takes on new meanings when it is seen as one of solving problems through group interaction. New conceptions and new skills are required if supervision is seen as working with groups rather than as controlling the work of a certain number of individuals.

Figure 5.3 / Three Types of Conflict. Type A occurs when the leader must choose one person for favored treatment. All the subordinates want the treatment, so they are in conflict with one another. Type B conflict occurs when the group members unite against the leader. This type tends to occur when the leader wishes to introduce a change. Type C occurs when the group is divided into two or more subgroups so cooperation is at a minimum.

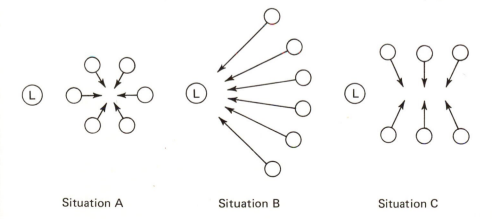

Situation A   Situation B   Situation C

Laboratory Exercise

Practice in Discussion Leadership

A. Preparing for discussion.

The instructor will:

1. Divide the class into groups of five or six persons.
2. Appoint one member of each group as a discussion leader.
3. Take leaders aside and instruct them to rejoin their groups and conduct a discussion on the topic, "What is the single most important economic gain a company would enjoy if employee morale improved?"

B. Discussion time: about 20 minutes.

C. Reports to class.

1. One at a time the leaders will report the conclusion reached by their groups. The instructor will summarize the items on the blackboard under each group's number.
2. How many of the group's members accepted their group's report? Indicate number under summarized report.
3. Allow members opportunity to criticize their group's report; summarize criticism.
4. Determine number of members who were bored, satisfied, or interested by the discussion.

D. Analysis of reports.

1. Determine number of common factors in group reports.
2. Discuss relative merits of group reports.
3. Discuss the values of specific items, such as reduced training costs due to less labor turnover, and general or vague items, such as production increases because of higher morale.

E. Evaluation of discussion leadership functions.

1. General discussion of what the various leaders did—both good and bad.
2. What could a leader do to increase the interest and satisfaction of members in the discussion?
3. What could a leader do to improve the quality of contributions?
4. What could a leader do to move discussion along?
5. What could a leader do to make participation more nearly equal for all members of a group?

Suggested Readings

Bass, B. M. *Leadership, psychology, and organizational behavior.* New York: Harper, 1960.

Cartwright, D., and Zander, A. *Group dynamics* (3rd ed.). New York: Harper & Row, 1968, Chs. 7, 13, and 23.

Jones, E. E., and Gerard, H. B. *Foundations of social psychology.* New York: Wiley, 1967, Chs. 6, 11, and 15.

Laird, D. A., and Laird, Eleanor C. *The new psychology for leadership.* New York: McGraw-Hill, 1956.

Likert, R. *New patterns of management.* New York: McGraw-Hill, 1961.

Thibaut, J. W., and Kelley, H. H. *The social psychology of groups.* New York: Wiley, 1961.

6

Supervisory Leadership

Autocracy, Democracy, and Laissez Faire

The Search for Definitions

The terms *autocracy*, *democracy*, and *anarchy* (*laissez faire*) describe various forms of government. In general, one thinks of an autocracy as strict and inconsiderate, as an arbitrary rule imposed by one person. Democracy carries a favorable connotation, and we think of it as fair to people and considerate of them. Anarchy is often considered the absence of leadership, representing a hands-off (laissez-faire) policy likely to end in chaos.

The specific definition of these terms, however, is a complex matter involving many differences of opinion over the meanings inherent in them. For example, one may argue that democracy means majority rule, protection of minorities through a bill of rights, equality before the law, a method for choosing leaders, a method for making reforms, or some combination of these conditions.

Definitions involving several conditions do not lend themselves to simple experimental designs. In order to investigate in the laboratory the way a form of government or of leadership influences behavior, and to allow the testing of single variables, clear-cut single distinctions must be used. For example, one may distinguish forms of leadership in terms of the amount of freedom permitted, the degree of efficiency attained, the manner in which leaders obtain their positions, or any other measurable difference.

After somewhat arbitrarily making certain limiting and specific definitions, the laboratory investigator of leadership must request still another concession. This is the privilege of testing leadership with only one *level* of difference present: that between the leader and the group members. In government and in industry, hierarchies involving as many as five or six levels may be included, and because these various levels exert upward and downward influences, they must be excluded for the time being so they do not cloud the factor investigated.

The Location of Authority

Lewin selected the location of authority as a critical experimental variable.[1] Theoretically, authority could be located in (1) the leader (autocracy); (2) the group (democracy); or (3) the individual (laissez faire). Figure 6.1 shows how these three pure locations might be illustrated as the vertices of a triangle. In practical situations these three locations of authority are not likely to occur in pure states. The sides of the triangle represent mixtures that might occur in real life situations.

In the initial research, experimenters served as leaders and boys (about 10 years old), who were induced to join a club, served as group members.[2] Experimental

Figure 6.1 / Differences between Various Types of Leadership. The location of authority or the place where decisions are made differs in pure democracy, autocracy, and laissez faire situations. These extreme locations are shown as the vertices of a triangle. Intermediate locations are also possible, and these can be described as falling on the sides of the triangle. Majority-rule democracy would seem to fall between pure group decision and autocracy because it implies both participation and imposition of a majority decision upon a minority. A paternalistic leader is both autocratic, in that he makes decisions, and laissez faire, in that he considers the wishes of individuals, and so may be described as being a point on the base of the triangle. Since a leaderless discussion involves discussion but does not make for organized action, it may be described as a condition between pure democracy and laissez faire. Any leader may be described by his placement on this triangle. (After K. Lewin. The dynamics of group action. *Educ. Leadership*, 1944, *1*, 195–200.)

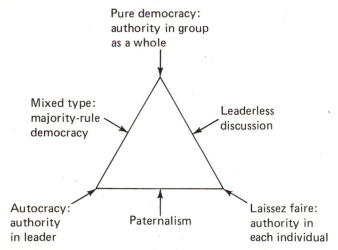

[1] Lewin, K. The dynamics of group action. *Educ. Leadership*, 1944, *1*, 195–200.

[2] Lewin, K., Lippitt, R., and White, R. K. Patterns of aggressive behavior in experimentally created social climates. *J. soc. Psychol.*, 1939, *10*, 271–301; Lippitt, R. An experimental study of the effect of democratic and authoritarian group atmospheres. *University of Iowa Studies in Child Welfare*, 1940, *16*, 43–195; White, R., and Lippitt, R. Leader behavior and member reaction in three "social climates". In D. Cartwright and A. Zander (Eds.), *Group dynamics*, Evanston, Ill.: Row, Peterson, 1953.

tests of the three pure locations of decision making yielded results clearly favoring group decision, both regarding satisfaction and measure of production or group effectiveness, whereas individual decision making generally resulted in chaos and little satisfaction. These laboratory findings became the stimulus for a great deal of research and for many practical applications and misapplications. Since autocracy was inferior to democracy, decisions imposed by leaders were regarded as poor leadership methods. However, if autocratic leaders cease controlling as in the past, they do not necessarily become democratic but merely nonautocratic. Many tend to become permissive and hence follow the laissez faire style. If one type of control is surrendered, the group must be organized in a different way to coordinate effort. Group decision represents a new type of control but is not likely to arise without training. In this sense it is an invention and could not have been found by studying group activity. Thus the elimination of autocracy in supervisors, teachers, or parents does not necessarily replace it with something better. As illustrated in Figure 6.2 pressures to move away from autocracy can lead to laissez faire or permissiveness.

Experiments with boys demonstrated that group activities could effectively be controlled by having members make the decisions for the club activities (naming the club, determining activities, task assignments, etc.). In other experiments food habits were changed more effectively by group decision than by persuasion of the leader.[3]

Figure 6.2 / Avoiding Autocracy Because of Social Pressure Is Not the Solution. The avoidance of autocracy does not produce democracy since democratic leadership is not the opposite of autocratic. There are two directions away from autocratic styles. Both autocracy and democracy (as defined in the text) limit freedom, but in one case the limitation is imposed by the leader, while in the other, it is agreed upon by the group.

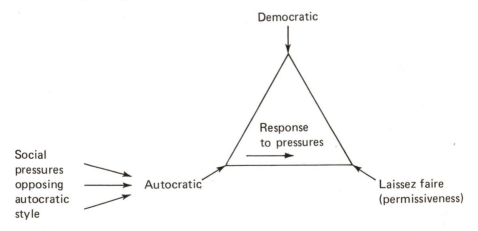

[3] Lewin, K. Group decision and social change. In T. M. Newcomb and E. L. Hartley (Eds.), *Readings in social psychology.* New York: Holt, 1947, pp. 330–344.

Figure 6.3 shows the results of an industrial study which illustrates how production was greatly increased by inviting workers to set their own production goals, and Figure 6.4 shows how a change in work methods was successfully introduced without the usual distrust when workers were given the opportunity to participate in the planning. These experiments had a great impact on the thinking of organizational psychologists and modern management. Some of the developments will be discussed further in Chapter 21.

Group Decision vs. Participation

In the early experiments on group decision, trained psychologists conducted the meetings so there was a tendency to overlook the need for skills since all discussion

Figure 6.3 / Effect of Team Decision. When a team of workers decided to attain a specific goal, their production showed a sharp increase, which was maintained despite the fact that the team's performance was already above the plant average. (Courtesy of A. Bavelas.)

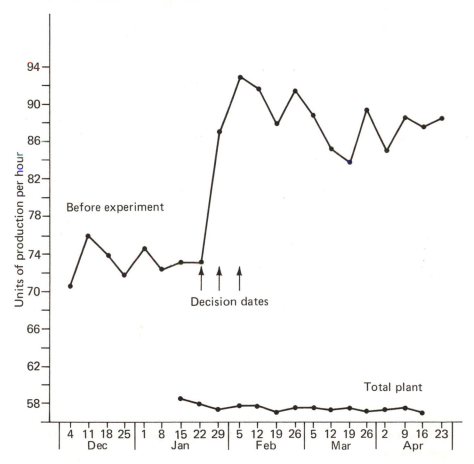

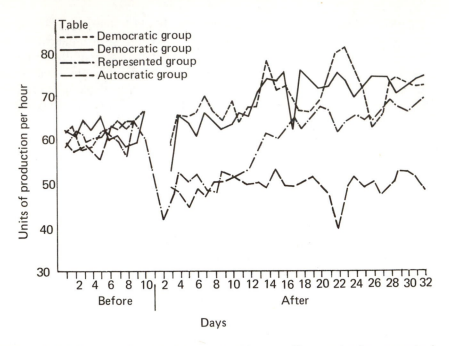

Figure 6.4 / Overcoming Resistance to Change. The production records for each of the four groups studied are shown before and after the job change. The curve of the autocratically handled group shows a sharp drop in production when the change is made, and recovery does not occur during the period studied. The two democratically handled groups show rapid recovery and reach a production level on the new job that exceeds the old one. Production of the group that participated through its representatives shows a sharp drop and recovery gradually occurs. The gaps in the curves of the democratically and autocratically led groups indicate the period during which they were paid on a time-work basis. (After L. Coch and J. R. P. French, Jr., Overcoming resistance to change. *Hum. Relat.,* 1948. *1,* 512–532. Permission granted by the Plenum Publishing Corporation.)

leaders possessed them. A supervisor who tries to practice goal setting in his group may be incorrectly perceived as being dissatisfied with his group or as trying to sell them on setting higher goals. The untrained supervisor of a group is also likely to fear losing control and so permits participation on an important matter only if he retains veto power. As a result, group participation has become heavily loaded with manipulative or deceptive approaches in which employees are allowed to discuss matters, but not really make decisions. What is called participative management today includes practices ranging from having a chance to express views to having a vote. In our modern society most people favor democracy, but, at the same time, they are afraid to practice it without some safeguards. People are inclined to favor having a "say-so" when on the receiving end but are hesitant when on the giving end.

An illustration of what happens under the influence of such ambivalent feelings occurred in a large corporation. Coffee drinking was getting out of hand because employees were taking coffee breaks when policy did not permit them. Attempts to restrict this freedom caused employees to sneak out of the building without coats in winter. This lead to colds, and sickness costs money. When the violations became intolerable, top management personnel held a meeting in which they reached the decision to permit all employees a 20 minute coffee break. (This is a top management decision because paying employees for nonwork involves a change in policy). The next step was to determine whether this should be given in the morning or afternoon. The sensible time was afternoon. One member remarked that employees would also choose the afternoon to have their coffee, so why not let them make the decision. This was agreed upon, ballots were printed, and employees were given the chance to vote on whether the coffee break that they were to receive should be given in the morning or afternoon. The vote showed 80 per cent voting in favor of the morning coffee break. So the decision to have the coffee break in the afternoon "where God intended it to be" caused participation to do more harm than good in this case.

Clarification of the Group Decision Concept

Leader-Group Relationship

In order to utilize group decision effectively in industry it must not be confused with popular definitions of democratic or participative approaches. As initially tested the group decision concept assumes a face-to-face meeting of the leader with members in which the leader (a) poses a problem and (b) leads the discussion, but the group makes the decision. The problem concerns a matter that participants understand and in which they have an interest. The size of the group is assumed to be 12 or fewer. If the concept is to be adapted to larger groups or participants who cannot meet, certain modifications in procedure are needed.

Unanimous Agreement

The purpose of discussion in the experiments was to reach unanimous agreement. If cooperative effort in the implementation of a decision is to result, differences must be resolved. A majority decision imposes its will on the minority so that the group is divided. Thus the voting type of democracy must not be confused with group decision. Failure for groups to reach agreement is less likely to occur than imagined because discussion tends to resolve differences once the disagreement is clarified. The results of the experimental studies are based on unanimous agreement.

Distinction between Group Leader and a Supervisor

In the initial experiments the leader was not only an adult, but a psychologist as well. His authority was not restricted by higher management, unions, or other work groups. Furthermore, he had no emotional investment in favoring certain solutions over others. This means that practical life situations introduce variables not present in laboratory experiments.

Location of Decision vs. Strictness

Autocracy is often associated with strictness, and laissez faire with leniency. The location of authority, however, does not necessarily determine whether standards for work will be high or low. An autocrat can be strict or lenient, and individuals may set lenient or strict standards for themselves. Figure 6.5 illustrates how the high and low standards might be included in the concept by changing the triangle to a prism. Thus some autocratic leaders might expect higher standards of performance than others; some individuals may work harder doing what they want to do than others; and some groups might set higher goals than others. If group decision makes a group more productive than autocracy, it demonstrates that high standards are more easily achieved through group decision than through autocracy, not that one is *necessarily* associated with the other.

Implementing Group Decision

Experiments demonstrated that when groups rather than leaders made a decision, behavior was more cooperative and initiative was higher. Members worked on the task regardless of the leader's presence, with greater pride in their work, better group cohesiveness, greater satisfaction with the task, and more positive feeling for the leader. Whether the decision to engage in the activity selected was the best one cannot be determined, and for the purpose of the experiment this aspect of the de-

Figure 6.5 / Differences in the Efficiencies of Groups Form a Third Dimension. A prism is here used to picture this aspect of group functioning and at the same time to describe the various locations of a decision-making function. It follows that efficiency or standards can be high or low in any type of leadership. An important problem is to determine which type of leadership can achieve high standards most easily.

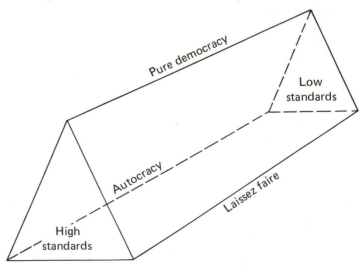

A manager who shares the planning function with subordinates generates job interest and effective execution of the decision.

Courtesy of Boeing Company

cision was irrelevant. However, in many practical situations decision quality must be considered. It is essential therefore that a distinction be made between the objective goodness of a decision (its quality) and the degree to which the participants like it (its acceptance).[4]

Determinants of Effective Decisions

Quality and Acceptance

The tests in life situations indicate that participation in making decisions is more likely to cause the group to implement its decisions than those supplied by the leader. We might speak of this dimension of the decision-making function as *acceptance*. People are more likely to accept the decisions that they feel responsible for, as a result of having participated in making them.

The risk involved in the use of group decision is that the decisions may lack objective quality and be influenced too much by feelings. High-quality decisions require an effective use of objective facts. Decisions made by experts or by experienced and capable leaders can generally be trusted to respect facts and protect quality.

A decision lacks effectiveness if it does not have the emotional support of those who must execute it or if it ignores or fails to respect relevant objective facts. The formula

$$ED = Q \times A$$

describes this relationship. Effective decisions (ED) are a product of the degree to which the decision has quality (Q) (which concerns the objective facts) and acceptance (A) (which concerns the feelings of the persons who must execute the decisions).

In the light of this analysis we are confronted with an interesting practical problem. To be effective, decisions should have both high quality and high acceptance, but the procedures for gaining quality and acceptance conflict. The method for achieving quality puts the decision-making function in the leadership where there is access to information, advice, and expert opinion; whereas the method for gaining high acceptance puts the decision-making function in the membership. Must one of these objectives be sacrificed for the other?

This conflict in methods is a management dilemma that has plagued organizations for centuries. Traditionally, achieving quality was regarded as the first step. The leaders protected quality by making the decision themselves. Once this was done they were left with the problem of executing the decision. The oldest method for gaining acceptance was through the use of fear. Later on, paternalists gained acceptance through loyalty. Perhaps the most common method in present practice is persuasion. A successful leader, it is argued, must be a good persuader. Participative approaches often are invoked to gain acceptance, but the leaders still hold on to the right to make the final evaluation and decision. Consultative managers, at best,

---

[4] Maier, N. R. F. *Problem-solving discussions and conferences.* New York: McGraw-Hill, 1963.

are open to suggestions and, at worst, attempt to manipulate the group members to come around to their ways of thinking. All these changes in management styles stop short of giving up the decision-making function from fear either of endangering quality or losing control.

Despite the fear of risking quality by permitting group decision it is not uncommon for managers to admit that they frequently make second-best decisions because the highest-quality decision is not acceptable. Compromises are common resultants of conflicts in interest between superiors and subordinates.

Suppose we had to decide on the best way to do a particular job and that four solutions were possible, each differing from the standpoint of engineering excellence. On the basis of this much information, perhaps everyone would be inclined to choose the best method. Suppose, however, that the persons who had to perform the job liked the best method the least. In the light of these feelings it might be wise to choose a lesser-quality method in order to gain acceptance.

How Q and A Interact. In a large power plant the job of cleaning furnaces was a trouble spot for management because of grievances and turn-over. A four-man crew had to work inside the furnace and use specific cleaning tools. The job procedure had been worked out by time-and-motion engineers who had to consider the facts listed below.

1. Two men shouldn't need the same tools at the same time.
2. The men shouldn't get in the way of each other.
3. Duplicate tools should be minimized because of space limitations.
4. The number of times a tool is picked up and put down should be minimized because these motions are not productive.

A method for the team was developed based upon these factual considerations, and the men were trained to follow the method.

Over the years the men complained about the job. Since they were not work-methods engineers, no one listened. After being trained in group decision the foreman called a meeting and asked the men what was wrong with their team. They agreed that one man had more of the dirty work than the others, and that this was a source of dissension. After the men voiced criticisms about the job, the discussion became more constructive. Various changes were suggested and evaluated. The ideas finally developed into a modified job procedure.

This new procedure was analyzed by the time-and-motion experts. Their report indicated that the modified work procedure would cut efficiency to 67 per cent of its original value. Nevertheless, the new method was put into effect with the result that it took four men *two* rather than *four* days to clean a furnace.

Analysis in terms of quality and acceptance would indicate that the first method had high quality and low acceptance, whereas the modified method had lower quality (67 per cent vs. 100 per cent), but that the acceptance rose enough to more than offset the reduced quality.

The increased production makes the new method more effective, despite the fact that one might agree that the engineers had the best answer from the quality point of view whereas the men had the best answer from the acceptance point of view. A decision's effectiveness, quality, and acceptance should be differentiated to facilitate communication about what is best.

The importance of quality and acceptance will undoubtedly vary with the nature of the problem. Perhaps a consideration of differences in problems will suggest an approach that will avoid the management dilemma and propose a method for avoiding the conflict in methods for gaining quality and acceptance.

Classification of Problems

Q/A Type Problems. Some problems are of such a nature that persons who have to execute decisions regarding them have no emotional interest in any particular decision. Decisions about where the company buys its raw materials, how much it charges for services or products, what is the best rate of expansion, and decisions on many technical engineering matters are readily accepted by subordinates. If they were involved in such decisions, they perhaps would complain about wasting their time.

The nature of solutions to such problems, however, may be highly important with respect to the quality dimension. Decisions pertaining to pricing a product or a service, or adapting growth rate to markets and economic conditions can mean success or failure for a company. Problems for which quality is important and acceptance creates little or no problem, belong to this type, and can continue to be solved at the leadership level.

A/Q Type Problems. Many problems have a great variety of possible solutions and the differences in their objective quality are negligible. Who should work overtime, who should get the corner office vacated by a retiring vice president, who is to be sent to a training program, what constitutes tardiness, and what are proper methods for discipline are questions management decides largely because decisions must be made, rather than because a particular decision is regarded as important. However, such decisions involve a good deal of feeling. Generally speaking, they involve the issue of *fairness*. Feelings rather than objective facts determine what is fair. Thus acceptance becomes the important dimension.

It is with problems of this type that management decisions are frequently challenged. The most common word in picket lines is "unfair." If problems of this type were solved by group decision the possibilities for gains in acceptance are great, whereas the risks to quality are minimal. In such instances the interests of superiors and subordinates or management and labor are least likely to conflict. Both sides favor fairness; the question is how to accomplish it. The actual conflict is often within the group. If a new truck is obtained, which driver should get it if several want it? This conflict in interest can be more effectively resolved through group discussion than in the marshalling of factual information. As a matter of fact, groups will not agree on the solution so that the most satisfactory solution will vary from one group to another even when the facts are the same. Such decisions are tailored to fit the values of the group members.

lower left

Θ/Q, A *Type Problems.* Some decisions have to be made among alternatives that are equally good from a quality point of view; furthermore, these decisions often make little difference to those who execute them. For example, if telephone lines have to be built from point A to point B a decision has to be made regarding which end to begin with. If the foreman decides to begin at A the crew might ask why not begin at B. He then feels obligated to point out why it is better to begin at A, which is hard to do when the alternatives have equal objective merit. If he holds a group-decision meeting, half the crew may vote for A and half for B. Since it really makes no difference, they don't discuss the problem to resolve a difference, but find the problem interesting from the point of view of winning the debate. Such problems can best be handled by flipping a coin.

upper right

Q, A/O *Type Problems.* With the above three classes of problems eliminated, a class of problems remains in which both quality and acceptance are important although their relative importance may vary. Such problems include standards for tardiness, production goals, improving service, increasing safety, improving work methods, and introducing labor-saving methods. These problems frequently involve (a) conflicts in interests (real or apparent) between superiors and subordinates; (b) utilization of expert opinion; and (c) complex patterns of variables that create issues of fairness.

Two procedures are available. On the one hand, the leader can make the decision to protect quality, but if he follows this plan he needs persuasive skills in order to obtain as much acceptance as possible. On the other hand, the group-decision method insures acceptance, but the leader must have certain conference skills in order to optimize the quality of the decision. These conference leadership skills are not in the form of manipulation and subtle controls, but methods for (a) upgrading the discussion procedure, (b) processing the information, and (c) selecting a solution. A group of persons has certain resources that, if effectively utilized, make group thinking more effective than that of a superior individual in the group, such as the leader. However, the group product also may be inferior because of interpersonal rivalry and self-interests. How and when to use the group for improving decision quality will be discussed later in connection with problem solving. Improving decision quality becomes especially important at higher levels in the organization where a great deal of talent lies latent. As organizations increase in size and technical complexity, it becomes more essential to use group resources effectively. Individuals working alone cannot process information and generate the ideas needed. For the present, our concern is with the potential uses of group decision to gain acceptance, cooperation, and improved communication.

The Problem Chart

Since the needs for quality and acceptance of decision vary, the leader may visualize problems as occupying a position on a chart, such as shown in Figure 6.6. To determine the method to follow in reaching a decision, the leader may rate the importance of quality and acceptance separately. A rating of zero to nine can desig-

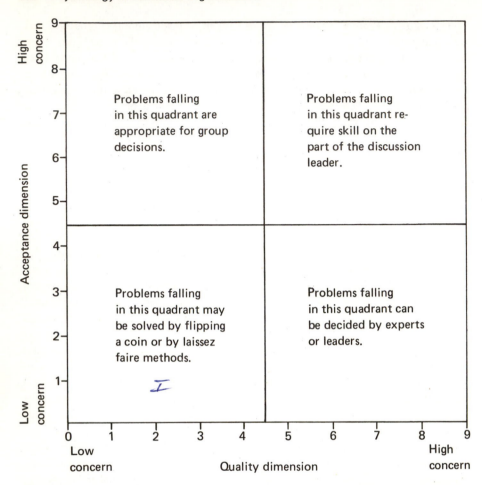

High concern

8 –

7 –

Problems falling in this quadrant are appropriate for group decisions.

Problems falling in this quadrant re- quire skill on the part of the discussion leader.

6 –

Acceptance dimension

5 –

4 –

3 –

Problems falling in this quadrant may be solved by flipping a coin or by laissez faire methods.

Problems falling in this quadrant can be decided by experts or leaders.

2 –

1 –

Low concern

0   1   2   3   4   5   6   7   8   9

Low concern

Quality dimension

High concern

Figure 6.6 / Classifying Problems According to the Acceptance and Quality Dimensions. Problems may be rated in terms of the two dimensions essential for effective decisions. Each problem then becomes a point on the chart and falls in one of the four quarters. The method to be followed in solving the problem depends on the quarter in which it falls. This is a simple method which may aid the beginner in deciding on the appropriate decision-making procedure.

nate the importance of both quality and acceptance for an effective solution. These two ratings will locate the problem on the chart.

The location of the problem will suggest the most appropriate method to follow. A/Q type problems fall in the upper left quarter of the chart, Q/A type problems in the lower right quarter, the O/Q, A problems in the lower left quadrant, and the Q, A/O problems in the upper right.

Supervisory personnel will not usually agree regarding the way the same problems are classified. Some estimate the quality dimension more highly than others.

With training the awareness of the acceptance dimension increases, as does agreement. After training managers classified 43.8 per cent of their problems as A/Q type and only 22.6 per cent as of the Q/A type.[5]

Adapting Group Decision to Operating Conditions

Some adaptations are required to bring the group-decision method somewhat closer to the day-to-day operating needs of a company. As discussed below, these should assist the practicing supervisor in relating the method to problems on the job as well as clarify for him the problem areas that lend themselves to the approach.

Group Decision as a Supervisory Method

A leadership style should be considered a method and not a description of a person. Mr. Jones may handle a problem on vacation scheduling democratically by conducting a group-decision conference, he may behave autocratically in setting up an improved housekeeping plan by making the decision without inviting discussion, and he may behave in a laissez-faire manner in allowing employees to select work companions. The reason for pointing out the difference between types of leaders and methods is that many supervisors feel they must accept the concepts of democratic leadership completely in order to use it at all. They resist using the method because they feel they haven't the time; they fear the method would backfire in some cases; or they feel that the method would sometimes become too involved for their level of skill. Objections to group decision that are based on special cases where the method seems inappropriate need not prevent its use in other instances, providing we separate the method from the person. The most democratic supervisor is the one who uses the group-decision method on the greatest number of problems. Supervisors would become more democratic if they sought new instances in which group decision could be used instead of looking for conditions under which it could not be used.

Accountability

In describing the experiments on leadership styles the location of *authority* was the distinguishing feature. For practical purposes it seems better to distinguish the styles on the basis of the location of the *decision-making function.* The supervisor does not relinquish his responsibility when he shares a problem with his group and asks them to help solve it. He is still accountable to his superiors for results. When he chooses to use group decision he should be willing to accept responsibility because he believes the decision will be more effective.

The Area of Freedom

In a typical industrial set-up there is a hierarchy of management personnel. A somewhat simplified example of this hierarchy is illustrated in Figure 6.7. The figure

[5] Maier, N. R. F., and Hoffman, L. R. Types of problems confronting managers. *Personnel Psychol.*, 1964, *17*, 261–269.

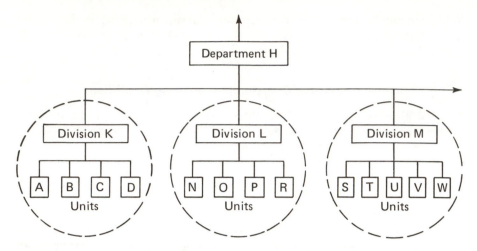

Figure 6.7 / Organizational Chart of a Typical Department. The relationship between departments, divisions, and units is shown by the connecting solid lines. This chart shows only a small department within a company. The broken lines, each enclosing a division and several units, represent potential discussion groups in which the division supervisor acts as the leader. Each unit supervisor is the leader of groups of rank-and-file employees, not shown in the chart. All management personnel are potential participants in one grouping and leaders in another.

shows only the relationship between the units and divisions in a particular department. Each square describes a position held by a particular individual, who in turn reports to the person above him in the chart. For example, the first-line supervisor who is in charge of Unit B reports to Division Supervisor K, who in turn reports to the head of Department H. In a similar manner a figure might show how the several department heads report to a works manager, who then may report to a vice president. The person in charge of each management position shown has certain tasks to perform and certain decisions to make. The unit supervisors are in charge of a crew of workers, and although each unit may perform different functions—ranging from clerical to drill press work—they are alike in that they supervise the work of nonmanagement personnel. It is at this level that the actual production job is done.

Unit supervisors have to deal with disciplinary problems, scheduling work loads and vacations, maintaining quality, meeting production schedules, housekeeping, and so on. Division supervisors are in charge of a group of unit supervisors. The three divisions pictured may be thought of as handling of materials, assembly, and manufacturing. Each division supervisor must plan and integrate the work of his units, see that standards between them are comparable, coordinate the work of his division with that of the others, and so forth. In higher levels in the organization the problems encompass a wider segment of the company. The department head must deal with problems on a department-wide basis, hence must think more in terms of principles and less of specific details.

In holding group-discussion meetings, supervisors ordinarily would meet only with their immediate subordinates,[6] and the problem shared would be one they had the authority to solve. It is important to keep in mind that supervisors cannot have a group decision on matters over which they have no authority. If they have the authority to make a decision they can accept the group decisions as *the* decision, but they cannot let their group decide the problems of another level in the organization.

In order to clarify the area open for group decisions, the diagram shown in Figure 6.8 has been constructed. The circle represents the limitations imposed by the job. A supervisor is a group leader only insofar as the job he supervises is concerned. Problems about religion, hair styles, or politics, for example, would not be matters for group decision because they would fall outside the circle. Activities unrelated to the specific supervisor's responsibility also are outside the circle. Thus, drill press operators cannot decide to become material handlers or to change the shift on which they would like to work.

However, even when considering problems falling inside the circle that define the job activity, there still are certain restrictions on the area open for group decisions. Within a supervisor's job territory some activities have been taken from him or

Figure 6.8 / The Areas of Freedom for the Practice of Democratic Leadership. The circle represents the limitations which the job situation imposes upon activity. *C. Po.* and *C. Pr.* represent the limitations imposed by company policies and company practices, respectively; *U.C.* and *L* represent activity areas removed by union contracts and legislation, respectively; and *E* represents problem areas solved by experts. The remaining area falls within the authority of a given level of supervision, and problems in this area may be solved by group techniques. (From N. R. F. Maier, A human relations program for supervision. *Indust. and labor relat. Rev.*, 1948, *1*, 443–464.)

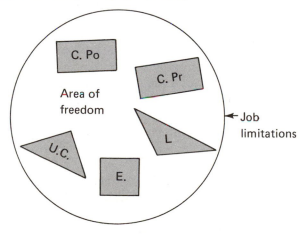

---

[6] Usually no more than 12 are in a group. When the number is larger, there usually are group leaders or nonsupervisory leaders who may be considered as another level in our organizational chart.

greatly limited. Higher management has established company policies and practices which are felt at all job levels, and supervisory as well as group decisions cannot contradict these. Company policies (*C. Po.*) and company practices (*C. Pr.*) reduce the area of a supervisor's decision-making functions and are thus shown as rectangles in Figure 6.8. Similarly, union contracts (*U. C.*) cannot be violated or altered by group decisions. Laws (*L*), such as those governing the length of the workweek, child labor, minimum wages, or establishing the rights of employees to hold union membership, also restrict the freedom of action at all levels of management. The square labeled *E* refers to experts. Most companies have taken some of the technical aspects of the supervisor's job from him and have turned them over to specialists. Lighting engineers, time-study men, personnel assistants, and safety engineers are a few of the specialists whose job is to supplement the activities of supervisors throughout the plant. The area within the circle and between these limiting geometrical figures is designated as the *area of freedom*. Problems falling within this area are the ones to consider for group decision. Since all problems of a company fall within the area of freedom of one group or another, all decisions can be group decisions, though all groups do not participate in all decisions.

The Supervisor as an Expert

In making good decisions, effective use must be made of available facts. Often a supervisor has access to sources of information or has had training and experience that are valuable in reaching good decisions. An autocratic leader can utilize this advantage of superior knowledge, but what happens when decisions are group decisions? In order not to impose his views on a group, a skilled discussion leader gives his group the benefit of his knowledge by the way he states the problem and the manner in which he supplies the facts.

Suppose a group-decision meeting is held to determine what color the walls shall be in a women's lounge. A knowledge of such things as the amount of light reflected by various colors, the opinions of interior decorators on color combinations, and cost differences arising because some color combinations would require making changes in the drapes is relevant. The discussion leader can supply the group with this information, using charts and samples, as the various points come up and the group asks about them. If the leader is open-minded and sincerely wishes the group members to make the decision, he will find them much interested in facts.

In using the group-decision approach a supervisor should consider himself having two parts to play.[7] In one role he is the discussion leader and has the job of conducting a good discussion. In the other role he is an expert and has information that may be of value. Before supplying information he might explore the group's knowledge, since various members might be able to supply the essential facts. However, when he does supply information himself, he should be careful not to do so in a way that indicates his own preference for the decision to be taken. A city council, for example, can make a wise decision about the design of a new bridge, providing they have the benefit of an engineer as consultant. It would be this ex-

[7] Maier, N. R. F. *Principles of human relations.* New York: Wiley, 1952.

pert's role (*a*) to point out problems, such as relationship between cost and load, style and cost, style and type of rock formation, and (*b*) to ask good questions about the needs and objectives of the citizens. He need never, and should not, express his own choice because he then reflects a bias and so becomes a party to a possible controversy. Similarly the supervisor, in his role of expert, should conduct himself as a resource person.

If we think of experts as individuals with knowledge greater than that of the persons with whom they deal, the supervisor becomes an expert on several counts. He knows more about company plans, company policies, what other units are doing, past records, methods, and his area of freedom. In dealing with new employees he knows more than they do about specific jobs, and when he teaches them he functions as an expert.

Often supervisors can phrase problems to make them fall within the area of freedom. For example, if Mrs. Collins knows that her unit has been allotted 500 dollars to redecorate the lounge, she can put the problem to her group as follows: "We have been given up to 500 dollars to redecorate the lounge. Let's discuss the matter and decide how we want to spend it."

Many decisions must consider limitations that can be clarified in the statement of the problem. A few examples will illustrate.

(*a*) Two men from our crew can be gone at one time during the deer-hunting season—now how should we arrange our schedule?

(*b*) During this overtime period we have to have one skilled and two semiskilled operators in attendance. What is the fair way to distribute overtime so as to accomplish this?

(*c*) This job involves the duties shown in this job description. We want to work out a good way to transfer workers so as not to lose valuable training.

Selection of Problems

Group decision makes its greatest contribution when the acceptance of decisions becomes important for their effective execution. The conservative use of group decision therefore should be in the solution of problems that primarily involve acceptance. Whenever emotions are present and attitudes within a group conflict, the use of group decision should be seriously considered. Problems involving work changes, fair treatment, fair standards, and job security are loaded more with feelings than with facts, hence readily lend themselves to group decision. It is important for the leader to evaluate problems in terms of their importance to employees. Availability of iced tea may become an important issue to a group of employees whereas a supervisor may consider it a big fuss over nothing.

In the selection of problems for group decision one should also consider their possible ramifications. Wash-up time in a unit may create a problem for the whole department. If the area of freedom is properly clarified, such difficulties can be avoided; nevertheless problems differ in the degree to which they involve other issues.

Discussion Leadership

Both the degree of acceptance of a decision by group members and its objective quality depend upon the skill of the discussion leader. Experimental tests show that the leader performs a valuable function when he serves merely as the chairman.[8] He becomes even more valuable when he asks good qustions, sets the example of listening and trying to understand, and becomes less inclined to sell his ideas.[9] The principles and methods discussed in the chapters on attitudes and frustration can serve as aids to the leader in dealing with feelings, and his ability to do so becomes a primary skill area. A group's respect and interest in facts is elicited when true feelings can be communicated and understood. A group's problem-solving activity, which requires a consideration for factual matters and goals, places no great demands on the leader's capacity. His major difficulties are to refrain from dominating and to inhibit his tendency to make suggestions, supply alternatives, and manipulate the group by indicating the ideas he favors. Relaxing and letting the group pick up the problem is an important leadership skill and is easiest to do when the leader has no fear that the group will reach the wrong solution. Because of his emotional involvement in outcomes it is often difficult for him to distinguish between solutions and problems. As a matter of fact, many supervisory problems turn out to be "How can I get my ideas accepted by my subordinates?"

A problem is properly isolated when it is formulated in terms of the desired goal and the obstacles that lie in its path. Group decision is the process of finding and agreeing on solutions. Presenting a solution and trying to sell it to subordinates is the authoritarian approach and it needs to be inhibited when conducting group discussions.

The use of group decision therefore represents a change in the role of the discussion leader, and the use of the method with a few basic skills will be adequate for solving problems of the A/Q type. With the acquisition of additional skills in discussion leadership, further gains can be made. To achieve the maximum potential gains, special training in group decision methods is highly desirable. These further gains are not in the form of getting the group to cooperate but in raising the problem-solving level of the group process, which often means that the leader's thinking also will be upgraded.

Time Requirements

The initial reaction to using group decision on the job is that a great deal of time will be needed. It is desirable therefore to consider the possibility of spending one or two hours per week for such meetings. Most supervisors do not find this excessive. If the meetings effectively solve one or two problems each month, considerable progress can be made over a year.

[8] Maier, N. R. F., and Solem, A. R. The contribution of the discussion leader to the quality of group thinking: The effective use of minority opinions. *Hum. Relat.,* 1952, *5,* 277–288.

[9] Maier, N. R. F. The quality of group decisions as influenced by the discussion leader. *Hum. Relat.,* 1950, *3,* 155–174; Maier, N. R. F., and Hayes, J. J. *Creative management.* New York: Wiley, 1962.

To here
7/28/79

Training Needs

Basic Leadership Skills

The skills essential to the group-decision type of discussion must be consistent with the concept. Sometimes it is thought that if the leader cannot dominate a discussion, as in autocratic leadership, he will be left without a function. However, a different set of skills is needed for group-decision leadership, and it is possible that in complexity they exceed those essential to autocratic leadership. The following are some skills that seem to be essential:

1. *The ability to state a problem in such a way that the group does not become defensive, but instead approaches the issue in a constructive way.*
Stating the problem in terms of the situation, in terms of fairness, or in terms of common objectives are successful approaches. It is important that the leader share a problem with his group (for example, how to make the job more safe) rather than pass judgment on them (how to get the employees to be more careful). He should not suggest alternatives to choose from, indicate his preference for a solution, or criticize suggestions made by employees. In many instances he would show more skill if he had no preconceived idea of what should be done.

2. *The ability to supply essential facts and to clarify the area of freedom without suggesting a solution.* Ordinarily this aspect of leadership requires little time, and it is important that the problem can be turned over to the group as quickly as possible. Any facts overlooked can easily be supplied later. The most frequent fault encountered in training discussion leaders is the leader's tendency to make a long preliminary speech.

3. *The ability to draw persons out so that all members will participate.* This technique requires leaders who are able to (*a*) accept contributions (using an easel helps); (*b*) make reluctant individuals feel their ideas are wanted and needed; (*c*) prevent talkative individuals from dominating without rejecting them; (*d*) keep the discussion moving forward; (*e*) accept feelings and attitudes of all participants as valid considerations; (*f*) protect individuals that other group members might attack verbally; and (*g*) accept conflict in the group as good and essential to the resolution of the problem. Complete acceptance of decisions can occur only when there has been full participation, and this can take place only when the leader uses his position to encourage the expression of and respect for all points of view.

4. *The ability to wait out pauses.* This is one of the most difficult skills to practice. Pauses trap the leader into continuing to talk, calling on persons, asking leading questions, and suggesting his own ideas. The same pause that makes the leader participate *too much* should instead be used to cause the group members to enter the discussion. If the leader can out-wait the first few pauses (which may seem painfully long) he will have made a great advance in stimulating discussion. Calling on individuals puts them "on the spot" and they may not be ready to contribute. Participation should not be forced, but should occur naturally.

5. *The ability to restate accurately the ideas and feelings expressed, and in a more abbreviated, more pointed, and more clear form than when initially expressed by a*

member. In performing this function the leader demonstrates that he is paying attention, understands what is said, and accepts the views and the person who expresses them. Acceptance of ideas means that the leader neither agrees nor disagrees, but respects the right of the group members to contribute.

6. *The ability to ask questions that stimulate problem-solving behavior.* This skill is highly important in conducting discussions for solving complex problems. Questions from the leader cause all group members to think about the same thing at the same time. If the questions are good ones, they direct exploration along fruitful lines, as well as prevent the thinking from persisting in areas where failure is repeatedly experienced.[10] Questions become bad when the group sees them as threatening (cross-examination) rather than helpful.

7. *The ability to summarize as the need arises.* This skill is important since it can be used to (*a*) move the discussion along, (*b*) indicate progress, (*c*) restate the problem in a new form (in the light of discussion), and (*d*) point up the facts that differences exist in the group and that these differences are part of the problem. Summarizing at the end of a discussion also serves to check on understanding, commitments made, and the responsibilities entailed.

The need for practicing the skills. A little experience with training student and supervisory groups makes it apparent that these skills improve with practice. Discussion procedures and role-playing cases, such as those described in the laboratory exercises, are designed to furnish opportunities to practice and apply the principles of leadership. A person can also improve his skills by practicing discussion leadership on his job. If he critically evaluates his performance in relation to discussion outcomes and is sensitive to the satisfaction of those participating, he can continue to improve over a long period of time. Since most problems can be successfully handled with a minimum amount of skill, ample opportunities to improve through real-life practice present themselves.[11]

The ability to deal with deadlock. Failure to reach unanimous agreement is much less common than usually anticipated. A conflict situation was described (page 118) in which all 30 groups reached unanimous agreement. Nevertheless, anticipated failure to resolve differences tends to create anxiety in the leader so that he uses persuasion. Searching for added alternatives or making failure to reach agreement a problem for the group to solve are effective ways to deal with competing alternatives or individual hold-outs.

Essential Attitudes

Skills must be supplemented by appropriate attitudes. Discussion leadership seems to require a respect for the rights and feelings of others. One must be concerned more with understanding than with judging.

[10] Maier, N. R. F. An aspect of human reasoning. *Brit. J. Psychol.,* 1933, *24,* 144–155; The behavior mechanisms concerned with problem solving. *Psychol. Rev.,* 1940, *47,* 43–58.

[11] A more complete treatment of leadership skills will be found in N. R. F. Maier, *Problem-solving discussions and conferences.* New York: McGraw-Hill, 1963.

Some research shows that a leader's behavior and his effect on the outcome of discussions are influenced by experimental variations in the leader's attitude.[12] In one part of the experiment the attitude of the leaders was manipulated in a role-playing situation by telling them that they were foremen conducting a discussion either (*a*) with other foremen or (*b*) with their employees. The problem was the same in each instance, but the difference in the mental set of the leader caused him to be more permissive and open to suggestions when dealing with peers than when dealing with subordinates. As a result, satisfaction and free participation were greater when the leader felt his group to be his peers rather than his subordinates.

In another study[13] a leader who took a helpful attitude toward his group caused participants to be more satisfied with discussion than a leader who assumed a negative nonconstructive attitude. Failure to obtain a difference in the quality of decisions seemed to be due to the fact that when the leader's behavior was too bad certain group members took over some of his functions. Members summarized ideas, clarified issues, and corrected misstatements when the leader purposely was inadequate.

The experiments suggest that a leader with a given amount of knowledge and training will do his best job of conducting a discussion when he respects the ideas and feelings of the group members, has no favored solution in mind himself, and considers it his job to perform the functions of leadership.

Social Perception

People communicate not only with language but with actions, voice intonations, and facial expression as well. Frequently a person's spoken words actually misrepresent what he thinks or feels. In any group discussion a good deal of potential communication is lost because members fail to respond to nonverbal expressions. It is the leader's responsibility to become sensitive to the feelings of persons so that he can conduct himself in accordance with the group's condition at the moment.

Sensitivity to the feelings of others can be developed, but one must learn what to observe, and there is no simple formula to follow. This leader-sensitivity is analogous to what a car driver must learn in properly applying the brakes. In an emergency he does not use a formula and apply a particular force for a particular speed; rather, he applies the force as the car can take it. From the response of the car he can sense a slippery pavement or a soft shoulder, and in order to become a good driver he must respond to this *feedback* the car gives him.

A conference leader cannot concentrate on the agenda and expect to conduct a satisfying meeting. The group will feed back reactions to him in many ways, and no single behavior will have a consistent meaning. He must get the meaning of these signs from their context, just as we get the right meaning for a word from the way it is used.

---

[12] Solem, A. R. The influence of the discussion leader's attitude on the outcome of group decision conferences. Doctoral dissertation, University of Michigan, 1953; Solem, A. R. An evaluation of two attitudinal approaches to delegation. *J. appl. Psychol.*, 1958, *22*, 36–39.

[13] Heyns, R. W. Effects of variation in leadership on participant behavior in discussion groups. Doctoral dissertation, University of Michigan, 1948.

Practice in sensing when persons like or dislike each other, when they are satisfied or dissatisfied with decisions, when participants are bored, hurt, or hostile during a discussion, and so on, are important aspects of leadership training. Role playing and evaluative analysis of past discussions are effective ways for increasing sensitivity.

Industrial Examples of Group Decision

When a supervisor changes his approach from supplying decisions (and often having to spend considerable time persuading subordinates) to sharing a problem, the social climate shows a radical change. In some instances subordinates become suspicious, but if the supervisor is sincere in inviting their help or in finding a fair solution, discussion begins. In simulated life situations differences both in the quality and in the acceptance of decisions among leadership styles clearly favor leaders that invite the group to make the decision.[14]

Evidence from life situations is less easily obtained because the given problem cannot be duplicated to allow a comparison of solutions obtained under different methods. However, instances of practices do serve as case studies in which crucial behaviors can be identified.[15]

The modifications (e.g., area of freedom, problem classification) imposed by adopting the group-decision concept to practical situations clearly have not destroyed the way group behavior is influenced by it. The case studies reported are included to show how the dynamics of behavior are changed when decision making is transferred to the group.

Efficiency in a Repair Crew

The *production index* of a telephone repair crew is expressed in terms of the average number of visits per man per day. The company average at one time was 10.8. The best crews had a score of 12.5, the poorest 8.5. After training in group decision the foreman of a crew with a production score that ranged between eight and nine for the past six months called his 12 men to a meeting. He asked whether they had any ideas on how their work could be better coordinated. He wished to know whether there were obstacles that might be overcome if the group sat down and discussed various phases of the job. In his presentation of the problem he avoided any criticism of the relative standing of his crew. The group agreed that such a discussion would be worthwhile, and their attitude was one of a sincere desire to help.

The group readily came up with criticism about the organization of the job. For example, the group agreed that there were too many *repeats*. A repeat is defined as a further report of trouble from a station (customer) within 30 days after a repair-

[14] Maier, N. R. F. *Problem solving and creativity: In individuals and groups.* Studies 23, 26, 29, 30, 31, 33, 34, and 35. Belmont, Calif.: Brooks/Cole, 1970; Maier, N. R. F., and Sashkin, M. Specific leadership behaviors that promote problem solving. *Personnel Psychol.,* 1971, *24,* 35–44.

[15] Maier, op. cit. fn. 7.

man has visited the job. Repeats measure the quality of service in that they either show that the repair job was not properly done or that the instrument went out of commission a second time for some new cause. A new cause (chance) cannot easily be prevented, but the first indicates inadequate workmanship. Thus the frequency of repeats is used as the *quality index*. The company practice is to send a more highly skilled workman on a repeat, assuming that if the first man failed to correct the difficulty, a more skilled man might succeed. The group felt that this procedure was wrong because it did not permit a man to learn new things, or to know the outcome of his efforts.

In order to solve this problem the group recommended that on all repeats the man who previously visited the station should be sent back, and that the foreman should meet him there to help him locate the difficulty. This suggestion was particularly interesting because the men were actually asking for training. Furthermore, by having the foremen visit the job, they were protected from unfair evaluation.

Another item was then brought up for consideration. This was time wasted in travel. The company practice was to send a man on a new assignment as soon as he became available. Thus jobs were assigned according to the order in which they were received and the repairman's availability. The purpose of this procedure was to keep the number of *subsequents* as low as possible. (A subsequent is second or third call from a customer before a repairman arrives.) The percentage of subsequents was used as the *service index*.

The crew recommended that the district in which they worked be divided into 10 territories. A map was used to make up these divisions, so that about an equal amount of work would be required in each. There were 12 men in the crew, and 10 men were to be given territories. The remaining two men were to be *floaters*, who would cover the district. The plan was that floaters would make up for irregular fluctuations in the repair load.

In addition, provision was made for such marked changes in load as occur after storms, fires, etc. It was agreed that although 10 men were to work primarily in their own territories, they could be moved into adjacent territories. By this procedure, more than half the crew could be pulled into a trouble area and leave the rest to cover their own and an adjacent territory.

The men spent the remainder of the meeting discussing assignment of territories and floaters. Two men liked driving and wanted to be floaters. At the end of the meeting the men expressed pride in the territories assigned them and acted as if they owned them.

During the next two years the effectiveness of the plan was also reflected in the objective records as follows:

1. Repeats, which previously averaged over 17 per cent of all service calls, now were held down to an average of 4 per cent.
2. Subsequents, which previously occurred about 20 per cent of the time, also fell to 4 per cent.

3. The number of visits per man per day rose from an average of 8.5 per cent to an average of 12.5 per cent, while the company average remained below 11.

The interesting aspect of this case is the way the quality of the work procedure was upgraded. Job experience introduced facts that cut travel time and motivated learning. How much improved productivity was due to greater acceptance vs. higher decision quality cannot be determined.

A Problem of Inclement Weather

The head of a department in a large utility company came to work on a day when the weather was such that it might be called a blizzard. He observed that gas company workers were on the job but discovered that his company linemen were in the garage playing pinochle. The union contract stipulated that the men were not required to work outside during inclement weather. However, a decision as to whether a specific day was to be judged inclement was required. In a management seminar dealing with group decision, the department head pointed out that such decisions could not be left to the crews. Differences of opinion were voiced and a decision to put this problem to a test was reached. It was agreed that in two garages the foreman would make such decisions, whereas in two other garages the crews would decide. A total of 16 crews were involved. Since borderline days are infrequent it took considerable time to make a convincing test. At the end of four years the department head was convinced that the difference favoring the group-decision groups was not due to chance.

Feedback during the test period revealed some interesting sidelights. Crews that made group decisions to work during bad weather, instead of feeling sorry for themselves, kidded the crews that decided not to work for being sissies. However, when different foremen made conflicting decisions, the crews that worked were critical of the foremen.

When one considers the position of the foreman the outcome of the experiment ceases to be surprising. Men tend to protect themselves from exploitation and foremen have learned that when they make decisions on borderline cases they run the risk of being charged with being unreasonable or of having a grievance filed. To play safe, the foremen make lenient decisions.

Employee Grievance

Mrs. G. was given a voluntary transfer from her job at the University laundry to a job at the University hospital which had somewhat different working conditions in that in making the change she went from a salaried to an hourly wage. Mrs. G. was told that she would lose nothing in the transfer. However, she soon learned that her vacation accrual was only 1½ days per month on her new job for her length of service, whereas it was two days per month on the old one. When she learned this she complained, and after some deliberation the personnel office ruled that she could keep her two days accrual since she had been promised equivalent benefits.

However, this decision created a problem. Miss L. found that she had as much seniority as Mrs. G. but received less vacation, and so filed a grievance. It was clear that if Miss L. won her case there would be others. How could personnel go back on its word with Mrs. G. or how could they persuade Miss L. to withdraw her case?

A meeting was held which included Mrs. G., Miss L., two other employees who were concerned with the outcome, the department head and his assistant, the union president, the personnel manager, and his assistant. The personnel manager put the problem to the group as follows: "We have a problem in that Mrs. G. is getting more vacation time than other hourly employees with the same seniority. A grievance has been filed by Miss L., stating that she feels Mrs. G. is receiving preferential treatment, and we will probably get many more grievances on the same question. The hospital policy is to accrue 1½ days per month when you have as much seniority as Mrs. G., but, through what we now feel was a misunderstanding, and a mistake on our part, Mrs. G. is getting two days per month. Now, could you ladies think of any way to solve our problem?"

After 25 minutes of discussion, with all taking part, Mrs. G. suggested that she give up the extra half-day she was getting per month. The group-decision approach accomplished in a single meeting what would have taken upwards of six months to accomplish via the channels usually followed, and the solution did not result in loss of face for anyone. The personnel staff, initially reluctant to try the method, was both surprised and pleased. Mrs. G. felt more accepted in her new job because of her willingness to give up a special privilege.

Higher Management Decisions

The foregoing examples illustrate participation at lower levels of management. The reason for these selections is threefold. (1) Group decisions made with subordinates in management positions are not as crucial a test of the effectiveness of the group-decision procedure as are decisions made with rank-and-file employees because the former are expected to respect management goals and consequently evidence of good quality decisions is not especially surprising; (2) Problems and decisions at higher levels of management require consideration of many details, hence are difficult to describe; (3) The benefits of such decisions are more difficult to appraise in terms of production standards and services rendered. However, this does not mean that the group-decision method is not needed or is inappropriate at higher levels. As a matter of fact, it is at these levels that a good deal of talent might be marshalled for creative decision-making. An example of the use of group decisions in higher management will illustrate its possibilities and some of the difficulties in reporting their value.

One case involved the briefing of an airline company officer, Mr. A., who was assigned to represent his company in working out a new or supplemental contract with a municipal airport to determine charges for the various services and facilities. All airlines serving the city are represented in such cases and a favorable contract for a particular airline depends upon the number of flights, the amount of freight carried, the amount of space used, and so on. A contract that was favorable to an airline handling a good deal of freight might be unfavorable to one having many short passenger trips. Each airline representative is inclined to strive for a contract that favors his company, but the type of contract favorable in one city might be unfavorable in another. Thus, each airport represents a unique situation, which changes from time to time, necessitating the negotiation of new contracts. Furthermore, the contracts agreed to for one airport are of concern to those who must represent the company at another airport.

Persons involved in these negotiations have their own territories, and all report to the same superior. In this instance, Mr. X was Mr. A's superior. In the past, Mr. X's involvement in negotiations was that of supervising the work of the subordinate involved by being available for consultation and giving approval to certain concessions or changes in procedure.

On the occasion in question Mr. X decided to use the group-decision approach. His subordinate Mr. A had a pending contract situation so instead of having him in for a briefing Mr. X called a conference of all of his subordinates. The meeting included eight subordinates (A through H) but a ninth, Mr. I, was on vacation.

The group discussed the specific problem situation Mr. A faced, and it soon became evident that any contract he concluded would be of concern to them. Thus Mr. A learned how any contract he negotiated would raise problems for his fellow representatives. They, in turn, became sympathetic with his problem, exchanged ideas, and discussed various alternatives. Mr. X was surprised and impressed with the degree of involvement in alternative possibilities and with the plans of action that emerged.

When Mr. A went to the city concerned for contract negotiations he felt better briefed than on previous occasions. He also found himself better qualified than his competitors to discuss the issues, and had no occasion to call his superior and check on his next move. The preliminary discussion had briefed him on all eventualities.

The resulting contract was regarded by Mr. X as highly favorable to the company; he felt Mr. A had done an excellent job; and all his fellow representatives, except Mr. I, praised the contract. Mr. I felt that certain factors had not been given adequate consideration. Whether this criticism stemmed from the decision's quality which his presence might have upgraded, or whether it was due to lack of acceptance because he had not influenced the outcome could not be determined.

Summary

The examples make it clear that workers approach a problem constructively if it is relevant to their jobs and does not threaten them. The contrast between what occurs and what is anticipated often is striking. This observation is frequently voiced by persons who give the group decision method a trial. They go into the situation with certain fears and expectations that are in sharp contrast to what actually happens. As they gain experience they become more relaxed and look forward to surprises. They learn it is best not to have a solution in mind. It has been shown experimentally that the obvious preference by a power figure for a particular alternative tends to strengthen another.[16]

[16] Worchel, S., and Brehm, J. W. Direct and implied social restoration of freedom. *J. Person. soc. Psychol.,* 1971, *18,* 294–304.

Group Decision Is Not	Group Decision Is
1. Abandoning control of the situation.	A way of controlling through leadership rather than force.
2. A disregard of discipline.	A way of group discipline through social pressure.
3. A way of giving each individual what he wants.	A way of being fair to the job and all members of a group.
4. A way of manipulating people.	A way of reconciling conflicting attitudes.
5. A way of selling the supervisor's ideas to a group.	Permitting the group to jell on the idea it thinks will best solve a problem.
6. Sugar-coated autocracy.	A way of letting facts and feelings operate.
7. A matter of collecting votes.	Pooled thinking.
8. Consultative supervision in which mere advice is sought.	Cooperative problem solving.
9. A way of turning the company over to employees.	A way of giving each person a chance to participate in things that concern him in his work situation.
10. Something anyone can do if he wishes.	A method that requires skill and a respect for other people.

Table 6.1 / Clarification of Group-Decision Leadership

Because the group decision method is confused with many supervisory practices now in vogue, it is essential that basic distinctions be clarified. Table 6.1 identifies 10 leadership concepts that frequently have been mistaken for group-decision leadership.

Why Group Decision Works

All the factors mentioned in Chapter 5 as improving morale are utilized in group decision. The principle of participation is carried to its logical conclusion, since it is applied to the points of decision making and enforcement. The principle of mutual sacrifice is fully used, because fairness is determined by the way members of a group see it. Freedom and tolerance are present to a high degree, and when restricted they are restricted by the group, not by the power invested in the leader. Progress is experienced when one perceives movement toward a goal. A group's goal is more real than a supervisor's goal, hence the experience of progress is more real in group decision. Further, when groups specify goals and participate in ways to measure them, the experience of progress can become apparent without being mixed with the anxiety always present when someone is checking up.

Psychologically these factors add up to sound motivation, clarification of attitude differences, security of group membership, constructive social pressure, prevention or removal of misunderstanding, good two-way communication, and respect for human dignity. Simple procedures that utilize many principles are efficient procedures.

When group decision is used as a problem-solving procedure, its effectiveness depends upon the more thorough exploration of the problem, discovery of a greater variety of obstacles, utilization of a larger amount of information, and generation of a greater variety of points of view. Problem solving as a management skill will be discussed in Chapter 22.

Laboratory Exercise

Role Playing: The Case of the New Truck

(Students are asked not to read the case materials before participating in the laboratory exercise.)

A. Preparation for role playing.

The instructor will:

1. Read General Instructions (E.1) to class as a whole.
2. Place data regarding name, length of service, and make and age of truck on chalkboard for ready reference by all.
3. Divide class into groups of six. Any remaining members should be asked to join one of the groups and serve as observers.
4. Assign roles to each group by handing out slips with the names Walt Marshall, George, Bill, John, Charlie, Hank. Ask each person to read his own role only (E.2). Instructions should not be consulted once role playing is begun.
5. Ask the Walt Marshalls to stand up when they have completed reading their instructions.
6. When all Walt Marshalls are standing, ask that each crew member display conspicuously the slip of paper with his role name so that Walt can tell who is who.

B. The role-playing process.

1. The instructor will start the role playing with a statement such as the following: "Walt Marshall has asked his crew to wait in his office. He is out now. Apparently he wants to discuss something with the men. When Walt sits down that will mean he has returned. What you say to each other is entirely up to you. Are you ready? All Walt Marshalls please sit down."
2. Role playing proceeds for 25 to 30 minutes. Most groups reach agreement during this interval.

C. Collection of results.

1. Each foreman in turn reports his solution. The instructor summarizes on the chalkboard by listing the initials of each repairman and indicating with arrows which truck goes to whom.

2. A tabulation should be made of the number of persons getting a different truck, the crew members considering the solution unfair, and the foreman's evaluation of the solution.

D. Discussion of results.

1. Comparison of solutions will reveal differences in the number of persons getting a different truck, who gets the new one, the number dissatisfied, etc. Discuss why the same facts yield different outcomes.
2. The quality of the solution can be measured by the trucks retained. Highest quality would require the poorest truck (Hank's) to be discarded. Evaluate the quality of the solutions achieved.
3. Acceptance is indicated by the low number of dissatisfied repairmen. Evaluate solutions achieved on this dimension.
4. Locate the new truck problem on the Problem Chart (Fig. 6.6).
5. List problems that are psychologically the same as the new truck problem. See how widely the group will generalize.

E. Materials.

1. General Instructions

Each group of six persons will be working on the same thing at the same time and members of each group will be asked to participate in solving a job problem. (This procedure is called "multiple role playing" and combines role-playing and "Phillips 66" to give a new kind of participation experience.)

Assume that you are repairmen for a large utility. Each day you drive to various locations in the city to do repair work. Each of you drives a small truck and you take pride in keeping it looking good. You have a possessive feeling about your trucks and like to keep them in good running order. Naturally, you like to have new trucks too, because a new truck gives you a feeling of pride.

Here are some facts about the trucks and the men in the crew that reports to Walt Marshall, the supervisor of repairs:

George	17	years	with	the	company,	has	a	2	year old	Ford	truck	
Bill	11	"	"	"	"	"	"	5	" "	Dodge	"	
John	10	"	"	"	"	"	"	4	" "	Ford	"	
Charlie	5	"	"	"	"	"	"	3	" "	Ford	"	
Hank	3	"	"	"	"	"	"	5	" "	Chevrolet	"	

Most of you do all of your driving in the city, but John and Charlie cover the jobs in the suburbs. (The instructor should write the above facts on the chalkboard so that they are visible to all during the role play.)

You will be one of the persons mentioned above and will be given some further individual instructions. In acting your part in role-playing, accept the facts as well as assume the attitude supplied in your specific role. From this point on let your feelings develop in accordance with the events that transpire in the role-playing process. When facts or events arise that are not covered by the roles, make up things which are consistent with the way it might be in a real-life situation.

2. Role-playing Instructions

Walt Marshall—Foreman of Repair Crew

You are the foreman of a crew of repairmen each of whom drives a small service truck to and from his various jobs. Every so often you get a new truck to exchange for an old one, and you have the problem of deciding to which of your men you should give the new truck. Often there are hard feelings because each man seems to feel he is entitled to the new truck, so you have a tough time being fair. As a matter of fact, it usually turns out that whatever you decide, most of the men consider wrong. You now have to face the issue again because a new truck has just been allocated to you for assignment. The new truck is a Chevrolet.

In order to handle this problem you have decided to put the decision up to the men themselves. You will tell them about the new truck and will put the problem in terms of what would be the fairest way to assign the truck. Don't take a position yourself, because you want to do what the men think is most fair.

George

When a new Chevrolet truck becomes available, you think you should get it because you have most seniority and don't like your present truck. Your own car is a Chevrolet, and you prefer a Chevrolet truck such as you drove before you got the Ford.

Bill

You feel you deserve a new truck. Your present truck is old, and since the more senior man has a fairly new truck, you should get the next one. You have taken excellent care of your present Dodge and have kept it looking like new. A man deserves to be rewarded if he treats a company truck like his own.

John

You have to do more driving than most of the other men because you work in the suburbs. You have a fairly old truck and feel you should have a new one because you do so much driving.

Charlie

The heater in your present truck is inadequate. Since Hank backed into the door of your truck it has never been repaired to fit right. The door lets in too much cold air, and you attribute your frequent colds to this. You want a warm truck since you have a good deal of driving to do. As long as it has good tires, brakes, and is comfortable you don't care about its make.

Hank

You have the poorest truck in the crew. It is five years old, and before you got it, it had been in a bad wreck. It has never been good, and you've put up with it for three years. It's about time you got a good truck to drive, and you feel the next one should be yours. You have a good accident record. The only accident you had was when you sprung the door of Charlie's truck when he opened it as you backed out of the garage. You hope the new truck is a Ford since you prefer to drive one.

Suggested Readings

Barnlund, D. C., and Haiman, F. S. *The dynamics of discussion.* Boston: Houghton Mifflin, 1960.

Dill, W. R., Hilton, T. L., and Reitman, W. R. *The new managers.* Englewood Cliffs, N.J.: Prentice-Hall, 1962.

Maier, N. R. F., and Hayes, J. J. *Creative management.* New York: Wiley, 1962.

Marrow, A. J., Bowers, D. B., and Seashore, S. E. *Management by participation.* New York: Harper & Row, 1967.

Odiorne, G. *How managers make things happen.* Englewood Cliffs, N.J.: Prentice-Hall, 1961.

Stagner, R. *Psychology of conflict.* New York: Wiley, 1956.

Zelko, H. P. *Successful conference and discussion techniques.* New York: McGraw-Hill, 1957.

7

Individual Differences

Introduction

That people differ from one another is especially obvious from their physical appearance. That differences exist in their abilities is also a commonly recognized fact. The full importance and nature of the variation among people, however, is not generally appreciated. Many believe that practice makes perfect; yet no amount of practice on the part of one man will make him as proficient in his work as less practice will make another. We also hear people classified as bright or dull, good or poor workers, easy-going or hot-tempered. The implication in each of these pairs of characteristics is that a man falls into either one of two categories.

In industry, a common practice is to pay men by the hour. This indicates that a man's time is what counts rather than how much he accomplishes. Paying for time spent encourages men to put in their time rather than to produce according to their abilities. If a man falls below a certain level of performance, he may be discharged, but frequently the discharge is based upon factors unrelated to production. The fact that one man may be capable of producing as much as two or more other men, and require no more equipment than each of them, is not sufficiently appreciated by the average employer.

Since marked differences in ability do occur, proper selection alone would greatly increase production. Once the most capable available men are selected, pains can be taken to keep them and to utilize their superior ability. Because superior individuals can do quite satisfactory work without much effort, they ordinarily need not exert themselves to keep their jobs. Inducements must be offered to encourage them to produce more in accordance with their ability. This is not a simple problem, since their associates may object to having their own lesser abilities exposed. The objections of less capable men to superior performance are based largely upon the fact or the impression that they will suffer thereby. It has been the experience of labor that, when men are paid for the amount they produce, some men have made a lot of money. When this has occurred, they have often found that management is likely to lower the piece rate. This practice has become a cause of labor's objection to superior performance. If managers wish to utilize individual differences, they must do it in a way that will avoid opposition from labor in general. Although the improper utilization of man's ability may provoke opposition, it does not follow that differences in ability should not be recognized and used.

The Nature of Individual Differences

The Normal Distribution Curve

If we subject any aspect of man to measurement, we find that the measured trait is distributed in the population in a particular fashion. Further, all traits are distributed in a very similar manner whenever the traits are measured in individuals selected at random; that is, so that they are representative of the general population. The measured trait may be height, strength of hand grip, intelligence, ability to memorize, speed of reacting to a signal, honesty, or emotional stability. Regardless of whether one measures physical characteristics, mental traits, personality traits, sensory capacities, or muscular coordination, the manner in which each is distributed in the population forms a bell-shaped pattern as illustrated in Figure 7.1. The height of the curve represents the frequency with which the various scores plotted on the

Figure 7.1 / Normal Distribution Curve. The height of the curve indicates the frequency with which the various scores shown on the base line appear in a population. Half of the people make scores which fall in the narrow band in the middle. The other two quarters make scores which are spread over a wide range, both above and below the middle band. If the middle half is divided into two quarters, the population is divided into two groups of equal size.

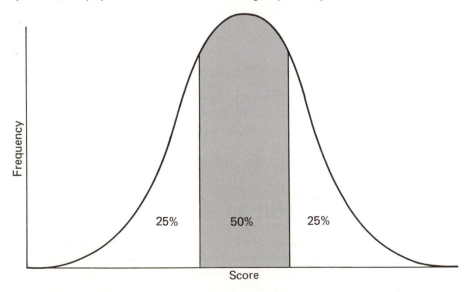

base line occur in a population. This is the theoretical normal distribution curve for individual differences. It is characterized by symmetry about a center, which is the average or mean.

The shaded portion includes 50 per cent of the total population. Mathematical procedures are available for marking off such parts of a curve. The population represented in the curve can be thus divided into four equal parts. We can therefore refer to individuals as being in the first, second, third, or fourth quarter of the population in regard to the particular trait measured. The greatest variation in individual ability occurs within the first and fourth quarters. In the two middle quarters, the individuals are more closely bunched and are more homogeneous. Because the middle half of the people are very much alike in ability we are likely to overlook the fact that a wide range in ability occurs in both the upper and lower quarters. It is these exceptional performers that are most frequently misunderstood, and it is through a proper appreciation of the upper quarter that potential gains can most easily be achieved.

When sufficiently large numbers of people are tested, when these are selected at random, and when the test is not too easy or too difficult, the plot of the actual measurements obtained corresponds to the theoretical curve. In other words, the distribution curve describes the manner in which ability is distributed in a group when selective and chance factors are excluded and a good measuring instrument is used. When conditions do not substantiate this distribution there is good reason to investigate further to discover the cause.

The importance of any individual's score must always be judged by its position in the distribution curve. This position gives an idea of how rarely or how commonly this degree of ability occurs. The fact that a man can inspect 200 parts in an hour has little meaning, but the fact that only 3 per cent of the men can do better than that shows clearly that he is superior. To find another who would do as well would not be easy. Human ability, for the psychologist, is always a relative matter. To appreciate any one individual, we must know how he compares with the population as a whole.

Practical Implications

Since about half of the people are near average in ability such individuals are likely to be represented in any small group of employees. It is these employees that a supervisor is most likely to understand, and it is their performance that gives him the notion of what he can expect in the form of a day's work. The lower as well as the upper 25 per cent often will be misunderstood because they are rare and because some of them will be very much above or below average in ability. Often both superior and inferior producers are classified as "loafers": the superior ones because they do not keep busy and the less gifted because they accomplish less than is expected of them.

A supervisor may transfer or discharge the superior "loafer" and then find too late that two, three, or even four workers are needed to cover the job. A job that keeps an average worker busy will allow considerable leisure for one of superior ability. In some cases there may be nothing for him to do, a state of affairs that frustrates the supervisor who must keep him busy. When there is no limit to the amount of work to be done, workers of superior ability become problem employees if they refuse to do more than a certain amount.

Persons below average in ability are problems because they respond to the fore- man's urge for more work by reducing quality, ignoring safety, or becoming hostile. Furthermore, other employees may slow down so that the poor producer's work no longer is out of line.

The first step in meeting the problem of individual differences in ability is to recognize them and to accept the differences as facts. To expect the same from all workers can at best lead to a condition in which the slowest one sets the pace for all.

The concept of a normal distribution can serve a valuable positive purpose when it is used to give a supervisor some notion of unfavorable conditions in his group. Although the production figures of small groups cannot be expected to form a smooth distribution curve, certain trends can be expected. Let us examine an actual situation and see how this knowledge may be an aid.

A foreman in the telephone industry, when asked about the productivity of his crew, pointed out that six men were above average in productivity, each doing four installations per day; six men were below average, each doing three per day; and none was average since no man did three and a half installations. It is apparent that half of the workers cannot be equally superior even if only twelve men are involved. At least one or two should be able to do more than four installations if six can do four per day. It also follows that some of them should do less than three if six can do three per day. However, this condition can be explained by assuming that those who are unable to do three per day had been discharged or transferred. But most interesting is the fact that no installer completed between three and four jobs, since the ability to do approximately three and a half installations must be present in some who are doing three.

The discrepancies indicate the need for determining: (1) why installers turn in only complete jobs (see Chapter 16); (2) why some either hold back on produc- tion or are not interested in doing more; and (3) how workers who have difficulty in doing three installations are treated. If superior workers hold back on production to protect low producers, it would be more efficient to accept low production. How poor must a worker's production be before being considered unfit for the job? The answer to this question involves supervisory attitudes, the notions of fairness in a group of employees, and some further consideration of individual differences.

Another illustration will throw some light on this question, but the problem of fairness discussed in Chapter 6 must not be forgotten. In a toll-ticket–sorting unit the production figures for a group of 13 women on a particular day were as follows: 610, 790, 910, *1005, 1060, 1090, 1150, 1195, 1255,* 1405, 1595, 1780, and 2098. Note that the production of six women (scores italic) falls between 1005 and 1255, a range of less than 300 units. This is the middle part of the distribution curve where we find people to be very much alike in ability. The production of four superior performers has a spread of more than 600 units, and that of the three low performers ranges from 610 to 910.

The question now is whether or not the employee with production at 610 should be removed. Perhaps the lowest scorer already has been removed. One must not overlook the fact that eliminating the poorest producer always leaves another. How bad is a production of 610 when it is seen in relationship to a distribution curve?

Since scores near the average are always the ones most alike, it is reasonable to suppose that the concentration of scores between 1000 and 1300 centers on the average for this kind of activity. Roughly 1150 would be about the center of distribution. A woman producing 610 units will be 540 units below average; while one woman producing 2098 units will be 948 units above. As a matter of fact the woman producing 1595 units is just as superior as the one producing 610 units is inferior.

In this instance the poorest performers already have been removed by one method or another. To continue removing the poorest performer eventually will cause anxiety on the part of others, and this condition leads to morale problems. Large differences in productivity are a healthy condition because they stem from the fact of abilities spread over a wide range. As long as the superior producers are definitely farther above the central grouping than the less gifted producers are below, a good selection of employees is indicated. This favorable condition is more readily apparent when the production figures are graphically presented as in Figure 7.2. Here we see that the superior performers more than offset the low production of the less capable workers.

When tests are not used to select employees, the distribution of abilities approaches what may be expected from the general population. For example, finger

Figure 7.2 / Production Scores of a Small Group of Workers. The slowest worker is less of a problem when it becomes apparent that superior workers more than make up the deficiency. Since every group must have a slowest worker, study of the distribution of production scores reveals when this condition is acceptable and when it needs correction. In this example the slowest worker does not deviate enough to be classified as unsatisfactory.

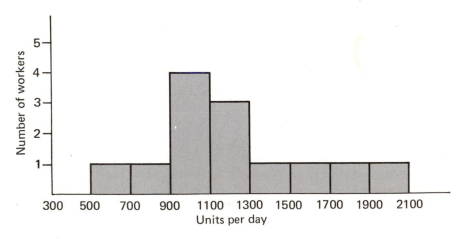

dexterity is an important ability for radio assemblers. Figure 7.3 shows the manner in which this ability is distributed in the population as a whole (solid line) and among 42 radio assemblers (broken line). In this instance, ability was measured by the time required to place 100 pegs in the O'Connor Finger Dexterity Test Board. A low score therefore means superior ability. Note that this group of 42 radio assemblers differs from the population as a whole only by a small shift in the curve as a whole toward the right or upper range. The average time for people in general is 7.99 minutes as compared to 7.35 minutes for the assemblers. Supervisors are often misled in supposing that the degree of selectivity in their group is greater than it really is.

Sex and Race Differences

Whether or not the distributions of ability between sexes and races differ and whether or not differences reported are due to biological, cultural, or educational factors are questions that cannot be answered at this time. For practical purposes the answers would have little value. The differences within a race and within a sex would show normal distributions and if any differences in shape between these distributions did occur it would have to be slight. (Visualize another distribution curve superimposed on the one in Figure 7.1 but placed slightly to the left.) It follows that even if the average male were slightly superior in some ability to the average female, it would still allow, for example, 48 per cent of the females to

Figure 7.3 / Distribution of Scores on O'Connor Finger Dexterity Test. The solid line shows the distribution for people selected at random and the broken-line curve shows the distribution for the radio assemblers. Although finger dexterity is an important aptitude for this work, it will be noted that the ability of the assemblers (average time 7.35 minutes) is only slightly better than that of the population as a whole (average time 7.99 minutes). (From Joseph Tiffin, *Industrial psychology,* 3rd edition. © 1952, by permission of Prentice-Hall, Inc., Englewood Cliffs, N.J.)

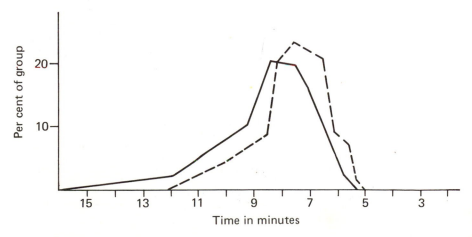

be superior to 50 per cent of the males—and the cause of the difference would be undetermined.[1] The function of employee selection should be to screen for job ability. Race and sex offer no meaningful clues for selection since individual differences are the important variables.

The value of psychological tests for measuring differences in ability has come under severe criticism because ethnic groups are placed at a disadvantage, particularly if verbal tests are used.[2] A test that places a particular group at a disadvantage obviously is not a valid instrument.

Variations in Normal Distributions of Human Abilities

The Range of Ability in Different Occupations

Although the abilities of an unselected group of people tend to be distributed as in the normal distribution curve, some variations do occur. These are variations in the spread of the scores. For some abilities, the highest score may be only 1½ times as great as the lowest score; for others, the highest score may be as great as 26 times the lowest. A large variation may occur even when individuals with similar training are compared.

Figure 7.4 illustrates how ability to produce may be distributed in three different occupations. Usually, the actual accomplishments in gainful occupations do not have as wide a range as occurs in the general population. Markedly inferior workers are eliminated, and superior workers lack motivation. Nevertheless, the productive performances of different workers are not as much alike as is usually supposed. For example, it has been found that for polishing spoons the ratio is 1 to 5, and that for loom operation it is 1 to 2.[3] In looping hosiery, the production of 199 employees ranged from three pairs to 84 pairs per hour.[4] These production figures, however, included those of inexperienced individuals. When the output of fully experienced persons only was studied, the range was from 30 to 84 pairs per hour. These differences in production among hosiery workers showed little fluctuation.

Generally speaking, the spread of a distribution curve is greater for complex than for simple abilities. When the range is great, it is particularly important to encourage the superior individuals to remain with the company, since their ability is an important factor in total production. The low producing workers either should be transferred to a simpler type of operation where the distribution is less widely spread and where varying degrees of ability show minor differences in production,

---

[1] Bardwick, J. M. *Psychology of women: A study of biocultural conflicts.* New York: Harper & Row, 1971.

[2] Kirkpatrick, J. J., Ewen, R. B., Barrett, R. S., and Katzell, R. A. *Testing and fair employment: Fairness and validity of personnel tests for different ethnic groups.* New York: New York University Press, 1968; Miner, J. B. *Personnel Psychol.* London: Collier-Macmillan, 1969; Anastasi, A. Some implications of cultural factors for test construction. In A. Anastasi, (Ed.). *Testing problems in perspective.* Washington, D.C.: American Council on Education, 1966.

[3] Hull, C. L. *Aptitude testing.* New York: World Book, 1928, p. 33.

[4] Tiffin, J., and McCormick, E. J. *Industrial psychology* (4th ed.). Englewood Cliffs, N.J.: Prentice-Hall, 1958, pp. 25–27.

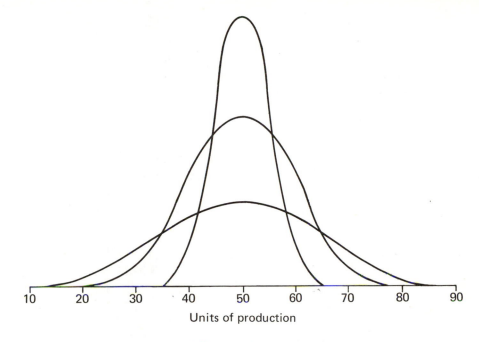

10   20   30   40   50   60   70   80   90

Units of production

Figure 7.4 / Three Normal Distribution Curves. Normal distribution curves may differ in the extent to which the ability measured is spread. The tallest curve shows that the range from lowest to highest score is less than the ratio of 1 to 2; the flat curve indicates a range in scores of more than 1 to 4. In simple occupations there is less of a spread in ability than in complex occupations.

or be placed in occupations very different from those in which they are at a disadvantage.

Differences in Experience Confuse the Picture of Individual Differences

Practice does not equalize productive ability. Differences in ability to learn a task may actually increase the spread. Great emphasis on the number of years of experience as a qualification for a job is a mistake. That length of experience is not a satisfactory basis for choosing employees is shown in Figure 7.5.[5] Applicants for stenographic positions were divided into three groups: (1) those with five or more years' experience; (2) those with one to five years' experience; and (3) those with less than one year's experience. The figure shows that, when the experience was matched, a wide range in ability still occurred. The average ability for each group is indicated. Although the more experienced stenographers had a slightly higher average, the difference in no way made up for the wide variation in ability between individuals.

[5] Paterson, D. G., and Darley, J. G. *Men, women, and jobs.* Minneapolis, Minn.: University of Minnesota Press, 1936, p. 94.

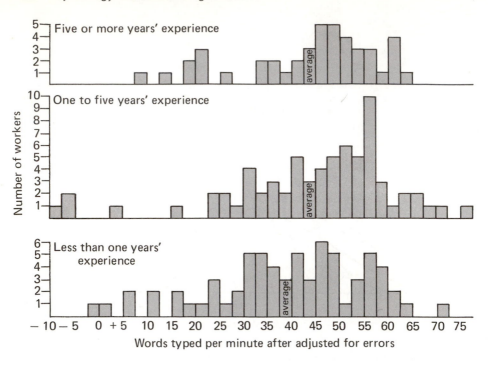

Figure 7.5 / Range in Skill of Three Groups of Typists. The typists are classified according to length of experience. It will be seen that the variation of ability within each group far exceeds the difference in skill which accompanies experience. (After D. G. Paterson and J. G. Darley, *Men, women, and jobs.* Minneapolis, Minn.: University of Minnesota Press, 1936, p. 94.)

Since each person has an inborn capacity for learning to do certain kinds of work better than others, attempts should be made to train him on jobs that best suit his natural talents. Experience can develop the potentialities, but how much it will develop them depends on the original endowment. In comparing human performances, it is well to match experience in order to bring out the original differences in ability because they give an indication of future performance. For instance, suppose one individual can do exactly as much as another but does so with a lesser degree of experience. In such a case, we can expect the former to surpass the latter when both have added the same amount of experience. It is therefore wiser to employ the person with less experience rather than the one with more. For many industrial purposes, individual differences in ability are far more important than varying degrees of experience.

Figure 7.6 shows how three different men might profit from experience. All will eventually reach a ceiling so that experience will not improve them further. However, sharp differences among individuals will occur in the height of the ceiling, the steepness of the curve of improvement, and the degree of proficiency revealed before training. Ordinarily, persons who have the most proficiency at the outset will

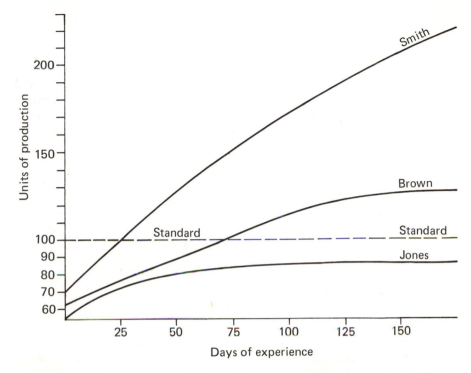

Figure 7.6 / Curves Showing Rates of Improvement with Experience. Although all people profit from job experience or training, some profit more than others. The hypothetical curves of Jones, Brown, and Smith differ in: (a) the points at which they begin; (b) the steepness of the progress; (c) the height at which the curves level off to indicate the ceiling of their progress; and (d) the length of time over which improvement will occur.

improve the fastest, will improve over a longer period, and will reach the highest final level. These trends are shown in Figure 7.6 for Jones, Brown, and Smith. Jones will never be a satisfactory worker since his performance levels off before it reaches standard. Brown becomes a satisfactory employee after about 70 days experience, and Smith after about 25 days. Early performance is somewhat of an indication of how much skill employees will be able to develop.

Not only will the steepness of improvement and the overall period of improvement vary from one person to another, but variations will also occur because of the nature of the job. Jobs involving complex skills will permit improvement over longer periods of time than will simple jobs. One might say that, where job failures are most likely to occur, most attention should be placed upon individual differences in ability to improve.

Deviations from Normal Distributions

Although the measurement of a given trait may be adequate for testing both extremes of ability, a normal distribution curve is not always obtained. When this occurs, we know either that we are dealing with a special group of people or that some factor is operating to influence our measurement of ability.

Bimodal Distribution Curves

If one measured the strength of hand grip in a mixed group of 10- and 15-year-old boys the distribution curve would have two high points. Normal distribution curves are obtained from either group, but the curve for 10 year-olds would be shifted somewhat to the lower end. The two humps obtained from the measurements of the combined group represent the averages for the two ages. A theoretical bimodal curve is shown in Figure 7.7.

Bimodal distribution curves reveal that we have actually measured a combination of two different populations. Similar curves would be obtained if we measured the intelligence of a group of college students combined with a group of children. If two extremely different groups were combined in this manner, the distribution would result in two entirely separated curves. The bimodal effect is due to incomplete separation.

In certain departments of industry (see Chapter 19), a bimodal distribution curve for intelligence reflects that persons of average ability are discouraged and find jobs elsewhere. This occurs when workers of superior intelligence are given more desirable work within the department. The less gifted are content to remain, but the average employees in the department are not satisfied with their positions and so seek other work. The remaining workers cease to be representative of the industrial population as a whole, since a selective factor has operated to eliminate persons with a specific degree of intelligence. If it is found that the individuals of below-average intelligence are doing satisfactory work, this selective factor is desirable. The intelligence test can then be used for selecting individuals having the desired degree of mental ability.

Because bimodal distributions occur only under special conditions, people cannot be divided into categories or classified into types. If people were either honest or

Figure 7.7 / Bimodal Distribution Curve. Curves of this type are obtained when two different populations are combined, or when a selective factor, which eliminates persons of average ability, operates in a single population.

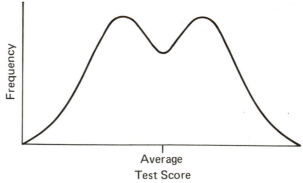

dishonest, wise or foolish, good workers or poor workers, bimodal curves would be the rule rather than the exception.

Skewed Distribution Curves

Bimodal distribution curves differ from normal curves in that the middle group of scores is not the most frequent one. Deviations also can occur because of increases or decreases in the number of individuals falling at either end of the curve. Such curves are described as *skewed* in that they are nonsymmetrical and the high point does not lie in the center.

Three examples of skewed distribution curves are represented by solid lines in Figure 7.8. Curves A and B are both skewed to the right, but Curve A represents a selective condition in which low scores are abundant, while Curve B represents a condition in which low scores have been eliminated. To determine whether a skewed condition is favorable or not one must know what the total population looks like.

In order to produce Curve A one would have to select from a large population, shown by the broken-line Curve X, retaining primarily the lower-scoring individ-

Figure 7.8 / Skewed Distributions. Curves A, B, and C represent skewed distributions and indicate operation of a selective factor, serving either to exclude or include scores as they approach extremes. Curves A and C are skewed in opposite directions, and represent select populations taken from a large population, shown as Curve X. Curve B is skewed toward the upper end, as is Curve A. This type of curve can be derived from a smaller population, such as represented by Curve Y and is produced by weeding out persons with progressively lower scores.

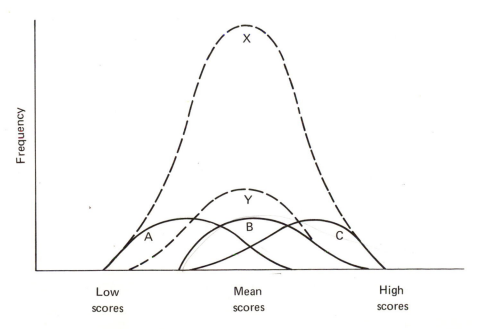

uals and rejecting those with progressively higher scores. To produce Curve B, one could take a given population, such as represented by Curve Y, and weed out the low-scoring persons, being progressively more strict as scores fell below average. Curve B would represent a favorable employment condition in that it showed that the poorest workers were most inclined to leave; while Curve A would represent an unfavorable condition in that average and poor producers are relatively more frequent than in the total population and that high-producing individuals are entirely lacking.

Curves also may be skewed toward the left; for example, Curve C is skewed toward the lower end and represents a favorable condition. Thus skewness indicates the operation of a selective factor, but its desirability cannot be determined unless one knows its relation to the total population. The objective of employment tests is to produce a select population of workers, which would be indicated if their production scores showed distributions such as those represented by Curves B and C. However, these are more extreme than our present selection methods can produce. The differences are exaggerated for clarity.

Select populations are highly desirable in industry, since they tend to be more homogeneous and specifically adapted to do a particular kind of work. The best vocational guidance would be that which placed each individual in the kind of work which gave him his most favorable position in the distribution curve. This kind of guidance would actually fit the person to the job. Since people are most contented when they are doing work they can perform fairly proficiently, this procedure would not only increase the productive capacity of a company but would increase work satisfaction as well.

Measuring the Relationship Between Human Abilities

Introduction

In industry, one of our main concerns is the ability to produce. For this reason, it is desirable to learn whether certain specific abilities are related to competence in a given job. If marked relationships are found, and the specific abilities are measured, we can select superior individuals on the basis of such tests. The degree to which the tests are selective will in part be indicated by the magnitude of the relationships existing between the test scores and job performance.

Successes in various jobs may also show relationships with one another. If these are known, they may aid in properly transferring workers from one job to another when conditions demand. Even a worker's interests may be related to success. Generally speaking, people tend to have more ability in tasks for which they have special interests than in tasks for which interest is lacking.[6]

Correlation Coefficients

To demonstrate the relationship between two sets of measurements, we may plot one against the other on a graph. A hypothetical graph or scattergram of this nature is

[6] Pervin, L. A. Performance and satisfaction as a function of individual-environment fit. *Psychol. Bull.*, 1968, *69*, 56–68.

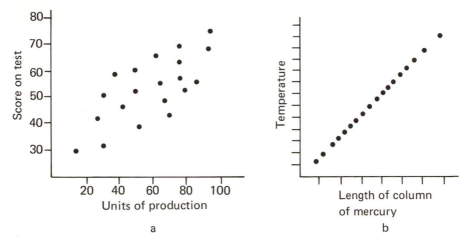

Figure 7.9 / Scattergrams Showing Relation between Two Measures. (a) Relationship between test score and production. Each dot represents an individual, and the position of the dot indicates his production and test score. (b) Relationship between temperature and length of column of mercury. When the dots fall into a straight line, the relationship between the two variables is perfect.

shown in Figure 7.9a. Each dot represents an individual. The production score for each individual can be read by noting his position along the horizontal axis, while his test score can be found by reading its value from the vertical axis. This type of *scatter diagram* can be made whenever we have two sets of measurements on the same group of individuals.

If a perfect relationship exists between two sets of scores, the dots arrange themselves in the straight line shown in Figure 7.9b. When a linear relationship of this type exists, a scientific law can be formulated, and prediction is perfect. Such a relationship exists between the length of a column of mercury and the temperature.

Another straight-line relationship occurs when the dots arrange themselves at right angles to the line of dots shown in Figure 7.9b. In this case, the highest score on one test would go with the lowest score on the other test, the second highest with the second lowest, and so on. This arrangement of dots would express an inverse relationship, such as is found between the volume of a gas and its pressure.

When the relationships are less than perfect, the dots merely tend to fall about a straight line, within an elliptical area, as in Figure 7.9a. If the long axis of the ellipse is in the direction of increasing scores on both axes (e.g., lower left to upper right) the relationship is positive; if the axis is at right angles to this, it indicates an inverse relationship and the relationship is negative. The more extreme elliptical arrangements indicate high relationships. The most extreme relationship occurs when the short diameter of the ellipse is zero, and such an ellipse becomes a straight line. If no relationship exists between two tests, the dots do not tend to group about an axis. The scatter of dots thus appears circular rather than elliptical.

From inspection of scatter diagrams, we can see whether or not relationships exist, whether they are small or large, and in what direction the measures are related. By means of statistical formulae, we can express the degree of relationship by a value known as the *correlation coefficient.*

The procedure for obtaining a correlation coefficient need not concern us here but can be found in any textbook on elementary statistics. Our present concern is with the meaning of various correlation coefficients. When a perfect relationship is found, the value of the coefficient is 1; when no relationship exists, the value is 0. Values between 0 and 1, such as .2, .5, .8, indicate varying degrees of relationship. Since relationships may be positive (direct) or negative (inverse), the correlation coefficients are given a plus or minus sign so that the correlation values range from −1 to +1. Figure 7.10 shows six scatter diagrams with the correlation coefficients given to indicate degree and direction of each relationship. An experienced person can judge with considerable accuracy the magnitude of such coefficients by inspecting a scatter diagram.

When dealing with the relation between human traits or abilities, perfect relationships are never obtained. For example, relationships exist between height and body weight, intelligence and school grades, performance on certain tests and ability on a job, but none of these relationships is perfect. Relationships between +.5 and +.7, however, are frequently obtained. This is the extent to which body weight and height are related. Individual exceptions would occur, but we could do better than chance if we utilized a measure of one trait to predict a measure of the other. The number of exceptions increases as the correlation coefficient decreases.

Industrial Applications of Correlated Performances

Any industrial tests will be worth using which correlate .3 or better with performance on a job, and such tests will be superior in predictive value to nonpsychological procedures, such as the use of photographs and general impressions. A combination of tests, each of which measured something different and all of which correlated with job performance, would greatly increase the accuracy of prediction. Correlation coefficients of .6 or better are highly important, and any test which correlates with job performance to this degree is about as good as can be expected. A little study of a scatter diagram of test scores plotted against job performance, shown in Figure 7.11, shows how the exclusion of individuals with test scores below a certain level would eliminate a large percentage of poor performers on a job.[7]

Another useful application of the scatter diagram arises if workers had to be shifted from one job to another. Suppose one had a knowledge of the correlation of performance on various pairs of jobs in an industry. If more workers were needed on some jobs and could be spared from others, one could shift workers between

---

[7] A variety of examples of the effectiveness of tests in the selection of employees will be found in C. H. Lawshe, Jr., *Principles of personnel testing.* New York: McGraw-Hill, 1948; Cronbach, L. J. *Essentials of psychological testing* (2nd ed.). New York: Harper, 1960, pp. 324–356; Tiffin, J., and McCormack, E. J. *Industrial psychology* (5th ed.). Englewood Cliffs, N.J.: Prentice Hall, 1965, Chs. 5–9; E. A. Fleishman (Ed.). *Studies in Personnel and Industrial Psychology.* Homewood, Ill.: Dorsey Press, 1967, Section I.

Figure 7.10 / Scattergrams Illustrating Different Correlation Coefficients. By means of a statistical formula, correlation coefficients can be calculated to express these relationships. Positive relationships range from +1.00 to 0 while negative or inverse relationships range from 0 to −1.00. (Redrawn from Fig. 5.8, *Psychology and human performance,* by Robert M. Gagné and Edwin A. Fleishman, copyright © 1959, Holt, Rinehart and Winston, Inc. By permission.)

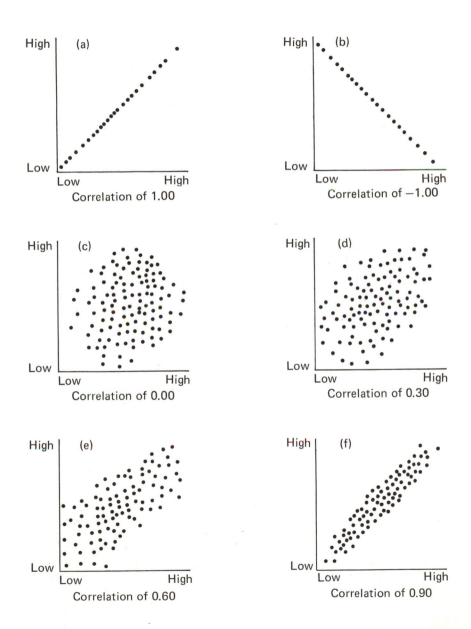

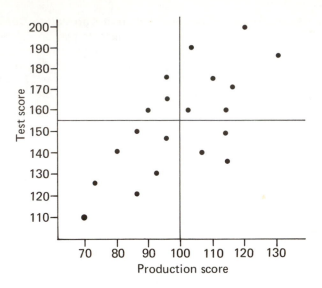

Figure 7.11 / Using Tests to Screen Workers. In this example the highest scorers tend to be the best producers. Among the 10 best producers, seven are also among the best scorers. If such test scores were used to hire new employees, one could increase the proportion of high producers and decrease the proportion of low producers.

correlated jobs and expect them to occupy similar positions in the distribution curves. Thus, if Job *A* correlated with Job *B,* it would be safe to transfer workers from the *A* to the *B* job with a good probability that the transferred workers would be about as successful on the new job as on the old.

When workers do poorly on one job, it is advisable to shift them to jobs which are uncorrelated or negatively correlated. In two jobs which are uncorrelated, a person's performance on the one will probably be different from that on the other. Thus if a person does very badly on one job, it is probable that he will not do so badly on the other. When a negative correlation exists, one may actually expect the person to be in a superior part of the distribution curve after the change.

Psychologists have constructed lists of jobs which they speak of as *job families,* occupations which demand similar patterns of activity.[8] Through job analysis the relative importance of each activity is determined and consideration is given to the time that would be saved in training if transfers were made from one job to another. Jobs which require (1) similar activities, (2) the same worker characteristics

[8] Shartle, C. L., *et al.* Occupational analysis activities in the war manpower commission. *Psychol. Bull.* 1943, *40,* 701–713; Shartle, C. L. *Occupational information, its development and application* (3rd ed.). Englewood Cliffs, N.J.: Prentice-Hall, 1959; *Estimates of worker trait requirements for 4000 jobs as defined in the dictionary of occupational titles.* Washington, D.C.: U.S. Dept. of Labor, Bureau of Employment Security, 1958; Mosel, J. W., Fine, S. A., and Boling, J. The scalability of estimated worker requirements. *J. appl. Psychol.,* 1960, *44,* 156–160.

or traits, (3) corresponding machines, tools, and instruments, and (4) work on the same kinds of material (for example, wood) are placed in the same family. With the advent of the computer, systematic comparisons between large numbers of jobs have become feasible. Thus simple clustering and factor analysis techniques are now being employed in a statistical approach to the development of job families.[9] When shifts in workers become necessary, manpower is efficiently utilized if the transfers are made within the job family. Correlation of performance on jobs within the job family serves as a check on the degree of relatedness in each family. Future work along these lines may become a great aid in vocational training as well as in reeducation of displaced workers.

Career Ladders

Job families permit lateral transfers when the grades of the jobs are the same (e.g., equal pay). When jobs at different levels show correlations they supply valuable information for promotion. This vertical linking of jobs has been described as the development of *career ladders*. This is a rather new development that holds considerable promise for training and developing employees along different lines of advancement in an organization.[10]

Summary

This treatment of individual differences will have achieved its purpose if it (1) reduces the tendency of the reader to judge the abilities of others in the light of his own abilities, (2) encourages him to look for special talents in employees, (3) stimulates him to make comparisons in terms of relative abilities, and (4) makes him analyze jobs and duties in terms of human abilities. An understanding attitude toward individual differences on the part of the supervisor will be recognized by subordinates, since such an attitude leads to the kind of personal attention to which employees have referred in the morale studies (see Chapter 5).

Ability and Performance

What a person is capable of doing and what he actually does are not necessarily the same. The term *ability* refers to a person's potential performance, whereas the term *performance* refers to what a person actually does under given conditions. How a person performs on a job depends both upon his ability and his willingness or motivation. We may express the relationship between these factors by the following formula:

$$\text{Performance} = \text{Ability} \times \text{Motivation}$$

[9] Dunnette, M. D., and Kirchner, W. K. A checklist for differentiating different kinds of sales jobs. *Personnel Psychol.*, 1959, 72, 421–430; Hemphill, J. K. *Dimensions of executive positions: A study of the basic characteristics of the positions of ninety-three business executives.* Columbus, Ohio: Bureau of Business Research, Ohio State University, 1960; Orr, D. B. A new method of clustering jobs. *J. appl. Psychol.*, 1960, 44, 44–59.

[10] Fine, S. A. *Guidelines for the design of new careers.* Kalamazoo, Mich.: Upjohn Institute, 1967; Miner, J. B. *Personnel psychology.* New York: Macmillan, 1969.

According to this formula, performance has a value of zero if either ability or motivation is absent, and increases as either factor rises in value.

In order to measure a person's ability, it is necessary to get him to perform.[11] As long as motivation is the same for all individuals in a group, variations in their performance records reflect differences in ability. Ordinarily, test situations are conducive to uniformly good motivation, so that test performance scores become measures of ability. Psychological test scores are regarded as measurements of ability because of this assumed constant in motivation. When there is reason for believing that the motivating conditions have been disturbed, the test scores have little meaning.

It is of interest to examine the effects of motivation on the shape of curves based on distributions of production in a work situation. If all persons were motivated maximally one would expect the distribution of production to follow the normal curve, except insofar as some low producers might have been eliminated. The effect of lowering motivation would then be one of merely displacing the curve to the left without altering its shape. Figure 7.12 shows three curves, A, B, and C, representing the conditions of low, medium, and optimum motivation, respectively.

Suppose we now consider the possibility that persons with differing ability might have varying degrees of motivation. One possibility is to postulate that persons of low ability tend to have low motivation; those with average ability tend to have average motivation; and those with superior ability tend to have optimum motivation. If these conditions were in fact the case, then the distribution curve of pro-

Figure 7.12 / Effects of Motivation on Curves of Production. Curves A, B, and C represent the effects of low, average, and optimum motivation on the production of a given unselected population. Increasing everyone's motivation to the same degree merely moves the production curve from left to right.

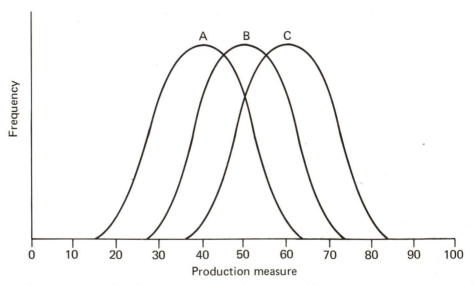

11 Vroom, V. *Work and motivation.* New York: Wiley, 1964.

duction would be more widespread than the ability to produce. The production curve would range from about 15 units (the low-ability end of the low motivation curve) to about 85 (the high-ability end of the optimum motivation curve). Thus we would expect the distribution curve to approach the shape of Curve X in Figure 7.13. However, this widespread curve does not describe the practical findings, so the abovementioned relationship between ability and motivation must be rejected.

Let us therefore make the opposite assumption and postulate that persons with low ability tend to have optimum motivation; those with average ability tend to have average motivation; and those with superior ability tend to have low motivation. If these conditions existed one would expect the production curve to range roughly between 35 (the low-ability end of the high-motivation curve) and 65 units (the high-ability end of the low-motivation curve). This narrow range (Curve Y of Figure 7.13) corresponds more closely with actual findings. The range in production measures invariably is narrower than that of ability scores. That the lower end is curtailed by selection is understandable, but the absence of high producers poses a problem even if one supposed that some of them had been promoted.

The evidence indicates that persons of low ability are highly motivated unless they become discouraged. Pressures to keep up with others are sufficient to motivate most persons. However, persons with superior ability can keep up easily so there are no social pressures to motivate them. Thus the potential for increasing produc-

Figure 7.13 / Effects of Differential Motivation. Curve X would describe the distribution of production if persons of lesser ability tended to be least motivated and persons of great ability tended to be optimally motivated. However, if persons of lesser ability were most highly motivated, and persons with great ability were least motivated, a curve approaching that of Y would result. This curve most accurately describes prevailing conditions.

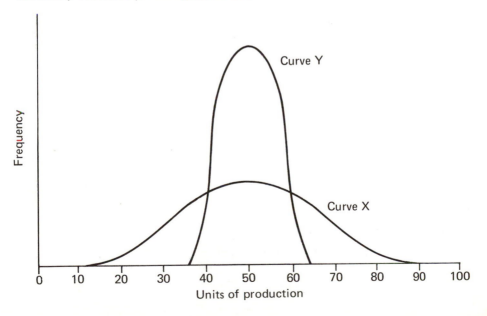

tivity by motivation procedures lies in tapping the efforts of superior workers, while persons with low aptitudes can be helped most by additional training or lateral transfers. Yet supervisors unfortunately are inclined to seek production improvements by trying to motivate the low producers and, as a consequence, quality decreases and errors or accidents increase. A person who already is doing his best can produce more only by taking shortcuts. If pressures are too great they lead to frustration and a further deterioration in performance. Thus the greatest possibilities for increasing production seem to lie in the direction of finding ways of motivating persons with superior talents.

Curves of Restricted Production

Another type of curve is frequently found when actual production in a factory, rather than ability to produce under carefully controlled conditions, is measured. A theoretical distribution curve of this type is shown in Figure 7.14. This curve shows

Figure 7.14 / Curve of Restricted Population. This curve is cut off sharply because individuals who have the ability to produce the greatest amounts limit their production to 110 units or less. The result of this restriction in production is that a large number of individuals produce a maximum amount. (After A. Ford, *A scientific approach to labor problems.* New York: McGraw-Hill, 1931.)

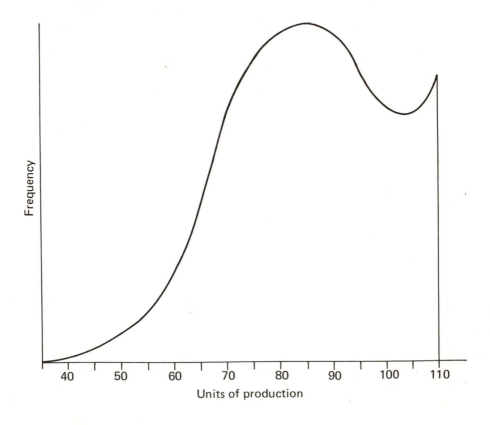

that the expected superior producers are conspicuous by their absence. The curve is sharply cut off because the superior individuals are producing a lesser amount than their ability warrants. Instead of being at the extreme right, these cases form a cluster which is indicated by the sharp rise at the right end of the curve. Apparently, there exists among the workers an agreement not to produce more than a certain number of units. It is at this amount of production that the curve is sharply cut off. One study revealed that 40 percent of the workers were performing at a production level of 120 per cent, when 100 per cent was supposed to represent average.[12]

This condition, known as *restricted production,* tends to arise when there is hostility toward the company, fear or distrust of company objectives, job insecurity, or group pressures to protect low standards. In one survey[13] employees were asked to answer the question: "When a man takes a job in a factory how much work should he turn out?" Table 7.1 shows how the responses were distributed among the four alternatives offered. Nearly half gave a favorable response, but 40 per cent held the opinion that average performance was proper. The other 11 per cent gave evasive responses which suggested that the situational circumstances would be factors.

The reasons given by the workers who felt that production should not exceed average are shown in Table 7.2. The first five classifications reveal an opinion that high production would act against them. Opinions that may be classified as "distrust of management" (Items 1 and 3) account for 41 per cent of the reasons. Social pressure from other employees (Item 2) accounts for 23 per cent. Fear of unemployment (Item 5) is not a big factor (given by 7 per cent) but could change with economic conditions. The 8 per cent who indicate physical breakdown either fear that the pace will continue to be speeded up or that they now have difficulty making average. Even if we assume the latter to be the case, it appears that a large number of workers are controlling their output. However, we must not overlook the fact that an even larger body of workers do not hold these attitudes (Table 7.1) so that if the evidence of restricted production is clear-cut it means that a strong minority group is influencing the production of many others.

One worker described in *Harper's Magazine* the means used in his factory to eliminate the "eager beaver" tendency to produce more than his fellow workers

Table 7.1 / Workers' Opinions on How Much Work a Man Should Turn Out

Opinion	Percentage
As much as he can	49
Average amount	40
That depends	8
No opinion	3

Data from *Factory Mgmt. and Maint.,* Jan. 1946, p. 83.

[12] Georgopoulos, B. S., Mahoney, G. M., and Jones, N. W. A path-goal approach to productivity. *J. appl. Psychol.,* 1957, *41,* 345–353.

[13] Opinion Research Corporation. What the factory worker really thinks. *Factory Mgmt. and Maint.,* 1946, *104,* 83–84.

Table 7.2 / Workers' Opinions about What Would Happen if They Produced More

Reasons Given	Per Cent
1. Production quotas would be raised by management	30
2. He would become unpopular with his fellow workers	23
3. Piece rates would be reduced	11
4. Worker would break down physically	8
5. Would cause unemployment	7
6. Nothing; worker would not make more money	7
7. Other replies	14

Data from *Factory Mgmt. and Maint.,* Jan. 1946, p. 83.

considered adequate. At first, gentle hints were employed; if these were not success-ful, glue might be found on the handle of his locker door or his clothing might be found knotted at the end of the day. The writer also indicated that some workers had been known to suffer "accidental" falls, with resulting sprained wrists and so on, while en route to lunch. The idea that the new or eager worker did not have to produce more than standard did eventually get across.[14]

Thus restricted production implies more than lack of motivation of superior in-dividuals; it indicates motivation to hold down production. Piece-rate work, ordi-narily designed to motivate workers to produce, is most subject to this condition because it shows up differences in ability. Salesmen working on commission bases have a wide range in earning. In 1960 some salesmen of a large business machine organization earned as little as 5000 dollars while others earned 100,000 dollars. To reduce the discrepancy in earnings it is not uncommon to have a decreasing scale of commission percentage. This not only reduces the earnings of the superior salesmen but their motivation as well.

Without some precautions the earnings of superior factory workers would sur-pass that of their foremen, which would discourage employees from seeking super-visory positions and also could easily lead to a reexamination of piece rates. It is therefore not unusual for a union contract to include a statement to the effect that rates and work standards cannot be altered unless there has been a change in the job itself, thus requiring establishment of a new set of standards.

The actual extent of restricted production is unknown. There is reason to believe that it is considerable. For example, the standard for bricklayers varies, but seldom exceeds 350 bricks per mason per day. It is also well known that a superior brick-layer can lay well over 2000 bricks without lowering quality. This might require more effort than would be considered comfortable but a mason of this caliber would also feel little job satisfaction if required to limit his production to 350.

The solution to the problem of unused ability created by various forms of re-stricted production requires cooperative problem-solving. To hold either labor or

[14] Bradshaw, C. Sure, I could produce more. *Harper's Mag.,* 1947, *194,* 396–401.

management responsible evades the basic issue. Workers do not restrict production because they are unwilling to do a good day's work, rather, they fear to do it. Where workers are frustrated, restriction is a form of retaliation. Distrust and conflicting interests are involved and these are states of mind that will not be altered by legislation. Instead, the differences must be resolved along lines suggested in Chapter 6.

Laboratory Exercise *OMIT*

Discussion: The Case of Viola Burns

(Students are asked not to read the case materials before participating in the laboratory exercise.)

A. Background information.
  1. The instructor will read the background material supplied and will have three members of the class act out the parts of Randall, Birdsall, and Viola Burns from the script (section D).
  2. The class is to divide into groups of three or four.
  3. Discussions.
     a. Free discussion. Half of the groups should serve as consultants and try to reach agreement on one of three alternative decisions:
        1. *Encourage* Viola to take the new job.
        2. *Insufficient Information* has been given for making a decision.
        3. *Discourage* Viola from taking the job by indicating she is needed in the old job.
     b. Developmental discussion. Half the groups should serve as consultants and follow the discussion steps below.
        1. Develop list of Viola's duties on present job.
        2. Determine which she does well.
        3. Develop list of duties on new job.
        4. Determine which of these we know Viola can do well and which ones we have doubts or insufficient information about.
        5. Determine which three duties the new boss will consider most important.
        6. Try to reach agreement on one of the three decisions.

B. Reports to class as a whole.
  1. Reports from the groups following the unstructured (*free*) discussion pattern and those following the structured (*developmental*) pattern should be tabulated separately.
  2. The instructor should tabulate the number of votes for the three alternatives, using headlines (Encourage, Insufficient Information, and Discourage) for each group.
  3. The totals for the free and developmental groups should be compared.

4. The proportion of unanimous decisions reached for the two discussion procedures should be indicated.

C. General discussion.

1. The two discussion methods have been found to yield different results,[15] and this will probably be duplicated in class results. Why should the same facts discussed with two procedures yield different outcomes?
2. Why were such a large proportion of decisions unanimous?
3. There are two sources of error in decisions regarding promotion: (1) the tendency to favor promotions when the person makes a favorable impression; and (2) an inclination to use promotion as a reward for past performance. Which discussion procedure tends to reduce these sources of error? Discuss.

D. Case materials.[16]

1. Background.

Viola Burns was hired directly upon her graduation from high school and placed in the payroll office as a typist. She was intelligent, quick, cheerful, energetic, and had a pleasing manner but looked delicate and somewhat unprepossessing at first sight and was somewhat lacking in self-confidence. The paymaster had asked for a woman who was good at figures, could type with reasonable speed and accuracy, and do shorthand. Viola more than met these qualifications.

There were twenty women in the paymaster's office, and Viola readily made friends with all of them. She not only adapted herself quickly to the job but evidently enjoyed the work. She was usually the first to arrive in the morning and was frequently spoken to for her failure to quit work at noon or at night. She became an asset to the department head and within a year had demonstrated to the employment manager that she was in line for promotion. Consequently when Mr. Randall received a requisition for a secretary to one of the sales executives, Viola Burns immediately came to his mind. He went to the paymaster, Mr. Raymond Birdsall, and suggested Viola's release for transfer.

2. Script.

RANDALL: Ray, I have a requisition from Jim Wagner's office for a bright woman to replace Agnes Brown who is leaving to be married. I think Viola Burns is just the person for the job.

---

[15] Maier, N. R. F., and Maier, R. A. An experimental test of the effects of "developmental" vs. "free" discussions on the quality of group decisions. *J. appl. Psychol.*, 1957, *41*, 320–323. Maier, N. R. F. Prior commitment as a deterrent to group problem solving. *Personnel Psychol.*, in press.

[16] Case taken from *Social Problems in Labor Relations*, by P. J. W. Pigors, L. C. McKenney, and T. O. Armstrong. Copyright, 1939. McGraw-Hill Book Company, Inc. Used by permission.

BIRDSALL: Hey, Randall, that woman is practically indispensable to me. She's one of the best employees I ever had. You don't think I'm going to let her go, do you?

RANDALL: How much are you paying, Ray?

BIRDSALL: One hundred twenty-nine dollars.

RANDALL: But you're not going to stand in her way if she has a chance for a better job and more money, are you?

BIRDSALL: Well, maybe I could pay her more money myself.

RANDALL: Maybe you could, Ray. But you're limited to the top rate for her present job classification. You can't pay her what she may eventually receive as a private stenographer.

BIRDSALL: No, of course not. Damn it all, the good people always go. I sometimes wonder if I'd be better off to take women that aren't quite so good, so I could keep 'em around here after I've spent time and money training them.

RANDALL: Well, here's your chance to decide. If I take Viola, you'll need someone to replace her. Tell me what you want and I'll find just the right candidate for you.

BIRDSALL: Well, I suppose there's only one answer. You'll have to take Viola. After all, I've got to give her the break. But you find another woman as good as she is, if you can. I guess I'm better off to hire bright women even if there is a chance that I may lose them.

(*Later in the day, Viola Burns was called to see Mr. Randall in his office.*)

RANDALL: Good morning, Ms. Burns. Have a chair. I have a suggestion to make which I believe will please you. Do you know Ms. Brown in Mr. Wagner's office?

BURNS: Not very well, but I know who she is.

RANDALL: Well, she's leaving us very soon—getting married—perhaps you have heard? I have suggested that you be considered to take her place. But whether or not you get the job depends on three conditions. The first is Mr. Birdsall's consent to release you; the second, your own willingness to give it a try; and the third, Mr. Wagner's acceptance. Now I want to tell you something about this job before you make up your mind. If you do well you would become Mr. Wagner's private stenographer, and be the only person in his office. This is quite a change from your present job and you might feel rather lonesome. Mr. Wagner's work requires a considerable amount of detail. You would handle his correspondence, keep his files, and run the office when he is out of town. This would involve contact with customers in person as well as over the telephone. If you should be transferred to this job you would receive a slight increase in salary at once, and more later if you do well. Do you think you would like to try this job?

BURNS: Really, I don't know, Mr. Randall. It sounds like a lot to learn, and so different from what I've been doing. I'd hate to fail. You know more about it than I. Do you think I could do it?

RANDALL: I'm very sure you can do it if you want to.

BURNS: Is there much dictation?

RANDALL: Yes, there's a good deal. But I'm sure you can handle that part of it. And, of course, Ms. Brown would be with you for a couple of weeks to show you the ropes. How about it, would you like to give this a try?

BURNS: Well . . . it's awfully hard to say, Mr. Randall. Could I think it over and let you know later?

RANDALL: Certainly, Viola, just let me know in a day or so when you've made up your mind.

(*At the end of two days, Mr. Randall had heard nothing further from Ms. Burns. He spoke to Mr. Birdsall during the lunch hour.*)

RANDALL: Oh, by the way, Ray, has Viola said anything to you about taking the job at Wagner's office?

BIRDSALL: No, she hasn't, but I certainly hope she'll make up her mind about it pretty soon. She's not much good to anybody since you spoke to her. She goes around looking like she's lost her last friend. She even cries about it. I believe she feels she ought to take a chance but hates to leave the department and her friends.

Suggested Readings

Anastasi, A. *Individual differences.* New York: Wiley, 1965.

Bardwick, J. M. *Psychology of Women: A study of bio-cultural conflicts.* New York: Harper & Row, 1971.

England, G. W., and Paterson, D. C. Selection and placement—the past ten years. In H. G. Heneman, Jr., *et al.* (Eds.), *Employment relations research.* New York: Harper, 1960.

Fleishman, E. A., and Bartlett, C. J. Human abilities. *Annual review of psychology,* 1969, *20,* pp. 349–380.

Marshall, R. *The negro worker.* New York: Random House, 1967.

Miner, J. B. *Personnel psychology.* New York: Macmillan, 1969.

Thorndike, R. L., and Hagen, E. *Measurement and evaluation in psychology and education.* New York: Wiley, 1955.

Tiffin, J., and McCormick, E. J. *Industrial psychology* (5th ed.). Englewood Cliffs, N.J.: Prentice-Hall, 1965.

8

Measuring
Proficiency

Introduction

The recognition of differences in the abilities of individuals immediately suggests the desirability of measuring the amount of work that they do on a job. Such measurements would not only bring to light the existing differences in ability but would serve other purposes as well. They would make it possible to differentiate between superior and inferior workers and thus permit analysis of their respective abilities. By measuring the characteristics of workers differing in productive capacity, it would be possible to determine whether specific traits are present to a different degree in efficient and inefficient workers. These traits or characteristics might have to do with personality, intelligence, muscular coordination, sensory capacity, or body structure. A knowledge of the desirable characteristics would be very helpful in selection and placement of workers.

In measuring proficiency in work, one must distinguish between merit and production. Merit is a far more general aspect of proficiency than production, since it includes productivity on the job as well as other characteristics which make a person a valuable employee. It is also necessary to distinguish between production on jobs in which the number of units produced accurately represents how much a person has accomplished and production on jobs in which the accomplishment is complex and may not even involve direct contact with specific units of production. This chapter describes methods for measuring these different aspects of work and shows how each is related to proficiency.

Measurement of Work on Production Jobs

A production job is characterized by the fact that quantity is the only variable which must be considered when we wish to measure the amount produced. Counting the number of items produced is all that is required. Sometimes the parts produced can be delivered and recorded; in other cases, various types of counting devices are available or can be designed. A satisfactory counting device is one which cannot be manipulated by the worker without his producing the desired item. Designing effective counters for the various operations is an engineer's problem and often requires ingenuity and inventive ability.

In actual practice, the items produced vary in quality, so that one cannot do justice to a person's output by mere counting. If a standard can be set up which demands that the product be of a certain quality in order to be acceptable, then this quality variable can be dealt with. Inspection methods which require that minimum standards be met take care of such qualitative features and permit measurement in terms of quantity, provided proper adjustments are made for defective production. All unsatisfactory items represent a waste in material. The amount of loss, after salvage value is considered, can be translated into its equivalent of production units.

For example, suppose that each part which does not pass inspection represents a waste in material equivalent to one-half the value of the work expended in producing a good part. A worker who produced 90 good parts and ten unsatisfactory parts would then be credited with producing 85 parts. If, however, the faults in the unsatisfactory parts can be corrected, such as errors in typesetting, unsatisfactory units represent partial production. Suppose the average worker can correct twice as many units as he can produce. In this case each unsatisfactory unit would have a value of .5. The worker in our illustration would then be credited with producing 95 parts.

Whenever quality can be reduced to quantity by adjustments of this sort, individual production can be designated by a single score. Careful study of various kinds of work will suggest possible means for translating qualitative into quantitative features. To the extent that this can be done, measurement of work can be put on a purely production basis.

When people work in groups or teams, production must be measured by the team score. In such cases employees should be matched and team spirit encouraged. The employees should have a voice in selecting teammates, and the company should cooperate in making desirable changes in the makeup of the group, since one slow or uncooperative individual can destroy the efficiency of the whole team.

Measurement of Work on Nonproduction Jobs

Rating Scales

A *nonproduction job* is one in which the quality of the work plays a predominant part; this merely means that a complex pattern of quantities is involved in each unit of production. When a person's productiveness depends upon a variety of considerations, it is impossible to use simple quantitative procedures. The work of a fireman, a policeman, a supervisor, or a schoolteacher are examples of jobs which do not easily lend themselves to simple quantitative measurement. In such cases, it has been necessary to resort to human judgments to secure a measure of success on a job. Human judgments are subject to error, but if the source of the error is known, the judgments can become surprisingly trustworthy. But when we resort to this method, we are actually measuring more than production; we are really measuring a person's merit or value to the company. Although productive ability is a very important aspect of merit, it must be recognized that merit is a more inclusive concept. A convenient expression for this relationship may be shown by the following formula:

$$\text{Merit} = \text{Production} \pm \text{Indirect contributions}$$

Rating is a technique by means of which we evaluate members of a group by comparing them with one another. Thus, a foreman might be asked to give each of his subordinates a letter grade of A, B, C, D, or E, according to the degree of proficiency and value on the job. This procedure seems little more than the usual method of passing an opinion on an employee, yet it is a distinct step forward. Since the mere introduction of a grading system requires the raters to take some care in observing the work of the people, it encourages them to make comparisons. As soon as they make such comparisons, the raters are less inclined to use themselves as a model and are more likely to use the average person in the group as a standard. As pointed out in Chapter 7, an individual's ability has true meaning only when it is expressed in terms of its relation to the abilities of other people.

Problems of Merit Rating

Rating scales in common practice are designed so that one form can appraise workers in a variety of jobs. A company may have three basic forms, one for the hourly-paid, one for salaried, and another for supervisory employees. This means that the traits measured might be in such general terms as quality of work, quantity of work, dependability, attitude, and safety. An example of a simple rating form is shown in Figure 8.1.

A supervisor's rating form might include such job dimensions as leadership, planning, job knowledge, ability to train, emotional stability, productivity of unit, administration of safety, and communication skills. Most scales require the rater to assign a numerical value or a letter grade to each dimension to indicate judgments ranging from very superior to poor or unsatisfactory. Rating forms in actual practice differ considerably. The number of traits rated varies from as few as five to as many as 20 and the number of grade steps range from three to eleven.

It will readily be conceded that certain problems, inconsistencies, and errors creep into measures based upon human judgments. A knowledge of some of these deficiencies helps introduce certain refinements.[1]

---

[1] Additional information regarding rating scales may be found in: Cronbach, L. J. *Essentials of psychological testing* (3rd ed.). New York: Harper, 1970; Ghiselli, E. E., and Brown, C. W. *Personnel and industrial psychology* (2nd ed.). New York: McGraw-Hill, 1955, Ch. 4; Strauss, G., and Sayles, L. R. *Personnel: The human problems of management*. Englewood Cliffs, N.J.: Prentice-Hall, 1960, pp. 527–540.

Figure 8.1 / Merit Rating Form

Name _____ Dept. _____ Date _____

Div. _____ When Assigned _____

Job Grade _____

Quality of work accuracy, economy, neatness, etc.	Consistently Superior ☐	Sometimes Superior ☐	Consistently Satisfactory ☐	Usually Acceptable ☐	Consistently Unsatisfactory ☐
Quantity of work	Consistently Above Standard ☐	Often Above Standard ☐	Meets Standard ☐	Sometimes Below Standard ☐	Consistently Below Standard ☐
Dependability punctuality, judg- instructions	High in all Respects ☐	High in some Respects ☐	Satisfactory ☐	Sometimes Undependable ☐	Consistently Undependable ☐
Attitude toward company, other employees, supervisor	Inspires Others to Work as Team ☐	Quick to Volunteer or Help Others ☐	Cooperative as General Rule ☐	Works well with Some & Not Others ☐	Works poorly with Others ☐
Safety respect for rules, influence on others	Leads in Promoting Safety ☐	Goes Out of Way to Be Safe ☐	Respects Rules ☐	Sometimes Violates Safety ☐	Disregards Safety ☐

Comments:

Instructions:
1. Rate all employees on one factor before going to next factor.
2. Consider only performance on present job.
3. Place check mark in square that best describes employee.

The Halo Effect

A common source of error in rating is the *halo effect*.[2] If raters have a generally favorable impression of a person they tend to rate this person generously, whereas if they have an unfavorable impression they tend to be hypercritical. Evidence for halo effect comes from two sources: (1) different raters disagree on their estimates of individuals when confronted with the same information; and (2) the ratings given a particular individual on a series of unrelated traits or characteristics show a striking correlation. First impressions, personal likes and dislikes, a tendency to generalize strengths or weaknesses of one behavior trait to other traits, and judgments influenced by the age or length of service of the employee[3] are the bases for the halo effect. It is not uncommon for a rater to assign approximately the same value to all traits.

The effects of this type of error can be reduced by having several observers rate the same workers. Various raters are likely to have different prejudices, and when they rate the same group of people independently, the various bases of the halo error tend to cancel one another. The superior individuals are the most likely to receive the highest average rating because superior performance tends to be a consideration common to all the raters. Obviously, this method can be practiced only when several raters are in a position to know the employees and their work well enough to pass judgment. Raters who have slight contact with the work of a group only introduce an additional source of error.

When it is not possible to have several supervisors rate the same individuals, it is frequently desirable to have workers rate one another. If they pass honest judgments, this procedure may be effective. Honest judgments, however, depend upon the cooperation of the employees, and this exists only in plants which foster interpersonal trust.

An effective method for reducing the tendency to give an individual the same rating on a number of traits is to require the rater to mark all employees on one trait before rating any on the next. In rating all subordinates successively on the same characteristic the rater has to focus attention on a particular trait or function and the various individuals are compared within this one dimension. Tests with this method[4] show that ratings given to an individual become more diversified. This improved procedure thus achieves a result similar to that accomplished by increasing a rater's skill.

In order to facilitate use of this procedure, the rating forms should have the names of the employees listed under each trait, thus supplying a page for each trait rather than a page for each employee. For record-keeping, however, this method

---

[2] Thorndike, E. L. A constant error in psychological rating. *J. appl. Psychol.*, 1920, *4*, 25–29.

[3] Tiffin, J., and McCormick, E. J., *Industrial psychology* (5th ed.). Englewood Cliffs, N.J.: Prentice-Hall, 1965.

[4] Stevens, S. M., and Wonderlic, E. F. An effective revision of the rating technique. *Personnel J.*, 1934, *13*, 125–134.

requires that the data be transferred from the rating form to the employee's file by a clerk, and this extra step tends to deter use of the procedure.

Since the nonproduction job requires consideration of a number of types of contributions that an employee may make, the process of rating should include measures of the various dimensions of the job. For example, a saleswoman may be judged not only in terms of her sales volume and the cost of her errors for which objective measures may be available, but also for her effect on customers and her knowledge of the product. Certain aspects of her performance, indirectly associated with her production, should also be considered in merit rating. These considerations might include her helpfulness to and congeniality with other sales personnel because of the effect such traits have on their work performance; her dependability in showing up for work on time because this may be important in planning for adequate coverage; her relations with her superiors since this trait influences their assignments and peace of mind; and her care of the stock because this activity both aids other sales personnel and simplifies inventory.

In many types of work these indirect aspects of production become so important that overall merit rather than productivity as such becomes the essential measure. As a matter of fact, they are so pertinent to the value of an employee that they often overshadow the importance of production. Employees are more likely to be discharged for being troublemakers than for being incompetent. It is therefore not unusual to find that rating procedures are used with employees who work on production jobs. Such traits as getting along with other workers, spirit of cooperation, and dependability have become so essential that the method of merit rating rather than productivity is applied to both production and nonproduction jobs. These indirect traits also influence judgments of promotability and estimates of supervisory talent. Although certain traits may be important in maintaining good interpersonal relationships it is essential not to lose sight of the fact that productivity is the real goal, and that the indirect merit traits should influence this goal in some way but not become a substitute goal.

Differences in Standards

Another source of error lies in the fact that all raters do not use the same standards. Some tend to rate all individuals relatively high, while some are inclined to be perfectionists and give few or no high ratings. Because of such differences, an "A" rating, for instance, does not always have the same meaning.

Attempts to correct this error have led to the use of order-of-merit ratings. By this method the rater is asked to list the employees in rank order from best to poorest. This is somewhat difficult and time-consuming, particularly when large groups are involved. Also, it does not take into account the possibility that the quality of the individuals may show considerable differences in the various departments. The person in the middle position of one department may actually be superior to one in the highest position in another department. As long as departments differ in the quality of the people they employ, it is difficult to know whether persons are rated high because of their own superiority or because of the inferiority of their associates.

Because this method is relatively time-consuming and also introduces other diffi-culties, it is not widely used. However, since the training of raters and the defining of standards help to bring the judgments of different raters closer together, the ad-vantages of the order-of-merit method can be achieved, at least in part, in other ways.

Importance of Defining Duties

A third difficulty arises because traits such as leadership, dependability, safety, and even productivity do not have the same meaning to all raters. To reduce this error the functions must be defined in terms of on-the-job behaviors, and illustrations should be supplied. The meanings of the various ratings should also be illustrated. As one goes from simple to complex jobs the problem of defining essential traits becomes even more difficult. Job analysis, to be discussed shortly, is a great aid in isolating essential behaviors to observe.

Definitions should avoid descriptions of persons and objectively define specific activities. Phrases such as "gets work done on time," "follows safe practices," "no-tices things to do without being told" describe behavior. However, this causes a tendency to include a larger number of characteristics on the rating form, which leads to certain disadvantages, which will be discussed shortly.

Number of Steps in Scale

A rating scale should have no more steps than raters can reliably differentiate, yet should have enough to make the needed number of distinctions. Ordinarily one might suppose that the fewer the steps the easier the job of rating and the greater the accuracy. However, one study revealed that optimum accuracy was reached with a nine-point scale.[5] This optimum number of steps may be expected to vary with the skill of the raters and with the complexity of the trait or function rated, but nine may safely be considered as the largest number that should be used.

Another study revealed that raters are less willing to use a form requiring a two-point distinction than one requiring four distinctions.[6] People want to make quali-fying evaluations, and when the number of steps is small, the number of borderline cases is large. Borderline cases are the ones that make the decisions difficult.

Odd vs. Even Steps in Scale

Most scales in use fall within the limits described and have four, five, or six steps. However, there is some question about whether an odd or an even number of steps is preferable. When an even number of steps is used, the procedure advocated is first to divide a group into the best and the poorest halves. Next, each of these is again divided, yielding four groups. If six distinctions are desired, the two extreme groups are again split.

[5] Champney, H., and Marshall, H. Optimal refinement of the rating scale. *J. appl. Psychol.*, 1939, *23*, 323–331.
[6] Ghiselli, E. E. All or none versus graded response questionnaires. *J. appl. Psychol.*, 1939, *23*, 405–413.

The character of the normal distribution curve suggests an odd number of steps. Most people's scores will fall in the center of the curve, and they are the ones who are much alike in ability. A classification for them is needed to avoid making many borderline distinctions. A scale with an even number of steps requires that the middle group be separated, obliging the rater to make distinctions among the large group of people who are the most alike.

Number of Traits Rated

The number of traits rated will naturally depend upon the complexity of the job. However, the overall evaluation obtained from a few traits differs little from that obtained if many traits are used. One study showed that ratings on three traits (job performance, quality of work, and health) yielded the same results as ratings on 12 traits;[7] another obtained equivalent results from six traits after factor analysis had collapsed 14 seemingly independent traits.[8]

Considerations other than the accuracy of ratings, however, must sometimes be taken into account. If employees and supervisors feel that ratings on a few items do not properly describe an employee, it may be desirable to use more items in order to achieve the confidence of the raters as well as of those rated.

Rating Average Performers First

In most practical rating situations, from eight to 15 employees are involved. Since both superior and inferior abilities are rare, such individuals are not likely to be properly represented in all groups. For example, the best producer in one group might be quite inferior to the best producer in another group. If one followed the common-sense rating procedure of using the extreme performers as points of orientation or as the ones to rate first, these two individuals would receive similar ratings.

The most dependable point of orientation is the group of near-average persons. Such persons are much alike and are sufficiently numerous so that a few will be present in any group. These are the individuals on whom standards are based and they should be thought of as satisfactory employees. Approximately half of a small group of people are similar with respect to any particular trait under consideration. Thus, in a group of ten employees there should be four, five, or six persons who are most difficult to distinguish from one another with respect to each of the traits rated, be it productivity, dependability, or safety. These individuals should be rated as satisfactory (a rating of "3" on a five-point scale) on the trait under consideration. Once the middle ratings are assigned, the task of assigning ratings of one and two steps above as well as one and two steps below the typical persons is relatively easy.

Weighting of Functions

Once employees have been rated on the way they perform various functions, the problem of combining the several ratings of a given individual into one score still

---

[7] Ewart, E., Seashore, S. E., and Tiffin, J. A factor-analysis of an industrial merit rating scale. *J. appl. Psychol.,* 1941, *25,* 481–486.

[8] Bolanovich, D. J. Statistical analysis of an industrial rating chart. *J. appl. Psychol.,* 1946, *30,* 23–31.

remains. If a five-point scale has been used to evaluate traits, A, B, C, and D, and the values 5 through 1 have been used to indicate the best to the poorest performances, one could obtain a composite score by merely adding the numerical ratings. All traits or functions would be treated as equal in importance, and no differential weightings would be involved. A rating form with four items would then produce a range in possible scores between 20 and 4.

It is possible, however, that Functions A and B are more important than Functions C and D. In such a case one could multiply the ratings on Functions A and B by some constant value, such as two. This would weight the first two functions, making the range in score fall between 30 and 6 in our example. Another possibility would be to require minimum scores on certain functions. Thus, a worker who rates less than average in a certain important category might automatically be given a zero rating in this function, or even be regarded as entirely unsatisfactory because of failure in the performance of an essential duty.

Group Decision Applied to Merit Rating

In one company supervisors tended to give high ratings to employees on high-skill jobs and low ratings to employees on low-skill jobs. This meant that supervisors were judging employees in part by the jobs they held, whereas the purpose of rating was to determine the proficiency with which they performed on their jobs.

An experiment was designed to evaluate procedures for correcting this supervisory fault.[9] Twenty-nine supervisors were randomly divided into three groups. One group of nine was used as a control and given no training; a second group of nine was involved in a group decision as to what to do about the problem; and a third group of 11 was given a lecture on how to improve their rating skills. Measures of rating performance (indicating extent to which rating was influenced by job grade) were obtained before as well as after these attempts to improve the ratings were made.

The results showed that only the group-decision group improved significantly. There was no improvement in the control group, and the improvement in the lecture group was not statistically significant.

Refinements of Merit Rating

Forced-Choice Method

Because merit rating plans reflect inaccuracies, persistent attempts are made to improve the method of using human judgments to evaluate employees. One of these is the *forced-choice* procedure.[10] By this method sets of four phrases or adjectives pertaining to the job are presented on a form. The rater is asked to indicate which

---

[9] Levine, E., and Butler, J. Lecture vs. group decision in changing behavior. *J. appl. Psychol.*, 1952, *36*, 29–33.

[10] Sisson, E. D. Forced choice—the new Army rating. *Personnel Psychol.*, 1948, *1*, 365–381; Richardson, M. W. Forced choice performance reports. In M. J. Dovher and V. Marquis (Eds.), *Rating employee and supervisory performance.* New York: American Management Assn., 1950, pp. 35–46.

of each set of four is most characteristic of the person rated and which is least characteristic. Examples of sets used for army officers are shown in Figure 8.2. In each set of four items, two are favorable and two are unfavorable. However, the rater does not know that only one of the favorable items is associated with success and only one of the unfavorable items with failure. The scoring takes into account only the checking of favorable and unfavorable items associated with good and poor performance. For example, a checkmark gives a plus value only when a crucial good trait is checked as most characteristic and when a crucial poor trait is checked as least characteristic. Checking the alternative items that only "appear" favorable or unfavorable has no effect on the score, yet permits the rater to express his likes and dislikes.

Among the variations of the forced-choice procedure are approaches that present blocks of two, three, four, or five statements, all either favorable or unfavorable, but

Figure 8.2 / Sets of Items in Forced-Choice Rating. The rater is asked to evaluate a subordinate by checking in each set of four items: (a) the one most characteristic of him; and (b) the one least characteristic of him. In each set of four items, one is related to success and another to failure, but the rater does not know the diagnostic items.

Job Proficiency	most	least	Personal Qualifications	most	least
A. A go-getter, always does a good job.			Immature.		
B. Cool under all circumstances.			Modest but not retiring.		
C. Doesn't listen to suggestions.			Nervous.		
D. Drives instead of leads.			Cooperative.		
A. Always criticizes, never praises.			Unassuming.		
B. Carries out orders by "passing the buck."			Follows rather than leads.		
C. Knows his job and performs it well.			Has attitude of superiority.		
D. Plays no favorites.			Tactful.		
A. Cannot assume responsibility.			Cool-headed.		
B. Knows how and when to delegate.			Commands respect.		
C. Offers suggestions.			Overbearing.		
D. Too easily changes his ideas.			Indifferent.		

which discriminate among employees to differing degrees. The form using four favorable statements from which the rater is asked to choose the two most descriptive of the ratee was found most effective by Berkshire and Highland.[11] In addition to yielding high validities and acceptable reliability, this form appeared to be the most resistant to bias and was one of the two forms best liked by the raters.

The forced-choice method has proved its value over standard rating methods in that it produces more objective evaluations, yields a more nearly normal distribution, can be machine-scored, and the ratings are related to valid indices of good and poor performance.

In order to use this method, however, the following prerequisites are needed: (1) a separate group of descriptive items for each job; (2) trained personnel available to develop the rating form; (3) fair agreement on the criterion of success and failure; and (4) willingness on the part of supervisors to pass judgment on employees even if they cannot tell whether they give one person a more favorable rating than another.

Attempts to improve the value of this method and to make it more acceptable to raters continue.[12] Much of the research is associated with selection of officers in the military. Forms that require the rater to choose items that are the *most* descriptive of the person are more acceptable than forms that require the rater to choose both the *most* and the *least* descriptive items. Thus the method becomes less objectionable when the rater is required only to make a judgment on items that are *most* descriptive of a person.

Forms also may be more acceptable if the rater is allowed to rate the degree to which an item selected from alternatives applies to the person rated. At least this was found to be the case when the form was used for self-rating.[13] Apparently the act of choosing an item that has little relevance to a person, even if it has more relevance than its alternative, makes the rater feel he is making a judgment that is untrue. It appears that further improvements and simplifications are needed if the forced-choice method is to replace the less sophisticated rating method in industry. Attempts to conceal from the rater whether or not he is giving favorable or unfavorable ratings may reduce bias but at the expense of cooperation. Yet this cooperation is essential to successful merit rating.

Check Lists

To make employee evaluation as specific as possible, lists of good and bad behaviors on a job have been developed, and supervisors are asked to check the descriptions that apply to a particular employee. This check-list procedure[14] has been refined so

[11] Berkshire, J. R., and Highland, R. W. Forced-choice performance rating: A methodological study. *Personnel Psychol.*, 1953, 6, 355–378.

[12] Berkshire and Highland, *op. cit.*; Berkshire, J. R. Comparisons of five forced-choice indices. *Educ. psychol. Measmt.*, 1958, 18, 553–556.

[13] Waters, L. K., and Wherry, R. J., Jr. *Evaluation of two forced-choice formats.* Project MR005, 13–5001, Subtask 2, Rep. No. 10. Pensacola, Fla.: U.S. School of Aviation Medicine, 1961.

[14] Probst, J. B. *Measuring and rating employee value.* New York: Ronald, 1947.

that the items form a scale: each item has a value depending upon its importance.[15] Scale values are derived from preliminary research in which the pooled judgments of persons familiar with the job are used. Such persons are asked to arrange the potential items in seven piles, in terms of their importance. Examples of items and their scale values for sales personnel are shown in Table 8.1. Only items on which the judges agree are finally used. A scale of this kind ordinarily contains about 50 items with scale values ranging between 10 and 70.

In rating a person, the rater is asked to place a plus ($+$) sign, a minus ($-$) sign, or a question mark ($?$) in front of each item, depending, respectively, on whether he feels the item applies, does not apply, or there is doubt. The actual rating is the average of the scale values of all items checked with a plus sign. Since the scale values do not appear on the form, the rater does not know how highly he has rated a given person.

This method, like the forced-choice method, has definite merits in that it objectifies the rating procedure and also demands the same prerequisites.

Field Review

The field review is an approach to evaluating employee proficiency in which a member of the personnel department cooperates with the supervisor in developing employee ratings. The personnel specialist interviews the supervisor at the place of work, posing questions on an employee's performance, such as, "What are his strengths?" "Should he be promoted?" The personnel specialist later studies the notes and writes a tentative summary to be checked with the supervisor, who is invited to make additions or corrections. The supervisor is responsible for the final rating which is then prepared, but he is aided by a trained person in its preparation and is freed of considerable detail work.

This technique requires very competent personnel analysts plus support throughout the line, including top management. However, the field review is advantageous in that supervisors frequently prefer to give oral ratings rather than the more usual written evaluations. Then too, since the ratings are prepared by experts they tend to be more readily comparable and more easily reviewed.[16]

Table 8.1 / Scaled Items Appearing on Rating Form for Salesmen

Item	Scale Value
_____ He is somewhat in a rut on some of his brand talks	32
_____ He tends to keep comfortably ahead of his work schedule	56
_____ He is a good steady worker	46
_____ He is weak on planning	29
_____ He is making exceptional progress	69

[15] Richardson, M. W., and Kuder, G. F. Making a rating scale that measures. *Personnel J.,* 1933, *12,* 36–40.

[16] Harrell, T. W. *Industrial psychology,* (rev. ed.) New York: Rinehart, 1958, p. 67.

Critical Incident Technique

The critical incident technique developed by Flanagan[17] is less a rating method than a procedure for collecting relevant data about employee performance. However, once a large number of incidents are recorded for each of the jobs under consideration, they can be analyzed to determine which are critically associated with superior performance and which are associated with employee unsuitability, thus providing a basis for a scientifically constructed rating scale. This system provides standards for raters' judgments, accumulates observations of behavior upon which various raters can agree (rather than dealing with vague generalities or trait names which can be variously defined), and frequently helps decrease the influence of personal bias. In one study,[18] 16 critical job requirements were developed for hourly employees of the Delco-Remy plant. Through use of forms drawn up for the purpose, the time required by the supervisors for recording their observations usually took less than five minutes per day. In one study managers were asked to report instances of behaviors associated with good vs. poor salesmen.[19] Out of 135 reported instances, 96 were obtained that could be used to relate to job successes. Of these 61 were related to effective performance and 35 to noneffective performance. On the basis of these critical incidents an evaluation form was developed. The form included statements such as "follows up quickly on requests from customers," and the managers indicated the degree to which it describes a particular salesman by checking a five point scale ranging from *strongly agree* to *strongly disagree*. The job of chain store managers has been effectively analyzed by similar methods in order to appraise managerial effectiveness.[20] A major advantage of the method is that the behavior record of an employee is more complete and does not depend on recall, which may be incomplete and subject to moods. It is claimed that the record of the critical incidents also can serve as a basis for employee counseling because "specifics" rather than general evaluative judgments are involved. Widespread use of the method is hindered by the cost since critical incidents even for similar jobs (selling different products) would have to be developed.

Some Persistent Problems

Conflicting Interests

The need for performance appraisal is indicated by the fact that approximately half the companies included in a survey use some form of merit rating plan.[21] Despite

[17] Flanagan, J. C. The critical incidents technique. *Psychol. Bull.*, 1954, *51*, 327–358; Flanagan, J. C. A new approach to evaluating personnel. *Personnel*, 1949, *26*, 35–42.

[18] Flanagan, J. C., and Burns, R. K. The employee performance record: A new appraisal and development tool. *Harvard Bus. Rev.*, 1955, *33*, 95–102.

[19] Kirchner, W. K., and Dunnette, M. D. Using critical incidents to measure job proficiency factors. *Personnel*, 1957, *34*, 54–59.

[20] Dunnette, M. D. Managerial effectiveness: its definition and measurement. *Studies in Person. Psychol.*, 1970, *2*, 6–20.

[21] National Industrial Conference Board. Personnel practices in factory and office. *Studies in personnel policy, no. 145.* New York: Author, 1954.

the apparent need and the research that has been done to refine rating, few companies take advantage of the knowledge gained. One study showed that 32 per cent of the companies surveyed offered no training at all, while few gave what might be regarded as adequate training.[22]

Confidence in the rating results is also lacking. One study[23] showed that 52 per cent of the employees felt the ratings should not be considered in making promotions and an additional 42 per cent felt that the rating should count only 25 per cent toward the decision. Managers, too, resist filling out the forms and dislike the task of playing God.[24]

Attempts to make the ratings more objective have not solved the problem of acceptance. Attempts to reduce human error have made rating procedures less meaningful to the supervisors who must use them. Furthermore, little progress has been made in evaluating the critical subordinate behaviors.[25] This involves the problem of finding an acceptable criterion for successful performance. We will return to this question later in the chapter.

Communicating the Appraisal

When an appraisal must be discussed with the employee the superior soon discovers that the employee accepts praise but reacts defensively to criticism. Thus in striving to let the employee know where he stands, the interview makes him feel rejected or that the appraisal has been unfair.[26] In order to avoid trouble in an interview, superiors tend to be overly generous with the result that the appraisal has less value as a measure of proficiency and therefore serves less as a basis for promotion or pay increases.

In many companies the practice of discussing the appraisal with the subordinate is followed throughout the various levels in the organization. When this is done the objective is to improve the subordinate's performance by getting him to correct weaknesses and letting him know his strengths. (Other techniques for developing subordinates will be discussed in Chapters 20 and 22.)

Behind this approach are two misleading assumptions: (1) that employees want to know where they stand; (2) that an employee will improve if he is told his weaknesses. Employees may say they want to know where they stand; but they do not like to be criticized and they frequently show resentment when supervisors tell them where they stand. In order to help supervisors to make their evaluations de-

[22] Spicer, L. G. A survey of merit rating in industry. *Personnel,* 1951, *27,* 515–518.

[23] Van Zelst, R. H., and Kerr, W. A. Workers' attitudes toward merit rating. *Personnel Psychol.,* 1953, *6,* 159–172.

[24] MacGregor, D. M. An uneasy look at performance appraisal. *Harvard Bus. Rev.,* 1957, *35,* 89–94.

[25] Kipnis, D. Some determinants of supervisory esteem. *Personnel Psychol.,* 1960, *13,* 377–391.

[26] Kay, E., French, J. R. P., Jr., and Meyer, H. H. A study of threat and participation in an industrial performance appraisal program. *Mgmt. developm. employee relat. Ser.* New York: General Electric, 1962; Meyer, H. H., Kay, E., and French, J. R. P., Jr. Split roles in performance appraisal. *Harvard Bus. Rev.,* 1964, *43,* 124–129; McGregor, *op. cit.;* Maier. N. R. F. *The appraisal interview.* New York: Wiley, 1958.

fensible, they are instructed to stick to facts or instances in these discussions. Supervisors have found that when they keep careful records so as to be able to do this they are accused of spying and carrying a "black book."

The second assumption implies not only that employees will correct their weaknesses when they know them, but also that they can correct them if they wish. As stated above, employees often challenge the supervisor's evaluation and thus admit no reason for changing. Some employees show their resentment of criticism by going to the opposite extreme in changing their behavior. One department head asked his assistant not to interrupt him with a problem when he was in conference. His assistant corrected this behavior: he never again entered his superior's office. Anyone who has raised children is familiar with this exaggerated form of correction in response to criticism.

Still more involved is the problem of changing people once their weaknesses are pointed out to them. No one expects a child to increase his intelligence if told that he is deficient, yet we often try to get employees to make wiser judgments by telling them to think things through. Suppose, however, that we are very careful, and suggest changes only when the new behavior is under a person's voluntary control. Immediately differences of opinion arise as to what a person can control. Can a person be more aggressive, show more initiative, see jobs that need to be done, make decisions a bit faster, or speak more distinctly if he is told he should? We all know that in some instances these things can be accomplished easily, but in other instances a personality change seems to be involved. If some people started suddenly to keep a neat desk there might be reason for alarm.

Superior and Subordinate Viewpoints

When employees feel they have been unfairly appraised or unjustly criticized, is this purely a defensive reaction or is there a basis for honest disagreement? It is not uncommon for subordinates and their superiors to disagree on the question of what constitutes satisfactory job performance. In a study of middle-management communication[27] both the superior and his subordinate were interviewed in detail regarding the subordinate's job. Fifty-eight pairs of managers in five representative large organizations participated. Each job was examined from the point of view of the man who supervised it and that of the man who occupied it. Four areas were explored: (1) the actual duties required by the job; (2) the kinds of skills, knowledge, training, personality, and so on essential to good performance; (3) the anticipated changes in the job in the near future; and (4) the kinds of obstacles or problems that the person met in performing the job. The interviews were analyzed and rated on a five-point scale to indicate the degrees of agreement, 0 indicating little or no agreement and 4 indicating high or full agreement. Special precaution was taken not to treat oversights, differences in ways of breaking down the job, and the number of details mentioned as disagreements. Despite the fact that the superior

[27] Maier, N. R. F., Hoffman, L. R., Hooven, J. J., and Read, W. H. *Superior-subordinate communication in management.* Research Study 52. New York: American Management Assn., 1961.

selected the subordinate job that was to be analyzed, the lack of agreement is striking. Table 8.2 shows the percentage of the 58 pairs studied that fell into each rating category.

Agreement decreases as one goes from the first job area to the last. Except for the area of job duties, the low agreement categories (0 and 1) include more pairs than the high agreement categories (3 and 4). Since a person's notion of the "job duties," "job requirements," and "obstacles faced" would influence the rating of a job performance, one can see that a superior's evaluation of a subordinate's performance would have to differ from that of the subordinate. Thus it seems that the prevalent feeling that an appraisal made by a superior is unfair might have more than an emotional basis. Until the two agree on the above job areas there is bound to be disagreement in appraising or rating performance. The use of job descriptions and previous experience of the superior on the subordinate's job does not remove the discrepancy.[28] Clearly, the definition of job success is a complex question on many nonproduction jobs, yet proficiency has little meaning until this problem is settled. Finding an objective criterion of job success is essential to developing tests to select personnel, and it is also essential to training employees to perform more effectively. Yet should one assume that an answer can be found? If so, can one hope to make further improvements in executing a job when a new approach to the job might violate the old standards of performance?

Job Analysis as an Aid to Production Measurement

Introduction

Since a knowledge of the job is an essential factor in measuring or appraising performance, let us turn our attention from people to their jobs.

A job description describes the duties of a particular position, states the conditions of work, rate and method of pay, and factors relevant to training and promotion. The *job specification* is a description of the requirements an individual worker is expected to possess for a given job. Thus the job description and specification supplement each other.[29] The job description with its specifications sets forth what the job entails and what is expected of the worker.

All companies do not have job descriptions for the various positions since occupancy of a position also teaches a worker what is expected of him. In larger organizations a job analyst usually prepares job descriptions and specifications since the relationships between workers and management are likely to be more formalized. When job descriptions are desired it is best to have experts work with both the worker and the supervisor to prepare acceptable descriptions.[30]

[28] Read, W. H. Upward communication in industrial hierarchies. *Hum. Relat.*, 1962, *15*, 3–15.

[29] For occupational descriptions in general, see: Shartle, C. L. *Occupational information: its development and application* (3rd ed.). Englewood Cliffs, N.J.: Prentice-Hall, 1959.

[30] Scott, W. D., Clothier, R. C., and Spriegel, W. R. *Personnel management.* New York: McGraw-Hill, 1961. Chs. 9 and 10; Otis, J. L., and Leukart, R. H. *Job evaluation.* Englewood Cliffs, N.J.: Prentice-Hall, 1954; Prien, E. P., and Ronan, W. W. Job analysis: A review of research findings. *Personnel J.*, 1971, *24*, 371–396.

Table 8.2 / Comparative Agreement between 58 Superior-Subordinate Pairs on Four Basic Areas of the Subordinate's Job

	0 Almost No Agreement on Topics	1 Agreement on Less Than Half the Topics	2 Agreement on About Half the Topics	3 Agreement on More Than Half the Topics	4 Agreement on All, or Almost All, Topics	Mean Rating
1. Job duties	3.4%	11.6%	39.1%	37.8%	8.1%	2.35
2. Job requirements (subordinate's qualifications)	7.0	29.3	40.9	20.5	2.3	1.82
3. Future changes in subordinate's job	35.4	14.3	18.3	16.3	15.7	1.62
4. Obstacles in the way of subordinate's performance	38.4	29.8	23.6	6.4	1.7	1.03

Reprinted by permission of the publisher from AMA Research Study No. 52, *Superior-subordinate communication in management*. © 1961 by the American Management Association, Inc.

Job evaluation describes the process of grading jobs so that pay rates reflect the demands made upon the employee. The value of a job increases as requirements in skill, education, intellectual demands, physical requirements, and amount of responsibility increase, and as safety, working conditions, and health factors decrease. Thus the same job with an added element of risk or less favorable working hours carries an increased value which is reflected in a pay differential if job evaluation is used to set the rates.

Different procedures are used in evaluating the various jobs in a company, but most depend on some form of rating.[31] Once the key jobs have been rated and standardized with other companies, various jobs that may be specific within the company can be compared with the key positions. It should be emphasized that the job value refers to the job requirements and does *not* concern itself with the degree to which an individual meets these requirements.

As in the case of job descriptions a job analyst should seek the aid of supervisors and workers in arriving at acceptable job ratings. Both job descriptions and evaluations lean upon a job analysis. The objective of *job analysis* is to determine the detailed requirements a worker should have for a particular job.

Negative Aspects of Job Analysis

Job analysis tends to stereotype the job and may reduce the freedom of the employee to make decisions and to improve the work method. It assumes that the best work method is the same for all individuals. With the advent of participative approaches to management subordinates are seen as occupying role prescriptions (see Chapter 21) and job flexibility is increased. However, the extent to which such flexibility is an asset will vary with the job.[32] Since subordinates and superiors do not fully agree on the job requirements participative approaches should reduce differences and clarify the need for flexibility.

The Job Profile

Ratings can be improved if the job is analyzed to some degree and the ratings applied to different aspects of the job. This procedure can be carried much farther if the analysis is in terms of the abilities required to do the job. A simple method for such an analysis is the use of the job profile. A card is prepared, listing all the human traits which have a bearing on the job. Persons familiar with the job then rate the importance of each trait.

In one study[33] six activities that seemed to revolve around the duties of super-

---

[31] Patton, J. A., and Littlefield, C. A. *Job evaluation.* Homewood, Ill.: Richard D. Irwin, 1957; International Labour Office. *Job evaluation.* Geneva, Switzerland: La Tribune de Genève, 1960.

[32] Filley, A. C., and House, R. J. *Managerial process and organizational behavior.* Glenview, Ill.: Scott, Foresman, 1969.

[33] Rothe, H. F. Matching men to job requirements. *Personnel Psychol.,* 1951, *4,* 291–301; see also E. A. Fleishman (Ed.), *Studies of personnel and industrial psychology.* Homewood, Ill.: Dorsey, 1967, pp. 5–13.

visors were selected on the basis of hundreds of interviews with supervisors. In chronological order these were:

1. Plans an activity.
2. Decides to do or not do a certain thing.
3. Organizes a group of persons to carry out the plans decided upon (delegates).
4. Communicates the program to the organization.
5. Leads the organization toward the established goal.
6. Analyzes the progress toward the goal.

These six activities were then rated in their importance for various supervisory positions, thus yielding job psychographs or job profiles for supervisory positions at several levels in the organization.

Figure 8.3a shows the job profiles for the positions of Section Supervisor, General Supervisor, and Superintendent. Note that the demands of the various supervisory behaviors increase as one goes from lower to higher positions.

Figure 8.3b shows how the merit ratings of John Doe, in his present position of Section Supervisor, can be made into a personal qualifications profile. If we assume that Mr. Doe has the adequate job knowledge, his profile shows that he has five of the six other qualifications needed to become a general supervisor, but has not yet qualified as a superintendent.

By matching job and personal qualifications profiles one can combine merit ratings and job analysis results to improve job placement. It will also be apparent from the above illustration that this analysis of the foreman's job presupposes a leader quite different from that described in Chapter 6. If one used job analysis as a means for specifying desired supervisory behavior it would be difficult for new types of leaders to satisfy the qualifications and job specifications.

The Empirical Method

The psychographic method analyzes a job in terms of human traits, but it does not escape direct dependence upon human opinions, even though the opinions may be those of experts. To avoid this source of error, it is necessary to use more time-consuming procedures. The empirical method largely escapes the element of human opinion by comparing extremes.

Suppose we select for study a group of 60 men in a certain occupation. These men are then rated by supervisors (or individuals who have observed their work) on a five-point scale according to their proficiency. The score of each man is the average of the supervisors' ratings. Thus far, the method utilizes the relatively crude rating procedure.

The next step is to divide the men into three groups, according to the scores attained. The one-third achieving the highest ratings are labeled superior workers; the third obtaining the lowest scores are labeled unsatisfactory workers; and the middle third, making intermediate scores, constitute the average workers. Conceding that errors in ratings have occurred, these divisions have placed some men

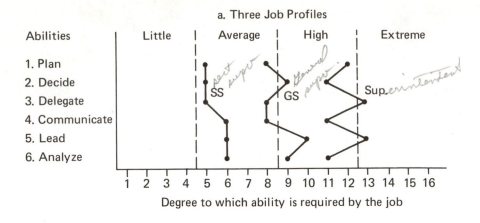

a. Three Job Profiles

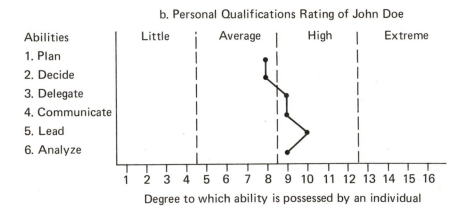

b. Personal Qualifications Rating of John Doe

Figure 8.3 / Job Profile and Personal Qualification Rating. Figure 8.3a shows the profiles of Section Supervisor (Profile SS); General Supervisor (Profile GS); and Superintendent (Profile Sup.). These progressively higher positions require increasing amounts of the essential abilities. Figure 8.3b shows the qualifications of John Doe, whose qualifications meet five of the job requirements of a general supervisor. By making profiles of jobs and personal qualifications employees can be readily matched for jobs. (After H. F. Rothe, Matching men to job requirements. *Personnel Psychology,* 1951, *4.*)

in the middle group who belonged in either the lowest or the highest groups, and placed some men in the two extreme groups who should have fallen in the middle group. The placing of unsatisfactory individuals in the superior group or of superior individuals in the unsatisfactory group would occur very seldom. If we now ignore the middle group, and consider only the superior and unsatisfactory groups, we have two distinctly different samples of employees.

The third step is to study carefully the mental, physical, and personality traits of these two groups. Any trait associated with success on the job should appear in different degrees in the two groups, and, within each group, this trait should appear to a fairly uniform degree. By subjecting the groups to various measurements and tests, we may obtain many bases for comparison. The results frequently reveal that supervisors cannot always choose the important traits associated with success.

This method not only permits us to locate objectively the more important behaviors, but also to determine their relative importance. The scores on the most important traits would show the most clear-cut differences in the two samples, and these could be given more thorough consideration. A knowledge of the important factors gives the rater a definite basis on which to judge, thereby increasing the accuracy of proficiency measurements.

Job analysis, however, has importance beyond that of improving rating procedures. Once a job is analyzed in terms of the traits essential to success, tests can be devised to measure these traits. By utilizing the results of these tests people can be placed on jobs which best fit their particular abilities. The use of tests for selection and placement of employees is discussed in the following chapters.

Role Prescriptions

A person may be regarded as having a repertoire of behaviors so, as the situation warrants, he plays the roles of spouse, parent, subordinate, or superior. These roles are influenced by custom and past experience which create expectancies. Each person behaves according to his role perception, but is judged by the role perceptions of persons with whom he relates.

A person who performs a particular job has duties specified by the job description. However, his performance is not only judged by how well he does these duties but by how it relates to what is expected of him. These expectations determine the role prescription and this includes more than a description of the job. Role prescriptions for the same type of work (e.g., salesperson) might be expected to vary between countries having cultural differences, but perceived roles can differ within a company. Such expectations as giving help to associates, willingness to take suggestions, and being loyal to the company may be included even if unrelated to getting the job done. These expectations influence performance appraisal since such judgments are based on the relationship between what is expected and what actually occurs.

A supervisor may be given an unfavorable rating for practicing group decision with his subordinates if such behavior is in conflict with the role prescription in the company. Role expectations are developed from past experience and can lead to conflict when organizational changes are introduced (see Chapter 21).

The Criteria of Successful Job Performance

The first question raised in any study of job success is, "What is good performance?" Is there a correct answer to this question or is it purely a matter of opinion? Since the superior appraises his subordinates and determines an employee's merits, should the psychologist listen to him or should he investigate the nature of success regardless of the superior's opinion? In middle management positions there is lack of agreement between superiors and subordinates on various basic questions (see Table 8.2). When there is widespread disagreement between responsible superiors and subordinates should one settle for an average? These and many other questions constitute what is called the *criterion problem.*

Since most readers have had the experience of getting grades in school, we may profitably use the concept of "successful" college performance to illustrate the complexity of the criterion problem. It will be conceded that teachers do not always agree with one another on the grades they give and that their students are in even greater disagreement with them. To explore this question one may examine the goals of higher education. Among those that have been listed[34] are the following:

1. Necessary skills in writing, speaking, and listening
2. Self-reliance through ability to think clearly
3. Understanding of one's self and one's relationship to others
4. Growing convictions based on the search for truth
5. Understanding and appreciation of our cultural, social, scientific, and spiritual heritage
6. Intelligent approach to local, national, and world problems leading to responsible and responsive citizenship and leadership in life
7. Some practical understanding of another language
8. Professional competence based on high ethical standards in preparation not alone for the immediate job but for a lifetime of responsible leadership in professional activities
9. Healthful development of the body

Most readers undoubtedly will accept some if not all of these objectives, but it would be too much to hope that they would reach agreement on the relative importance of each. It is doubtful whether these goals have the same meaning to all educators, and it is probable that each of the nine items is made up of several more primary goals. This means that even the objectives are vague. Furthermore, it is likely that these several goals are not attainable by the same methods so that in striving for some goals others would thereby be sacrificed.

Can success in college be scientifically measured under such indefinite conditions? Despite the lack of a satisfactory solution, school grades are given and used as the criteria for college success. Similarly, industry uses merit ratings as measures of success; even though they are subject to error, the crude measure is better than none at all. In the meantime efforts to objectify the concept of success continue. The mere recognition of the fact that opinions of success are human judgments, made from particular points of view, represents progress. When value judgments are acknowledged as personally biased, tolerance increases and some of the conflicts can be resolved.

[34] Dressel, P. L., and Associates. *Evaluation in higher education.* Boston: Houghton Mifflin, 1961.

Since the objective of a business enterprise is to make money it has been suggested that in this instance the criteria of success should be a measure of a man's worth, hence should be reduced to a dimension of dollars and cents.[35] A single measure of success such as monetary worth would be the ideal type of criterion since this quantitative measure could then be correlated with scores on various kinds of psychological tests. Such a measure would be in operation if the salaries of baseball players reflected their worth. However, the problem of equating batting averages with home runs, runs batted in, fielding records, and so on, suggests the number of difficulties involved. Even if these were surmounted, salaries would be influenced by a player's popularity with the fans, his bargaining ability, the specific needs of a ball club during a particular year, and the club's ability to buy players.

Evidence shows that salary, when corrected for tenure, is a better index of executive success than peer ratings and position in the hierarchy.[36] The index is further improved when it incorporates predicted salary increases. However, these combined measures remain at odds with peer ratings. At present, most researchers feel that the goal of a single measure is impractical and believe that the eventual criterion will be multidimensional.[37]

Practical Considerations

The various criteria in common use include quantity of work, quality of work, learning time, tenure, absenteeism, and safety. Each can be quantified and related to other measures and little is gained by an attempt to reduce them to a single measure. As a matter of fact, the importance of each dimension varies from one job to another.

The desire to quantify can also lead to errors. One would not be justified to regard one salesman as superior to another because his sales volume was greater than another's, since their territories might offer differing opportunities. Nor could it be assumed that one secretary was more proficient than another if she turned out more work, because the dictation given by one boss might be more difficult to handle than that given by another. Differences in the same measures are often subject to what is called *contamination,* which means that the measures are influenced by variables other than the one measured.

Before any dimension of success is acceptable as a criterion it should have stood the test of *reliability.* This means that the measures should be relatively constant and not vary from one occasion to another. Thus the measures of a group of workers made on two separate occasions should correlate highly with one another. Where

---

[35] Brogden, H. E., and Taylor, E. K. The dollar criterion: applying the cost accounting concept to criterion construction. *Personnel Psychol.,* 1950, *3,* 133–154; Bass, B. M. Ultimate criteria of organizational worth. *Personnel Psychol.,* 1952, *5,* 157–174.

[36] Hulin, C. L. The measurement of executive success. *J. appl. Psychol.,* 1962, *46,* 303–306.

[37] Dunnette, M. D. A note on the criterion. *J. appl. Psychol.,* 1963, *47,* 251–254; Fisk, D. W. Values, theory and the criterion problem. *Personnel Psychol.,* 1951, *4,* 93–98; Georgopoulos, B. S., and Mann, F. C. *The community general hospital.* New York: Macmillan, 1962, Ch. 5; Ghiselli, E. E. Dimensional problems of criteria. *J. appl. Psychol.,* 1956, *40,* 1–4; Nagle, B. F. Criterion development. *Personnel Psychol.,* 1953, *6,* 271–287; Ruch, C. H., Jr. A factorial study of sales criteria. *Personnel Psychol.,* 1953, *6,* 9–24.

production measures are used as the criterion the correlations between two work samples often exceed .9. Low correlations indicate contamination and operation of chance factors.

The Criteria for Promotability

Merit rating forms frequently include a space for evaluating an employee's promotability.[38] This suggests that the appraisal of an employee's competence on his present job is related to his competence on a higher-grade job. Chapter 7 pointed out that success on one job is related to success on another *only* when the two require similar abilities. This being so, promotability cannot be appraised unless it is considered in relation to a specific job opening. Even if the duties on the higher-level new job are closely related to those on the old job (such as a promotion from supervisor of a small group to supervisor of a large group, or from first-line supervisor to second-line supervisor), the higher position is likely to make more demands on abilities common to both jobs. This means that unused capacities will have to be appraised when the positions are similar, and unobserved abilities will have to be appraised when the positions are different. Thus the problem of promotion is similar to the problem of placement in that abilities and job requirements have to be matched. The difference is that in making a decision on a promotion one has the employee's past record to turn to, which, incidentally, may be an advantage or a disadvantage, depending on how it is used.

Two major sources of error creep into making promotions. The first is the tendency to treat a promotion as a reward for above-average performance on the present job. If this practice were consistently followed it would lead to staffing each job grade with average and below-average performers. This would occur because superior workers would be removed from the job as soon as an opening occurred and would continue to be promoted through the job grades until they became located in positions for which they lacked aptitude. Less capable workers would be kept in their jobs because they failed to demonstrate superior performance and their discouragement would merely depress their limited aptitude.

Supervisors are inclined to be unhappy with this conclusion because they feel that promise of promotion is a way of motivating employees, and indeed it is. However, must one mortgage future performance in order to motivate present performance?

The second source of error resides in the fact that we tend to favor promotion for persons we like. Promotion is regarded as desirable and it is only human to want to be kind to those we like. Obviously this practice does not increase efficiency and a company could not successfully compete if this practice prevailed. Family-owned businesses often fail when the management is kept in the family, and favored treatment dominates good judgment.

As a matter of fact, one may do a person a disfavor by promoting him. Many

---

[38] Taylor, E. K., Parker, J. W., and Ford, G. L. Rating scale content. IV. Predictability of structured and unstructured scales. *Personnel Psychol.*, 1959, *12*, 247–266.

persons hold jobs in which they are unhappy because they cannot afford to give up a high job grade for a lower one in which they would be comfortable. Proper placement makes for greater true job satisfaction than the paycheck.

In the laboratory exercise at the end of Chapter 7 the *Case of Viola Burns* is considered. The question of whether or not she should be promoted is raised for group discussion. Most groups favor promotion and commit the two errors described above. The description of Viola indicates that she is shy and introverted and would not fit into a sales office. Yet because she has done a good job in the payroll office and gives a favorable impression to the readers of the case, their usual decision is to promote her.

Promotability thus is not a characteristic of the person, but represents a relationship between his ability and the requirements of the job under consideration: the degree of congruence between personality and a job profile (see p. 199). The most promotable person for a given job opening then would be the person whose personal qualifications best matched the requirements of the job; and the degrees of matching of a group of candidates might be quite different from their relative merits on their present jobs. The only justification for devoting space on a rating form to the trait of promotability is to indicate unused potential so that various persons might be appraised for more demanding positions in the company. For the same reasons a space for suggestions for lateral transfers might also be included in each employee's personnel file.

Laboratory Exercise

Role Playing: Sensitivity to Deception in an Interview[39]

A. General preparation

1. The General Instructions (D.1) should be read to everyone. The information regarding points received for each question should be placed on the chalkboard.
2. Two persons will be selected as role players, one assigned the role of Professor Parker, the other, one of the two roles of Cohen, a student (in one of his roles Cohen is honest; in the other, dishonest). Cohen's given name should be either Walter or Sheila.
3. Other class members will act as observers and be prepared to judge whether or not Cohen is honest.
4. Two chairs and a table should be arranged in front of the room to simulate an office.

[39] From N. R. F. Maier, Sensitivity to attempts at deception in an interview situation. *Personnel Psychol.*, 1966, *19*, 55–56.

B. The role-playing process
1. When the role players have had time to read their parts, they should put aside their role instructions.
2. Professor Parker should be in his office and shortly thereafter Cohen should be instructed to approach Parker and begin the role play.
3. Role playing should be continued until a decision is reached.
4. Leader should tabulate observers' opinions on whether: (a) decision was too lenient or too strict; and (b) whether Cohen was honest or dishonest. Parker's opinion also should be indicated, but Cohen should not reveal the role played.
5. Repeat with a different Parker and the other Cohen, assigning the alternate student role.
6. If the group interest is high and time permits, the process might be repeated with a third pair of role players.

C. Discussion
1. The identity of persons playing the honest and dishonest Cohens should be withheld for the time being.
2. The judgments of the observers for the different interviews should be compared.
3. Evidences of honest and dishonest actions on Cohen's part should be explored to determine whether or not agreement exists among observers.
4. A discussion of what Parker might have done to obtain more reliable evidence should be conducted.
5. The roles of the Cohens should be revealed at this point.
6. A list of the things learned from the case should be posted on the chalkboard.
7. Relevance to employment interviews should be explored.

D. Materials

1. General Instructions.

Walter (or Sheila) Cohen is a student in a college course taught by Professor Parker. The mid-term consisted of five questions, each worth 20 points. Cohen received the following scores on the five questions:

Question 1	15 points
Question 2	14 points
Question 3	13 points
Question 4	12 points
Question 5	9 points
Total	63

The grade was a *D*, seven points below a *C*. He/she was particularly concerned with the small number of points received for Question 5. At the next class meeting Cohen asked Professor Parker whether they could discuss a possible error in grading the test. Professor Parker asked for the blue book in order to be able to recheck the grading. It was then agreed that Cohen should come to Professor Parker's office the following day at 2 pm.

At the agreed upon time Cohen arrives and knocks on Professor Parker's door.

2. Role for Professor Parker

You asked your assistant to check Cohen's paper. After looking it over he reported that he had been over generous on the first two questions. However, on Question 5, which had two parts, he had given 9 points to Cohen's answer to the first part. He felt certain that the second part of the answer was not there when he had graded the paper originally, but had been added later.

After your assistant left you looked over the exam and found that the answer to the first half of the question ended about three-fourths of the way down the right page of the blue book. Then in a less firm hand, but clearly present, there was the comment "see over". It seemed unlikely that the reader would have missed this comment, particularly since he knew the second part of the question had not been answered. The answer to the second part of the question as it now stands is very good and would have received 10 points. It is the best section on the exam. This adds to your suspicion that it may have been added later. Cohen only needs seven points to raise his grade to a *C*.

It is not uncommon for students with *D* grades to try to get their grades raised. However, you don't like to see dishonesty practiced to achieve these ends.

It's about time for Cohen to arrive.

3. Role for Walter (or Sheila) Cohen (a).

You usually do not complain about your grades, but a *D* is going to look bad on your record. You feel that an error has been made in grading, especially on Question 5. There were two parts to this question. You finished the first part, leaving a little space at the bottom of the page in case you might wish to add something, and turned over the page to have a fresh space for the second part of the question. On examining your blue book you feel quite sure that the grader may have forgotten to turn over the page. The last question was one that you knew most about, yet you received the poorest grade on it. This oversight on the part of Professor Parker seems the most plausible explanation. At least you'd like to know what was wrong in your treatment of the question.

Before giving the blue book to Professor Parker you added a note "see over" at the end of the page on which you had answered the first part of Question 5. This will help the reader find the answer to the second half of the question and prevent the same oversight a second time.

4. ROLE FOR WALTER (OR SHEILA) COHEN (b).

You usually do not complain about grades, but a *D* is going to look bad on your record. You feel that you can make a case for an error having been made in grading on Question 5. There were two parts to this question. You had finished the first part, leaving a little space at the bottom of the page in case you might wish to add something. You forgot to answer the second part of the question. When you got the exam back you found you could answer this part of Question 5 without looking at your notes.

Since you need to improve your grade you decided to answer the question, using the same ball point pen you had used during the exam. You feel quite sure that you can make a case that the grader had forgotten to turn over the page and didn't see your answer to the second part of the question. You can claim that the last question was one that you knew most about, yet you received the poorest grade. Thus you can suggest a possible explanation. At least you will tell him that you'd like to know what was wrong in your treatment of the question.

Before giving the blue book to Professor Parker you added a note "see over" at the end of the page on which you had answered the first part of Question 5. You did this with pencil to show it had been added. This will help the reader find the answer to the second half of the question, and you can say you did this to prevent a second oversight.

Suggested Readings

Barrett, R. S. *Performance rating.* Chicago: Science Research Associates, 1966.

Cemach, H. P. *Work study in the office.* London: Current Affairs Ltd., 1960.

Fleishman, E. A. *Studies in personnel and industrial psychology* (rev. ed.). Homewood, Ill.: Dorsey, 1967, Chs. 10–17.

Guion, R. M. *Personnel testing.* New York: McGraw-Hill, 1965.

McFarland, D. E. *Personnel management: Theory and practice.* New York: Macmillan, 1968.

Rowland, V. K. *Evaluating and improving managerial performance.* New York: McGraw-Hill, 1970.

Ronan, W. W., and Prien, E. P. *Perspectives on the measurement of human performance.* New York: Appleton-Century, 1971.

Shartle, C. L. *Occupational information: Its development and application.* Englewood Cliffs, N.J.: Prentice-Hall, 1959.

9

OMIT

Selection and Placement

Limitations in the Use of Psychological Tests

Psychological tests are widely used by industry as an aid in the selection and placement of employees. Since blacks, compared to whites in general, have less schooling and perform less well on most psychological tests, the tests tended to exclude them from jobs that they might otherwise be capable of performing.

In 1964 the Civil Rights Act was passed which prohibited the use of tests which discriminated against minority groups. This act limited the use of tests to those measuring ability and which were "not designed, intended or used to discriminate because of race, color, religion, sex, or national origin."

The search for employment tests that could be regarded as "culture free" followed this legislation. Tests that depended upon educational and language requirements were regarded as discriminatory.[1] However, when the samples are matched for educational attainment and age, the nonverbal tests still contain a cultural bias since many of them measure a spatial factor (e.g., tests using blocks) which has been shown to be biased.[2]

In 1971 a unanimous Supreme Court decision (Duke Power case) ruled: "If an employment practice which operates to exclude Negroes cannot be shown to be related to job performance, the practice is prohibited." This decision clearly disqualifies the use of general intelligence tests and educational qualifications as prerequisites to employment or promotion, and requires that the relationship between a test score and job performance be established. Tests and educational requirements

[1] Dreger, R. M., and Miller, K. S. Comparative studies of Negroes and Whites in the United States. _Psychol. Bull.,_ 1960, _57, 361–402;_ Equal Employment Opportunity Commission. _Guidelines on employment testing procedures._ Washington, D. C.: E.E.O.C., 1966; Owens, W. A., and Jewell, D. O. Personnel selection. _Annual Review of Psychology,_ Palo Alto, Calif.: Annual Reviews, Inc., 1969, _20,_ pp. 419–446.

[2] Moore, C. L. Jr., MacNaughton, J. F., and Osburn, H. G. Ethnic differences within an industrial selection battery. _Personnel Psychol.,_ 1969, _22,_ 473–482.

designed to select persons who have abilities to move ahead in the organization (selection for careers as compared to specific jobs) would have difficulty in meeting these requirements.

The U. S. District Court for the Northern District of Georgia (United States, et. al., *v.* Georgia Power Company) subsequently ruled that aptitude tests are lawful, but the high school educational requirement is unlawful. In this case the decision to allow aptitude tests was influenced by documented evidence showing a relationship between certain aptitude test scores and successful performance on the job. The evidence supplied by the Georgia Power Company apparently made the difference between a favorable ruling regarding the use of specific tests in this case as compared to the Duke Power case.

These limitations on the use of testing will undoubtedly result in improved selection methods because the burden of proof now rests on the employer, and he will be less inclined to listen to salesmen who make false claims about the tests they offer.[3] Instead, industry will be more ready to cooperate in the development of better tests and to take a new look at promotional procedures. However, even if tests are developed that relate more accurately to success on the job for which employees are hired, they still may be unfair. Insofar as this occurs, the quota system (hiring a certain percentage of a minority group) can be followed, and the test still will be useful in selecting the best qualified from each group. Thus the quota system does not preclude the use of sound selection methods.

Another development that may restrict the use of tests for employment purposes is based upon the charge that it is an invasion of privacy.[4] Personality tests and physical examinations are regarded as the major offenders. A considerable degree of the fear of tests is based upon a misunderstanding of how tests are used and an assumption that they are more revealing than they actually are. Regardless of the justification of such attacks they represent a constraint and point up the importance of accurately reporting the limitations of a testing instrument and recognizing the need for ethical contracts.[5]

The field of testing is a technical branch of psychology, and a complete treatment of the subject is not possible in a general survey such as this. Therefore, we shall confine our discussion of psychological tests to showing how they are used to analyze jobs in terms of ability, and to a general treatment of the nature of tests.

How Test Scores Define Ability

The use of psychological tests in industry presupposes that a satisfactory *criterion* for success on a job is available. In the preceding chapter, methods for arriving at

---

[3] Stagner, R. The gullibility of personnel managers. *Personnel Psychol.*, 1958, *11*, 347–352; Dunnette, M. D. Use of sugar pill by industrial psychologists. *Amer. Psychologist*, 1957, *12*, 223–225.

[4] Gallagher, C. E. Why house hearings on invasion of privacy. *Amer. Psychologist*, 1965, *20*, 881–882.

[5] Brayfield, A. H. Testimony before the Senate subcommittee on constitutional rights and the committee on the judiciary. *Amer. Psychologist*, 1965, *20*, 888–898.

such criteria were discussed. Since both test results and measurements of job perform-ance are expressed quantitatively, the degree of correlation between the two meas-ures can be determined. After such correlations are obtained, it is possible to define the desired abilities in terms of a test score. This is an important advantage, since it replaces ambiguous and subjective descriptions of human abilities with objective and quantitative scores. For example, an intelligence test score revealing an I.Q. of 100 has a meaning which does not depend upon a particular person's definition of intelligence.

Well-constructed tests measure some aspect of human ability. As long as such tests succeed in measuring the abilities related to success, it is irrelevant whether or not one agrees with the name given to the ability measured. If we know what work-ers should accomplish with their abilities, tests can be constructed to measure the de-sired abilities. By this procedure, psychological tests become objective instruments for measuring even the most elusive human traits.[6]

Test Reliability

Norms have been developed for the standard tests which permit interpretation of the score of an individual in terms of the frequency with which it occurs in an un-selected population. In addition, many tests have norms for various types of work groups (select populations). Standard tests also have had their *reliability* measured, which means that if the proper procedures for administering and scoring them are followed, the test scores of a group of people will tend to be consistent when given on different occasions or by different testers. Thus scores of a test administered to the same group on two occasions should correlate highly if chance factors have been largely eliminated. The reliability coefficient of tests thus becomes an index to in-dicate the degree to which the test score is an accurate one (of whatever it meas-ures).

An elastic tape measure would have less reliability than a steel one and a tape measure with numbers difficult to read would lead to more scoring errors than one with legible numbers. Measures of human ability are more subject to uncontrolled variations than physical measurements so that test reliability becomes an important consideration in psychological measurement. Thus, two persons making scores of 60 and 63, respectively, might be regarded as equal if fluctuations of three points commonly occurred when the same test was repeated.

Test Validity

The chief requisite of any test is its validity[7]—the extent to which the test measures what it purports to measure. Although an instrument may be called a test of "intel-ligence" or "supervisory competence," such titles mean little or nothing unless the instrument predicts the employee's subsequent performance with reference to defi-

---

[6] For detailed discussion see J. C. Nunnally, *Psychometric theory.* New York: McGraw-Hill, 1967; Bock, R. D., and Wood, R. Test theory. *Annual Review of Psychology,* Palo Alto, Calif.: Annual Reviews, Inc., 1971, *22,* pp. 193–224.

[7] Sparks, C. P. Validity of psychological tests. *Personnel Psychol.,* 1970, *23,* 39–46.

nite criteria of job success within the organization. No test is valid for every purpose. The use of psychological tests in industry presupposes that a satisfactory criterion, or knowledge of the various criteria currently used for job performance within the organization, is available. In the preceding chapter, methods of arriving at such criteria were discussed.

The validity coefficient is used to express the degree to which the instrument measures a specific criterion (or multiple criteria). This statistic is obtained by administering the test to unselected job applicants and correlating their test scores with measurements of their subsequent job performance (*predictive* validity); or by correlating test scores with job performance of persons already employed (*concurrent* validity). Since both test results and measurements of job success are expressed quantitatively, the extent of the relationship can be determined.

Basic research on test validation is sorely needed in business and industry. Often the cost of validating procedures is considered prohibitive, with the result that industrial users frequently employ tests that lack validity.

Validity coefficients (correlation between test scores and job performance of a particular group) are included in the manuals of well-constructed tests. The usefulness of any test validation findings is determined by the extent to which the populations tested are similar to those from which the company's employees are drawn, and the degree to which the criteria of job success are identical.

In developing or choosing tests, the concept of *face validity* can conceal pitfalls for the unwary. Essentially, face validity refers to the apparent validity of tests or test items that appear to be logically related to, or bear superficial resemblance to, job activities. In actuality, such items frequently do not sample relevant abilities and thus have low validity. Perhaps the chief value of face valid items lies in their capacity to arouse involvement since testees quickly notice similarities between job and test situations.[8]

All jobs require the functioning of a pattern of abilities. Some of these abilities are phases of intelligence, others are forms of motor coordination, and still others may be associated with personality. Certain tests in each of these areas may show definite relations with job success. A person who qualified on all the diagnostic tests would have a better chance of succeeding than one who qualified on some of the tests. Use of a number of tests thus serves to give a more complete picture of job requirements.

Factors Which Influence the Value of Psychological Tests in Selection

The Degree of Relationship between Test and Criterion

The results of tests which are highly correlated with the criterion of success on a job are obviously more valuable for selecting employees than are tests less highly correlated. For this reason, it is important to strive for highly refined tests and more

---

[8] Additional sources for information on statistical foundations of testing: Anastasi, *op. cit.;* Cronbach, *op. cit.;* Ghiselli, E. E., and Brown, C. W. *Personnel and industrial psychology.* New York: McGraw-Hill, 1955, pp. 186–217.

complete batteries of tests for specific types of work. The extent to which improvement in selection varies with the size of the correlation coefficient can be learned from statistical tables.[9] Let us suppose that in a particular work situation 50 per cent of the employees are satisfactory when no tests are used. Suppose further that the number of applicants is such that 50 per cent of them must be hired. What effect will selection tests that yield different sized correlation coefficients have on the number of satisfactory employees?

Table 9.1 shows that if the only variable is the degree of correlation, a test that correlates .3 with job performance would raise the number of satisfactory employees from 50 to 60 per cent, while a test that correlates .8 with job performance would raise the number to 80 per cent.

The Nature of the Relationship between Test and Criterion

When the relationship between tests and the criterion holds only for a limited range of test scores the degree of correlation for the test as a whole is lowered by the inclusion of the whole range of scores. However, this does not preclude the usefulness of the test for the range in which it correlates with the job. This requires the examination of the scatter diagram to determine whether or not *critical scores* are in evidence.

Figure 9.1 illustrates three types of relationships, with decreasing correlation coefficients of .53, .42 and .11, respectively. Diagram A shows a typical scatter diagram in which the relationship between test score and job performance extends throughout the range. The ten top scoring individuals (see encircled area) have an average performance of 5.4 while the lower ten have an average performance of 3.6. With a relationship of this type one could raise employee performance from 4.5 to 5.4 by selecting persons with the highest test scores. There is no evidence of a critical score.

Diagram B illustrates a relationship in which the correlation coefficient is lower because the relationship between test score and performance only extends to scores up to about 55. Note that scores exceeding 55 (enclosed in circle) show no relation-

Table 9.1 / Effect of Variations in Correlation Coefficients on Number of Satisfactory Employees

Different Correlations with Selection Ratio Constant	Per Cent Satisfactory	Per Cent Improvement
No test: 50% hired	50	0
Test with r = .3: 50% hired	60	20
Test with r = .6: 50% hired	70	40
Test with r = .8: 50% hired	80	60

Samples from Taylor-Russell Tables (see footnote 9).

[9] Taylor, H. C., and Russell, J. T. The relationship of validity coefficients to the practical effectiveness of tests in selection. *J. appl. Psychol.,* 1939, *23,* 565–578. The complete tables are reprinted in Tiffin, J., and McCormick, E. J. *Industrial psychology,* (5th ed.). Englewood Cliffs, N.J.: Prentice-Hall, 1965, pp. 649–657.

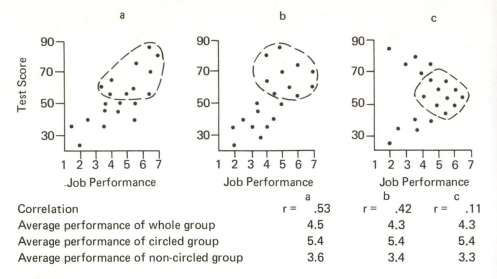

	a	b	c
Correlation	r = .53	r = .42	r = .11
Average performance of whole group	4.5	4.3	4.3
Average performance of circled group	5.4	5.4	5.4
Average performance of non-circled group	3.6	3.4	3.3

Figure 9.1 / Types of Relationship between Test Scores and Performance.
Scattergram *a* shows a typical relationship between test scores and performance. The correlation coefficient is .53. The trend is one in which high performance tends to be shown by persons making high scores. Scattergram *b* shows a type of relationship between test scores and performance that yields a lower correlation (r = .42), yet which can be just as helpful for selection. Scattergram *c* shows a relationship between test scores and performance that yields a correlation coefficient approaching 0 (r = .11), yet inspection of the diagram suggests that the best performers make scores between 50 and 65.

ship with performance. If such a relationship were obtained, applicants who scored 55 or better could be expected to be satisfactory. The average performance rating of the ten persons scoring 55 or better is 5.4, in contrast to the average of 3.4 for those scoring less than 55. Thus with a lesser correlation and this type of relationship a good selection can be obtained (raising performance from a rating of 4.3 to 5.4) by using a *minimum* score as a prerequisite to job placement. Scores above this minimum would have no further merit so that selection from among these should be based on other evidence. The use of *minimum* test scores therefore can materially improve the value of a test when this type of relationship is obtained.[10]

Diagram C shows a relationship in which the correlation coefficient approaches zero. The characteristic of the high performers (enclosed in circled area) is that their test scores tend to fall between 50 and 65. When such a relationship exists it would be possible to select persons scoring within this range and thereby obtain a performance average of 5.4 instead of 4.3, by rejecting those with an average of 3.3. This improvement is possible despite the fact that the correlation coefficient is only

[10] Kipnis, D., and Glickman, A. S. The prediction of job performance. *J. appl. Psychol.*, 1962, 46, 50–56.

.11. These situations are atypical, but illustrate the need to examine the qualitative features of relationships between test scores and performance. Such relationships call for the use of *maximum* and *minimum* cutting scores.

The Proportion of Satisfactory and Unsatisfactory Employees

If a small proportion of employees is satisfactory on a job, it follows that methods of selection may eliminate a large number of potentially unsatisfactory employees, thereby greatly increasing the proportion of satisfactory ones. On the other hand, if most employees are satisfactory when selected at random, there is less room for improvement by selection methods.

Table 9.2 contains some examples of how the extent of improvement in employee selection varies with the per cent of satisfactory employees. In this case the comparisons are made by assuming that the test used showed a correlation coefficient of .5 and that 50 per cent of the applicants were to be hired.

This table shows that if 10 per cent of the employees are satisfactory when no tests are used, a test which correlates .5 with the criterion of proficiency would raise the proportion of satisfactory employees to 17 per cent (70 per cent improvement), provided one out of every two applicants could be rejected. If 80 per cent of the employees were previously found satisfactory, however, a similar test would raise the proportion of satisfactory employees to 91 per cent (14 per cent improvement), assuming again that one out of two applicants could be rejected. Thus the extent of improvement varies with the ratio between satisfactory and unsatisfactory employees.

The need for selective methods increases as the problem of finding satisfactory employees becomes more difficult. It is in elimination of unsatisfactory employees that the testing program has the most to contribute. Jobs differ considerably in the ease with which satisfactory employees are found to fill them, and, in general, this selection problem varies with the complexity of the occupation. Thus complex occupations have more to gain from employee-testing than simple ones. It must be pointed out, however, that oftentimes the number of "unsatisfactory" employees is low because the employer regards his employees as satisfactory even when they are

Table 9.2 / Values of Test as Related to Number of Satisfactory Employees

Per Cent Satisfactory with No Test: 50% Hired	Per Cent Satisfactory When Test with r = .5 Is Used: 50% Hired	Per Cent Improvement in Satisfactory Employees
10	17	70.0
30	44	46.7
50	67	34.0
70	84	20.0
90	97	7.8
100	100	0.0

Samples from Taylor-Russell Tables (see footnote 9).

relatively ineffective. A rise in standards has the same effect as an increase in the complexity of a job, because the ability requirements are extended.

The Selection Ratio

Other things being equal, the effectiveness of employee selection can be increased by reducing the proportion of applicants hired for a job. It is apparent that if all applicants are hired, tests would have no value. Tests increase in value the more applicants there are from which to choose. Thus, the smaller the proportion of applicants hired, the more valuable the test.

The extent of the influence of the selection ratio (per cent of persons hired from among those tested) is illustrated in Table 9.3. In this table we will assume that 50 per cent are satisfactory when no test is used and that the test used has a correlation coefficient of .5 with job performance.

If 50 per cent are satisfactory when no tests are used and all persons are hired, even when a good test is used, there obviously can be no improvement in the percentage of satisfactory employees. If, however, we hire 80, 50, or 20 per cent, respectively, the percentage of satisfactory employees rises from 50 to 78. The last column in the table shows the extent of improvement as selectivity is increased.

The selection ratio adopted will naturally vary with the available labor supply. By testing all applicants, employers can be more selective and place prospective employees in occupations to which their particular talents are most suited.

The Nature of Human Abilities[11]

The abilities involved in almost any kind of work are not only numerous, but varied in kind. Each is highly specific, so that one cannot even speak of muscular coordination without specifying the kind of coordination. Add to this problem the fact that each job involves a pattern of abilities and traits, and that this pattern varies from job to job. A skilled carpenter, for example, must have several kinds of muscular coordination; considerable ability to learn; the ability to judge distances, make meas-

Table 9.3 / Influence of Selection Ratio on Number of Satisfactory Employees

Selection Ratio	Per Cent Satisfactory When Test with r = .5 Is Used	Per Cent Improvement
100%	50	0
80%	57	14
50%	67	34
20%	78	56

Samples from Taylor-Russell Tables (see footnote 9).

[11] For a discussion of factors affecting human abilities see E. A. Fleishman, and C. J. Bartlett, Human abilities. *Annual Review of Psychology,* Palo Alto, Calif.: Annual Reviews, Inc., 1969, *20,* 349–380.

urements, figure out angles; a certain amount of endurance and strength; good balance; adequate eyesight; the ability to plan work for himself and his assistants; the ability to get along with his assistants and his employer; sufficient interest and perseverance to learn the job and keep at it; caution to avoid accidents; a sense of responsibility and honesty, so that he will use proper materials even where they do not show; and many other abilities and traits. This list of characteristics includes personality traits, mental traits, physical traits, and sense-organ traits. Some of the abilities are dependent upon experience; others are quite independent of experience and depend purely upon good development and heredity.

The impracticality of measuring each specific ability essential to a given type of work is apparent. For most purposes, a cross-sectional measure of certain areas of ability will serve. A psychological test therefore frequently gives a composite picture of a number of abilities. The method is similar to that used in the measurement of physical traits, where, for example, we know that a child's height is dependent upon the length of his legs, his trunk, his neck, and his head, yet for most purposes we are satisfied to indicate his growth rate by combining all these measures. When accepting the overall body measurement, it is important to realize that all parts of the body do not grow at the same rate and develop at the same time, and that two children of the same height are not necessarily alike in body proportions. Similarly, it is important to understand that most psychological tests give a composite measure of a number of functions and that equal scores do not indicate identical abilities.

Different tests are designed to measure aspects of several areas of ability. In some cases, varied factors make up an area and the tests become relatively specific; in others the tests measure a large area because the factors are related. Tests are also designed to measure functions that are influenced by learning, and others that are native or natural to the person. Finally, some tests must be administered individually, whereas others are designed so that large groups may be tested at the same time. The equipment necessary for administering the tests varies greatly; some tests require elaborate instruments; others are purely the paper-and-pencil variety. To interpret test results properly, it is essential that these distinctions between tests be made. The assumption that a composite test score measures something highly specific, or that a relatively specific test measures a large pattern of abilities, has led to much misinterpretation. Failure to distinguish between tests influenced by learning and those not so influenced has led to the fallacious comparison of experienced and inexperienced individuals. Since each test is designed for a given purpose, it performs a specific function.

Types of Tests

Individual and Group Tests

People must be tested individually when some performance on an instrument or a piece of apparatus must be measured, or when the time for the completion of a task must be recorded. Tests for car-driving ability, ability to assemble small pieces of equipment, and insight in fitting blocks together are examples of test situations requiring individual administration. Such tests permit a greater variety of observations and measurements than do group tests. For the skilled tester, these casual observations often supply added information which may be useful. Some individual tests have the added virtue of not requiring language ability, so can be used with illiterate or foreign-speaking populations. One can reduce errors by observing whether the person tested is in the proper condition to do himself justice.

The great advantage of group tests lies in the economy of their administration and attempts are constantly being made to devise group tests which will measure the same things as are measured by certain individual tests. Group testing is entirely satisfactory for measuring attitudes, mental abilities, and information, since these functions can be reduced to language.

Aptitude Tests

Aptitude tests are designed to measure a person's potential for succeeding in certain tasks. Aptitude, therefore, refers to a man's abilities before he is trained in a specific task. His aptitude thus depends upon the abilities he has developed through heredity and growth and the extent to which these have been improved through exercise and experience in general.

The purpose of aptitude testing is to obtain, before training, an indication of how well a man will perform a job after training. People with the same training will show great differences in their performances on a job; the cause of these differences lies in the dissimilarities in aptitude. Aptitude tests are therefore so designed that certain kinds of experience do not influence the score attained. Figure 9.2 shows four different aptitude tests, each designed to measure a different specific ability. In some instances, items of information are included in the test, but in such cases exposure to the information is so common that individuals with the necessary aptitudes would have acquired it.

For example, the MacQuarrie Test of Mechanical Ability has the following seven parts: (1) tracing with a pencil through gaps in straight lines; (2) tapping three times in each of a number of circles with a pencil; (3) putting a penciled dot in small circles that are irregularly spaced; (4) copying straight line drawings; (5) locating the positions of objects in figures that are the same shape but a different size from a given pattern; (6) counting blocks that are pictured in piles where some blocks are hidden by others in the piles; and (7) pursuing with the eyes wavy lines that cross several other lines. Applicants would have no previous training on these activities and practically all people in a given culture would have had the necessary preliminary general training to understand instructions, to hold a pencil, and to write. Despite these background similarities, large differences in test scores would be obtained from a group of people, and these are the differences that aptitude tests are designed to reveal.

Aptitude tests also include measures of bodily structure and the various aspects of sensory functions, such as vision, hearing, and balance.[12] These are clearly dependent

[12] Fleishman, E. A. Psychomotor selection tests: Research and application in the United States Air Force. *Personnel Psychol.,* 1956, *9,* 449–468.

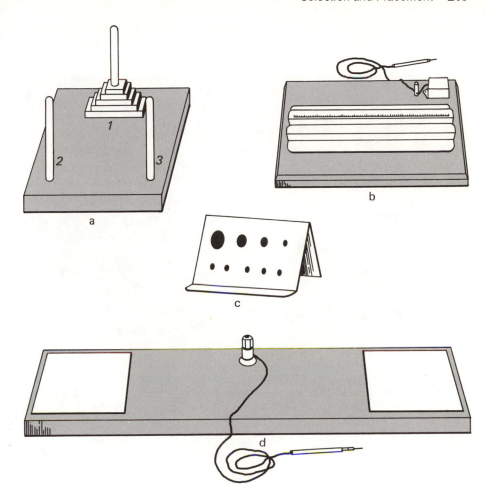

Figure 9.2 / Examples of Aptitude Tests. *a. Pyramid Puzzle.* The pyramid problem involves moving the blocks to a designated post without placing a larger block on a smaller one. Demonstrates problem solving. *b. Steadiness Tester— groove type.* Calibrated. Sides are electrified to activate buzzer or electric counter. *c. Steadiness Tester—hole type.* Conventional hole type with terminals for completing electric circuit to activate buzzer or counter. *d. Tapping Board.* Stainless steel metal plates at each end completes circuit when stylus contacts each successive plate. (*All* equipment made by Lafayette Instrument Co.)

upon developmental factors and are largely unchanged by practice or experience.

Various capacities to learn or to develop skills or to be inventive are considered aptitudes in that they determine how much one can profit from experience. The ability to acquire knowledge is largely measured by intelligence tests, provided age, cultural factors, and education are equated.

Passing the dexterity and eye tests are crucial for this applicant because the job she is applying for involves the use of intricate wire-bonding equipment and microscopic machinery.

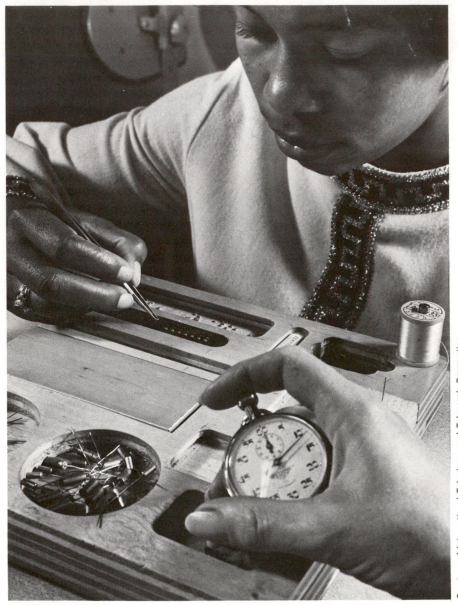

Courtesy of International Telephone and Telegraph Corporation

The majority of tests now in use in industry are aptitude tests.[13] Most industries give the specific training that is needed, but they wish to have some knowledge of an applicant's potential before making an investment in his training. For example, the telephone industry can hardly expect operators to be trained in the public schools. Rather, such an industry depends upon the schools to give a general background training in such skills as reading, speaking, and arithmetic, and then selects graduates on the basis of school grades, interview data, and test performances. Some companies do not even use the specific training given by high school business courses and actually train typists themselves.

Achievement Tests

We may think of abilities as two kinds: (1) aptitudes or abilities developed without special training; and (2) achievements or abilities which contain the modifications that are induced by special training or practice.[14] Since most jobs require some training, the ability to do a job is an achievement. We may express the relationships as follows:

$$\text{Achievement} = \text{Aptitude} \times \text{Training}$$

Achievement as here used must be differentiated from accomplishment. The production accomplished (performance) depends not only upon the ability to do a job but also upon the motivation to do it (see Chapter 13). Production failures arising from inferior aptitudes, poor training, or low motivation have quite different remedies.

Since achievement tests measure a trained ability, one must not assume that differences in scores are measures of amounts of practice. Rather, an achievement test measures the resultant of aptitudes and training experiences. No activity is purely a matter of training, since all learning extends, integrates, or modifies the behavior an individual brings to the training situation.

Achievement test performance improves with training on the job. Two people who show equal ability in performance on one occasion may be quite different in performance on a later occasion. For example, a person with one year's experience may show the same achievement as one with three years' experience. The fact that the person with the lesser experience equals the achievement of that of the other indicates that the former has superior aptitude. Two years later, it may be expected that the person with the lesser experience will surpass the achievement of the other.

As experience increases, the returns in the form of improvement diminish, but the original difference in aptitude remains the same. Employers frequently err when they choose people with the greatest amount of experience.

---

[13] Super, D. E. (Ed.). *The use of multifactor tests in guidance.* Washington, D.C.: Amer. Personnel and Guidance Assn., 1958.

[14] Cronbach defines aptitude tests as instruments used to forecast success in some future assignments, and achievement tests as instruments used to examine a person's success in past studies or performance. Cronbach, *op. cit.,* p. 31.

Achievement tests are used when hiring applicants for a job that requires training which the company cannot provide. When carpenters, toolmakers, and lathe operators are needed, one cannot be satisfied with their potential skills or take the pains to train them for industry in general. The employer therefore advertises for men skilled or experienced in certain operations and wishes to select those most qualified at that particular time. Since people who wish to obtain employment frequently claim experience they do not have, it is desirable to have tests which differentiate the qualified from the unqualified.

The most accurate way to measure achievement on any job is actually to try people out on the work. In some cases this would mean the adoption of a system of temporary employment for a probationary period. This method is obviously costly, both because it involves excessive employment and because of the damage to machinery and injury to workers which it entails. The next best thing is to devise tests which will measure certain essential qualifications.

Since the purpose of an achievement test is to measure how well a person can do a given job, the test frequently duplicates many of the operations and problems confronting the worker on the job. In testing punch-press operators by means of a miniature and hazardless facsimile of the actual machine, experienced punch-press operators scored definitely higher than untrained persons and workers skilled on other machines.[15]

Trade tests perhaps are the most familiar type of achievement test. Such tests frequently are of the pencil-and-paper variety and consist of a group of questions which have been found to differentiate between trained and untrained workers. For any trade there exist specific tools, a jargon, problem situations, and standard procedures around which an examination might be built. A good trade test not only separates experienced from inexperienced personnel, but also differentiates within the group of experienced personnel.[16] A written trade test may hope to measure the amount of trade knowledge, but it would not measure a worker's speed or accuracy on the job.

Achievement Tests May Measure Aptitude

Since achievement is the result of both aptitude and learning experience, if training is held constant any differences in performance among a group of people will be due to aptitude. Thus if an achievement test in typing is given periodically to a group of students in a typing class, any differences in speed occurring on a given test will be due to individual variations in aptitudes (providing practice and motivation have been controlled). If one plotted the learning curves of individual learners, the steepness of the curves would reflect the aptitudes, and the heights of the curves, at any given stages of development, would reveal the levels of achievement

15 Tiffin, J., and Greenly, R. J. Experiments in the operation of a punch press. *J. appl. Psychol.*, 1939, 23, 450–460.

16 Descriptions of tests and test sources of interest to industrial users may be found in: Anastasi, A. *Psychological testing.* New York: Macmillan, 1954, pp. 39–42; Dorcus, R. M., and Jones, M. H. *Handbook of employee selection.* New York: McGraw-Hill, 1950; Tiffin and McCormick, *op cit.*

(see Figure 7.6, p. 163). However, one must not assume that typing speed alone determines progress. Copying a passage, for example, relates to only one aspect of a secretary's job, but the other aspects are also susceptible to measurement.

Supervisors can learn much about the past training and aptitudes of new employees by carefully observing their progress. Aspects of the job which are difficult for some may be easy for others, and this means that each will profit most if given the kind of help he most needs.

Similarity between Achievement Tests and Training Devices

If proficiency on an achievement test improves as skill on the job increases, practice on the achievement test may cause an improvement in job performance.

The miniature punch press described on the preceding page as an achievement-test may also be considered a training device insofar as practice on it will develop essential job skills. Similarly, devices which duplicate the situation of gunners in air combat have been used not only to measure skills but also to train personnel under safe conditions. Likewise, the *flight simulator* is an intricate apparatus which duplicates the essential operations in piloting a plane and is extensively used for training pilots. Experience on a flight simulator significantly shortens the training period for airplane pilots, and is without hazard. It is particularly valuable in training pilots in instrument flying.

Tests used for car and truck drivers simulate aspects of real-life conditions, but with fewer hazards and more accurate scoring methods. Many of these tests are valuable training tools. Some training situations are adaptations of role-playing procedures (see Chapter 12). For example, in training sales personnel, the trainee may be asked to play the part of the salesperson, while the trainer acts as the customer and presents the salesperson with some typical problems encountered in the job. In training telephone operators and commercial representatives, the trainees from time to time are placed in situations simulating real-life ones, with respect to both customers and equipment, to give them the "feel" of the work. If trainers or supervisors used artificial situations of this sort to test abilities at the outset and at various stages of training, they would, in essence, be using a training procedure as an achievement test.

A simulated exercise initially developed for training managers has been successfully used to measure managerial performance.[17] The role-playing cases following many of the chapters of this text initially intended for training likewise reflect the interpersonal and leadership skills and attitudes of the participants.

Interviews and Other Selection Devices

Application Blanks and Biographical Data

Application blanks are almost universally used in industry. Various responses on these blanks are related to job success as well as to length of service, but unless these

---

[17] Meyer, H. H. The validity of the in-basket test as a measure of management performance. *Personnel Psychol.,* 1970, *23,* 297–307.

relationships are known they cannot aid the employment manager in his selection. Usually the interviewer appraises the responses in terms of his own judgment, which means that he places more emphasis on certain responses than on others. Thus the process of appraising implies that some aspects of an employee's application form are given more weight than others.

For this assessment to have an objective value it is necessary to determine which items in a person's history are related to desirable characteristics in job performance and assign a weight to them in terms of their relevance.[18] Such factors as tenure, salary, absenteeism, and quality of work might be related to certain biographical items in varying degrees. The purpose of weighting is to yield a single score to which the most relevant items contribute the greater number of points. By properly weighting the items on the application blank the correlation between the single score and the performance criterion can be maximized.

Unfortunately, the weighting pattern and the relevant items that should be considered vary for different jobs so that each job must be separately analyzed.[19] One study showed that secretaries who were still on the job two years after hiring showed the following biographical information: they tended to be over thirty-four years old; had children in high school; and lived within the city. Women not having these characteristics were more likely to have left the company.[20] The same study showed that the previous salary of the secretaries yielded no information of value.

The use of biographical data has been particularly valuable in the selection of salesmen[21] and it is often difficult to prejudge the items that will be critical. For example, in selecting teenage boys for door-to-door salesmen it had been assumed by the company that the needy would be the best candidates.[22] Actually it was found

---

[18] Welch, J., Stone, G. H., and Paterson, D. G. How to develop a weighted application blank. *Research and Technical Report 11.* Industrial Relations Center, University of Minnesota, Dubuque, Iowa: William C. Brown, 1952; England, G. W. *Development and use of weighted application blanks.* Dubuque, Iowa: William C. Brown, 1961; Mahoney, T. A., Jerdee, T. H., and Nash, A. N. Predicting managerial effectiveness. *Personnel Psychol.,* 1960, *13,* 147–163; Siegel, L. *Industrial psychology* (rev. ed.). Homewood, Ill.: Irwin, 1969, Chapter 5.

[19] Kirchner, W. K., and Dunnette, M. D. Applying the weighted application blank techniques to a variety of office jobs. *J. appl. Psychol.,* 1957, *41,* 206–208; Scollay, R. W. Personal history data as a predictor of success. *Personnel Psychol.,* 1957, *10,* 23–26; Dunnette, M. D., Kirchner, W. K., Erickson, J., and Banas, P. Predicting turnover among female office workers. *Personnel Admin.,* 1960, *23,* 45–50; Smith, W. J., Albright, L. E., and Glennon, J. R. The prediction of research competence and creativity from personal history. *J. appl. Psychol.,* 1961, *45,* 59–62; Walther, R. H. Self-description as a predictor of success or failure in foreign service clerical jobs. *J. appl. Psychol.,* 1961, *45,* 16–21; Lockwood, H. C., and Parsons, S. O. Relationship of personal history information to the performance of production supervisors. *Eng. Industr. Psychol.,* 1960, *2,* 20–26.

[20] Fleishman, E. A., and Berniger, J. Using the application blank to reduce office turnover. In E. A. Fleishman (Ed.), *Studies in personnel and industrial psychology.* Homewood, Ill.: Dorsey, 1961, pp. 30–36.

[21] Harrell, T. The validity of biographical items for food company salesmen. *J. appl. Psychol.,* 1960, *44,* 31–33; Kornhauser, A., and Schultz, R. S. Research in selection of salesmen. *J. appl. Psychol.,* 1941, *25,* 1–5; Kurtz, A. Recent research in selection of life insurance salesmen. *J. appl. Psychol.,* 1941, *25,* 11–17.

[22] Appel, V., and Feinberg, M. R. Recruiting door-to-door salesmen by mail. *J. app. Psychol.,* 1969, *53,* 362–366.

that those who seemed to be the least in need of money were most likely to succeed. Table 9.4 shows the responses on three of seven critical items found to be diagnostic on the application blank. The last line shows that an average of 63.4 per cent positive responses to seven critical items were obtained from boys who became successful, whereas the average score for those who failed was 42.7 per cent.

An additional factor also was experimentally tested; 483 sales applicants were divided randomly into two samples. One (control) group was sent the merchandise as usual, the other (screened) group was sent a questionnaire to be returned before the merchandise was sent. Failure to return the questionnaire screened out 45 per cent without reducing the number of successful applicants. The single act of returning the questionnaire was an extremely effective factor for reducing failures from 91 per cent to 45 per cent on a job in which failure was the predominant outcome.

The employment manager who keeps an active file which relates biographical data and job performance will find it a source of helpful information in decisions he must make in subsequent hiring. This biographical information should be viewed as data supplementary to that obtained from the testing program.[23]

Scholastic Success as a Predictor

Employers have long looked at college grades to evaluate prospective employees, but little research has been done to establish scholastic success as a valid selection criterion. Williams and Harrell[24] studied graduates of MBA programs to determine predictors of success in business. They found that grade point averages for undergraduate courses and for required courses in the business school did not have significant correlation with the success criterion (salary adjusted for length of time out of school). However, grades in elective courses in business school were significantly correlated with success. Distinction in chosen areas of academic or administrative interest in college were an indication of probable success in business.

Table 9.4 / Discriminating Questions on Application Blank

Questionnaire Reponse	Successful (Per Cent)	Unsuccessful (Per Cent)
Has bicycle	75	52
Goes to shows with parents	64	43
Saves money earned	57	38
Average of seven items	63.4	42.7

From V. Appel, and M. R. Feinberg, Recruiting door-to-door salesmen by mail. *J. appl. Psychol.*, 1969, *53*, 362–366. Copyright 1969 by the American Psychological Association, and reproduced by permission.

[23] Owens, W. A., Glennon, J. R., and Albright, L. E. Retest consistency and the writing of life history items: A first step. *J. appl. Psychol.*, 1962, 42, 329–331.

[24] Williams, F. J., and Harrell, T. W. Predicting success in business. *J. appl. Psychol.*, 1964, 48 (no. **3**), 164–167.

References and Recommendations

References and letters of recommendation are frequently required of job applicants despite their many apparent deficiencies. Table 9.5 shows correlations of rating from different respondents' and supervisors' rating of job performance. Only two sources of recommendation had any correlation with performance even when a standardized recommendation questionnaire was used, and these correlations were low. A non-standardized letter would perhaps lead to even less correlation since it allows a respondent to mention only those aspects of a former employee's performance and personality that he cares to mention.

Standardized or Patterned Interviews

In practice, most firms employ selection interviews—one survey indicated that 99 per cent of the companies contacted routinely do so—despite the fact that the use of the interviewing technique as a selection tool is open to serious question. Conflicting opinions are rife with regard to its usefulness and an extensive review of the literature[25] shows highly variable findings.

"Nearly everyone uses this costly, inefficient, and usually invalid selection procedure ... (although) nothing in the recent literature may be cited to give strong support to the use of the personal interview as a prediction tool."[26] Since interviewing is time consuming, expensive and thus far lacking in widely accepted standards, companies could profit considerably from any improvement in its effectiveness.

The standardized or patterned interview represents an attempt to raise the validity of the interviewing procedure.[27] The interviews are structured to lead to a more systematic collection of data and to follow a similar pattern for all applicants so that comparisons can be made. The interviewer is trained to follow a specific plan

Table 9.5 / Correlation between Recommendation Scores and Performance

Source of recommendation	N	r
Personnel officers	102	.02
Supervisors	188	.19*
Co-workers	311	.09
Acquaintances	182	.20*
Relatives	12	−.16

*significant at 0.05 level.

From J. N. Mosel and H. W. Goheen, The employment recommendation questionnaire: III. Validity of different types of references, *Personnel Psychol.*, 1959, *12*, 474.

[25] Scott, W. D., Clothier, R. C., and Spriegel, W. R. *Personnel management* (6th ed.). New York: McGraw-Hill, 1961, Appendix A, p. 565. Wagner, R. The employment interview: A critical summary. *Personnel Psychol.*, 1949, *2*, 17–46; Mayfield, E. C. The selection interview —a re-evaluation of research. *Personnel Psychol.*, 1964, *17*, 236–260; Ulrich, L., and Thrumbo, D. The selection interview since 1949. *Psychol. Bull.*, 1965, *63*, 100–116.

[26] Dunnette, M. D. Personnel management. *Annual Review of Psychology*. Palo Alto, Calif.: Annual Reviews, Inc., 1962, *13*, pp. 285–314.

[27] Harrell, T. W. *Industrial psychology* (rev. ed.). New York: Rinehart, 1958, pp. 82–87.

for the time spent with the applicant. Often he works from a job description, and he may fill out a printed form which contains rating scales for the traits he is to observe. The ratings provide permanent records that are more useful in the subsequent comparison of applicants than are the rather haphazard notes obtained from non-patterned interviews. The validity of the items included in the standardized interview should be determined in the same way as those included in tests or weighted application blanks.[28]

Another attempt[29] to improve the value of the interview is to make a rating (five-point scale) after each question and thus make a series of small decisions before the total one. This Q by Q interview has been shown to increase the reliability of the interview (the degree of agreement between raters), but whether the validity (accuracy) of decisions reached by this means is improved remains to be determined.

Fraser stresses the need for refining the interview and for developing skills.[30] Two prerequisites are: (a) that the interviewer knows what he's looking for, and (b) that he can recognize it when he sees it. Since experienced interviewers do not agree in their appraisals of candidates, research must determine sources of error and determine the type of training that is needed. Even persons observing the same interview use the same behaviors to prove opposite conclusions.[31] Actually the judgments are more accurate when the interview is heard on a tape recorder than when observed, indicating that the presence of the interviewee serves as a distraction.[32] However, exactly the opposite results were obtained in predicting grades in a statistics course.[33] The Q by Q interview was used to predict success in the statistics course study, and deception was not an issue, but the reversal of results (both significant) indicates that behavior cues influence the judgments either negatively or positively.

Bias in Interviews

The prevalence of an ineffective procedure, such as the unstructured interview, indicates that some need other than good selection is satisfied by the interview. People like to see what they are buying, not because they can better judge its merits, but because they want to see if they like it. This also seems to be true in hiring employees. In an organization the employment manager serves as gatekeeper and must pass an opinion on whoever is admitted. He must not only select good applicants

[28] Gagné, R. M., and Fleishman, E. A. *Psychology and human performance.* New York: Holt, 1959, pp. 375–376; Fear, R. A., and Jordan, B. *Employee evaluation manual for interviewers.* New York: Psychological Corp., 1943; Fear, R. A. *The evaluation interview.* New York: McGraw-Hill, 1958; McMurray, R. N. Validating the patterned interview. *Personnel,* 1947, *23,* 263–272.

[29] Asher, J. J. Reliability of a novel format for the selection interview. *Psychol. Repts.,* 1970, *26,* 451–456.

[30] Fraser, J. M. *Employment interviewing.* London: Macdonald & Evans, 1966.

[31] Maier, N. R. F., and Janzen, J. C. The reliability of reasons used in making judgments of honesty and dishonesty. *Perceptual and Motor Skills,* 1967, *25,* 141–151.

[32] Maier, N. R. F., and Thurber, J. A. Accuracy of judgments of deception when interview is watched, heard and read. *Personnel Psychol.* 1968, *21,* 23–30.

[33] Asher, J. J. How the applicants' appearance affects the reliability and validity of the interview. *Educ. & Psychol. Measurement,* 1970, *30,* 687–695.

but must also please the supervisors to whom he sends them. Whether or not he is aware of this dual role, he cannot escape the criticisms that may be directed toward him.

People have positive and negative first impressions, which are known to be unreliable yet often are unavoidable. It is only natural for a supervisor to feel that if he needs a new employee why not hire one he likes—someone who is "his kind" of person. The more psychologists try to objectify the interview procedure the more they interfere with this emotional bias and thus destroy interest in the improved method. The same thing occurs when attempts are made to remove the halo effect in rating procedures (pp. 185–186).

An investigation by Ghiselli and Barthol[34] offers some support for the view expressed above. They found that higher management "approves of supervisors whose attitudes seem to be similar to those traditionally held by higher management." This means that people who are most like their superiors are most apt to be advanced. This same bias undoubtedly operates in employment interviews. The effect of these biases is to create in the organization an image of a desirable personality in which the individual members might change but the personality of the image would be rather stable.

If bias is here to stay we need to find ways not to eliminate it but to maximize its beneficial effects and minimize its undesirable ones.

The interview is at its best when it is used not to judge ability but to learn and understand the viewpoint and thinking of another person. This approach stems from nondirective counseling[35] and can be adapted to many interview situations. It is least appropriate in the employment interview since the interests of the applicant and the interviewer conflict: the applicant wants to get an offer and the interviewer wants to screen. Placement interviews are not as subject to this conflict because both parties can be interested in assigning the individual to a job in which his abilities will be most effectively utilized. This common interest, when established, improves the reliability of the applicant's statements. Nondirective interviewing and its relevant skills are discussed in detail in Chapter 20.

Premature Employment Decisions

Decisions regarding employment seem to be colored by the fact that people are solution-minded, hence liable to make premature decisions. Some of the researches at McGill University show that decisions regarding hiring versus not hiring are made early and that subsequent data tend to be used only to test the initial decision.[36] This tendency operates regardless of the order in which relevant information is supplied. In these studies three types of information were given to the decision

[34] Ghiselli, E. E., and Barthol, R. Role perceptions of successful and unsuccessful supervisors. *J. appl. Psychol.*, 1956, *40*, 241–244.

[35] Rogers, C. R. *Counseling and psychotherapy.* Boston: Houghton Mifflin, 1942.

[36] Webster, E. C. Decision making in the employment interview. Montreal: Industrial Relations Research Centre, McGill University, 1964; Springbett, B. M. Factors affecting the final decision in the employment interview. *Canad. J. Psychol.*, 1958, *12*, 13–22; Anderson, C. W. The relation between speaking times and decision in the employment interview. *J. appl. Psychol.*, 1960, *44*, 207–268.

maker: biographical data (application form), description of personal appearance, and the interview notes. Regardless of which material was supplied first, the decision made after a scrutiny of the initial information tended to correspond with the final decision in 73 per cent of 177 cases. Further, an initial rating of rejection was more likely to be upheld than one of acceptance. The interviewer's behavior also is different in cases of acceptance and rejection. Once an interviewer has decided to reject an applicant he talks less and is less friendly, and the applicant is made to feel uneasy. The applicant's subsequent reactions thus tend to reinforce the interviewer's initial judgment.

If all sources of information are to play a more important part in the selection process, employment decision makers must find ways to delay their decisions. When decisions are made too early, subsequent information tends to be classified as black or white. This approach to information evaluation excludes the gray region between the extremes, which region should be thoroughly explored before the final classification step is taken.

A decision is like a theory in that it gives specific meanings to factual information. These meanings restrict the varied interpretations that the same data might have if different theories were operating. Once a decision is made, it functions to screen and evaluate information. Bruner has used the term "gating" to refer to this selective attention given to new information which progresses until the final stage when further information is gated out.[37]

Contribution of Interview to Assessment

Data, no matter how objectively they are obtained, do not organize themselves; only human beings bring meaning to facts. The interviewer, according to Fraser,[38] is in a position to integrate objective facts about a person and make a personality assessment. This interpretive aspect of human judgment can be either a fault or a virtue. It requires both skill and insight to make it a virtue; ability to withhold judgment until the objective data are assembled is difficult. This conclusion is supported by the longitudinal investigation in the Bell System Management Progress study.[39] Skilled interviewers (psychologists) having access to biographical data, and covering topics related to work goals, attitudes on social issues and hobbies were able to contribute information on individual assessments which subsequently were found to be related to progress in management. Variables reflecting career motivation, dependency needs, work motivation, and interpersonal skills were found to be related to individual differences in salary increases.

The Need for Observant Supervisors

Supervisors must not assume that the problem of selecting and placing employees is a job purely for the personnel department. The relating of jobs and people gives one statistical trends and cross-sections of many people, but each individual possesses

---

[37] Bruner, J. S. On perceptual readiness. *Psychol. Rev.,* 1957, *64,* 123–152.
[38] Fraser, *op. cit.*
[39] Grant, D. L., and Bray, D. W. Contributions of the interview to assessment of management potential. *J. appl. Psychol.,* 1969, *53,* 24–34.

a unique combination of abilities. An observant supervisor deals with large samples of individual behaviors and can see each person as a whole. For this reason the army sergeant is often better able than the psychiatrist to judge a soldier's ability to stand up under fire. A supervisor is in a position to observe and discover special talents and interests and to distinguish between deficiencies in aptitudes and poor attitudes. Changes in behavior are important, and the skilled supervisor is sensitive to them and able to understand their meaning. The judgment of qualified persons should not be overruled by tests.

Value of the Employee's Record

Test data are used not only for employment purposes but also for transfers and promotions. In attempting to match abilities and job requirements they serve the same purposes as in hiring. However, an additional source of information is available when a job change is involved: the employee's record in the company. Invariably this information is used and, when properly interpreted, can be of great value. As a matter of fact, it is more complete than test information because it includes the whole man's performance in a life setting, not just cross-sections of certain abilities measured under test conditions. The rating of a man's job performance incorporates not only his pattern of abilities, but also his motivation, an indication of his attitudes, personal and interpersonal adjustments, and the impressions he made on his supervisors.

Since employee ratings often are used as the criterion of success, a test constructor is quite satisfied when he finds a battery of tests that correlates with merit ratings. Despite this fact it is not uncommon for managers to accept a tester's judgment instead of relying on the record. When job changes involve different abilities, the test may be a source of information, but insofar as similar activities are involved the record is more reliable. Further, the record provides information about a particular person and permits specific predictions, whereas a test merely indicates the probabilities of success. People change surprisingly little, so a good record of an employee's past is invaluable as a predictor of his future actions.

In promoting people through the management ranks, executives wish to have certain assurances when making decisions since poor choices may have serious consequences. Frequently they call in consultants to test and interview their management personnel and then ask for assessments and recommendations. Granted that reputable consultants have certain skills, nevertheless their opinions, at best, are based upon limited knowledge gained over a short period of time. These opinions should not be used as a substitute for an employee's performance record. Nor should the consultants be shown the performance record as an aid in their appraisal because this will bias their assessment. When outside consultants are used, their assessment of an individual and his record should be treated as supplementary data gained from different situations. Conflicting appraisals should not be viewed as suggesting conflicting decisions, but rather as posing a problem that requires further exploration.

When outside consultants assess managers, serious emotional problems can be created which may color the interviewer's assessment. Are those who fear the assessment the least capable, the most sensitive, the most ambitious, the least informed of the limitations of assessment, or the least stable? As yet no one knows the answer. Regardless of the effect of calling in specialists, the skilled interviewers must reassure the interviewee and help him gain confidence in the value of the assessment. All parties gain when the assessment leads to job placement in which the amount of responsibility is commensurate with the employee's ability and interest in using it effectively. But regardless of the values to be gained from assessment, the initiation of such a program should be carefully thought through in order to avoid widespread anxieties.

Management assessment can be a valuable supplement to other biographical data if used in accordance with its unique contribution. A good interviewer can learn about a person's ambitions, concerns, important needs, and set of values. These understandings can aid in interpreting the employee's record and test data, and they can aid the person interviewed to better self-understanding and more realistic self-assessment.

Areas of Human Abilities

The characteristics of people may be divided into four general areas: (1) mental abilities; (2) muscular or motor coordinating functions; (3) personality characteristics or traits, including temperament and emotionality; and (4) physical and sensory capacities. Little or no relationship appears to exist among these four areas of ability, so that all must be sampled in any overall description of an individual. Each area is also made up of a large number of highly specific abilities which, on the whole, are unrelated; but different combinations of them may be closely associated in the performance of specific tasks.

The relative importance of these areas varies greatly, depending upon the nature of the job. Occupations which require persons to work without close supervision, and which necessitate judgment and resourcefulness, or occupations which demand planning, clerical operations, computations, and the like, clearly depend on the mental abilities.

When occupations require routine operations of a repetitive nature, or when speed is an important factor, the motor abilities become important. If trade knowledge, as well as manipulative ability, is required, then both mental and motor abilities influence performance.

Positions which involve dealings with others, such as supervisory work, instruction, and personnel management, make demands on certain personality traits. Since many of these positions require knowledge and judgment as well, mental abilities are also implicated.

Specialized work which calls for unusual strength, endurance, or agility requires certain body builds for the attainment of high degrees of proficiency. It is not surprising that some occupations have been found to be better adapted to women's hands than to men's. Forms of work which demand close or far vision, keen judgments of distance or color, acute hearing, or fine development in some other sensory capacities depend largely upon the special sensory abilities associated with the task. Since many of these rather special forms of work demand manipulation, motor abilities are also involved to varying degrees.

Clearly, the analysis of jobs in terms of abilities is rather complex. However, once the essential abilities are known, the pertinent measurements of the applicant can be made, and people can be effectively fitted to occupations which suit their abilities. At present, the psychological analysis of jobs and measurement of human abilities have progressed sufficiently to make their use a sound investment.

Laboratory Exercise

Matching People and Jobs

A. Developing a test for a specific job.
  1. Divide class into teams of five or six.
  2. Each team will develop a test to measure one specific ability for the job of Directory Assistance Operator in a telephone company.

B. Team assignment.
  1. Assume that one third of the employees hired will become Directory Assistance Operators. You wish a test that will aid in selecting the best third of those available.
  2. Description of the Directory Assistance Operator's duties are as follows: Customers contact directory assistant operators to obtain the telephone numbers of persons not yet listed, whose listings have changed, or whose number is unknown to the customer. These operators look up the requested number in telephone books issued daily and transmit numbers to the customers. A number must be found quickly so that the customer is not kept waiting. It is often necessary to look under various spellings of the same name since customers frequently give incorrect spellings.
  3. The instructor should serve as a resource person and be ready to supply information but not solutions.

C. General Procedure.
  1. Make a list of the abilities that seem relevant to success on the job.
  2. Rate the importance of these abilities on a five-point scale.

D. Specific Procedures.
  1. The instructor will assign procedures 2a and 2b to different teams.
  2. Alternate Procedures.
     a. Select a high-rated ability and develop a test to measure it. Only the materials available in the room are to be used. Telephone directories may not be furnished. The test should permit quantitative scoring and may be an individual or a group test.

b. Select a high-rated ability that is susceptible to a rating by means of an interview. Develop a patterned interview format as well as a method for scoring.

E. Demonstration of instruments.

1. Each team should be given a chance to demonstrate their test on one of the other groups.
2. The instructor should impose time limits in accordance with time available and class interest.

F. Developing a test battery.

1. The various tests when combined form a test battery. The instructor should lead discussion on which tests would make up the best battery.
2. If time permits telephone directories could be supplied and the ability of class members to obtain telephone numbers of persons named by the instructor could be written down. Using a time limit success could be measured by the number of correct responses.
3. The above scores should be related to test results. Use as time permits.
4. What part of the job was not measured by the test with telephone directories? Discuss.

Suggested Readings

Albright, L. E., Glennon, J. R., and Smith, W. J. *The use of psychological tests in industry.* Cleveland, Ohio: Howard Allen, 1963.

Buros, O. K. (Ed.). *Tests in print.* Highland Park, N.J.: Gryphon, 1961.

Buros, O. K. (Ed.). *The sixth mental measurements yearbook.* Highland Park, N.J.: Gryphon, 1965.

Cronbach, L. J. *Essentials of psychological testing* (3rd ed.). New York: Harper, 1970.

Dunnette, M. D. *Personnel selection and placement.* Belmont, Calif.: Wadsworth, 1966.

Horst, P. *Psychological measurement and prediction.* Belmont, Calif.: Wadsworth, 1966.

Lawshe, C. H. and Balma, M. J. *Principles of personnel testing* (2nd ed.). New York: McGraw-Hill, 1966.

Super, D. E., and Crites, J. O. *Appraising vocational fitness.* New York: Harper, 1962.

Wasmuth, W. J., Simonds, R. H., Hilgert, R. L., and Lee, H. C. *Human resources administration: Problems of growth and change.* Boston: Houghton Mifflin, 1970.

10 The General Nature of Psychological Tests

The Mental Abilities

Mental abilities include learning, memory, flexibility in thinking, seeing relationships (commonly called insight), alertness, speed of thought processes, and creative or inventive reasoning. Since there is some relationship between all these functions, it is possible to give a composite measure of this group of abilities without greatly misrepresenting any one of them. The term *general intelligence* is now commonly used by psychologists to designate this group of abilities.

Intelligence Tests

Since the score on an intelligence test tends to correlate to a greater degree with each of the more special abilities listed above than each of them is correlated with any of the others, the intelligence score is regarded as the most representative single measure of mental development presently available. The intelligence test score is closely associated with success in school and obviously measures the abilities essential for school and college work. It is particularly predictive with subject matter requiring more than memory. Since general intelligence progressively increases in the child as he grows older, it is possible to compare mentally defective adults with children and treat them as retarded in their mental development.

Mental age is a concept that has developed as a measure of mental growth. The average child of a given chronological age is able to perform certain functions, such as obeying simple commands, building certain structures from blocks after a demonstration, and interpreting pictures or telling stories about them. If the child tested shows an overall ability to perform the crucial operations of, say, the average eight-year-old, he is then said to have a mental age of eight years, regardless of whether his chronological age is six, eight, or ten years. Mental age therefore indicates the extent of mental development and increases as long as the child continues to grow. Figure 10.1 shows the course of development of three individuals. All three, at some stage, reach a mental age of eight, but one arrives at this level of maturity at the age of four, another at the age of eight, and the third at the age of 16.

The steep curve in Figure 10.1 describes the development of a superior individual. At every stage of development this individual has a mental age approximately twice as great as his chronological age. The middle curve describes the development of an average person; his mental age corresponds with his chronological age. Below-average individuals show retarded growth at all stages of development, and as a consequence the chronological age exceeds the mental age, as shown in the bottom curve. Although an individual's mental growth may show spurts and deviate some-

Figure 10.1 / Relationship between Mental Age and Chronological Age for Differing Rates of Development. The height of the curves indicates the level of development attained at various chronological ages. Three individuals differing greatly in mental potential may have similar mental ages, but differ in the age at which a given level of maturity is reached. The I.Q. indicates the rate of development and is represented by the steepness of the curves. (From *General Psychology* by J. P. Guilford © 1939 by Litton Educational Publishing, Inc. Reprinted by permission of Van Nostrand Reinhold Company.)

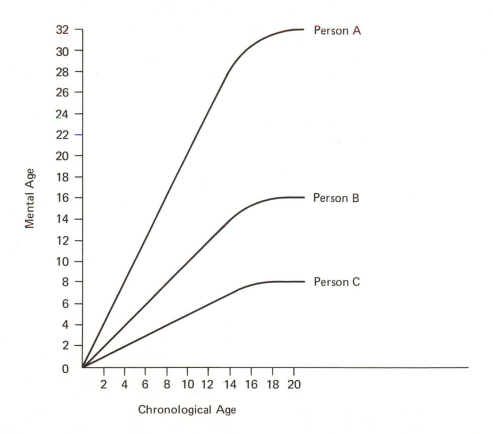

what from the straight-line relationship shown in the figure,[1] it is important to recognize that individuals differ markedly in the general slope of their developmental curves.

The *I.Q.*, or *intelligence quotient*,[2] is the ratio between a child's mental age (M.A.) and his chronological age (C.A.). In order to avoid fractions, the ratio is multiplied by 100. The formula for determining the I.Q. thus is:

$$\text{I.Q.} = \frac{\text{M.A.}}{\text{C.A.}} \times 100.$$

If a child passed the equivalent of the eight-year-old test at the age of six, his I.Q. would be 133; if he passed it at the age of eight, his I.Q. would be 100; and if he passed it at the age of ten, his I.Q. would be 80.

The mental age of the average child continues to increase until the age of about 15 or 16, so that, in using the formula for adults, the chronological age is always treated as if it were one of these figures. For example, in one well-known test, all persons of fifteen and over who passed no more than an eight-year-old test would have an M.A. of eight and an I.Q. of 53 ($8/15 \times 100$).

As measured by conventional intelligence tests, mental ability develops most rapidly during childhood and adolescence. Research of a longitudinal nature has indicated that some growth occurs during adulthood.[3] In later years, however, a decline of tested intelligence is apparent.[4] This is especially evident in tasks which require psychomotor speed and certain types of abstract thinking.[5]

It is important not to lose sight of the fact that intellectual accomplishments are not purely a matter of general intelligence. It is obvious that the adult has many intellectual superiorities over the 16 year old. These superiorities are largely the contributions of experience. An inventor must have both intelligence and knowledge. A supervisor or a toolmaker improves enough through experience to counterbalance other losses due to age. A professor is still able to teach college students and to think more accurately in his specialized field than are his students, even when the I.Q.'s of some members of his class surpass his own. Social judgment, responsibility, carefulness, and perspective are important traits which improve with the experience of living.

Barring unusual circumstances (health, motivation, emotional factors, or environmental causes[6]), the I.Q. is a comparatively stable measure. In general, the intel-

[1] Cronbach, L. J. *Essentials of psychological testing* (3rd ed.). New York: Harper, 1970. Lord, F. M., and Novick, M. R. *Statistical theories of mental test scores.* Reading, Mass.: Addison Wesley, 1968.

[2] Terman, L. M., and Merrill, M. A. *Measuring intelligence.* Boston: Houghton Mifflin, 1959.

[3] Bayley, N. On the growth of intelligence. *Amer. Psychologist,* 1955, *10,* 815–818; Bradway, K. R., Thompson, C. W., and Cravens, R. B. Pre-school IQs after 25 years. *J. educ. Psychol.,* 1958, *49,* 278–281.

[4] Wechsler, D. Intelligence changes with age. *Pub. Hlth. Rep.,* 1942, Suppl. No. 168, 43–52.

[5] Dibner, A. S., and Cummins, J. F. Intellectual functioning in a group of normal octogenarians. *J. consult. Psychol.,* 1961, *25,* 137–141.

[6] Bayley, *op. cit.;* Sontag, L. W., Baker, C. T., and Nelson, V. L. Mental growth and personality development. *Mongr. Soc. Res. Child Develop.,* 1958, *23,* (No. 2).

ligence test is most suitable for measuring school-age children of all levels of ability and adults who are average and below average in mentality. It is more difficult to devise satisfactory tests for highly superior adults, since an I.Q. of 140 or over occurs in only about one-half of 1 per cent of the population. Superior children can always be compared with older children, but superior adults must be studied in relationship to one another. Standard intelligence tests therefore are relatively inadequate for differentiating the highly superior individuals. Although intelligence tests would show engineers and research men in industry to be highly superior, they would not be very effective in distinguishing the ingenious and creative men from the rapid learners, or, necessarily, in differentiating those individuals who will be highly successful from those whose careers will be mediocre.[7]

To answer some of the more perplexing problems involved in the measurement of mental ability, many researchers are actively developing less traditional approaches designed to take into account the impact of experience, situational conditions, and other factors on intelligence.[8]

Cattell[9] divides general intelligence into two factors: fluid intelligence and crystallized intelligence. Fluid intelligence is seen as biologically determined—best measured by speed tests or at adulthood by culture-fair tests (tests giving no advantage to educational background)—quite constant, and apparent in tests that involve adaptation to new situations. Crystallized intelligence, in contrast, is seen as a result of earlier learning, best measured by power tests (in which speed of response is not important), and varying with recent or present interests and exercise. Cattell contends that these two factors show little discrepancy during school years, but that serious mistakes can result from ignoring them when faced with the task of selecting from groups that vary in age and distance from school activities.

Despite interest in the concept of general intelligence, the chief trend for some years has been toward more specific tests. Much research has been addressed to determining the different factors which make up intelligence. When broken down in this way, the mental abilities turn out to be such functions as verbal comprehension, word fluency, number facility, memory, visualizing or space thinking, perceptual speed, induction, speed of judgment, analogic reasoning, symbol perception, planning, sequential reasoning.[10] Examples of test items designed to measure specific mental abilities, known as *primary abilities,* are shown in Figure 10.2. Each contributes to general intelligence.

[7] Terman, L. M. The discovery and encouragement of exceptional talent. *Amer. Psychologist,* 1954, *9,* 221–230. Reprinted in D. E. Dulany, Jr. (Ed.), *Contributions to modern psychology.* New York: Oxford University Press, 1958, pp. 51–56.

[8] Hunt, J. McV. *Intelligence and experience.* New York: Ronald, 1961; Liverant, S. Intelligence: A concept in need of re-examination. *J. consult. Psychol.,* 1960, 24, 101–110; Siegel, I. E. How intelligence tests limit understanding of intelligence. *Merrill-Palmer Quart.,* 1963, 9, 39–56; Cronbach, L. J., and Gleser, G. C. *Psychological tests and personnel decisions* (2nd ed.). Urbana, Ill.: University of Illinois Press, 1965; Nunnally, J. C. *Psychometric theory.* New York: McGraw-Hill, 1967.

[9] Cattell, R. B. *Abilities: Their structure, growth, and action.* Boston: Houghton Mifflin, 1971.

[10] See D. E. Super and J. O. Crites. The expanding list of primary abilities. In *Appraising vocational fitness.* New York: Harper, 1962, Table 2, Ch. 5.

Figure 10.2 / Sample Items from Tests of Primary Mental Abilities. The first five factors shown on these two pages are from *SRA Primary Mental Abilities— Ages 11 to 17 Manual.* © 1958, Thelma Gwinn Thurston. Reproduced by permission of the publisher, Science Research Associates, Inc. The last factor is from D. M. Andrew, D. G. Paterson, and H. P. Longstaff, *Minnesota Clerical Test.* Reproduced by permission. Copyright 1933, renewed 1961 by The Psychological Corporation, New York, N.Y. All rights reserved.

Check the sums of the columns below. If the answer is right, mark the space in the **R** row. If the answer is wrong, mark the space in the **W** row.			
	17	35	63
	84	28	17
	29	61	89
	140	124	169
Right	=	=	=
Wrong	=	=	=

a. Number Factor. A number factor, N, is involved in the ability to perform arithmetic calculations rapidly and accurately. It does not involve the reasoning ability which is important in solving story problems in arithmetic but appears to be restricted to the simpler processes of numerical calculation, such as addition and multiplication.

In each of the following lines mark the word that means the **same** as the first word.				
quiet	blue	still	tense	watery
safe	secure	loyal	passive	young

On the blanks below write several **four-letter** words which **begin** with **M**. One word you might write is **most**. Go ahead and write more **four-letter** words which **begin** with **M**.

_____

_____

_____

_____

b. Verbal Factors. One verbal factor, V, is found in tests involving the understanding and use of words, such as tests of vocabulary, reading comprehension, or giving words of opposite meaning.

Another verbal factor, namely, *word fluency* or, W, is tested by asking the subject to think of isolated words at a rapid rate as well as by such tasks as anagrams, crossword puzzles, rhyming, and recalling words that begin with the same letter or have a common prefix or suffix. Factor analysis shows that this is separate from V.

> In the row of figures below, mark every figure which is **like** the first figure in the row. Do not mark the figures which are made backward.
>
> A   B   C   D   E   F
>

c. Space Factors. One space factor, S, is involved in tests in which the subject manipulates objects in space in his imagination. This ability is involved in many mechanical tasks and in working with mechanical drawings and blueprints. There are several space factors.

> Now study the series of letters below. In each series decide what the next letter should be and mark the letter in the answer row at the right.
>
> c d c d c d   a b c d e f
>
> a a b b c c d d   a b c d e f
>
> a b x c d x e f x g h x   h i j k x y

d. A Reasoning Factor. A reasoning factor, R, occurs in tasks that require the subject to find and apply a rule or general principle in a mass of data.

> In the first row the correct first name has been marked. Mark the correct first name for each last name. Mark only one name in each row. Go right ahead.
>
> Last Name   First Name
>
> | | | | | | |
> |---|---|---|---|---|---|
> | Preston | Fred | John | Mary | Nancy | Ruth |
> | Brown | John | Mary | Nancy | Ruth | Walter |
> | Smith | Fred | John | Mary | Nancy | Walter |
> | Davis | Fred | John | Nancy | Ruth | Walter |

e. A Rote Memory Factor. A rote memory factor, M, is measured by tests which call for rapid memorization. This can be measured readily by giving the subjects a fixed amount of time to study a list of names, such as *Ruth Preston,* presented on flash cards and then asking the subjects to pick out the correct first name for each of a list of last names.

> **Instructions**
>
> On the inside pages there are two tests. One of the tests consists of pairs of names and the other of pairs of numbers. If the two names or the two numbers of a pair are *exactly the same* make a check mark (√) on the line between them; if they are *different,* make no mark on that line. When the examiner says "Stop!" draw a line under the last pair at which you have looked.
>
> *Samples* done correctly of pairs of *Numbers*   *Samples* done correctly of pairs of *Names*
>
> 79542_____79524   John C. Linder_____John C. Lender
>
> 5794367_√__5794367   Investors Syndicate_√_Investors Syndicate

f. A Perceptual Speed Factor. A perceptual speed factor, P, is found in tests which require the rapid and accurate picking out of a particular detail so that pairs of objects can be labeled as like or unlike. This ability is involved in many routine clerical operations.

Many mental abilities have been identified through application of the factor-analytic technique,[11] bringing the recognition that these abilities may perhaps be best described as a hierarchy, ranging from narrow factors present in highly specific tests to very broad or general factors.[12] Guilford's three-dimensional structure of intelligence model postulates 120 specific abilities, 80 of which have been identified; good tests for many of them have been developed.[13] Although it is unlikely that all the significant factors which make up intelligence have been defined, many abilities have been well established and some fairly pure measures of these are available. Inspection of the different kinds of test items will reveal that some items would be more relevant to certain jobs than others.

By identifying and analyzing the many elements that comprise intelligence, better selection and vocational guidance will undoubtedly be achieved. But there also is a danger that something may be lost. Combinations of abilities produce relationships between them. Thus, AB is made up of A and B, plus the relationship between A and B. A house is made of many bricks, but a pile of bricks is not a house. It is possible that we may lose certain relations between abilities if we pay too much attention to the elements that are related. Will an anagram expert's performance be a mere combination of word fluency and visualization, or will the relationship between the two give him an added advantage? Will inventive ability turn out to be an elementary ability, or is it dependent upon the elements with which it is combined? These are problems research psychologists must confront.

Industrial Uses of Intelligence Tests

A great variety of intelligence tests is available for industrial purposes.[14] There are group tests, individual tests, self-administered tests, and performance tests. All are correlated with one another, but their scores are not interchangeable. Some are more applicable to particular occupational groups than are others. The various tests sample different mental abilities in different proportions; thus, some samplings fit the demands of a given occupation more closely than others. Frequently the test used by a company is selected because of its simplicity of administration rather than its particular merit.

Proficiency in most forms of office work shows relationships with intelligence test scores, and correlations between .34 and .57 are very common.[15] One study

---

[11] Davis, F. B. *Utilizing human talent.* Washington, D.C.: Amer. Council on Education, 1947; Davis, P. C. A factor analysis of the Wechsler-Bellevue Scale. *Educ. Psychol. Measmt.,* 1956, *16,* 127–146; Guilford, J. P. A revised structure of intellect. *Reports from the Psychological Laboratory of Southern California,* 1957, No. 19; Guilford, J. P. Three faces of intellect. *Amer. Psychologist,* 1959, *14,* 469–479; Guilford, J. P., and Hoepfner, R. *The analysis of intelligence.* New York: McGraw-Hill, 1971.

[12] Vernon, P. E. *The structure of human abilities.* New York: Wiley, 1950, pp. 22–23; Moursy, E. M. The hierarchical organization of cognitive levels. *Brit. Jour. Psychol., Statist. Sect.,* 1952, *5,* 151–180.

[13] Guilford, J. P. *The nature of human intelligence.* New York: McGraw-Hill, 1967.

[14] See O. K. Buros (Ed.), *Tests in print.* Highland Park, N.J.: Gryphon, 1961; Buros, O. K. (Ed.). *The sixth mental measurement yearbook.* Highland Park, N.J.: Gryphon, 1965.

[15] McMurry, R. N. Efficiency, work-satisfaction and neurotic tendency: a study of bank employees. *Personnel J.,* 1932, *11,* 201–210.

found correlations ranging from .40 to .65 between clerical employees' ratings and a fifteen-minute mental test.[16] In another, an intelligence test was found more diagnostic for choosing stenographers than was a test for stenographic achievement.[17] Of the management traits measured in a third study, intelligence correlated most highly (.85) with the occupational levels of workers on eleven different jobs.[18] The abilities making for proficiency in mill supervisors, public utility employees, and salesgirls, and the abilities essential in a great variety of other occupations have also shown significant relationships with intelligence. Table 10.1 shows the relationship obtained in a variety of occupations when proficiency and intelligence scores are correlated.

Ghiselli's review of the literature published prior to 1955 indicates that group mental tests do predict future performance for many jobs, but that the efficiency of these predictions varies greatly, ranging from high to very low. The average correlations for group mental tests and job proficiency for electrical workers, managerial and professional groups ranged from .35 to .47; for supervisors, assemblers, and

Table 10.1 / Correlations between Proficiency Measures and Intelligence

Occupation	Coefficient Correlation	Investigator
Proficiency of cashiers	.57	Clarke
Production of machine bookkeepers	.56	Hay
Ratings of clerical employees	.35	Hay
Ratings of machine skills	.40	Anderson
Ratings of all utility plant workers	.68	Wadsworth
Grades in training course in engineering subjects	.50	Bolanovich
Ratings of cotton mill supervisors	.37	Harrell
Ratings of aircraft industry foremen		Shuman
Plant A	.39	
Plant B	.05	
Plant C	.66	
Efficiency ratings of office supervisors	.51	Holmes

From Anderson, R. G. Test scores and efficiency ratings of machinists. *J. appl. Psychol.,* 1947, *31*, 377–388; Bolanovich, D. J. Selection of female engineering trainees. *J. educ. Psychol.,* 1944, *35*, 545–553; Clarke, W. V. The evaluation of employment tests. *Personnel,* 1937, *13*, 133–136; Harrell, T. W. Testing cotton mill supervisors. *J. appl. Psychol.,* 1940, *24*, 31–35; Hay, E. N. Predicting success in machine bookkeeping. *J. appl. Psychol.,* 1943, *27*, 483–493; Holmes, F. J. Validity of tests for insurance office personnel. *Personnel Psychol.,* 1950, *3*, 57–69; McMurry, R. N. Efficiency, work-satisfaction and neurotic tendency: A study of bank employees. *Personnel J.,* 1932, *11*, 201–210; Shuman, J. T. The value of aptitude tests for supervisory workers in the aircraft engine and propeller industry. *J. appl. Psychol.,* 1945, *29*, 185–190; Wadsworth, G. W. Tests prove worth to a utility. *Personnel J.,* 1935, *14*, 183–187.

[16] Tiffin, J., and Lawshe, C. H., Jr. The adaptability test: A fifteen-minute mental alertness test for use in personnel allocation. *J. appl. Psychol.,* 1943, 27, 483–493.

[17] Shellow, S. M. An intelligence test for stenographers. *J. Personnel Res.,* 1926, 5, 306–308.

[18] Ghiselli, E. E. The validity of management traits in relation to occupational levels. *Personnel Psychol.,* 1963, 16, 109–113.

clerks, from .20 to .34; and for repairmen, sales personnel, packers and wrappers, service occupations, and machine workers, from .00 to .19.[19]

It is apparent that mental abilities are related to success in all types of work requiring judgment, knowledge of the job, and understanding of fairly complex relationships.

On the whole, jobs requiring dexterity, strength, and routine mechanical operations show little or no relation to intelligence. For instance, mental test scores and job proficiency correlated below .15 for pottery decorators, welders, meat-packing workers, and electronic-parts assemblers.[20]

As a matter of fact, the lower levels of intelligence are sometimes more satisfactory for these jobs. In a simple assembly operation, a negative correlation was found between the amount produced and intelligence scores.[21] Tiffin and McCormick[22] reported instances in which persons below average in intelligence were among the best in production. Such individuals were superior on tests of motor ability.

In one company turnover was greatest among salesmen who made high scores on the Wonderlic Personnel Test of Mental Ability.[23] Later in our discussion of labor turnover (Chapter 19), we shall see that job satisfaction is closely associated with intelligence, and that the most desirable amount of intelligence varies considerably even from one factory job to another. It is important, therefore, for the intelligence level to be related to the complexity of the job.[24] When necessary, more use should be made of individual rather than group tests.

Mechanical-Relations Tests

Among the tests of mechanical ability we find some that measure primarily the mental aspect of mechanical relations, whereas others measure primarily certain muscular or motor abilities. It is necessary, therefore, to distinguish between two types of tests of mechanical ability. Here we are concerned with tests which measure the understanding or comprehension of mechanical relationships. For convenience, we have called them *mechanical-relations tests.* Mechanical tests which measure, to a large degree, the motor aspects of mechanical ability will be discussed in the next section.

The intelligence of some people is such as to make them particularly adapted to working with machinery; in contrast, others have an intelligence that makes them more adapted to dealing with literary subjects. Mechanical tests of intelligence are formulated to give more weight to the former kind of intelligence than to the latter;

---

[19] Ghiselli E. E. The measurement of occupational aptitude. *Univer. Calif. Publ. Psychol.,* 1955, *8,* 101–216.

[20] *Guide to the use of the General Aptitude Test Battery.* Washington, D.C.: U.S. Govt. Printing Office, 1958.

[21] Tiffin, J., and Greenly, R. J. Employee selection tests for electrical fixture assemblers and radio assemblers. *J. appl. Psychol.,* 1939, *23,* 240–263.

[22] Tiffin, J., and McCormick, E. J. *Industrial psychology* (4th ed.). Englewood Cliffs, N.J.: Prentice-Hall, 1958, pp. 121–122.

[23] Albright, L. E., Smith, W. J., and Glennon, J. R. A follow-up on some "invalid" tests for selecting salesmen. *Personnel Psychol.,* 1959, *12,* 105–112.

[24] Simon, L. M., and Levitt, E. A. The relation between Wechsler-Bellevue I.Q. scores and occupational area. *Occupations,* 1950, *29,* 23–25.

for this reason these tests may be regarded as a more specific kind of intelligence test than are the tests of general intelligence. Because a great deal of industrial work is mechanical in nature, it is often desirable to use this more specific type of test of intelligence in industry.

Various kinds of mechanical-relations tests are available, both individual and group.[25] Most of them show a high correlation with each other, so it may be supposed that mechanical comprehension is rather general in nature. The common form of the test is designed to determine whether a person has insight into mechanical functions. Some of the tests present pictures of pulleys or gears, and the person tested must describe which way one wheel turns when another turns clockwise. Care is taken not to require mathematical computations, since the inclusion of such items would make the test a measure of achievement rather than of aptitude.

In other forms, a person is required to name the functions of various parts of a machine. Such questions presuppose a general knowledge of shop machinery; but when all people tested have a shop background, the questions really measure comprehension rather than knowledge. Still other tests require that parts of unfamiliar mechanisms be assembled. This task requires insight into the relationship of the various pieces and thus resembles a puzzle. Often the parts are blocks which have to be fitted together to produce an end product of specified shape. In the latter case past familiarity with machinery is entirely excluded as a helpful factor.

Inventive mechanical ability is tested by showing an applicant how a particular gadget functions and requiring him to draw diagrams to show how the inside mechanism must be arranged in order to work the way it does. For example, he may be shown how the movement of one lever activates another lever in a peculiar fashion and be asked to draw the inside mechanism that makes possible this particular action.

The selection of repairmen, troubleshooters, merchandise packers, and many machine operators can be greatly improved by the use of well-selected mechanical ability tests.[26] The proper test battery to use for a given job is the one that proves itself the most selective.

Creative Ability

For many years it was generally believed that high intelligence test scores indicating superior learning ability were indicative of the highly creative person since differences in mental ability were assumed to be quantitative. Recent studies, however, support the neglected theory that mental processes of a higher order than learning exist.

Creative persons appear to differ more in kind than in degree from good learners. Creative ability seems to require a certain amount of intelligence but beyond this

---

[25] Bennett, G. K., and Cruikshank, R. M. *A summary of manual and mechanical ability tests.* New York: Psychological Corp., 1942; Super and Crites, *op. cit.*

[26] Shartle, C. L. A selection test for electrical troublemen. *Personnel J.,* 1932, *11,* 177–183; Vernon, P. E., and Parry, J. B. *Personnel selection in the British forces.* London: University of London Press, 1949, p. 230; Stead, W. H., and Shartle, C. L. *Occupational counseling techniques.* New York: American Book, 1940, Ch. 6; Wolff, W. M., and North, A. J. Selection of municipal firemen. *J. appl. Psychol.,* 1957, *35,* 25–29.

minimum individuals vary greatly in creative ability.[27] Research with gifted children show them to vary greatly in originality, particularly in their perception of problem situations.[28] Torrance[29] has developed a number of tests and training exercises that support the notion that productive (creative) thinking and reproductive (recall of past learning) thinking are qualitatively different.[30] In the second case an old solution is used to solve a new problem; in the first, the solution to the new problem is a reorganization or an integration of parts of old solutions (learnings). In experimental studies in which subjects were given information to learn, they utilized this information differently when required to recall it than when required to use it in a problem situation.[31] If some individuals react to a problem by trying to recall the solution from their past learnings (as students do when taking an exam) while others react to the problem as something new and try to make up a solution, different kinds of mental processes are to be expected.

Recall depends upon associative bonds formed during learning. However, another process, that of the *fragmentation* of associative bonds, also occurs. Once learned sequences are fragmented, spontaneous reorganizations of old learnings can occur so that *new* combinations are created. Individuals differ widely in which of these processes (reproducing or reorganizing) dominates in problem situations, but the evidence reveals marked individual differences in the way stored information is treated.[32]

It has been shown that the search for uniqueness[33] can be influenced by training, and creativity is even improved when the person is told he has the reputation of being creative and because of it has been approached by his associates to solve a problem.[34] Guilford[35] has developed a variety of specific tests of creativity and distinguishes between *convergent* and *divergent* processes in creativity. The convergent process is one in which different things must be brought into an organized pattern (dividing a list of words into a certain number of classes) and the divergent process in which one starts with specific things and with them makes as many further things

[27] Creativity, intelligence don't necessarily correlate, admen told. Report on speech presented by D. W. McKinnon at Sixth Annual Creative Workshop held by *Advertising Age.*

[28] Getzels, J. W., and Jackson, P. W. *Creativity and intelligence: Explorations with gifted children.* New York: Wiley, 1962.

[29] Torrance, E. P. *Encouraging creative behavior: Experiments in classroom creativity.* Englewood Cliffs, N.J.: Prentice-Hall, 1965.

[30] Wertheimer, M. *Productive thinking.* New York: Harper & Row, 1959.

[31] Maier, N. R. F., Thurber, J. A., and Janzen, J. C. Studies in creativity: V. The selection process in recall and problem-solving situations. *Psychol. Reports,* 1968, *23,* 1003–1022.

[32] Maier, N. R. F., Julius, M., and Thurber, J. A. Studies in creativity: Individual differences in the storing and utilization of information. *Amer. J. Psychol.,* 1967, *80,* 492–519.

[33] Torrence, *op. cit.;* Christensen, P. R., Guilford, J. P., and Wilson, R. C. Relations of creative response to working time and instructions. *J. exp. Psychol.,* 1957, *53,* 82–88.

[34] Colgrove, M. A., Stimulative creative problem solving: Innovative set. *Psychol. Reports,* 1968, *22,* 1205–1211.

[35] Guilford, J. P. Intelligence: 1965 model. *Amer. Psychol.,* 1966, *21,* 20–26; Kettner, N. W., Guilford, J. P., and Christensen, P. R. A factor analytic study across the domains of reasoning, creativity, and evaluation. *Psychol. Mono.,* 1959 (No. 279); Hendricks, M., Guilford, J. P., and Hoepfner, R. Measuring creative social intelligence. Los Angeles: University of Southern Calif., 1969, Report #42.

as possible (make many structures out of a given set of lines). There is evidence that high scores on measures of divergent process are associated with superiority in science.[36]

The abilities associated with so-called creative functions seem to be rather specific so that it is difficult to develop a test that will satisfy various criteria of creativity. Generally speaking, tests that have been developed are difficult, but a task can be made difficult by being long, requiring fine distinctions, or requiring a new idea. In studying the way different individuals utilized learned information in a problem situation, none of the types of processes investigated were found to correlate with various tests of creativity.[37] People generally agree about which persons are creative, but the characteristics of creative thinking are difficult to pinpoint. One author reports rating by peers as a valid measure of an individual's creativity.[38] If people utilize stored information differently, creativity is not developed by supplying more information.[39] Rather the development of creative solutions requires that nonhabitual kinds of thinking be utilized. Reorganizing old experiences is not necessarily a difficult task, merely a different approach.

The need for creativity in industry is most obvious in departments concerned with research and development. In one study[40] a correlation of .31 between scores on Remote Associates Test[41] and supervisory ratings of creativity in engineers was obtained. This test requires one to think of the word that is related to three other seemingly unrelated words supplied (e.g., base, snow, dance, ——) and will thereby relate them (e.g., ball). For research scientists' scores on this test the correlation coefficient with ratings of creativity was only .13.[42] Foreign born scientists tended to score poorly on the test, revealing the dependence of the score on language facility. In another study items from the Guilford Creativity Battery[43] were used, and out of 42 different test scores only four were significantly related to creativity ratings.[44] Among tests of creativity now being used by industrial concerns are the AC Test of Creative Ability[45] and the Owens Creativity Test for Machine Design.[46]

---

[36] Cropley, A. J. Divergent thinking and science specialities *Nature, 1967, 215, 671–672.*

[37] Maier, N. R. F. *Problem solving and creativity: In individuals and groups.* Belmont, Calif.: Brooks/Cole, 1970, Parts 1–4.

[38] Buel, W. D. The validity of behavioral rating scale items for the assessment of individual creativity. *J. appl. Psychol., 1960, 44,* 407–412.

[39] Mednick, S. A. The associative basis of the creative process. *Psychol. Rev.,* 1962, *69,* 220–232; Maltzman, I., Belloni, M., and Fishbein, M. Experimental studies of associative variables in originality. *Psychol. Mono.,* 1964, 78 (No. 3).

[40] Datta, L. E. Remote Associates Test as a predictor of creativity in engineers. *J. appl. Psychol.,* 1964, *48,* 183.

[41] Mednick, S. A., and Mednick, M. T. *Remote Associates Test.* Boston: Houghton Mifflin, 1967.

[42] Datta, L. E. A note on the Remote Associates Test, United States culture and creativity. *J. appl. Psychol.,* 1964, *48,* 184–185.

[43] Beverly Hills, Calif.: Sheridan Psychological Services, Inc.

[44] Mullins, C. J. *Prediction of creativity in a sample of research scientists.* WADC Technical Documents Report PRL, Lackland Air Force Base, Texas.

[45] Harris, R. H. and Simberg, A. L. *AC* test of creative ability. Chicago: Education-Industry Service.

[46] Owens, W. A. Owens' creativity test for machine design. Ames, Iowa: Iowa State Univer. Press.

At present there is confusion about the meaning of creativity. Certainly studies of creativity in different fields should not be generalized until common elements in the processes involved are securely established. Further, problem solving and creativity should be differentiated. Three basic types of problem-solving behavior can be distinguished: (1) trial and error; (2) adapting old solutions to new situations; and (3) forming original solutions by reorganizing past learning. Only the last process should be regarded as creative or productive problem solving.

Perhaps the best measure of the creative person in an organization is his record for innovation and originality. One can make fairly accurate judgments of this ability, and for the present these should be considered in relationship with tests of creativity. The creative person, unfortunately, may also be regarded as a problem employee because he is likely to think differently from his group and tends not to be a conformer.

Motor Coordination

Differences between Motor Abilities

The motor functions, such as dexterity, manipulative activity, and muscular control in general, are unrelated to the mental functions. Thus it is not surprising to find that a very intelligent person may be all "hands and feet" when it comes to assembling a simple piece of machinery or operating a lathe.

Though not commonly known, it is a fact that the various motor tests show little or no relationship with one another.[47] In one study, the average correlation between a large number of motor tests was found to be only +.15.[48] A summary of many studies[49] indicated that the motor abilities could be divided into 11 fairly independent groups as follows:

1. Control precision (e.g., moving lever to precise setting)
2. Multilimb coordination (e.g., packaging with both hands)
3. Response orientation (e.g., reaching out and flicking switch on signal)
4. Reaction time (e.g., pressing key in response to bell)
5. Speed of arm movement (e.g., gathering objects and tossing in pile)
6. Rate control (e.g., holding rod on irregular moving rotor)
7. Manual dexterity (e.g., rapidly placing blocks in a form board)
8. Finger dexterity (e.g., manipulating small objects)
9. Arm-hand steadiness (e.g., threading needle)
10. Wrist-finger speed (e.g., tapping speed)
11. Aiming (e.g., placing dots in circles)

Since the motor abilities are highly specific, the individual tests are relatively simple, and administration does not require a great deal of time. A good sample of the

[47] Cronbach, *op. cit.;* Fleishman, E. A., and Hempel, W. E., Jr. A factor analysis of dexterity tests. *Personnel Psychol.*, 1954, 7, 15–32.

[48] Garfiel, E. The measurement of motor ability. *Arch. Psychol.*, 1923, 9 (62), 32.

[49] Fleishman, E. A. The description and prediction of perceptual motor skill learning. In R. Glaser (Ed.), *Training research and education*. Pittsburgh: University of Pittsburgh Press, 1962.

pattern of motor abilities can be obtained fairly quickly. Most of the tests involve equipment, however, and must be given individually. A few have been reduced to pencil-and-paper performance and can be given to groups. For example, such a test may require the applicants to put dots in circles arranged on a sheet of paper. In some cases the score is based on the number of circles filled out in a specified period of time.

Characteristic Motor Tests

Typical dexterity tests require the applicant to place pegs in small holes arranged in various patterns. The arrangement of the holes determines the relative importance of finger and arm movements. Precision tests may require the testee to plunge a stylus accurately into a hole each time it is mechanically uncovered. Some tests merely record the speed with which one can tap a stylus on a metal disk and activate an electrically controlled counting device. Tests of rhythm require the applicant to duplicate, by tapping a telegraph key, a pattern which is presented on a phonograph.

The use of a device that measures the speed with which a person can react to a signal is one of the oldest tests in use. This *reaction time* varies with the type of stimulus used and the conditions under which it is given, as well as with the person tested. Short reaction times are helpful in most activities which require alertness.

Tests of motor coordination are usually more elaborate. They require a person to synchronize different movements of the two hands or of the hands and feet. A person may be asked to cause a beam of light to follow a given course when the horizontal movement is controlled by one lever and the vertical by another lever. The arrangement of the task is unusual in that it does not duplicate learned activity. In more simple arrangements, a person may be required to turn, as rapidly as possible, a small crank with the right hand and a large one with the left hand.

When the purpose is to test aptitude, the task required is usually one that does not duplicate some form of work. Insofar as a test situation simulates a kind of work, it tends to become an achievement test. In some instances motor tests are purposely designed to duplicate some of the activities required on a given job. Such tests are achievement tests and may be used to select experienced men. They may be used for testing aptitude, however, if they are given to people with no experience or with the same amount of experience. When such tests distinguish between good and poor operators who possess the same degree of experience, they are highly satisfactory tests for aptitude.

Typical Results

Since the motor abilities are highly specific it is possible for one test to be closely related to one manual job and poorly related to another. For women operating garment machines, the correlations between job success and a paper-folding test, a card-sorting test, and a dexterity test were .52, .35, and .21, respectively.[50] However, the test for finger dexterity, which was the poorest test for the machine operators,

---

[50] Treat, K. Tests of garment machine operators. *Personnel J.,* 1929, *8,* 19–28.

showed a correlation of .37 with output records for simple electrical assembly jobs.[51]

Sometimes superficial similarities (face validity) between jobs and tests are misleading. For example, a test involving the use of tweezers to pick up and place pins might be supposed more related to the efficiency of workers in a watch factory than a test of finger dexterity in which the same pins are handled with the fingers. Nevertheless, the tweezer dexterity test showed no correlation with skill ratings, whereas the finger dexterity test showed a .26 correlation. Despite the fact that the better of the two correlations was low, there was a significant difference between the average score for superior workers and that for mediocre workers.[52] The tweezer dexterity test was, however, related to the productivity of women doing put-in-coil work.[53] In this instance the correlation was .57, but the finger dexterity test gave a correlation of only .25. Similarly, the aptitudes of bus drivers and drivers of heavy trucks are sufficiently unlike to warrant use of different sets of tests.[54]

The MacQuarrie Test of Mechanical Ability (see p. 218) measures a group of abilities including speed, accuracy of tracing, tapping, dotting, copying, letter location, block identification, and visual pursuit. The Dotting Items correlate in the vicinity of .30 with proficiencies of can packers, merchandise packers and power sewing machine operators; but approach zero when correlated with efficiencies of calculating machine operators, index clerks, and lamp shade sewers. The Pursuit Items show good correlations with proficiencies on such jobs as power sewing machine operators (.51) and calculating machine operators (.43), but have little relationship with card punch operators, put-in-coil jobs, and pull-socket assembly.[55]

Tests which predict quality of performance may have little or no value in predicting speed of production.[56] Thus it is highly necessary for the individual or firm using psychomotor tests to specify the nature of the activity to be predicted, and to know whether speed or quality of production is more important to the particular operation.

Test Batteries

Since many jobs require a number of rather specific abilities, best results can be obtained by combining a number of specific tests and forming a *test battery*.[57] Each test should be related to a measure of job performance, but the tests should not be

[51] Hayes, E. G. Selecting women for shop work. *Personnel J.,* 1932, *11,* 69–85.

[52] Candee, B., and Blum, M. Report of a study done in a watch factory. *J. appl. Psychol.,* 1937, *21,* 572–582.

[53] Stead and Shartle, *op. cit.,* p. 235.

[54] Roche, M. Le laboratoire psychotechnique des transports routiers. *Travail Hum.,* 1952, *15,* 265–276.

[55] Stead and Shartle, *op. cit.*

[56] Otis, J. L. The prediction of success in power sewing machine operating. *J. appl. Psychol.,* 1938, *22,* 350–366.

[57] *Guide to the use of the General Aptitude Test Battery.* Washington, D.C.: U. S. Govt. Printing Office, 1958; Fleishman, E. A. Psychomotor selection tests: Research and application in the United States Air Force. *Personnel Psychol.,* 1956, *9,* 449–468; *The use of multifactor tests in guidance.* Washington, D.C.: American Personnel and Guidance Assn., 1957; Hall, R. C. Occupational group contents in terms of the DAT. *Educ. Psychol. Measmt,* 1957, *17,* 556–567.

related to one another because, to the extent that they were related, one test would merely duplicate the function of one of the others. For example, two tests with validity coefficients of .60 and .50 would have a combined coefficient of correlation of .78, providing the two tests were entirely unrelated to each other. If, however, the tests showed an intercorrelation of .80, their combined value would be no greater than that of the better of the two tests used by itself.[58]

In a recent study a large number of test items were combined to form a test battery which was used for substation operators. The full test required four hours and 20 minutes to administer, and was surprisingly effective in 90 per cent of the cases.[59]

Some Limitations

It is more difficult to obtain tests that correlate highly with job performance for complex jobs than for simple jobs. For one thing, the criterion of success on complex jobs is often more difficult to establish, and it is not uncommon for supervisors to differ considerably in what they expect from a person. Actually, the failure to agree on the criterion of job success may be our good fortune. Perhaps our hopes and faith in the future will be better served if success is not conceived of as an absolute and establishable fact.

All relationships between job performance and test scores are limited by the fact that motivational and attitudinal factors as well as ability to do the job influence performance.[60] The practical user of tests in selecting workers should always keep these limitations in mind. As a matter of fact, trainability for a job and the aptitudes necessary to maintain proficiency on a job are not the same.[61] An employer who trains his employees should therefore use somewhat different tests than one who is merely concerned with present job performances.

Personality Traits

The Nature of Personality

Contrary to popular usage, personality should not be regarded as a "something" which characterizes the inner self, such as the spirit of the individual, or as a force within man which makes him what he is. Like general intelligence, the term refers to a group of abilities or traits. For this reason, each of the specific traits pertinent to performance on a job must be measured separately.

The personality traits include such characteristics as honesty, cheerfulness, persistence, dominance, emotionality, adjustment to life, sociability, relation between

[58] Stead and Shartle, *op. cit.,* p. 128.

[59] Goguelin, P. Etude du poste d'électricien de tableau et examen de selection pour ce poste. *Travail Hum.,* 1951, *14,* 15–57.

[60] Richards, T. W. Mental test performance as a reflection of the child's current life situation: A methodological study. *Child Develop.,* 1951, *22,* 221–223; Cronbach, *op. cit.:* Portu, A. *Predictors of organizational leadership.* Unpublished doctoral dissertation, Stanford University, 1961.

[61] Brown, C. W., and Ghiselli, E. E. The relationship between the predictive power of aptitude tests for trainability and for job proficiency. *J. appl. Psychol.,* 1952, *36,* 370–372.

emotion and reason, and cooperativeness. Some authors also include mental and physical characteristics among personality traits, but when they do so, they use the term to refer to all human traits. Since we have divided all the traits into four areas, our use of the word is more limited and so has a more specific meaning.

There is no question that mental and physical traits influence many personality traits, but modifications of personality arise because this group of traits is subject to change through experience, and the mental and physical factors influence this experience.

We have already seen what frustration may do to emotional adjustments (see Chapter 4). A man of small stature if frustrated because of his physical inferiority may become aggressive and carry a "chip on his shoulder." Women if frustrated in business because of differential pay rates, may become dissatisfied and defensive. Many develop traits of resignation, making their adjustment in that way. Childhood insecurity, problems of the only child, difficulties arising when one boy is dominated by several sisters, and many other family situations have an influence on personality development.

Intelligent people often have difficult emotional adjustments to make. Highly intelligent children have an easy time in school, are praised by teachers and envied by contemporaries, but they face difficult adjustment problems when they enter the adult world. They tend to have ideas about doing things in a better way, but their efforts are unappreciated because their bosses do not like to be "shown up"; they are critical of less intelligent associates and become unpopular; they cannot find friends of like ability because highly intelligent people are rare; so they are lonely.[62] These and many other experiences leave their mark, and they will make either good adjustments or highly inadequate ones. Children of low intelligence also have special problems of adjustment. Since they experience inferiority in school and in later years, they have to find ways of adapting themselves so that their demands and expectations will conform to their abilities.

In all aspects of life, the unusual or exceptional individual has the most difficult adjustments to make. Very often the inability to make human adjustments drives people to apply themselves exclusively to their work. Work is their escape, and the resulting application frequently results in great success in fields in which human relations are relatively unimportant.

Personality traits are also dependent on heredity and on the functional condition of the body. Heredity determines the potentialities of personality development, but experience can influence their course. That some people, through heredity, are more likely to become neurotic and maladjusted than others is generally agreed, but that some will remain relatively normal, no matter what their life-problems turn out to be, is a matter of debate.

The functions of the endocrine glands play an important part in human general makeup and determine physical and mental growth as well. For instance, inadequate functioning of the thyroid gland makes one easily tired, sluggish, and unable to

[62] Hollingworth, L. S. *Children above 180 I.Q. Stanford-Binet.* New York: World Book, 1942, pp. 258–262 and 271–283.

concentrate, while overfunctioning results in restlessness, irritability, and worry. Extreme malfunctions of this gland produce marked bodily symptoms and interfere with both mental and physical growth. The parathyroid glands have a quieting function, so that excessive secretions produce lassitude, while deficient amounts induce overexcitement.

In general, the glands regulate the chemistry of the body, and a proper balance in their function is essential if people are to have the personality traits normal for them. There is no reason to believe that one can control personality by the injection of glandular secretions. Rather, certain maladjustments are due to glandular unbalance which can be corrected by medical treatment.

Other bodily conditions also influence our reactions. Hungry or tired people are more irritable and more likely to be uncooperative. Well-fed and rested people are more generous and congenial.

The Measurement of Personality Traits

The methods of measuring personality and personality traits fall into four types: the experimental method, the rating procedure, the questionnaire form, and the projective test. Each has its limitations for industrial use, but a discussion of them is worthwhile both because it adds to an understanding of problems involved and because it indicates the conditions under which the methods are invalid. Short-cut methods, such as an analysis of photographs, handwriting, or any physical characteristics, are entirely unsound and have been completely discredited by research.

The experimental method measures individual reactions to specifically arranged test situations. For example, honesty has been measured by determining whether children will record all their errors when grading their own examinations.[63] If the grading is done the day after examination, under the pretext of helping the teacher, the child does not suspect that a previous record has been obtained, and the test becomes a realistic situation. This duplication of a real-life situation is highly desirable, since certain personality traits vary considerably with the type of situation. Attempts to measure persistence have ranged from situations requiring the endurance of pain (electric shock) to continued attempts to solve difficult problems. Up to the present, this approach has been used largely to explore the nature of personality traits and to determine the conditions which influence the expression of various traits. Its practical use as a method for objective measurement of specified personality traits must await further developments.

In industrial studies this procedure has been limited primarily to the study of emotional reactions. The lie detector is an instrument which accurately records some of the emotional reactions (physiological changes) to certain stimuli; it does not indicate the kind of emotion. Other tests of emotionality involve a situation in which the applicant is put to work on some motor-coordination test and then is suddenly frightened by having the floor drop from under the person or by being confronted with flashes of light or loud noises. How the individual reacts under

[63] Hartshorne, H., and May, M. A. Studies in deceit. Part 1 of *Studies in the nature of character*. New York: Macmillan, 1928, p. 51.

such conditions is a measure of fright reaction. By measuring the emotional behavior under conditions of stress, one can detect individuals who are easily upset by noise, danger, and pressure of work. Since some individuals completely lose their skill and judgment under emotional stress, tests of emotion are highly desirable for occupations in which this behavior is detrimental. As will be seen in the discussion of accidents, tests of emotionality can be used to good advantage in reducing accident rates.

The psychological examiner frequently observes many personality traits when individually testing for other abilities. Cooperative behavior, persistence, poise, and tendencies to make excuses can be observed. Although such observations are not standardized, the experienced tester soon learns to use them to advantage. The skilled interviewer also can make pertinent personality observations, a source of supplementary information which should not be overlooked.[64]

The rating method utilizes other people's estimates of a given individual's personality traits. The procedure was described in our discussion of rating proficiency on a job. By using a list of pertinent personality traits, a group of people can rate any given individual who is known to them. Since, unfortunately, prospective employees cannot always be rated, this method is largely limited to placing more effectively those already employed. In some instances recommendation forms are so arranged that applicants must be rated by the persons who recommend them. When this is done, it is desirable that the same persons recommend several employees, for then the raters are required to make comparisons. When hiring young people from trade schools, such data can be furnished by teachers who are in a position to rate several prospective workers.

The great virtue of the rating procedure lies in the fact that a wide range of traits can be explored with very little time and effort. The method presupposes, of course, that the employer already has determined the traits which best suit specific jobs. The limitations of the rating method discussed in Chapter 8 apply equally to the rating of personality traits.

The questionnaire method of testing personality has been used very widely, largely because it is simple to administer. The applicant is required to fill in a form by answering a series of questions, usually with "yes", "?", or "no." From the responses, some understanding of the person is achieved. Widely used questionnaires are concerned with measures of emotional adjustment and tendencies toward introversion or extroversion. Since emotional adjustment is essential to cooperative behavior and morale, these questionnaires or scales are often useful in detecting problem employees.

Poorly adjusted people tend to exaggerate their troubles, so that their behavior is not in keeping with the situation. They feel they are unlucky, excessively criticized, lonely, and misunderstood. They have little confidence in other people, do not enjoy the company of others, and have family conflicts. In general their health is poor; they have no appetite and sleep poorly. Selected questions would have diagnostic value in detecting poor adjustment.

[64] Fraser, J. M. *Employment interviewing.* London: MacDonald & Evans, 1966.

To discourage attempts to beat the test, questions have been made as innocuous as possible, the tests have been called personality inventories or temperament scales, forced-choice items (see pp. 189–191) have been developed, and questions whose ostensible content is not the actual basis for scoring have been used.[65] One must also take into account the fact that the individual tested does not know how he will react to certain new situations the questionnaire may raise. When filling out a test form the person is not emotionally aroused or frustrated, so is more inclined to give logical or "reasonable" responses.

Despite attempts to improve the questionnaire method such precautions have been found to be somewhat inadequate.[66] In one experiment,[67] students were asked to fill out a questionnaire designed primarily for detecting poorly adjusted individuals in industry.[68] The students were first asked to answer the questions honestly, and then to answer them again under the assumption that they were applying for a job. It was found that there were more answers of the good-adjustment type under the second condition. In another study,[69] retail sales applicants distorted their scores, whereas industrial sales applicants did not. In this case, the Edwards Personal Preference Schedule[70] was used in an actual employment situation. It is apparent, therefore, that persons applying for a job can give favorable slants to their responses. Development of methods for spotting *faked* scores will offset some of this disadvantage. In one study the keys constructed to detect fakers on three forced-choice personality inventories were able to identify 91 per cent of the fakers, while only 6 to 9 per cent of the nonfakers were thus misclassified.[71] On the other hand, if the instrument being used has been carefully validated so that a certain *pattern* of responses is significantly related to successful job performance in a given situation, the "truth" or "falsity" of the subject's answers is of little importance with reference to prediction.[72]

The use of personality questionnaires as selection devices and the attempts of test developers to conceal the purpose of these instruments may encourage the view that psychologists are tricky, which in turn may cause subjects to become even

[65] Couch, A., and Keniston, K. Yeasayers and naysayers: Agreeing responses as a personality variable. *J. abnorm. soc. Psychol.,* 1960, *60,* 151–173.

[66] Wesman, A. G. Faking personality test scores in simulated employment situation. *J. appl. Psychol.,* 1952, *36,* 223–229; Borislow, B. The Edwards Personal Preference Schedule (EPPS) and fallability. *J. appl. Psychol.,* 1958, *42,* 22–27; Dicken, C. F. Simulated patterns on the Edwards Personal Preference Schedule. *J. appl. Psychol.,* 1959, *43,* 372–378; Hedberg, R. More on forced-choice test fakability. *J. appl. Psychol.,* 1962, *46,* 125–127.

[67] The study was made by W. J. Giese and F. C. Christy, and is reported in Tiffin and McCormick, *op. cit.,* pp. 180–181.

[68] Humm, D. G., and Wadsworth, G. W. *The Humm-Wadsworth Temperament Scale* (1940 revision.). Los Angeles: D. G. Humm Personnel Service.

[69] Hedberg, R. "Real-life" faking on the Edwards Personal Preference Schedule by sales applicants. *J. appl. Psychol.,* 1962, *46,* 128–130.

[70] Edwards, A. L. *Manual for the Edwards Personal Preference Schedule* (rev. ed.). New York: Psychological Corp., 1959.

[71] Norman, W. T. Personality measurement, faking, and detection: an assessment method for use in personnel selection. *J. appl., Psychol.,* 1963, *47,* 225–241.

[72] Albright, L. E., Glennon, J. R., and Smith, W. J. *The use of psychological tests in industry.* Cleveland, Ohio: Howard Allen, 1963, p. 126.

more evasive in their responses.[73] In any case, popular writers have offered various suggestions for faking on these tests.[74] However, an experiment designed to test the effectiveness of Whyte's rules for cheating on personality tests[75] found that differences occasioned by giving dishonest answers were not great enough to be significant when supervisors chose applicants for the job, despite the fact that respondents were able to bias their scores. This finding, plus the fact that nearly half (42.5 per cent) of the subjects did better on the inventory by being honest, raises doubt as to the efficacy of these rules.

The Minnesota Multiphasic Personality Inventory,[76] originally designed for clinical diagnosis, is among the questionnaires most frequently employed in personnel selection. Data from this instrument must be treated in a configural, rather than a cookbook fashion, since the shape of the profile obtained is more important than the level of single scores.[77] Thus interpretation by highly competent examiners is imperative. Many other instruments of the self-report variety are currently available.[78] The purposes for which the questionnaire is to be used as well as the requirements of the specific situation will, of course, determine eventual choice.

Scales designed to measure rather specific personality traits also are available.[79] Among the traits isolated, for example, are (1) shyness, (2) cycloid trait (easy and frequent changes in mood), (3) ascendancy (as opposed to submission in social situations), (4) depression (lonely, low spirits, worries over possible misfortunes), (5) rhathymia (carefreeness), (6) nervousness (easily disturbed, inability to relax, nervous manner), (7) general drive (quick in action, rushes into work), (8) meditative thinking (analyzes others, serious, philosophic), (9) masculinity (as opposed to femininity in attitudes and interests), (10) lack of inferiority, (11) will control, and (12) radicalism. The scales are based upon research[80] which led to the isolation of primary traits, as distinct from compound traits. Such traits as persistence

[73] Cronbach, *op. cit.*, p. 453.

[74] Whyte, W. J., Jr. How to cheat on personality tests. Appendix to *The Organization Man.* Garden City, N.Y.: Doubleday, 1957; Gross, M. L. *The brain watchers.* New York: Random House, 1962.

[75] Shaw, M. E. The effectiveness of Whyte's rules: "How to cheat on personality tests." *J. appl. Psychol.,* 1962, 46, 21–25.

[76] Published by University of Minnesota Press, 1943; New York: Psychological Corp., 1945.

[77] Hathaway, S. R., and Meehl, P. E. *An atlas for the clinical use of the MMPI.* Minneapolis: University of Minnesota Press, 1951; Welsch, G. S., and Dahlstrom, W. G. *Basic readings on the MMPI in psychology and medicine.* Minneapolis: University of Minnesota Press, 1956; Drake, L. E., and Oetting, E. R. *An MMPI codebook for counselors.* Minneapolis: University of Minnesota Press, 1959.

[78] For excellent critical reviews, see: Cronbach, *op. cit.,* pp. 464–499; Super and Crites, *op. cit.,* pp. 514–586.

[79] (a) *The Guilford-Martin Inventory of Factors G A M I N;* (b) *The Guilford-Martin Personnel Inventory;* (c) *The Guilford-Martin Temperament Profile Chart;* (d) *Guilford's Inventory of Factors S T D C R.* Beverly Hills, Calif.: Sheridan Supply Co., 1943; (e) *Guilford-Zimmerman Temperament Survey.* Beverly Hills, Calif.: Sheridan Supply Co., 1949; (f) *The 16 P. F. Test.* Urbana, Ill.: Institute for Personality and Ability Testing, 1950.

[80] Cattell, R. B. Personality theory growing from multivariate quantitative research. In S. Koch (Ed.), *Psychology: a study of a science. III. Formulations of the person and the social context.* New York: McGraw-Hill, 1959, pp. 257–327; Guilford, J. P. *Personality.* New York: McGraw-Hill, 1959.

and honesty have been found to be compound rather than unitary. For example, persistence in enduring pain is quite different from plodding or keeping at a task. Similarly, honesty may vary greatly from one situation to another, so that we may speak of different kinds of honesty. The isolation of primary personality traits will lead to much greater refinement in personality measurement.

Personality inventories are of greatest value in situations in which they are regarded by the subject as providing a basis for gaining information or aid for which he has genuine need. In such instances these instruments are not viewed as invading privacy, thus faking and other types of resistance are held to a minimum.

In industry the questionnaires are most adequate when used to achieve better placement with personnel already employed. Under these conditions there is no motivation to fake responses since improved placement is in the interest of the employee as well as the company.

Projective tests require that the subject respond to ambiguous stimuli by giving them meaning or structure. The vague or incomplete nature of the material permits the individual to project himself into the situation. In the Rorschach Test, for instance, the subject is asked to locate and describe images in inkblots—much as one sees figures in clouds. In the Thematic Apperception Test he responds to rather indistinct drawings by making up a story; telling what has led to the present scene, what is now happening, and what the outcome will be. These two tests are among the most frequently used projective instruments.

Others, however, involve drawing a person or copying geometric figures from cards as accurately as possible on the first trial, later embellishing these figures in any fashion that makes them more pleasing. The subject may also be asked to develop appropriate captions for cartoons; to supply endings for short stories; or to complete sentences such as:

Today I . . . .
I particularly like . . . .
Bosses usually . . . .

The chief characteristic of a projective test is that the individual imparts meaning to the stimuli with which he deals. Thus these instruments are especially useful in identifying personal reactions, personality patterns, or behavioral styles which may determine the way a person frequently responds in real-life situations. These tests were originally developed for use in clinical diagnosis and require skill in administration and interpretation. In the hands of an inexperienced tester, they may become more a test of the projections of the tester than of the subject. In the hands of psychologists skilled in their use, however, valuable insights can be generated which can then serve effectively as a framework against which other test findings and biographical material can be compared.

One value of projective tests is that they can obtain a global view of personality since the respondent can react freely without being forced to use special categories or degrees of response ordinarily imposed upon him by the nature of other instruments used to assess personality. This breadth of response can be helpful, but it makes the statistical handling of test results very difficult. The projective tests have neither the mystic power to locate all the inner workings of the personality attributed to them by psychiatrically-oriented movies or television programs, nor the complete lack of power attributed to them by those who insist that a test must be statistically perfect.

Occupational Differences in Personality

Most personality inventories measure emotional adjustment and the ability to relate satisfactorily to others. As such they may seem relevant to many occupational groups. However, one must distinguish between productivity and job satisfaction in making these analyses. In a study of unskilled factory workers, personality variables (worry, depression, neurotic tendencies) were unrelated to production but showed a .45 correlation with job adjustment as measured by the supervisors' judgments of employees as sources of concern.[81] Because occupations differ in the extent to which people must interact with one another, it is of interest to determine the degree of relationship between job proficiency and standard personality measures. Ghiselli and Barthol[82] have brought together the results of many investigations. Table 10.2 summarizes the results for various occupational groupings. It will be seen that personality measures are relevant in all the groups, as shown by Column 3, but the magnitudes of the relationships are somewhat disappointing (.14 to .36). As a matter of fact, the same occupational groups, when studied by different investigators, give a greater range of correlation coefficients than the range obtained by comparing different occupational groups. The last column shows the range of correlations ob-

Table 10.2 / Correlations between Personality Inventories and Various Occupational Groups

Occupation	No. of Studies	No. of Cases	Average Correlation	Approximate Range of Correlations
General supervisor	8	518	.14	–.10 to +.40
Foreman	44	6433	.18	–.20 to +.50
Clerical workers	22	1069	.25	–.05 to +.65
Sales clerks	8	1120	.36	+.15 to +.45
Salesmen	12	927	.36	.00 to +.80
Protective workers	5	536	.24	+.20 to +.35
Service workers	6	385	.16	–.40 to +.50
Trades and Crafts	8	511	.29	+.15 to +.50

Modified from E. E. Ghiselli, and R. P. Barthol. The validity of personality inventories in the selection of employees. *J. app. Psychol.,* 1953, *37,* 18. Copyright 1953 by the American Psychological Association, and reproduced by permission.

[81] Heron, A. A psychological study of occupational adjustment. *J. appl. Psychol.,* 1952, *36,* 385–387.

[82] Ghiselli, E. E., and Barthol, R. P. The validity of personality inventories in the selection of employees. *J. appl. Psychol.,* 1953, *37,* 18–20.

tained by different investigators for each of the eight occupational groups studied, and the first and second columns show the number of studies and cases, respectively, from which coefficients of correlation were obtained. Because of the inconsistency of results, it is clear that generalizations must be carefully made.

Table 10.2 reveals that the studies of sales clerks and salesmen almost invariably show a positive correlation, and in some instances it is strikingly high. A single test designed to measure empathy, the ability to put oneself in another's position, showed a rather striking relationship with the success of new-car salesmen.[83] This test gave a validity coefficient of .71 with the manager's rankings of the ability of salesmen and a coefficient of .44 with their sales record. The test was not useful for selecting salesmen of used cars; in this instance the corresponding correlations were only .17 and .12.

The results obtained from clerical groups differ considerably, indicating that the value of a personality test in the selection of clerks must take into account the extent to which social interaction is required in the job. In the protective occupations the results are consistent but the magnitude of the relationships is consistently low. For the trades and crafts the relationships are consistently positive and fairly good, suggesting the advisability of including personality measures in test batteries for skilled workers.

Service workers show the greatest discrepancy, with correlations ranging from −.40 to +.50. It is probable that the stress placed upon cooperation and good public relations varies considerably in different companies, and this may account for the wide range in results. Friendliness may be regarded as an asset because it makes for good public relations, or as a detriment because it takes up time. The value of personality measures for selecting service workers therefore must be examined in the light of service requirements.

Use of Personality Tests in Selection of Supervisors

Personality inventories might be expected to be especially effective in selecting foremen and supervisors. However, Table 10.2 reveals rather poor average relationships between success in these activities and personality measures. The tendency to fake results on questionnaires can explain low correlations but not inconsistent findings. These can be explained in part by recognizing the fact that success in a supervisor has unlike meanings in different companies. The Bernreuter Personality Inventory was found to have questionable value in differentiating good and poor foremen in an oil refinery,[84] but it did differentiate between them in a steel manufacturing concern,[85] although not as well as did tests of mental functions.

---

[83] Tobolski, F. P., and Kerr, W. A. Predictive value of the empathy test in automobile salesmanship. *J. appl. Psychol.*, 1952, 36, 310–311.

[84] Sparks, C. P. Limitations of the Bernreuter Personality Inventory in selection of supervisors, *J. appl. Psychol.*, 1951, 35, 403–406. For a critical appraisal, see W. H. Whyte, Jr., The fallacies of "personality" testing. *Fortune*, Sept., 1954, 117–121, 204–208.

[85] Poe, W. A., and Berg, I. A. Psychological test performance of steel industry production supervisors. *J. appl. Psychol.*, 1952, 36, 234–237.

The comparisons of successful and unsuccessful foremen often yield certain personality differences. In one study, care was taken to match the successful and unsuccessful foremen in skill and job knowledge.[86] When this was done the unsuccessful group tended (1) to withdraw from others, (2) to be indifferent to the actions of people, and (3) to show antagonisms in their dealings with people. Meyer[87] compared successful and unsuccessful work-group leaders in a utility and obtained similar differences. He found the social attitude to be the most distinguishing feature. Successful leaders were more likely to perceive others as individuals who had feelings and goals of their own, while the unsuccessful leaders saw things in terms of their own goals and situations. He also found that unsuccessful leaders were more inclined to engage in combative sports although the successful leaders actually participated more in sports in general.

Another interesting approach to the relationship between personality and supervisory skill is to examine the way superior versus inferior supervisors see themselves. Using the forced-choice method, Ghiselli and Barthol[88] developed 64 pairs of adjectives, both members of each pair about equal in social desirability. Half of the pairs contained adjectives describing desirable traits and half, undesirable ones. First-line supervisors were asked to select from the favorable list of pairs the adjective that best fit them and from the unfavorable list the adjective that least fit them.

In eighteen of the pairs shown in Table 10.3, low-rated and high-rated supervisors checked opposite adjectives; eleven were in the favorable category and seven in the unfavorable category. These self-perceptions reveal some interesting differences in attitudes and values as well as suggesting some possible personality differences that should be explored.

Personality seems to play a more important part in the success of higher levels of supervisors. A study of leadership in which top officeholders were compared with nonofficeholders showed officeholders to be more dominant, more self-confident, less neurotic, less introverted than the others.[89] However, these traits may indicate merely that persons with certain traits were chosen to be leaders rather than indicate that the traits were relevant to success once they were chosen.

In another investigation the personality traits of executives and supervisors of a large chain grocery were compared.[90] The executives averaged significantly more (1) sociable, (2) free from depression, (3) emotionally stable, (4) happy-go-lucky, (5) active, (6) ascendant (socially bold), (7) self-confident, (8) calm and composed, (9) objective, (10) agreeable, and (11) cooperative than the super-

---

[86] Shartle, C. L. A clinical approach to foremanship. *Personnel J.*, 1934, *3*, 135–139.

[87] Meyer, H. H. Factors related to success in the human relations aspect of work-group leadership. *Psychol. Monogr.*, 1951, *65*, 1–29.

[88] Ghiselli, E. E., and Barthol, R. Role perceptions of successful and unsuccessful supervisors. *J. appl. Psychol.*, 1956, *40*, 241–244.

[89] Richardson, H. M., and Hanawalt, N. G. Leadership as related to the Bernreuter Personality Measures: III. Leadership among adult men in vocational and social activities. *J. appl. Psychol.*, 1944, *28*, 308–317.

[90] Guilford, J. S. Temperament traits of executives and supervisors measured by the Guilford Personality Inventories. *J. appl. Psychol.*, 1952, *36*, 228–233.

Superior Supervisors See themselves as:		Inferior Supervisors See themselves as:
energetic	vs	ambitious
loyal	vs	dependable
kind	vs	jolly
planful	vs	resourceful
clear-thinking	vs	efficient
enterprising	vs	intelligent
progressive	vs	thrifty
poised	vs	ingenious
steady	vs	sociable
appreciative	vs	good-natured
responsible	vs	reliable
Do not see themselves as:		**Do not see themselves as:**
noisy	vs	arrogant
affected	vs	moody
shallow	vs	stingy
unstable	vs	frivolous
nervous	vs	intolerant
opinionated	vs	pessimistic
self-pitying	vs	hard-hearted

After E. E. Ghiselli, and R. P. Barthol, Role perceptions of successful and unsuccessful supervisors. *J. appl. Psychol.,* 1956, *40*, 241–244. Copyright 1956 by the American Psychological Association, and reproduced by permission.

Table 10.3 / Items Differentiating High- and Low-Rated Supervisors

visors. However, when ratings of success among the executives were studied, only four factors were related to success: sociability, lack of inferiority feelings, cooperativeness, and masculinity. Success among supervisors showed a somewhat similar trend, the significant factors for them being emotional stability, calmness and composure, and cooperativeness.

At present the ratings of supervisors depend on how they please their superiors and carry out their orders, as well as on the productivity of their groups. Some superintendents like to see their supervisors keep busy and so evaluate them more on how many disturbances they settle or suppress than on how many they prevent. The influence of the criterion used and the relationship obtained with a personality measure is illustrated in a study by Van Zelst.[91] He used as his personality measure the Empathy Test which measures the ability to put oneself in another's position. The test scores of 64 union leaders (business agents of five A.F. of L. building

[91] Van Zelst, R. H. Empathy test scores and union leaders. *J. appl. Psychol.,* 1952, 36, 293–295.

trades unions) correlated .38 with percentage of votes received; .55 with scores on a supervisory test; .64 with ability to settle disputes; and .44 with enforcement of rules and regulations. The combined measures yielded a correlation of .76 which suggests that the empathy test may have more value in selecting leaders than a personality inventory. However, which of the four measures is the best criterion of union leadership? At the present time, opinion plays a dominant role in the selection of a criterion of leadership.

Harrell[92] approached the problem of personal qualifications associated with success in executive positions by following up three classes receiving M.B.A. degrees from Stanford University. While on campus the students had been given a large variety of tests, including various personality scales. Earnings after five years was used as the criterion of success. Comparing the upper with the lower third in earnings, differences in 13 out of 55 comparisons were significant. Using data only from those employed in large companies, the high earners showed significant differences in personality and social interest when compared with low earners. The differences for the high earners were in the desirable (well adjusted) direction. Specific measures showed them to be higher in energy levels, to have greater self confidence, to be more socially bold, and to be more ready to make decisions.

Trends in Personality Testing

Of late, much attention has been given to the problem of selection of managerial personnel.[93] The use of projective techniques such as the Rorschach and Thematic Apperception Test, has become more widespread despite the fact that these techniques do not lend themselves to quantitative analysis. This trend has resulted in the development of semiobjective approaches to scoring[94] and in recognition of the need for additional validation studies.[95] Newer approaches such as Goldner's "method of attack" in problem solving[96] and Bion's Leaderless Group Discussion,[97] when used as an observation technique for persons applying for a given position,

[92] Harrell, T. W. The personality of high earning MBA's in big business. *Personnel Psychol.*, 1969, *22*, 457–463.

[93] Gellerman, S. W. Seven deadly sins of executive placement. *Mgmt. Rev.*, 1958, *47*, 4–9; Taylor, E. K. The unsolved riddle of executive success. *Personnel*, 1960, *37*, 8–17; Stark, S. Executive personality and psychological testing. *University of Illinois Bull.*, 1958, *55*, 15–32; Michael, W. B. Differential testing of high-level personnel. *Educ. Psychol. Measmt.*, 1957, *17*, 475–490.

[94] Nevis, E. C., Wallen, R. W., and Stickel, E. G. *The thematic evaluation of managerial potential.* Cleveland, Ohio: Personnel Research and Development Corp., 1959; Harrower, M. R., and Steiner, M. E. *Large-scale Rorschach techniques.* Springfield, Ill.: Charles C. Thomas, 1945; Piotrowski, Z. A., *et al.* Rorschach signs in the selection of outstanding young male mechanical workers. *J. Psychol.*, 1944, *18*, 131–150.

[95] Taylor, E. K., and Nevis, E. C. The use of projective techniques in management selection. *Personnel*, 1957, *33*, 463–474.

[96] Goldner, R. H. Individual differences in whole-part approach and flexibility-rigidity in problem solving. *Psychol. Monogr.*, 1957, *71* (21).

[97] Bion, W. R. The leaderless group project. *Bull. Menninger Clinic*, 1946, *10*, 77–81; Bass, B. M. The leaderless group discussion. *Psychol. Bull.*, 1954, *51*, 465–492.

may hold promise. If further findings are positive, such techniques, which cover a broad range of behavior, may provide bases for integrating personality measurement with that of other cogent ability areas. The continuing search for the bases of individual differences in personality is being carried on by some researchers in the areas of interests and personal choice.[98] Instruments soon should be developed which will take into account the way behavior is influenced by the situation in which the individual finds himself.

In general, personality tests may be helpful in selection and placement, but they frequently do not survive rigorous validation procedures. Despite the usefulness of current tests for clinical purposes, authorities seriously question their automatic inclusion in batteries for personnel purposes and suggest that well-developed biographic inventories may prove more useful for organizations at present.

The Measurement of Vocational Interest

Interests are largely a matter of personality and can readily be measured by means of interest questionnaires. Some men would rather work indoors than outdoors; some like to deal with people, others prefer working with machinery; some crave responsibility, others strive to avoid it. By matching interests and vocations, it is quite apparent that job satisfaction, at least, can be increased.

Two well-known questionnaires for measuring interests are the *Strong Vocational Interest Blank*[99] and the *Kuder Preference Record.*[100] As in other questionnaires, the respondents can fake the results if motivated to do so.[101] Interest tests are of value to industry not only because an employee who likes his work is a satisfied employee but also because people like to do the things they do well. Some experimental proof of this common-sense relationship is available. Grades of students in engineering courses correlated .66 with measures of interest in the physical sciences[102] and ability in seven fields of interest, as measured by the seven components of the Kuder test, showed an average correlation of .42.[103] Interest tests, like personality inventories, differentiate between successful and unsuccessful sales-

[98] Brayfield, A. H. Vocational counseling today. In E. G. Williamson (Ed.), *Vocational counseling—a reappraisal in honor of Donald G. Paterson.* Minneapolis: University of Minnesota Press, 1961; Dunkleberger, C. I., and Tyler, L. Interest stability and personality traits. *J. counsel. Psychol.*, 1961, 8, 70–84; Tyler, L. Research explorations in the realm of choice. *J. counsel. Psychol.*, 1961, 8, 195–201; Kuder, G. *The Kuder Preference Record—Personal, Form A.* Chicago: Science Research Associates, 1948.

[99] New York: Psychological Corporation.

[100] Chicago: Science Research Associates.

[101] Cross, O. H. A study of faking on the Kuder Preference Record. *Educ. Psychol. Measmt.*, 1950, 10, 271–277; Garry, R. Individual differences in ability to fake vocational interests. *J. appl. Psychol.*, 1953, 37, 33–37; Kuder, G. F. Identifying the faker. *Personnel Psychol.*, 1950, 3, 155–167; Abrahams, N. M., Newman, I., and Githens, W. H. Faking vocational interests: Simulated versus real life motivation. *Personnel Psychol.*, 1971, 24, 5–12.

[102] Laycock, S. R., and Hutcheon, N. B. A preliminary investigation into the problem of measuring engineering aptitude. *J. educ. Psychol.*, 1939, 25, 280–289.

[103] Wesley, S. M., Corey, D. Q., and Stewart, B. M. The intra-individual relationship between interest and ability. *J. appl. Psychol.*, 1950, 34, 193–197.

men.[104] An interest in people seems essential in supervisors,[105] but this interest also seems desirable for success in many other activities.[106]

The Strong Vocational Interest Blank and the Kuder Preference Record were originally designed to tap the interest patterns of professional and semiprofessional people. The Minnesota Vocational Interest Inventory developed in 1961 is designed to tap interest patterns of craftsmen and semiskilled workers. This instrument is of considerable value to industry since it deals directly with levels at which large numbers of workers are recruited.[107]

The Measurement of Physical and Sensory Capacities

Variations in Body Structure and Their Importance

Some occupations require rather special physical structures. For certain kinds of heavy work, such as pig-iron handling, a strong, stocky build is desirable. In other cases, as in jobs which require a great deal of walking or running, a wiry build is preferred. Small rather than large hands may be an advantage in fine assembly work. Although the relation of body build to occupational proficiency has not been explored to any great extent, employment managers react to such factors in their selection of applicants. The validity of their opinions, however, should be determined in order that the correct aspects of body structure may be considered in selection.

Body structures can easily be measured by a set of scales and a tape measure. Various proportions, such as the relation between weight and height, length of trunk and legs, length and width of hand, and total height and width of shoulders, should also be considered. The strength of various muscle groups can also be determined with simple measuring devices. Since strength varies for different parts of the body, strength of hands, arms, legs, and back must be differentiated. The relation of strength to body weight is also important, particularly in occupations involving much walking and climbing.

The Significance of Sensory Differences

The important sense in most jobs is vision. It is necessary, therefore, to determine not only a worker's visual capacity in general, but how well the vision is adapted to the job in particular. Thus, for close work persons who tend to focus their eyes relatively close produce significantly more than those who tend to focus farther away. The use of glasses to adapt the eyes to the special work resulted in increased production in hosiery loopers.

In one investigation of textile workers, nine out of 15 different visual tests were

---

[104] Bills, M. A. A tool for selection that has stood the test of time. In L. L. Thurston (Ed.), *Application of psychology*. New York: Harper, 1952; Webster, E. C., Winn, A., and Oliver, F. A. Selection tests for engineers: some preliminary findings. *Personnel Psychol.*, 1951, *4*, 339–362.

[105] Meyer, *op. cit.*

[106] West, E. D. The significance of interpersonal relations in job performance. *Occupations*, 1951, *29*, 438–440.

[107] Minneapolis: University of Minnesota Press.

found to be related to successful inspection of cones of rayon yarn.[108] It was found that 35.6 per cent of the inspectors failed three or more of these tests, and only 6.7 per cent of these were above average standard in job performance.

Many operations also require accurate judgments of distance. Distance perception (under 30 feet) is largely a matter of binocular vision and can be accurately measured. Many accidents in industry, caused by faulty vision, can be prevented. Hiring people who do not wear glasses does not protect the employer against workers with defective vision. Because people who wear glasses have at least had their vision tested, they may actually be a safer risk.

Since night and day vision depend upon different types of receptors in the eyes, people who are alike in day vision may be highly unlike in night vision. Work which requires vision under dim illumination must therefore take this fact into account. Bus and truck drivers who have accidents primarily at night may be defective in night vision.

Color vision varies greatly, particularly among males, and color-vision tests are necessary to detect deficiencies when jobs require color differentiation. Many partially and totally color-blind people are unaware of their defect.[109]

Visual acuity also varies with age, and many people fail to recognize the gradual reduction in ability to see at close range. Glasses can correct these changes, but the only way to be certain that employees are obtaining these corrections is to have periodic examinations made at the plant.

Other senses play vital roles in certain specialized jobs. Hearing perhaps is next to vision in importance, but deficiencies are more readily apparent.[110] In conversation one can make adjustments for hearing difficulties, but this can lead to inefficiency in an office situation. Even differences that occur within the normal range of hearing will determine whether or not a telephone operator must have a message repeated. Exceptional auditory sensitivity has been shown to be an asset to inspectors of electrical equipment. Some persons were able to hear defects in motors and compressors when the equipment was running, whereas most could not make the necessary distinctions.

The sense of smell is essential to food and wine tasters and to perfume testers, and success in these occupations undoubtedly depends on exceptional acuity. One study showed that a random sample of persons were unable to differentiate between cheeses made by different processes, but that connoisseurs could not be deceived by substitutes.[111] The sense of touch is important for lens grinders, and sense of balance is important to people who work aloft.

---

[108] Ayers, A. W. A comparison of certain visual factors with the efficiency of textile inspectors. *J. appl. Psychol.*, 1942, *26*, 812–827.

[109] Kuhn, H. S. Articles bearing on industrial eye problems. *Transac. Amer. Acad. Opthal. Otolar.*, 1946, *50*, 175–178; Tiffin, J., and Wirt, S. E. Near vs. distance visual acuity in relation to success on close industrial jobs. *Suppl. Transact. Amer. Acad. Opthal. Otolar.*, 1944, *48*, 9–16; Tiffin and McCormick, *op. cit.*, pp. 145–156.

[110] Licklider, J. C. R. Basic correlates of the auditory stimulus. In S. S. Stevens (Ed.), *Handbook of experimental psychology.* New York: Wiley, 1951, Ch. 24.

[111] Personal communication with Dr. L. K. Riggs, National Dairy Research Laboratories, Inc.

It is desirable for supervisors to observe and analyze the jobs they supervise to determine whether or not special sensory capacities may be an asset. Most jobs make no special demands, and a person who falls within the normal range or has the minimum requirement may be as effective as a person with a high degree of sensitivity. However, certain jobs will permit a person gifted in a specific capacity to perform easily a task that is difficult for the average person. A central office worker who had an unusual sense of touch was able to adjust electrical contacts without going through the usual trial-and-error adjustments made by other workers. Circus performers have an exceptional sense of balance and can perform acts which the average person could never learn.[112]

The Significance of Differences in Perception

Visual perception is dependent on the way the brain organizes the nervous impulses which come from the eyes. Whether or not one will see a particular part of a complex object is therefore a matter of perception as well as of visual acuity. Even more common differences in perception arise when a picture contains many objects. Which details will be seen depends on the way the elements are grouped, what the subject is looking for, and the like. Asking people to tell what they see in an inkblot brings out a great variety of reactions. Experiments on perception have shown that the eye may report a detail as perfectly as does a film, but the detail may fail to be experienced by the observer. Two observers of the same picture will describe widely different versions of its details. A person's ability to observe defects in inspection work, see the conditions leading up to an accident in time to prevent it, or detect the snapping of a thread in weaving depends upon his perception as well as upon his vision.

People differ greatly also in the rapidity with which they perceive. A brief exposure (flash) will permit some people to identify a complex object, whereas others do not have time even to recognize any part of it. Fast readers are usually rapid perceivers because they can recognize words by rapidly scanning. Slow perceivers are handicapped in situations in which only a momentary glance at an object is available. This is invariably the case when objects are in motion, and motion often is a factor in industrial work.

Another aspect of perception especially important in many industrial operations is the size of the visual field. For example, some automobile drivers see only the street, while others see the houses along the street as well. In tests in which the

---

[112] For detailed discussions of sensory functions, see the following: Brant, H. F. *The psychology of seeing.* New York: Philosophical Library, 1945; Luckiesh, M., and Moss, F. K. *The science of seeing.* Princeton, N.J.: Van Nostrand, 1937; Hirsh, I. J. *The measurement of hearing.* New York: McGraw-Hill, 1952; Stevens, S. S., and Davis, H. *Hearing: Its psychology and physiology.* New York: Wiley, 1938; Pfaffman, C. Taste and smell. In S. S. Stevens (Ed.), *Handbook of experimental psychology.* New York: Wiley, 1951, pp. 1143–1171; Jenkins, W. L. Somesthesis. *Ibid.,* pp. 1172–1190; Wendt, G. R. Vestibular functions. *Ibid.,* pp. 1191–1223; Geldflard, F. A. *The human senses.* New York: Wiley, 1953; Tufts College Institute for Applied Experimental Psychology. *Handbook of human engineering data for design engineers* (2nd ed.). Medford, Mass.: Tufts College, 1952; Rosenblith, W. A. (Ed.). *Sensory communication.* New York: Wiley, 1961; Brindley, G. S. *Physiology of the retina and the visual pathways.* London: Edward Arnold Co., 1960.

exposure to the visual object is too brief to permit eye movement, some people recognize detail far off to the side of their point of fixation, whereas others can see detail only at the point at which they are looking. Obviously, work which involves a large field of vision will be ill adapted to a person with a small perceptual field, even though his visual acuity may be highly adequate.

Perception is largely a matter of training, but many differences are inherent in people and cannot be eliminated by experience. To the extent that the differences are biological, industry must solve the problems by employee selection. Training will influence the kind of detail that will be recognized but it cannot correct basic differences in perceptual speed and in the size of the visual field. Persons trained in the Chinese language will see details in a Chinese character that others will miss because their familiarity with the characters makes them react to details which are necessary for reading. For the same reason, a man trained in a given job can be made responsive to the kind of defect he is set to perceive. Speed of perception can be improved by training only insofar as it teaches people to see groupings of objects rather than individual objects. Thus, a person can speed up his reading by learning to react to groups of words rather than to single words. Even after training, however, people differ widely in their manner of perceiving.

Many tests incorporate aspects of perception since organization of sensory data is involved in any type of response. The importance of qualitative differences in individuals tends to be neglected in the more specific tests. The projective tests, however, may owe much of their value to perception variables.

Laboratory Exercise

Discussion of the Criterion Problem

A. Obtaining a criterion of a successful professor.
1. Criterion is needed if tests are to be developed.
2. Problem is first to determine the activities making for success.

B. Procedure.
1. Divide the class into two groups of no more than 10 students each. (If more than 20 students are in class, duplicate groups should be formed.)
2. Each group should be asked to select a discussion leader and a recorder.
3. A group report should be prepared and should consist of a list of characteristics that represents the group's best effort at reaching agreement.
4. Instructions for groups:
   a. Group I should develop a list of characteristics which makes for success, and another list which contributes to failure.
      1. Discussion should be used to explore various suggestions.
      2. Agreement should be sought on five traits that make for success and five traits associated with failure.

    b. Group II should work individually at the outset.
1. List all of your past professors.
2. Rearrange them in the order of merit.
3. Cross out the middle third.
4. Choose no more than three traits that characterize the top group.
5. Choose no more than three traits that characterize the lower group.
6. The group leader will conduct discussion to determine five traits most common to top rated professors and those most common to low rated professors.

C. Reports to class as a whole.

1. The leader of Group I should report his group's conclusions on the nature of a criterion for a successful professor.
2. The recorder of Group I should report some of the difficulties encountered.
3. The leader of Group II should report his group's conclusions on the nature of their criterion.
4. The recorder of Group II should report the difficulties encountered.

D. Discussion problems for class as a whole.

1. Discuss the similarities and differences in the reports from the two groups.
2. Determine the extent to which the procedures used may have influenced the outcome.
3. To what extent does industry have the same problem of obtaining criteria? Can basic generalizations be made?
4. Discuss the degree to which the development of tests in industry may be handicapped by difficulties with obtaining criteria.
5. Discuss how a knowledge of the criteria would influence a professor's behavior. If a knowledge of such criteria causes persons to try and beat them, do they cease to be objective measures?

Suggested Readings

Anastasi, Anne. *Psychological testing* (2nd ed.). New York: Macmillan, 1961.

Brown, F. G. *Principles of educational and psychological testing.* Hinsdale, Ill.: Dryden, 1970.

Buros, O. K. (Ed.). *The seventh mental measurement yearbook.* Highland Park, N.J.: Gryphon, 1971.

Buros, O. K. (Ed.). *Personality tests and reviews.* Highland Park: N.J.: Gryphon, 1970.

Buros, O. K. (Ed.). *Tests in print.* Highland Park, N.J.: Gryphon, 1961.

Fiske, D. W. *Measuring the concepts of personality.* Chicago, Ill., Aldine, 1971.

Glaser, G. C. Projective methodologies. In P. R. Farnsworth, O. McNemar, and Q. McNemar (Eds.), *Annual review of psychology* (Vol. 14). Palo Alto, Calif.: Annual Reviews, Inc., 1963, pp. 391–423.

Horst, P. *Psychological measurement and prediction.* Belmont, Calif.: Wadsworth, 1966.

Jenkins, J. J., and Paterson, D. G. (Eds.). *Studies in individual differences.* New York: Appleton, 1961.

Lork, F. M. and Novick, M. R. *Statistical theories of mental test scores.* Reading, Mass.: Addison Wesley, 1968.

Nunnally, J. C. *Psychometric theory.* New York: McGraw-Hill, 1967.

Wood, Dorothy A. *Test construction: development and interpretation of achievement tests.* Columbus, Ohio: Charles E. Merrill, 1960.

11 The Design of Jobs and Man-Machine Systems

Introduction

The three preceding chapters dealt with the problem of analyzing jobs in terms of human abilities. By selection of individuals who possess the abilities most essential to a given job, productivity on that job is increased without driving the workers to expend more energy than before. A person unadapted to a job uses a good deal of energy for unproductive purposes and receives none of the satisfactions associated with proficiency.

In this chapter the problem of job analysis is approached from the other side. How can a job be altered so that it will better fit the nature of human abilities? People differ in the degree to which they possess abilities, but they also have a great deal in common. Certain kinds of activities are unnatural for the way a person is constructed. Any change in a task which makes it better fit the human organism should increase the productivity and job satisfaction of all humans. The problem, then, is to fit jobs to people rather than people to jobs. Therefore, we shall now discuss people, primarily from the point of view of the ways in which they are more alike than different.

This approach should produce an increase in production without increasing the human energy expended. In this way, the method differs from the "speed-up," which attempts to increase production by increasing the energy output. Failing to differentiate between these two procedures is to miss entirely the importance of the contribution proper design of jobs can make to modern industry.

Equally important, consideration of the workers in the design of jobs can reduce their frequent alienation from their work and even produce a renewed sense of satisfaction and pride in work. The potential gains for companies and society in the mental health of workers are great.

Early Approaches

The first systematic attempt to discover the principles for designing jobs to fit the abilities of individuals may be traced to the work of Frederick W. Taylor.[1] He believed that the application of his principles of management, which went beyond merely changing work patterns, would benefit management, workers, and society in general. However, the desire for immediate gains resulted in partial applications and misapplications of his principles. Resistance by workers and unions to "speed-up" methods produced frequent failure to achieve the benefits he visualized.

Taylor originally conceived of scientific management as the cooperative effort by management and workers to determine the one best way to do a job, to select workers capable of doing the job that way, and to provide incentive pay for those selected who would work in the prescribed manner. Management was to provide the proper tools and sufficient material to work effectively. Information was to be collected from the workers and also by means of careful experimentation. This total personnel approach to the design of work systems has only recently been revived, as we shall see, in the most advanced approaches to these problems.

Taylor described one of the earliest applications of his principles in the coal yards of the Bethlehem Steel Company as "developing the science of shoveling. You . . . give each workman each day a job to which he is well suited and provide him with just that implement which will enable him to do his biggest day's work."[2] He put to experimental test with "two or three first-class shovelers" the question of what the optimum shovel load would be to obtain maximum productivity without overworking the employee. After about four months of experimentation, one conclusion was that, regardless of material being shoveled, a 21-pound load was optimal. The company accepted this figure, provided the necessary number of the eight to ten different types of shovels required for different types of coal, improved their planning and measurement of the work by adding more staff, and selected the best workers on the basis of performance. The result, including the cost of new equipment and additional staff, was a reduction in the cost of handling a ton of coal "from between seven and eight cents to between three and four cents . . . $78,000 a year." The men received increased wages of approximately 60 per cent more than they had been earning.

Taylor's followers and copiers, however, chose to concentrate on only two aspects of this approach, the determination of the "one best way to do a job" and the use of incentive pay to ensure conformity to the prescribed method of working. Moreover, systematic experimentation to determine the best way of working was replaced by systematic observation, analysis, and intuition—intuition which was often creative, but frequently unpsychological.

Examples of this approach to job design abound in the brilliant work of Frank and Lillian Gilbreth, a husband-and-wife team, who together revolutionized the work of many occupations. Gilbreth had learned the trade of bricklaying, an occu-

[1] Taylor, F. W. *Principles of scientific management.* New York: Harper, 1947.
[2] *Ibid.,* p. 57.

pation which had been passed from one generation to the next with little alteration. While serving as contractor on a building project, he analyzed the job and found that 18 separate movements were made in laying each brick.[3] By organizing the work pattern, he was able to reduce the movements to five and increase a bricklayer's production from 120 to 350 bricks per hour.

His method, in this case, involved a careful study of the position of the workman's body in relation to the wall, as well as of the accessibility of the mortar and bricks to the work. He found that the mason was frequently required to work at different levels and that he had to stoop constantly to reach his materials, lowering and raising his 200-pound body to pick up each four-pound brick. As a result of these observations, scaffolding was designed which could easily be moved up in small stages as the wall grew in height. This scaffold held two tables, on which mortar and bricks were arranged. The tables were placed so that the materials were within easy reach of the bricklayer. These arrangements completely eliminated stooping, which is unproductive but energy-consuming. With a deep mortar box placed on one side and bricks on the other, the tradesman was trained to use both hands simultaneously in obtaining mortar and brick and then in bringing them together. An assistant was assigned the job of sorting and supplying the bricks and mortar. A part of the helper's job was also to arrange the bricks on a frame in neat piles and place them, with their best edges up, at the proper place on the scaffolding. The bricklayer thus was saved the time of disengaging each brick from its pile and examining it for the best edge before laying it. By making mortar of the right consistency, it was possible to embed the brick properly with a pressure of the hand and so eliminate tapping with the trowel. The entire pattern of activity was greatly altered and simplified by (1) elimination of unproductive and energy-consuming activity, (2) transfer of simple aspects of the work to the helper, and (3) use of labor-saving equipment to give the bricklayer a comfortable level at which to work.

This example illustrates the Gilbreths' principal contributions to the study of job design: elimination of waste movements, retention of the shortest movements, and simplification of work patterns, by assigning different functions to different people, consistent with their abilities. *Motion and time study* as it is practiced today owes its start principally to the general approach and specific methods developed by the Gilbreths. A survey of current American industrial practices indicates that the most important consideration used in dividing operations among workers is still minimization of the time required to perform the operation.[4]

The Scope of Motion and Time Study

Breaking Down Jobs

Some jobs require a combination of activities rarely found together in the makeup of most men. For example, positions that demanded both research and administrative

---

[3] Gilbreth, F. B. *Motion study*. Princeton, N.J.: Van Nostrand, 1911, p. 88–89.

[4] Davis, L. E., Canter, R. R., and Hoffman, J. Current job design criteria. *J. industr. Engng.*, 1955, *6*, 5–10.

abilities might be very hard to fill. But if the duties of such positions were divided, the resulting research and administrative positions might each be filled by specialists. Similarly, the breaking-down of complex mechanical jobs in a factory permits the utilization of more specialized abilities. In this way a larger proportion of the potential work force is eligible to perform each of the simpler jobs adequately and thus becomes somewhat interchangeable. This breakdown of jobs into smaller and specific units, so that each worker performs a few simple and routine operations, is one characteristic of modern production methods developed from motion-and-time analysis. (It should be noted here that the advantages gained from "deskilling jobs" frequently are offset by their unfavorable effects on the motivation of the workers themselves.)

Finding The Best Way

Another function of motion and time study has been to determine the most efficient way to execute a given operation and to induce people to work that way. Persons left to their own devices are not likely to perform a manual operation in the most effective manner, no matter how much they practice. Once having learned one system, they would resist changing to the superior method. The way a person performs a task has a great effect on the final efficiency attained, and this final efficiency may be quite independent of actual manipulative ability.[5]

Analysis of an inspection job revealed that most workers tended to put their attention on the wrong aspect of an operation.[6] In visually examining tin plates for defects, the natural tendency for inspectors was to watch what they were doing; as a result, they watched the plate they were handling, which was, of course, in motion. This misplaced attention interfered with proper inspection, because it was difficult to see defects while the plate was moving. Altering the operation so that the plate inspected was not in motion greatly improved the inspector's efficiency.

Tool Arrangement

Motion and time analysts have also examined the arrangement of workplaces to eliminate waste effort in finding tools and handling materials. By rearranging the work space and having a convenient place for every tool used, the job was often greatly simplified. Each tool was given a special place within easy reach, the most frequently used tools being most conveniently located, and the heaviest ones closest to the operator.

Proper tool arrangement enables the worker to develop automatic habits, because the same movement is always made to obtain a particular tool. The mere need of a tool calls up the special movement; without thinking, the worker makes the proper reach. Considerable time is saved by eliminating the time wasted in searching for misplaced tools.

[5] Seashore, R. H. Work methods: an often neglected factor underlying individual differences. *Psychol. Rev.,* 1939, *46,* 123–141.
[6] Tiffin, J., and Rogers, H. B. The selection and training of inspectors. *Personnel,* 1941, *18,* 14–31.

Time and effort spent in reaching for tools is also decreased if all operations with a given tool are carried out before the next tool is used. For example, if a large number of bolts are to be used to fasten two pieces of metal together, the naïve procedure is to drill each hole and secure each bolt separately, thus completing all operations with one bolt before going on to the next. The more efficient method would be to mark all drill holes; then drill all the holes; next put in the bolts and fasten the nuts by hand; and, finally, tighten all the nuts with a tool. Reducing the number of times tools are changed is one of the simplest and commonest methods of eliminating waste motions.

Designing Tools, Chutes, and Conveyors

A fourth area for potential improvement in productivity and efficiency is proper design of tools for each job. Following Taylor's illustration of the benefits gained from the proper shovels for coal handling, many ingenious improvements have been introduced to relieve the worker of unnecessary activities. Drills suspended from springs within easy reach, special wrenches and screwdrivers, and all manner of other gadgets and conveniences suggest themselves when the job is analyzed. In addition to special tools and ways for mechanizing them, knee and foot pedals have been introduced, for example, to operate vises and other mechanisms requiring strength but not fine control. Chutes and conveyor belts are used to replace carrying, transporting, and delivering movements.[7]

Fatigue Reduction

Other factors often contributing to excessive energy expenditure and inefficiency involve uncomfortable workplaces and inconvenient work positions. The untrained supervisor is inclined to confuse comfort with loafing. However, if jobs are designed to permit sitting, the energy saved can be used for productive purposes.[8] In addition, an unnecessary source of irritation for the worker is removed.[9] Similarly, methods analysts have improved productivity by placing work benches at heights appropriate for the amount of lifting required.[10] Recent anthropometric studies of workers' physical measurements have provided information for equipment designers to plan work spaces which will fit comfortably most of the people likely to fill the jobs.[11]

Plant Layout and Environment

Finally, attention is also given to the design of offices and plants to reduce movement. Operations related to one another should be physically related.[12] Lighting,

[7] Barnes, R. M. *Motion and time study* (5th ed.). New York: Wiley, 1963.

[8] Gilbreth, F. B., and Gilbreth, L. M. *Fatigue study*. New York: Macmillan, 1919, pp. 104–108.

[9] Koskela, A. Ergonomics applied to office work. *Ergonomics*, 1962, *5*, 263–264.

[10] Bedale, E. M., and Vernon, H. M. *The effect of posture and rest in muscular work*. Industr. Fat. Res. Bd., 1924, Rep. No. 29.

[11] Dempster, W. T., Gabel, W. C., and Felts, W. J. L. The anthropometry of the manual work space for the seated subject. *Amer. J. Physical Anthrop.*, 1959, *17*, 289–317; Hertzberg, H. T. E. Dynamic anthropometry of working positions. *Hum. Factors*, 1960, *2*, 147–155; Thomson, R. M., Covner, B. J., Jacobs, H. H., and Orlansky, J. *Arrangement of groups of men and machines*. Washington, D.C.: Office of Naval Research, Dec., 1958, ONR Rep. ACR–33.

[12] Barnes, R. M. *Work methods manual* (5th ed.) New York: Wiley, 1963.

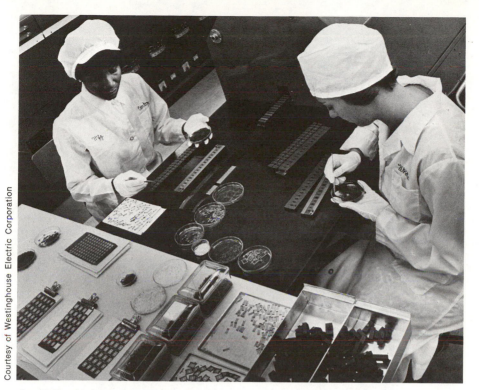

Carefully designed worktables are important, as are well-designed chairs. Both prevent fatigue and enable the worker to perform more naturally and efficiently.

noise, ventilation, plans to avoid congestion during shift changes, and facilities for eating, rest pauses, and medical care are also properly considered. Concern by time-and-motion analysts for the personal implications of plant design is limited presently to ensuring the availability of physical comforts (rest rooms and water fountains), but the impact on social groupings and labor relations is ignored.[13] Nevertheless, architects interested in factory design are beginning to study industrial sociology and group behavior as well as production needs.

General Principles of Motion Economy

Reliance on the ingenuity of motion analysts in developing the principles of motion economy has resulted in a variety of such "principles." Despite differences in specifics analysts tend to agree on the basic ideas. The Gilbreths were the first to develop a set of principles and described 16 of them.[14] Lowry and his associates considered

---

[13] See Reed, R., Jr. *Plant layout: Factors, principles and techniques.* Homewood, Ill.: Richard D. Irwin, 1961.

[14] Gilbreth, F. B., and Gilbreth, L. M. A fourth dimension for measuring skill for obtaining the one best way. *Soc. for industr. Eng. Bull.*, 1932, No. 11.

some laws more basic than others and describe five laws and eight corollaries.[15] Barnes grouped 22 principles under several general headings which refer to work situations or functions, such as arrangement of work space, design of tools, and relation of motion to body.[16] Interestingly, the few principles on which most analysts now agree are those which treat the person most like a biological and psychological being and least like a machine.

Some examples and illustrations of principles concerned with workers' movements are discussed in the following pages. They are stated broadly, so that specific applications must be made for each job.

Symmetrical Movements

The right and left halves of a person's body are mirror images of each other. This means that movements of the two hands or arms are most simple when they are symmetrical. Thus, a movement to the right with the right hand and a movement to the left with the left hand are very naturally made simultaneously. At the same time, a pair of such movements does not disturb balance, whereas movement of either one alone does.

For example, a supply of bolts on the left and a supply of nuts on the right will make their assembly a symmetrical pattern. Other illustrations include: turning one knob counterclockwise with the left hand while turning another clockwise with the right; throwing a switch to the left with the thumb of the left hand while throwing another to the right with the thumb of the right hand; and using corresponding fingers of the two hands at the same time.

The notion of symmetrical movements can be extended to include the use of both hands and feet. If jobs are expertly designed, feet or knees can perform duties that neither cause fatigue nor interfere with hand movements. In this way, use of the feet and knees becomes a pure gain, since they can do heavier work than the hands. In fact, it is easier to flex all muscles together (legs pulled up, arms in, hands clenched, body curved) than to extend one limb and flex others. Furthermore, the hand grip is stronger when other muscles are allowed to work at the same time than if the others must be relaxed.

Accessible Work Space

Because of his bodily structure a person seated at a table can describe half-circles on the table top with a piece of chalk. The semicircles drawn from the right and left arms will overlap and the two half-circles will be small (radius 12 to 14 inches) or large (radius 24 to 26 inches) depending on whether the forearm or the full arm has been used. The spaces enclosed by the lines are the work areas available to a person without disturbing his posture. The spaces in the larger half-circles involve use of the full arm and consequently work that requires access to this greater area is more fatiguing than that confined to the smaller half-circles. The overlapping

[15] Lowry, S. M., Maynard, H. B., and Stegmerten, G. J. *Time and motion study formulas for wage incentives* (3rd ed.). New York: McGraw-Hill, 1940.

[16] Barnes, *Motion and time study, op. cit.*

areas constitute the work space available to both hands and consequently delimit the space in which the hands can work conveniently together, as required in assembly work.

Let us take a simple example and see how this layout may be applied to a job. Suppose one wishes to assemble a set of 18 different cards, arranged in sequence *A* through *R*. The printer delivers them in packages of like cards. The cards as delivered from the printer can be arranged in bins as shown in Figure 11.1. If a card box is placed in a depression in the two-hand area, the cards can be slid over the table surface into the box. The hand operations would then follow the sequence: left hand obtains Card *A* while right hand obtains Card *B*, Card *A* being slid into box just ahead of Card *B*; left and right hands perform same function for Cards *C* and *D*, *E* and *F*, *G* and *H*, and so on until the full set is assembled. If strings protrude from the sides of the box, the strings can be tied with the two hands and the assembled set lifted out and dropped into a chute.

This illustration also incorporates two other principles—it utilizes symmetrical movements and eliminates the manipulative act (p. 278) of picking up the cards. Job applications of the motion principles often represent ingenious integration of a number of basic principles.

Integration of Movements

Rhythm is important to patterning and combining movements into the behavior sequences. If jobs can be arranged to set up a natural rhythm, they are easier. However, some groupings or sequences of movements are easier than others, so that merely combining the movements with the smallest elemental times may not produce the shortest cycle operation. For example, two stroke movements of two different fingers require more time when made by fingers of one hand than when made

Figure 11.1 / Typical Bench Layout for Assembly Work. A deck of 18 cards can readily be assembled in the proper order by means of the arrangement shown above. The right and left hands simultaneously reach for cards in corresponding positions (Pairs AB, CD, EF, etc.) and slide them across the table into the box placed in a depression in the two-handed area. (Modified from J. Munro Fraser, *Psychology: general, industrial, social.* Sir Isaac Pitman and Sons, Ltd., London, 1951, p. 185.)

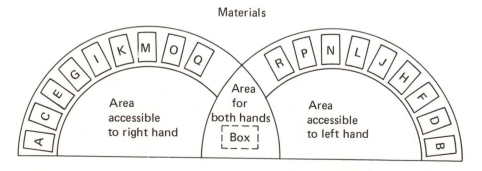

Materials

by fingers of two hands. Manufacturers of typewriters fail to utilize this fact fully. Considering the frequencies and sequences of letters in the words used in the English language, the present keyboard does not permit the maximum number of strokes that require the alternate use of the hands.[17]

Sequences in which completion of one movement leads naturally to the beginning of the next are also conducive to rhythmic performance. In analyzing the movements of a violin bow it was found that the attack on an accented note was better if an up-beat movement preceded it.[18] An up-bow movement permitted the performer to "hook" into the down stroke and thereby attain a greater initial acceleration (shown by photographing the motion).

Distribution of Work

The amount of energy and movement required of the various limbs should be distributed according to their inherent capacities. Leg muscles are strong and should be used to operate heavy loads. For most people one arm is stronger and more skillful than the other; therefore the strong limb should do the greater share of the job. This would mean that jobs or machines would differ for right- and left-handed persons. Further, fingers vary in dexterity and strength; demands made upon them should be adapted to their capacities.

When the present typewriter keyboard is examined in these terms, it is found that (1) the right hand does only 43 per cent of the work, (2) the first finger of the right hand does too much and the second finger too little, (3) the second finger of the left hand does too much work, and (4) the little fingers are expected to operate the loads controlled by the shift lock, shift key, and back spacer.[19] Keyboards designed to correct these deficiencies have been built, but the problems created by making the change have been too great to permit their adoption. Electrically powered typewriters, with the less perfect keyboard but with light loads, have largely replaced the standard machines.

Circular Movements

Another factor in efficient motion design is the replacement of straight-line movements with circular ones. A circular movement of the hand between the two points is made more easily than a back-and-forth movement between the points, particularly if this movement must be made at high speed. Suppose, for example, that three coins are flipped from the back of the hand and then caught one after the other by three successive downward sweeps of the same hand. The downward sweeps may be part of a spiral movement, or they may be three separate downward thrusts. The former pattern can be executed easily at high speed, since it has a continuous course

---

[17] Lahy, J. M. French psychologists improve typewriting. *Industr. Psychol.*, 1926, *1*, 333–337.

[18] Lemke, L. Improvement in playing the violin through instruction in phrasing. Doctoral dissertation, University of Michigan, 1945.

[19] Hoke, R. E. *The improvement of speed and accuracy in typewriting.* Baltimore: Johns Hopkins Press, 1922; Conrad, R., and Longman, D. J. A standard typewriter versus chord keyboard—an experimental comparison. *Ergonomics,* 1965, *8*, 77–88.

and requires no sudden stops at the low and high points. Starting and stopping movements waste energy. Well-executed acts of skill never involve jerky movements. Even the rapid up-and-down bow movements required in playing the violin are executed by circular arm and wrist movements.

Jobs should be laid out and machines designed so that limb movements can follow a curved course. Starting and stopping and zigzag movements should be replaced whenever possible. When this is accomplished certain other benefits are achieved. The momentum of one movement can flow into another, thereby removing the effort required to stop the first movement and start another. By effectively utilizing curved movements, inertia becomes an asset rather than a waster of energy.

Sometimes it is difficult or impossible to utilize the principles of motion to the degree desired. In such cases, alternate ways to improve methods should be consid-

Figure 11.2 / Bolt and Washer Assembly. Two assemblies are performed at the same time. Washers are moved across the table into recessed slots, and bolts are placed through washers. Lock washers (placed in the slot first) hold the other washers in place; the two complete assemblies are then lifted from their slots and dropped into chutes (shown to the right and left of the slots). The arms then continue their motion to the outside bins containing lock washers, and the next pair of assemblies is begun. (Redrawn from R. M. Barnes. *Motion and time study* [3rd edition]. New York: Wiley, p. 232. By permission of the author and publisher.)

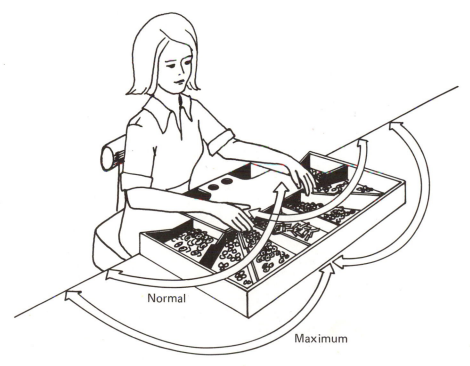

Normal

Maximum

ered. For example, when jerky or zigzag movements cannot be replaced by curved movements, it is sometimes desirable to slow down an operation in order to escape the tiring effects of inertia. In other instances, conveyors and chutes can replace straight-line movements for moving an object from one point to another.

Elimination of Manipulative Movements

Picking up and handling objects requires a certain amount of precision, and jobs should be so designed that these requirements are simplified or reduced. Gross movements are the more primitive, and the progress of human maturation and development is one of achieving greater differentiation of muscle control, until highly detailed and specific movements can be made.[20]

If fine and detailed movements represent a higher stage of development than gross movements, it follows that they are the more complex. Therefore reducing the number of required fine movements produces some of the greatest savings in work methods. From the discussion of the assembly of decks of cards (p. 275) it will be recalled that the cards were transported by being slid across the table rather than by being picked up. Smooth table surfaces therefore can be used to eliminate grasping and handling movements. Recesses cut into work space permit the assembling of sequences without handling.

When handling movements cannot be replaced by more primitive movements, attempts should be made to make the part, tool, or control lever easy to grasp and hold. This leads to research in the design of handles, knobs, and wheels (see p. 290).

Trends in Motion and Time Study

Synthetic Elemental Times

While direct observation and analysis of jobs is still the predominant method in use by time-study analysts, two trends are apparent in the innovations in this field. The more important is the development of "synthetic" times for elemental movements. By timing the same element in a large variety of jobs or in controlled laboratory situations, a standard time is established for that element, which may then be applied to the development of time standards for new jobs in which that element appears. For example, the Methods-Time Measurement Association has set .00002 hours as the time it takes to reach three-quarters of an inch or less to pick up and grasp an object by itself.[21]

In using predetermined elemental times, the analyst describes a new job in terms of its basic elements, such as *therbligs* (Gilbreth spelled backward), then assigns

[20] Coghill, G. E. *Anatomy and the problem of behavior.* London: Cambridge University Press, 1929; Pratt, K. C., Nelson, A. K., and Sun, K. H. The behavior of the new-born infant. *Ohio State Univ. Stud. Psychol.,* 1930 (10); Halverson, H. M. An experimental study of prehension in infants by means of systematic cinema records. *Genet. Psychol. Monogr.,* 1931, *10,* 107–286.

[21] Maynard, H. B., Stegmerten, G. J., and Schwab, J. L. *Methods-time measurement.* New York: McGraw-Hill, 1948.

the appropriate times to each. The sum of the assigned times, as in the older forms of time study, becomes the standard time for the operation.

This method has the obvious advantage that once the analyst has determined the best method of doing a job, a proper standard time can be established for the job immediately. He does not have to wait until men are trained in the method and have acquired the necessary skill to maintain a steady flow of production. Since the times are already "leveled," the analyst is freed from having to judge the workers' performance.

A similarly derived system of detailed synthetic time standards is the Work-Factor System. Four basic variables are assumed to affect the performance of a given motion: the body member (arm, leg, etc.) which does the act, the distance moved, the weight or resistance involved in the motion, and the manual control required by the motion's function.[22] Tables of standard times for movements of seven different body members, under four different conditions of manual control, over a variety of distances, and with differently weighted objects are provided in Work-Factor Units (equal to .00001 minute). These data are then applied to the design of jobs and to the timing of standard jobs.

A somewhat different, but in total very similar, approach is that of Basic Motion Study. The authors of this system identify as basic motions any movement of a body member which starts and stops.[23] They identify four classes of such motions with subcategories within each. Each subcategory is influenced by such variable factors as distance, visual control needed, precision required, and force exercised. Standard times for these movements have been developd in laboratory studies and applied to job situations.

All these systems of predetermined times make the same questionable assumption: a total job is the sum of its elemental movements. Their authors claim, however, that their systems are more precise, therefore less liable to error, because they define smaller elements in more specified contexts of the job requirements.

Work Simplification

A second trend is an attempt to overcome the resistance frequently expressed by workers to the application of time-and-motion study to their jobs. The basic assumption in this approach, usually called *work simplification,* is that if workers participate in improving their working methods and in setting standards, they will accept the changes more readily.[24] The usual procedure in work simplification is to have time-study experts train workers and foremen in the principles and methods of motion economy and then to encourage them to apply the methods to improve their jobs. The motivational advantage of having workers make decisions about the way

[22] Quick, J. H., Duncan, J. H., and Malcolm, J. A., Jr. *Work-factor time standards.* New York: McGraw-Hill, 1962.

[23] Bailey, G. B., and Presgrave, R. *Basic motion timestudy.* New York: McGraw-Hill, 1958.

[24] Lehrer, R. N. *Work simplification.* Englewood Cliffs, N.J.: Prentice-Hall, 1957; Mogensen, A. H. *Common sense applied to motion and time studies.* New York: McGraw-Hill, 1932.

they do their work is clearly consistent with the assumptions of group decision for gaining acceptance, outlined in Chapter 6. This fact may account for the fairly wide-spread adoption of work simplification procedures in American industry and its many successes reported. A survey of companies using work simplification programs indicated annual savings of from $200 to over $1000 per employee trained, and ratios of savings to training costs of 5 to 1 or more.[25]

It is not clear, however, whether the successes are due to application of the principles of motion economy or to the motivation and ingenuity workers apply when given a chance to decide how they should do their work, and management goes along with their recommendations. In any case, the involvement of workers in improving their work methods seems desirable.

Limitations of Motion and Time Study

Despite the seeming success of motion-and-time methods in thousands of industrial situations, the critics are numerous. The criticisms take many forms, including doubt about the precision of the measurements themselves, questions about the validity of the assumptions underlying them, and the listing of instances in which application of the methods created new organizational problems, often of greater magnitude than those it was employed to solve.

Criticisms of the Methodology

Once a job motion has been established, the time required by the average worker has to be known so that proper pay rates are set. Determination of time standards relies on measurements made, often to the hundredths of a second. Even among successive ratings of experienced raters, however, discrepancies of the order of 15 per cent have been found from one rating to the next. Even worse, these raters disagreed with one another's simultaneous ratings of the same workers by an average of 20 per cent.[26] The magnitude of these discrepancies under highly controlled conditions are about the same as those reported by Gomberg in comparisons of the results of company-appointed and union-appointed time-study men.[27]

An additional source of error is introduced into time-study measurements by the fact that people work at different rates of speed. To compensate for such differences in setting a standard for "normal" production, the analyst applies a "leveling" or "rating" factor to the times recorded.[28] The leveling factor reflects the analyst's judgment that the worker timed was working "15 per cent faster than normal" or

[25] Lehrer, *op. cit.*

[26] Nadler, G. An analysis of the differences in the study from films of operations and the actual operator. *Report of the 3rd Annual Motion and Time Study Work Session,* Purdue University, May, 1946; Mundel, M. E., and Margolin, L. *Report of the 4th Annual Motion and Time Study Work Session.* Purdue University 1948.

[27] Gomberg, W. *A trade union analysis of time study.* Chicago: Science Research Associates, 1948.

[28] Barnes, R. M. *Motion and time study, op. cit.*

"20 per cent slower than normal," or the like. By applying the leveling factor to the observations—reducing the time taken by slow workers or increasing the time of fast workers—he produces a "normal time," the time it should take "a qualified, thoroughly experienced operator" working at "a pace that is neither fast nor slow" to complete a work cycle.[29]

Careful research has confirmed the logical assumption that the subjective leveling factor is an added source of error in time-study measurements. Ghiselli and Brown[30] reported a study in which time measurements before leveling revealed that "the most rapid worker was 67 per cent faster than the slowest worker." Even after the leveling factor was applied, however, the standard time set on the fastest worker was 53 per cent higher than that set on the time of the slowest worker. If the leveling factor were completely accurate, the two standard times should have been identical. Lifson,[31] in another study, found that experienced time-study analysts rating the same group of workers (1) varied by as much as 30 per cent on the average, (2) set different rates for the same workers, and (3) overrated slow workers and underrated faster ones. The last explains why workers usually want standards for incentive pay set on the slowest worker.

While the amount of error in time measurements uncovered by these studies is not large in absolute terms, it assumes considerable importance from the way time standards are applied. Often wage rates for different jobs are established on the basis of time studies. If the workers' perceptions of the relative difficulty of two jobs differ from the time-study results, much resentment and resistance to the introduction of standards can be expected.

Criticisms of Motion and Time–Study Assumptions

The assumption that behavior can be analyzed by breaking it down into basic elements is known as the atomistic approach to psychology and has been challenged strongly by the *Gestalt* (configurational) approach, which contends that the whole act cannot be understood by an analysis of its parts. The function of any behavioral element is influenced by its relationship to other elements in the total behavioral pattern.

A series of laboratory studies by K. U. Smith[32] using the Universal Motion Analyzer has shown that elemental times vary according to their position in a sequence. The time it takes a worker's hand to move from one point to another will be different if he first pushes a button than if he first turns a knob. While the refined categories of synthetic time systems recognize this fact in part, they do not take account of the total pattern of behavior into which the elements are formed by the worker.

[29] Niebel, B. W. *Motion and time study*. Homewood, Ill.: Richard D. Irwin, 1958, p. 265.

[30] Ghiselli, E., and Brown, C. *Personnel and industrial psychology* (2nd ed.). New York: McGraw-Hill, 1955, p. 73.

[31] Lifson, K. A. Errors in time-study judgments of industrial work pace. *Psychol. Monogr.*, 1953, 67, No. 5.

[32] Smaders, R., and Smith, K. U. Dimensional analysis of motion: VI. The component movements of assembly motions. *J. appl. Psychol.*, 1953, 37, 308–314.

A recent carefully controlled series of experiments by two German investigators showed that workers' actual performance on certain jobs deviated sharply from standards set on the basis of predetermined elemental times.[33] Their studies confirm the *Gestalt* position that analysis of jobs by fragmentation cannot lead to correct reconstruction of the total performance pattern any more than the study of all the pieces of a building can give one the knowledge necessary to construct the building.

Other studies have provided experimental evidence which casts doubt on certain additional motion-and-time assumptions about workers' behavior. One experiment demonstrated that travel time was approximately the same over a considerable range of distances.[34] It appears that the hand accelerates more rapidly in moving a long distance than in moving a short one. However, the amount of travel time over a fixed distance varied considerably, depending on the type of manipulation which preceded or followed the movement.[35] The context within which the behavior occurs influences the time it takes.

In another study, complexity was shown to have little effect on the workers' performance.[36] Where complex tasks can be organized into manageable patterns, complexity is no barrier to good performance.

Loss of Motivation and Job Interest

Another factor often overlooked by motion analysis is the type of motivation produced in the worker when jobs are fractionated in the name of efficiency. Several writers have contended that when jobs are oversimplified, workers become bored and feel alienated from their work.[37] There is a danger that the emphasis on simplicity in designing jobs can produce boredom, with its costs in accident, wasted materials, poor quality work, absenteeism, and turnover. (The effects of boredom will be discussed in Chapter 16.)

One Best Way Open to Question

A final important criticism of the basic assumptions of motion-and-time study concerns the "one best way" of doing a job. The assumption that a job can be done effectively in only one way ignores individual differences. Because people differ in their aptitudes, it is reasonable to assume that they may work better using efficient but different methods. We need only to look at sports champions to realize that each

[33] Schmidtke, H., and Stier, F. An experimental evaluation of the validity of predetermined elemental time systems. *J. industr. Engng.*, 1961, *12*, 182–204.

[34] Chapanis, A., Garner, W., and Morgan, C. T. *Applied experimental psychology.* New York: Wiley, 1949.

[35] Wehrkamp, R., and Smith, K. U. Dimensional analysis of motion: II. Travel-distance effects. *J. appl. Psychol.*, 1952, *36*, 201–206.

[36] Rubin, G., von Trebra, P., and Smith, K. U. Dimensional analysis of motion: Ill. Complexity of movement pattern. *J. appl. Psychol.*, 1952, *36*, 272–276.

[37] Blum, F. H. *Toward a democratic work process.* New York: Harper, 1953; Morse, N. C. *Satisfaction in the white collar job.* Ann Arbor, Mich.: Institute for Social Research, University of Michigan, 1953; Walker, C. R., and Guest, R. H. *The man on the assembly line.* Cambridge, Mass.: Harvard University Press, 1952.

reached the top by adopting a style of play which fit his particular abilities. In an industrial study, it was found that the fastest workers in a sheet metal factory actually did the job differently than the average workers. The average workers could not be taught the method used by the superior workers because they did not have the necessary minimum aptitudes required.

Training unskilled workers to use a single method in their work has the advantage of bringing everyone to a moderate level of performance. But insisting that superior workers use the same method deprives a company of the high productivity of the outstandingly able workers whose rare pattern of abilities may be better suited to a different method. The simpler the job, the more likely there is to be a "one best way" to do it, which fits the similarities among men. The more complex the job, the more individual differences in patterns of abilities will permit several successful work methods. In some instances the best method may be one suited only to a limited number of persons. In any case, the concept of the best method must be considered in terms of "best for whom."

The Problem of Acceptance

Any change or improvement in work arrangements may be resisted by employees not only because it is new, but also because it is frequently a threat to their security. The mere fact that management favors a new method arouses distrust and fear, and the intensity of these emotions is related to the degree to which workers distrust management. Distrust and resistance are increased whenever management attempts to impose changes without gaining the workers' acceptance.[38] The need for skills in conducting discussions of problems involving changes in the work situation will become apparent in the exercise given at the end of this chapter. A detailed analysis of the forces operating in resistance to change appears in Chapter 13.

Organizational Problems Arising from Time-Study Applications

The application of time standards in industrial firms has been criticized for ignoring their effects on the relations among work groups. Whyte[39] documents numerous instances in which payments to workers based on time-study standards disrupted relations between work groups and created considerable labor-management strife. Jaques has made the point that workers have a fairly clear idea about what constitutes a fair pay rate for different jobs.[40] If wage rates assigned to such jobs on the basis of time standards conflict with accepted rates, antagonism and resistance can be expected. Workers evaluate the adequacy of their wages in comparison to the pay received by other workers with similar qualifications.[41] If the rates set by time standards run counter to the social system of the factory, they can produce more long-term problems than they are worth in immediate production.

While motion-and-time study has proved beneficial in increasing job performance

[38] Gotterer, M. G. Union reactions to unilateral changes in work measurement procedures. *Personnel Psychol.*, 1961, *14,* 433–450.
[39] Whyte, W. F. *Money and motivation.* New York: Harper, 1955.
[40] Jaques, E. *Equitable payment.* New York: Wiley, 1961.
[41] Patchen, M. *The choice of wage comparisons.* Englewood Cliffs, N.J.: Prentice-Hall, 1961.

and in establishing performance standards, it obviously cannot be applied uncritically. Establishing acceptable wage rates for different jobs seems to be the most controversial issue.

Modern Approaches to the Design of Jobs

A Biopsychological Approach

What has been needed for years and neglected both by psychologists and engineers is a coherent theory of human skilled performance based on biological and psychological considerations. In very simplified form, Smith[42] contends that workers organize their motions in terms of the space they see around them. This space is organized geometrically with respect to the vertical and horizontal axes of the body, corresponding, respectively, to the line of postural erectness and to the right-left symmetry of the body.

The basic and most primitive movements are postural, keeping the body erect in response to variations in gravitational stimulation. These are the first types of movements an infant learns. Travel motions—movements of body members—are organized, on the other hand, "mainly according to the bilateral symmetry of the body, with right and left members working together or in opposition." However, these movements must be integrated within the postural base. For example, when a tool or object is placed beyond a worker's normal reach, he wastes energy restoring himself to an erect position, since he cannot perform his job while off balance. Less obvious, however, is the conclusion that his arm movements are probably better controlled in the horizontal plane than in the vertical, so that tools and materials should be placed around the perimeter of his normal working area rather than suspended above him.

Manipulative motions ("fine manipulation of the terminal members of the body or the receptor systems of the head") form the third class of movements identified. These actions are learned, not as a series of discrete and unrelated events, but as an integrated pattern of perceptual-motor actions occurring within specific space-time relationships.

The importance of the space-time control of a worker's skilled performance is often overlooked in the design of equipment. For example, with the demands placed on pilots of jet and space craft, mechanical and electronic assistance was thought to be helpful in control of the craft. Much to everyone's surprise, however, laboratory experiments revealed that people are less effective in tracking targets when their actions are given an electronic boost than when they tracked unaided.[43] The explanation for this poorer performance with electronic aid lies in the delayed effect of what the tracker did, which breaks down the fine perceptual-motor integration required for the job.

[42] Smith, K. U., and Smith, W. M. *Perception and motion.* Philadelphia: Saunders, 1962.
[43] Cherinkoff, R., Birmingham, H. P., and Taylor, F. V. A comparison of pursuit and compensatory tracking under conditions of aiding and no aiding. *J. exp. Psychol.,* 1955, *49,* 55–59; Lincoln, R. S., and Smith, K. U. Systematic analysis of factors determining accuracy in visual tracking. *Science,* 1952, *116,* 183–187.

All the principles of motion economy stated earlier are consistent with Smith's principles as outlined here. Many "principles" still listed in motion-and-time–study books, as well as the basic assumptions criticized earlier, are consistent neither with the theory nor with experimental evidence. The most important contribution Smith's theory makes to job design is to provide a framework consistent with psychological evidence.

The Changing Nature of Work

With the development of complex equipment, engineering technology, and the utilization of computers, programmed cycles are taking over much of the work formerly performed by human beings and changing the kind of work that is allocated to employees.[44] One type of decision that had to be made was the allotment of functions according to the superiority of either *man* or *machine*. Table 11.1 shows some of the ways in which the human being excels and some in which the machine excels. The superiority of computers for handling data has even encouraged researchers in this field to investigate mathematical models for decision making and solving problems such as discovering a principle underlying orderly events so that future events can be predicted.[45] Some believe that machines can be made to do creative thinking. However, human beings are still needed to operate machines and

Table 11.1 / Comparison of Functions of Man and Machines

Advantages of Man over Machine	Advantages of Machine over Man
1. Able to handle unexpected events whereas machines cannot adapt to unanticipated contingencies.	1. Information that can be stored is very large whereas man's capacity is relatively limited in the information it can handle in a unit of time.
2. Can organize bits of information into meaningful wholes (perception) whereas machines cannot perceive	2. Little or no decrement in function over long periods of time, whereas man is subject to muscular fatigue, lapses in attention and sensory decrement.
3. Can accomplish similar results by alternative means whereas machine may fail because of injury to part of it.	3. Are excellent and rapid computers whereas man is slow and subject to errors.
4. Can change programs easily whereas a programmed machine is relatively inflexible.	

Based on A. Chapanis, On the allocation of functions between man and machines. *Occup. Psychol.*, 1965, *39*, 1–11.

[44] Fitts, P. M. Engineering psychology and equipment design. In S. S. Stevens (Ed.), *Handbook of experimental psychology*. New York: Wiley, 1966.

[45] Johnson, E. S. An information-process model of one kind of problem solving. *Psychol. Monogr.*, 1964, 78 (5819), 1–30; Dreyfus, H. L. What computers can't do: A critique of artificial reason. New York: Harper & Row, 1972.

to decide what goes into the machine. They also are the sources of many errors that computers are accused of making.

The amount of automation to be introduced is not fully dependent upon the development of superior machines since human beings make the decision regarding allocation. The need for jobs, boredom created by automation, foreign competition, and social attitudes therefore will influence the extent of automation.

Man-Machine Systems[46]

When designing equipment engineers speak of systems which have *inputs* and *outputs*. Materials are inputs when they enter the factory and the product is the output. Some systems are open loops in that they have no controls. For example, a window is broken which turns on a burglar alarm. It continues to ring even after the police arrive. The purpose of controls is to introduce some kind of regulation, such as a home that has the temperature controlled by a thermostat. When the temperature falls below a certain point the furnace will be activated. The heat generated by the furnace will in turn cause the furnace to shut off. Thus the thermostat regulates the furnace to operate only to achieve a desired temperature. In this case we speak of a closed loop system because the product produced sends a message (feedback) to the thermostat. Before the thermostat was invented a human being regulated the furnace.

In fully automated plants a person is needed only when something goes wrong, but in many work systems a human being is needed to interpret the feedback messages and to make adjustments to meet changing needs. A familiar example of a man-machine system is a truck and driver as illustrated in Figure 11.3. The driver has many *inputs* which are displayed to him by dials, sounds, the visual picture of the highway, sensations from the steering wheel, etc. He responds to these messages by moving levers or pedals. The things he does to the operation of the machine are his *outputs*. The sensation of his movements, the response of the machine and the message from the visual displays are the feedback which influence his subsequent outputs. Transportation is the output of this man-machine system, while wages, training, gasoline, company officers, etc., represent inputs.

The human being is a remarkable part of the man-machine system that will not readily be replaced, even though there are instruments that measure more accurately (e.g., speed) than sense organs can. Instead human responsibilities become greater as the sophistication of machines increases because the whole system fails when the controller is inadequate. The research problems for the engineer involve developing improved ways of supplying information (for inputs to man) and designing controls that are most adequate for him. The task of the engineering psychologist is to test human ability to process information when supplied in different forms and to operate controls of different design. Also important is the environment in which the person must operate. By working together the engineer and psychologist are in a position to best integrate man-machine systems.

[46] DeGreene, K. B. (Ed.). *Systems psychology,* New York: McGraw-Hill, 1970; Fleishman, E. A. (Ed.). *Studies in personnel and industrial psychology.* Homewood, Ill.: Dorsey, 1967, Section 9.

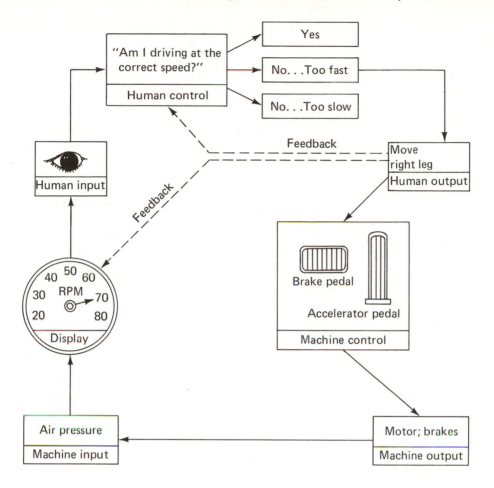

Figure 11.3 / A Man-Machine System. (Reproduced by permission from L. Siegel, *Industrial psychology* [rev. ed.] Homewood, Ill.: Irwin, 1969.)

Inputs

Visual and auditory messages are most common, but the choice of the input *channel* depends not only upon human sensory development, but also upon the work environment. Auditory displays in a noisy environment would have disadvantages but would have an advantage over visual displays if the operator has to move about. Under certain circumstances the olfactory channel may serve the best function. Depending on the need for precision, speed of response, need for vigilance, etc., improvements in messages or displays are sought. Much of the design, therefore, will be specific for the type of equipment developed, but certain common elements can be isolated and so permit generalizations.

Dials are common to the operation and control of many machines. A dial may have a pointer on a vertical, circular, or horizontal scale. Which is least subject to error in readings? The horizontal was found to be best, the vertical poorest. The reason suggested is horizontal eye movements are easier than vertical.[47] Subsequent experiments further complicated the problem by revealing that (1) the finer the gradations, the longer the reading time; (2) there are optimum lengths of dial markings; and, (3) the type of dial which is read most quickly and accurately for quantitative information (e.g., altitude in feet), is least good for qualitative information (e.g., whether the engine is too hot).[48] The common-sense assumption that dials should be built to present as much information as possible was invalidated by the last experiment.

Many situations require dial readings merely to determine whether everything is in order (check-reading). Thus, aircraft instrument panels must not only be examined for quantitative and qualitative readings but for check-readings as well. Power plants have similar groups of dials that must be examined to see that nothing has gone wrong. Are there groupings of pointer patterns that are superior to others?[49] In one experiment the six 16-dial panels in Figure 11.4 were tested. Each panel was exposed for a brief period and deviating dials had to be located by observers. (The dial second row, second from the left deviates 90 degrees in each display.) The dial patterns in the top half of the figure are of three types: ungrouped, subgrouped, and subgroup rotated 45 degrees, and they were compared with the same patterns, but with dials having extended pointers (lower half). The number of errors obtained for the six patterns are shown below each. It is apparent that the big gain comes from extending the pointer. Viewing the dials from an angle or from the front had no significant effect on errors.

Out-Put and Control Devices

Fitts and his coworkers have made continuous study of the relationships of the display of information and the design and arrangement of controls to pilot performance in military aircraft. Errors made by pilots in operating controls and in reading instruments were collected. They were then grouped into categories based on a psychological analysis of the causes of the errors. For example, 50 per cent of the operating errors involved confusion of one control with another (e.g., confusing flap and wheel controls), producing an unexpected and undesired change in the airplane's performance. Much of this confusion centered around the lack of uniform arrangements or operating characteristics of the controls, difficulty in distinguishing among different controls due to their identical shapes or close placement, and application of

[47] Graham, N. E. The speed and accuracy of reading horizontal, vertical, and circular scales. *J. appl. Psychol.*, 1956, 40, 228–232.

[48] Kappauf, W. E., and Smith, W. M. A preliminary experiment on the effect of dial graduation and size on the speed and accuracy of dial reading. *Annals N. Y. Acad. Sci.*, Jan. 31, 1951, Article 7, 51; Thomas, D. R. Exposure time as a variable in dial reading experiments. *J. appl. Psychol.*, 1957, 41, 150–152; Elkin, E. H. Effect of scale shape, exposure time, and display-response complexity on scale reading efficiency. *Techn. Rep.*, Wright Air Development Command, 58–472, Feb., 1959, 1–15.

[49] Dashevsky, S. G. Check-reading accuracy as a function of pointer alignment, patterning, and viewing angle. *J. appl. Psychol.*, 1964, 48, 344–347.

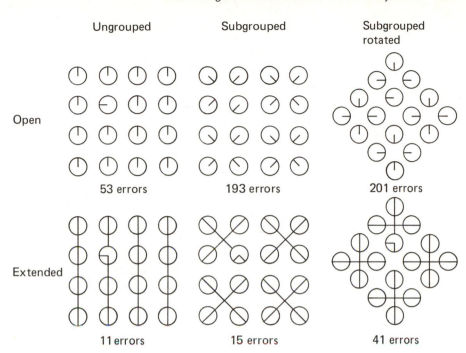

Figure 11.4 / **Extending Pointer Significantly Reduces Errors in Each of the Three Patterns.** (Adapted from S. G. Dashevsky, Check-reading accuracy as a function of pointer alignment, patterning, and viewing angle. *J. appl. Psychol., 48,* 1964, 344–347. Copyright 1964 by the American Psychological Association, and reproduced by permission.)

habitual sequences of control operation at inappropriate times. Recommended solutions to the first two types of problems focused on changes in control design, establishing standard places for controls, and making them easily distinguishable.[50]

Analysis of errors made in many industrial situations would reveal numerous instances where job design is incompatible with the way workers are accustomed to act. Such analyses could lead to a redesign of parts of the equipment to make them compatible with well-learned work habits. Control devices, for example, are too often designed to operate in a direction opposite to the normal way. We have all experienced the problem of which way to turn off the hot water in a strange house, sometimes with scalding effects. Controls are frequently paired with an instrument

[50] Fitts, P. M., and Jones, R. E. Analysis of factors contributing to 460 "pilot error" experiments in operating aircraft controls. In H. W. Sinaiko (Ed.), *Human factors in the design and use of control systems.* New York: Dover, 1961, pp. 332–358; Fitts, P. M., and Jones, R. E. Psychological aspects of instrument display. I. Analysis of 270 "pilot error" experiences in reading and interpreting aircraft instruments. In H. W. Sinaiko (Ed.), *op. cit.,* pp. 359–396.

to restore the equipment to its normal operating condition, as indicated by a return of the instrument needle to a desired position. The experimental evidence indicates clearly that the control should be designed so that the needle moves in the same direction as the knob turns. For example, to restore the needle in Figure 11.5 to an upright position, the control should be turned to the left, not toward the needle.[51] While workers could be trained to make the adjustment by turning the control knob to the right, they would be likely to make the more habitual counterclockwise movement if they were excited, thus possibly producing an accident. The considerable experimental evidence for the existence of many such "population stereotypes," that is, almost universal ways of responding to instruments, has been reviewed by Loveless.[52]

In order to make appropriate responses to inputs the response alternatives should be readily distinguishable. This problem is acute when there is a large array of controls and quick responses are required. In a study of aircraft controls[53] tactual discrimination was essential. Various knob shapes were developed and eleven of them were readily identified by touch. The shapes included spheres, cylinders, triangles, arcs, and cones.

Analysis of job "errors" could also be useful in pointing out specific training needs. The effectiveness of skill training can be enhanced substantially by concen-

Figure 11.5 / Display-Control Relationship. Needle has been displaced from normal operating position. To restore it to its normal position, the control device should be designed to move in the counterclockwise direction—the direction the needle must move—as indicated by the arrow.

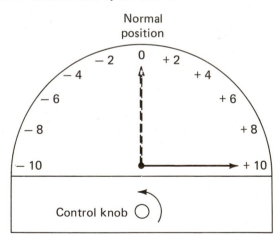

[51] Fitts, P. M., and Seeger, C. M. S-R compatibility: spatial characteristics of stimulus and response codes. *J. exp. Psychol.*, 1953, 46, 199–210.

[52] Loveless, N. E. Direction-of-motion stereotypes: A review. *Ergonomics*, 1962, 5, 357–383.

[53] Jenkins, W. O. Tactual discrimination of shapes for coding aircraft-type controls. In P. M. Fitts, *Psychological research on equipment design*. Washington, D.C.: Government Printing Office, 1947.

trating on those aspects of the job which research has demonstrated to be especially difficult to learn.[54]

Monitoring Automated Equipment—Vigilance

The advent of automation in industry has created many jobs that require workers to monitor constantly banks of instruments, watch for occasional deviations in dial readings, and react appropriately and quickly to remedy the situation indicated. Modern oil refineries, petrochemical plants, and electric power plants now operate automatically, with self-correcting feedback devices to handle slight deviations in subparts of the process.[55] The men who staff these plants can do little, if anything, to improve productivity when the equipment is operating normally. When something goes wrong, however, they must make the necessary adjustments as quickly as possible or serious damage to the entire production system may occur.

Since these events occur infrequently and at irregular intervals, the question arises of how long a person can maintain adequate attention with no loss in the speed and accuracy of his response. This problem of vigilance[56] has been investigated extensively in connection with maintaining effective performance of radar operators. Experiments have shown that the speed and accuracy of responding to infrequent signals diminish rapidly, as early as the first half-hour of viewing under difficult conditions. Alternating operators, improving the distinguishability of the signal, and providing the operator with information about his performance reduced the impairment in performance. However, anticipation of a telephone message about the job and the addition of more signals served again to reduce effective performance.[57]

An interesting sidelight was the discovery of an optimum effective temperature range—that is, temperature-humidity combination—for performance, below *and* above which errors showed a marked increase.

The efficiency of automated production systems is measured by the least amount of "down-time," that is, unproductive time.[58] The assumption that operators can maintain a consistently high level of performance over an entire eight-hour working day is open to serious question. Experimental study of the optimal conditions for work, such as rotation among different jobs, could yield important dividends in operating efficiency and worker satisfaction.

Computer Operations

A wide variety of principles derived from experimental research has been applied to the design of jobs as illustrated in the description of the installation of the control

---

[54] Parker, J. F., Jr., and Fleishman, E. A. Use of analytical information concerning task requirements to increase the effectiveness of skill training. *J. appl. Psychol.*, 1961, *45*, 295–302.

[55] Mann, F. C., and Hoffman, L. R. *Automation and the worker.* New York: Holt, 1960.

[56] For bibliography see D. R. Davies, and G. S. Tune, *Human vigilance performance.* New York: American Elsevier, 1970.

[57] Mackworth, N. H. Researches on the measurement of human performance. In H. W. Sinaiko (Ed.), *op. cit.*, pp. 174–272; Mackworth, N. H., and Mackworth, J. P. Visual search for successive decisions. *Brit. J. Psychol.*, 1958, *49*, 210–221.

[58] Mann and Hoffman, *op. cit.*

console of a large digital computer.[59] The designer has the task of identifying "an order of importance and a frequency of use (of the various dials and controls) . . . and the ease or difficulty for the operator in searching for, acquiring, and transmitting back information to the machine" and then applying "rigorously the relevant advice and knowledge available from ergonomic research."

Illustrative of the wide range of types of applications made and the research on which they were based are the following:

a) Instruments and their related controls are grouped and color-matched according to similarity. This system increases the faculty of identifying controls and enhances the accuracy of activating the correct ones.

b) In one part of the console four lamps, usually off, glow amber and are announced by one "ding-dong" of a chime to signal that attention is needed within the next five minutes. Use of a chime as a general alarm to notify the operator to look for a light signaling specific trouble is based on research.[60] Experiments showed that operators' speed and accuracy in reacting to peripheral danger signals (like the amber lights) was improved when a master tone (a chime) was introduced to announce the error, even though the peripheral signals were easily seen.

c) The engineer decided that vertical control panels would be least expensive to produce. Within these limitations, the findings of anthropometric studies of the sitting height, and vertical and horizontal reach (of the population likely to operate the console) were used to design a main central section 42 inches wide with side limbs positioned 15 degrees beyond a right angle from it and a desk height in front of it 28 inches from the floor.[61]

This example of the cooperation of a human factors specialist with the engineers responsible for equipment design illustrates the advantages that can accrue to industry when the workers' characteristics as well as the engineering requirements are considered *before* the equipment is built. This type of cooperative effort at the design stage avoids many personnel problems that arise after machines are installed and can then be remedied only at considerable expense. In designing automated plants, Mann and Hoffman have pointed to the necessity of considering the total system (including the types of jobs and the grouping of personnel) in order to provide the optimal man-machine relationships for efficiency and worker satisfaction.[62]

Human Decisions

The task of the operator in a man-machine system is to translate data supplied (input) into a form that is usable by the machine (output). This means he must evaluate inputs and make decisions or choices. These decisions range from "Did I or did I not receive a signal?" to "Which response is called for?" under the changed

[59] Shackel, B. Ergonomics in the design of a large digital computer console. *Ergonomics,* 1962, *5,* 229–241.

[60] Siegel, A. I., and Crain, K. Experimental investigations of cautionary signal presentations, *Ergonomics,* 1960, *3,* 339–356.

[61] Floyd, W. F., and Roberts, D. F. Anatomical and physiological principles in chair and table design. *Ergonomics,* 1958, *2,* 1–16.

[62] Mann and Hoffmann, *op. cit.*

circumstances. Factors that influence the time for such decisions include the complexity, amount and clarity of the input; the number of alternate responses; the degree of risk involved; probability distributions; and fatigue. A great deal of research is involved in determining the optimum conditions that prevail for a given system and cannot be covered in this volume.[63] At the present state of knowledge it has become apparent that wiser choices are made if the operator has a good and explicit knowledge of the task. This justifies the great amount of training and knowledge required of astronauts. It is interesting to note that fatigue increases decision time but does not affect the reaction time once the decision is made.

Considerable research has compared group vs. individual risk-taking. After discussion, persons seem more ready to take risks. The change through discussion is called the *risky shift.* Factors that influence this change have to do with divided responsibility, social pressure, nature of the instructions, and type of risk.[64] Since risk-taking has both advantages and disadvantages and since groups are often interdependent on a decision that is made, the problem is of special interest. Comparisons of other aspects of individual and group problem solving will be discussed in Chapter 22.

Designing Jobs for Groups of Men

Airport control towers offer an example of an interdependent work system. As an aircraft approaches for a landing, a control tower operator directs the activities of the pilot, observing his progress on a radarscope. In a large airport many aircraft continually arrive and depart, and at least two tower operators share the responsibility for their direction. The close cooperation required among the operators has been carefully studied in a series of experiments in which the tower operations were simulated in a laboratory setting.[65] The major conclusion from a number of studies comparing individual to two-man performance is that the teams are more effective than individuals, but that their efficiency per person is less. Team performance requires coordination between the members, which diverts each from his principal task of controlling the aircraft.[66] Thus the job of each includes the ability to cooperate with the other member. This consideration accounts for the fact that the

[63] Schum, D. A. Behavior decision theory and man-machine systems. In K. B. DeGreene, *op. cit.;* Simon, H. A. *Models of man.* New York: Wiley, 1957; Miller, D. W., and Starr, M. K. *The structure of human decisions.* Englewood Cliffs, N.J.: Prentice-Hall, 1967; Hulbert, S. F., and Burg, A. Human factors in transportation systems. In K. B. DeGreene, *op. cit.;* Lee, W. *Decision theory and human behavior.* New York: Wiley, 1971.

[64] Kogan, N., and Wallach, M. A. Risk taking as a function of the situation, the person, and the group. *In new directions in psychology III.* New York: Holt, Rinehart & Winston, 1967; Vinokur, A. Distribution of initial risk levels and group decisions involving risk. *J. Person. soc. Psychol.,* 1969, *13,* 207–214; Clark, R. D. III, and Willems, E. P. Where is the risky shift? Dependence on instructions. *J. Person. soc. Psychol.,* 1969, *13,* 215–221.

[65] Fitts, P. M., *et al.* Some concepts and methods for the conduct of system research in a laboratory setting. In G. Finch and F. Cameron (Eds.), *Symposium on Air Force human engineering, personnel and training research.* Washington, D.C.: National Academy of Science —National Research Council Publication 516, 1958.

[66] Kinkade, R. G., and Kidd, J. S. *The effect of team size and intermember communication on decision-making performance.* Wright-Patterson Air Force Base, Ohio: WADC Technical Report 58–474, April, 1959.

effectiveness of a team may be different from the performance expected from a combination of their individual abilities to do the job.

A faulty approach to training for such jobs may be traced to thinking of them only in individual terms. Teaching each worker how to do his job before he is put on the team often produces poorer team performance than when the team learns to work together as a unit. Work patterns learned individually frequently interfere with a person's ability to work in the group. Thus, training of a team should be done on a unit basis, so all members know what they are to do and what they can expect from one another.

Job Design and Worker Satisfaction

The limited research to date has generally led to the conclusion that the classical principles designed to reduce production time (make jobs as simple as possible; divide job units into the smallest possible units; put as much of the job under machine control as possible) are precisely those which (1) make the workers most dissatisfied with their jobs; (2) increase spoilage; (3) alienate workers from the company's goals; and (4) produce apathetic citizens.[67] Furthermore, when such simple jobs are placed together, the work groups thus formed appear to be the most militant and aggressive supporters of union-management conflict, often initiating wildcat strikes and other production-delaying tactics.[68] The costs of such labor strife are rarely attributed to the design of jobs, but may well offset the immediate advantage gained from oversimplification.

Faced with the fact that an adequate theory of job design is lacking, much can still be done to reduce boredom. Proposals will be made in Chapter 16. Other facets of workers' motivation, interests, and satisfaction will be discussed in Chapters 13 and 14. Proper consideration of all sides of the worker's position in the industrial environment can maintain a productive and satisfying society.

Laboratory Exercise

Role Playing: The Case of the Change in Work Procedures

(Students are asked not to read the case materials before participating in the laboratory exercise.)

A. Preparation for role playing.

The instructor will:

1. Divide class into groups of four persons. Assign extra persons to various groups as observers.

[67] Walker and Guest, *op. cit.;* Argyris, C. The individual and organization: An empirical test. *Admin. Sci. Quart.,* 1959, *4,* 145–167.

[68] Sayles, L. *Behavior of industrial work groups.* New York: Wiley, 1958; Singleton, J. W., and Druth, A. Interface: Man and machine: Two scientists look ahead. *Prospectives in Defense Mgmt.* June, 1969, 27–35.

2. Read General Instructions (E. 1) aloud to all.
3. Assign roles. Each person is to read his instructions only.
4. Request role players Jack, Walt, and Steve to wear name tags so that Gus, the foreman, can call them by name.
5. Ask all Guses to stand up when they have finished reading their roles. Indicate that they may continue to refer as needed to the data supplied with their instructions.

B. The role-playing process.

1. When all the Guses are standing, the instructor will remind the Jacks, Walts, and Steves that they are waiting for Gus in his office. When he sits down and greets them, this will indicate that he has entered his office, and each should adopt his role.
2. At a signal, all Guses are seated. All groups role-play simultaneously.
3. 25 minutes is required for the groups to reach a decision. If certain groups have trouble, the instructor may ask Gus, the foreman, to do the best he can in the next minute or two.
4. While groups are role playing, the instructor will write a table on the chalkboard with the following column headings: (1) group number, (2) solution, (3) problem employees, (4) expected production, (5) method used by foreman, and (6) sharing of data.

C. Collecting results.

1. Each group should report in turn while remaining seated as a group. The instructor will enter in Column 1 the number of the group called on to report.
2. Each Gus reports the solution he intends to follow. The solutions may be of three types: (*a*) continuation of old method (i.e., rotation through all positions); (*b*) adoption of new method with each person working his best position; (*c*) a compromise (new method in the morning, old in the afternoon); or (*d*) integrative solution containing features of old and new solutions (e.g., each man spends more time on best position; two men exchange positions and third works on his best position; all three exchange but confine changes to work their two best positions). The instructor will enter type of solution in Column 2 and add notes to indicate whether a trial period is involved, a rest pause is added, etc.
3. Each Gus reports whether he had any special trouble with a particular employee. If so, the initial of the problem individual is entered in Column 3.
4. Jack, Walt, and Steve report whether production will stay the same, go up, or down as a result of the conference. The estimates of Jack, Walt and Steve should be recorded as "0," "+," and "−" signs in Column 4.
5. Group observers report on the way Gus handled the group and how the group responded. Enter a descriptive term in Column 5 for Gus's method (e.g., tried to sell his plan, used group decision, blamed group, was arbitrary and somewhat

abusive, etc.). If no observers were present in a group, data should be supplied by the group itself. For leading questions about method, see "Instructions for Observer" (E. 2).

D. Discussion.

1. Discuss differences obtained and see if these can be related to the attitude and the method of Gus.
2. List the kinds of resistance encountered. Classify them into fear, hostility, introduction of boredom, etc.
3. Discuss the proper method for dealing with each of these kinds of resistance. (See Chapter 13 for analysis of resistance to change in this case.)

E. Materials.

read aloud to class

1. GENERAL INSTRUCTIONS

You work in a plant that does a large number of subassembly jobs, such as assembling fuel pumps, carburetors, and starters. Gus Thompson is foreman of several groups, including the one with which we are concerned today. Jack, Walt, and Steve make up your particular group, which assembles fuel pumps. The assembly operation is divided into three positions or jobs. Since the three jobs are rather simple and each of you is familiar with all of the operations, you find it desirable to exchange jobs or positions. You have worked together this way for a long time. Pay is based on a team piece-rate and has been satisfactory to all of you. Presently each of you will be asked to be one of the following: Gus Thompson, Jack, Walt, or Steve. In some instances an observer will be present in your group. Today, Gus, the foreman, has asked Jack, Walt, and Steve to meet with him in his office. He said he wanted to talk about something.

2. INSTRUCTIONS FOR OBSERVERS

(May be omitted if desired)

Your job is to observe the method used by Gus in handling a problem with his men. Pay especial attention to the following:

a. Method of presenting problem. Does he criticize, suggest a remedy, request their help on a problem or use some other approach?

b. Initial reaction of members. Do group members feel criticized or do they try to help Gus?

c. Handling of discussion by Gus. Does he listen or argue? Does he try to persuade? Does he use threats? Or does he let the men decide?

d. Forms of resistance expressed by the group. Did members express fear, hostility, satisfaction with present method, etc.?

e. What does Gus do with the time-study data? (1) Lets men examine the table; (2) mentions some of the results; or (3) makes little or no reference to the data.

Best results are obtained if Gus uses the data to pose the problem of how they might be used to increase production.

3. ROLES FOR PARTICIPANTS

Role for Gus Thompson, foreman

You are the foreman in a shop and supervise the work of about 20 men. Most of the jobs are piece-rate jobs, and some of the men work in teams and are paid on a team piece-rate basis. In one of the teams, Jack, Walt, and Steve work together. Each one of them does one of the operations for an hour and then they exchange, so that all men perform each of the operations at different times. The men themselves decided to operate that way and you have never given the plan any thought.

Lately, Jim Clark, the methods man, has been around and studied conditions in your shop. He timed Jack, Walt, and Steve on each of the operations and came up with the following facts:

	Time per operation			
	Position 1	**Position 2**	**Position 3**	**Total**
Jack	3 min.	4 min.	4½ min.	11½ min.
Walt	3½ min.	3½ min.	3 min.	10 min.
Steve	5 min.	3½ min.	4½ min.	13 min.
				34½ min.

He observed that with the men rotating, the average time for all three operations would be one-third of the total time or 11½ minutes per complete unit. If, however, Jack worked in the No. 1 spot, Steve in the No. 2 spot, and Walt in the No. 3 spot, the time would be 9½ minutes, a reduction of over 17 per cent. Such a reduction in time would amount to saving of more than 80 minutes. In other words the lost production would be about the same as that which would occur if the men loafed for 80 minutes in an eight-hour day. If the time were used for productive effort, production would be increased more than 20 per cent.

This made pretty good sense to you so you have decided to take up the problem with the men. You feel that they should go along with any change in operation that is made.

Role for Jack

You are one of three men on an assembly operation. Walt and Steve are your team mates and you enjoy working with them. You get paid on a team basis and you are making wages that are entirely satisfactory. Steve isn't quite as fast as Walt and you, but when you feel he is holding things up too much each of you can help out.

The work is very monotonous. The saving thing about it is that every hour you all change positions. In this way you get to do all three operations. You are best on the No. 1 position so when you get in that spot you turn out some extra work and so make the job easier for Steve who follows you in that position.

You have been on this job for two years and you have never run out of work. Apparently your group can make pretty good pay without running yourselves out of a job. Lately, however, the company has had some of its experts hanging around. It looks like the company is trying to work out some speedup methods. If they make these jobs any more simple you won't be able to stand the monotony. Gus Thompson, your foreman, is a decent guy and has never criticized your team's work.

Role for Steve

You work with Jack and Walt on an assembly job and get paid on a team piece-rate. The three of you work very well together and make a pretty good wage. Jack and Walt like to make a little more than you think is necessary, but you go along with them and work as hard as you can so as to keep the production up where they want it. They are good fellows; often help you out if you fall behind; and so you feel it is only fair to try and go along with the pace they set.

The three of you exchange positions every hour. In this way you get to work all positions. You like the No. 2 position the best because it is easiest. When you get in the No. 3 position you can't keep up and then you feel Gus Thompson, the foreman, watching you. Sometimes Walt and Jack slow down when you are on the No. 3 spot and then the foreman seems satisfied.

Lately the methods man has been hanging around watching the job. You wonder what he is up to. Can't they leave guys alone who are doing all right?

Role for Walt

You work with Jack and Steve on a job that requires three separate operations. Each of you works on each of the three operations by rotating positions once every hour. This makes the work more interesting and you can always help out the other fellow by running the job ahead in case one of you doesn't feel so good. It's all right to help out because you get paid on a team piece-rate basis. You could actually earn more if Steve were a faster worker, but he is a swell guy and you would rather have him in the group than someone else who might do a little bit more.

You find all three positions about equally desirable. They are all simple and purely routine. The monotony doesn't bother you much because you can talk, daydream, and change your pace. By working slow for a while and then fast you can sort of set your pace to music you hum to yourself. Jack and Steve like the idea of changing jobs, and even though Steve is slow on some positions, the changing around has its good points. You feel you get to a stopping place every time you change positions and this kind of takes the place of a rest pause.

Lately some kind of efficiency expert has been hanging around. He stands some distance away with a stop watch in his hand. The company could get more for its money if it put some of those guys to work. You say to yourself, "I'd like to see one of these guys try and tell me how to do this job. I'd sure give him an earful."

If Gus Thompson, your foreman, doesn't get him out of the shop pretty soon, you're going to tell him what you think of his dragging in company spies.

Suggested Readings

Barnes, R. M. *Motion and time study* (5th ed.). New York: Wiley, 1963.

Gagné, R. M. (Ed.). *Psychological principles in system development.* New York: Holt, 1962.

Goldberg, W. (Ed.). Information systems and decision making. In *Behavioral approaches to modern management.* Gothenburg, Sweden: Gothenburg Studies in Business Administration, 1970.

Holding, D. H. (Ed.). *Experimental psychology in industry: Selected readings.* Baltimore, Md.: Penguin Books, 1969.

McCormick, E. J. *Human factors engineering* (3rd ed.). New York: McGraw-Hill, 1970.

Meister, D. *Human factors: Theory and practice.* New York: Wiley, 1971.

Morgan, C. T., Cook, J. S., Chapanis, A., and Lund, M. W. *Human engineering guide to equipment design.* New York: McGraw-Hill, 1963.

Shils, E. B. *Automation and industrial relations.* New York: Holt, 1963.

Walker, C. R. (Ed.). *Modern technology and civilization.* New York: McGraw-Hill, 1962.

12

Training in Organizations

Introduction

Training should include supervised practice on a job as well as classroom instruction. Experience alone develops job knowledge and skills, but poor methods and skills are also acquired from experience. A student left to his own devices would improve his skill on a typewriter, but it is doubtful that he would discover the touch system. Before elaborate machines were designed and errors did little or no damage, experience alone was considered adequate. Although training (apprenticeship) was accepted for the trades, companies had to be convinced that a training program for unskilled work paid for itself in improved performance,[1] including gains in production, decreased breakage, absenteeism, and turnover. With advances in technology acceptance of training for operators as well as management personnel is quite general. As a matter of fact companies need to be cautioned against extravagant claims that are often made by those who market programs. Campbell refers to the overemphasis of packaged programs as training "fads."[2]

It is important at the outset to distinguish between training objectives and training methods. The method that is best for one objective may be entirely inadequate for another. Sound-slides and movies have their promoters; programmed learning has its advocates; and participative approaches (including discussion methods, case studies, and role playing) have theirs. But to contend that one method is superior to another, regardless of what is taught, is to miss the basic problem of training: that of teaching something specific. The objectives must determine the method. The

[1] Greenley, R. J. Job training. *Nat. Assn. Manuf. Labor Relat. Bull.*, 1941, *35*, 5–8; Lawshe, C. H., Jr. Eight ways to check the value of a training program. *Factory Mgmt. and Maint.*, 1945, *103*, 117–120. Lindahl, L. G. Movement analysis as an industrial training method. *J. appl. Psychol.*, 1945, *29*, 420–436; Kelly, R. W. and Ware, H. F. An experiment in group dynamics. *Adv. Mgmt.*, 1947, *12*, 116–119; Chaney, F. B., and Teel, K. S. Improving inspector performance through training and visual aids. *J. appl. Psychol.*, 1967, *51*, 311–315.

[2] Campbell, J. P. Personnel training and development. *Annual Review of Psychology*, 1971, *22*, pp. 565–602.

value of a program should be examined in terms of the relationship between the objective of the program and what is *learned* by the trainees. Too often a program is judged by its content or by *what* is taught. This approach protects the trainer or teacher, since a class's failure to learn becomes the pupils' fault.

The degree to which trainees like a course or training program may also be misleading, since what persons get from a program may not always correspond with the training objective. However, interest and enthusiasm are assets to learning, and insofar as they affect learning, the program that does an efficient teaching job must arouse them.

Failure of a program to produce results might mean any of the following: (*a*) the training was a waste of time; (*b*) the method used was ineffective; (*c*) the training objective was not a basic one; (*d*) supervisors and trainers did not agree on how the job should be done; (*e*) the measuring procedure was ineffective; or (*f*) the training was discontinued before measurable gains were made.

Finding training methods appropriate to the training objective is of concern to line supervisors as well as to teachers and training supervisors. Regardless of how much training is done in a company before an employee reports to a particular supervisor, this supervisor still must do some training. Actually, giving assignments, inspecting work, and upgrading performance should be thought of as training. Furthermore, the line supervisor should agree with the training content so that he reinforces rather than inhibits the desired behavior. Involving management personnel in setting training needs and goals is an essential way to obtain their acceptance of the program.[3]

Aspects of Learning

Skilled Labor Versus Job Skill

Industrial jobs are commonly divided into skilled and unskilled work. When used in this sense, the term *skilled* refers to jobs requiring trade knowledge, *unskilled*, to jobs requiring no special training. The trades require both the learning of certain manipulations and the acquisition of information or knowledge. Carpenters, masons, electricians, and toolmakers thus possess knowledge as well as the ability to perform certain activities. These two aspects of learning are quite independent of each other. A person could possess trade knowledge to such a degree as to be able to tell others all the steps in constructing a building, yet be unable to saw a board at right angles. Another person might be able to perform all the necessary acts efficiently but be unable to construct the building. Knowing how a job should be done and being able to carry out the necessary operations are quite different learnings. In the trades, these two aspects of work are possessed by the same individual, but, in a large number of factory operations, only the manipulative ability is required of the worker; this is called *unskilled labor*.

[3] Zerfoss, L. F., and Maier, N. R. F. Improving staff procedure in training. *J. indust. Train.*, 1952, *6*, 5–16.

To the psychologist, an act of skill is a learned pattern of movements. It refers to activity on the job and is quite independent of trade knowledge. A skillful worker, therefore, is not to be confused with one who has a trade and belongs to a class known as *skilled labor*. It is the *unskilled* worker, in the industrial sense, who does most of the manipulative work and has the opportunity of becoming skilled in the psychological sense.

Although there is no sharp theoretical distinction between so-called skilled and unskilled labor, a clear-cut distinction has been made in union circles. With the development of industrial unions, the distinction has become less pronounced. As further specialization in the division of labor occurs, supervisors will possess the knowledge and workmen will possess the ability to perform the operations. Emphasis on skill in manipulation will increase the importance of training in this kind of work; it will also increase industry's respect for so-called *unskilled labor*.

Training activities in large companies not only include the various kinds of job training discussed above, but also supervisory training and executive development. Each of these programs involves a variety of learnings, and since the best method of teaching depends upon the kind of learning involved, it is important to study the various aspects of learning in general. Different combinations of the six aspects of learning discussed below may be involved in the several training activities of a company, and for this reason the program should not determine the method. In setting up training procedures for a given program, a first step is to determine which aspects of learning are relevant to the training objectives.

Associative Learning

The formation of associations takes place in all types of learning, and it is through their formation that man's behavior is modified by experience. However, some learning situations are almost entirely dependent upon the process of connecting experiences with one another. We experience objects with our sense organs and we experience responding to the stimulation they produce. When any of these experiences becomes linked with any other, so that one of them arouses or recalls another, associative learning has taken place.

The essential condition for an association between two experiences is that the experiences occur simultaneously or in close succession. Seeing a man with a dog causes me to associate the two, so that on later occasions the dog reminds me of the man. Meat placed in a dog's mouth causes him to salivate but this relationship between the taste of meat and salivation *grew* in the dog and is an unlearned response. However, if I ring a bell and then put meat in the dog's mouth, I build up an association in the dog between the bell and meat experiences. On later occasions the sound of the bell causes the dog to salivate because of the association that links the bell and meat experiences. This change in the dog's behavior is acquired through experience and represents simple associative learning, in contrast to trial-and-error learning which always involves some selection in activity. The term *conditioned response* also is used to designate associative learning, particularly if a response or movement rather than an idea is aroused by a sensation.

Through a repetition of the same combination of experiences, the associations accumulate and become more stable and permanent. Although some individuals form associations more quickly than others, all continue to profit by further repetition. There is, therefore, no final or complete stage of learning. Even if performance is no longer improved by repetition, the benefits of practice show up in less rapid forgetting.

Although all forms of learning involve formation of associations, only some may be said to be confined to this aspect of learning. Job activities that depend most heavily upon pure associative learning are those that require memorization. Examples of routine learnings are spelling, recalling telephone numbers, learning to read a new language (excluding pronunciation), restating company rules and procedures, recalling names and addresses, memorizing postal regulations, and all aspects of job information that require little understanding or judgment.

Selective Learning[4] (Operant Conditioning)

In selective learning a person must not only connect experiences, but must find out which things to connect. Through trial-and-error persons learn what action on their part lead to what kind of results. The problem is to learn to make responses that lead to the desired results.

Practical situations demand two types of selection: *sensory* and *motor*. In *sensory* selection the problem for the learner is to discover the conditions under which to express certain responses. For example, you may know that you should stop your car whenever a red light flashes at a certain rhythm and that a constant green light means that you may continue. What should you do when new conditions arise such as: a constant red light, a red light flashing very rapidly, a flashing green light, an alternating red and green light, and so on?

If you were rewarded for stopping when any kind of flashing light appeared and punished for stopping for a steady light, you could select the essential condition and learn that flashing lights require you to stop. This kind of learning requires more than contiguity—it also requires that pleasant or unpleasant consequences be connected with the response.

Unless selection is controlled, the connection between a given stimulus and a response may be left to chance. In one experiment an attempt was made to make cats fear rats. Cats placed in a box were given an electric shock as soon as they moved toward a rat that was introduced into the box from the opposite side.[5] The several cats received different educations from this training: (1) some learned to fear rats and avoided them in a room; (2) some learned to fear the box and struggled when placed near it; and (3) the rest feared neither the box nor the rat alone but were afraid when the rat was in the box. In this experiment the electric shock introduced the fear response, but the stimulus selected and connected with it was left to chance.

[4] Noble, C. E. Outline of human selective learning. In E. A. Bilodeau and I. M. Bilodeau (Eds.), *Principles of skill acquisition.* New York: Academic Press, 1969.
[5] Kuo, Z. Y. The genesis of the cat's responses to the rat. *J. comp. Psychol.*, 1930, *11*, 1–35.

While a father is giving his child a bath the child stands up in the tub, slips, and falls. What has the child learned? He may connect this unhappy experience with his father, the water, the bathroom, or standing in the tub. All factors were present at the time of the fall, but which one is selected in the association process determines what the child will avoid in the future. What do employees connect with disciplinary action, with accidents, with strict inspection, and the like? Most situations permit various possible connections, and good training should not leave this to chance.

Problems requiring *motor* or movement selection are the more typical kinds of trial-and-error learning situations. They are characterized by the fact that they require the learner to discover what responses to make to a situation.[6] A cat locked in a box must discover that pulling a string will open a door, a child placed on a toilet must find out what he must do in order to regain his freedom, an employee must learn how to do a job to get praised or what not to do to escape reprimand. In this type of learning a good many responses may be made to a general situation and, in order to learn what to do, the individual must unwittingly make the correct or desired response during his stay in the situation. If a child never urinates while on the training seat, the first requisite to learning is missing.

For learning to take place, the desired response must be in the individual's repertoire and must be connected or associated with the consequence. If the consequence is pleasant the person is motivated to repeat the behavior; if the consequence is unpleasant he has reason to avoid the action. In order to influence or control this learning in people, we often give rewards or punishments in conjunction with certain behaviors, hoping that the desired association will be made. Thus the child is freed from the training chair and praised when the desired response occurs. The following mistakes, however, are commonly made: (1) the child is released before the desired response occurs, because he cries; (2) his stay on the training seat is made so pleasant with toys that release is no longer a reward; and (3) the release and praise are given so long after the response occurs that no connection is made between response and reward.

Responses that are seldom made are necessarily the ones that are most difficult to master. Dogs have a hard time learning to push levers upward in order to get food, but readily learn to push them down. The reverse is true for pigs. Motion and time study simplifies learning when the responses required come naturally or are in the person's more immediate repertoire. In associative learning this difficulty is not present because the desired response is under the trainer's control. He can cause a person to connect a sound with a light because he can expose the person to both, one after the other; and he can cause a dog to salivate in response to a bell because he can initiate the response, at will, by placing meat in the animal's mouth.

[6] Thorndike, E. L. *Animal intelligence.* New York: Macmillan, 1911; Adams, D. K. Studies of adaptive behavior in cats. *Comp. Psychol. Monogr.,* 1929, 6; Guthrie, E. R. *The psychology of learning.* New York: Harper, 1952; Guthrie, E. R., and Horton, G. P. *Cats in a puzzle box.* New York: Rinehart, 1946.

Sensory Discrimination

Many learning situations demand that a person respond in a certain way to one signal (stimulus) and in another way to a different signal. Whether to express a response or to withhold it raises a similar problem. When the stimulus signals are very different, the problem of training is primarily a matter of building up the proper associations. However, when two objects are very much alike, a different kind of difficulty is introduced. The ability of the sense organs (eyes, ears, nose, and so on) to make distinctions limits what an individual can learn. A child with poor vision may be unable to learn to read because he cannot differentiate between letters, a color-blind man may make mistakes in matching fabrics, and a competent employee may make a mistake because of incorrectly hearing an assignment. Training methods not only should create situations that make optimum use of the sense organs (through such devices as lighting, glasses when needed, and contrast) but should train people to use the sense organ most useful for discrimination. A defect in a surface might be felt more easily than seen, a good piece of equipment might be selected more accurately by how it sounds when tapped than by how it looks, and a sound mounting for a motor might be detected with the sense of touch (vibration) more readily than with the sense of hearing.

The problem of aiding the ability to discriminate may even be extended to training persons where to look for differences. How does one most readily detect the year and make of a car? A comparison of tail lights may be a useful clue. Different clues would be needed for making differentiations from different angles.

Acquisition of Skill

Acquiring an act of skill requires not only a particular combination of movements in a specified sequence, but also a given intensity of movement. In juggling balls, the balls must be tossed in a certain sequence, *and* they must be tossed at the proper height and in the proper direction. Of all the movements one is capable of making, only certain ones should be made and these must be performed with a given intensity. As learning progresses, the selected movements become more specific and closely knit, while interfering movements are dropped. The degree of skill is indicated by the stability of the pattern and the extent to which unessential and disturbing movements have been eliminated. Because such learning requires the discovery and selection of proper movements, it is a form of so-called trial-and-error learning. One aspect of learning is trying out movements, making mistakes, and trying some more.

The acquisition of skill differs from other forms of trial-and-error learning in that it is largely dependent on the muscle sense,[7] as well as other senses. This means

---

[7] Small sense organs, located in the muscles, tendons, and joints, give a person the "feedback" by which he senses his posture and movement. This sense, known as *kinesthesis,* is essential to posture, walking, talking, and all other skilled activities. Although it is perhaps our most important sense, it is not popularly appreciated because the organs are not visible.

that the response is an end product for most forms of learning, but for acts of skill the muscular response serves also as a stimulus for further activity and in this capacity it becomes a *means* to an end. When muscular activity serves as a guide to further behavior, the quantitative aspect of movement becomes highly important. In all learning, some kind of response is eventually made, but how it is accomplished is not always important. For instance, a string which opens a door may be pulled in a great variety of ways, and either the right or left hand may be used. This kind of response must be distinguished from one in which a specific pattern of muscular activity results in string-pulling.

All of us have experienced muscle sense when running down a flight of stairs in the dark. Our reliance on the muscular sense becomes very apparent when an error in the pattern of movements is made. We have the "feeling" of having reached the floor and step forward. If the floor is a step farther down, the final movement is completely inadequate for the situation.

Understanding and Insight

At one extreme, a person may learn parrot-fashion and make correct responses without experiencing any deeper relationships; at the other extreme, he may learn something with complete insight and understanding. Appreciating the point of a joke involves more than knowing the meaning of each word. To understand something is to see a rich pattern of relationships in a situation or a passage, and these relationships give the situation a complex organization and structure. Intelligence enriches understanding and insights, and a person may be superior in these respects without being superior in ability to memorize.

Problems that permit understanding and insight are more readily solved than those that must be solved entirely by trial and error.[8] It has been shown that learning material that permits organization and understanding not only results in much better retention, but what is learned can also be applied and used in other situations.[9] Training methods that encourage insight and organization therefore will increase retention, improve judgments, and permit a more widespread application of knowledge.

Changing Attitudes

Ordinarily the subject of developing or changing attitudes is not included under the topic of learning. Nevertheless, attitudes constitute an important segment of acquired behavior. One reason for giving them a separate or unique treatment is their failure to change as readily as habits. Attitudes contain a heavy loading of emotion either pleasant or unpleasant; consequently they are associated with visceral responses, involving heart and circulatory changes, glandular secretions (especially

---

[8] Köhler, W. *Gestalt psychology.* New York: Liveright, 1929; Wertheimer, M. *Productive thinking.* New York: Harper, 1945.

[9] Katona, G. *Organizing and memorizing: Studies in the psychology of learning and teaching.* New York: Columbia University Press, 1940.

from the adrenal glands), and inhibition of digestive processes. The fact that internal organ responses, not directly under voluntary control, are involved explains in part why attitudes cannot be changed by choice. Their close association with frustration also makes them a special case of acquired behavior. Insofar as attitude problems are associated with many learning situations, it is important to recognize them as such and to deal with them in accordance with their nature (see Chapters 3 and 4).

Training Procedures

Rules for the Formation of Associations

Since all learning requires associations, rules describing conditions that favor this process are of general value. However, associative connections are more important to some job situations than to others, and the value of specific associative bonds may differ.

1. *Frequency of repetition influences the number or strength of associations.* This is one of the oldest rules of learning and requires no elaboration. It is most fundamental for memorization tasks, less relevant to attitude change. Its effect on pure memorization and understanding are different in that repetitions make simple associations stronger or more stable while they merely increase the opportunities to gain understanding. Once a relationship is understood, further repetitions are boring rather than helpful.

Trial-and-error learning profits from repetition in two ways; (*a*) repetitions increase opportunities for selection; and (*b*) they permit the stabilization of the essential associations. For many trial-and-error learning situations the selective aspect of the problem is the big difficulty, and once it is achieved, further repetitions add little. Acts of skill profit greatly from repetitions because a whole chain or sequence of movements must be tied together. Learning the correct response in a sequence of choices, such as the route from one city to another, profits from repetition for a similar reason. Doubling the number of required associations approximately doubles the number of repetitions necessary to reach a given level of proficiency. However, the time requirement is four times as great because each complete repetition takes twice as long.

Repetition is perhaps the most commonly employed device of learning. One sees it applied, almost ruthlessly, in advertising, propaganda, and training films. Although the principle is basic to memorization, there is more to learning and to inducing the buying of a product than the formation of associations.

2. *Attention and intention are important mental sets for learning.* Although some learning may occur without conscious effort, it is an asset to learning if the experiences to be associated are dominant in consciousness and if there is an intent to learn. Intent increases attention, and attention in turn determines the experiences that will be most vivid to the learner. Learning gains result from anything that increases intention, such as motivating the person to learn, and from any procedures that make the relevant events or objects stand out in consciousness. Common methods for making experiences stand out are increasing the size, intensity, duration,

and distinctness of the stimulation. Introducing movement and sudden changes in intensity and size also increases the attention-getting properties of stimulus objects.

3. *Distributed or spaced repetitions are superior to massed or accumulated repetitions for most standard learning conditions.* Numerous experiments have demonstrated that a given number of repetitions spaced over a period of days results in more learning than the same number of repetitions massed in a short period of time. The optimum interval between repetitions varies somewhat, but generally speaking, intervals as long as a day or more are optimum.[10] This principle of making learning more economical by spreading the effort over a period of time holds for memorizing passages, learning routes (mazes), and acquiring skills (for example, typing and archery), but it does not apply to ideational learning. The extent of the advantage is greater for difficult (long) tasks than easy ones. Under extreme conditions, massed trials produce inattention and boredom, resulting in a pure waste of time. However, no simple formula describes the way massed and spaced distribution of effort works, since differences in motivation, interest, and even age influence the outcome. Massed practice is actually favored insofar as (*a*) some of the activity serves the purpose of a warm-up period and (*b*) long intervals produce too much forgetting between trials.[11]

The application of the principle of spaced learning to training may seem a simple one, but frequently certain practical conditions do not permit the trainer to set up ideal conditions. When an employee is hired he is not willing to spread his learning time over a period of months by working an hour or so at a time. Practical solutions of the following types may be feasible; (*a*) alternate job training with some useful but simple activity (e.g., filing); (*b*) alternate training on very different aspects of the job; (*c*) employ high school students on a part-time basis and use the part-time employment for training.

The last method is used extensively in some banks and not only supplies trained employees for work after graduation, but permits both employees and supervisors to get acquainted before permanent employment is arranged. A telephone company trained some operators on a half-time basis and others on a full-time basis. Both groups showed similar progress, and as a result it was found unnecessary to make any changes in the overall duration of the training period when half-time training was introduced.

4. *Whole learning generally is favored over part learning.* This means that learning a complete meaningful unit is better than breaking the material into parts and learning them separately. Generally speaking, a four-stanza poem is learned more economically if it is repeated as a unit than if it is memorized stanza by stanza. A chapter studied as a whole gives a reader a better sense of organization and allows him to form more meaningful interrelationships than the same amount of time devoted to studying it in sections.

[10] Woodworth, R. S. *Experimental psychology.* New York: Holt, 1938, Ch. 9.
[11] Hovland, C. I. Human learning and retention. In S. S. Stevens (Ed.), *Handbook of experimental psychology.* New York: Wiley, 1951, pp. 613–689.

A complex task is first learned as a general impression of the whole thing, like seeing a large painting as a mass of bright color. As repetitions are permitted, more detail is noticed. In the painting, one sees objects not noticed at first. Gradually, as repetitions continue, the minutest details acquire meaning. Figures in the painting formerly perceived as background may now add variety and subtleties.

Training programs should make use of the principle of repeating wholes by going over the entire program from the point of view of the overall relationships and then, on subsequent coverages, working into the more and more specific relationships. A supervisor should not expect perfection of any part of a beginner's work. Rather, many parts should mature together toward perfection as the finer details are mastered.

5. *Recitation or active repetitions are superior to passive reading or listening to another read.* One may have heard the Lord's Prayer many times and still be unable to recite it, but a few repetitions, in which the learner is required to recite the prayer, will force rapid learning. Reciting demands attention and concentration, locates weaknesses or gaps in learning, uses the process of recall, and demands the making of the very responses that will be required when the learning is utilized later on. These advantages apply to memorizing, and to selective learning as well. A person learns a route through a city much better when driving his own car, and receiving help when it is needed, than when riding with someone else. Learning an act of skill also is favored by activity, but for additional reasons which will be discussed later.

Since recitation cannot occur until there is some learning produced by other methods, it is necessary to mix passive training methods with active ones. This means that the active learning procedure must be accompanied by coaching.

6. *Uniqueness facilitates learning.* If a list of nonsense syllables (such as "zif") are to be learned and three numerals are included in the list, the numerals will be remembered better than the nonsense syllables. Likewise, if a nonsense syllable is included in a list of numbers it will be remembered better than the numbers. The same principle applies to other types of content. The material that is different from the rest of the content stands out and is better remembered.

7. *Short-term memory shows rapid decrement.* If given a number a person forgets it unless he repeats it over and over or unless he gives it some meaning. If repetitions of the number are prevented the recall of the number fades rapidly during an 18-second period. This phenomenon is called short-term memory and represents recall of experience before it has been stored.

8. *Grouping aids memory.* Some meaningless numbers (telephone) or letters (i.e., government agencies) can be remembered better when grouped. An eleven-digit telephone number would require a considerable number of repetitions to be memorized as a sequence. However, if given the meaning that the first number is the long distance dialing number, the next three are the area code, the next three are the local exchange and the last four are the individual's number, the memory task is simplified even for short-term memory. Grouping is a method for imposing organization and meaning into material to be learned.

Aids to Selective Learning

In order to produce or control selective learning the trainer must have some way of encouraging or discouraging responses. This is a problem in motivation. Reward and punishment are common ways for motivating behavior. Reward need not be in the form of a material object; praise and even having a response called "correct" are effective. Punishments also need not produce physical pain to teach an individual what to avoid, since reprimand and the word "wrong" are effective. Selection can be accomplished by (*a*) excluding undesirable behavior (negative selection), (*b*) including only desirable behavior (positive selection), or (*c*) a combination of both.

The following principles facilitate the selection aspects of learning.

1. *The use of positive selection methods is recommended to trainers.* A comparison of the merits of rewards and punishments as selectors involves a vast amount of conflicting and varied experimental data; nevertheless, certain distinctions and general statements supporting this conclusion can be made.

(*a*) Although training and discipline sometimes are difficult to distinguish, it is important to differentiate between such problems as teaching new employees their jobs and teaching employees to get to work on time.

(*b*) Most comparisons of the effects of reward and punishment involve two behavior possibilities, thus making avoidance of one synonymous with choosing the other.

(*c*) Most of the jobs that require selective learning are more concerned with what to do than with what not to do, and for this reason positive selection is the more economical.

(*d*) Bad habits can be eliminated by practicing them, if during this practice they are consciously repeated as wrong.[12] To avoid a bad habit, one must know when one is doing it.

2. *Knowledge of results is essential to selection.* A training period in target practice led to no improvement because the trainees were not given their scores until the end of the period. They could not select the proper responses because it was impossible for them to know what they did correctly and when. This feedback of results should be immediate, while the experience of the action made is still clear. The trainee must learn to discriminate between acts that lead to different results if he is to learn to control them. Failure to supply effective feedback will oblige the learner to use cues that are available to him and which may be misleading. However, the feedback should be suited to the particular stage of learning. Supplying more information than the trainee can handle will only confuse him.[13]

Feedback also influences the motivational state of the trainee. Knowledge of results in the form of scores produces the experiences of success and failure which can influence the amount of effort expended. The motivational effects on perform-

---

[12] Dunlap, K. *Habits, their making and unmaking.* New York: Liveright, 1932.

[13] Ammons, R. B. Effects of knowledge of performance: A survey and tentative theoretical formulation. *J. gen. Psychol.*, 1956, *54*, 279–299.

ance should be distinguished from the way the learned content influences performance.[14] Motivation can influence what is learned only insofar as it controls attention and intention. Variations in performance due to effort expended are motivational and will be discussed in Chapter 14.

3. *Cause-and-effect relationships should be made clear and meaningful.* Learning to operate the controls of a machine is easier if one knows something of the internal mechanisms.

4. *Individual instruction is needed to determine whether or not each learner is reacting to the proper aspect of the situation (sensory selection) and whether any are having difficulty in making the desired response.* This requires two-way communication and interpersonal relations skill as well as insightful observation skills on the part of the trainer.

5. *Social facilitation enhances dominant responses only.* An audience improves the performance of a person but may impair learning[15] because the presence of observers enhances the emission of dominant responses. In the early stages of learning, wrong responses dominate so that the impairment is greatest during this period.

Cautions Regarding Discrimination Problems

It is important to recognize the part played by individual differences in sensory capacities. Before spending time training an employee, one should be satisfied that he can make the sensory distinctions required. The first step in training inspectors might be to determine whether or not the trainees can differentiate satisfactory and unsatisfactory items. A common error in training is for the trainer to talk too much and fail to observe what the trainees see and what they are reacting to.

Training methods should conform to the sensory capacity involved. All learning requires a reaction to some sort of sensory stimulation. If vision is involved, then visual aids are appropriate. Thus one can teach social relationships, the internal workings of a blast furnace, or the way to read a dial, with the aid of movies, blackboards, and models. However, sound movies, records, and auditory demonstrations would have to be used to teach pronunciation, proper tone of voice to use on the phone, the meaning of sound signals, and the like. Because people can both read and hear words, much training utilizes visual and auditory methods. If a person has both read a passage and heard it spoken, double associations are formed and he can recall items from it by two different routes, visual and auditory.

Aiding the Acquisition of Skill

The basic dependence of acts of skill on the muscle sense make it a unique problem in training. The associations required are those between sensations of movement and their execution. This means that the trainer cannot manipulate or control

---

[14] Locke, E. A. Effects of knowledge of results, feedback in relation to standards, and goals on reaction-time performance. *Amer. J. Psychol.,* 1968, *81,* 566–574; Fleishman, E. A. Individual differences and motor learning. In R. M. Gagne (Ed.), *Learning and individual differences.* Columbus, Ohio: Merrill, 1967; Porter, L. W., and Lawler, E. E. *Managerial attitudes and performance.* Homewood, Ill.: Dorsey, 1968.
[15] Zajonc, R. B. Social facilitation. *Science,* 1965, *149, 269–274.*

a necessary component of the training. One person can teach another that pushing a switch turns off a motor by demonstrating the relationship between the two events. Both events are under the trainer's control. However, he cannot teach another to juggle balls by demonstration because he cannot give the other person the sensations from the muscles involved. Teaching by imitation is greatly overrated.[16]

In order to utilize effectively the specialized nature of motor-skill learning, somewhat different training methods are needed from those required in the acquisition of knowledge. The principles stated below are derived from the fact that skill is a form of trial-and-error learning in which the muscle or kinesthetic sense plays a unique role.

1. *Doing, not observing, is basic to forming the associations needed in the development of skill.* The trainer must arrange for trainees to execute the skilled act, at the outset, as best they can. Time for demonstrations should be kept at a bare minimum. When danger and damage to equipment are possible, safe methods (training devices) for practicing the desired acts off-the-job should be used (see p. 318). Role playing is a method for off-the-job training in leadership skills.

2. *The trainer performs his most useful function by aiding trainees in the selection of movements.* He must be able to recognize correct movements by the way they "look" so he can inform the learner whether or not he is improving.

3. *Guiding the movements of another (as guiding a child's hand in helping him to write) has some value in communicating the general idea during the early stages.* However, guidance alters the sensations of movement because part of the muscle load is carried by the trainer.

4. *Directing attention to the "feel" of correct movements makes the reliance on this sense more conscious.* It has been shown that, even in learning to relax, people profit from training in which they learn to recognize a state of relaxation from the "feel."[17]

5. *Controlling perception has been found to be a helpful device in some training situations, and its possibilities should be further investigated.* How should an information operator in the telephone company perceive and visualize a name in order to recognize it most quickly in the directory? Should a painter view a paintbrush as an extension of his hand or as a tool in his hand to produce the best stroke? Should a singer view the vibrato as a fast trill, as a single act, or as something else? These are questions coaches and trainers might ask when attempting to assist others in developing skills.

Experimentally, foremen have done a better job of conducting a discussion when they viewed or thought of the participants as peers than when they viewed them as subordinates.[18] Seeing people as equals makes leaders more tolerant and permissive.

---

[16] For a report of experiments on the acquisition of skills required for control of sensitive equipment see: Smith, K. U., and Sussman, H. Cybernetic theory and analysis of motor learning and memory. In E. A. Bilodeau, and I. M. Bilodeau (Eds.), *Principles of skill acquisition.* New York: Academic Press, 1969.

[17] Jacobson, E. *Progressive relaxation.* Chicago: University of Chicago Press, 1939.

[18] Solem, A. R. The influence of the discussion leader's attitude on the outcome of group decision conferences. Doctoral dissertation, University of Michigan, 1953.

6. *The speed at which the movements in an act of skill are executed during train-ing should match, as early as possible, the pace desired for the finished performance.* Since the nature of the sensations from the muscles not only depends upon the particular muscles involved, but also upon their rate of contraction and relaxation, the sensation of the correct pattern of movement can be achieved only if the action is properly paced. To hurry an act of skill or to slow it down results in inaccuracies and accidents.

Judgments must be used in applying this principle to various training situations. Slow motions may be needed at times to permit a trainee to discover some of the finer details. For this reason a musician may play a new cadenza slowly at first in order to recognize and play each of the notes. If, however, he wants to memorize the passage as a sequence of movements, he must progress beyond the point of responding to individual notes, and he can best do this if he learns the movements as a sequence at the pace desired for the final execution.

7. *Recognizing and dealing with tenseness is important to the trainer of skills.* A perfect act of skill utilizes only the muscles essential to the act. All other muscles should be relaxed or utilized only to the extent that posture is required. A nervous or worried person tends unnecessarily to tense muscles not involved in a job activity. These partially contracted muscles send sensations to the brain and not only con-fuse the problem of learning but also disturb the execution of the act of skill.

Trainers should be understanding and considerate of feelings if they wish to reduce undesirable muscle tensions in learners who, because they are in a strange situation, frequently are in an anxious state. Expecting reasonable improvement rather than perfection should determine the trainer's objective.

8. *In order to keep up interest in learning a task, proper incentives for improve-ment are important.* Evidence from a number of investigations indicates that moti-vation increases not only the *willingness* to do more, but also the *ability* to do more. Greater attention further improves the selection process and thereby increases the skill.

9. *In many instances of learning, a person reaches a stage in which apparent progress ceases.* Periods of this sort are known as *plateaus* in learning. Sometimes a plateau seems to be inherent in the nature of the task, sometimes the method of learning is a factor, and sometimes the plateau appears to be due to reduced appli-cation.[19] Whatever the cause, it is important that the trainee shall not become dis-couraged by his seeming lack of improvement. He can be told that the plateau is temporary, that with a little more application it will soon pass. The mere knowledge that the phenomenon is characteristic of learning and not a unique characteristic of his own is all that is necessary to prevent an attitude of "giving-up."

10. *Attention to what one does is important in the early stages of learning.* After an act of skill is well learned, it is performed with little or no conscious attention to its various phases. During the early stages, however, there are so many things to watch that it is often confusing. The instructor can be of great aid in assisting the

[19] Book, W. F. *Learning to typewrite.* New York: Gregg, 1925, Ch. 15; Batson, W. H. Acquisition of skill. *Psychol. Monogr.,* 1916, *21,* 1–92.

learner to put his efforts in the right place. Always the "correct" movements should be emphasized. To draw attention to "wrong" movements is harmful, in that it deprives the correct movements of necessary attention.

When movements have to be made in rapid succession, attention should be placed on the rhythm. In typing the letters t-h-e, the pattern rather than the elements is stressed. To promote the experience of the pattern, the same combination is repeated many times in succession. A smooth act of skill is no more a mere aggregation of muscular movements than a triangle is a cluster of points.

Attention to the end result of the action pattern also tends to guide the execution of a pattern. We throw a baseball or drive a tennis ball where we look. Always, the attention must be well ahead of the movements, otherwise each separate unit becomes connected with the attention rather than with the preceding movement. In order to gain rapid and smooth performance, the pattern cannot be split into separate parts without necessitating separate acts of attention.

It follows that a unit of skill cannot be divided into parts which can be learned separately. This breaking-up of a task into parts is feasible only when the parts are actually separate units of performance. Thus, posture in golf can be separated from the drive, whereas juggling a ball with one hand cannot be separated out of a pattern which utilizes both hands. In dividing jobs for production purposes, it is important that effective movement units be retained. Ordinarily, one thinks of a manufacturer's product in terms of the number of physical parts from which it is assembled. From the point of view of skill, one should think of the product as the assembly of units or patterns of skill.

Better Learning through Understanding

Learning with understanding is superior to rote learning in that retention is greater and the learning transfers to new situations. For example, if a student understands how to find the area of a parallelogram he can use this understanding to find the area of many other geometrical figures. Some methods of teaching stimulate insights while others encourage rote learning.[20]

1. *Training materials should be organized around principles.* Sequences of illustrations, breakdowns of subject matter, comparisons of data, and visual aids should be presented to point up the basic principles. If shortcuts in arithmetic are learned as rules, opportunities to use them are overlooked, they are not used with confidence, and the rules are readily forgotten. For example, one might teach the rule that a number can be multiplied by 25 merely by dividing by four and adding two zeros. If one understands, however, that multiplying by 25 is the equivalent of multiplying by $100/4$, then one can divide by four either before or after multiplying by 100, depending on which is easier. Further, one also knows how to multiply by 50, by $33\frac{1}{3}$, and so on. But if a person does not understand a rule, it may be inappropriately used.

2. *Discussion and free exchange of opinion should be encouraged.* Discussion

[20] Wertheimer, M. *Productive thinking.* New York: Harper, 1945; Katona, *op. cit.*

helps stimulate insightful experiences because extra time is spent examining various relationships. It takes more time to explore, analyze, and test ideas than to present them.

Discussion also requires the trainees to take an active role, and the extra energy called up for this purpose serves as an aid to understanding. Understanding is always an active rather than a passive process since the person must impose organization on the sensations supplied to his senses. The leader plays an action-provoking role when he asks stimulating and exploratory questions.

There are a variety of discussion methods and each has its purpose. Discussion designed to create understanding should be of the developmental variety.[21] The objective of developmental discussions is learning and problem-solving, rather than catharsis, acceptance of change, or resolution of conflicts.

3. *Periodically checking on the growth of trainees is essential because understanding declines rapidly when a person falls behind others in his thinking.* Trainers can profit from conducting discussions because they are made aware of the degree of comprehension and understanding achieved by their group members. When in possession of this knowledge they can adapt statements and questions to the level of development the groups have attained.

4. *Requesting trainees to use their own words to summarize or restate a problem, restate another's viewpoint, and the like, aids learning because these assignments demand understanding.* Only when there is understanding, hence communication, can the same idea be accurately expressed in different words by several people. Requesting group members to judge the accuracy of an interpretative statement made by one of them extends this procedure into a discussion process.

Changing Attitudes

Chapters 3 and 4 dealt with attitudes and frustrations, respectively, and such skills as listening, permissiveness, and acceptance were discussed. These skills, and the methods of responding to feelings by reflecting them, to be discussed in Chapter 20, may be regarded as effective ways for dealing with the feelings, attitudes, and frustrations of individuals. In Chapter 6 a method for achieving acceptance and agreement in groups was discussed. To complete the picture for dealing with attitudes as a training problem only a brief statement of methods is needed.

1. *Permissive discussion methods, designed to encourage full expression of feelings and viewpoints, influence attitudes constructively because group members learn what others think and feel.* Individuals tend to adopt the attitudes of their group, and permissive discussions make the prevailing attitudes known. This influence of a group's attitude on individual attitudes is called *social pressure.*

2. *When frustrations are present, procedures designed to release hostile expression should be used.* Attitudes that dominate during frustration are nonconstructive and often destructive, and can change only if the state of frustration is reduced.

[21] Maier, N. R. F. *Principles of human relations.* New York: Wiley, 1952, Ch. 3; Haiman, F. S. *Group leadership and democratic action.* Boston: Houghton Mifflin, 1950.

3. *As previously suggested, the method known as role playing is especially suitable to attitude training.* This method permits the trainer to place a trainee in a great variety of situations, so that he can better appreciate how situations influence the attitudes and actions of others. A first-line foreman can be given the role of company president, black worker, employee with least seniority, worker with most seniority, or typist. In these different roles he will experience some of the attitudes, feelings, and problems engendered by the situation. Such experiences make for greater understanding and tolerance.

4. *Pleasant experiences create favorable attitudes whereas unpleasant experiences create unfavorable attitudes.* Anything in a training situation that produces positive experiences tends to train attitudes in the direction of generosity. Good relations with supervisors cause attitudes toward a company to become more generous, thus resulting in more favorable opinions.[22]

Evaluation of Training Methods[23]

The Lecture Method

Lecturing is an economical training method because it permits one trainer to cover a considerable amount of information with a number of persons. Many people learn more from hearing lectures than from reading, although for others the sight of a word facilitates learning better than the sound. Good lectures aid understanding and selective learning, but no lecture is efficient in helping people make simple associations unless it is conducted as a drill session. Lectures are of little value in changing attitudes, developing job skills, or training in human relations skills. However, lectures have more effect on attitudes than the written word.[24]

The aspects of a training program that lend themselves to lectures are those involving principles and presentation of background information. Some companies have their officials talk to new employees and present the company history and its policies to them. Such talks give employees an impression of the company and of the officials. Some feeling for the history is communicated, and some idea of policy is gained, but if examinations were given, the speakers would be greatly disappointed by what was learned.

Subject matter that requires the learning of speech sounds, intonations, phrasing, and so on, is better taught by lectures and voice sounds than by the printed word. Similarly, more content is learned from poems well read aloud than read to oneself.

Sound Motion Pictures

The original cost of a sound movie is high, but since it can be used with many audiences it is a relatively inexpensive investment for large companies. Many com-

[22] Maier, N. R. F., and Solem, A. R. Audience role playing: A new method in human relations training. *Hum. Relat.,* 1951, *4,* 287–294.

[23] Although research has not been carried to the point of permitting an exacting evaluation of certain training procedures, it seems desirable to give the reader some general idea of their relative merits. The following evaluations are the author's opinions and should be considered as such.

[24] Wilke, W. H. An experimental comparison of the speech, the radio and the printed page as propaganda devices. *Arch. Psychol.,* 1934, No. 169.

Lectures and demonstrations are effective for presenting information and visual relationships to groups.

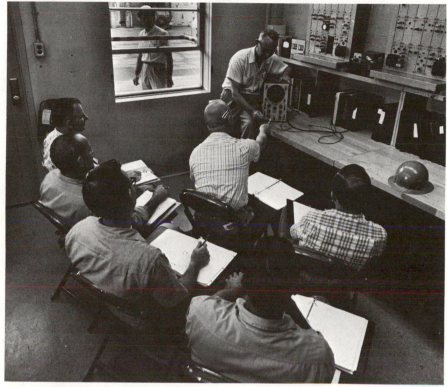

Courtesy of E.I. du Pont de Nemours & Co., Inc.

Supervised training on the job is effective for developing skills.

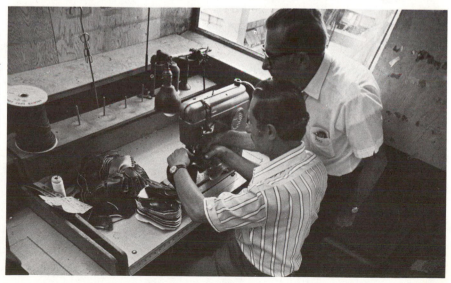

Frank Siteman, with cooperation of Stride-Rite Corporation

panies make their own films and also purchase films made by other companies. As a result, a randomly selected film library is likely to teach philosophies or values that are inconsistent with one another. By careful selection, however, a set of films consistent with a particular company's point of view may be assembled, but it will not be a complete resource for training.

A film's greatest value is in visual learning. A movie can show what actions lead to what ends, how something works, and how different functions relate to one another. In this way, too, one can often teach the overall picture of a company operation even more effectively than by means of an actual trip through the plant. The sound film can be better than a lecture and demonstration combined.

A movie cannot teach any job skills, and its value for teaching interpersonal skills is grossly exaggerated. Human relations *principles* can be presented in movies, as in lectures, though the drama and emotional appeals they contain testify more to their superiority as an entertainment medium than as a teaching device. A movie might fail to train, yet serve to convince management that the company needs a training program. Unfortunately, management might settle for purchasing the film and using it to do the training job!

Demonstrations, Visual Aids, and Sound Film Strips

Direct demonstrations, visual aids for slap-on boards, and sound film strips are less expensive ways of accomplishing what is achieved by a movie. Like the movie, their main value is in aiding visual learning and associating sounds with visual descriptions. Demonstrations and visual aids permit somewhat greater flexibility, since they can be adapted to the interests and level of the audience. However, this may also be a disadvantage in that the trainer is given a certain amount of leeway. If his judgment and understanding are of lesser quality than those of the producer of the training material, he can use this leeway to reduce the value of the material.

One of the values of using so-called "canned" training material is that the prearrangement of materials prevents trainers from introducing their own pet notions. Although this approach eliminates some of the benefits of more personal approaches to training, it is preferable to poor training.

On-the-Job Training and Simulation

Insofar as motor skills are required, the training facilities should be a duplication of the job situation. Supervised training on the job is ideal when the job requirements permit low initial performance. If a certain level of proficiency is needed before work in the actual situation is to begin, off-the-job training, in which the actual jobs are set up for the use of trainees (vestibule schools), is often used. In other cases, facsimiles of the jobs are set up, with hazards removed and opportunities for drill increased. In these improved situations trainees can learn to climb utility poles without going high enough to injure themselves in case of failure; they can operate telephone equipment, with coaches serving as customers, and not disrupt service; sales personnel can be questioned by trainers, acting as clients, to see if they have mastered their knowledge of the product; and pilots can get practice in instrument flying and in handling emergencies by being enclosed in a simulated cockpit.

A unique feature of on-the-job training and its equivalent in the vestibule school is that it is training through doing. Another feature is that instruction is primarily individual. Even if several persons are trained simultaneously, each receives opportunities to practice and each should receive individual help on any particular difficulty or weakness.

Job Rotation

A frequently used training method in industry is known as job rotation. The objective is to broaden an employee's exposure as well as experience. College recruits are often rotated among jobs, departments, and company locations before they are given a more permanent assignment. The rotation method also is used to broaden the experience of managers who are being groomed for executive positions.

The Case Method[25]

The case method was developed at the Harvard School of Business and is one of the first deviations from the standard teaching method in that the teacher or trainer is not the source of knowledge. Instead, learning occurs through participation in discussions and problem analysis. The idea of using case discussion evolved from legal training methods where cases are used as a basis for argumentation. The objective of finding the correct solution (which an authority supplies in traditional teaching) is replaced by the objectives of using facts effectively and of developing a convincing rationale for a position or decision.

Executive training programs frequently use the case method. A complex situation typical of a real-life problem is presented to a small group. The case becomes the theme for discussing "What to do?" "How could the problem have been prevented?" and "What are some of the policy issues involved?" The case method gives trainees practice in problem solving, and utilizes the benefits of discussion. It does not increase interpersonal skills materially, but many of the cases stimulate inquiry into effective leadership styles. One important insight gained from case discussion is discovering that there is no one correct answer or solution and that the best solution is often a matter of opinion or personal preference.

Discussion Methods

Insofar as participation is a motivating force, the use of discussion introduces motivation and involvement. It stimulates understanding, influences attitudes, and can give practice in problem solving. Because considerable time is consumed by a limited subject matter, the coverage is thorough, but there is a sacrifice of systematic organization and of wide coverage of content. If lectures or other methods of presentation are used to cover information for which there is general acceptance, while discussion methods are used to deal with content for which acceptance is limited, both coverage and acceptance can be effectively and economically accomplished. The use of discussion methods for participative problem solving will be discussed in Chapter 22.

[25] Glover, J. D., and Hower, R. M. *The administrator: Cases on human relations in business* (4th ed.). Homewood, Ill.: Richard D. Irwin, 1963; McNair, M. P. *The case method at the Harvard Business School.* New York: McGraw-Hill, 1954.

Programmed Instruction

Pressey[26] invented a method of teaching by exposing a statement with a blank in the frame of a machine. The learner would fill in the blank and then see the correct answer by turning a crank. He would be required to continue a lesson until he mastered all of the items. It would be similar to students taking a sentence-completion type examination in which they could compare their response with the correct one. The so-called *teaching machine* is an apparatus that exposes frames of the programmed sequence to be learned and the correct answers in another frame. This approach fitted Skinner's learning theory regarding repetition and immediate reward (reinforcement), and his support of this type of teaching gave it considerable status and many applications.[27] In more complicated programs the type of wrong answer exposes remedial material that the person can study.[28]

Programmed training permits the individual to learn by himself so that differences in the rate of learning neither hold up fast learners nor stigmatize slow ones. Teaching school subjects in which the correct answer is not a matter of dispute lend themselves to programming. The expected superiority of the method for industry[29] has not been supported by studies in which it was compared with the lecture-discussion method for teaching statistics and insurance fundamentals. It is evident that training for dealing with job problems is not the same as mere memorization of answers such as is required on examinations.

The Incident Process[30]

Instead of presenting a group of trainees with a rather detailed account of a situation as required by the case method the procedure in the incident process is to describe an event that requires action. For example, a good employee wants special treatment. What should the supervisor do? Before coming to a decision the group members are allowed to ask the trainer some questions. Since the incident usually is a real one, the trainer can answer pertinent questions.

Will the trainees seek out and obtain relevant information? This method offers training in getting vital facts and becomes a game in detective work. It is not skill

---

[26] Pressey, S. L. A simple apparatus which gives tests and scores—and teaches. *School & Society*, 1926, *13*, 373–376.

[27] Skinner, B. F., The science of learning and the art of teaching. *Harvard educ. Rev.*, 1954, *24*, 86–97; Skinner, B. F. *The technology of teaching.* New York: Appleton-Century-Crofts, 1968.

[28] Hughes, J. L. (Ed.). *Programmed learning: A critical evaluation.* Chicago: Educational Methods, Inc.; Milton, O., and West, L. J. *Programmed instruction: What it is and how it works.* New York: Harcourt, Brace & World, 1961.

[29] Goldberg, M. H., and Dawson, R. I. Comparisons of programmed and conventional instruction methods. *J. appl. Psychol.*, 1964, *48*, 110–114; Hedberg, R., Steffan, H., and Baxter, B. Insurance fundamentals—a programmed text versus a conventional text. *Personnel Psychol.*, 1965, *18*, 165–171; Nash, A. N., Muczyk, J. P., and Vettori, F. L. The relative practical effectiveness of programmed instruction. *Personnel Psychol.*, 1971, *24*, 379–418.

[30] Pigors, P. J., and Meyers, C. A. *Personnel administration: a point of view and a method.* New York: McGraw-Hill, 1961; Pigors, P. J., and Pigors, F. *Case method in human relations: The incident process.* New York: McGraw-Hill, 1961; Champion, J. M., and Bridges, F. J. *Critical incidents in management.* Homewood, Ill.: Richard D. Irwin, 1963.

training in ways to obtain information from a person because the leader is ready and willing to answer any question; rather the skill requirement is in asking relevant questions. (Will they discover he has an artificial limb?)

The next stage of the discussion requires the participants to make the decision and supply a rationale for it. These may be individual reports which become the subject for discussion in the third stage.

Finally, the leader tells what actually happened and why. This report may reveal background facts and considerations the participants failed to elicit during the first period. The values of this part of the process are similar to those in case discussion.

Business Games[31]

The most elaborate training procedure is known as the Business Game. Like war games, business games simulate a complex realistic situation in which groups compete with one another and the effects of decisions made by one group have an effect on the others.

For example, two or more teams may represent competing business organizations in which decisions have to be made regarding production schedules for some months in advance. Decisions involving cost of storing; excess production versus inability to meet demands; cost of changing schedules, frequent adjustments versus long-range plans; possible gains versus losses from risks; and many other realistic considerations are introduced. The decisions are then processed—often by data processing equipment—and facts relating to market changes are used to feed back the consequences of each group's decision to them. The groups then are confronted with the next step in the decision process.

Business games invite a good deal of emotional involvement. The learning gained perhaps is the development of a better appreciation of the range of factors that must be considered in making wise decisions, dangers involved both in risk-taking and conservativeness, and the value of cooperative discussions. Business or economic principles as such are not taught; the emphasis is on gaining intellectual sophistication.

The-In-Basket[32]

The in-basket method refers to a series of matters or decisions an executive finds on his desk. How will he dispose of them? Trainees are confronted with a rush situation, limited information, and a list of action-demanding items an executive might find in the in-basket. Disposing of matters by delegating, replying by mail, setting

---

[31] Kibbee, J. M., Craft, C. J., and Manus, B. *Management games: a new technique for executive development.* New York: Reinhold, 1961; Greene, J. R., and Sisson, R. L. *Dynamic management decision games.* New York: Wiley, 1959; Andlinger, G. R. Business games—play one. *Harvard Bus. Rev.,* 1958, 38 (March–April), 115–125; Rawdon, R. *Learning management skills from simulation gaming.* Ann Arbor, Mich.: Bureau of Industrial Relations, University of Michigan, 1960; and Cohen, K. S., *et al. The Carnegie Tech management game.* Homewood, Ill.: Richard D. Irwin, 1963.

[32] Hemphill, J. K. (Ed.). Proceedings of the Conference on the Executive Study. *The in-basket technique.* Princeton, N.J.: Educational Testing Service, 1961.

up meetings, delaying action, and deciding who should do some of the urgent things, are possibilities open to him. The fact that actions must be taken places the emphasis of this type of training on the "doing" process. However, the doing involves primarily mental skills rather than interpersonal skills.

This technique reveals the kinds of decisions executives make under pressure and could serve a useful purpose in the selection of personnel, which, incidentally, was its original purpose. The training value resides largely in the subsequent discussion; members report their decisions to small groups which evaluate each member's report.

The needs for delegation, the failure to consider all the alternatives, the importance of taking a look at the larger picture, and the detrimental effects of hasty decisions appear. A variety of self-insights are reported by trainees. All persons have an opportunity to learn what they may have overlooked in their own decisions.

Role Playing

The role-playing method requires trainees to project themselves into a simulated interpersonal situation and play the parts of the persons and situations assigned to them. Role playing can be limited to practice in the skills of interpersonal relations and of conference leading. If this is done, attitudes are constructively influenced, the skills needed for effectively dealing with people are upgraded, and sensitivity for the feelings of others is increased. If role-playing cases are built around issues and industrial problems, such as the Laboratory Exercise in the preceding chapter, the benefits of the case method are combined with the benefits of role playing.[33]

To make the most of the time required in role-playing procedures, principles of behavior and of skill should first be learned by other methods. With a knowledge of principles as a background, good and poor practices become more than opinions for discussion.

Role playing has been shown to be effective in improving two important components of sensitivity: observation and empathy.[34] Sensitivity is heightened by placing supervisory and management personnel in roles in which they experience attitudes and problems of people in situations different from their own.

Role playing can also be used to develop self-insight and therapy. In such cases the interaction processes and the feelings of the participants are more carefully analyzed and a greater degree of skill is required of the trainer.[35] When used to solve personal adjustment problems of the participants it becomes therapeutic and is known as psychodrama.[36]

[33] Maier, N. R. F., Solem, A. R., and Maier, A. A. *Supervisory and executive development: A manual for role playing.* New York: Wiley, 1959.

[34] Smith, H. C. *Sensitivity to people.* New York: McGraw-Hill, 1966.

[35] Bradford, L. P., and Lippitt, R. Role-playing in supervisor training. *Personnel,* 1946, *22,* 358–369; Corsini, R. J., Shaw, M. E., and Blake, R. R. *Role-playing in business and industry.* New York: Free Press, 1961; Culbertson, F. M. Modification of an emotionally held attitude through role playing. *J. abnorm. soc. Psychol.,* 1957, *54,* 230–233.

[36] Moreno, J. L. *Who shall survive?* Beacon, N.Y.: Beacon House, 1953.

Role playing in all its forms differs from the above-mentioned participation methods in that it carries the training into the action phase. It is one thing to decide that a subordinate should be told "in a nice way" how he can improve, and quite another thing to execute this decision. Deciding to delegate responsibility is still a long way from the act of delegating. Even making a decision and communicating it to others require very different skills. Interpersonal skills, emotional control, and sensitivity to feelings are central to role playing, and, when followed by discussion, the benefits derived from it are incorporated.

T-Group Training[37] *(OMIT)*

The T-group (also known as sensitivity training) had its origin at the National Training Laboratories in Bethel, Maine and is a product of a school of social psychology known as *Group Dynamics*. The basic objective of the training (T) is to improve group interaction and communication by having participants develop an understanding of the impact they have on others. A person knows how others affect him, but he often has little knowledge of how others see him or how he affects them. A basic assumption made is that one cannot understand others until he understands himself. This is a rather common assumption in psychology but there is no experimental evidence to support it and this author is inclined to doubt its validity.

The procedure is to organize groups of about 12 persons and have them meet for two or three hours daily for a period of two or more weeks. (Some concentrated programs are scheduled for a long weekend, eight or ten hours each day.) The trainer's function is to pass responsibility for discussion subject matter to the members. It matters little what is discussed, just so long as interaction occurs. Before long the members' conversation turns to themselves and the leader finds ways to encourage the expression of feelings and opinions about personal reactions to one another. The discussion soon becomes surprisingly frank, and these reactions become the main subject. A member often finds himself talking about some of his innermost feelings with the others, who show a surprising interest. Gradually people open up and show themselves for what they are and find that bonds between them become stronger.

The inherent need for persons to be understood, the effects of authority on their freedom of expression, and the freedom of exploring what another meant by something become topics of discussion. The trainer might comment on unobserved expressions of feelings by making a statement such as, "I wonder if John is as sure of what he said as he wants us to believe," or he might say, "It seems that Bill has been very quiet this afternoon. Have some of you noticed that?"

Persons within an organization who must communicate and work with one another are being sent to hide-outs for T-group training. Some are hurt by the frankness, others strongly endorse the experience. Much depends upon the skill of the

[37] Tannenbaum, R., Wechsler, I. R., and Massarik, E. *Leadership and organization: A behavioral science approach.* New York: McGraw-Hill, 1961; Bradford, L. P., Gibb, J. R., and Benne, K. D. (Eds.). *T-group theory and laboratory method.* New York: Wiley, 1964; Gordon, T. *Group centered leadership.* Boston: Houghton Mifflin, 1955.

trainer and various trainers are not in agreement as to the extent to which the leader should facilitate the insights or to what extent he should do nothing and thereby frustrate the group into taking action.

T-group training and some of the role-playing methods have similar objectives— to facilitate interpersonal and group interaction. The former stresses freeing the individual from the shell he has built around himself so that he can better communicate with others; the latter stresses development of an understanding of others so as to penetrate their shells and make them feel free to communicate. The former tends to train participants; the latter, the leader. Perhaps the methods supplement each other; perhaps they are different attempts to do the same thing.

A good deal of controversy centers on T-groups largely because they have become as much a fad as a training method.[38] The fact that no obvious skills are required of the trainer permits persons who have once participated to feel competent to conduct training sessions. It is one training procedure where a little knowledge can be harmful rather than merely ineffective.

Desensitivity Training

As a result of increasing emphasis on the minority rights and feminist movements, it has become difficult to communicate because suspicion can give an innocent or humorous comment an offensive meaning. Failure to speak to someone because of absentmindedness can be interpreted as rejection. The "hidden agenda" referred to in sensitivity training indicates a goal that a person is assumed to be concealing and as a result his apparently generous remarks may be seen as deceptive. For example, knowing that a member of the school board is a real estate broker would cause one to interpret his comments regarding the purchase of property for a new school in a different light than the same comments made by a different member. Sometimes this background knowledge clarifies remarks, but the perception of ulterior motives that are inaccurate or that do not exist distorts communication. The objective of sensitivity training is to increase trust, not suspicions.

With the increasing awareness of discrimination in our society, it is inevitable that nonexisting discriminations will be perceived. Hypersensitivity causes a person to perceive rejection when it isn't there and encourages him to use rejection as an explanation for his own failures.

As insensitivity can cause one to overlook the presence of true feelings and hence fail to perceive unspoken messages, hypersensitivity causes one to perceive false feelings and makes for polarization. It would not be too difficult to discuss the misunderstood motives, the imagined hidden agendas, and the dangers of hypersensitivity in conjunction with discussions of increased awareness of oneself and one's interpersonal impact. This analysis of group process would amount to desensitivity training.

[38] House, R. J. T-group education and leadership effectiveness: A review of the empiric literature and a critical evaluation. *Personnel Psychol.*, 1967, *20*, 1–32; Campbell, J. P., and Dunnette, M. D., Effectiveness of T-group experiences in managerial training and development. *Psychol. Bull.* 1968, *70*, 73–104.

The Training of Trainers

The potential benefits inherent in proper teaching are demonstrated by an experiment conducted under actual factory conditions.[39] Approximately eight hours of special training were given to the people who taught the operation of a stitching machine. The training emphasized (1) techniques of establishing favorable social interrelations, (2) methods for increasing motivation, and (3) procedures by which the trainer could guide and lead rather than push the workers. The training did not attempt to modify the former method of teaching the technical aspects of the work. The basis of the instruction, therefore, may be regarded as one which influences the work environment by changing the attitudes of the trainer toward his job of teaching and toward his trainees. The discussion method was used entirely.

Figure 12.1 shows the results of a trainer's effectiveness in teaching the stitching operations. The two solid lines show the progress of two new operators over a

Figure 12.1 / Learning Curves of Six Beginners. These employees were trained by the same instructor as he received special training in the handling of employees. The curves show that the rate of learning increases as the instructor receives more special training. (Courtesy of A. Bavelas.)

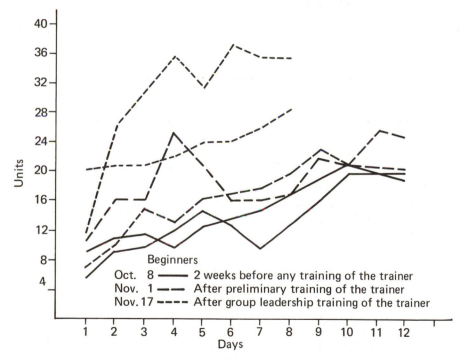

[39] This experiment was conducted by Alex Bavelas of the Massachusetts Institute of Technology.

12-day period before the trainer received the special training. After four hours of this training he taught two other operators. The progress made by these operators is shown by the two broken lines. Finally he taught two operators after receiving his full special training (eight hours). The progress made by these operators is shown by the two dotted lines. It is clear from these curves that the rate of improvement of workers is directly related to the amount of instruction their trainer has received. Despite the fact that individual differences in learning are marked, the benefits of the special training are so great that they predominate over the natural variations in aptitude.

In this experiment, the training of trainers was confined to certain aspects of the teaching of workers. If striking improvements can be shown by this limited instruction in interpersonal relations skills, learning progress must be greatly influenced by the motivation and attitudes instilled by the trainer. Discussion regarding goal setting has been shown to increase motivation for improvement and to lower turnover.[40]

Laboratory Exercise

Discussion Methods and Problem Solving

A. Preparation.

The instructor will:

1. Divide class into committee groups of approximately five persons each.
2. Inform groups that they will be given four problem-solving assignments.
3. Request groups to work as a unit and present one report.
4. Ask groups to select a leader who will coordinate activities as he sees fit.

B. Discussion Topic I.

1. Assignment for all groups: To make up as many words as they can from the letters in the word "industrial."
2. Allow about three minutes' time.
3. Each group reports in turn on its total number of words, and the instructor records scores on the chalkboard.

C. Discussion Topic II.

1. The instructor will place nine dots on chalkboard, arranged in three rows of three dots each. This makes a square of dots three to a side and one in the center.
2. Assignment for all groups: To solve the problem of passing through all nine dots, using only four straght lines and without raising the pencil from the paper. Retracing is not permitted, but a dot may be passed through by more than one line.

[40] Konwin, V. A motivational approach to training. *Train. Devel. J.,* 1967, *21* (3), 26–31.

6 chickens lay 6 eggs in 1½ days
6   4   4   12   (3) days

3. Allow about 20 minutes for solving the problem.
4. Groups report their solutions to the instructor on a slip of paper, and if the solution is correct, are credited with solving it. (In case of doubt regarding the correct solution, resolve this problem in discussion. Some group will find the solution, and, when found, there is no doubt about its correctness.)

_3 3 3_
_6 6 6_

D. Discussion Topic III.

1. Assign for all groups the following arithmetic problem: If a chicken and a half can lay an egg and a half in a day and a half, how long will it take six chickens to lay 12 eggs?
2. Allow five minutes for discussion.
3. The instructor will obtain individual reports from each group member and record group scores in terms of the number of persons giving each of several answers.

I Illustrates that group pressure can cause incorrect answer to be reported.

E. Discussion Topic IV.

1. A supervisor has an extra sum of money in his budget for pay increases. He could distribute this money by: (a) giving all employees an equal lump sum; (b) giving each worker an equal percentage increase in pay; (c) giving increments recognizing differences in need (e.g., dependents, illness in family); (d) giving higher increases to the better workers; and (e) giving increases relative to length of service. The assignment for each group is to reach a decision on the weight (expressed in per cent) to give to each of the five criteria.
2. Each group should report on the weight assigned to the five categories.
3. The instructor will tabulate group results under five headings: (a) lump; (b) per cent; (c) need; (d) merit; and (e) seniority.

Pressures to agree tend to bring individuals together so that agreement within groups is obtained.

F. Evaluation of discussions.

1. Groups are to analyze the interaction processes in each of the four problem-solving discussions. Each group should:
   a. Settle on the characteristic contribution made to each topic by the discussion approach.
   b. Agree on the topic for which discussion time was most worthwhile.
2. Allow between five and 10 minutes for this discussion.
3. The instructor will obtain group reports and tabulate decisions for points _a_ and _b_.

G. General discussion questions.

1. In some discussions, participants act primarily to supplement each other; in others, they check on each other; and in still others, they stimulate each other. Did you have each of these experiences? If so, what determined the type of interaction?
2. Did the role of the participants change from one discussion to another? Why?

3. Which topics introduced the greatest and smallest degree of difference in opinion? Why?
4. Was the difference in opinion always attitudinal or emotional in nature?
5. What topic involved social pressure to the greatest degree?
6. In which topic did discussion contribute the most? In which did it contribute the least?

Suggested Readings

Bradford, L. P., Gibb, J. R., and Benne, K. D. (Eds.). *T-group theory and laboratory method.* New York: Wiley, 1964.

Campbell, J. P. Personnel training and development. *Annual Review of Psychology,* 1971, *22,* pp. 565–602.

Gagne, R. M. (Ed.). *Learning and individual differences.* Columbus, Ohio: Merrill, 1967.

Krech, D., Crutchfield, R. S., and Livson, N. *Elements of psychology.* New York: Knopf, 1969, Chs. 20–22.

Maier, N. R. F. *Principles of human relations.* New York: Wiley, 1952.

McGehee, W., and Thayer, P. W. *Training in business and industry.* New York: Wiley, 1961.

O'Day, E. F., Anderson, W., Kulhavy, R. W., and Malczynski, R. J. *Programmed instruction techniques and trends.* New York: Meredith Corp., 1971.

Silvern, L. C. Training: Men-man and man-machine communications. In K. B. DeGreene (Ed.), *Systems psychology.* New York: McGraw-Hill, 1970.

13

Basic Principles in Motivation

Introduction

Although motivation is a critical determinant of behavior it is often regarded as a panacea. If behavior is deficient a diagnosis must be made before a remedy is sought. An employee may be ineffective because he lacks essential aptitudes, because he has not been adequately trained, because his motivation is low, or because he has a poor job attitude (due to personal or social maladjustment). Any one of these deficiencies could account for limited merit on the part of the employee, but the remedy would differ depending on the location of the deficiency. The remedy for deficient aptitude is good selection and placement; for inadequate training, better or additional training; for low motivation, finding additional ways to motivate; and

Figure 13.1 / Relationship between Factors Influencing an Employee's Merit. Diagnosis of the problem area is the first step required if an employee's behavior is deficient. Starred entries indicate these possible problem areas, and each area requires a different solution. Only problems that are diagnosed as motivational in nature can benefit from motivational approaches.

Aptitude $*^1$ X Training $*^2$
(natural ability)

Achievement X Motivation $*^3$
(ability to do a job)

Performance X Job attitude $*^4$
(amount of production)

Merit

for poor attitude, the search for factors that are at the root of the negative job and social adjustment. Figure 13.1 brings together the relationships discussed in previous chapters and the location of the possible deficiencies for diagnostic purposes are starred. (The multiplication sign indicates that the relationships are interactive rather than additive.) This chapter is concerned with the contribution of motivation to behavior.

The Nature of a Motivating Situation

The Relation between Needs and Incentives

A motivating situation has both a subjective and an objective aspect. The subjective side is a condition in the individual which is called a *need, a drive, a motive* or a *desire.* The objective side is an object outside the individual which may be called the *incentive* or *goal.*

When the natures of the need and of the incentive are such that obtaining the incentive satisfies and therefore removes the need, we speak of the situation as *motivating.* For example, hunger is a need and food is an incentive. The food is of such character that, when obtained, it satisfies the hunger need. If both food and hunger are present in an animal's experience, the animal will carry out activity which brings the two together, provided the activity is in his repertoire. If we place food at the end of a pathway, a hungry rat will work for the food if it has previously learned the relationship between food and pathway. Similarly, human beings will work if they have learned that such activities obtain incentives which satisfy their needs.

Initially both a need and the proper incentive must be present to arouse behavior. Thus the hunger need and the food incentive are both necessary to produce eating behavior. Hunger and water or thirst and food also are combinations of need and incentive but they are ineffective because they are improperly paired. Needs by themselves may produce restless behavior, but such general behavior is in contrast to motivated behavior that is goal-oriented or pointed toward an incentive. However, restless behavior may lead to discoveries; and when a need is associated with a satisfying discovery, future need conditions arouse memories that are called *anticipated goals.* For example, the restlessness of a hungry cat causes it to wander into a field of corn, where by chance it discovers a mouse. After this, the hunger state causes the cat to recall the incentive and so the cat now goes to the field and hunts in anticipation of a mouse. Most of man's motivated behavior is guided by anticipated incentives. Anything associated with the goal object may serve as a cue for it.

The strengths of both needs and incentives vary from time to time and from individual to individual. Hunger, for example, can be increased by lengthening the period of food deprivation. Presentation of the same incentive, therefore, will produce stronger motivation in individuals in whom the need is intense than in individuals in whom the need is slight. Hungry animals will take more punishment to obtain food than will partly satisfied animals; similarly, hungry men will take greater risks to obtain food than will well-fed men. The same degree of hunger will be associated with different degrees of motivation when various food incentives are used. A child will do more for a piece of candy than he will for a slice of bread. It is clear, therefore, that the intensity of motivation can be altered either by changes in the need or by changes in the incentive.

Nature of Adaptive Behavior

Behavior that brings the individual to a need-satisfying incentive is adaptive. Because such behavior makes sense we often refer to it as purposeful. Many adaptive responses are of a purely routine nature, and we may be unaware of the fact that they are need-satisfiers. We dress in the morning, go to a certain place for breakfast, get to our job, do our work, and so on, without really making decisions, forgetting that these habits are learned ways of reaching objectives or goals.

We become especially conscious of the need-satisfying nature of our behavior under two conditions: (1) when two or more possible behaviors lead to different incentives, sometimes even satisfying different needs; and (2) when an obstacle blocks or prevents the learned behavior from being expressed. The first is a choice situation and requires a decision; the second is a problem situation and requires a solution.

Motivated behavior is in contrast to frustrated behavior (see Chapter 4) in that it points to or is directed toward an anticipated need-satisfying incentive. If the desired incentive is not obtained, failure is experienced; if it is obtained, success results. Behavior is adaptive when the anticipated goal satisfies the need.

Behavior is not necessarily unadaptive when there is a failure to reach the anticipated goal. For example, an employee might work fast to gain attention and praise from his supervisor but instead have an accident and be reprimanded for carelessness. However, if the employee persists in repeating behavior that leads to failure, his behavior can rightly be called unadaptive. Motivated behavior, then, is a *means* to an end and is evaluated in terms of the end it achieves. It differs from frustrated behavior, which often is an *end* in itself because the consequences of such behavior do not influence its basic character. Motivated behavior is terminated when the incentive (consequence of behavior) is achieved, but frustrated behavior is terminated when it spends itself.

The Study of Needs

Innate Needs

Some needs are inherent in the nature of the organism and occur in all animals. These needs may be called *natural* or *innate,* since their appearance is quite independent of past experience. In animals hunger, thirst, maternal drives, sex, and perhaps curiosity are generally regarded as constituting the basic needs. With the possible exception of curiosity, for which future research may also identify specific physiological mechanisms, each of these needs can be shown to be associated with a form of internal stimulation.

Acquired Needs

The *acquired* needs are dependent upon experience. If other boys in the neighborhood have bicycles, our son acquires a need for one and will work hard to satisfy this need. Needs for such incentives as indoor plumbing, a certain standard of living, and pleasant working conditions are acquired by the experiences the environment offers. A good example of an acquired need in industry is the coffee break that has created problems for many industrial managers. Acquired needs are just as real and intense as the natural needs; they differ only in the way they were obtained.

The acquired needs cannot be localized in specific parts of the body. This is not surprising, because they are acquired through experience and probably are attributable to changes in the nervous system. Such changes are primarily caused by modifications in the function of the brain. Animals with the most highly developed brains show the greatest number of acquired needs.

From the very nature of the acquired needs, it follows that people cannot revert to methods of living that are more primitive than the ones to which they are accustomed without experiencing deprivation. To argue that workers are better off today than were their predecessors a century ago and therefore should be more satisfied is quite beside the point. Since people had fewer acquired needs a hundred years ago, the same conditions which now represent deprivation did not do so then. To speak of modern advantages as luxuries, hence unessential, is to deny the reality of acquired needs.

By the very nature of human strivings for satisfactions, civilization must move forward, never backward. Too much deprivation produces frustration and releases the undesirable forms of behavior discussed in Chapter 4. As more and more people acquire new needs to be satisfied, a greater number experience these possibilities and so acquire the needs in turn. The accumulation of needs in man serves to drive the desired standard of living upward.

Acquired Needs as Sources of Misunderstanding

Because acquired needs originate in past experiences, people will differ considerably in the needs they develop and respect. A person who needs tea in the afternoon will respect the time and effort another person takes for obtaining tea, but might disapprove of this person's request for smoking facilities. People understand behaviors that satisfy needs with which they are familiar, and for this reason there is acceptance and respect for behaviors that satisfy innate needs. Time off for meals is never questioned. Parents are understanding when their children want food, but they question the need to follow current fads in dress.

We would be willing to concede that when a dog chooses water and passes up food it is more thirsty than hungry, but we might be unwilling to conclude that our son's need for entertainment exceeded that for food if he used his lunch money to buy a comic book. When persons choose to satisfy their needs in a different order of importance than we ourselves do, we tend to question their judgment, even their intelligence, rather than recognize a difference in needs.

It follows that groups that deviate most in experience will have the greatest differences in needs and hence show the least understanding of one another and experience the poorest communications. The following pairs of groups are dissimilar in their social experiences and as a result they should differ in their acquired needs: parents and children; management and labor; supervisors and employees; long-service employees and new employees; rich people and poor people; and Americans and Japanese. Each member is critical of the choices made by the other, and frequently communication between them is handicapped. This failure to understand the changes and differences in acquired needs causes each generation to long for the "good old days."

Social Needs

Like most other animals, human beings are social creatures. A person feels the need to belong or to be a member of a group. The family is the original social group, and every child, early in life, experiences the need to be wanted and loved. Problem children are likely to be rejected children, and rejected children are likely to be poorly adjusted. Rejection is sensed by a person not only through the specific behaviors of authority figures, but also through their attitudes, be they parents[1] or supervisors. It appears that one's attitude toward another person cannot be successfully hidden in any close relationship.

The need to be wanted and to belong continues throughout life. Problem employees usually feel unwanted and rejected at home or on the job. Older employees often begin to feel insecure when retirement approaches, because they fear they no longer are needed. Good adjustment depends upon having this need satisfied. Companies frequently encourage clubs and social activities to increase opportunities for belonging to some group. Union membership frequently serves this function.[2]

An important activity in this direction is the proper induction of new employees, and newly transferred or promoted employees. Such persons leave a situation in which they have a known position and status and enter one in which they alone are strangers. Anything that is done to bridge this gap not only will reduce turnover but will also influence an employee's final attitude toward the situation. A first impression **is** often a lasting one.

Social needs, in addition to a need to affiliate[3] or belong, include such intangibles as status and pride. The need to feel oneself a person of consequence, which we may call the *ego* need, expresses itself in many ways. In order to achieve social status and gain the respect and admiration of others, people will work, compete, and deny themselves many of the more obvious incentives. People may choose lower-paying white-collar jobs instead of higher-paying blue-collar jobs, and a change in title will sometimes give a person more satisfaction than a raise in pay. Ingham inter-

[1] Baldwin, A. L., Kalhorn, J., and Breese, F. H. Patterns of parent behavior. *Psychol. Monogr.,* 1945, *58,* 1–75.

[2] Walker, C. R., and Guest, R. H. *The man on the assembly line,* Cambridge, Mass.: Harvard University Press, 1952.

[3] Schacter, S. *The psychology of affiliation.* Stanford, Calif.: Stanford University Press, 1959.

viewed many employees and found that those with high social needs tended to work for small companies where informal social relations were common, whereas those financially motivated chose large companies where the pay was higher for the same work.[4]

Face Saving

The problem of saving face is an aspect of a social need that is so important in business that it requires special attention. A company may spend a good deal of money to cover a mistake made by an officer in order to protect his feelings and the reputation of the company. One company had an old-type machine custom-built rather than purchase the more efficient modern design on which they could have had immediate delivery and a saving of thousands of dollars. The problem arose because the junior engineers had disagreed with the head engineer over the merits of the old machine. Since he had insisted that the old machines were superior to the new models, a new model could not be purchased without his losing face.

Many disputes between labor and management are face-saving problems. What begins as a difference of opinion over a small matter becomes a heated issue over who is right. This makes the dispute a matter of principle rather than the resolution of the issues debated. Walk-outs listed in the records as due to a foreman's disciplinary action against an employee, to a company's exercising its right to put devices on trucks to record stops along the road, or to a dispute about overtime, are unintelligible until one recognizes these factors as origins of disagreements. The actual walk-out is caused by the inability of either of the disputing parties to back down.

Face-saving situations also are common in our day-to-day dealings with individuals. When one says to another, "I told you so," he is gaining prestige at another's expense. A person will quit a good job rather than apologize, and a supervisor will discharge a good worker if the worker shows him up in front of other people or questions his right to give an order.

Recognizing a face-saving problem for what it is not only makes it possible to prevent differences from being made personal issues, but also helps a manager to deal with such occurrences. Prevention is accomplished by keeping problems impersonal and objective. When problems do become face-saving situations, the resolution becomes a matter of finding a way for each to have an out and seeing that neither claims a victory over the other.

Personality and Needs

Certain needs are associated with personality; among these are fear of failure, and the needs for affiliation, achievement, and power.[5] These needs are fairly stable char-

---

[4] Ingham, G. K. *Size of industrial organization and worker behavior.* London, England: Cambridge University Press, 1970.

[5] For an overview of theory and research, see: McClelland, D.C., *et al. The achievement motive.* New York: Appleton, 1953; Atkinson, J. W. (Ed.). *Motives in fantasy, action, and society.* Princeton, N.J.: Van Nostrand, 1958; McClelland, D.C. *The achieving society.* Princeton, N.J.: Van Nostrand, 1961; Schacter S. *The psychology of affiliation.* Stanford, Calif.:

acteristics which influence the way various individuals respond to challenges, risks, and group tasks. Scores on tests used to measure such needs are treated as unrelated variables. For instance, scores on one measure of the need to achieve and on a questionnaire measuring the fear of failure show some individuals high on both motives, others low on both, while the majority have scores higher on one than on the other.[6] In short, these needs, with those for affiliation and power, may occur together. These motives are different but not, of necessity, mutually exclusive.

The personality differences in needs reveal themselves in an interesting manner when persons choose work partners. A laboratory experiment[7] revealed that persons with high achievement-need scores and low affiliation-need scores tend to select a competent nonfriend as against a less competent friend, whereas persons with low achievement-need scores and high affiliation-need scores tend to choose a friend.

Persons who have a high need for achievement are attracted to challenging tasks, the most attractive being those giving them an even chance of success. Persons high in fear of failure, avoid such tasks since easy tasks are not threatening, and difficult ones permit an excuse. High need-achievers tend to assume responsibility for outcomes (success or failure) whereas low need-achievers are more inclined to ascribe outcomes to external factors.[8]

Supervisors must learn to react to differences in the way competition, hazards, threats of discipline, and pressure affect different individuals. The same methods that motivate some people may frustrate others. These differences may be even more relevant to problems of executive development.

Is There a Need Hierarchy?

Is there a possible ordering of the variety of needs described above? Maslow[9] has proposed that needs can be ordered from lower to higher, and that as each need level is satisfied the needs at the next level begin to determine the behavior. His sequence is as follows:

1. Physiological needs (hunger, thirst, etc.)
2. Safety needs (security, health, etc.)
3. Belonging and love needs (identification, affection, etc.)

Stanford University Press, 1959; Kagan, J., and Lesser, G. S. (Eds.). *Contemporary issues in thematic apperceptive methods.* Springfield, Ill.: Charles C Thomas, 1961; McClelland, D. C., and Winter, D. G. *Motivating economic achievement: Accelerating development through psychological training.* New York: Free Press, 1969; Atkinson, J. W., and Feather, N. T. (Eds.). *A Theory of achievement motivation.* New York: Wiley, 1966.

[6] Atkinson, J. W., and Litwin, G. H. Achievement motive and test anxiety conceived as motive to approach success and motive to avoid failure. *J. abnorm. soc. Psychol.,* 1961, *63,* 552–561.

[7] French, E. G. Motivation as a variable in work-partner selection. *J. abnorm. soc. Psychol.,* 1956, *53,* 96–99.

[8] Feather, N. T. Valence of outcomes and expectation of success in relation to task difficulty and perceived locus of control. *J. Person. soc. Psychol.,* 1967, *7,* 372–386; Rotter, J. B. Generalized expectancies for internal vs. external control of reinforcement. *Psychol. Monogr.,* 1966, *80* (No. 609).

[9] Maslow, A. H. *Motivation and personality.* New York: Harper, 1954.

4. Esteem needs (prestige, success, self-respect, etc.)
5. Need for self-actualization (desire for worthwhile accomplishments, self-fulfill-
   ment, personal growth, etc.)

According to this point of view the deprivation of satisfaction of lower-level needs prevents emergence of behaviors influenced by higher-level needs. It does not follow, however, that satisfactions of lower-level needs insure the functioning of those at the next level; rather, potential higher-level needs emerge and influence behavior only after there is opportunity for satisfaction of lower-level needs. Although there is little direct research support for this ordering of needs, in general it is consistent with findings of studies on motivation. Industrial studies using the hierarchy as a model will be discussed in the next chapter.

Are Satisfaction and Dissatisfaction Opposites?

The existence of a need hierarchy does not necessarily mean that the various need levels are latent or innate. It is possible that as needs are satisfied new ones are acquired. Thus as employees gain job security and good living wages, they acquire other needs. Managers who experience high job satisfaction mention such sources as advancement, responsibility, recognition, and achievement most frequently. However, when they talk about events associated with poor job attitudes, they do not mention a lack of satisfaction in these areas. Instead the items brought up most frequently are criticisms of company policy, supervision, interpersonal relations, and salary.[10] It seems that dissatisfactions are not due to a denial of the sources of satisfaction, which raises a problem for the assumption of a hierarchical ordering of needs. The evidence indicates that (1) the satisfaction of needs, (2) the failure to satisfy needs, and (3) the sources of dissatisfaction should be carefully differentiated in studies of need satisfaction.

A person in a life situation experiences a combination of all three conditions, and the resultant of the forces varies from day to day. The factor of frustration must also be evaluated since deprivation of strong needs may cause frustration, whereas deprivation of less intense needs motivates. One study showed that employees most disappointed with promotions had the poorest motivation to learn while the moderately disappointed groups had the best motivation.[11] Dissatisfaction also may arise when need satisfaction occurs but is regarded as unfair. A study of absenteeism[12] revealed that men who felt they should be receiving more pay showed significantly more absences than those who felt their pay was fair. However, the actual pay had no relation to absences.

A person may be satisfied with a promotion until he learns that someone else received a better promotion. The study of satisfaction is a complex one and there

[10] Herzberg, F., Mausner, B., and Snyderman, B. B. *The motivation to work.* New York: Wiley, 1959.

[11] Sirota, D. Some effects of promotional frustration on employees' understanding of, and attitudes toward, management. *Sociometry,* 1959, *22,* 273–278.

[12] Patchen, M. Absences and employee feelings about fair treatment. *Personnel Psychol.,* 1960, *13,* 349–360.

is more to it than the postulation of needs. We will again meet this problem when we consider the effects of reward and punishment.

Dealing with Needs

The presence of unsatisfied needs in people does not mean that they must all be gratified. This state of affairs is not only impossible but undesirable, since without active needs people could not be motivated. However, it is important to know the needs of an individual if we wish to understand his behavior. Extreme deprivation,[13] such as occurs in starvation, not only increases the food interest and does physical damage, but important psychological changes also occur. These include loss of sense of humor, moodiness, unsociability, and various anxieties. Rejection and deprivation of the need to belong produce various kinds of poor adjustment, including delinquency, and also reflect themselves in physical ailments.

Cases of extreme need-deprivation are not the common problem for supervisors; rather, they are concerned with evaluating individual differences. The objective is to treat each person in accordance with his needs. An understanding of differences in needs among individuals in a group requires the same methods already discussed in connection with attitudes and frustration. The person with the needs is in the best position to communicate them, but this requires an understanding listener. The key to the nature of the need is to discover *why* a person wants something.

Surveys (see Chapter 5) can determine the need differences within and between work groups. Thus white- and blue-collar workers differ in some of their aspirations, as do young and old workers, skilled and unskilled, and successful and unsuccessful.[14] Survey designs and analyses should permit determination of the *why* behind the expressed wants and dissatisfactions. A knowledge of differences in group needs is important for evaluating improvement or benefit.

It is also desirable to know prevailing needs in order to negotiate union contracts realistically rather than politically. A good union contract should give consideration to the needs of all employee groups. Shortening the wage-progression schedule increases wages for short-service employees but neglects those with long service, and some retirement plans have value only to employees who remain with the company until they reach retirement age.

The Study of Incentives

Real Incentives

Incentives, when obtained, tend to satisfy needs. Eating food eliminates the state of hunger; drinking water removes sensations of thirst; nursing the litter relieves the tensions produced by glands distended with milk; sexual behavior alters the physiology of the glands; and the exploration of a new area removes curiosity.

[13] Guetzkow, H. S., and Bowman, P. H. *Men and hunger.* Elgin, Ill.: Brethren Publishing House, 1946.

[14] Gellerman, S. W. *Motivation and productivity.* New York: American Management Assn., 1963, Ch. 19.

The acquired needs, similarly, are satisfied by the attainment of specific objects. A couple may be satisfied by the purchase of the house they have picked out, and an employee may be satisfied when the desired promotion materializes. However, in the case of acquired needs, it frequently is difficult to determine whether the incentive received is the real need-satisfier or whether an apparent need (one expressed to cover up some other need) has been pacified. Furthermore, a simple need may have a number of satisfying incentives. For our purpose we shall think of the real incentive as the one that is the main determiner of the behavior under consideration.

Substitute Incentives

When real incentives cannot be attained, a person often will accept substitutes. Finding substitutes for real incentives prevents frustration, creates extra opportunities for setting up motivating conditions, and extends need-satisfactions to a greater number of people. The childless couple may shower love on a dog; the small boy may accept a cooky in place of candy; and the worker may accept a raise in pay rather than a promotion. In each case the substitute must have some relation to the real incentive, and its effectiveness is relative to its need-satisfying properties.

The importance of considering the relation between needs and possible incentives can be made apparent by an illustration. Suppose a job as supervisor opened up in a plant. Immediately several employees might feel that they wanted it, and all but one would have to be denied the satisfaction of this desire. However, closer examination would reveal that, although several workers wanted the position, their reasons for wanting it might vary. Table 13.1 shows the different needs seven such persons might have. Each employee sees something different in the job, and although all may want it, each wants it for a personal reason. Furthermore, the substitutes from which each would derive satisfaction would differ. Thus, increases in take-home pay, various forms of recognition, more suitable work, and better supervision might each become a substitute for a promotion, depending upon the nature of the need. As a matter of fact, some of the substitutes may have as much or even more need-satisfying potentials than the initial so-called real incentive. Certainly some of the substitutes are more practical from the company's viewpoint, and they might reasonably be given without even thinking of them as consolation-incentives.

Table 13.1 / Substitutes for Position of Supervisor

Person	Condition	Need	Substitute
A	Has five children	Food, clothing, etc.	More overtime
B	Wears overalls to work, spouse a school teacher	Prestige	Cleaner work
C	Dependent on others	Recognition	Praise
D	Buying house	Job security	Assurance of steady work
E	Bored with job	Responsibility	More complex job
F	Dislikes boss or group	Escape	Lateral transfer
G	Seniority	Face saving	Chance to suggest candidate

Many promotion problems can be solved by first exploring the needs of various employees by means of interviews or discussions. Some employees actually do not wish a new job, yet are disturbed when it is given to someone else. They may object to being bypassed or overlooked. Others are satisfied if they have opportunities to make suggestions, to learn how promotions are handled, or to talk about their needs and expectations. Failure to receive a particular promotion creates a face-saving problem for some employees because they imagine that others wonder why they didn't get it. A closer examination of such problems will suggest various ways in which face-saving opportunities can be created.

Positive and Negative Incentives

In the sense that incentives satisfy needs, they have a *positive* or attracting influence and lead to pleasure. Unpleasant objects have an opposite effect, so we tend to move away from them. Such objects may be called *negative* incentives. These do not satisfy needs, unless one wishes to say that the body has a need to escape from pain. Because people tend to move toward positive incentives and away from negative incentives, we may think of them as being pulled toward certain activities and pushed away from others. There are, therefore, two ways of influencing behavior; one associated with reward, the other with punishment.

Both methods are logically possible. People will do a job to obtain rewards and they will do it to avoid punishment. People will pay their utility bills before the tenth of the month to gain a discount, or they will do so to avoid a fine. However, the two methods do not have the same psychological effect, and this difference may be overlooked. In one experimental situation, for example, when children were told to stop playing with a particular toy, they obeyed, but many cried and did not resume play with other toys; however, when told to play with a different toy, the children also stopped playing with the particular toy but were not emotionally disturbed and continued to play with other toys.[15]

Before deciding whether to use reward or punishment as a motivator, one should analyze the situation. To what extent does the situation demand avoidance behavior and to what extent does it demand positive action? Most training problems require learning *what to do* rather than *what not to do*. If a person knows the correct job method, how to do the job incorrectly need not be learned. There may be hundreds of incorrect methods. Many disciplinary problems could be translated into the substitution of desirable for undesirable behaviors.

In a study of productivity of railroad workers, the foremen of low-producing groups were seen by their workers as assigning personal blame and/or exacting penalties when someone failed to do a good job. Nonpunishing behavior, on the other hand, was more characteristic of the foremen of high-producing sections.[16]

---

[15] Meyers, C. E. The effect of conflicting authority on the child. In K. Lewin, C. E. Meyers, *et al.* (Eds.), *Authority and frustration.* Iowa City, Iowa: University of Iowa Press, 1944, Part 2.

[16] Kahn, R. L. Psychology in administration: a symposium. III. Productivity and job satisfaction. *Personnel Psychol.*, 1960, *13*, 275–287.

Dangers in the Use of Punishment

Although punishment is effective in motivating avoidance behavior, this training objective can be lost because some uncontrolled factors may have introduced unwanted conditions.[17] Some possible undesirable effects are briefly given below.

1. Punishment may frustrate the person punished and thereby produce the hostile and childish behavior discussed in Chapter 4. Uncooperative and emotionally unstable individuals are most likely to be frustrated by punishment and are the very persons most likely to receive it.

2. The wrong association may be formed when one person punishes another. This produces avoidance of things other than those intended, such as the avoidance of getting caught.

3. Threat of punishment highlights what *not* to do, thus suggesting an action not previously considered by the individual so threatened. When you are told, "Don't think of how the roof of your mouth feels," you are unwittingly made aware of these sensations and actually do what you are requested not to do. "Don't kill a child," is an instruction given to drivers who have neither the desire nor the intent to kill a child. On the other hand, a sign "School—Children Crossing" is a positive instruction and suggests the desired action. One company displayed over the time clock a list of 22 different violations and the punishment that went with each. It is doubtful whether any employee could have thought of so many ways to cause trouble.

4. In the use of punishment, the objective often is to stop or prevent behavior rather than to train an avoidance response. Inhibiting is not constructive training but rather a destructive or a surgical (cutting out) approach. It is more constructive to substitute an alternative response for a poor one. When possible, training in "do this" should replace "don't do that."

5. Punishment and the thought of being punished create a hostile state of mind, thereby setting up an unfavorable attitude. All things, events, and experiences occurring during this state of mind become associated with it. Employees who are punished for poor workmanship are prone to develop unfavorable attitudes toward the job. The reverse is true for reward.[18]

6. The threat of punishment creates fear and reduces the acceptance of ideas. Experimental evidence supports the belief that fear-arousing approaches designed to change behavior may effectively arouse fear but accomplish less change in behavior than a moderate and reasonable approach.[19]

The fact that dangers are often inherent in the use of punishment does not indicate that it should never be used. Rather it suggests that punishment be used appropriately. Positive forms of motivation should be sought to replace negative

[17] Church, R. M. The varied effects of punishment on behavior. *Psychol. Rev.*, 1963, *70*, 369–402.

[18] Dinsmoor, J. A. Punishment: I. The avoidance hypothesis. *Psychol. Rev.*, 1954, *61*, 34–46.

[19] Janis, I. L., and Feshbach, S. Effects of fear-arousing communications. *J. abnorm. soc. Psychol.*, 1953, *48*, 78–92; Hovland, C. I., Janis, I. L., and Kelley, H. H. *Communications and persuasion*. New Haven, Conn.: Yale University Press, 1953.

ones; but until positive ways to control behavior are found, the old negative ones must be retained.

Why Positive Motivation Is Difficult

If punishment has so little justification, why has it stood the test of time so well? One reason is that we punish not to train, but to vent anger. Our attention is attracted to situations when something goes wrong and then we are irritated. As a consequence, we have neither the time nor the patience to make a constructive response. At such times the use of positive methods is contrary to our natural tendencies. It is a fact that persons are inclined to punish when frustrated.[20] Interpersonal skills should ideally be developed to the point where one does not become irritated when things go wrong: first, because one does not succeed in hiding irritations; and second, because the attempt to hide them is bad for the person who tries, and confusing to the person on the receiving end of the relationship. At least that is the finding in child-parent relationships.[21]

The prevalent use of punishment is due also to the fact that the negative approach is simpler than the positive. One doesn't have to know how to improve a job in order to find fault with the way it is done. Thus, we may find fault with secretaries, foremen, and violinists without being able to show them how to do better. The positive approach assumes that a person knows not only what is wanted but how it can be accomplished.

Activities as Incentives

Incentives are generally regarded as need-satisfiers so that when it is found that some object has incentive value it is customary to assume the existence of a need. This approach to behavior makes attainment of the incentive the end-product of the activity, while the activity itself serves merely as a means. However, some activities are enjoyed and continued for their own sake, not for what they lead to.[22] One can continue walking because it is enjoyable, not because it takes one to a restaurant for food or to friends who satisfy social needs. Exploratory activity might be explained by assuming curiosity needs, but the desire to explore is created by the situation and it seems unnecessary to assume that an inner craving must precede the activity of exploring something new. To reduce the joy of all activity to curiosity, affiliation needs, or achievement needs tends to overlook the possibility that certain activities may simply be interesting. Some activities are boring and we perform them only if they lead to need-satisfiers, but it also seems obvious that some activities are attractive in themselves and that a person will perform them even if they lead to a loss in need-satisfaction or to punishment.

[20] Watson, G. A comparison of the effects of lax versus strict home training. *J. soc. Psychol.,* 1934, *5*, 102–105; Maier, N. R. F. *Frustration, op. cit.*

[21] Baldwin, Kalhorn, and Breese, *op. cit.;* Durkin, H. E., Glatzer, H. T., and Hirsch, J. S. Therapy of mothers in groups. *Amer. J. Orthopsychiat.,* 1944, *14*, 68–75.

[22] Henle, M. On activity in the goal region. *Psychol. Rev.,* 1956, *63*, 229–302; Klinger, E. Development of imaginative behavior: Implications of play for a theory of fantasy. *Psychol. Bull.,* 1969, *72*, 277–298.

In studying the most satisfying aspects of managers' jobs, investigators[23] found that the six most frequently mentioned sources of satisfaction were: (1) achievement, (2) recognition, (3) the work itself, (4) responsibility, (5) advancement, and (6) salary. Note that the work itself is in third position. The report describes instances of satisfactions gained from the work itself, regardless of achievement and recognition. Work that required creativity, was challenging, contained variety, and that permitted an opportunity to do the job from beginning to end was deemed most satisfying.

The postulation of needs for such sources of satisfaction would confuse the issue rather than clarify it. A person might be unable to describe a satisfying job unless one had previously been held. Joy in activity, it would seem, does not always indicate that a need is being satisfied any more than boredom implies unsatisfied needs.

Perhaps the greatest gap in our understanding of motivation results from failure to explore the interests and joys of an activity as a *goal* because of the tendency to define satisfaction as need-fulfillment. This causes one to treat behavior as a means to an end when there is reason to believe it can be an end in itself. A study made on a national sample of employed men found that even if there were no economic necessity for working most men would work anyway. To the typical man in a middle-class occupation, working means *having something to do*.[24]

Choice Behavior

Choice behavior occurs when there is a conflict between two conditions of motivation. If persons are motivated in one way only, there is no doubt about what they will do. But when two motives are present at the same time, two forms of actions tend to be brought to expression. In the end, one wins out, but in the meantime the persons have the experience of making a decision.

Conflict in Motivation

There are three basic types of conflict situations.[25] Each is represented by a separate diagram in Figure 13.2. The *first type* is a conflict between two positive attractions. If the employees of a factory are offered a choice between a certain increase in the rate of pay or hospital, sickness, and old-age benefits, they will have to choose between two attractive goals. Eventually, the alternative that seems to offer the greater total need-satisfaction will be chosen. It must be recognized, however, that needs are an individual matter and that all men would not necessarily make the same choice.

The more evenly balanced the attracting forces, the more difficult it will be for one force to win out to produce a decision. If analysis does not produce a choice, then it is futile to continue the state of indecision. Flipping a coin would be an aid to many who have difficulty in choosing in such cases. There isn't much to lose when all possibilities are satisfying.

[23] Herzberg, Mausner, and Snyderman, *op. cit.*
[24] Morse, N. C., and Weiss, R. S. The function and meaning of work and the job. *Amer. Sociol. Rev.,* 1955, *20,* 191–198.
[25] Lewin, K. *Dynamic theory of personality.* New York: McGraw-Hill, 1935, p. 123.

Situation: Type 1

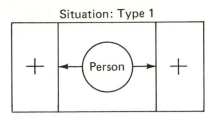

Situation: Type 2

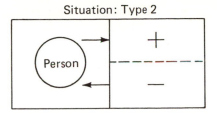

Situation: Type 3

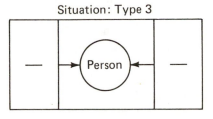

Figure 13.2 / Three Basic Types of Conflict in Motivation. Type 1. The person must choose between two or more different incentives, each of which satisfies a need. Type 2. The person must choose between going toward and going away from something that has attracting and repelling qualities. Type 3. The person must choose which of two unpleasant behavior routes to follow. (Modified from K. Lewin, *A dynamic theory of personality.* New York: McGraw-Hill, 1935.)

The two incentives involved in a conflict may either satisfy the same need (e.g., two kinds of food) or different needs (e.g., food and water). The important element in this type of conflict is that two or more different behaviors are aroused and block each other.

The *second type* of conflict in motivation arises when positive and negative incentives are associated with the same action. People avoid a course of action that leads to a negative incentive, but, if a positive incentive is also present, they will be impelled both toward and away from the goal object. If these opposing forces are approximately equal, a conflict in motivation occurs. For example, because work on the night shift interferes with the normal mode of living, men do not choose it. Rather than force the choice in order to staff this shift, one could increase the pay rate. At a certain differential pay rate, the proper proportion of men would be induced to choose the night shift.

All people can be caused to choose unpleasant incentives if thereby they attain more pleasant ones. This procedure does not utilize coercion but allows choice, and the action is determined by the positive aspects of the goal.

The reverse of the above situation may also occur. Robbing a bank offers attractions in the way of finances, but connected with this behavior is the possibility of an unpleasant prison term. In all cases the conflict is resolved in terms of the relative intensities of the repelling and attracting forces.

The *third type* of conflict involves two negative incentives acting from opposite directions. The individual in this case must choose between the lesser of two evils, such as the unpleasantness of being changed from one job to another and being discharged. This type of choice situation has no positive aspect and is actively unpleasant.

Assisting Others in Decision-Making

Insofar as authority figures are in a position to introduce rewards and punishments into a situation, they can influence the choices others will make. Rewards will cause people, be they children or employees, to choose to do unpleasant things; and punishments, if wisely used, will discourage choices they otherwise are inclined to make. Supervisors, parents, and friends can assist in making wiser decisions by encouraging persons with choices or problems to discuss alternatives with them. Accepting needs, rather than evaluating them, and asking exploratory questions (see Chapter 20) encourages frank discussion and analysis.

When supervisors confront subordinates with a choice in connection with new jobs, the subordinates are not likely to be free agents. Rather they are inclined to feel they must accept the suggestion or offer. Employees frequently accept transfers and even promotions they do not want because they fear they will be bypassed in the future if they turn down an "opportunity." Superiors should be aware of this problem, and, if it is possible, they should give a subordinate a choice between two possible job changes. Giving another person a choice between two alternatives is always desirable, even if the person *must* choose one of them. Employees will accept a transfer more readily if they can participate by choosing between two or more jobs or locations. Giving an employee a choice between transferring or quitting is not a reasonable choice.

A Choice Always Involves the Self

The need which is present in every motivating situation is located in the individual who is behaving. It follows, therefore, that behavior is oriented with reference to the self. Ordinarily, one speaks of self-oriented behavior as selfish. It would be more apt to distinguish between social and antisocial behavior.

If one chooses activities which raise the standard of living for everyone, he is called a benefactor, yet he has satisfied his own needs. It is only when he satisfies his needs by depriving others of the satisfaction of their needs that he receives social disapproval. It is such behavior that society calls selfish.

Because choice behavior depends upon a person's needs, it is not surprising that a great many people look out for their own personal interests. To expect labor to struggle for the interests of the farmer, industry to encourage unions, and Americans to be glad to pay taxes is to expect a good deal. Resolutions of conflicts between groups and between individuals depend upon finding common goals. However, fears and distrust must first be removed. Workers will do a good day's work when they see it is in their interests, and managers will institute reforms when such action is in line with their needs.

Resistance to Change

Countermotivation

Many misunderstandings arise because employees object to changes, such as the introduction of new machines and methods, adoption of higher standards growing out of improvements, and new policies. Often the changes are such that employees will benefit from them, yet they hesitate to accept them. Unions, for example, have frequently opposed work simplification programs and improved work methods, and it has therefore been claimed that they oppose efficiency. The forces operating in resistance to change may be regarded as countermotivations because they exert an influence in the direction opposite the intended or more obvious motivation. It is in the countermotivations that the obstacles to change are to be found. In order to overcome resistance to change, the forces acting upon the individuals must be analyzed and dealt with in accordance with their nature.

Analysis of Case of Change of Work Procedure

Let us examine the case described in the laboratory exercise at the end of Chapter 11 and study the kind of forces at work in resisting the change. The three men on the subassembly jobs exchanged work positions every so often; this was their way of working. In Figure 13.3 this rotation method is called "Old Method." The time-study man, however, made an analysis of the work and found not only that each man had a best position, but that no two men had the same best position. He therefore recommended to the foreman that each man work continuously on the position for

Figure 13.3 / Interacting Forces in a Proposed Change. The forces (arrows) are those set in motion when a foreman suggests a change in work methods. The direction of the forces (to right or left) is determined by the positive (plus signs) and negative (minus signs) motivational conditions aroused or removed, and act upon the crew (circle), determining whether or not they will move from left to right.

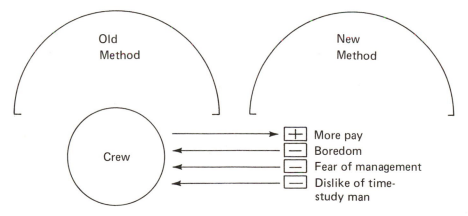

which he was best suited. This method of work is called "New Method." The problem as seen by the foreman is to get the men to move from the "Old" to the "New." The crew (shown as a circle) is on the side of the old method, and since the men work on a piece-rate basis they stand to gain by making the change to the new method. The arrow pointing to the plus sign indicates a force operating in the direction of change.

However, the men object to making the change, not because of a disinterest in money, but because they anticipate boredom by the new method, fear rate cuts or layoffs, and feel hostile toward the time-study man. These three factors are pictured as arrows pointing away from the new method and represent three forces opposed to change. Whether or not the men change depends on how these forces summate and what changes may be introduced in them as a result of discussion.

The Foreman's Problem

Since the foreman favors the *new* method and the crew favors the *old,* a conflict between them is created if he tries to get them to adopt the *new* method. The more he pushes for his solution the more the crew tends to resist.

Two aspects of the resistance should be differentiated: emotional (fear and hostility) and situational (repetitive work). If the discussion remains at the emotional level, problem solving is hindered. The alternatives are limited to winning or losing. The leader needs to use skills to dissipate fears and hostility if the situation is to improve. However, if the discussion centers on the work situation and ways of reducing boredom, new possibilities emerge. These include: (1) two men rotating while leaving the slowest worker on his best position; (2) all men rotating between their two best positions; (3) rotating as before, but spending more time on their best positions; and (4) combinations of these. Such solutions are called *integrative* because they incorporate the facts about the causes of boredom (which the men emphasize) as well as the facts obtained from the time study (which the foreman emphasizes). A compromise solution would be a point between *old* and *new* such as working the *old* method in the mornings and the *new* method in the afternoons.

The integrative solutions have high quality because they deal with more of the facts, whereas the *old* solution ignores the facts of individual differences and the *new* ignores the repetitive nature of the work. They have been shown to have the highest acceptance[26] (measured by faith in the solution). Acceptance, it will be recalled (Chapter 6) is a measure of the way persons feel about a solution and hence influences their motivation to implement it. The greater acceptance is due, in part, to the removal of distrust since the crew need not fear a solution they participated in developing, and in part to the dissipation of hostility toward the time-study man, because they have used his data to achieve their own solution. Thus the emotionally-based negative motivational forces cease to be countermotivations. Al-

[26] Maier, N. R. F., and Hoffman, L. R. Acceptance and quality of solutions as related to leader's attitude toward disagreement in group problem solving. *J. appl. behavioral Sci.,* 1965, *1,* 373–386.

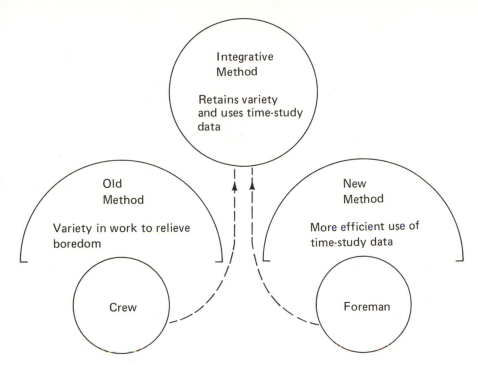

Figure 13.4 / The Emergence of New Alternatives. Conflicts may be resolved by the generation of alternatives that integrate facts favoring each of two conflicting alternatives. Feelings tend to polarize people in conflict and make resolutions difficult.

though an integrative solution may not be the solution the leader had in mind, it can be one that has high acceptance and achieves high quality. The emergence of an integrative solution from conflict is shown in Figure 13.4.

Persons trained in group decision are more likely to be successful foremen in achieving high quality and high acceptance because they are less inclined to persuade or argue and more inclined to be considerate and to entertain ideas contributed by the group.[27] Thus the group-decision approach as well as leadership skill is very important in motivating persons to adopt new ways.

The Level of Aspiration

Success and Failure as Regulators

Success and failure are forms of reward and punishment in that they satisfy or deny certain ego needs. What constitutes success or failure is a relative matter, and the

---

[27] Maier, N. R. F. An experimental test of the effect of training on discussion leadership. *Hum. Relat.*, 1953, 6, 161–173; Maier, N. R. F., and Sashkin, M. Specific leadership behaviors that promote problem solving. *Personnel Psychol.*, 1971, 24, 35–44.

psychological process that determines whether a particular action gives the satisfaction of success or the disappointment of failure is one's *level of aspiration.*[28]

Suppose a person is asked to roll marbles into a hole from a distance of 20 feet and to continue practice until able to make a score of nine successes in 10 trials. In terms of actual achievement, the person would suffer continual failure and soon give up. However, this is not the way people operate. Regardless of the instructions given, each adopts a criterion in terms of ability to achieve success. It might be getting one marble out of 10 in the hole. If this leads to persistent failure, the level of aspiration might be lowered to one out of 20 marbles. As the performance results in repeated successes, the level of aspiration is raised so that some failures are introduced. The difficulty of the situation and the ability of the individual largely regulate the level which a person's aspiration will reach. Success tends to raise the level and failure to lower it.

The level of aspiration functions as a regulator of success and failure and serves to protect the ego from frustration, while at the same time it keeps the goal ahead of actual achievement. Under conditions of normal and healthy functioning, a person never achieves the goal because the aspired-to goal moves ahead as it is approached. This permits the person to continue to exert effort. When the motive to achieve and the fear of failure are about equal, motivation is highest when the chances of succeeding are about equal to the chances of failing.[29] This amounts to competing with equals. So effective is the level of aspiration in serving as a realistic motivational objective that it was possible to predict the success of hosiery work trainees by their level-of-aspiration scorings obtained during employment testing.[30]

Culturally imposed experiences of success and failure of males vs. females and of whites vs. blacks also seem to influence levels of aspiration as measured by an activity similar to a pin-ball game.[31] On the basis of 20 previous trials, the person is asked to estimate the score he will make on successive sets of five trials. Comparison of black and white ninth grade students (low socioeconomic level) showed the black male estimates to be based largely on chance, with large shifts in estimates, whereas the white males were influenced more by previously made scores and their estimates were more stable and realistic. Females of both races were more cautious and less aspiring than males. The authors suggest that the black is less inclined to believe that competence brings future reward and to be unrealistic with regard to the relationship between performance and expectation. Because females have learned that their ambitions are not as readily fulfilled as those of males they tend to protect themselves from failure by setting their sights lower.

[28] Hoppe, F. Erfolg und Misserfolg. *Psychol. Forsch.*, 1930, *14*, 1–62; also Lewin, K. *Dynamic theory of personality, op. cit.*, pp. 250–254; Starbuck, W. H. Level of aspiration. *Psychol. Rev.*, 1963, *70*, 51–60.

[29] Atkinson, J. W. Motivational determinants of risk-taking behavior. *Psychol. Rev.*, 1957, *64*, 359–372.

[30] Heller, F. A. Measuring motivation in industry. *Occup. Psychol.*, London, 1952, *26*, 86–95.

[31] Strickland, B. R. Aspiration responses among Negro and white adolescents. *J. Person. soc. Psychol.*, 1971, *19*, 315–320.

The Influence of Social Pressure on Level of Aspiration

When persons are members of a group, their levels of aspiration are influenced by the performance of other members. Those below average in performance adopt levels of aspiration too high for their abilities; those above average, adopt levels that are too low. In order to keep the level of aspiration of each individual commensurate with ability, only individuals of similar ability should compete with one another.

In the industrial situation, the demands for production are usually calculated in terms of average performance. Low producers, therefore, are under pressure, since their levels of aspiration tend to be raised by the superior work of the others. They become dissatisfied with their jobs and may quit, or they may rationalize their poor performance by blaming conditions outside themselves. They find fault with their tools, their associates, or their foreman. People with inferiority complexes are likely to have levels of aspiration too high for their ability.

In a job for which 60 units per hour was standard, turnover increased as the worker's performance approached 60, and reached a peak for the group that produced between 55 and 59 units.[32] At 60 units the turnover fell off sharply. The study left little doubt that the turnover was caused by job dissatisfaction, and it is significant that the dissatisfaction was greatest for those just below standard. Apparently this group had set 60 as its goal, and after exerting a great deal of effort, had failed. Those with definitely inferior ability were sufficiently far from standard so that the figure 60 ceased to raise their sights. It appears that a specific group objective has an influence for raising a level of aspiration significantly only when it is close enough to an individual's potentiality to be a realistic possibility. In other words, a production goal must be a felt possibility before it can exert a significant influence.

In contrast, workers with superior abilities tend to acquire levels of aspiration too low for their abilities. As a result they experience success without exerting themselves. They tend to be self-satisfied and are content to take things easy while less capable ones exert themselves. Industry suffers a great waste in potential production because it does not adequately utilize the abilities of superior workers. It is true that such individuals do highly satisfactory work, but in terms of potential ability their accomplishment is low. Thus, industry tends to motivate inferior individuals, some to the point of frustration, while neglecting to tap the latent talent of the superior ones (see discussion of restricted production in Chapter 7).

Although the level of aspiration is influenced by previous personal successes and failures and by the group standards, persons with like personal and social experiences are by no means similar in their aspirations. Two influences accounting for these differences are possible. One appears to depend upon personality variables. Persons showing greater anxiety about failure (see p. 334) show larger variations

---

[32] Coch, L., and French, J. R. P., Jr. Overcoming resistance to change. *Hum. Relat.,* 1948, *1,* 512–532.

in their levels of aspiration than those with lesser anxieties.[33] It appears that fear of failure causes persons to set their aspirations either defensively high or defensively low rather than setting them realistically. Differences in affiliation needs also may cause variations in the influence of social pressure.

The other influence is more intellectual and depends upon judgment.[34] Although judgment is unfavorably influenced by emotional involvement and ego needs, the mere absence of such emotional factors does not assure realistic judgment. It is important to distinguish between poor judgments due to intellectual deficiencies and those due to emotional problems, since the method for dealing with the two causes necessarily differs. This need to diagnose is especially great in evaluating executives, because their decisions affect so many people.

Team membership also influences the goals set. Although groups and individuals set similar goals, groups seem somewhat less optimistic about reaching them (divided responsibility) and failure to reach the goal leads to lesser feelings of failure.[35]

Relationship between Motivation and Performance

Figure 13.5 shows three possible relationships between performance and motivation. The solid line represents a relationship in which increased motivation leads to improved performance in equal increments. This possibility is unrealistic in that it

Figure 13.5 / Possible Relationships between Motivation and Performance Levels. (After V. H. Vroom, *Work and motivation.* New York: Wiley, 1964.)

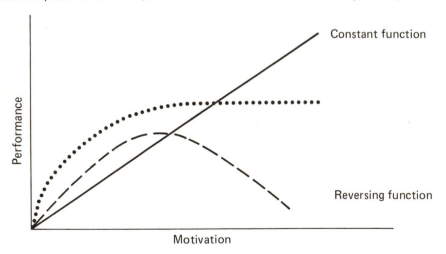

[33] Atkinson, J. W. (Ed.). *Motives in fantasy, action, and society, op. cit.*

[34] Frank, J. D. Individual differences in certain aspects of the level of aspiration. *Amer. J. Psychol.,* 1935, *47,* 119–128; Some psychological determinants of the level of aspiration. *Ibid.,* 285–293; Influence of level of aspiration in one task on level of aspiration in another. *J. exp. Psychol.,* 1935, *18,* 159–175.

[35] Zander, A., and Medow, H. Individual and group levels of aspiration. *Hum. Relat.,* 1963, *16,* 89–105.

fails to recognize the existence of a performance ceiling that is limited by ability. The dotted line represents a negatively accelerated relationship in which a performance ceiling is reached. This is a commonly accepted relationship. However, there is the possibility that strong motivation may retard performance in some instances. Motivation produced by social facilitation has been shown to impair learning, especially in the early stages.[36] Thus curves based on group performance on a variety of tasks might average out the negative and positive effects of increased motivation.

The literature on performance under conditions of high motivation reveals conflicting results. Increasing motivation sometimes is associated with an improvement in performance, sometimes with a decrease. The nature of a task used to measure performance is often crucial. High motivation would tend to increase the speed of running but might impair decision making. The curve represented by the broken line reflects reduction in performance with increased motivation and might accurately describe the influence of motivation in pressure situations.[37]

Attempts to oversimplify the relationship between motivation and performance also overlook the individual differences in reaction to high motivation. Persons high in need achievement and those high in fear of failure differ in risk-taking situations.[38] Furthermore, pressures that motivate some people frustrate others, and when the frustration threshold is passed, behavior deteriorates rather than improves.

Motivating Economic Achievement

Assuming that economic achievement requires initiative which is promoted by high achievement needs, McClelland and Winter designed a training program for businessmen in communities in India.[39] The training was geared to stimulate economic achievement. Need achievement (*n*Ach) tests were given at the beginning and end of the course and significant changes were obtained in the scores. With regard to such personal values as: (1) cautious fatalism; (2) respect for powerful "others"; (3) traditionalism; (4) conforming to caste rules; and (5) submissive conflict avoidance, no changes occurred. Thus the effects of training seemed to have influenced specific values but did not generalize to related ones to justify claims for personality changes. Nor was there evidence to justify the conclusion that the changes in need-achievement scores caused any changes in entrepreneur behavior since business training was also involved.

Accelerating economic achievement in underdeveloped countries by altering needs such as achievement, fear of failure, affiliation, etc., remains an interesting but unproven prospect. Also troublesome is the fact that eight different measures of need-achievement used by various experimenters fail to correlate significantly.[40]

---

[36] Zajonc, R. B. Social facilitation. *Science*, 1965, *149*, 269–274.

[37] Vroom, V. H. *Work and motivation.* New York: Wiley, 1964.

[38] Atkinson, J. W. Motivational determinants of risk-taking behavior. *Psychol. Rev.*, 1957, *64*, 359–372.

[39] McClelland, D. C., and Winter, D. G. *Motivating economic achievement.* New York: Free Press, 1969.

[40] Weinstein, M. S. Achievement motivation and risk preference. *J. Person. soc. Psychol.*, 1969, *13*, 153–172.

Laboratory Exercise ———————————————————

Role Playing: The Case of the Storm Windows

(Students are asked not to read the case materials before participating in the laboratory exercise.)

A. Preparation.
1. Arrange a table at the front of the room. (This should be in addition to the instructor's desk.)
2. Place four chairs around two or three sides of the table so that all occupants face the class as well as each other.
3. The instructor will choose a person to play the role of George Brown, the foreman. He is to leave the room and study the "Instructions for George Brown" (E.1). CAUTION: He must not be familiar with the script that will be used (E.3) and he should not return until instructed to do so.
4. The instructor will select four persons to occupy the seats at the table; see that each has a copy of the script (E.3); and assign the parts of Jack, Steve, Dave, and Bill in a clockwise direction.
5. A fifth person is chosen to take the part of Foreman Brown, who makes an entrance in the middle of the script. He takes a copy of the script and stands ready to go to the table and act this part when the time comes. He is an alternate of Mr. Brown who has left the room.

B. Reading the script.
1. The instructor will read aloud to the class and the actors the preliminary material, labeled "Situation" (E.2).
2. He then gives the signal for the reading of the script.
3. Reading proceeds to end, "Curtain."
4. The instructor thanks the actors for their help, asks the four workmen to remain seated at the table, and asks the person who has read Mr. Brown's part to join the class.

C. Role playing with a new George Brown.
1. Jack, Steve, Dave, and Bill read the last six speeches, just preceding Mr. Brown's entrance, to get in the mood for repeating the situation.
2. They are to dispense with the script as soon as the new Mr. Brown enters, but to continue the business of eating lunch. As soon as Brown enters they must make up their own lines.
3. The instructor signals role player George Brown to enter the room, points out to him who is playing the role of Jack, and asks him to proceed as he sees fit.
4. Role playing should be allowed to continue to a point where the decision reached by the role players terminates the interview or where something else

happens that requires an interruption. The instructor should feel free to discuss progress or offer suggestions during these interruptions.

5. If subsequent interviews are implied in the decision, such as having a discussion with the employees as a group, role play such meetings.

D. Discussion.

1. Use class discussion to evaluate the process observed. How do the observers feel about the decision?

2. List all the things Jack did in the role playing that indicated he had a problem which was more than a dislike of window washing. Distinctions should be made between (*a*) the status of the job; (*b*) the number of times Jack did the work; (*c*) the influence of "kidding" on Jack; and (*d*) Jack's statement to the men about what he would do.

3. Analyze face saving and insubordination as employee behaviors, and determine extent of agreement in the class.

4. Evaluate face-saving problems of Foreman Brown and consider what he can do to avoid them.

5. Determine whether the class considers this a problem between the foreman and his crew or between the foreman and Jack. (Free exchange of views should be encouraged, and differences in opinion sought.)

6. See if class can agree on some rule that will guide them in determining when a problem involves the group and when it does not.

E. Materials for the case.

1. INSTRUCTIONS FOR GEORGE BROWN

You are a foreman in the Plant Department in the Telephone Company and have your headquarters in a small town. The department is located in a two-story frame building, which contains the operating equipment. Your crew is required to maintain the central office equipment, repair lines, install phones, etc. A total of four men report to you and this number is entirely adequate. There is no handyman or janitor in the group because there are practically no upkeep problems. If a door lock needs repairing, someone fixes it when he has a spare moment. Often you fix little things if the men are busy. However, now and then certain jobs have to be assigned. The accepted practice you have followed is to give these assignments to the man with least seniority. This procedure is followed quite generally in the company, and no one has ever questioned it as far as you know. You put in your share of dirty work when you were new. One of these special jobs that comes up periodically is the washing and putting up of storm windows in the fall and taking them down in the spring. There are 12 windows on the first floor and 12 windows on the second. The windows are stored in the basement. There is a new aluminum ladder there that you just got. That ought to make the job easier.

The time is late October. It's getting chilly but today is a nice day. It is a good day to put up the storm windows. Jack, Steve, Dave, and Bill are in the other room having lunch. They bring their lunch and have coffee in thermos bottles. You got them this table and they seem to like eating together.

Jack has the least seniority, so you are going to ask him to do the job. Since you've had no replacements for some time, Jack has done this job several years and knows the ropes. He's a good fellow and cooperates nicely.

In giving Jack the assignment it is suggested that you take Jack to your office. You may greet the group as a whole, but take Jack to the instructor's desk which will be your office.

✓ Instructor read to class

2. SITUATION

Telephone crew men work out of a small building that contains central equipment which serves the community. Although Jack has been on his job five years, he has the least seniority of anyone in his group. Many of the unpleasant jobs around the place fall to him because he is the newest man. One of these is washing and putting up the storm windows each year. There are 12 windows on the first floor and 12 on the second. Jack has made no complaints about it.

However, during lunch one day when he is sitting around with the other members of the group the conversation turns to the storm window job.

E3 ↘

3. SCRIPT [41]

JACK: Boy, that hot coffee really tastes good.

STEVE: Yeah, it's getting chilly outside. Almost had a real frost last night.

DAVE: Yeah! Time to finish my fall plowing in the south forty.

BILL (*reading from paper*): Here's a special on storm windows that looks good. It's time to start thinking of them. By the way, Jack, seems to me we ought to be getting them put up here, too.

STEVE: Sure, Jack, get out the [Windex] and shine 'em up.

JACK: Aw, quiet—you guys are always riding somebody.

DAVE: What's the matter, don't you like the job?

BILL: Takes all your brains to do it, don't it, Jack?

STEVE: That's a real stiff job! You have to figure which one to wash first and which end is up.

JACK: Why don't you dry up?

DAVE: What's the matter, Jack? Don't you like the job?

BILL: Ah, it can't be that! He's been doing it for years. He must like it.

JACK: You know well enough I don't like it.

STEVE: Well, you keep doing it, don't you?

JACK: I'm going to get out of it, though.

DAVE: This I must see!

BILL: What are you gonna do—jump the seniority list?

---

[41] Written by H. F. Shout, The Detroit Edison Company. In N. R. F. Maier, *Principles of human relations*. New York: Wiley, 1952.

JACK: I don't know, but I think it's time somebody else did it.

STEVE: Not me!

DAVE: You don't hook me on it either, I had my turn.

JACK: For how long—one time, that's all you ever did it.

BILL: And that was enough too, wasn't it, Dave?

STEVE: What's the matter, Jack, can't you take it?

JACK: Sure I can take it. I have for five years.

DAVE: Looks like you're gonna make it six years, too.

JACK: Not me—I'm through doing all the dirty work around here.

BILL: What do you mean—dirty? You get your hands clean don't you?

STEVE: Who do you think's gonna put 'em up—Brownie himself?

JACK: I don't care who does it but not me any more.

DAVE: Aw, you talk big but you can't make it stick.

BILL: Yeah, Jackie, you're just asking for trouble.

(*Mr. Brown, foreman, enters.*)

BROWN: Hello, fellows. (*Greetings from the group.*) Say, Jack, could I see you for a minute? I don't want to break up the lunch session. (*Looks at some papers in his hand.*)

DAVE: Oh no—it's time we were getting back on the job anyway.

JACK: Yes, sure, Mr. Brown. (*Picks up paper bag and waxed paper and throws in basket.*) Anything wrong?

BROWN: No, Jack, not at all. I just wanted to remind you about the storm windows. (*Laugh from group at the table.*)

JACK: What about 'em?

BROWN: It's starting to turn cold, Jack. I think we ought to get 'em up. Don't you think so?

DAVE: This is where we came in, fellows, let's go. (*All but Jack leave.*)

JACK: Yeah, I guess *somebody* ought to put 'em up.

BROWN: Will you take care of that, Jack—anytime this week you can manage it.

JACK: I wanted to talk to you about that, Mr. Brown. I'd rather not do it this year.

BROWN: Do what—put up the storm windows?

JACK: Yes, Mr. Brown, I'd rather not do it.

BROWN: Well, Jack, it won't take you any time at all. I'll get you some help to get 'em out when you're ready.

JACK: It isn't that—I just don't want to do it again. I've had it for five years. It's not fair!

BROWN: Well, now—I know how you feel, Jack. I know it's a chore—but somebody has to do it.

JACK: If you don't mind—count me out this time.

BROWN: But I do mind, Jack. We've got to do what's part of our job. And you're the newest man here. Be a good fellow.

JACK: I've been the goat around here for five years. Let somebody else do it for a change.

BROWN: Now, Jack, the others had their turn.

JACK: For how long? Dave did it once and so did Bill. I don't think Steve ever had to put 'em up. Why pick on me?

BROWN: Nobody's picking on you. We just have to do our jobs, that's all.

JACK: Well, it's not part of my job—it's not in my job description.

BROWN: It is part of your job, and I think we have a right to expect you to do it.

JACK: Count me out.

BROWN: Now, be yourself, Jack. I don't want to be unreasonable about this thing, but after all.

JACK: Well, I think I've done my share.

BROWN: We can try to work something out on this next year but suppose you take care of it this time.

JACK: No, Mr. Brown, I just don't feel I ought to do it.

BROWN: Jack, I think I'll have to say you've got to do it.

JACK: I'm sorry, but I'm not going to do it this time.

BROWN: It's an order!

JACK: Not to me it's not.

BROWN: You'll take an order, Jack, or get out.

JACK: You're not firing me. I quit and you can give your dirty job to some of those other guys. I'm through.

(*Curtain*)

Suggested Readings

Atkinson, J. W., and Birch, D. *The dynamics of action.* New York: Wiley, 1970.

Cofer, C. N., and Appley, M. H. *Motivation: theory and research.* New York: Wiley, 1964.

Gilmer, B. von H. *Industrial and organizational psychology.* New York: McGraw-Hill, 1971.

Hall, J. F. *Psychology of motivation.* New York: Lippincott, 1961.

Herzberg, F., Mausner, B., and Snyderman, B. B. *The motivation to work* (2nd ed.). New York: Wiley, 1959.

Maslow, A. H. *Motivation and personality.* New York: Harper, 1954.

McKeachie, W. J., and Doyle, C. L. *Psychology* (2nd ed.), Reading, Mass.: Addison-Wesley, 1970, Ch. 7.

14

Motivation and Work

The Needs that Money Satisfies

Money, in itself, has no incentive value. Since our economic structure has made money a medium of exchange, however, it can be used to obtain the real incentives. Money is sought after in our society because of what it represents. Chimpanzees have been trained to work for poker chips which they found they could exchange for food. As a result of this experience, the poker chips became sought after and saved. The chimpanzees even begged from one another to obtain them, and learned the difference between the high- and low-value chips.[1] In humans, the exchange value of money has become so ingrained that they sometimes appear to be seeking money for its own sake rather than for what it represents.

Before we can understand humans' interest in money, we must appreciate the fact that although people in different income brackets receive the same kind of currency in their pay checks, they are not working for the same things and so are motivated quite differently. The order in which different amounts of income satisfy needs is, roughly:

1. basic necessities of life (food, shelter, clothes, and the like)
2. necessities for health and education
3. luxuries (mostly acquired needs)
4. social position
5. power.

The person who accumulates millions seeks power, and this need is real. People in lower income brackets wonder why the wealthy person should seek more wealth

[1] Wolfe, J. B. Effectiveness of token-rewards for chimpanzees. *Comp. psychol. Monogr.,* 1936, *12,* 1–77.

than is necessary for bodily needs and comforts. They do not understand the motivation to increase wealth because they have not tasted the power and influence one may achieve with money. Many people have said that they will stop working for money when they have obtained a certain amount. Such people failed to realize that they would develop other needs in the meantime and that these new needs would make them continue to struggle. The chimpanzees learned only that poker chips bought food and water. They stopped working when they had accumulated a set of 20 or 30 chips.

That money represents the satisfaction of different kinds of needs becomes apparent if we speculate a moment on what people would do if they could not obtain social position and power by means of money. In such a case these needs would most readily be satisfied by service to society. The success of a person would become a matter of social, rather than financial, status. Instead of competing with one another for money chips, people would compete for other socially recognized indicators of merit. In the Bennington College community, where liberal leanings became associated with prestige, the girls developed nonconservative values, the most capable leaders showing a greater degree of liberalism than the less capable ones.[2] Prestige is not necessarily associated with wealth; rather, our social structure has given money a prestige value. The real factors are prestige and the experience of success. Making money thus becomes an aspiration; once it attains this status, we must continue to make money in order to avoid experiences of failure. With repeated success in the accumulation of wealth, the level of aspiration rises; as a consequence, there is no limit to the game.

Methods of Pay and the Values They Create

There are a number of possible methods by which wages may be distributed, each having its unique effect on motivation and values. Since no single or pure method is universally accepted, the effects in actual practice are mixtures. A discussion of each method, however, will reveal its influence on behavior and help to clarify why reactions to wage procedures are so varied.

Pay in Terms of Production

Payment in terms of the amount produced motivates workers to exert and improve themselves for the production of goods. This method emphasizes individual differences, making superior ability a virtue. Efficiency and the production of goods become outstanding values, whereas culture and leisure come to be regarded as wasteful. Security tends to be a matter of individual responsibility, and the standard of living varies greatly among individuals doing the same kind of work. As strength and alertness decline with age, productivity also declines. Respect for old age is not encouraged by this pay method; the white-haired employee in the shop is not treated with consideration and addressed with respect by the more productive generation.

---

2 Newcomb, T. M. *Personality and social change.* New York: Dryden, 1943, p. 149. See also A. H. Maslow, *Motivation and personality.* New York: Harper, 1954.

Although piece-rate methods use wages as an incentive to greater production, they do not necessarily motivate people to maximum effort.[3] If morale is bad, superior workers fear the reactions of average workers, who do not like the unfavorable light in which they are made to appear. Guarantees that the company will not change rates or discharge part of the labor force if production rises must accompany the scientific use of piece rates. When properly introduced, pay in terms of production is not opposed by labor.[4] As a matter of fact, labor frequently supports such a program.

Experimental tests have shown increased production with the introduction of incentive wage plans. In one study[5] a change from an hourly to a bonus rate resulted in an immediate production increase of 46 per cent and some additional advances during the next 15 weeks. The introduction of a piece-rate system resulted in another immediate increase of 30 per cent. The two changes combined resulted in a production more than 100 per cent above the initial figure. In general, employees regarded the piece rate as the fairest method of pay; there was less lost time and fewer instances of "troublesome" conduct when it was in use. But associated with it there were signs of greater stress such as disagreements among workers, more fault finding with materials, and criticism of working conditions that interfered with productive activity. In one study, opposition to a group incentive came primarily from persons who did not understand the plan.[6] Large work groups also were more opposed than small ones.

However, incentive pay cannot be evaluated in isolation because the effect of a monetary incentive depends upon the way other basic needs are satisfied,[7] the economic situation of the worker, and the type of work. It perhaps has its greatest value in monotonous work and is least valuable in machine-timed jobs and jobs paced by factors beyond the worker's control (production lines, electric substation attendants, watchmen, and so on.) The emphasis on earnings would perhaps have least value for service jobs since it might motivate poor service and strain public relations. The use of incentive pay would also create problems with groups in the company not operating on a piece rate.

Perhaps the greatest obstacle to incentive methods of pay is the employee's fear of the consequences of increased production. A survey showed that 40 per cent of the manual workers believed a worker should turn out the average amount of work but not more. Of these, 41 per cent were of the opinion that management would raise standards or cut rates if production increased, and 23 per cent feared they

---

[3] Adams, J. S., and Rosenbaum, W. The relationship of worker productivity to cognitive dissonance about wage inequities. *J. appl. Psychol.,* 1962, *46,* 161–164.

[4] Davis, N. M. Some psychological conflicts caused by group bonus methods of payment. *Brit. J. Indust. Med.,* 1953, *10,* 18–26.

[5] Wyatt, S. Incentives in repetitive work: A practical experiment in a factory. Indust. Health Res. Bd. Rep. No. 69, London, 1934.

[6] Campbell, H. Group incentive payment schemes: the effect of lack of understanding and of group size. *Occup. Psychol.,* 1952, *26,* 15–21.

[7] Mace, C. A. Incentives: Some experimental studies. London: Indus. Health Res. Bd. Rep. No. 72, 1935; Skinner, B. F. *Science and human behavior.* New York: Macmillan, 1953, Ch. 25.

would be unpopular with the other workers if they did more than the average amount of work.[8]

Pay According to Time Spent

The method of paying wages by the hour or the day fails to recognize the fact that individuals differ in ability. One person can put in time as well as another, so all people become equal. As a consequence, the superior individual is not encouraged to exert beyond the point of a comfortable pace. Social pressure and the possibility of discharge might motivate substandard performers, but these factors then become negative incentives. This daily-wage method wholly fails to use pay as an incentive to production but uses it only to get persons to report for work and put in their time.

To obtain any individual exertion, other incentives must be used; in actual practice, these are invariably present in one form or another. The policy of making promotions in terms of merit, for example, utilizes to some degree the principle of pay in terms of merit or production. However, this practice can lead to poor placement since the job on the next level may require different abilities. Promotion can only be an effective reward if the new job utilizes the individual's strengths and makes no great demands on weaknesses. If promotion is an indiscriminate reward for good performance on the present job, employees tend to become stranded on jobs they are least able to perform. Other nonfinancial incentives will be discussed later in the chapter.

Bonus methods combine day wages with piece work. It is significant that bonuses distributed at the end of the year are too remote to be highly effective, for the effectiveness of an incentive varies inversely with its remoteness. Thus, the use of short-range merit bonuses suggested by Costello and Zalkind might be expected to influence employee behavior more than an annual plan.[9]

The method of payment by the day does not penalize old age. Neither differences in age nor differences in experience and ability influence pay; for this reason, older workers, as well as those who are less experienced or of inferior ability, favor it over piece rates. In many ways, it promotes a kind of equality, but it is an artificial form of equality.

Perhaps the strongest factor in making this method of pay acceptable is that it cannot be abused by management. Favoritism, discriminatory rates, and competition between workers to obtain personal increases are difficult to practice when the job determines the rate. Fear of abuses by management is a form of negative motivation in influencing a choice in favor of hourly wages. On the positive side, there is security in knowing what the wages will be, regardless of inefficient supply lines or daily fluctuations in ability to produce. The fact that superior producers must make up for the wages paid the below-average producers might be argued both ways. Persons of superior ability always have to carry more than their share of the social

[8] What the factory worker really thinks about productivity, nationalization of industry and labor in politics. *Factory Mgmt. and Maint.*, 1946, *104*, 81–88.

[9] Costello, T. W., and Zalkind, S. S. Merit raise or merit bonus: A psychological approach. *Personnel Admin.*, 1962, 25 (6), 10–17.

burden, regardless of the specific economic arrangement followed. The question is, "What is the fairest way to do this so as to recognize merit and not degrade persons with less ability?"

The Seniority Method of Pay

Payment of wages in terms of length of service offers security in old age and makes a person's declining years pleasant and comfortable. Individual differences in ability are not recognized, since all people have the same ability to age. Like day-wage procedures, this method of pay does not induce people to exert themselves unless other motivating factors are added.

Practiced on a limited scale, this method would encourage young people of superior ability to seek employment in organizations in which ability to produce was a factor. The less qualified people would remain in occupations where seniority pay methods were used, since they could wait for promotions as well as others. Practiced universally, it would not permit people of superior abilities to go elsewhere to find a means to capitalize on their talents. As a consequence, such workers could not escape this method of remuneration, and the total effect would be one of reducing labor turnover for all groups of employees.

It is sometimes argued that a person's worth to a company increases with experience and therefore the seniority method approaches pay in terms of merit or production. Although an employee improves with experience, this improvement extends over a relatively short period (two years or less), and as already pointed out (Chapter 7), individual differences in aptitude usually more than offset differences created by training. However, some seniority increases would be justified on this basis.

In order to guard against the undesirable effects of seniority privileges, some companies follow the civil service procedure and give periodic increases within a job classification, but require a person to pass tests or qualifying examinations to become eligible for a higher job classification. This practice limits the progress that can be made purely on the basis of seniority and actually combines merit with seniority pay practices.

Pay on the Basis of Need

None of the above methods takes into account a person's needs. In actual practice, this factor is given some consideration. It is not uncommon for one man to be paid a little more than another because he has a larger family. If pay were determined purely on the basis of need, it would tend to equalize the standard of living of all people.

Since this method of pay would not encourage individual initiative, in this respect it would function the same as do the methods based on day rates or seniority. It would, however, tend to create security, for individual misfortune would become the responsibility of society. Since government has taken the step to make a person's need a factor determining spendable income through tax deductions, relief benefits, and social security legislation, it is less necessary for industry to consider it.

Table 14.1 / Effect of Methods of Remuneration

Pure Pay Methods	Behavior Motivated	Ethical Value	Major Objection	Group Favored
Production	Increased production	Recognizes individual differences	Creates insecurity	Capable employees
Time	Reporting for work	Prevents favoritism by equalizing wage rates	Merit not recognized	Insecure and below average ability employees
Seniority	Long service in a given company	Represents a form of advancement all can expect and control. Security in old age	Discriminates against new employees	Employees with long service
Need	Extending family responsibilities	Equalizes standard of living and gives security to all	Fails to motivate job behavior	Employees with large families

Values Associated with Method of Pay

The motivational effects, as well as the desirable and undesirable ethical values of each of the four basic methods of pay, are summarized in Table 14.1. Regardless of how management might feel about each method, claims for each will be made at one time or another by some group of workers. Good producers feel unjustly treated if less competent workers receive as much or more pay than they do. Other employees feel abused if they are not paid when their machines break down and they cannot produce. Line crews for a utility may play cards in a truck or at the garage during a storm and still feel that it is fair to receive full pay. They feel that because they put in their time the company should pay them for it. Demands for portal-to-portal pay reflect the feeling that the company purchases employees' time, and as long as they are on company property they should be compensated.

One also hears employees talk about giving a company the best years of their lives and because of this they expect to be compensated at rates in excess of others, regardless of productivity. The alleged fairness of seniority rights is an honest and understandable feeling and must be respected.

Cost-of-living increases, wages adjusted to a cost-of-living index, and farm price supports are ways in which the value of the economic need has been recognized. These considerations are a far cry from the law of supply and demand that at one time was a basic determiner of wages as well as of commodity prices.

Proper Methods of Remuneration

There Is No Fair Method

The fact that all four pure methods of pay are actually in use suggests that each has a value for society as a whole. The last column of Table 14.1 shows the group that tends to be favored by each method. People on low paying jobs desire and make demands for decent standards of living despite their lack of productivity. Superior producers have higher levels of aspiration and make demands for extra pay for their superior services. Old employees feel justified in being rewarded for their accumulated wisdom, while people with large families demand more because they must have it. We recognize and appreciate the justice in each of these demands because all these values have arisen in our society.

Since values that exist in society cannot be ignored by organizations, it follows that the best method of remuneration will depend on the ethical standards a given society wishes to perpetuate. Industry can influence these values by its method of remuneration, but it cannot arbitrarily decide on one method entirely to suit its own purpose and interests.

Practical Considerations

The psychological analysis of different pure methods of pay does not yield a solution to the problem of the best criterion of remuneration, not only because of varying notions of fairness and the differences in the incentive value of money, but also because pay is seen as a livelihood and represents income rather than compensation.

In modern society it is not uncommon for employees to feel that they own a job when they have one and are entitled to jobs if they do not. Furthermore, a decent standard of living, regardless of productivity, is accepted as a right. It is not surprising, therefore, that a review of the literature on compensation as a method of motivation in industry failed to support a particular plan or theory.[10]

Financial incentives may influence the level at which one intends to perform, but the intention determines the performance.[11] Thus setting a goal is an intention, and method of pay might influence it. However, the resulting performance would tend to match the goal set. Using "The Changing Work Procedure Case" analyzed in Chapter 13 (Laboratory Exercise, Chapter 11) two methods of pay were experimentally compared: group piece-rate and hourly. Under the piece-rate method the foreman was more likely to get his preferred solution adopted, and the production intentions were higher than when the pay rate was hourly. However, when an innovative solution was developed by group discussion the production-intention was highest and the frequency with which these solutions were developed was unrelated to the method of pay. Discussion influences intention, but the method of pay can serve a persuasion function. Nevertheless, problem solving is the better intention producer.[12]

The wage plan which may be effective for a commercial concern may be quite inadequate for an industry employing unskilled and temporary workers. Similarly, changes in social legislation, economic security, and labor organizations alter the needs of employees, and wage plans must be changed accordingly. Because of these varying considerations, wage plans must be evaluated in terms of motivating conditions as they exist. A knowledge of motivation, therefore, is a prerequisite for the evaluation of such plans.

The most successful plans in profit sharing have involved employee participation, which seems to be essential to obtaining a plan that is perceived as fair. Both the Scanlon[13] and Nunn-Bush[14] plans owe some of their success to the relationship established between management and workers.

Fringe benefits play an important part in labor-management negotiations. When employees find some company offering a desired benefit that their company does not give, they are inclined to register dissatisfaction. To deal with this criticism one personnel director has suggested what might be called the *Green Stamp Plan*. The company would offer a basic package and a number of credit points (stamps), for which the employee could select, from a number of electives, additional benefits to the extent of his credit points. Thus employees with different needs and responsibilities could select the benefits most suitable to their tastes and personal situations. Although this would be a flexible plan, it has not as yet appealed to any companies.

10 Opsahl, R. L., and Dunnette, M. D. The role of financial compensation in industrial motivation. *Psychol. Bull.,* 1966, 66, 94–118.

11 Locke, E. A., Bryan, J. F., and Kendall, L. M. Goals and intentions as mediators of the effects of monetary incentives on behavior. *J. appl. Psychol.,* 1968, 52, 104–121.

12 Maier, N. R. F., and Hoffman, L. R. Financial incentives and group decision in motivating change. *J. soc. Psychol.,* 1964, 64, 369–378.

13 Lesier, F. G. (Ed.). *The Scanlon plan.* New York: Wiley, 1958.

14 Nunn, H. L. *Partners in production.* Englewood Cliffs, N.J.: Prentice-Hall, 1961.

Extrinsic Versus Intrinsic Motivation

In recent years industry has increased the proportion of earnings paid to workers as wages and at the same time has increased the number of fringe benefits. Retirement plans, life and health insurance, rest pauses, and vacations with pay have been added to wages as rewards for workers. Each of these incentives is intended to influence satisfaction with working for a particular company rather than to increase the satisfaction of the work itself. As a matter of fact, individuals are motivated to get through work so they can reach the desired incentives. To enjoy them the employees must be away from work. Behavior that is motivated by what it leads to is influenced by extrinsic incentives.

Figure 14.1 / Intrinsic and Extrinsic Motivation. Work and play generate different kinds of motivation. Extrinsic motivation is produced by giving people rewards (reinforcements) for doing something. The top part of the figure shows the positive incentives (plus signs) that follow work. Persons must perform the work to reach the incentives. Play has no such rewards and instead offers negative incentives (shown as minus signs) which must be experienced in order to reach the play activity. Thus, extrinsic incentives clearly favor the work activity (as shown by arrows) over play. To offset this imbalance we must consider the intrinsic motivational variables which are derived from the activity. What makes play more interesting than work? The lower half of the figure shows that work activity contains many negative incentives. Finding ways to remove negative incentives and ways to introduce positive incentives, as found in play, would be the best way to increase work satisfaction.

Extrinsic Incentives

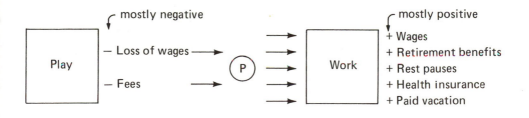

Intrinsic Incentives

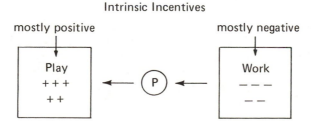

Examples of extrinsic incentives used in industry. These influence choice of job. Job satisfaction, however, requires intrinsic incentives.

Frank Siteman photos

Retirement benefits

With cooperation of U S M Corporation

Company cafeteria

Company sports programs

Tanner L. Ottley

Vacations with pay

Wages

Medical department

With cooperation of Stride-Rite Corporation

In contrast, play activity achieves none of the extrinsic incentives associated with work. Rather, one often must pay fees to play and suffer a loss in wages. These represent negative incentives. Thus, with regard to the obvious extrinsic incentives, there is strong motivation to work and adequate motivation to avoid play. This motivational pattern is shown in the top half of Figure 14.1.

Since this analysis of work and play does not explain why people prefer play to work, certain incentives must have been overlooked. In order to explain the motivation to play it seems best to regard it as having a purpose or a goal in itself. Play is often defined as activity engaged in for the functional pleasure it affords. It has no ulterior motive.[15]

An activity that is satisfying in itself has intrinsic motivation. A comparison of play and work activity indicates that work has more negative than positive intrinsic incentives, whereas play has more positive than negative incentives. The lower half of Figure 14.1 illustrates how the intrinsic motivational forces push the person away from work and in the direction of play.

In order for work to compete with play for people's time, most of the incentives used in industry have been extrinsic. It would seem that more attention should be given to developing intrinsic motivation on the job. What can be done to remove some of the negative signs in the work situation and to introduce some plus signs? How to make work situations more like play situations becomes a question that can lead to generation of new forms of motivation.

Certainly one cannot claim that the hours for play are more favorable. Early hours for fishing and late hours for playing cards are not frowned upon, but would be sources of complaint in work situations. Similarly, energy expenditure does not explain the preference for play over work because a person often expends more energy in play than a company would dare expect. Rules and regulations are present in both work and play situations, yet in one they are taken as regimentation while in the other they are regarded as essential.

Some of the factors favoring play seem to be more freedom in the choice of activity, freedom from criticism, less organizational structure, choice of companions, fewer status factors, less superior-subordinate conflict, and more opportunity to be oneself. It is also true that some people would rather work than play. This is indicated by the fact that wealthy persons, who are not in need of the extrinsic factors associated with work, may devote long hours to work. Usually their jobs are a challenge and contain the abovementioned favorable factors. People who have jobs they enjoy and which, at the same time, offer them the extrinsic factors are indeed fortunate.

Finding ways to incorporate more intrinsic motivation into the work situation requires innovation.[16] Nonfinancial incentives and methods for increasing job interest are forms of intrinsic motivation that lie in the direction of making work

[15] See review by E. Klinger, Development of imaginative behavior: Implications of play for a theory of fantasy. *Psychol. Bull.*, 1969, *72*, 277–298.

[16] Herzberg, F. One more time: How do you motivate employees? *Harvard Bus. Rev.*, 1968, *46*, 53–62.

more like play. Additional gains can be accomplished if the play situation is used as a model for making practical adaptations suited to each particular work situation.

Nonfinancial Incentives

The Use of Praise

Praise is a form of ego satisfaction, and adults as well as children can readily be motivated with it. Too often, reprimand is the more natural procedure. Supervisors tend to expect good work, so they neglect to comment on such behavior but react to errors because they are frustrating in a program of work.

A number of experimental studies have shown the effects of praise and reprimand on the quality and quantity of work of college students. These results are combined and averaged together in Table 14.2. It will be seen that praise of their work produced improved work in 87.5 per cent of the students and resulted in poorer work in only .5 per cent. Various expressions of disapproval of work done caused from 11.9 to 66.3 per cent of the students to do better, the number varying with the form of disapproval, while poorer results occurred in from 10.7 to 65.1 per cent of the cases. It is clear that praise for past efforts is distinctly superior to any form of disapproval of work done.

Only one method of disapproval improves results more than it curtails them. This is private reprimand. All the other procedures listed in Table 14.2 cause the overall performance to decline. It is significant to note that the negative incentives fail to yield the intended results in proportion to the degree to which they damage the ego. Reprimand, ridicule, and sarcasm injure the ego in the order named, and they produce progressively poorer results. Public disapproval is more degrading to the individual than is privately expressed disapproval; thus, in the case of each of the three forms, the public form is more harmful in terms of improvement in work than is the private form.

A comparison of work and play situations will reveal that praise and recognition

Table 14.2 / Comparison of Positive and Negative Incentives

		Percentage Showing		
Incentive	Order of Merit	Better Results	Same Results	Poorer Results
Public praise	1	87.5	12.0	0.5
Private reprimand	2	66.3	23.0	10.7
Public reprimand	3	34.7	26.7	38.7
Private ridicule	4	32.5	33.0	34.5
Private sarcasm	5	27.9	27.5	44.7
Public ridicule	6	17.0	35.7	47.3
Public sarcasm	7	11.9	23.0	65.1

Modified from *Psychology for business and industry* by H. Moore. Copyright 1939, McGraw-Hill. Used with permission of McGraw-Hill Book Company.

for good performance are more common in play than in work situations. In a game such as tennis, players praise their opponents for good shots and console them for poor shots.

Effects of Praise

To understand the variable effects of praise, it is essential to explore some of its functions and objectives. One is related to learning. Learning requires differentiation between correct and incorrect responses. Thus rewards may serve merely to indicate correct responses, while punishment may indicate incorrect responses. Actually, any stimulus that is not highly distracting may act either as a "punishment" or a "reward," depending on whether it accompanies responses which are designated as right or wrong.[17]

A second influence of praise is its effect on attitudes and morale. A ballplayer who is booed may suffer a loss of confidence, whereas cheers would build him up. Supportive behavior by teammates may act favorably on morale whereas critical comments tend to isolate the individual. The source of praise may affect the recipient's attitude quite differently, but in either case, praise indicates acceptance of and liking for the person.

The third effect of praise is its influence on motivation. Praise often serves as a reward and makes the activity that leads to it attractive, while criticism can cause the individuals to avoid activity that leads to it. However, to serve in these capacities the activity praised or criticized must be under the individual's control, that is, one must have a choice between alternative behaviors. Thus the motivational effects can influence the attractiveness of activities that lead to praise, providing, of course, the person has ego needs that are satisfied by the praise. If the praise is perceived as recognition of work and effort, it satisfies, and as already pointed out, recognition is high on the list of job satisfiers.

Finally, the effect of praise as an evaluation of the person or of a behavior must be included as a unique effect. As Farson[18] has pointed out, praise may have a distinctly negative value in this context. Inherent in the use of praise is the process of passing judgment. When one person passes judgment on another, he can be seen as taking the role of a judge or superior person. Thus if one person praises or criticises another, a superior-subordinate relationship may be implied, and, if the recipient does not accept this relationship, the comment may be resented.

Each of the four possible effects can occur, depending upon the situation and the relationship between giver and recipient. Praise seems to have its greatest value when given and received as recognition, and is not perceived by either party as an attempt to control the behavior of the recipient. When pay is perceived in this light its influence on performance and satisfaction is greatest.[19]

[17] Bernard, J., and Gilbert, R. W. The specificity of the effect of shock for error in maze learning with human subjects. *J. exper. Psychol.*, 1941, 28, 178–186.

[18] Farson, R. E. *Praise reconsidered: some questions about the functions of praise.* Rep. #16. La Jolla, Calif.: Western Behavioral Science Inst., 1962; Farson, R. E. Praise reappraised. *Harvard Bus. Rev.*, 1963, 41, 61–66.

[19] Opsahl and Dunnette, *op. cit.;* Vroom, V. H. *Work and motivation.* New York: Wiley, 1964.

Knowledge of Results

In Chapter 12 it was found that in order for an individual to show selective or discriminatory learning, one had to experience *what led to what*. Interests and motivation also seem to depend on a knowledge of what occurs as a consequence of behavior. A person would soon give up driving a golf ball if darkness prevented seeing where it went. In many situations the learning and motivating aspects of the problem are so combined that their separate influences on improvement cannot be differentiated. Apparently both are aided by a knowledge of results, but frequently knowing how and to what extent such knowledge influenced each is desirable. Several experiments involving the acquisition of knowledge have shown that rates of improvement are at least 25 per cent greater, and that interest is also greater, when a person is able to see what he is accomplishing.[20] It also has been shown that previously acquired skill is lost when reports of errors and progress are withheld.[21] Knowledge of results encourages both social and self-competition; failure to supply desired feedback may produce frustration.[22]

In one experiment two groups of students were given a series of mental tasks requiring both accuracy and speed. One group was told to do its best; the other was told its results and urged to better them.[23] A total of 120 tests were made on the two groups. The final results showed that the group in which the individuals had knowledge of their scores did 16.5 per cent better than the group which was urged to do its best.

Similar results were obtained in an experiment which required students repeatedly to lift a weight by flexing a finger and to continue until the finger was exhausted.[24] Eleven such tests were made at intervals of 48 hours. When the subjects knew the number of lifts their efforts had produced on previous occasions, they were able to make a greater number of lifts than when they had no knowledge of their previous scores.

The extent to which improvement in these experiments is a matter of knowledge of results and of self-competition, cannot be determined. Certainly keeping score is essential to competition, but whether knowledge of results introduces something additional has been questioned.[25]

[20] Ammons, R. B. Effects of knowledge of performance: a survey and tentative formulation. *J. gen. Psychol.*, 1956, *54*, 279–299; Bilodeau, E. A., and Bilodeau, I. McD. Variations of temporal intervals among critical events in five studies of knowledge of results. *J. exp. Psychol.*, 1958, *55*, 603–612; Macpherson, S. J., Dees, V., and Grindley, G. C. The effect of knowledge of results on learning and performance. *Quart. J. exp. Psychol.*, 1948, *1*, 68–78; Rao, K. V., and Russell, R. W. Effects of stress on goal-setting behavior. *J. abnorm. soc. Psychol.*, 1960, *61*, 380–388.

[21] Bilodeau, E. A., Bilodeau, I. McD., and Schumsky, D. A. Some effects of introducing and withdrawing knowledge of results early and late in practice. *J. exp. Psychol.*, 1959, *58*, 142–144.

[22] Annett, J., and Kay, H. Knowledge of results and skilled performance. *Occup. Psychol.*, 1957, *31*, 69–79.

[23] Book, W. F., and Norvelle, L. An experimental study of learning incentives. *Ped. Sem.*, 1922, *29*, 305–362.

[24] Arps, G. F. Work with knowledge of results versus work without knowledge of results. *Psychol. Monogr.*, 1920, *28*, 1–41.

[25] Chapanis, A. Knowledge of performance as an incentive in repetitive, monotonous tasks. *J. appl. Psychol.*, 1964, *48*, 263–271.

Knowledge of results is essential to goal setting. In experiments using complex mental arithmetic tasks it was found that supplying scores aided the person in setting realistic goals.[26] Such knowledge, therefore, influences the *level of aspiration* (see Chapter 13) and the resulting benefits can be attributed to motivation.

Knowledge of results also influences team performance by facilitating communication and problem solving.[27] This is especially important when teammates must coordinate their activities. In one study,[28] military defense problems were used with 13-man flight crews. Two study teams that received feedback data and were given discussion opportunities improved an average of 42 per cent while two control teams improved only slightly more than 2 per cent. The opportunity to analyze results served not only to improve team work but also to sustain motivation.

However, when group results are based on the summation of individual results group feedback has little value. In an experiment in which individuals were grouped in teams, only slight improvement resulted from team-score feedback, but much greater improvement occurred when both team and individual scores were supplied.[29] Superior performers improved most from the information and showed a greater concern for personal success and failure than slow performers. When the task was changed so as to reduce the chances for success, the slow performers improved and showed more concern for group results. The fact that slow and fast performers respond differently to these conditions indicates that dependence upon one another is important in attempts to upgrade team performance by motivational approaches.

Competition

Individuals compete with one another not only for incentives when these are limited in number, but also for the mere satisfaction of winning. When prizes or monetary rewards are not at stake the motivational factor must be based on some form of ego need. The person who wins may gain status or social prestige, or experience need-achievement, but one must also consider that the loser experiences failure and may lose status. Thus each competitive situation can create both satisfaction and deprivation. One may argue that both effects have motivational possibilities since each competitor exerts himself, but the fact that these opposed effects may interfere with cooperation must not be overlooked. Sometimes the forces at work in competitive situations conflict with those involved in morale building.

The efficacy of competition has been questioned by several studies. Greater productivity was achieved by groups of students encouraged to work cooperatively on problem-solving tasks (both puzzles and a human relations problem) than was obtained by those encouraged to work competitively.[30] A study designed to clarify

[26] Locke, E. A., and Bryon, J. F. Goal-setting as a determinant of the effect of knowledge of score on performance. *Am. J. Psychol., 81,* 1968, 398–406.

[27] Smith, E. E., and Knight, S. S. Effects of feedback on insight and problem solving efficiency in training groups. *J. appl. Psychol.,* 1959, *43,* 209–211.

[28] Alexander, L. T., Kepner, C. H., and Tregoe, B. B. The effectiveness of knowledge of results in a military system-training program. *J. appl. Psychol.,* 1962, *46,* 202–211.

[29] Zajonc, R. B. The effects of feedback and probability of group success in individual and group performance. *Hum. Relat.,* 1962, *15,* 149–161.

[30] Deutsch, M. An experimental study of the effects of cooperation and competition upon group processes. *Hum. Relat.,* 1949, *2,* 199–232.

these results found that noncompetitive, as compared to competitive conditions, favored attentiveness and involvement for both groups and individuals. But in this case, working in groups (rather than individually) was significantly related to development of high quality solutions under both competitive and noncompetitive conditions.[31]

If self-serving behavior can be assumed to set up competition in conference groups, as appeared to be true in the 72 decision-making conferences studied in an industrial setting, competitive groups did not complete as many items on their agenda as did more cooperative (less self-serving) groups.[32]

The competition in play situations is usually healthy and motivates without causing hard feelings. Imagine a game of cards in which scores were not kept and no winner determined. Competition is involved in many play situations and is one of the basic motivating factors. However, disgrace for losing is seldom present, and facesavers are furnished. The loser is credited with putting up a good fight and is praised for his sportsmanship; a poor showing is explained by bad luck or an off-day. In many games, chance plays a great part in determining the winner, and one can lose without feeling inferior. The experience of winning also is distributed among the members of a group because Lady Luck has no favorites.

When winning is a matter of skill, interest declines as soon as the same person begins to win consistently. If motivation is desired in competition, an element of uncertainty is necessary. One need merely reflect on how a sports event loses interest when the outcome is known and the game is seen as a movie. Games and sports introduce uncertainty by having players compete with equals, limiting competition to .equally graded leagues, making a certain difference in score the objective of play, and setting up various kinds of handicaps. These methods tend to give everyone a more nearly equal chance and therefore distribute winning and losing more equitably.

The importance of success and failure in competition was nicely illustrated in a study involving eight groups of children working arithmetic problems.[33] This task was selected because the children already had mastered the essential skills and productivity (number of problems correctly solved) was easily measured.

Two conditions were tested: (1) each of two competing teams was declared the winner on a fictitious basis in an irregular sequence; and (2) one of two competing teams was fictitiously always declared the winner by an increasing margin.

Figure 14.2 shows the results of two groups of 18 and 19 boys, previously matched for ability, under the first condition. The trend over 12 daily tests shows a rather continuous improvement. The results for two groups of girls working under the same conditions show the same trend.

[31] Goldman, M., and Hammond, L. K. Competition and non-competition and its relation to individual and group productivity. *Sociometry*, 1961, *24*, 46–60.

[32] Marquis, D. G., Guetzkow, H., and Heyns, R. W. A social psychological study of the decision making conference. In H. Guetzkow (Ed.), *Groups, leadership, and men*. Pittsburgh: Carnegie Press, 1951, pp. 55–67.

[33] Bujas, Z., Kopajtic, N., Ostojčić, A., Petz, B., and Smolić, N. An experimental contribution to the psychology of competition in public schools. *Acta Instituti Psychologici*, 1953, *18*, 1–14.

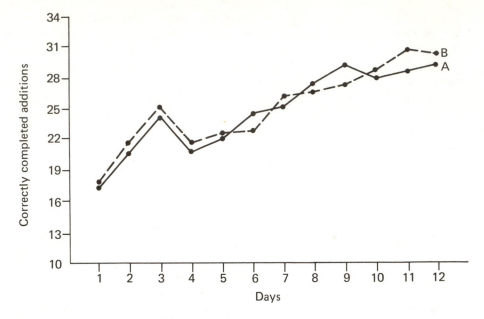

Figure 14.2 / Effects of Competition When Fictitious Victories Are Randomly Awarded to Both Teams. The average number of problems correctly solved by the two teams of boys shows a rather progressive improvement over 12 successive daily tests. (Team A contained 19 boys and Team B, 18 boys.) The progress of two teams of girls showed similar trends. (From Z. Bujas, N. Kopajtić, A. Ostojčić, B. Petz, and N. Smolić, An experimental contribution to the psychology of competition in public schools. *Acta Instituti Psychologici,* 1953, No. 18.)

However, when one team was consistently declared victorious the results were quite different, as shown in Figure 14.3. Here we find the victorious group (B) reaching a plateau while the losing group (A) shows a decline from its best performance. The two groups begin with equal performance but separate after the fifth day. In this instance repeated failure reduces motivation and repeated success fails to sustain motivation. Two groups of girls tested under the same conditions showed similar trends.

When effort exerted by the losing group fails to show gains, motivation declines. It is possible that the fallacious feedback creates a distortion between effort expended and victory, and that this is an artifact influencing the motivational condition. However, if this were an important factor, the motivational effects of the first condition should have been less pronounced.

Limitations of Competition

A typical example of competition in industry is that of giving prizes to first, second, and third place winners in sales campaigns. In order to distribute the opportunities for winning, breakdowns of territory are sometimes arranged. However, winning is

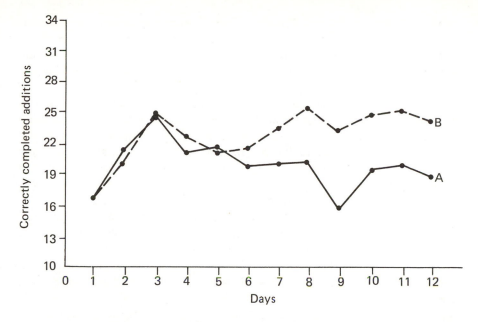

Figure 14.3 / Effects of Competition When One Team Was Fictitiously Always Declared the Winner by an Increasing Margin. The average number of problems correctly solved by two teams of boys shows the winning team (B) leveling off, while the losing team (A) shows the effects of discouragement. (Team A contained 22 boys and Team B, 21 boys). (From Bujas, *et. al., op. cit.*)

the rare and exceptional experience, hence such competition motivates only a few. Group competition has been used in connection with safety records. Frequently the motivation is so high that records are distorted, and *winning* instead of *safety* becomes the objective. In such safety drives accidents often go unreported, and injured workers have been kept on the job so as not to have time-lost accidents.

Few foremen have the authority or the desire to promote competition in order to increase production. They claim the union would object, and this is probably true. Such competition would be frowned upon by workers because it would be regarded as a trick to exploit them. Further, it would degrade slower workers, if not actually threaten their job security. Thus the introduction of competition can make work more like play or more threatening, depending on how it is done.

If supervisors do not attempt to introduce competition but are concerned with job interest only, competitions arise spontaneously. These the supervisor can permit. Indeed, if no steps are taken to criticize poor work records, and instead attempts are made to spread out the experience of winning, these spontaneous competitions can help a supervisor make work seem more like play. The use of group decision will help dictate how extensively this can be done. It is also important to recognize that there is little likelihood of suspicion if employees compete for records or scores that do not reflect production. These measurable items include attendance, punctuality, quality, safety, suggestions, housekeeping, and waste. At all times it is important to be aware of the problem of fairness, and factors making for pressure and relaxed states should be examined. A certain amount of pressure is motivating and pleasant, but too much is frustrating.

Before setting up a competitive situation managers should examine the possible motivational forces it will release. Since competition requires some kind of scoring method, motivation to obtain a high score is created. This means that people will not only be motivated to perform better, but also to find other ways to improve the score. If amount of production is used as the criterion, workers may seek shortcuts which can reduce quality, increase accidents and waste, cover errors, or create problems for competitors; or it can lead to broken rules, falsified records, and poor service to customers. Thus the score, rather than the production the score was designed to measure, becomes the goal. A fair criterion, one that cannot be faked, thus becomes a requirement in effective motivation through competition.

The goal should also be examined to determine whether or not it conflicts with other desirable objectives. Some goals are exclusive of one another, at least under certain conditions. For example, individual versus group results, helping a less able worker versus making a good personal record, competitive versus cooperative behavior, personal pride versus consideration for others, and job satisfaction versus fear of failure are pairs of objectives, both of which may be desirable, but attempts to increase one might reduce the other.

Experience of Progress

Keeping score is an important part of any game. Without measured results or scores there could be no effective competition, and knowledge of results would be limited. Scoring is also essential to creating the experience of progress.

It is sometimes claimed that job performance on nonproduction jobs cannot be objectively measured. However, a little speculation and job analysis would reveal a variety of possibilities. The telephone industry has done a great deal in developing indices for measuring results on service jobs. For example, the effectiveness of a repair crew is measured in several dimensions each determined monthly: (*a*) production—the number of visits per worker per day; (*b*) quality—percentage of repairs that required two or more visits within a month; and (*c*) service—percentage of times a customer called twice before a repairman arrived. Other work groups have comparable indices for scoring quantity, quality, and service. These measures are in addition to records of tardiness, absenteeism, accidents, and a morale index based upon a questionnaire.

Indices of this kind, when used to measure rather than to criticize, are a source of interest to employees. All groups wish to know whether or not they are making progress, and employees watch the monthly or weekly charts of performance. New employees can readily be made to feel that their efforts are rewarded because they can see their improvement, but older employees do not have as much opportunity to experience progress. It is for groups who have already learned their jobs that nonthreatening scoring methods can be used to make work more like play. When employees participate in designing fair methods of scoring, they can experience moving from one aspect of the job to another and experience progress by licking one problem after another.

One of the limitations here is that the more effectively a job is mastered the more difficult it becomes to progress. Extra effort does little to reduce accidents, improve quality, or increase production if these are already near optimum. If effort spent is to be rewarding, improvement must show up clearly in the results. This suggests that progress charts should have units of improvement spaced farther and farther apart as perfection is approached. Figure 14.4 illustrates this method of charting so as to magnify progress. It is clear that Curve A communicates the fact of improvement more effectively than Curve B. This way of depicting progress is not deception if an improvement of from 96 to 96.5 is as difficult to achieve as an improvement of from 81 to 86. Progress is experienced by wage increases. Even when the income tax absorbs most of it, executives (as well as athletes and entertainers) are sensitive to small differences in pay. Obviously it is not what the money will buy, but rather its meaning as a measure of success that has incentive value.

Expectancy and Motivation

The belief that one's effort (Expectancy I) will result in effective performance is a motivational factor that influences performance. It influences motivation even more than the belief that effective performance will lead to certain rewards (Expectancy II).[34] Such expectancies give the task a valence that increases the motivation given the task. It is evident that both of these expectancies are more likely to be present in play than in work situations and that such beliefs or attitudes can be encouraged by managerial behavior.

It is also apparent that Expectancies I and II are more likely to influence persons in high positions than in low. Workers on the production line repeat the same acts; if one leaves a soft drink bottle in the door panel, it leads to no consequences as far as they are concerned. It is not surprising, therefore, that employee job motivation increases at progressive levels of management. Of course, one must not overlook the selective factor—motivation is an important trait in a person's promotability.

Experience of Achievement

Later in the chapter we will find that an important source of job satisfaction is gained from sensing achievement. One of the basic factors in achievement is the experience of task completion. Activities that have definite completion points create involvement, and motivational forces to complete the task are set up. Regardless of

[34] Arvey, R. D., and Dunnette, M. D. *Task performance as a function of perceived effort-performance and performance-reward contingencies.* Minneapolis, Minn.: Technical Report, Center for the Study of Organizational Performance and Human Effectiveness. University of Minnesota, 1970; See also J. P. Campbell, M. D. Dunnette, E. E. Lawler, III, and K. E. Weick, Jr. *Managerial behavior, performance, and effectiveness.* New York: McGraw-Hill, 1970; Porter, L. W., and Lawler, E. E. III, *Managerial attitudes and performance.* Homewood, Ill.: Irwin, 1968; Vroom, *op. cit.*

Figure 14.4 / Two Methods for Showing Progress. Curve A is the usual manner of showing progress in that the vertical axis shows equal steps. For skills that approach a ceiling there is little experience of progress once a certain proficiency is reached. Curve B is plotted against a vertical axis on which the magnitude of the steps decreases as difficulty in improvement increases. This method permits the curve to continue to climb upward.

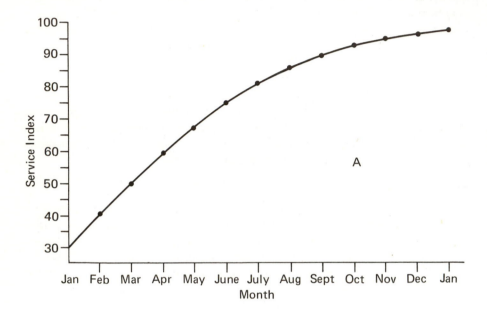

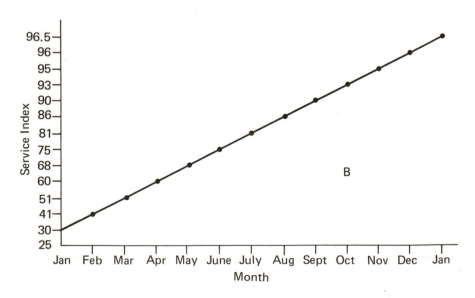

whether the task is pleasant or unpleasant, the completion of the task becomes a goal, and the closer a person gets to the goal the stronger the force. One asset of many play activities is that games have completion points. Methods for increasing the experience of task completion in various types of work situations are discussed in Chapter 16.

Social Factors in Motivation

In sports one observes what is called *social facilitation.* The enthusiasm of the performers influences the spectators, and the spirit of the spectators inspires the performers. It is recognized also that the enthusiasm of certain members of a team may spread to others so that the total motivation of a group is more than the sum of the individual motivations. Group membership therefore becomes a source of motivation, and it may operate to increase the group's productive effort or it may operate to motivate the group to restrict its production.[35] Interdependence of team members and pride in group performance are constructive factors in group performance.[36]

Whether or not the superior performance of an individual is an asset or a threat to other workers depends upon how the performance affects them. In play situations superior performers are more likely to be regarded as assets, while in work situations they are often seen as "rate-busters." The team situation seems to give the superior worker the opportunity to be helpful to associates; whereas, when working as an individual, superior performance may appear as a threat to the less able—particularly when the supervisor uses the high producer as an example.

Participation

A person who feels a member of a group must experience some form of participation. There can be varying degrees and several forms of participation, but it is generally accepted that participation in any form creates interest, and interest is a form of motivation. Participation also operates to remove countermotivation (see Chapter 13). Employee committees and union representatives are often asked to participate in management planning. The results invariably are in the direction of greater acceptance.[37] Of course, participation in decision making is the most complete form participation can take.

Group Decision

The effectiveness of group decision as a method for increasing group effort has already been discussed in detail in Chapter 6. It is perhaps the most effective motiva-

[35] Schachter, S., Ellertson, N., McBridge, O., and Gregory, D. An experimental study of cohesiveness and productivity. *Hum. Relat.*, 1951, *4,* 229–238; Darley, J. G., Gross, N., and Martin, W. C. Studies of group behavior: Factors associated with the productivity of groups. *J. appl. Psychol.*, 1952, *36,* 396–403.
[36] Berkowitz, L., and Levy, B. I. Pride in group performance and group-task motivation. *J. abnorm. soc. Psychol.*, 1956, *53,* 300–306.
[37] Jaques, E. *The changing culture of a factory.* New York: Dryden, 1952; Nunn, *op. cit.*

tional procedure developed in social psychology. Although the forces that operate in group decision have not been isolated, it is probable that those listed below are important in making it an effective group procedure.

1. *Participation is carried to the point of action.* Not only can members participate in a discussion, but they participate in determining what action should be taken. This is a form of intrinsic motivation.

2. *Countermotivations are removed.* Decisions sometimes are ineffective because there is a failure to accept them without reservations. When a group makes a decision there is more complete acceptance.

3. *An acceptable and specific goal is set.* It has been found that specific goals (e.g., 90 units) are more effective than general ones (e.g., improvement).[38] Goals set by outsiders may be specific but they are not as acceptable as specific group decisions. Specific and acceptable goals permit the clearest experience of progress.

4. *Social pressure is constructively utilized.* All people are sensitive to the opinions of others, but sometimes these judgments are injurious to them. The child who is ridiculed by his classmates for wearing shabby clothes is injured by social pressure, but the child who carries out his responsibilities as a class officer to gain the good will of classmates is positively motivated. Group discussion crystallizes the group judgment, and members feel positively motivated not only to contribute, but also to help others less able to do their share.

5. *The freedom and the right to participate give members recognition and ego satisfaction.* This in turn stimulates a sense of responsibility. There is nothing that develops the dignity of the individual and aids in emotional maturity as much as freedom and responsibility. Restriction is a form of regimentation and it stimulates dependent behavior.

Increasing Job Interest

Fitting People to Jobs

Play situations give people an opportunity to choose the game or sport in which they wish to participate. If all persons were required to play the same games, there is little doubt that play interest in general would suffer. Work situations do not permit this freedom of choice. An employee's selection of a position is determined by (*a*) the jobs available at the time a choice is made, (*b*) the location of job, (*c*) the wage rates of various jobs, and (*d*) previous educational opportunities. These factors often conflict with a person's interests and aptitudes. Anything a company can do in the direction of placing employees with their interests and aptitudes in mind should improve job performance because both ability and motivation will be utilized to a greater degree.

Making Jobs Important

Work is interesting and motivation is high when people see their duties as important. Motivation to do a good job declines when people do not understand the

---

[38] See Chapter 6; also J. R. P. French, Jr. Field experiments: Changing group productivity. In J. G. Miller (Ed.), *Experiments in social process.* New York: McGraw-Hill, 1950, pp. 81–96.

why of what they are doing or feel they make no contribution to the total effort.[39] Job training should encourage an understanding of each job and should show how its activities relate to the success of the company; company tours, films, and company meetings furnish employees opportunities to see how their jobs relate to company operations as a whole; and supervision should be aware of the need to respect the dignity of each individual.

During emergencies it is very characteristic for motivation to be extremely high. Utility executives are in full agreement that line crews can be depended upon during storms and after disasters. Certainly, an important factor in their unique motivation is the feeling of importance and of being needed that is afforded such employees by a crisis.

Job Enlargement and Job Enrichment

Job enlargement represents an approach designed to take some of the negative aspects out of work activity by introducing variety (combining two jobs) and some of the other features discussed above. Job enrichment, on the other hand, is more concerned with introducing some positive features in work activity (e.g., participation in goal setting). Both of these developments are primarily concerned with the intrinsic aspects of motivation rather than extrinsic and hence are in line with our emphasis on making work more like play. These and other methods for reducing boredom and increasing job interest are discussed in detail in Chapter 16.

What Employees Want in their Jobs

Needs of Rank-and-File Workers

The importance of nonfinancial factors in work is borne out by a number of investigations on the wants of employees. In one study, 325 women factory workers in England were asked to arrange ten items in order of their importance.[40] High pay was found to be only the sixth in importance. More important items were steady work and factors dealing with working conditions. In a similar study of 100 department store employees and 150 miscellaneous workers, it was found that the item of good pay was sixth and seventh for the two groups, respectively, in a list of 12 factors.[41] Opportunities to advance, to use their own ideas, and to learn, as well as steady work, were rated higher than good pay by these groups. Nonselling employees of a merchandising organization placed good pay in the twenty-first position in a list of 28 items.[42] Factors having to do with fair and considerate treatment tended to characterize the items thought to be the more important.

In a comparison of union and nonunion workers, the amount of pay tied with working conditions for fourth place in a list of 14 items among union employees

---

[39] Wickert, F. R. Turnover and employee's feelings of ego-involvement in the day-to-day operation of a company. *Personnel Psychol.*, 1951, *4*, 1–14.

[40] Wyatt, S. Langdon, J. N., and Stock, F. G. L. Fatigue and boredom in repetitive work. Indust. Health Res. Bd., 1937, Rep. No. 77, pp. 43–46.

[41] Chant, S. N. F. Measuring the factors that make a job interesting. *Personnel J.*, 1932, *11*, 1–4.

[42] Houser, J. D. *What people want from business.* New York: McGraw-Hill, 1938, p. 29.

and was in second place for nonunion employees.[43] The two groups of men differed to a marked degree on three items only. Union employees regarded fair adjustment of grievances and safety as highly important and put them in first and third places, respectively; whereas nonunion employees put these items in the seventh and ninth positions. Chance for promotion was given third place by the nonunion employees and sixth place by the union men.

Many items vary in importance, depending upon the conditions under which the employees are working. The desirability of a good boss is apparent when one does not have one. If promotions are made without regard to ability, this factor becomes the basis of a grievance. Women apparently feel the need for good working conditions, congenial working companions, and a good boss more than do men. It is particularly important to recognize this sex difference with the increase in the number of women in industry.

A recent survey of workers' self-ranking of their needs compared with their needs as judged by union leaders and supervisors revealed some interesting discrepancies.[44] The average rank given each of the 14 items is shown in Table 14.3. Security needs tended to rank high in all groups and were quite accurately judged by union leaders and managers. The greatest discrepancy in both the union leaders and supervisors' judgments of the worker needs had to do with social needs (Item 5, "getting along with coworkers," and Item 6, "getting along with supervisors"). Factory workers ranked these items fourth and fifth, respectively, whereas union leaders judged them to be 11.5 and 13, respectively, and supervisors judged them to be 11 and 12.5 respectively. Self-reported rankings of union representatives gave Item 5 a ranking of 2.5 and Item 6 a ranking of 13. It is apparent that social needs of employees continue to be underrated by both union representatives and supervisory personnel. The higher order need of self-actualization (indicated by Item 8, chance to do interesting work) ranks lowest (10.5) for factory workers but ranks third or higher in the self-rankings of others.

Needs of Managers

What people want from a job may reveal sources of satisfaction or avoidance of dissatisfaction. This was demonstrated in a study[45] in which engineers and accountants in management were interviewed in connection with company experiences that lead to major satisfactions and dissatisfactions. Each of 228 participants was interviewed in connection with at least one of each type of experience. It was found that this select group mentioned experiences of (1) achievement (41%); (2) recognition (33%); (3) work itself (26%); (4) responsibility (23%) and (5) advancement (20%) more often than salary (15%). This ordering places five satisfiers ahead of "salary" and indicates the importance of nonfinancial incentives. Even when salary is mentioned as a satisfier it is in connection with recogni-

[43] Hersey, R. B. Psychology of workers. *Personnel J.*, 1936, *14*, 291–296.

[44] Gluskinos, U. M., and Kestelman, B. J. Management and labor leaders' perception of worker needs as compared with self-reported needs. *Personnel Psychol.*, 1971, *24*, 239–246.

[45] Herzberg, F., Mausner, B., and Snyderman, B. B. *The motivation to work* (3rd ed.). New York: Wiley, 1959. See also L. E. Danielson, *Characteristics of engineers and scientists.* Ann Arbor, Mich.: Bureau of Industrial Relations, University of Michigan, 1960.

Table 14.3 / Self-Perceived Needs as Compared to Judgments of Managers and Union Leaders

Job Factors	Factory Employee's Self-ranking	Management's Ranking of Employees	Union Leaders' Ranking of Employees	Management's Self-ranking	Union Leaders' Self-ranking
1. Steady Work	1	2	1	1	2.5
2. High Wages	3	1	2	2	10
3. Pensions and	2	3	3	6	6
4. Not . . . work too hard	8	14	8.5	14	14
5. Getting along with coworkers	4	11	11.5	7	2.5
6. Getting along with supervisors	5	12.5	13	10	13
7. Chance to do quality work	7	12.5	14	4	4
8. Chance to do interesting work	10.5	6	11.5	3	1
9. Chance for promotion	12	7.5	8.5	5	7
10. Good working conditions	10.5	9	6.5	9	8.5
11. Paid vacations	10.5	10	6.5	12	12
12. Good unions	13	7.5	10	13	5
13. Good working hours	6	4	4	11	11
14. Chance for raise	14	5	5	8	8.5
n =	65	16	6	16	6

From Gluskinos, U. M., and Kestelman, B. J., Management and labor leaders' perception of worker needs as compared with self-reported needs. *Personnel Psychol.*, 1971, *24*, 239–246.

tion. "Job security" falls at the end of the list of 16 items, apparently indicating that steady work is taken for granted at this level of management. There were eight sources of dissatisfaction that exceeded the 10 per cent frequency. Four were in the top half of the list of sources of satisfaction and four in the bottom half, indicating that removal of some of these sources of dissatisfaction would not create satisfaction. However, "recognition," joy in the "work itself," "advancement," and "salary" appeared frequently in both columns, indicating that they remembered satisfaction when received and dissatisfaction when denied.

When the sources of satisfaction and dissatisfaction were added together the order of the first eight items was "recognition," "achievement," "work itself," "company policy," "salary," "advancement," "responsibility," and "technical supervision."

The source "interpersonal relations" was divided into several areas: subordinates, superiors, and peers. Relations with superiors was the largest source of dissatisfaction in the interpersonal relations category. When this source was added to "technical supervision" it became a major factor in dissatisfaction (35 per cent), but only a minor factor (7 per cent) as a source of satisfaction.

Factors Influencing Choice of Work

This study of college-educated personnel in management indicates that their job expectations and wants differ somewhat from rank-and-file workers in that a higher order of needs (p. 335) tends to play a more important part. Suppose we now turn to college students, who are preparing themselves for occupations, and examine the job characteristics that would influence them most in the *choice* of a job. Undergraduates were asked to check the five job factors in a list of 25 that would influence their choices the most. The list of items used was made up by the previous class of students and contains all the factors mentioned. The order of the items was varied for four semesters during which data were collected by the author.

Table 14.4 shows the per cent of male and female students who chose each of the items among the five characteristics they considered most important. They are listed in the rank order in which males placed them. Extrinsic factors, such as "opportunity to advance" and "good salary," were the two most important factors for both men and women, while intrinsic factors such as work that "challenges ability," contains "variety," and makes "use of talents" follow in third, fourth, and fifth positions. There is surprising agreement between the sexes, the correlation in the two rank orders being .86. Only two factors appear in the top ten choices of the males which are not in the top 10 for the females. These are having a work location that is a "good place to raise family" (seventh for males and twelfth for females) and "importance of job" (tenth for males and thirteenth for females). The two factors included in the top ten by women were "good work companions" (sixth for females and eleventh for males) and "good boss" (eighth for females and thirteenth for males).

The results suggest that the choice of job, whether for male or female, is determined most by two extrinsic factors, which apparently become relatively less important once a job is obtained. With this tendency already operating, it becomes apparent that college recruitment interviewers should not attempt to influence job

	Job Characteristics	Males	Rank Order[a]	Females	Rank Order	
			Per Cent of Time Chosen as One of Five Most Important Items in List			
1.	Opportunities for advancement	76.9	1	55.1	2	**
2.	Good salary	72.6	2	63.6	1	
3.	Challenges ability	50.0	3	54.2	3	
4.	Variety in the work	36.5	4	39.8	5	
5.	Make use of talents	33.3	5	40.7	4	
6.	High responsibility	32.7	6	18.6	10	**
7.	Good place to raise family	28.8	7	16.1	12	**
8.	Job security	27.6	8	32.2	7	
9.	Voice in decisions	23.1	9	22.9	9	
10.	Importance of job	17.9	10	14.4	13	
11.	Good work companions	16.7	11	34.7	6	**
12.	Status	15.7	12	8.5	16	*
13.	Good boss	14.7	13	23.7	8	*
14.	Free to choose hours	9.3	14	10.2	12	
15.	Liberal fringe benefits	8.3	15	7.6	18.5	
16.	Job requiring travel	6.4	16	6.8	18.5	
17.	Supervisory work	6.1	17	2.5	22.5	
18.	Good physical surroundings	5.8	18.5	11.9	14	
19.	Adequate equipment	5.8	18.5	7.6	17	
20.	Good hours	5.4	20	17.8	11	**
21.	Sabbatical leave	2.2	21	3.4	21	
22.	Can live near work location	1.9	22	4.2	20	
23.	Job location near recreation area	1.6	23	0.0	25	*
24.	Music	1.0	24	.8	24	
25.	Choice of dress	.3	25	2.5	22.5	

[a]Correlation of rank order for males and females is .86 (p = .01).
*Difference in percentages of males and females significant at .05 level.
**Difference in percentages of males and females significant at .01 level.

From data collected by N.R.F. Maier in 1963–1964: 326 males and 121 females.

Table 14.4 / Job Characteristics Desired by College Students

choices by extrinsic factors alone. They should explore more deeply to determine whether the job offered the recruit will provide intrinsic satisfactions, thereby improving job placement and reducing eventual turnover.

Theoretical and Practical Considerations

Herzberg's Two-Factor Theory

The factors contributing to satisfaction are largely those relating to the work itself, whereas those that produce dissatisfaction primarily concern the context in which the work is done. This leads to the classification of work variables into satisfiers and dissatisfiers: *motivators* and *hygiene factors,* respectively. This separation clearly establishes that satisfaction is not simply the absence of dissatisfaction. However, the division of the variables into two qualitatively different classes resulted in considerable controversy.[46] Since there is a tendency to blame others when frustration (dissatisfaction) is experienced, and to focus on task accomplishment when satisfaction is experienced, critical research is needed to determine whether the hygiene factors are causes or symptoms of frustration.

Solem[47] collected favorable and unfavorable experiences of managers on their present jobs. The 10 most frequently mentioned favorable experiences were: sense of accomplishment, stimulating work, pay and fringes, freedom to be responsible, high status job, pleasant associates, good company or organization, contact with higher management and others, opportunity for personal growth, and pride in subordinates. The ten most frequently mentioned unfavorable experiences were: incompetent and inconsiderate supervision, lack of support or help, incompetent higher management, poor planning and scheduling, poor working conditions, petty detail work, restriction of freedom, impersonal treatment, poor pay and fringes, and internal friction. It is evident that the tendency to blame is associated with unfavorable experiences. Nevertheless, the Herzberg distinction has greatly clarified many issues and with minor exceptions is in line with the differentiation between extrinsic and intrinsic motivation, the extrinsic being possible sources of dissatisfaction and job activity being the potential source of satisfaction.

Studies Based on the Need Hierarchy

The need hierarchy[48] (see Chapter 13) has served as a basis for comparing the motivations of different economic groups and personnel at different levels of management. A study of bottom and middle management personnel[49] revealed that some relationship exists between position in the organization and the need hierarchy, that higher positions led to more frequent satisfactions of the higher-level needs. The high-order needs are the least often satisfied, and self-actualization was regarded as an important need area seldom satisfied by persons in either bottom or middle management. Whether top management personnel experience satisfaction in this area was not determined but it would seem that such wants as personal growth, fulfillment, and worthwhile accomplishment would be among the most important factors in their motivation. In another study[50] the higher orders of needs were ful-

---

[46] House, R. J., and Wigdor, L. Herzberg's dual-factor theory of job satisfaction and motivation: A review of the evidence and criticism. *Personnel Psychol.*, 1967, *20*, 369–389; Burke, R. J. Are Herzberg's motivators and hygienes unidimensional? *J. appl. Psychol.*, 1966, *50*, 317–321; Bockman, V. M. The Herzberg controversy. *Personnel Psychol.*, 1971, *24*, 155–189; Wood, D. A., and Lebold, W. K., The multivariate nature of professional job satisfaction. *Personnel Psychol.*, 1970, *23*, 173–189; Hulin, C. L., and Waters, L. K. Regression analysis of three variations of the two-factor theory of job satisfaction. *J. appl. Psychol.*, 1971, 211–217; Herzberg, *et al., op. cit.*

[47] Solem, A. R. Unpublished data collected from 104 employed managers from varied organizations attending management programs.

[48] Maslow, A. H. *Motivation and personality.* New York: Harper, 1954.

[49] Porter, L. W. A study of perceived need satisfactions in bottom and middle management jobs. *J. appl. Psychol.*, 1961, *45*, 1–10.

[50] Porter, L. W. Job attitudes in management: III. Perceived deficiencies in need fulfillment as a function of line versus staff type of job. *J. appl. Psychol.*, 1963, *47*, 267–278.

filled more often in line than in comparable level staff positions. Ghiselli,[51] who has extensively studied managers in a variety of countries throughout the world, reported marked cultural differences in motives, goals, and attitudes, but in one respect there was a high degree of unanimity. More than anything else, managers the world over want to use their talents to the utmost, act independently, and realize themselves as individuals. He concluded that for managers, self-realization and autonomy are more important motivators than prestige, social satisfaction, and security.

The importance of the size of the company had an interesting influence on the need fulfillment of managers.[52] Lower level managers had more satisfaction in small than in large companies, whereas for higher level managers the reverse was true. The reason for the difference seems to lie in relative influence: a supervisor in a small company has fewer levels of management above him than an equivalent supervisor in a large company, but the span of control of a top level manager of a large company greatly exceeds that of a top level manager in a small company.

Although several studies of job satisfaction support the concept of the need hierarchy in a general way, many details need to be examined. Uncritical acceptance of evidence supporting the hierarchy may cause one to lose sight of important individual differences in perceptions and expectations.[53] To study job satisfaction, survey questions are designed so that a person is asked to give three responses to each item (e.g., Recognition, Job planning, Job responsibility, Opportunity to develop, Freedom, Accountability, etc.): (a) "how much is there now," (b) "how much should there be," and (c) "how important is it." The difference between (a) and (b) is the measure of fulfillment, whereas (c) measures the relative importance of various needs. Maslow's theory arranges the needs that exist in the person's frame of reference, but what exists in the environment and what is realistic are different dimensions. Individual differences in expectations, and the varied measures read into questionnaire items raise problems that make the need hierarchy difficult to test.

Wants Versus Choices

What people say they want and the choices they will actually make may not be the same. If we ask people (a) what accessories they want on a car, (b) how important is comfort, and (c) how much power they like in a motor, we may still not know much about the car they will purchase.

An industrial study[54] showed that the most disliked feature of a job in Plant X was that it was machine paced. However, 90 per cent of the workers on this job

[51] Ghiselli, E. E. Managerial talent. *Amer. Psychologist*, 1963, *18*, 631–642.

[52] Porter, L. W. Job attitudes in management: IV. Perceived deficiencies in need fulfillment as a function of size of company. *J. appl. Psychol.*, 1963, *47*, 386–397.

[53] Roberts, K. A., Walter, G. A., and Miles, R. E. A factor analytic study of job satisfaction items designed to measure Maslow need categories. *Personnel Psychol.*, 1971, *24*, 205–220.

[54] Walker, C. R., and Guest, R. H. *The man on the assembly line.* Cambridge, Mass.: Harvard University Press, 1952.

came from another factory and from jobs that were not machine paced. Workers may stay on jobs in which they are unhappy in order to have high pay and security. The choices of jobs made frequently do not reflect the things people want but rather the things they fear. Fear of unemployment, therefore, may be revealed by the choice of a steady job. However, removal of that fear may not create positive motivation or satisfaction; rather such a remedy is a method for avoiding trouble. In searching for factors that make for positive job satisfactions, one must go beyond the point of eliminating negative conditions. Only the satisfaction of needs can produce positive and constructive motivation.

A British study[55] revealed that two-thirds of the employees on a bonus system of payment were dissatisfied because of the strain created, yet they failed to report their nervousness to the medical department because they feared they might be removed from a bonus job. Such employees were in conflict because they disliked the pressure but felt the need for the extra money. Averaging the likes and dislikes of employees does not reveal the resultant of the various negative and positive forces that motivate the individual.

Union Demands Versus Employee Wants

One may well ask why workers strike for higher wages, fringe benefits, and shorter hours when these are not the items of greatest importance. The answer, in part, seems to be that if work is going to be unpleasant, employees will demand extra financial incentives to offset the undesirable conditions, and they will demand shorter hours to escape the unpleasantness for as long a time as possible.

Perhaps the most important factor in determining the nature of a union's demands is strategy. If a union demanded better supervision, more pleasant working conditions, and better working companions, it would be difficult to prove whether or not the company had lived up to the contract. Hours and wages are measurable and are independent of opinion. When they are factors in contract negotiations, there is no misunderstanding of what is demanded and what is received. Pensions, paid holidays, rest pauses, and an annual wage are also objective and make good bargaining issues. Although union demands may reflect dissatisfactions, the nature of the demand may not reveal their source or nature. Frequently employees do not know why they dislike a job, but they can be sure of the degree to which they dislike it.

A study[56] of 665 men and 639 women factory workers showed that two-thirds of the men and half of the women did not want their children to do the same kind of work they were doing. Instead of material benefits, the study of their hopes and attitudes revealed needs for status and security as well as such intangibles as self-respect and importance. It is clear that the intangible needs would be poor bargaining issues, and they would even be difficult to express as demands; nevertheless they might be the determiners of happiness.

---

[55] Davis, *op. cit.*

[56] Davis, N. M. The hopes of industrial workers for their children. *Occup. Psychol.,* London, 1953, *27,* 11–22.

Limitations of Status

The need for status and the need of workers to feel important create some interesting problems. Who is to generate the need-satisfiers and will there be enough to go around? How can we increase the status of all workers when status implies the ordering of people? Granted that material conditions can be improved and that the dignity of people can be increased, but is it unrealistic to assume that a classless society is possible and that such a society would generate the desired social need-satisfiers? Since social values are involved this would be a good discussion question.

A Word of Caution

One cannot discover from questionnaires, from the study of wants, or even from good interviews what produces the greatest satisfaction. One can locate dislikes more readily than satisfactions, but removal or correction of irritations is not the study of happiness. Happiness is a relative matter, and one can compare satisfactions only in the light of one's previous experience. The limiting factor is the unknown. How happy would certain conditions, not ever experienced by a person, make him? Most employees *could* not have recommended or requested group-decision methods in management. This way of leading groups first had to be invented before it could be experienced to any appreciable degree. Similarly, methods of interviewing, listening skills, improved work procedures, good lighting, employment tests, and so on have been developed experimentally, and their value has then been tested in terms of the results they produce. It is by this experimental method that new producers are discovered, and through this method that major advances are made.

Laboratory Exercise

Discussion Method: The Risk Technique[57]

A. Preparing for discussion.
   1. Divide class into discussion committees of five or six persons, each of which is to select a discussion leader. (In a small class, divide into smaller committees so that three or four committees may be obtained.)
   2. The discussion problem is as follows: "What are the risks a supervisor would take by practicing group-decision methods on the job with employees?"
   3. Each risk should be briefly worded in very specific terms.
   4. Each committee should divide its discussion into two phases:
      a. The listing of specific risks.
      b. The selection of the five most important risks.
   5. The instructor will indicate when time is up for each phase.

[57] From N. R. F. Maier, *Principles of Human Relations.* New York: Wiley, 1952.

B. Committee reports.

The instructor will receive the committee report. He will:

1. Call on each leader for a report.
2. Write summarized statement of the risks on the chalkboard.
3. Check with the committee to see if summary is accurate.
4. Summarize committee reports briefly.

C. Committee discussion: Second Assignment.

1. The instructor will ask each committee to discuss how their risks can be circumvented or reduced.
2. Allow about 20 minutes for evaluating each risk.

D. General discussion.

1. Each committee report should be handled as follows:
   a. The committee will state its conclusions on how their risks can be circumvented or reduced.
   b. The class as a whole should then discuss the pros and cons of the issues raised.
   c. When various aspects and opinions have been voiced, the instructor will summarize the degree of agreement or disagreement.
2. Take a poll to determine the number of persons whose opinion of the group decision method has:
   a. gone up
   b. gone down
   c. remained unchanged

Suggested Readings

Blum, M. L., and Naylor, J. C. *Industrial psychology: Its theoretical and social foundations.* New York: Harper & Row, 1968, Chs. 11 and 12.

Costello, T. W., and Zalkind, S. S. *Psychology in administration.* Englewood Cliffs, N.J.: Prentice-Hall, 1963, pp. 79–122.

Levenstein, A. *Why people work.* New York: Crowell-Collier, 1962.

Nosow, S., and Form, W. H. (Eds.). *Man, work and society.* New York: Basic Books, 1962.

Purcell, T. V. Work psychology and business values: A triad theory of work motivation. *Personnel Psychol.,* 1967, 20, 231–255.

Smith, P. C., Kendall, L. M., and Hulin, C. L. *The measurement of satisfaction in work and retirement.* Chicago: Rand McNally, 1969.

Veroff, J., and Feld, S. *Marriage and work in America: A study of motives and roles.* New York: Van Nostrand Reinhold, 1970.

Vroom, V. H. *Work and motivation.* New York: Wiley, 1964.

15

Fatigue and Leisure

Introduction

The Signs of Fatigue

For practical purposes, industrial fatigue may be defined as *a reduction in the ability to do work because of previous work.* This definition does not attempt to describe the nature of fatigue, but rather uses the result as its criterion. As soon as we attempt to determine the nature of fatigue, differences in opinion arise, for it is highly probable that the reduction in ability to do work is caused by a variety of changes, ranging from chemical to psychological. Previous activity of a particular part of the body alters its ability to continue to function, and some of the changes produced by this activity can be specifically localized.[1]

We may also approach the problem of fatigue by studying the "feelings" of fatigued persons. When people say they are tired, to what extent are they describing the localized changes that have taken place in their bodies? If the physiological changes always correspond with the psychological experiences, the two approaches might measure different aspects of the same thing. Unfortunately, the various evidences of fatigue do not always agree. On the one hand, a person may "feel" completely rested, but the work record may show a rapid decline. Under conditions of strong motivation, people may continue work for long periods of time without being aware of fatigue, whereas, under other conditions, they may feel fatigued before they begin to work. In activity such as reading,[2] a poorly motivated person

[1] Bartley, S. H., and Chute, E. *Fatigue and impairment in man.* New York: McGraw-Hill, 1947, Ch. 2; Karpovich, P. V. *Physiology of muscular activity.* Philadelphia: Saunders, 1959; Ryan, T. A. *Work and effort: The psychology of production.* New York: Ronald, 1947, Chs. 3, 4, and 5; Viteles, M. S. *Industrial Psychology.* New York: Norton, 1932, Ch. 21.

[2] Carmichael, L., and Dearborn, W. F. *Reading and visual fatigue.* Boston: Houghton Mifflin, 1947.

will show various signs of fatigue after a relatively short period of time. These signs include inefficient eye movements, closing the eyes, looking about, and periods of skimming alternated with serious reading. However, when properly motivated, the same person will show no decrement in reading ability even after six hours of continuous reading. In the next chapter the manner in which motivation complicates the problem of fatigue will be considered in detail.

There is every reason to believe that an individual's attitude is an important factor in the ability to do work, but the presence of this attitude cannot be detected by any physiological measures known at present. In Chapter 3 we pointed out how attitudes influence productivity and how they tended to cover up the expected

Biochemist at work. The extent to which work produces chemical and physiological changes in muscles, nerve tissue, and the blood and the problem of fatigue are concerns of biological chemistry and physiology.

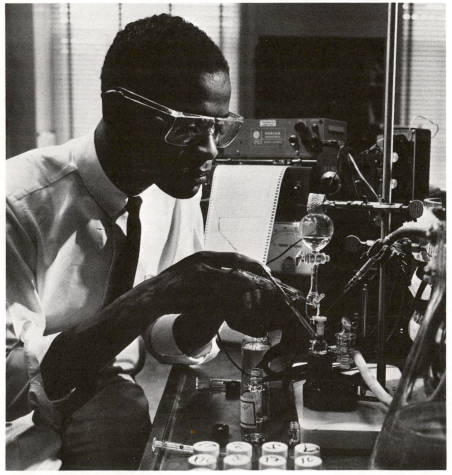

Courtesy of E.I. du Pont de Nemours & Co., Inc.

effects in experimental studies dealing with the influences of rest periods on work. Any study of fatigue must control not only the actual physical activity, but also the indefinite environmental factors which influence a worker's outlook and attitude toward the work. It has now become very apparent that emotional stability and mental hygiene cannot be divorced from fatigue, since emotional conflicts and attitudes are so closely related to fatigue that the latter cannot be defined without involving the other factors.[3] To the extent that fatigue involves the organisms as a whole, it is a psychological problem. To the extent that work produces chemical and physiological changes in muscles, nerve tissue, and the blood, the problem is the concern of both biological chemists and physiologists.

Complex Nature of Fatigue

The complexity of the fatigue phenomenon is illustrated by an interesting experiment done at the University of Zagreb in Yugoslavia.[4] An experimental group of 24 college students was confined in a lecture room all night without sleep and was kept active by reading, listening to music, dancing, and so on. At 6 A.M. the students went on a six-mile quick walk, after which they were tested for two hours. A comparable control group of 25 students was given the same tests after a normal night's sleep. With respect to subjective reports, 87.5 per cent of the experimental group rated their condition as "very tired" or "exhausted," and none reported "no fatigue" or "slight fatigue." In contrast, only 12 per cent of the rested group rated their condition as "very tired" and none rated it "exhausted," while 28 per cent reported "no fatigue" or "slight fatigue."

However, with respect to performance on 12 psychological tests requiring reasoning, spatial judgments, verbal tests, and locating printing errors, there were no significant differences between the groups. There is some suggestion that under conditions of fatigue other mechanisms and mental processes replace the initial ones so that the individual changes his method of carrying out a function and this substitution covers up the effects of fatigue. This conception was indicated by the fact that similar activities showed clusters of relationships in the control group, but these clusters were absent or unclear in the experimental group. The authors suggest that a variety of mental processes were used to perform similar intellectual functions in the experimental group, while the rested group showed this tendency to a lesser degree. Although the evidence is highly fragmentary, the idea is very suggestive and throws new light on the fatigue problem.

A similar phenomenon appears to occur in muscular effort when a person holds a certain load at a constant height. At first the person performs the task with the muscles best adapted to the task, then includes other muscle groups, and finally

[3] Bartley, S. H. Conflict, frustration and fatigue. *Psychosom. Med.*, 1943, *5*, 160–163; Cattell, R. B., and Schierer, I. *The meaning and measurement of neuroticism and anxiety.* New York: Ronald, 1960, Ch. 9 and 10; French, G. W. The clinical significance of tiredness. *Canad. Med. Assn. J.*, 1960, *82*, 665–671; Schwab, R. S., and DeLorno, T. Psychiatric findings in fatigue. *Amer. J. Psychiat.*, 1953, *109*, 621–625.
[4] Bujas, Z., Petz, B., Krković, A., and Sorokin, B. Analysis of factors in intellectual performance under fatigue and without fatigue. *Acta Instituti Psychol.*, 1961, *23*, 11–22.

muscles not at all involved at the outset become activated so that the work is done with a larger number of muscle groups. This occurs without a change in the work output.

It is possible that such changes in the integration of processes account for some of the difficulties in isolating the effects of fatigue in the organism as a whole. The body seems able to compensate for fatigue effects by spreading the work, in much the same way a person shifts a suitcase from right to left arms to prevent a work decrement that would occur if one arm did all the work. It is known that certain organs of the body can take over the functions of a diseased organ and serve as second and third lines of defense against loss of life.[5] The idea that a similar protection occurs to fight against physical and mental fatigue is an intriguing one worthy of more research.

Ergograph Studies of Fatigue

Method of Measurement

The work of Angelo Mosso,[6] an Italian scientist, has become one of the classics on the subject of fatigue. He developed an instrument, known as the *ergograph,* which made it possible to investigate the relation between fatigue and work in a relatively isolated part of the body. By studying the activity of a limited muscle group, he was able to induce fatigue in a short time. Thus he could study the phenomenon without complicating it greatly with such psychological effects as monotony and boredom, which are likely to accompany longer periods of work.

The principle of the ergograph is simple. The arm is strapped to a frame in such a way that it is kept comfortable but immobile. All fingers except the middle one are similarly immobilized. A string is then fastened to the free finger, which is to be put to work. By placing a load on the other end of the string, the free finger can be made to pull against it. The work of the finger is done by contracting and relaxing the muscles, which, in turn, move the load. Different rhythms of work are studied by having the finger contractions follow a pattern set by a metronome. Since the frequency of contractions is important, this factor must always be carefully controlled.

In order to obtain a graph of the work output, a recording device is fastened to the moving string. Each contraction carries a needle over a revolving drum which records the magnitude of successive contractions.

Results Obtained

The use of the ergograph has established a number of important relationships, each of which has definite applications to industry. Nine specific principles of fatigue are briefly summarized in the following paragraphs.

1. If the contractions with a given load are spaced one every two seconds or thereabouts, there is a gradual decrease in the amplitude of the contractions until finally

[5] Julius, S. *Mudrost nasega tijela.* Zagreb, Yugoslavia: Epoha, 1963.

[6] Mosso, A. *Fatigue* (trans. by M. Drummond and W. B. Drummond). New York: Putnam, 1904.

no further contractions can be made. With a six-kilogram load, this stage is reached in about one minute. Reducing the load will again permit contractions, but fatigue for this load is soon complete.

2. If the contractions for the same load are spaced at long enough intervals (10 seconds, for example), there is no apparent evidence of fatigue. A six-kilogram weight can be lifted almost indefinitely under these conditions.

3. If work is measured in terms of the total weight lifted through a given space, the amount of work the finger is capable of doing is greater for light than for heavy loads. Thus a three-kilogram load can be lifted definitely more than twice as often as a six-kilogram weight.

4. A given load lifted in a fast rhythm produces more fatigue per lift than the same load lifted at a slower rhythm.

5. The time for complete recovery (that is, until the optimum performance can be duplicated) increases rapidly as the period of work is increased. For example, the recovery time for 30 contractions may be as long as two hours, whereas the recovery time for 15 contractions may be 30 minutes. After the stage of complete inability to move the finger is reached, efforts to lift the weight produce more fatigue (in terms of recovery time) than do the actual lifts previously made. Generally speaking, the fatigue effects of each effort to contract increase rapidly as fatigue accumulates.

6. The activity of other sets of muscles reduces the ability of the finger to do work. Strenuous exercise preceding the test with the ergograph causes the stage of complete inability to lift the weight to appear more quickly than normally. Thus, the ergograph studies bear out the physiological finding regarding distribution of fatigue by way of the blood stream.

7. The ability of the muscle to do work is decreased by loss of sleep, mental activity, hunger, and anemia of the muscles. As a matter of fact, any condition that depresses or interferes with the nutritive state increases the susceptibility to fatigue.

8. The ability of the muscle to do work is increased by massaging the muscle, injecting sugar into the blood stream, and by good health and a well-nourished body.

9. The rate of fatigue differs greatly in different people, but the principles listed above apply alike to all.

Applications of Ergograph Findings

Energy Expenditure

The first five points listed in the previous section support the general conclusion that, with a given amount of muscular energy, more work can be done when this energy is spent gradually than when it is spent rapidly. There is a tendency, however, for people to work fast when they have a lot of energy available. This tends to influence the work performance, causing them to be extremely wasteful of their energy. Just as long-distance runners have to learn to keep their speed down and adjust themselves to a pace they have learned they can maintain, workers in industry should be be taught to spend their energy efficiently.

Another problem in the economical expenditure of energy lies in the fact that it is unnatural for people to rest before they are fatigued to an uncomfortable degree. Since recovery time increases rapidly as fatigue progresses, it is advisable for a worker to rest before fatigue has progressed very far or to work at such a pace that rest periods are unnecessary.

It has already been pointed out how the motion and time studies have utilized some of the ergograph principles by spacing or spreading the work. The Gilbreths[7] were strong advocates of fatigue elimination, and much of their effectiveness was attributable to their recognition of the problem of fatigue. In motion and time studies, fatigue was reduced by (1) lightening the load, (2) introducing rest periods, and (3) pacing the work. Since any one of these methods serves the same purpose, the procedure which is adopted depends on the nature of the work.

Because large shovels produce fatigue rapidly, they are inefficient. Small shovels induce fatigue slowly, but they transport little material in comparison with their own weight. Since production is measured by the amount of material handled, not by the weight lifted (shovel plus gravel), a shovel may be so small that it fatigues without producing results. Between the two extremes, there exists a shovel size which fatigues most slowly for the amount of material handled. The same applications may be made to other kinds of work. There is a most efficient hoe size for farmers, a most efficient hammer weight for carpenters, and a most efficient load for hod carriers.

On jobs in which the load to be handled is fixed, workers may work in pairs. For example, two people can handle more heavy lumber by working together than by working individually; at the same time, they are less likely to injure each other.

When it is impossible either to reduce the load or pair workers, periodic rest periods can serve the purpose of reducing fatigue. This was the procedure used in the handling of pig iron.

Much industrial work does not involve heavy loads, but instead requires rapid movements. In some cases the movements may be paced; in other cases rest periods should be imposed so as to distribute the work properly. Although the best procedure for setting the pace of a production line has not been determined, it probably should be fairly constant throughout the day, except during the first half-hour, when it should be slower to permit "warming up." It is fairly common practice to have the line move most rapidly in the early part of the day and to slow it down as the end of the work period is approached. This procedure is definitely contrary to the principles of fatigue. It is based upon the mistaken belief that workers should spend their energy when they have it available. Actually, it requires workers to spend most of their working time in a fatigued condition.

The General Characteristic of Fatigue

The sixth point of the ergograph results indicates that fatigue is general in nature. If activity of one set of muscles reduces the ability of others to do work, then re-

---

[7] Gilbreth, F. B., and Gilbreth, L. M. *Fatigue study*. New York: Macmillan, 1919.

covery must proceed most effectively when the person is completely relaxed. This suggests that work pauses for heavy muscular activity should not only be work stoppages, but periods of complete relaxation. Comfortable lounges might be made available for use during the lunch hour, and comfortable seats might be readily accessible during rest periods. Properly located drinking fountains would also help to conserve energy. Unfortunately, workers who have the most strenuous occupations too often have the least accessible facilities for relaxation.

Health and Nourishment

The seventh and eighth points of the ergograph results deal with the healthful state of the body. They suggest that an employee's living conditions outside the plant play an important part in his ability to work. Some of these conditions can be improved by adequate remuneration; others, by educational methods. A German investigator believes that the worker's travel time from home to work should be seriously considered.[8] This means that industry would have to consider locating its plants near residential areas or stimulate housing projects near its present plant locations. Furthermore, the applicant's address would become a condition of employment. Although there has been a sharp trend in the direction of decentralization of industry in this country, it must be conceded that most of the consideration given to a reduction in travel time has come from the employee rather than the employer. The German author recommends a maximum of 30 minutes in travel time each way. He also advises a nap of not more than 30 minutes during the day in order to reduce fatigue stresses. Naps exceeding 30 minutes should be avoided because they would interfere with the night's rest.

Services that reduce or eliminate causes of worry among employees are frequently introduced by progressive establishments. Such services include loans, hospitalization, and legal advice, all of which are made available to the employees at greatly reduced costs.

Since food intake reduces fatigue, it may be considered a practical substitute for, or addition to, rest. Company restaurants that sell good food at low prices encourage healthful eating habits and are sound investments.

Individual Differences

Fatigue is not merely related to strength since the rate of fatigue, and recovery times may differ for persons of like strength. In sports, the feeling of fatigue is influenced by the person's self-evaluation of his capacity.[9] This influence may be partly a matter of personality. Because of the varied individual differences in fatigue the work pace that suits one person may not be appropriate for another.

When people work in teams and are dependent on one another, it is advisable to match their susceptibility to fatigue as well as their ability. People should be care-

[8] Gärtner, H. Ermüdungsüberwindung vom Standpunkt der Hygiene. *Mensch u. Arbeit,* 1952, *5,* 156–170.
[9] Dimitrova, S. Dependence of voluntary effort upon the magnitude of the goal and the way it is set in sportsmen. *Internatl. J. Sport Psychol.,* 1970, *1,* 29–33.

fully selected for jobs requiring endurance. For example, in lifting the handles of a wheelbarrow and in starting it rolling, there are initial expenditures of energy which can be separated from the energy cost required to maintain its motion. For efficient utilization of energy, the barrow should be kept moving once it is started.[10] If long hauls are required, workers who can easily make the trip without a stop should be selected, because they can eliminate the energy loss occurring from stopping and starting the barrow after a rest pause.

An example of applying motion-and-time analysis to the above fatigue problem is the use of a rounded platform. This device would be placed at the point most economical for taking a rest. The worker would be trained to run the barrow onto the platform, the upward incline would stop the barrow and if the worker stopped it just beyond the hump, the decline would start the barrow after the rest pause. In this manner the laborer would be spared the extra work of starting and stopping the barrow to rest. A seat on the barrow handles would add to the restfulness of the work pause.

Limitations of Ergograph Findings

It is reasonable to question the supposition that the ergograph results will be applicable to industry. Laboratory and factory atmospheres are very different; also, completely fatiguing a finger is not the same as fatiguing the whole body to a lesser degree. However, although the situations are different, some similarity may exist. Considering the probable beneficial change in attitude which might accompany some of the practices mentioned, the total effect on the industrial worker might, in some instances, exceed that on the laboratory subject.

The ergograph principles should be verified in actual work situations with real job holders rather than laboratory subjects, not only because work on a job involves the whole body and takes up a good share of a person's working hours, but also because attitudes and motivation have such subtle effects on productivity. Employees like rest pauses not just because they want to rest, but because they want time for coffee, personal telephone calls, and sociability. Often they desire their coffee just after arriving for work or shortly before lunch. In such instances the rest period substitutes for breakfast or lunch. Using lunch periods for shopping and rest periods for lunch defeats the purpose for which these innovations were introduced.

Companies are reluctant to experiment with rest periods and coffee breaks because once a privilege is granted it is difficult to revoke if it proves to be ineffective. Many companies would grant more rest periods if they could be sure the privilege would not be abused. Management may also fear that granting one privilege would lead to more demands. The problem is further complicated by the belief that all employees are not entitled to the same amount of time off. How can the company give certain privileges to some and deny them to others without finding itself charged with discriminatory practices? Company restaurants, rest periods, attractive and comfortable restrooms, protection against hard cement floors, and stools to per-

[10] Crowden, G. P. *The physiological cost of muscular movements involved in barrow work.* Industr. Fat. Res. Bd., 1928, Rep. No. 50.

mit working while seated have been adopted to keep employees from quitting. Invariably, these changes have been found to pay dividends in increased production. In one instance just the installation of stools for women increased production 32 per cent.[11]

The ergograph finding that the detrimental effects of fatigue increase progressively is given some support by a practical investigation.[12] Its author advocates placing lunchtime one-third of the way through the workday to reduce cumulative fatigue.

Reactions to Sustained Work

Accidents and Fatigue

The relationship between hours of work and accidents was quite striking in industry when the hours of work were long and the accident rate was high.[13] With shorter hours, rest pauses, less heavy work, and a reduced accident rate due to accident prevention methods, this relationship is less evident. The earlier finding, that accidents among women are more often related to fatigue than among men, probably remains valid.[14]

Individuals differ in the way they compensate for fatigue so that whether or not fatigue influences accidents depends on the method of compensation as well as on the situation. Sustained effort may cause some to slow down, others to become more cautious, and still others to take a rest. Common effects are reduced coordination, inattention, and falling asleep. Whether or not these changes result in accidents depends upon the activity in which the individual is engaged as well as on the individual's method of compensation. Nevertheless, fatigue in one form or another is regarded as a physiological factor associated with accidents in aerospace studies.[15]

Impairment in High-Grade Performance

The concept that fatigue effects may be covered up by changes in the way a task is accomplished is further supported by studies of pilot errors in Cambridge, England.[16] These investigations indicate a disorganization of receptor-effector processes so that performance on a vigilance test shows greater variability after flying than before, at night than in the daytime, and after flights in jet than in piston-engined aircraft. This rise in variance will influence how well an aircraft can be held on its course and, although it might not affect the flying time, it could result in landing accidents.

---

[11] Mezerik, A. G. The factory manager learns the facts of life. *Harper's Mag.*, 1943, *187,* 289–297.

[12] Bornemann, E. Psychologische Wege zur Verminderung der Ermudung in Betrieb und Schule. *Mensch u. Arbeit,* 1952, *5,* 133–144.

[13] Vernon, H. M. *Industrial fatigue and efficiency.* London: Routledge, 1921.

[14] Vernon, H. M. *Accidents and their prevention.* London: Cambridge University Press, 1936.

[15] Directorate of Aerospace Safety. *Psychophysiological factors in major USA aircraft accidents.* Norton AFB, Calif.: USAF Study, 1962, 39–62.

[16] Fraser, D. C. Recent experimental work in the study of fatigue. In E. A. Fleishman (Ed.), *Studies in personnel and industrial psychology.* New York: Dorsey, 1961, pp. 473–478.

The Cambridge studies show that timing and the integrative functions are most readily affected by fatigue conditions and that their effect is most evident on tasks requiring high-grade performance and sustained attention and concentration.[17]

Loss of sleep may not impair a person's performance if the activity sustains attention. However, if the activity is not a demanding one the person tends to fall asleep. Thus, motivation may upgrade a person's performance and cover the lack of sleep, thereby masking the fatigue effects on performance.[18]

Hourly Production as a Measure of Industrial Fatigue

Characteristics of the Production Curve

When the amount of production is left largely to the individual and is not paced by the speed of the production line or of a machine, hourly production gradually falls off during both the morning and the afternoon work periods. Typical production curves for both morning and afternoon are shown in Figure 15.1. The work on

Figure 15.1 / Production Curves for Morning and Afternoon Work Periods. The solid line indicates production during the four morning hours; the broken line indicates production during the four afternoon hours. The warming-up characteristics are absent in the afternoon period, but the fatigue effects are more apparent than in the morning period.

[17] Takahuwa, E. The function of concentration maintenance (T.A.F.) as an evaluation of fatigue. *Ergonomics*, 1962, *5*, 37–49.
[18] Wilkinson, R. T. Effects of up to 60 hours sleep deprivation on different types of work. *Ergonomics*, 1964, *7*, 175–186.

which these curves are based is classified as medium-heavy.[19] The progressive falling off of production in both curves is attributed to fatigue and is characteristic of production trends on work which is not largely influenced by monotony effects.

The morning curve shows a rise during the first hour, known as the *warming-up period.* The exact cause of the warming-up period is not known, but unquestionably this phenomenon depends on a variety of factors. True warming up is usually understood to entail certain physiological adjustments. Muscles must be limbered up and a number of circulatory adjustments, such as changes in blood pressure and circulation, have to be made in accordance with the work pace. Thus a runner will exercise for a period before a race. Other factors, ranging from making the necessary tool arrangements to getting into a working attitude, also enter into the picture. The exact duration of this warming-up period is also unknown, but most probably it varies from job to job and from individual to individual. It is safe to assume that the period is definitely less than an hour and that in many instances it is a matter of minutes. The psychological aspects associated with getting started probably are more delayed in actual practice than are the physiological adjustments. A businesslike work atmosphere and a healthy state of mind contribute greatly to making the necessary psychological adjustments.

Between the second and third hours the combined production of a large group of men usually reaches its peak. Thereafter, production gradually falls off. It is this continuing decrease which reflects the presence of industrial fatigue.

The afternoon curve frequently shows no evidence of a warming-up period; if present at all, it is of shorter duration. Afternoon production ordinarily begins at a higher point than that which obtained at the end of the morning curve, showing the characteristic recovery one would expect because of rest and lunch. Thereafter, the curve falls off more rapidly than in the morning, indicating incomplete recovery during the rest pause. The final hour usually shows the lowest production of the day.

Part of the low production at the end of a day may be due to a tendency to quit early or to begin putting away tools. As in the warming-up period, some extraneous activities are performed, and the decrease in production is unrelated to fatigue. The general downward hourly trend, however, reflects the condition of lowered production because of previous work and justifies the characterization of *industrial fatigue.*

Another feature of some production curves is the *end spurt*. It consists of a rise in production at the end of a work period and appears only in some instances. It is possible that an end spurt always occurs, but that it is not always apparent because its influence is offset by fatigue effects, which are in the opposite direction. Evidence for the end spurt is most commonly found in work that does not require physical exertion. This temporary rise in production may be attributed to the motivation of approaching a goal, which in most cases is the end of the day. Production measured in 15-minute periods would probably show the presence of end spurts in many in-

[19] Goldmark, J., *et al.* Studies in industrial physiology: Fatigue in relation to working capacity: I. Comparison of an eight-hour plant and a ten-hour plant. *Publ. Health Bull.,* 1920 (106).

stances, whereas hourly measures are too crude to separate their effects from fatigue effects. In the next chapter this influence of an approached goal will be considered in detail.

The production curve thus reveals three characteristic features: the warming-up period, the end spurt, and the fatigue effects. Each is undoubtedly attributable to a complex set of factors, but all have basic causes which can be determined and which are worthy of investigation.

Hourly Production in Light and Rapid Work

Much of the work in industry may be characterized as light and rapid. Hourly production in typesetting is an example. What are the fatigue effects in this type of work? A comparison of typesetting in two Italian firms (A and B) is shown in Table 15.1.[20] The Italian workday is seven hours long and is interrupted by a two-hour lunch and rest period. In both firms the high point in production occurs during the second morning hour and the next highest point occurs during the first afternoon hour. Although the afternoon production begins at a fairly high point, it drops rapidly and reaches its low point at the end of the day.

In a British printing house, the workday was eight hours long, with one hour for lunch and a 10-minute period for tea in the afternoon. The morning production pattern (four hours) was similar to the Italian firms, but the afternoon pattern was different. The British firm showed no recovery after lunch but production rose during the second hour, which preceded tea, and was at its highest point (third hour) after tea. These gains occurred despite the fact that the tea period took five minutes from each of these hours. The last hours, as in the Italian firms, showed the lowest production.

Figures on errors for one Italian firm are also given in Table 15.1. These figures show that the number of errors increases whenever the production decreases, but the

Table 15.1 / Hourly Production in Two Printing Houses

Hour of Day	Percentage Production Firm A	Percentage Production Firm B	Percentage Errors Firm B
8–9	13.6	13.8	12.9
9–10	17.1	17.0	7.6
10–11	14.6	15.1	13.9
11–12	14.0	14.1	21.3
12–2		Lunch and Rest	
2–3	15.9	16.2	4.2
3–4	14.0	13.4	17.2
4–5	10.8	10.5	22.8

From B. Muscio, *Lectures in industrial psychology*. London: Routledge, 1920.

[20] From data cited by B. Muscio, *op. cit.*

changes are more marked in the case of errors than in the case of production. Since typesetting errors require considerable time for correction, actual or finished production is greatly lowered by frequent errors. If allowance is made for errors, it is evident that the actual production changes much more with fatigue than the tabulated production figures indicate.

Because errors and accidents probably have similar causes, the data on errors may also describe a kind of relationship between fatigue and potential accidents. The same condition which results in an error in typesetting may cause an injury in another kind of work.

Muscular Tension

Eyestrain and Conflict

Bartley[21] designed two experiments in which he produced eyestrain in a matter of minutes. In one, the observer was confronted with a flashing light, and as a result, the pupils of his eyes alternately dilated and constricted in rhythm to the flicker. When the frequency of the light flashes was too fast for the pupillary muscles to follow and too slow to produce the effects of a continuous light, eyestrain quickly appeared. Bartley called this a conflict situation. In the other experiment the eye muscles that control eye movement were used. In this instance the observer faced two bright lights, but was instructed to keep his eyes on a point midway between them. Since eyes tend to turn reflexively toward a bright light, it was difficult for the observer to look between the two lights. Here again conflict was present since the observer's eyes tended to turn toward the right and left lights simultaneously. Again fatigue was rapidly produced.

These results are in contrast to the findings of Carmichael and Dearborn[22] who obtained no evidence of visual fatigue after six hours of continuous reading. In the reading situation, eye movements were repeatedly made but conflict was not present. Instead, motivation and lighting were optimum. Further, it must be remembered that eye muscles are very strong and that they are taxed very little in performing the movements required for reading by a skilled person. Apparently the interval between periodic eye movements is adequate for recovery, as is the case for the heart muscle. Combining both researches on experimentally produced eyestrain and on reading, it is apparent that conflict or excessive demands on eye muscle activity must be carefully considered in evaluating fatigue-producing situations.

The reader may appreciate the fatiguing effects of a struggle between opposing sets of muscles if he will clench his fist and hold it up rigidly in front of his face. He will notice that holding his arm in a rigid position requires more effort of the muscles than if the forearm is moved back and forth. Muscles that pull against each other exert themselves a good deal, but accomplish little externally. To what extent does this condition of contractions of opposed sets of muscles occur in nervous ten-

[21] Bartley, S. H. A factor in visual fatigue. *Psychosom. Med.,* 1942, *4,* 275–396; Bartley, S. H. Conflict, frustration, and fatigue, *op. cit.*
[22] Carmichael and Dearborn, *op. cit.*

sion? The fact that the effects of eye movements involved in six hours of reading add up to much less than the effects of two minutes of looking between two bright lights makes it clear that we must look behind the external movements themselves to find the answer to our fatigue problems. Doing nothing but holding a pose may be hard work.

An Industrial Application

Some of the human relations aspects of the eye-fatigue problem became apparent in an office when a new billing machine was introduced. The machine was especially designed to cut down eye movements. On the old machine the eye had to sweep from left to right to compare two sets of figures, but on the new machine it was possible to maintain a fixed eye position for this comparison.

The first woman to operate the new machine complained of eyestrain after a few days, despite the fact that she was told eyestrain would decrease with the new machine. Matters became more serious when five other women, who soon were to receive identical billing machines, visited the manager and told him they did not want to be put on the new machines. They said they would quit rather than use them. The manager promised to look into the matter.

When the manager reported his problem to his superior he was told that a lot of money had been invested in the new machines and that they would have to be used. It was up to the manager to "sell" the new machines to the women, he said.

To meet this apparently insoluble problem, the following plan was evolved. The six employees who were to operate the new machines were asked if they would like to test various experimental methods of operating the new machines, the objective being to find a way to use them that was not fatiguing. They readily agreed to this proposal, and experimentation was begun as soon as the other five machines arrived.

The following three work patterns were tested, each one by two women on any given day: (1) do a complete page (about 10 minutes' work) and then rest for one minute; (2) rest for one minute after each half-page; (c) alternate rest and work periods of about one minute each.

Surprisingly, the findings showed that production remained the same for all three procedures, despite the large difference in the amount of rest. Furthermore, production was consistently but not strikingly higher on the new machines than it had been on the old ones. Since production was better on the new machines the operators decided they wanted to use them. They also argued that eye-rest pauses, in addition to the morning and afternoon breaks, were needed to abolish eyestrain. They preferred the frequent short units and settled on a routine of brief rests after each small unit of work (about one minute).

During the following year, no eyestrain was evident despite the fact that the manager frequently asked the operators whether another meeting was needed to explore the problem further. Production on the new machines continued slightly above that of the previous year. The question of whether the new machines that require fixation on one point are better than the old ones that required eye movements is, however, still unanswered.

Stress

Emotional problems create stress which is accompanied by failure to relax. Work performed with muscles that must pull against opposing muscles that are not completely relaxed creates a condition of conflict similar to eyestrain. This condition may account for the high incidence of fatigue in pressure situations.

Value of Rest Pauses

Effect on Production

The introduction of rest pauses in work does not make possible a comparison between work with and without such pauses, because spontaneous rest pauses inevitably occur, whether or not they are recognized. The question of interest to industry is whether or not externally introduced rest periods increase production.

The evidence clearly shows that increases of from 10 to 20 per cent are common.[23] For instance, the introduction of a 10-minute rest pause in the morning work period for women engaged in labeling resulted in a 20 per cent increase in production.[24] In another study, rest pauses of seven minutes, introduced in both morning and afternoon work periods, favorably changed the entire shape of the hourly production curves.[25] Other studies have used frequent and short rest periods. Favorable results have been found with a five-minute rest after each hour of work and even when a two-minute rest is alternated with three minutes of work.

The best distribution of rest pauses has not been determined for industry, but it may be expected to vary considerably with the type of work, length of the workday, length of the workweek, sex of the worker, and the level of motivation. Individual differences also will be a factor.

Although laboratory studies can never duplicate job conditions, some basic things can be learned from them. One experimenter tested six physically superior college students on the fatiguing effects of muscular activities that might be described as light-heavy work.[26] They worked one eight-hour day per week. The job was set up to fatigue the whole body and required the men to raise and lower weights by walking from and toward a machine. Work periods ranged from 25 to 60 minutes and rest pauses from seven to 16 minutes. On some tests the work period was held constant (e.g., 40 minutes) and the rest period was varied between seven and 16 minutes; on others the rest period was held constant and the work period was varied.

The results of the experiments demonstrated that between 16.7 and 20 per cent of the work period should be devoted to resting to obtain optimum results. Brief rest periods given after short periods of work were consistently better than the same

---

[23] For a detailed discussion see M. S. Viteles, *op. cit.,* pp. 470–482; Vernon, *op. cit.,* pp. 98–115.

[24] Vernon, H. M., and Bedford, T. *The influence of rest pauses on light industrial work.* Industr. Fat. Res. Bd., 1924, Rep. No. 25.

[25] Farmer, E., and Bevington, S. M. An experiment in the introduction of rest pauses. *Nat. Inst. Industr. Psychol.,* 1922, *1,* 89–92.

[26] Shepherd, G. Effects of rest pauses on production. *Personnel J.,* 1928, *7,* 186–202.

proportion of rest to work taken in longer periods. On two of the subjects the optimum distribution of rest was tested. Using 18.2 per cent rest for all test conditions, the greatest benefit of rest pauses was obtained when rest was distributed through the work period in one-minute stretches. Under these conditions there was no falling off in work at the end of the work period, which usually is the case for most work distributions. The experimenter points out that frequent rest pauses interrupting the work can perhaps only be applied to jobs having no organization and involving no planning.

Another interesting finding was that subjects left to their own devices failed to distribute rest pauses efficiently. However, the subjects could be trained to do this by being given practice in improved ways for distributing work and rest.

Unofficial Rest Pauses

Whether or not employees have rest pauses is not entirely under the control of the company. Employees can pace their work so that short rest pauses are continuously taken, they can pause at intervals, they can take washroom privileges, and they can cause machine breakdowns. Management can control only the rest pauses, and these result in decreased unofficial rest pauses.

Unofficial rest pauses actually reflect the employee's way of budgeting energy. When people work long days they pace their work differently and work more slowly than when they work short days. Vernon[27] studied the rest pauses taken by workers when they worked six- and eight-hour shifts. For the six-hour shifts the average rest per hour was 10.2 minutes and for the eight-hour shift it was 12.5 minutes. Thus the per cent of rest per workday was 17.0 and 20.8, respectively, for the six- and eight-hour shifts. However, the workers did not take the rest pauses on the hour as may be suggested by these figures. The distributions of rest and work periods for the two shifts are shown in Table 15.2. It appears that about each block of 16 or 17 minutes contains a rest and a work period. The problem for management is one of finding efficient work-rest distributions and motivating employees to accept them. Official rest pauses may be regarded as one of the ways in which management can influence the work-rest distributions.

Table 15.2 / Distribution of Unofficial Rest Pauses

Length of Shift	Average Work Period (Minutes)	Average Rest Period (Minutes)	Production Per Hour
6 hours	13.85	2.85	110
8 hours	12.98	3.42	100

From H. M. Vernon, The influence of hours of work and ventilation on output in tin plate manufacture. Industr. Fat. Res. Bd., 1919, Rep. No. 1.

27 Vernon, H. M. The influence of hours of work and of ventilation on output in tin plate manufacture. *Industr. Fat. Res. Bd.,* 1919, Rep. No. 1.

Some Practical Problems

It is quite generally agreed that the official rest pause should be introduced just before production begins to fall off. This opinion is based on the results of a number of investigations and corresponds to what one would expect from the ergograph results. Because rest periods may serve as interruptions and create unfavorable results, it may be desirable to permit the individual a certain degree of freedom in their arrangement. When a person is engaged in finishing a unit of work, an externally imposed pause may serve as an irritant because it disrupts the work pattern. Work patterns should be carefully studied and the rest pauses adjusted accordingly. Training individuals to space their rest properly may be the best solution to the problem of distributing rest periods in accordance with variations in jobs and differences in people.

One of the difficulties encountered in studying the specific effects of rest periods on production is the fact that an improved attitude toward the company is frequently associated with their introduction. As pointed out in Chapter 3, the effect of the better attitude tends to confuse the data, making it difficult to determine how much effect is attributable to rest gained and how much to the attitude factor. Although the total effect makes the use of rest pauses very desirable to the industrialist, the scientist is interested in separating and measuring the various sources of influence. It may be pointed out, however, that one of the most favorable conditions introduced in the Hawthorne plant[28] was that which included 15 minutes for lunch and rest in the morning and 10 minutes for rest in the afternoon.

The Effect of Length of Workday on Production

During the depression of the 1930s an attempt was made to distribute work among a large number of people by shortening the workday. During the war effort in the 1940s, on the other hand, an attempt was made to increase production by increasing the length of the workday. These procedures presuppose that production is a function of the number of hours worked. Considering the effect of fatigue on production, one may rightly question the validity of this supposition.

Excessively Long Hours

The story is told of a woman worker in a surgical-dressing factory who refused to follow the workday maintained by the plant.[29] The hours were from 6 to 8 A.M., 8.30 A.M. to 12.30 P.M., 1.30 to 5.30, and 6 to 8 P.M. Meals were eaten in the three free periods. The woman in question not only refused to work before breakfast, but also declined to return in the evening. When questioned, she claimed she stayed away because she could do more work if she worked only the eight hours. Investigation revealed that, in a month's time, this woman's output was 52,429 bobbins.

[28] Roethlisberger, F. J., and Dickson, W. J. *Management and the worker.* Cambridge, Mass.: Harvard University Press, 1939.

[29] Muscio, *op. cit.,* p. 73.

While she worked only 160 hours, the more cooperative workers put in 237 hours, yet not one of them produced as many bobbins. The average production of the three best workers was 48,529, while the production of the best worker was 51,641. Since it is unlikely that any one person can be that superior to the best workers in a group, it would appear that the shorter workday was the only plausible explanation for her superior productivity.

Another illustration concerns two groups of apple packers. Under pressure to get the work done, one grower permitted his employees to work 10 hours per day, while another limited the work of his employees to eight hours. The packing was on a piece-work basis in both instances. The results showed that the packers who worked eight hours averaged five cases per day more than those who worked 10 hours.

Under the pressure of the Second World War, England increased its workweek.[30] Before Dunkirk, the workweek was 56 hours; after Dunkirk it was increased to an average of 69.5 hours in the war industries. The first effect of this increase was a 10 per cent rise in production, but then production declined, and sickness, absenteeism, and accidents increased. By the end of a couple of months, the average workweek was 68.5 hours, but the average amount of time actually worked was only 51 hours, as compared with the period before Dunkirk when the average time worked per week was 53 hours. As a result, production was 12 per cent below that preceding Dunkirk. Six months later, the shorter week was restored, with the result that production steadily rose to a higher point than ever before.

This English experience throws grave doubts on the advisability of increasing production by means of overtime work. Working extra hours obviously results in some production, but its effects on subsequent production are likely to be considerable. Under stress of great motivation, these trends may be temporarily altered, but, eventually, undesirable effects may be expected.[31]

Optimum Workweeks

During the depression years of the middle 1930s, the Waverly Press went on a six-hour day.[32] The employees had the choice of working two three-hour periods or one six-hour period each day. They chose to work the six hours in one stretch. The first effect of the change from eight to six hours was a 5 per cent drop in production (from 100 to 95) and a doubling of errors. As the employees became accustomed to the new work pattern, however, the hourly production rose to 115, or 15 per cent above the normal level, and the errors were somewhat fewer than before the introduction of the six-hour day. With an hourly production of 115 per cent, the six-hour day yielded 690 production units, whereas the previous eight-hour day had yielded 800 units on the basis of eight hours of production at 100 per cent. Considering that errors were also reduced, this means that production for a six-hour

[30] *The Nation.* April 11, 1952, p. 412.
[31] Bartley and Chute, *op. cit.,* Ch. 2; Vernon, H. M. The influence of hours of work and ventilation on output in tin plate manufacture. *Industr. Fat. Res. Bd.,* 1919, Rep. No. 1.
[32] *Kalends.* Baltimore: Waverly Press, 1937, *3,* 5–8.

day was approximately the same as for an eight-hour day. A more efficient use of the six-hour day, such as interrupting it with a lunch period, might have made up for any slight difference that remained.

In a more detailed study, workweeks of 36, 40, 44, and 48 hours were compared.[33] The hourly output for the 40-hour week was found to be the most efficient, the production being 868 units. With the 44-hour week, hourly production fell to 839 units; and with the 48-hour week, it dropped to 793.5. For the 36-hour week, production was 834 units, which made this work pattern less efficient (per hour) than the 40- and 44-hour weeks, but more efficient than the 48-hour week. The inefficiency of the shortest workweek may have been due to loss in practice and improper work attitudes or to any number of other factors.

The differences in hourly production between the 40- and 48-hour weeks are not sufficiently great to make the total weekly production of the 40-hour week greater than that of the 48-hour week. Apparently, the 48-to-54 hour week is approximately the work pattern which yields the greatest weekly output. Only when the work period exceeds these hours is the decrease in hourly output sufficiently great to make the longer week less productive than the shorter week.

In deciding upon a most efficient workweek, it is desirable to distinguish between its effect on hourly production and its effect on weekly production. From the standpoint of efficiency, measured in terms of production per hour, a workweek of about 40 hours seems to be the optimum under existing conditions. But if there is a shortage of labor and the purpose is to get the maximum amount of goods produced with the manpower available, then a workweek in the vicinity of 50 hours is the optimum.

If there is an excess of labor and the goal is to spread the work, the reduction in either hours or days worked must be great enough to accomplish the objective, but this might require a reduction in weekly pay.

The Four-day Week

If the length of the work week is held constant and the number of days worked is varied, a new work pattern emerges. There has been an interest in the 40-hour, four-day pattern. This would take us to the 10-hour day which had been less productive than the eight-hour day for many types of work. Would the four-day week offset the fatigue of the long day? This, in part, would depend upon what the worker does with the time off. If used for long weekends, it could reduce the Monday absenteeism that plagues the automobile industry, but if workers still take an additional day off to achieve a four-day weekend, no reduction in absenteeism would occur. The low production figures for Monday obtained in industry can be attributed to absenteeism, to weekend recovery or to warm up. Will a longer weekend influence these factors? The fact that many workers took second jobs when a six-hour

[33] Miles, G. H., and Angles, A. The influence of short time on speed of production. *J. Nat. Inst. industr. Psychol.,* 1925, *2,* 300–302.

day was implemented[34] suggests that the shorter week may increase the number of multiple-job holders.

If a four-day week becomes widespread and causes families to take more weekend trips, absenteeism of children in schools would increase. This might necessitate schools adopting a similar plan of longer hours, but fewer days in school. Church attendance, already reduced by the Monday holidays, might also be affected by the four-day week. Thus a minor change in the work week might alter an established pattern of living and justly be called a revolution in social and economic values.

A clear-cut advantage associated with the four-day week is that it reduces travel to and from work where this is a fatiguing factor. For some industries scheduling would also be simplified.

In companies that have tried the four-day week the response has been generally favorable.[35] Some companies have initiated it to reduce turnover, unions have been consulted and react favorably, and generally speaking, employees like it, with the exception of women who have programs for the care of children. Experience with it seems to increase its desirability. The companies experimenting with the program are small and have found that scheduling work created no difficulties. In some companies the four-day week is reduced to as low as 34 hours, but pay is for 40 hours. In order to reduce the length of the "10-hour" day, rest pauses often are given up. From the fatigue point of view this would be an undesirable concession even though employees offer to give them up in exchange for a shorter day.

Research is needed to test productivity under controlled conditions so that case studies, which tend to be selected to prove a bias, need not be used as evidence. Since fatigue principles may be violated, the productivity losses resulting may be overcome by improved attitudes and morale. Thus, tests over a period of time are needed if one wishes to establish overall efficiency.

If the new pressures for a three-day work week are successful, some interesting changes in values may be expected. Work will cease to be the dominant activity, and leisure will take its place. If there is an excess of leisure people will use time on home projects. Thus there may be a return to the old style of living when both men and women were skilled in many arts and crafts. This could be satisfying or inefficient depending on one's values.

If the dominant part of the week becomes concerned with self-initiated activity, will job interest decline? Will the leadership of business change so that improvements and efforts to increase productivity will become inadequate? Since increased productivity is needed to finance leisure, could the trend toward a shortened work week become self-destructive? The alternative to escaping unpleasant jobs by shortening the work week would be to make the work more interesting. Some possibilities in this approach will be discussed in Chapter 16.

[34] Swados, H. Less work—less leisure. In E. Larrabee and R. Meyersohn (Eds.), *Mass leisure.* New York: Free Press, 1958, pp. 353–363; Northrup, H. R. The reduction in hours. In C. E. Dankert, F. C. Mann, and H. R. Northrup, *Hours of work.* New York: Harper & Row, 1965, pp. 1–16.

[35] Poor, R. (Ed.), 4 days, 40 hours: Reporting a revolution in work and leisure. Cambridge, Mass.: Bursk & Poor, 1970.

The Work Shift

Many industries are required to operate three shifts in order to give 24 hours of service; others use two or three shifts to increase the productive capacity of the plant. As capital investment per employee increases, it becomes more necessary to operate more than one shift to reduce overhead. This large investment in plant and machinery that is required for each employee creates a social problem that may become acute.

A study of British industries[36] revealed some of the problems and findings involved in the use of night shifts. When the same individuals alternately work both a day and a night shift, most of them are more productive on the day than on the night shift. The total result is that the day shift is more productive than the night shift. This corresponds to the general experience in this country. Contrary to what might be expected, however, the absenteeism of a given individual is about the same for both day and night shifts.

Various problems are created by the shifts. Most employees prefer the day shift, the expressed reasons being health, output, and social life. The investigators found general agreement among the workers that the feeling of fatigue was greater for the night than for the day shift. Failure to get enough sleep at home when working on the night shift was claimed by 42 per cent of the employees, and 75 per cent said they got less than eight hours of sleep. Daytime noise seemed to be a common interference with sleep.

More difficult than the problem of rest, however, was that of adjusting to the change in mealtime when changing shifts. Sixty-two per cent indicated this to be a problem, and 35 per cent said the adjustment required more than four days. Most employees mentioned loss of appetite and upset digestions in connection with shift changes.

Some of these adjustive problems were revealed in the production records. The plants covered included factories that changed shifts weekly, fortnightly, and monthly. Examination of production records of the fortnightly changes revealed that production was better on the second week than on the first week of the day shift. For the monthly changes there was a slight but continued improvement for each successive week of the day shift. However, the night shift schedules showed no such improvement. Because of physiological adjustment problems created, Bloom[37] argues against shift rotation, particularly on a weekly basis.

A study of two automated electric power plants in the United States revealed similar trends.[38] Answers of workers to the question of what caused the most trouble in making shift changes are shown in Table 15.3. In this study also the major problems had to do with making adjustments for sleeping and eating. The adjustment time varied from one to four days, with about 45 per cent in the two plants

[36] Wyatt, S., and Marriott, R. Night work and shift changes. *Brit. J. industr. Med.,* 1953, *10,* 164–172.
[37] Bloom, W. Shift work and the sleep-wakefulness cycle. *Personnel,* 1961, *38,* 24–31.
[38] Mann, F. C., and Hoffman, L. R. *Automation and the worker.* New York: Holt, 1960.

Area of Complaint	Percentage[1] of Shift Workers Mentioning This Area	
	Plant A (N = 42)	Plant B (N = 121)
Physical and Physiological		
1. Sleeping difficulties (getting enough rest, sleeping days, etc.)	84	67
2. Eating difficulties (scheduling meals, digestive problems, etc.)	45	47
3. Eliminative difficulties (irregular bowel movements, constipation, etc.)	6	5
4. Staying awake on the job (working at the time they had been sleeping)	3	8
Social		
5. Family life ("hardship on family," "making children understand I won't be home to play with them")	6	4
6. Social life and recreation ("letting friends know what shift I work," "no social life")	5	7
Miscellaneous	5	9
Did not answer	8	12

[1]Percentages add up to more than 100 since some respondents mentioned more than one complaint area.

From *Automation and the worker: A study of social change in power plants* by Floyd C. Mann and L. Richard Hoffman. Copyright © 1960 by Holt, Rinehart and Winston, Inc. Reprinted by permission of Holt, Rinehart and Winston, Inc.

Table 15.3 / Complaints about Shift Work

claiming that four days were required. The family reaction to shift work was negative in 61 and 79 per cent for Plants A and B, respectively.

Shift rotation is an attempt to distribute the hardship or inconvenience to all employees. Although the changes introduce an additional problem of adjustment, it does permit each family to live a normal life part of the time. It is possible that some of the problems created by three shift operations can be solved by making the night shift more attractive. Differential pay is only part of this picture. Persons who live out of phase with other people also have problems with shopping, recreation, and a social as well as a community life. When a large number of persons work on a night shift, the possibilities of developing a more nearly normal pattern of life should be explored. Perhaps the greatest immediate difficulty, at present, centers on the problems of daytime noise, which is most acute for families with children. Without shift changes, husbands and wives who work could more easily obtain jobs with similar hours. Whole communities might organize a social life around hours that suited their shifts. It now sometimes happens that husbands and wives find themselves working different shifts, and so they are denied a home life as well as a community life.

The Job of the Executive

Although the trends of lightening the physical work and shortening the workday apply to most employees, the executive's job has shown no such changes. Executives are working longer hours,[39] lunch periods are usually used for meetings, dinner meetings or obligations are frequent, and on some occasions breakfast meetings are held to increase scheduling opportunities for conferences. Conducting conferences and holding interviews are stressful activities because they require constant alertness.

Frequently there is little time for planning, which means that this may be done during the hours intended for sleep. Since unfinished work or work in the planning stage is hard to forget (see the *Zeigarnik Effect,* discussed in Chapter 16), this activity frequently becomes akin to worry.

The positions of executives are also less secure: they have no union steward to defend them; it is difficult for them to find other jobs at a comparable level on short notice; good performance is difficult to measure so that making a good impression rather than doing a conscientious job becomes a distractor. Thus work pressure, long hours, and little opportunity to escape from job worries can be seen as fatiguing.[40] However, if the jobs are satisfying, the need for leisure is less, because the work becomes more like play. The executives' perceptions of their jobs thus will determine, in part, the fatigue effects of long hours.

The executive's job does not lend itself to automation although data-gathering and processing may be simplified. Decision making, willingness to take risks, and generation of alternatives cannot be relegated to computers. With business consistently extending its trade on an international basis, functioning in a more restricted economic environment, and diversifying its products, the executive will hardly find in automation a means of job simplification. The only primary escape from pressure is delegation. More and more, decision-making functions will have to be moved farther down the line. Thus reforms in the executive's job must be sought in improved organizational climates (see Chapter 21).

Automation

With automation the pace of the work is controlled by the machinery, and heavy work is largely eliminated. In many instances the worker is present only to take action in the event that something goes wrong. In some modern chemical fabric plants employees are so scarce that they become lonely.

Lack of sleep and fatigue affect vigilance. Automation increases the cost of errors and the need for vigilance, and the difficulty of maintaining attention increases as improved mechanization reduces the probability of a failure.[41] Thus, an attendant

[39] Wilensky, H. L. The uneven distribution of leisure: The impact of economic growth on "free time." In E. O. Smigel (Ed.), *Work and leisure.* New Haven, Conn.: College and University Press, 1963, pp. 107–145.

[40] Schoonmaker, A. N. *Anxiety and the executive.* New York: American Management Association, 1969.

[41] Mast, T. M., and Heimstra, N. W. Effects of fatigue on vigilance performance. *J. engr. Psychol.,* 1964, *3,* 73–79.

must be ready to act when an incident occurs, but the required concentration is hard to maintain when action is required only a few times a day or even less often. Automatic safety controls often are built into the system, but usually an individual must make some adjustments.

In air transport, a similar type of vigilance is needed. In these cases emphasis is placed upon decreasing fatigue by reducing noise and vibration, introducing good temperature and humidity controls, giving attention to seating comfort, and having good illumination, which may be overlooked because the human element is so small a part of the operation. However, these fatigue-reducing conditions also encourage sleep, particularly if the employee has had inadequate rest. Automated plants often are confronted with a similar problem of reducing fatigue without promoting sleep.

Increasing the number of attendants might help, but this can lead to socializing, hence reduced attention. Thus, double-checking should be an independent process if it is to be safe.

Anticipation of automation also introduces job insecurity, and a good deal of preparation is needed to make an organization ready for change.[42] Loss of developed skills, boredom, loneliness, and reduced job satisfaction are problems created by automation and these states of mind affect fatigue as well as motivation. The problems of boredom and ways to reduce it are considered in the next chapter.

Leisure and Recreation

As incomes rise and working hours decline, off-the-job activities play a more important part in a worker's system of values. Paid vacations are becoming common and interest in long weekends is increasing.[43]

Leisure, on the one hand, can be an opportunity for satisfying the higher type needs, acquiring skills and knowledge which promote an individual's job potentials, strengthening family bonds, escaping the stresses of work, recuperating from fatigue, and preparing for retirement. The growing popularity of correspondence courses, specialized adult training, and so on, suggests that many people are using these hours to acquire new skills in line with those required by positions to which they aspire. Resting or taking part in activities designed to relieve the tensions built up on the job or to regenerate the individual's energy so that he may return to his job more zestfully is another positive approach. The do-it-yourself trend has made it possible to make articles ranging from original fabrics to furniture or entire houses after skill in the arts or crafts is developed during leisure hours. Both the do-it-yourself trend and the growing popularity of family camping dramatize the findings of a study in which 76.8 per cent of the 125 automobile workers questioned replied that they would spend more time with their families if their leisure time were in-

[42] Mann and Hoffman, *op. cit.*

[43] Faunce, W. A. Automation and leisure. In E. O. Smigel (Ed.), *Work and leisure.* New Haven, Conn.: College and University Press, 1963, pp. 85–106. Henle, P. Recent growth of paid leisure for U. S. workers. In W. Galenson and S. M. Lipset (Eds.), *Labor and trade unions.* New York: Wiley, 1960, pp. 182–203; Meany urges 35-hour work week. *The Detroit News,* November 12, 1963, 6–D; U.S. labor: Affluence vs. influence. *Newsweek,* November 25, 1963, 85–88.

creased.[44] Here leisure functions as a family unifier for the man whose work (and commuting schedule) requires that he be away from home a great part of the day. Wrenn[45] proposed that occupation (employed work) and leisure (nonemployed or voluntary work) be considered not as a polarity but as a fusion. This concept suggests that "work" not be restricted to employed activities and that unpaid work can fulfill a moral end (work considered as a virtue by society) and be satisfying at the same time. Working "out of the occupation" may have particular significance if the work one does for pay is not personally satisfying and makes one feel insignificant.

There is no guarantee that leisure will be constructively used. It can also be used to satisfy lower needs, development of tastes that conflict with job progress, breaking of family ties, increased fatigue and unhealthy distractions (e.g., increased drinking), and developing activities that cannot be continued in later life. Freedom from work in a work-oriented society can be an emotionally disturbing experience. It has been pointed out that suicides occur more frequently on weekends, holidays, and vacations.[46] The proper use of leisure is a concern for industry and society as a whole, and it requires training.

Since such training is not readily available, leisure time is frequently a source of negative experience to people in a culture which has valued work as a primary justification for man's existence.[47] A basic change in attitude is required before the use of leisure time can be deeply rewarding for the individual and for his society. When leisure can be accorded value similar to that historically given work by our industrial society, it is possible that the individual will be freer to utilize his total energies in both work and play.

Preparation for Retirement

Workers should learn to play and to develop various interests while they are still young so that these activities can replace work when it becomes too strenuous or when retirement is forced upon them. The leisure time now resulting from automation and from the changing work patterns of modern society can very profitably be used to prepare for retirement so that the individual will not equate the loss of his job with death or total uselessness, as is frequently the case.[48] Membership in various groups, be these religious, political, cultural, volunteer, or activity-based, begun during earlier years, both stabilize the individual's activities and maintain his self-concept upon retirement.

[44] Faunce, *op. cit.,* pp. 92–95.

[45] Wrenn, C. G. Human values and work in American life. In H. Borow, (Ed.), *Man in a world at work.* Boston: Houghton Mifflin, 1964.

[46] Wrenn, *op. cit.*

[47] Huizinga, J. *Homo ludens: A study of the play element in culture.* Boston: Beacon Press, 1955; Berger, B. M. The sociology of leisure. *Industr. Relat.,* 1962, *1* (2); Weiss, R., and Reisman, D. Some issues in the future of leisure. *Social Problems.* 1961, *9,* 78–86; Kaplan, M. *Leisure in America: A social inquiry.* New York: Wiley, 1960; Kerr, W. *The decline of pleasure.* New York: Simon and Schuster, 1962.

[48] Harlan, W. H. The meaning of work and retirement for coal-miners. In E. A. Friedmann *et al.* (Eds.), *The meaning of work and retirement.* Chicago: University of Chicago Press, 1954, pp. 53–98.

It is perhaps a mistake for retired persons to move to new locations if this will take them away from their friends and groups. Housing developments in Sweden stress the need for retired persons to live with varied age groups to keep their identity with society as a whole.[49]

Laboratory Exercise

Group Problem Solving: A Problem in Delegation

A. Procedure.

1. The instructor will read *Problem orientation* aloud (Section D.1). The situation described may be discussed for a few moments to ensure that the meaning of the delegation process is understood.
2. The class should be divided into groups of approximately five for discussion.
3. Groups should study the *Problem situation* (D.2) and clarify their impression of the company organization.
4. The *Discussion topic* (D.3) should then be studied. Group members should make a list of the various problems and issues this top management decision generated. Once the problems are isolated the discussion should turn to (1) the level at which the decision should be made and (2) whether the leader should make the decision or whether a group decision is recommended.
5. All groups will discuss the problem simultaneously and be prepared to report after approximately 20 minutes.

B. Report of results.

1. The leader should prepare the chalkboard showing five columns with headings indicating the organizational levels: Executive, General Administrative, Departmental, Sectional, and First Line, respectively.
2. Each group should report any additional decisions that top management should make beyond that of giving employees the coffee privilege. The instructor should briefly summarize these problems in first column under the heading, *Executive,* before going to the next column. The group reports also should indicate whether they recommend that the solutions be supplied by the leader (L) or through group decision (G.D.).
3. After each group has reported its conclusions for the first column, the same procedure should be followed in completing the remaining four columns.

[49] For further reading on aging and retirement the following sources are suggested: Barron, M. L. *The aging American: An introduction to social gerontology and social geriatrics.* New York: Crowell, 1961; De Grazia, S. *Of time, work, and leisure.* New York: Twentieth Century Fund, 1962; Heron, A. *Preparation for retirement: Solving new problems.* London: National Council for Social Service for the Preparation for Retirement Committee, 1961; Kleemeier, R. W. (Ed.). *Aging and leisure.* New York: Oxford University Press, 1961; Mathiasen, G. *Flexible retirement: Evolving policies and programs for industry and labor.* New York: Putnam, 1957; Tibbitts, C., and Donahue, W. *Social psychological aspects of aging.* New York: Columbia University Press, 1962.

C. Discussion of results.

1. After the tabulation is completed, the similarities and differences in reports should be noted and discussed. Attempts to resolve differences should be made.
2. General conclusions regarding the reasons for delegating or not delegating various problems should be discussed.
3. The value of group decision as well as its effect on upward and downward communication between the various levels should be explored.

D. Materials. *read aloud*

1. *Problem orientation:* When a decision is made by top management it generates a large number of problems in all parts of the organization. These problems will vary from one department to another because a top-level decision affects them in specific, and often different, ways. For example, decisions regarding mergers, expansions, and decentralization would influence the manufacturing department quite differently than the sales department. Certain of the problems created by top-management decisions might also be local in nature. The parking problem for employees might differ from one work location to another. Thus work sections or units find they have problems that are unique to them.

   Decisions made by top management also affect individuals in special ways. Moving the plant, for example, could constitute a hardship for one individual and a welcome change for another. It is essential to sort out the various types of problems and to place the responsibility for solving them at the most appropriate level. The more specific problems should be delegated farther down the line. The manager at each level must therefore select the portions of the problems he (1) will solve himself, (2) wishes to share with his subordinates, and (3) feels should be delegated to the lower levels.

2. *Problem situation:* Let us assume that a specific incident has occurred in a small electrical appliance company, which we shall call the Peninsula Home Appliance Co., Top management has made a decision to grant all nonsupervisory employees 30 minutes per day for a coffee break. The company management structure is not complex for it provides only five levels at which decisions are made. These are:

   a. Executive—consisting of president (as leader) and vice presidents, secretary, treasurer, etc.
   b. General administrative—operating vice president and several department heads
   c. Departmental—(manufacturing, sales, accounting, and personnel)—department head and his section heads
   d. Sectional (within each department)—section head and his supervisors
   e. First line—a supervisor and the workers who report to him.

   The company is located in several buildings in different parts of the city. The main office building houses the department heads and the officers of the company, as well as the accounting and personnel departments. Sales and manufacturing operate from several locations which vary in size. The main building has a company cafeteria. Restaurants are adjacent to some of the other buildings and, in a few of the locations, the nearest restaurant may be two or three blocks distant.

3. *Discussion topic:* The purpose of the discussion is (1) to determine the specific problems that this management decision creates and (2) to suggest at which levels of the organization each should be solved. Recommendations should then be made as to which of the specific problems should be decided by the leader at a particular level and which problems should be handled by group decision.

Suggested Readings

Bartley, S. H., and Chute, E. *Fatigue and impairment in man.* New York: McGraw-Hill, 1947.

Brouha, L. *Physiology in industry: evaluation of industrial stresses by the physiological reactions of the worker.* Oxford: Pergamon Press, 1960.

Dankert, C. E., Mann, F. C., and Northrup. H. R. *Hours of work.* New York: Harper & Row, 1965.

Dumazadier, J. *Toward a society of leisure.* New York: Free Press, 1967.

Hilliard, M. *Women and fatigue* (1st ed.). Garden City, N.Y.: Doubleday, 1960.

Kleemeier, R. W. (Ed.). *Aging and leisure.* New York: Oxford University Press, 1961.

Mackworth, J. F. *Vigilance and habituation: A neuropsychological approach.* Baltimore, Maryland: Penguin, 1970.

Ryan, T. A. *Work and effort.* New York: Ronald, 1947.

16 Psychological Fatigue and Job Interest

The Varieties of Psychological Fatigue

The term *psychological fatigue* designates the more elusive factors which cause work decrement. It includes the falling-off in efficiency of work commonly referred to as *mental fatigue,* as well as the phenomena known as *monotony* and *boredom.* The influence of attitudes and motivation on work decrement, also, should be considered under this category.

Insofar as true mental fatigue exists, the phenomenon may be a decrement in the functioning of nerve and brain centers. Monotony and boredom are influenced by the way a person views a task from time to time, causing the output to fluctuate rather than to fall off progressively. The manner in which a job is perceived or experienced is an individual matter, but certain kinds of tasks and work atmospheres are more likely to induce monotony and boredom than are others. These experiences are rather special forms of fatigue which are probably more psychological than physiological in nature.

Motivation is a factor in all forms of fatigue in the sense that the rate of fatigue for almost any type of task varies inversely with the intensity of the motivation. When motivation is low, fatigue effects appear early, but when motivation is high, evidence of fatigue may not be apparent until considerable physical exhaustion is manifest. Even though its symptoms are often vague and indefinite, the importance of psychological fatigue must not be overlooked. It is an important aspect of industrial unrest as well as of work decrement; it may even be responsible for the increase in nervous disorders in modern life. Mental conflicts and frustrations are so commonly associated with work that it is to the industrialist's interest to determine methods for reducing their incidence.

419

Fatigue, Motivation, and Energy Expenditure

A Motivation Theory of Fatigue

Work energy is not stored in a person in such a way that it can be drained off, as by opening a valve. Rather, it is more appropriate to think of this energy as inaccessible until motivation exists; even then only a given amount becomes available for a specific kind of activity. As a result, the energy for a given task may be depleted without greatly reducing the total supply. It is as if the energy were rationed and a particular job must have certain priorities if it is to get a good share of the energy. After a day at the office, a person may be too tired to work overtime, but if someone suggests a bowling game plenty of energy becomes available. The person's basic supply of energy is not depleted by work, but the portion allocated to a given task is expended. If many allotments are made, the total supply is reduced. Rationing then becomes more strict; higher priorities are needed or smaller allocations are made. Thus, the actual supply of energy is limited, but is seldom if ever depleted, because the rationing protects the basic supply. The depletion commonly experienced is the spending of an energy assignment. Motivation controls the distribution of energy; thus it is the key process in the rationing procedure.

Figure 16.1 describes the relationships between the total supply of energy, the portion allocated to a given task, the effect of motivation on the task allocation, and the relationship between fatigue, motivation, and energy expenditure. In each of the six conditions the large circle represents the total energy of an individual. This total energy is never entirely depleted, but the specified amounts assigned to various tasks can be used up. The smaller circles within the large circles represent allocations of energy for specific tasks, and their size indicates amounts of energy allocated. These amounts vary directly with the degree of motivation a particular task can arouse in an individual. Diagrams A and B represent energy allocations in two degrees of motivation for the same task in two different people, although the total supply of energy is the same for each. Diagrams C and D show that work on the tasks has been done; the shaded portions of the circles indicate that half the allocated energy has been spent. Spending half the allotted energy creates a relative degree of fatigue, and this fatigue is the same for Diagrams C and D, even though the amount of energy spent for Condition C is more than twice as great as for Condition D. Diagram E illustrates the condition in which a person expresses fatigue for Task I. However, when Task II, an activity with high motivation, is presented, energy for it is made available from the total reserve. The fact than an incomplete circle of energy is shown for Task II indicates stricter rationing conditions created by the reduced supply. Diagram F describes a condition in which many activities have been performed, each having enough motivation to obtain new allocations. Note that several circles are incomplete, indicating stricter rationing with the reduced total supply. When the total supply of energy has been reduced so that all tasks are curtailed, the condition of exhaustion is approached.

According to this view, high motivation makes more energy available, while low motivation releases a lesser amount of energy for the task at hand. It follows, then,

Figure 16.1 / Relationship between Energy Supply and Energy Available for a Task.

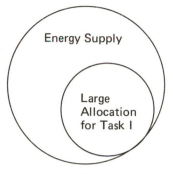

a. Condition of
high motivation.

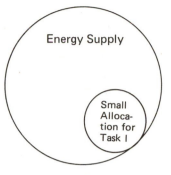

b. Condition of
low motivation.

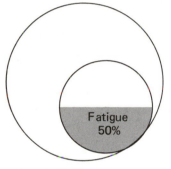

c. Average fatigue—
much work done.

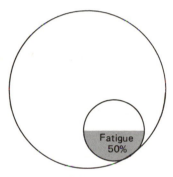

d. Average fatigue—
little work done.

e. Complete fatigue for
Task I. Energy for
Task II available
but reduced.

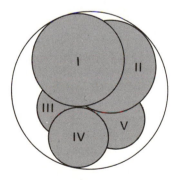

f. Energy allocated to several
tasks. With total supply
reduced, state of
exhaustion is approached.

that the problem of reducing fatigue can be approached either by making more energy available or by efficiently utilizing the quota of energy that has been made available. Motivation reduces fatigue by increasing the allocated energy supply, whereas such factors as rest periods and slower work pace reduce fatigue by causing the efficient expenditure of energy, regardless of the amount allotted. Since these two types of influence on fatigue are altogether different, we can understand why the curve of fatigue does not always follow the same trend. People sometimes perform heroic deeds and show surprising degrees of endurance without succumbing to fatigue. These exceptional feats appear superhuman only because we try to interpret them in the light of the more common and limited allotments of energy, while, actually, unusual amounts of energy were made available in such instances. The theory that fatigue is influenced in two distinctly different ways explains these unusual cases of human endurance and strength. Although this theory is still in its rough form, it represents an attempt to account for certain qualitative relationships between fatigue and energy expenditure. It also permits a distinction between fatigue and exhaustion which existing evidence seems to require.

Experimental Findings

Experimental support of the theory that energy is distributed according to the task motivation comes from an ingenious experiment with animals. Evidence from animal behavior in a problem of this kind is particularly convincing, since it shows that the phenomenon is a fundamental process; at the same time, the data are not distorted or confused by higher mental processes, which may alter the outlook on the task and indirectly influence the results.

In the experiment in question, rats were trained to run a certain distance along a path before they made a turn that led to food.[1] Figure 16.2 shows the apparatus used. Animals were required to begin at the starting point (S), make a right turn, and run to the sixth turning point before making a left turn, at the end of which they found food (F). The positions of the starting unit and of the food units were changed from trial to trial, but the distance between them was always the same. Since identical paths led off the main route at one-foot intervals, the only way for the rats to locate the correct turn was by learning to run a certain distance; that is, to recognize when they had spent a certain amount of energy. With motivation held constant (24 hours without food), the problem was learned with considerable accuracy.

Changes in motivation were then introduced. When motivation was increased by lengthening the period of food deprivation (48 hours without food instead of 24), the animals made the turn approximately one unit farther along the path; when the motivation was decreased below normal (12 hours without food instead of 24) the animals made the turn about one unit too soon. In other words, when the animals were highly motivated, they underestimated the energy they had ex-

[1] Crutchfield, R. S. Psychological distance as a function of psychological need. *J. comp. Psychol.*, 1939, *28*, 447–469.

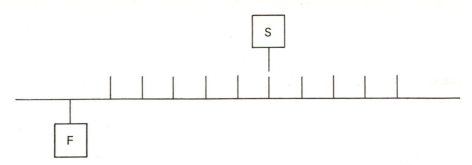

Figure 16.2 / Elevated Pathway Used to Measure Animals' Judgment of Distance. The positions S (start) and F (finish—food) were continually changed, but the location of F was always the sixth unit from S. Since all left-turning paths were alike, the animals had to learn to locate the path that led to F by means of the distance run. High motivation (hunger) did not make the animals overanxious as one might expect; rather, running about seven units under high motivation was confused with running about five units under low motivation, and both were confused with running the six units that the animals were trained to run under average motivation. The experiment indicates that motivation increases the amount of energy that is made available for a task; with more energy assigned to a task, distances run are underestimated.

pended; when they were poorly motivated, they overestimated it. If these errors in estimating energy expenditure can be produced by motivation, it appears that motivation influences the energy supply, and in this manner distorts the judgment of how much has been spent. In other words, spending half of a large amount of energy feels very much the same as spending half of a small allotment of energy.

In another experiment an ergograph was used to measure the ability of human subjects to do physical work under different conditions of motivation.[2] In one condition the subjects were required to apply maximum force for as many trials as possible, while in another they were required to apply as much force as necessary to keep each lift above a line drawn on the record sheet. The second condition thus specified the amount of energy expenditure which the subject must try to exert. Under the second condition less fatigue was apparent and more energy was available. The difference in energy expenditure for various persons working under the two conditions ranged from 14 to 68 per cent, with an average of 37 per cent. This experiment supports the view that with expectations defined, higher motivation occurred and increased the amount of energy made available for work.

This interpretation of motivation as a factor determining the supply of energy is consistent with the results of a number of other experiments which show a relationship between motivation and learning behavior, as well as with common experiences concerning the relation between motivation and industrial work. So-called "lazy"

[2] Wright, W. R. Some effects of incentives on work and fatigue. *Psychol. Rev.* 1906, *13*, 23–34.

people seem to have a deficiency in energy, yet we may be surprised at their endurance when sports are involved. Since their energy is available only for certain activities, it is a problem in motivation to make energy accessible for useful pursuits.

Work Decrement in Mental Operations

General Findings

Assuming that motivation can be kept fairly constant during a laboratory experiment, evidence shows that both speed and accuracy decrease as the work period continues.[3] Tasks such as mental multiplication of two- or three-place numbers, reciting the alphabet backwards repeatedly, and memorizing words or syllables produce evidences of fatigue within an hour. Also, signs of warming-up and end spurts often appear. It is apparent that in some mental tasks practice effects minimize the extent of fatigue and exaggerate the warming-up effects, but controlled experiments clearly show that the warming-up and work-decrement phenomena are as common in mental operations as they are in physical work.

As in the case of physical work, rest periods delay the onset of the work decrement. In general, frequent short rests seem more effective than a few long ones. Too long a rest period seems to be a disturbance in many forms of mental work because the person loses the continuity of the task or gets out of the mood for it. In general, pauses of about five minutes seem to be beneficial. The actual percentage of rest required for mental work is probably less than that for physical labor. Under optimal conditions, heavy physical work requires that at least 16.7 per cent of the time be spent in resting if the greatest efficiency is to be attained.[4] In actual industrial practice, this figure would undoubtedly be too low for hard physical work, but it would seem to be more than ample for common forms of mental work.

Bornemann emphasized the degree of involvement in a task as a factor in determining rest pauses.[5] He developed a method for measuring involvement and found that it is greater in office work (involvement ranges from 50 to 100 per cent) than in manual work (involvement ranges from 30 to 60 per cent). Although office work may not be fatiguing physically, the high degree of involvement introduces a new factor for consideration. The author recommends short breaks (five or 10 minutes) because recovery is rapid for fatigue effects resulting from psychological involvement in a task. In a military study it was found that 10-minute rest periods following each half-hour's duty facilitated detection of visual signals to a significant degree.[6] Here, too, a high degree of psychological involvement may be assumed since constant vigilance is necessary for performance of the task.

[3] A good summary of this work can be found in S. H. Bartley, and E. Chute, *Fatigue and impairment in man.* New York: McGraw-Hill, 1947, Ch. 15.

[4] Shepherd, G. H. Effect of rest periods on production. *Personnel J.,* 1928, 7, 186–202.

[5] Bornemann, E. Psychologische Wege zur Verminderung der Ermüng in Betreib und Schule. *Mensch u. Arbeit,* 1952, 5, 133–144.

[6] Gergum, B. O., and Lehr, D. J. Vigilance performance as a function of interpolated rest. *J. appl. Psychol.,* 1962, 46, 425–427.

Inspectors looking for occasional "rejects" among batches of items on a conveyor belt, sonar men listening for the "different echo," radar observers looking for targets on the screen, motorists checking the road for traffic signs, are all activities which involve receiving stimulus information, but for which few of the stimuli are signals for action. Such tasks require little muscular effort, and decrements in their function are attributable to mental fatigue.[7] Automation may be expected to increase such vigilance problems.

Physiological Changes in Mental Work

Muscular fatigue was never seriously questioned as a phenomenon because it was possible to demonstrate the presence of fatigue products when muscles were activated. If true mental fatigue exists, it is reasonable to assume that the fatigue products should be found in brain or nerve tissues. The discovery of fatigue products or other evidence of fatigue in nerve tissue was delayed for many years because the chemical changes in nerve metabolism were too small to measure. However, highly refined methods of measuring heat, oxygen consumption, and carbon dioxide production have made it possible to demonstrate increased metabolism when nerve tissue functions. It is now established that there is a resting metabolism, an activity metabolism, and reduced levels of nerve functioning with continued use.[8] It is the reduced functioning of the nerve with continued use that demonstrates fatigue. By reducing the magnitude of nerve responses, nerve tissue is protected from exhaustion.

Evidence of physiological changes produced by mental operations and unrelated to emotional factors has been reported by Ford.[9] He used an electronic indicator that he developed to measure changes in the functioning of the heart. Subjects lying in relaxed positions on cots were required to do mental arithmetic problems for a period of 27 minutes with alternating three-minute intervals of work and rest. To insure against changes produced by accompanying muscular contractions, electrical responses which even indicated twitches were taken from muscles. Under these carefully controlled experiments, it was found that : (1) the electrical output of the heart increased 6 per cent; (2) as work continued most subjects showed a decreased output which represents adaptation to the work load; and (3) most subjects showed a faster heart rate during mental work than during rest. The fact that mental work and rest pauses showed a difference demonstrates that mental effort, like physical effort, has an effect on the heart rate. That the relationship between work and rest for the last half of the experimental period differed from that of the first half is suggestive of the cumulative effects so commonly associated with true fatigue phenomena.

[7] Mackworth, J. F. *Vigilance and habituation: A neuropsychological approach.* Baltimore, Md.: Penguin, 1970; Alluisi, E. A. Sustained performance. In E. A. Bilodeau and I. M. Bilodeau, *Principles of skill acquisition.* New York: Academic Press, 1969.

[8] Brink, F., Jr. Excitation and conduction in the neuron. In S. S. Stevens (Ed.), *Handbook of experimental psychology.* New York: Wiley, 1951, pp. 50–93.

[9] Ford, A. Bioelectric potentials and mental effort: I. Cardiac effects. *J. comp. physiol. Psychol.*, 1953, 46, 347–351.

With the evidence of metabolism in nerves established and some physiological evidence apparent, the concept of mental fatigue has a more realistic basis.[10] The fact that many of the phenomena associated with mental work are subject to emotional factors and are influenced by attitudes, interests, and mental health, should not be overlooked.

Mental Blocking

Work which requires constant alertness and attention is subject to interferences known as *blocking*.[11] Most people have observed that, when adding a column of numbers, they reach momentary stages at which they repeat a sum over and over several times before they reach the next sum. Then, for a while, they find they can skip along from one number to the next in smooth succession until another block occurs. The same effect may be observed if one attempts to repeat over and over a word such as *banana*. The blocks are only a few seconds in duration, and several may occur per minute.

The phenomenon of mental blocking becomes objectively apparent when we measure the continuous results of mental work. If a person is asked to name a series of colors, give the opposites of a list of words, or add a series of sums, and if the responses are recorded on a revolving drum so that each response makes a mark, it is found that these marks are irregularly grouped. A few responses occur rapidly, then there is a delay, followed by another set of responses. Such records show that the responses are either very close together or fairly far apart.

The blocks or lapses in performance are associated with the making of errors. Mistakes in arithmetic tend to occur at the points where the blocks occur. Long blocks not only produce errors, but materially delay the speed of work. In industrial situations in which constant vigilance on the work is necessary, these blocks may cause accidents.

There are wide differences among people in the length of their mental blocks, as well as in the frequency with which these occur. The number of blocks range from two to six per minute in different people. Individuals who tend to perform slowly in experimental tests also are likely to be the ones who have long or frequent blocks.

Blocking probably functions as an automatic method of resting; for this reason an activity requiring attention can go on with only brief interruptions. Continued work, however, produces an increase in the length and frequency of blocking incidents, and this phenomenon probably accounts for the decrement in mental work

---

[10] Kalsbeek, J. W. H., and Ettema, J. H. Continuous recording of heart rate and the measurement of perceptual load. *Ergonomics,* 1963, *6,* 306–307 (Abstract); Cattell, R. B., and Scheirer, I. *The meaning and measurement of neuroticism and anxiety.* New York: Ronald, 1960, Chs. 9 and 19.

[11] Bills, A. G. Blocking: A new principle in mental fatigue. *Amer. J. Psychol.,* 1931, *43,* 230–245; Bills, A. G. Fatigue, oscillation, and blocks. *J. exp. Psychol.,* 1935, *18,* 562–573; Warren, N., and Clark, B. Blocking in mental and motor tasks during a 65 hour vigil. *Psychol. Bull.,* 1936, *33,* 814–815.

that gradually appears as the work period continues. Although mental blocking is a special phenomenon in itself, the fact that blocks increase in length and frequency makes it an aspect of psychological fatigue.

Monotony and its Relation to Efficiency

The experience of monotony is often regarded as the curse of modern efficiency. It is claimed that repetitive work makes robots of people and that it destroys such human values as pride in workmanship and individuality. There is a general belief that boredom and dissatisfaction are common in our present methods of production. To what extent these conditions are read into a situation by people who actually do not have to do the work, and to what extent a state of boredom really does influence production, are questions worthy of consideration.

Some Definitions

Both the terms *monotony* and *boredom* have been used to describe the undesirable effects of repetitive work. These terms have somewhat different connotations and should be more specifically defined. One writer[12] has pointed out that reading a book may be boring without being repetitious and that work which is repetitive but does not require attention might not be boring. He suggests the term *tedium* for the undesirable effects of repetitious activity. This use of the term is very close to the way the term *monotony* is used by the British investigators who have done most of the work on this subject.[13] For the purposes of this book, the terms *tedium* and *monotony* are employed to describe the state of mind caused by repetitive work. They refer to the experience of sameness without implying emotional distaste. The term *boredom* will be used as a more inclusive term, taking in the person's unfavorable outlook and feeling tone for the task he is performing.

It follows from this distinction that boredom will be affected more than monotony by the following factors: (1) the personality of the person; (2) the attitude and mood of the person; and (3) the perception of the task performed. This means that individuals might not agree on the task that was most boring; individual persons might show more boredom one day than another; and some people might become adjusted more readily to boring tasks than to monotonous ones.

In one interesting study, ten persons were rotated between five repetitive jobs.[14] They spent one month on each task, and were then asked to rate the jobs from zero to five according to the degree of boredom. The zero rating was for the job in which boredom was completely absent and the five for jobs in which it was always present.

---

[12] Baldamus, W. Incentives and work analysis. *University of Birmingham studies of economics and society,* Monogr. Al, 1951, 1–78.
[13] Wyatt, S., Fraser, J. A., and Stock, F. G. L. *The effects of monotony in work.* Indust. Fat. Res. Bd., 1929, Rep. No. 56.
[14] Wyatt, S., Langdon, J. N., and Stock, F. G. L. *Fatigue and boredom in repetitive work.* Indust. Health Res. Bd., 1937, Rep. No. 77.

On one of the jobs there was agreement: all ten persons assigned it their highest or second highest boredom ratings, and so it had to be rated as one of the two most boring jobs. Agreement ended at this point, however. The average boredom ratings given for the five jobs were 4.2, 2.4, 2.3, 1.7, and 1.7. Individual differences in the degree of boredom experienced are indicated by the average ratings given to the five tasks by each of the 10 persons. These ranged from 1.8 to 2.9. The authors of the study also pointed out that superior intelligence and extroversion tendencies increase a person's susceptibility to boredom. A study made in the United States demonstrated a relationship between boredom and poor adjustment.[15] These relationships indicate that boredom is a complex experience, influenced by personality and intellectual factors as well as by the activity performed. Before pursuing further the problem of boredom, it is desirable to relate the effects of repetitive activity to job performance. We may assume that the experience of either boredom or monotony might accompany such activity and that a claim for the mental state of monotony would be the more conservative opinion.

Industrial Findings

Monotony and boredom become specific topics under the general heading of fatigue only when it can be shown that performance of work which produces them results in work decrement. Further, this decrement must result from something other than muscular fatigue.

The British studies, in general, agree in indicating that the mental state of monotony is associated with definite fluctuations in the rate of working and with a fall in production. In one of the most exhaustive studies this relationship was demonstrated by showing (1) that production was low and variable during periods when boredom was experienced and (2) that the production of individuals who felt very bored was lower and more variable than that of individuals who did not feel bored.[16]

Monotony effects were most pronounced during the middle of the work period and disappeared in anticipation of the end of the work period, causing the end spurt in the production curve. During the state of boredom the workers were restless and felt under a strain; time seemed to pass slowly.[17] The extent of the monotony was dependent not only upon the repetitive nature of the task, but also upon the degree of attention required. Some of the findings of the British investigators have been questioned by investigators in this country.[18] The close relationship between the

[15] Smith, P. C. The prediction of individual differences in susceptibility to industrial monotony. *Amer. Psychologist,* 1951, 6, 361.

[16] Wyatt, Fraser, and Stock, *op. cit.;* Wyatt, Langdon, and Stock, *op. cit.*

[17] A good summary of industrial studies of monotony is given in Viteles, M. S., *Industrial psychology.* New York: Norton, 1932, Chs. 23 and 24; Ryan, T. A., and Smith, P. C. *Principles of industrial psychology.* New York: Ronald, 1954, pp. 411–421. Other studies of interest are S. Wyatt, Boredom in industry. *Personnel J.,* 1929, 8, 161–171; Lossagk, H. Experimenteller Beitrag zur Frage des Monotonie-Empfindens. *Indust. Psychotechn.,* 1930, 7, 101–107.

[18] Rothe, H. F. Output rates among butter wrappers: II. Work curves and their stability. *J. appl. Psychol.,* 1946, 30, 199–211; Smith, P. C. The curve of output as a criterion of boredom. *J. appl. Psychol.,* 1953, 37, 69–74.

experience of boredom and output was not reproduced; individual differences were very marked, and the slump in the middle of the day was not present. There is general agreement, however, that workers tend to slow down, talk, become restless, and show variable production when bored. The motivating effect of the end of the work period, causing an end spurt, was also found to be a characteristic of repetitive jobs.

The complicating factor in working with boredom is the failure of productivity and the state of mind to show a necessary, close relationship. In other words, both productivity and the mental state are influenced by a variety of factors, and although some of these factors may be common to both, each is influenced by special ones. It follows then that what workers think about while doing repetitive work is a condition that influences the way the work affects them. Letting the mind wander seems to be one way of escaping monotony. If daydreaming does not interfere with the ability to do good work, it is probably a useful adjustment, but if constant alertness is imperative, it may cause errors and accidents. Obviously, the best adjustment to repetitive work will vary with the nature of the job. We shall return to this question after analyzing the nature of boredom.

That a good deal of the loss in production in repetitive work is due to the specific condition of boredom rather than to a muscular fatigue is indicated by the facts (1) that afternoon monotony effects do not exceed those of the morning, as might be expected from accumulated fatigue, (2) that the anticipation of the end of the work period tends to abolish signs of monotony, and (3) that intelligent workers are more subject to monotony effects than are less intelligent ones. These facts indicate that a knowledge of the mental effects of repetitive work is highly important, since such information might suggest methods for eliminating this mental condition.

The Psychological Effects of Repetition

The Progressive Stages of Satiation

Much was learned about physical fatigue by performing experiments in which a few muscles were worked to the point of exhaustion. Is there a corresponding phenomenon for mental activity? Experiments along this line have actually been performed in the laboratory. By confining the activity to very simple operations and having them repeated indefinitely, marked changes in behavior were produced.[19] In these experiments the term *satiation* was used. Although the term *monotony* describes the initial stages of satiation, it does not lend itself to describing the process as a whole. For our purpose we may think of the process of satiation as the stages a person goes through in reaching mental exhaustion for a particular activity. Emotional components characteristic of boredom may also appear.

College students in a German university were used as subjects in the series of experiments in satiation. For one of the activities they were asked to draw vertical

[19] Karsten, A. Psychische Sättigung. *Psychol. Forsch.*, 1928, *10*, 142–154; these experiments are also described in K. Lewin, *A dynamic theory of personality*. New York: McGraw-Hill, 1935, pp. 254–257.

lines on a sheet of paper and to follow a certain pattern, such as alternately grouping the lines in twos and threes. As subjects filled one sheet of paper after another, the paper supply was replenished. They were never allowed to stop. Samples of the results are shown in Figure 16.3.

Gradually the quality of work declined until it was sometimes difficult to make out what had been done. Only the aspect of grouping into twos and threes seemed to connect the later stages of work with the earlier ones. After about four hours the average subject could no longer continue. This was the stage of complete satiation.

Similar results were obtained when persons were asked to read the same poem over and over. Variations in interpretation appeared, and as these ran out, different kinds of errors in reading and speech were made. Accent was changed, punctuation was ignored, and words were mispronounced. Words ceased to have meaning to the reader, and a listener would have had difficulty in understanding the poem. Finally, stuttering and choking on words occurred, until the stage of inability to talk was reached.

The stages of (1) variability, (2) reduction in quality, (3) difficulty in continuing to make the necessary movements, and (4) complete inability to go on with the work characterized the course of satiation.

Figure 16.3 / Changes in Task Performance Accompany Satiation. The first row shows vertical lines, alternately grouped in twos and threes, properly executed. The second and third rows show changes occurring in the stage characterized by variation. The fourth row illustrates reduced quality. The task is no longer executed according to the spirit of the assignment although the person could argue that he has grouped lines in twos and threes. Thereafter the performance deteriorates even more until the person is unable to write. When asked to complete the page, however, the ability to execute the task is restored, as shown in the last row of lines.

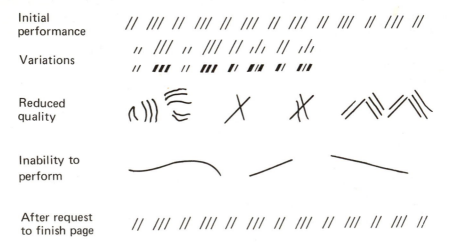

Satiation as a Psychological Condition

To demonstrate that the satiation could not be attributed to the fatiguing of the musculature involved, the experimenter merely changed the instructions. Subjects who could not write any more were told to finish the page or to write their names on the sheets, and their ability to write was restored as if by magic. Subjects who could no longer recite the poems were engaged in long conversations and showed no inability to use their vocal mechanisms. Changing the task to be performed, without changing the muscles involved, completely restored the use of the muscles.

Specific and General Aspects of Satiation

Another aspect of the experiment showed that variability in work delayed the onset of complete satiation. Individuals who were ingenious in finding variations in the execution of the task were able to continue longer. When the experimenter introduced variations in the task, the stage of complete satiation was postponed. For example, having subjects switch to grouping lines in threes and fours or in twos and fives, or giving the reader a different poem to read, served to lengthen the period of continued activity. However, each change in instruction became less beneficial, so that eventually a whole type of activity (such as line drawing or reading) was satiated. Variations prevented the satiation of a specific task, but they did so by spreading the satiation effects over a larger area thus depleting the energy supply (see Figure 16.1).

The Importance of the Experience of Progress

The experiment was next tried on a group of unemployed men who were paid a small sum per hour to serve as subjects. These men worked a full eight-hour day, and their work continued to be as neat and accurate at the end of the day as it was at the outset. Unlike the college students, they found the work highly pleasant. One asked if he could have the job on a permanent basis.

The difference in performance of workmen and college students was found to be due to the difference in the way the work appeared to them. For the unemployed men, the work period was fixed. As each hour passed, they moved along in the day and had earned more money. Analysis of the experiences of college students revealed that they tended to have the experience of marking time, going in circles, being on a treadmill; in other words, they experienced just "getting nowhere." The paper supply did not diminish, they did not approach an end, and their activity achieved nothing; yet they had to continue because they had consented to serve in the experiment.

The absence of the experience of a *goal* or an *end* toward which one moves seems to be the cause of satiation, a cause which depends completely upon the way one views the task. In this experiment a particular view of the task was encouraged by the situation, but in actual work a great deal of variation may be expected. The same task may appear quite unlike to people with varied backgrounds and different nervous systems. A particular person may not view a task in the same way on two occasions, or may react differently to two tasks that another feels are very similar. What appear to be unimportant modifications in the arrangement of a task may actually change the whole outlook of a group of dissatisfied workers.

Attitude toward the Task

It might be supposed that unpleasant tasks would be satiated more quickly than pleasant tasks. This assumption was not borne out by the experiments on satiation. On the contrary, pleasant and unpleasant tasks were satiated at the same rate, but more quickly than tasks for which there was no emotional feeling. This finding suggests that satiation is something more than mere dislike for a job. It is a condition of being disturbed because of the failure of an action to lead to anything, rather than because of the inherent nature of the task. It also appears that anything that can be done to remove emotional involvement in the task will be in the direction of reducing satiation. Perhaps daydreaming and music are helpful in industry because they dominate the person emotionally and so make the task a secondary, hence more neutral, activity. The physiological condition of the person also was found to influence susceptibility to satiation.[20]

Methods of Eliminating Boredom in Industry

The method of dealing with the problem of eliminating boredom will naturally vary for different types of work. In order to alter the way in which a job is experienced, it may be necessary to make changes in the work pattern. Although all jobs cannot be changed in the same manner, one or more of the suggested procedures should be applicable to most forms of repetitive work in industry.

Job Rotation and Job Enlargement[21]

If variability in a task delays the onset of satiation, it may be said that a change in work is as good as a rest, insofar as satiation is part of the general state of fatigue. As pointed out above, satiation becomes quite general in the sense that an area or type of activity may be satiated. For this reason any changes in work which are instituted must give the person the *experience* of doing something different. What one person regards as different may be the same old grind to another. When high degrees of skill are not at a premium, it is probably expedient to permit employees to exchange jobs for days or parts of days. Variability on the same job should also be permitted. Different ways of doing the job, fluctuations in pace, and other variations which the worker may adopt serve the purpose if they are not extensive enough to interfere with skill and to increase muscular fatigue. Rotating between simple jobs or positions on an assembly line or combining several simple jobs introduces variety by enlarging the job.

---

[20] Freund, A. Psychische Sättigung in Menstruum und Intermenstruum. *Psychol. Forsch.,* 1930, *13*, 198–217.

[21] Schoderbek, P. P., and Reif, W. E. *Job enlargement: Key to improved performance.* Ann Arbor, Mich.: Bureau of Industrial Relations, University of Michigan, 1969.

A few illustrations will suffice to show how this principle of variation may be applied. French[22] reported improvement in morale as a result of variation within a job. He had women working on a sewing operation fill out *pacing cards.* The cards divided the shift into hourly work periods, and the women were requested to indicate the hours of the day during which they wanted to work at slow, medium, and fast paces. They were encouraged to introduce variations in these paces and to try out a variety of plans. This planned variety in pacing had a beneficial effect on both attitude and productivity.

In a central office housing telephone equipment, the author found that two types of maintenance jobs, performed by women, were a constant source of difficulty. These were the jobs of the *solderers* and the *dusters.* The duty of the duster was to go over the equipment constantly to keep it clean; that of the solderer was to check the many wires and correct any loose or faulty contacts. Morale was poor; the workers fought; turnover was serious. The employees complained of being over-worked. Assuming the jobs to be monotonous and recognizing that the training problem was a minor one, the workers were given the opportunity to exchange jobs. All accepted the opportunity. Half of them dusted and half soldered, but every two hours they exchanged jobs. The two supervisors of the 20 employees agreed that conditions had improved and continued to improve for the following year at the least. Also interesting was the fact that the dusters now dusted as much on a half-time basis as they had previously on full-time. A similar though somewhat smaller improvement occurred with the solderers.

Jobs that are made less confining, and actually violate certain efficiency principles, may show production gains. In a telephone company office, six women sat at desks sorting toll tickets. Each hour a messenger came along and picked up their work. Eliminating the messenger, and permitting the sorters to go up a flight of stairs to deliver their own work, resulted in an increased productivity that permitted a one-third reduction in the size of the force, in addition to dispensing with the messenger's part-time service. This increased output occurred despite the fact that the sorters would often wait for each other and go upstairs in pairs. The change was made to eliminate job discontent and high turnover; the production gain was purely a byproduct.

The use of job rotation to counteract the boredom resulting from automation also should be considered. In training operators for their new jobs in a fully automated plant, rotation among the jobs was instituted. This practice was continued beyond the training stage and was found to be an important factor in the increased job interest the operators experienced in the modern power plant.[23]

The fact that the satisfaction to be derived from job rotation is frequently not anticipated by employees is an interesting phenomenon. A comparison of the feelings toward rotation of operators not removed to the new plant (and not having

[22] French, J. R. P., Jr. Field experiments: Changing group productivity. In J. G. Miller (Ed.), *Experiments in social psychology.* New York: McGraw-Hill, 1950, Ch. 6.
[23] Mann, F. C., and Hoffman, L. R. *Automation and the worker.* New York: Holt, 1960.

experienced job rotation) with operators moved to the new plant (and having experienced rotation) is shown in Table 16.1. The response of operators who experienced rotation shows 70 per cent "like rotation very much," whereas only 37 per cent of the operators who lacked the experience anticipated that they would like it, and 17 per cent indicated they would "dislike it a lot." Perhaps the concern about the new learning required dampens the expectations of those who have not experienced rotation, but it is also probable that job satisfiers cannot be prophesied.

Both job rotation and job enlargement contribute to job interest and job satisfaction because they increase job complexity. The power plant study demonstrated that the satisfaction from job rotation did not come from greater mobility and more contacts with fellow workers. The evidence indicates that job interest is a function of job content. If job enlargement and job rotation remain within the practical limitations of training cost, it seems advisable to incorporate one of these practices on jobs that require attention and cannot be reduced to simple habits. A survey of 276 companies revealed that less than 20 per cent of them have used some form of job enlargement.[24] Often its use is associated with lower levels of supervision where there has been enough delegation to permit making job changes. The infrequency of attempts to reduce boredom in industry indicates the richness of opportunities in this area of application.

Relating the Job to the Larger Picture

In general, the term *red tape* refers to activity which is experienced both as boring and as unnecessary. If employees do not understand what the detailed record is about, they react to it as unnecessary. Teaching the employees the meaning of their

Table 16.1 / Feelings about Job Rotation

	Percentage	
	New Plant (N = 35)	Old Plant (N = 109)
How would (do) you feel about doing these jobs in rotation with your own job?		
Like it very much	70 *	37
Like it fairly well	20	19
Don't care, don't like or dislike	5	14
Dislike it a little	2	6
Dislike it a lot	0	17
Not ascertained	3	7
	100	100

*Difference in percentages between the plants is significant.

From *Automation and the worker: A study of social change in power plants* by Floyd C. Mann and L. Richard Hoffman, p. 116. Copyright © 1960 by Holt, Rinehart and Winston, Inc. Reprinted by permission of Holt, Rinehart and Winston, Inc.

[24] Schroderbek, P. P. and Reif, W. E., *op. cit.*

work, how it fits into the total picture, how the records are arranged, and a number of other details would change much red tape into essential and important activity. Giving employees responsibility and opportunities for judgment is also very effective in accomplishing this end. Too often, the foreman tells a skilled workman exactly what to do on a repair job without telling him "why" or giving him a chance to get involved in the task. Assignments can become opportunities for involving the subordinates in problem solving if the superior welcomes their ideas on how they would like to do the job.

The Use of Pacing Methods and Automatic Work Habits

Our analysis has shown that repetitive work creates mental satiation and perhaps boredom as well, not because the activity is repetitive, but because it creates the experience of marking time. If one can change the experience, but leave the activity the same, boredom will partly disappear. This point suggests that repetitive work should be made entirely automatic whenever possible. A job that is "second nature" to a worker frees the mind for other things. One does not get bored with walking because one's thoughts can be on other things. However, if a person reacted to walking as picking up the feet and putting them down again, this activity would be most boring. Walking, however, leaves time for contemplation, daydreaming, and conversation.

Since many jobs are as automatic as walking, conversation and daydreaming should be encouraged in these cases. Industrial research has shown that monotony disappears when mind wandering is prevalent.[25] A survey in Germany revealed that about 90 per cent of the factory workers preferred repetitive, rhythmic tasks because these gave them a chance to think of other things while working.[26]

However, taking the mind from one's work may interfere with keeping up a work pace. It takes attention to keep going at a good speed. Industrial research has demonstrated that jobs which are repetitive in nature may benefit by external pacing methods. For example, production on a job involving the sorting of metal plates rose nearly 18 per cent when a metronome was used to set the pace.[27] The reader may also be aware of the fact that marching with a band is less fatiguing than walking without an externally imposed rhythm.

The Benefits of Industrial Music

Music piped into factories has become fairly common and therefore requires an evaluation.[28] Some of the first studies were made in England where we found the initial interest for dealing with monotony. The effects of musical programs on simple assembly operations showed production increases up to 6 per cent, when production on days with music was compared to that on days without music.[29]

[25] Wyatt, Fraser, and Stock, *op. cit.*
[26] Arendt, H. *The human condition.* Chicago: University of Chicago Press, 1958.
[27] Reinhardt, H. Rhythmus und Arbeitsleistung. *Indust. Psychotechn.,* 1926, *3,* 225–237.
[28] Benson, B. E. *Music and sound systems in industry.* New York: McGraw-Hill, 1945.
[29] Wyatt, Langdon, and Stock, *op. cit.*

Morning programs seemed most helpful, but the length of the programs (30 to 75 minutes) was not important. In a radio-tube assembly factory in which music was customarily played, the effectiveness of fast, slow, and mixed programs was studied.[30] The scrappage rate was found to be less when either fast or slow music was played than when there was no music or when fast and slow musical programs were alternated. Musical programs also had a beneficial effect on employee morale.

Subsequent studies tend to support the general finding that some production increases are obtained and that favorable effects upon employees' states of mind occur.[31] The increase in production varies considerably with the job and with the shift. A detailed study[32] reported production increases ranging from 4 to 25 per cent, with an average increase of 7 per cent for the day shift and 17 per cent for the night shift. Simple repetitive jobs that can be performed well while talking seem to benefit most by music. In one investigation no production increase was obtained.[33] The job studied was a complex one, in that judgment, thought, and working cooperatively with another person were required. Interesting, however, was the fact that the employees thought their production was better with music. An overview of research findings indicates that music seems to encourage young, inexperienced workers to increase production on routine jobs. No significant effects were found for older skilled workers.[34]

The general finding is that employees like music. At least 75 per cent strongly favor it and only 1 to 2 per cent oppose it. The findings on the kind of music to be used for different types of jobs indicate no sharp trends. It is probable that detailed studies along this line will yield little of importance. Slow music seems more desirable than lively music; variety is essential to keep young and older employees satisfied with the programs. Vocal music may be distracting for some jobs and some employees, and music with strong beats may disturb or aid depending on how it fits into the movement rhythms of a job. Spaced programs seem to be favored at present; it appears that the music should be on about 12 per cent of the time for the day shift and as much as 50 per cent of the time for the night shift.[35]

Although music may be beneficial for a number of reasons, one of the most favorable effects is its influence on boredom. It takes the mind from the work as well as frees the brain of the obligation of initiating the activity. Moreover, progress

[30] Humes, J. F. The effect of occupational music on scrappage in the manufacturing of radio tubes. *J. appl. Psychol.*, 1941, *25*, 573–587.

[31] Kerr, W. A. Effects of music on factory production. *Appl. psychol. Monogr.*, 1945, *5*; Smith, H. C. Music in relation to employee attitudes, piece-work production and industrial accidents. *Appl. psychol. Monogr.*, 1947, *14*.

[32] Smith, H. C., *op. cit.*

[33] McGehee, W., and Gardner, J. E. Music in a complex industrial job. *Personnel Psychol.*, 1949, *2*, 405–417; Newman, R. I., Jr., Hunt, D. L., and Rhodes, F. Effects of music on employee attitude and productivity in a skateboard factory. *J. appl. Psychol.*, 1966, *50*, 493–496.

[34] Uhrbock, R. S. Music on the job: Its influence on worker morale and production. *Personnel Psychol.*, 1961, *14*, 9–38.

[35] Smith, *op. cit.*

may be experienced by moving through the musical program, even if the job tends to give the experience of getting nowhere.

Psychological Effects of Incompleted Tasks

Introduction

Modern production methods are characterized by the division of the manufacture of the industrial product into many units or subassemblies. Each worker makes or assembles only a part, so that few employees have the experience of turning out a complete object. Is it essential to job satisfaction that the task be actually completed? The story is told of an industrial worker who, on his deathbed, was asked by his friends if he had a last request. "Yes," he replied. "Bring me a board with a screw driven halfway into it and let me drive the screw the rest of the way." All his life this man had worked on a production line and had driven screws part-way into a board; now he wanted the satisfaction of finishing one.

It is a common occurrence for a man to put off starting a job near the end of the day. This behavior indicates a general tendency to avoid starting something that cannot be finished. Since this is the case, it is unjust to regard the business of "stalling" at the end of the day as a fault.

These illustrations demonstrate that the drive to finish a task once it is begun presents a psychological problem of no minor concern to management. Since the problem has been carefully investigated in the laboratory, it is of interest to recount the results in some detail.

The Noncompletion of Tasks (The Zeigarnik Effect)

To obtain an index of the effect of preventing the completion of a task, one experimenter measured the influence of work interruption on memory.[36] Subjects were asked to perform a group of 20 tasks, such as modeling animals, stringing beads, and solving puzzles. Half of the tasks were allowed to go to completion, but the other half were interrupted and completion was prevented. At the end of the experiment, the subjects were asked to list all the things they had done. The incompleted tasks were remembered twice as frequently as the completed ones. Tests of memory, given some time later, showed the same difference. When a task was finished, it was easy to forget, whereas, when it was not finished, it lingered in the memory and even tormented the subject. When permitted to finish the incompleted tasks later, the subjects were greatly relieved and the memory difference disappeared.

Other aspects of the experiment made it clear that a certain energy system is built up when a task is being performed and that it is the strain of the unspent energy that influences the memory. A strong emotion tended to break up these strains, indicating that the energy system had its basis in emotional energy. Fatigue

---

[36] Zeigarnik, B. Über das Behalten von erledigten und unerledigten Handlungen. *Psychol. Forsch.*, 1927, *9*, 1–85.

tends to reduce the energy available for a task, so that when the experiments were performed under conditions of fatigue, there was less difference between the effects of completing and not completing tasks.

The Need to Complete a Task

In another experiment it was shown that there was a strong tendency to complete noncompleted tasks.[37] When the experimenter left the room on some pretext and then observed the subjects through a peephole, it was found that they furtively took from the desk the tasks they had not been allowed to finish. These tasks were hurriedly completed and put back in place. When the experimenter returned, the subjects acted as if they had been seated all the while. It was not pride that made them want another chance at the unfinished job; rather, it was a need to dissipate the energy system connected with the task. On a number of occasions, when the experimenter met children who had previously served in the experiment, they begged for permission to complete tasks that had been interrupted.

The experimental evidence demonstrates that the performance of a task sets up a psychological condition which demands its completion. The strength of this demand varies with the task, the stage of interruption, and the individual. More recent evidence indicates that tasks left uncompleted by one person may cause another to feel the need to complete them.[38] Unfinished tasks as such, depending upon how they are experienced, seem to have a disturbing effect and must be carefully considered in investigations of job satisfaction.[39]

Tasks which have a definite point of completion are the most affected by interruption. For example, when modeling a clay dog, the task is not finished until the animal has acquired all its parts. Interruption of such tasks invariably caused definite reactions. In contrast, the activity of stringing beads was often experienced as completed despite the interruption. A partly finished long string of beads may also be a completed smaller string. Some completed tasks were similar in their effects to other noncompleted tasks. Investigation revealed that such tasks, although completed, were experienced as incomplete. For example, a puzzle would be solved, but the subject might have missed the principle and feel that he was interrupted because he had not discovered how it worked.

The tendency to complete unfinished tasks which are either pleasant or unpleasant is greater than the tendency to complete emotionally neutral tasks, but the pleasantness or unpleasantness of the task does not influence the extent of the desire to

[37] Ovsiankina, M. Die Wiederaufnahme unterbrochener Handlungen. *Psychol. Forsch.,* 1928, *11,* 302–379.

[38] Henle, M., and Aull, G. Factors decisive for resumption of interrupted activities: The question reopened. *Psychol. Rev.,* 1953, *60,* 81–88; Horwitz, M. The recall of interrupted group tasks: An experimental study of individual motivation in relation to group goals. In D. Cartwright and A. Zander (Eds.), *Group dynamics.* Evanston, Ill.: Row, Peterson, 1953, Ch. 25.

[39] Atkinson, J. W. The achievement motive and recall of interrupted and completed tasks. *J. exp. Psychol.,* 1953, *46,* 381–390; Cartwright, D. The effect of interruption, completion and failure on the attractiveness of activities. *J. exp. Psychol.,* 1942, *31,* 1–16; Marrow, A. J. Goal tensions and recall. *J. gen. Psychol.,* 1938, *19,* 3–64.

complete it. The point at which a task is interrupted is a very important factor. Other things being equal, interruptions toward the end of the task create a stronger desire for completion than interruptions occurring toward the beginning. As the goal or end of the task is approached, the motivation to complete it rises and the tension created by interruption mounts.

Task Completion and Motivation

The experiments on task interruption clearly demonstrate that the completion of a task represents a strong goal or incentive. Anything that is done to permit experiences of task completion would represent a form of motivation and as such should be considered in connection with methods for increasing motivation on the job. Sometimes the very factors that induce efficiency unintentionally have introduced another form of inefficiency and job dissatisfaction through job segmentation. The problem now becomes one of obviating this created fault rather than rebelling against the more efficient patterns of movement.

Reducing Interruptions and Increasing Task Completion

Two approaches to the application of the experimental findings are possible: (1) to do what is feasible to prevent interruptions; and (2) to create additional kinds of completion experiences. Each method suggests a variety of innovations. Preventing interruptions not only means elimination of unnecessary interruptions but also reorganization of the situation so that the purpose of the interruption is viewed differently.

For example, a child is playing in the yard and his mother wants him to come in for lunch. For the good of the child and the convenience of the mother, his play must be interrupted. Frequently a child resists interruption and does not come when he is called. If force is used, an emotional scene rather than a pleasant lunch may result. Let us suppose, however, that the mother realizes that the child is pretending he is trucking freight to Chicago, and that she understands he is still a long way from Chicago, his destination, or a completion point in his activity. Under these circumstances she can point out that she owns a restaurant on the road to Chicago and can ask if the truck driver would like to stop for a meal. The child can now stop for lunch without his play being interrupted. Moreover, the mother makes capital of the situation in that the child now eats like a truck driver.

Interruptions can frequently be prevented by specifying stopping points. A child can be told that he will have to come home after one more ride on the merry-go-round; boys might agree to a five-inning baseball game and experience this point as the stopping place; poker players find it easier to quit at a reasonable hour if they set one additional hand as the completion point.

Another method of preventing interruption is to remind a person of an approaching appointment, thereby giving him a chance to come to a stopping place. In this case the burden of finding a good stopping point is left to the person interrupted. The reader will recall often looking over a task to see how much there is left to do, and may have looked ahead in reading this chapter to see how many more pages

Figure 16.4 / Methods for Introducing Completion Points. Method I illustrates repetitive activity that has no terminal point. Inspecting ball bearings delivered on a belt and dropped into a chute would be an example. If the inspected bearings are dropped into boxes that fill up, each full box becomes a complete unit. Method II illustrates a long job that may not be finished for days, weeks, or months. Such a job lacks completion experiences, too, even though it is not repetitive. If the job is planned and objectives are set for each hour or two, workers experience reaching these points as the completion of a succession of units. These units are the natural rest pauses and times for a stretch or a smoke.

remain. This will be particularly true when the reader has an engagement and must leave soon. If many pages remain, one settles for finding a paragraph that ends at the bottom of a page.

There are two ways to create new or additional completion points: (1) grouping small units into a bundle, such as combining sentences into chapters; and (2) dividing a long job into sections, such as getting a child to drink milk by serving it in a one-ounce rather than a four-ounce glass. These two methods of increasing the experience of completion are shown in Figure 16.4. Method I applies to repetitive assembly and inspection jobs where progress cannot be experienced because each unit is too small to be perceived as the completion of something. Method II applies to construction jobs that have a specific completion point, but one which is too far in the future to permit experiences of progress and the frequent satisfaction of finishing something. The size of the unit of work that seems most effective in industrial practice is one that requires one to 1½ hours to finish.[40]

Adapting Laboratory Findings to the Job

How to Avoid Interrupting the Worker

If the tendency to complete a task is a source of motivation, it should be constructively utilized. It is most characteristic of persons who become engrossed in their work. Constant frustration by interruptions forces such people to cease becoming engrossed in what they are doing. In one study, it was found that the typical foreman was repeatedly interrupted and engaged in approximately 400 to 600 different episodes during his working day.[41] Thus it would seem that one source of fatigue

---

[40] Cox, D., and Sharp, K. M. D. Research on the unit of work. *Occup. Psychol.*, London, 1951, *25,* 90–108.

[41] Walker, C. R., Guest, R. H., and Turner, A. N. *The foreman on the assembly line.* Cambridge, Mass.: Harvard University Press, 1956, pp. 123–124.

tension might well lie in the many interruptions that prevent task completion. On the other hand, when employees experience the satisfaction of completing tasks, they do not watch the clock, but are as insistent on finishing after hours a job once begun as they are on refusing to begin a job five minutes before quitting time.

Little changes in the layout of a job may do much to eliminate the frustration produced by the intrusion of others. Since a person may not be aware that these interruptions are the causes of friction, they continue undetected by management. In the painting department of one plant in Detroit, there was constant friction between inspectors and workmen. It was the practice of the inspectors to point out to the painters places they had missed and have them correct the oversights as they were discovered. After an analysis of the effect of noncompletion of tasks, the job was rearranged. A worker with a pail of paint was delegated to accompany the inspector and to fix up the places missed by the regular painters. This procedure eliminated the inspector's interruption of those workers. The result of this minor change in the inspection methods was to establish harmony in the whole department and to increase production.

One of the problems with telephone repairmen is their tendency to return to the garage before quitting time. There are a number of possible reasons for this action, but among them is the apparent reluctance to start jobs that cannot be finished. To test this assumption, each of a number of workers was given a few small jobs along with the larger assignments. (Previously the less experienced employees were given the small jobs.) As before, the workers were not expected to complete all assignments, but were always given enough work to keep them busy. The result of this change was that the little jobs were now taken care of before lunch and before quitting time, with no reduction in the number of routine or longer unit jobs.

It is common in industry for friction to arise between people working on different shifts. Part of this trouble is undoubtedly attributable to the fact that one worker must finish a unit begun by another.[42] This unit, the product of two people, is frequently below standard quality, and the worker who finishes it often blames the poor workmanship on the person who started the work.

Increasing the Experience of Completion

Management should be vitally concerned with having its employees experience their tasks as complete units or wholes. Dividing the job into sections does not destroy the unity of work, provided other units are set up. These units may be a box of 100 parts, the complete assembly of a unit of a radio, or the finishing of a set of orders. If paid for in terms of these arbitrary units, these activities can achieve the same status as building a complete radio. When a radio assembly is completed, its completion depends upon the fact that it is talked about and treated as a finished product. Another person may come along and consider it unfinished, because it has no case or because it has a case which is unpainted. Completion of a task is an experi-

---

[42] Roy, D. F. Work satisfaction and social reward in quota achievement: An analysis of piecework incentive. In W. Galenson and S. M. Lipsett (Eds.), *Labor and trade unionism.* New York: Wiley, 1960, pp. 361–369.

ence, which can be influenced by the way the job is set up. One or the other of the two basic methods for creating artificial units described in Figure 16.4 can be applied to practically any job.

Boredom in the plant department of the telephone industry is most pronounced in jobs concerned with maintenance of central office equipment. There is no challenge in diagnosing trouble, and the job is very confining since a person can work for hours within a space of a few feet. There is never a real experience of progress; when the job is finished, the worker just starts the whole operation over again. Outside workers, on the other hand, feel very little boredom even if they constantly do the same work over and over. They at least go from one spot to another.

In one office the frames on which the employees worked were subdivided by means of chalk lines. This is the application of Method I. The effect of the lines was to create blocks of work. Each square of work bounded by lines was given a tag with a red and a green side. When the red side was up, it meant that the work on the unit had not been done; the green showed that the job was finished. No tag meant that someone was working on that unit.

Each block required between one and two hours to complete. The worker made the choice of the unit on which to work. The selections made permitted progressive jumps from one end of the frame to the other, so that in a single day a worker not only worked in different parts of the room but progressed from one end to the other.

The benefits of this pattern of work were immediately apparent. No unit was ever left without a tag: once a person selected a block, he worked until it was finished. Every time a worker completed a unit he smoked a cigarette or stretched his legs. Even lunch and quitting time revealed no untagged units. The employees liked the plan and supervisors reported that complaints decreased and difficulty meeting work schedules was eliminated.

An application of Method II for creating extra completion units was tried out with telephone installers. It is characteristic for these installers to do three, four, or five complete installations per day, but not $3\frac{1}{2}$ or $4\frac{1}{2}$. In this case the installation job was divided into Units A, B, and C, representing work inside the house, at the pole, and between house and pole, respectively. Work records were kept on the number of units completed, and the foreman talked in terms of these units rather than of installations. In the 12-man crew on which this method was tested, it was found that production records of 10, 11, 13, 14, and 16 units occurred about as frequently as production scores of 9, 12, and 15 units. The first set of scores represents incompleted installations, the second set represents completed ones. The fact that workers responded to these arbitrary units as readily as to natural ones suggests that artificial units can become as realistic, as far as completion experiences are concerned, as units that are inherent in the nature of the job product.

Task Completion as a Subgoal

The experience of completing a task is a goal achievement and hence becomes a form of intrinsic motivation. Anything that is done to increase the number of completion experiences on the job represents the introduction of subgoals. The relationship between performance and goals and the negative relationship between performance and boredom is borne out by laboratory research.[43]

Job Enrichment

Job enlargement may be regarded as a way of removing boredom from work, and job enrichment, a way of adding interests or satisfiers to it. As discussed in Chapter 13, a job can be made more like play by either removing the negative features or introducing positive ones. Increasing completion experiences therefore represents a form of job enrichment. Herzberg has emphasized the introduction of more freedom and individual responsibility in jobs and recommends what he calls *vertical* job loading as contrasted with job enlargement which he terms *horizontal* loading.[44] Table 16.2 presents seven principles which may serve as guidelines, but how to adapt them to the job still requires some inventing.[45]

Participation in solving job problems and searching for ways to make work more interesting can facilitate job enrichment. Since certain job changes may increase

Table 16.2 / Herzberg's Job Enrichment Principles

Principle	Motivators involved
1. Removing some controls while retaining accountability	Responsibility and personal achievement
2. Increasing the accountability of individuals for own work	Responsibility and recognition
3. Giving a person a complete natural unit of work (module, division, area, and so on)	Responsibility, achievement, and recognition
4. Granting additional authority to an employee in his activity; job freedom	Responsibility, achievement, and recognition
5. Making periodic reports directly available to the worker himself rather than to the supervisor	Internal recognition
6. Introducing new and more difficult tasks not previously handled	Growth and learning
7. Assigning individuals specific or specialized tasks, enabling them to become experts	Responsibility, growth, and advancement

From F. Herzberg, One more time: How do you motivate employees? *Harvard Bus. Rev.,* 1968, *46,* 59.

[43] Locke, E. A., and Bryan, J. F. Performance goals as determinants of level of performance and boredom. *J. appl. Psychol.,* 1967, *51,* 120–130.

[44] Herzberg, F. One more time: How do you motivate employees? *Harvard Bus. Rev.,* 1968, *46, 53–62.*

[45] Ford, R. N. *Motivation through the work itself.* New York: American Management Assn., 1969.

challenge for some workers and frustrate others, it is important that job enrichment not be imposed by experts, yet experts may be needed to spark the ideas.

Problem solving discussions with subordinates could generate ideas that would enrich jobs. The fact that such discussions are seldom held in organizations indicates the untapped potential for making work more interesting.

Laboratory Exercise

Role Playing: The Case of the "Parasol Assembly"[46]

(*Students are asked not to read the case materials before participating in the laboratory exercise.*)

A. Procedure.
1. Eight persons are needed for this problem, one to play the part of the supervisor and the other seven to be subassembly workers.
2. If the room permits, arrange eight chairs in a circle, spaced to correspond to the positions of the workers shown in Figure 16.5. Chairs for observers should be arranged to form a circle or semicircle outside the ring of eight chairs. The desired pattern will simulate a "theater-in-the-round."
3. The instructor will select seven students to play the roles of the workers and ask them to take their places in the circle.
4. Name tags should be placed on each person to indicate which of the workers he is portraying.
5. The instructor will select a person to play the role of Helen Benton, the supervisor who is to remain apart from the group of workers until the role playing begins. The chalkboard should be used to show names of workers arranged in a circle.
6. The observers are to analyze the effectiveness of Benton's leadership.
7. The instructor will read the "General Instructions" (F.1) aloud to everyone. Permit a question period to clarify any points regarding work of this type. All persons should be encouraged to participate at this point.
8. Benton and the seven workers read their assigned roles (F.2, F.3).

B. The role-playing process.
1. The role players finish reading their instructions and put them aside.
2. The instructor checks to see whether the person playing Benton has any questions.
3. At a signal, Benton joins the group, who are seated in their work positions, and the case begins.

[46].Case taken from N. R. F. Maier, The quality of group decisions as influenced by the discussion leader. *Hum. Relat.,* 1950, *3,* 155–174, with the permission of the Journal.

4. Approximately three-fourths of an hour is necessary to role play this case.
5. If the instructor feels it is advisable to help the supervisor or to discuss some especially crucial aspect of the case, he should feel free to interrupt.
6. After an interruption the role playing continues, ignoring the interruption.

C. Analysis of quality of solution.

1. Observers discuss the quality of the solution in terms of its objective excellence, disregarding its acceptance by group members for the time being.
2. A high quality solution should (1) give workers who wish and are able to do more a way to do it; and (2) respect the fact of boredom and permit its reduction.

D. Analysis of general acceptance.

1. Determine which workers will cooperate with the new method, which are neutral, and which will cause trouble.
2. What could Benton have done to improve the acceptance? Discuss.

E. General discussion on questions.

1. How should Benton have stated the problem to her group to stimulate problem solving behavior?
2. How might Benton have made use of some of the differences of opinion in the group?
3. How could Benton have used the mention of such things as boredom, fear of breaking up the team, rotation, a bottleneck, etc., to raise the level of thinking or to prevent the group's thinking from staying in a rut?

F. Materials for the case.

1. GENERAL INSTRUCTIONS

Visualize a subassembly situation in which seven persons, working in a circle, assemble carburetors. The article enters the circle at one point, and each person adds his pieces and pushes the unit to the next worker, who adds his elements. When the unit leaves the circle, it is a completed carburetor. This work arrangement is diagrammed in Figure 16.5. It is called a "parasol" assembly because of the circular arrangement.

Suppose there are four such "parasol" subassembly stations, each one supervised by a supervisor. Suppose further that Station A assembles 85 units per day; Station B, 80 per day; Station C, 60 units per day and Station D, 50 units. It is a fact that Station D previously assembled 60 units. The supervisor was dissatisfied with the production and reprimanded the group. Following the reprimand production fell to 50 units per day. (Production scores should be posted on the chalkboard.)

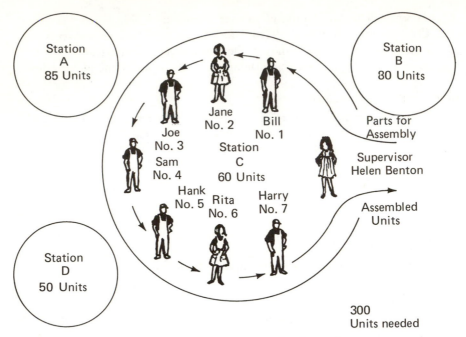

Figure 16.5 / Diagram of Four Subassembly Stations. The stations represent four groups of assemblers who work in teams and assemble carburetors. All groups do the same work and the combined output is 275 units, just 25 short of what is needed. The supervisor of Station C wishes to raise her group's production. There is a bottleneck at the No. 3 position. Work piles up here and the worker seems unable to keep up the pace. How can the problem be solved?

The assembly work is simple and requires a minimum of training for each step. The aptitude requirement is primarily good finger dexterity. The materials for each assembly position are located in bins which are kept supplied by material handlers. Thus each worker has his essential material at his elbow. The job has been analyzed by motion-and-time experts so that the positions are of equal difficulty. Pay is based on hourly rates.

The total factory production is dependent upon receiving the required number of assembled units from these four stations. The production is now so low that the factory production as a whole has had to slow down. The desired quota is 300 parts per shift for the four stations combined.

We are concerned with Station C producing at the rate of 60 units. The work piles up at the position of Joe. The unit must pass through him (Position 3) and he always has several piled up waiting for him. Supervisors on nonproduction jobs are not willing to accept Joe as transfer. Joe is a man of 60 with 30 years of service in the company. Emphasis on improving production has brought his deficiencies to light.

2. Role for the Supervisor, Helen Benton

You are the new supervisor of Station C and have been instructed to get production up. The job has been analyzed by motion-and-time-study experts and the amount of work at each position is practically the same. The No. 3 position (Joe's position) is, however, slightly easier than the others in that one less motion is required. Undoubtedly the previous supervisor put Joe there to reduce the bottleneck. You have received training in group decision methods and are going to try to work out your problem by this method. You have therefore stopped the production line for a discussion. You understand that what you do is your problem. You cannot pass Joe to another foreman. You find Joe a likeable person and it is your impression that Joe gets along well with the other men in the unit.

3. Roles for Assembly Workers

Bill, No. 1

You find you can easily do more work but have to slow down because Joe gets behind. In order not to make him feel bad you hold back. You don't want to get Joe into trouble.

Jane, No. 2

You and Bill work closely together and you usually are waiting for your part from Bill. This waiting for the part is more prevalent in the latter part of the day than in the beginning. To keep busy you often help out Joe who can't keep up. However, you are careful not to let the supervisor catch you helping Joe because she might let Joe go.

Joe, No. 3

You work hard but just aren't as fast as the others. You know you are holding things up, but no matter how you try you get behind. The rest of the workers are fine people and have more energy than you do at your age.

Sam, No. 4

Joe has trouble keeping up and you sometimes grab Joe's part and finish it for him when the boss isn't looking. Joe is a bit old for the pace set and he feels the strain. For you the job is easy and you feel the whole job is slowed down too much because of Joe. "Why couldn't Joe be given less to do?" you ask yourself.

Hank, No. 5

You feel a bit uneasy on this job. There isn't enough to do so you have to act busy. If only Joe could speed up a bit. Why don't they move him out of the group? Is the company so blind that they can't see where the production trouble is?

Rita, No. 6

You are able to keep up with the pace, but on the last assembly job you were pressed. Fortunately Joe is slower than you are so he keeps the pressure off you. You are determined that Joe not be moved off the job. Somebody has to protect people from speed-up tactics.

Harry, No. 7

You get bored doing the same operations over and over. On some jobs you get variety by working fast for a while, then slowly. On this job you can't work fast because the parts aren't fed to you fast enough. It gets you down to keep doing exactly the same thing over and over in slow motion. You are considering getting a job some place where they can keep a person busy. Maybe this new supervisor will get things going.

Suggested Readings

Ford, R. M. *Motivation through the work itself.* New York: American Management Assn., 1969.

Friedman, G. *The anatomy of work.* New York: Free Press, 1961, Chs. 3, 4, and 7.

Katzell, R. A. Personal values, job satisfaction, and job behavior. In H. Borow, *Man in a world at work.* Boston: Houghton Mifflin, 1964.

Meade, R. D. Time on their hands. *Personnel J.,* 1960, *39,* 130–132, 142. Reprinted in H. W. Karn and B. Von H. Gilmer (Eds.), *Readings in industrial and business psychology.* New York: McGraw-Hill, 1962.

Schroderbek, P. P., and Reif, W. E. *Job enlargement: Key to improved performance.* Ann Arbor, Mich.: Bureau of Industrial Relations, University of Mich., 1969.

VanBergen, A. *Task interruption.* Amsterdam, Holland: North Holland Publ. Co., 1968.

Viteles, M. S. *Industrial psychology.* New York: Norton, 1932, Chs. 23 and 24.

17

Accidents and Their Prevention

Approaches to Accident Prevention

The prevention of accidents may be approached from the point of view of the engineer or of the psychologist. The method of the engineer is to remove the hazard from the work by changing the operation of dangerous machinery, designing and installing safety devices, and inspecting the safety of the building and the machinery with a view to structural or functional changes. Simple improvements include enclosing moving parts, such as belts and gears; using paints to make stationary and moving parts more readily distinguishable; attaching guards so that the body cannot come in contact with rotating saws; designing safety goggles; and building floors or platforms to reduce chances of falling, slipping, or receiving electric shock. This approach has been a major factor in the reduction of industrial accidents in modern factories.

The psychological approach involves correction of the human factors in accidents. Training employees to use safety methods, and to become aware of hazards, developing attitudes of cooperation, reducing fatigue, and properly selecting people for their occupations are psychological aspects of accident control.

Since workers must use safety devices, the engineer's approach also gives rise to psychological problems. For this and other reasons psychological problems cannot be separated from purely mechanical ones.

Mechanical Safety Devices

The designing of safety devices is largely an inventor's problem, and some operations must be greatly altered to permit safe procedures. Like the motion-and-time engineer, the safety engineer must have originality and mechanical ingenuity. However, certain general principles apply to most situations and serve as points of departure

Hazardous jobs can be made safe through the use of protective clothing and other devices.

Courtesy of Shell Oil Company

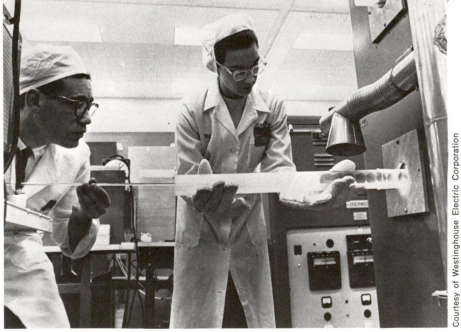

Courtesy of Westinghouse Electric Corporation

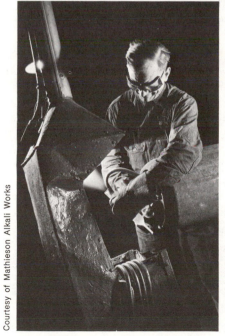

for further improvements. A common safety method is the use of guards which do not admit a part of the body but do admit material to be brought next to the cutting edges of machinery. Another approach is the use of contact switches which break the electric circuit, so that the hands must be occupied with pressing buttons if the machine is to remain in operation. Protective devices, such as special gloves, glasses to protect the eyes, and tools to hold the part to be cut or drilled are familiar safety aids. Analysis of the type of accident associated with a particular job will suggest the danger points and raise specific problems for solution.

The purpose of safety devices is to eliminate the danger points; each one may be designed to remove a specific hazard. For this reason every safety mechanism may be different from every other. But safety devices have certain common features as well as certain specifications which must be met if they are to be satisfactory. The three most important psychological concomitants of all mechanical safety devices are discussed below.

Good Safety Devices Cannot Be Disengaged

A psychological problem arises when employees are required to use safety devices, for many workers like to do the job in the old way and fear they will be thought timid if they seem afraid to take chances. They feel that the gadget slows production, and that they are experienced enough to get along without it. Because of such reactions, workers must be educated to respect safety methods. Moreover, safety devices should be designed in such a way that they cannot be disengaged. The device which interrupts the electric current and prevents a machine from running when the hands are not on the safety button is of such a character. Operators circumvent the safety feature of this device, however, by using pieces of stick to keep the electric button depressed.

The best kind of safety device is one so arranged that the workers must use it in order to produce. When this arrangement is impossible, psychological motivation must be introduced. When workers are trained from the outset to operate a machine with a safety device, this problem is less likely to arise. New employees can learn the safe way to work without overcoming old habits.

Good Safety Devices Are Foolproof

A second requirement for a safety device is that it be foolproof. A device that is only 50 per cent safe may actually increase the number of accidents because the worker may consider the machine safer than it really is and become less cautious than before the device was installed. People tend to adjust themselves to the degree of danger they know to be present, and if danger is made less apparent by safety devices, the number of accidents may be increased.

Since people adjust to danger, existing points of hazard should be made more obvious. Safety devices which guard completely against one type of accident may leave other sources of danger untouched. The use of safety devices may actually change the form of accident in a factory by protecting the worker from one hazard and, at the same time, making him unaware of others. Hazards which remain should always be made clear to the workers while they are being trained so that they will not over-estimate the value of any safety measures. When the hazards are clearly evident, the accidents that do occur tend to be unrelated to the nature of the hazard.[1]

Good Safety Devices Do Not Interfere with Production

Safety devices which interfere with work are unsatisfactory both because workers resist using them and because management objects to the loss in production. It should be the goal of safety engineers to so construct safety devices that they do not handicap the work pattern. Actually, the work pattern may be improved by the motion analysis involved in planning such devices. With the development of proper devices, production may be expected to increase because workers can apply themselves entirely to their work instead of having to divide their energies between personal care and work, a situation which rapidly induces fatigue.

Indirect Safety Measures

Elimination of Fatigue

That fatigue is most conducive to accidents when it is extreme is indicated by the difference in the effect of long and short days on the accident rates of men and women. Vernon cites the case of a shell factory in England that changed from a 12-hour day to a 10-hour day. This change did not materially alter the accident rate among men, but it reduced the accident rate among women by more than 60 per cent.[2] In this country women are being employed extensively in industry, and their accident record is about 45 per cent higher than that of men. A good deal of this high accident rate among women is attributable to accidents which occur after the seventh hour of work.[3] It is probable that some of the fatigue in women is due to the fact that they have more home responsibilities before and after work than do men.

The relation between fatigue and accidents is not limited to the purely physical aspects of fatigue that result in loss of skill, but includes such psychological factors as absent-mindedness and inattention that arise from boredom.

The weekly accident trend is often a mirror image of the production trend. Both the beginning and the end of the week show high accident frequencies.

Good Lighting

Accidents are about 25 per cent greater under artificial lighting than under natural lighting, but these figures are influenced by seasonal variations. Day- and night-shift work also involve differences other than lighting. There is no question about the fact that automobile accidents occur most frequently at dusk and that night driving is

[1] Keenan, V., Kerr, W., and Sherman, W. Psychological climate and accidents in an automotive plant. *J. appl. Psychol.*, 1951, *35*, 108–111.

[2] Vernon, H. M. *Accidents and their prevention.* London: Cambridge University Press, 1936.

[3] Mezerik, A. G. The factory manager learns the facts of life. *Harper's Mag.*, 1943, *187*, 289–297.

more hazardous than day driving.[4] That poor lighting may cause other forms of accidents is generally agreed, but careful industrial studies with specified illumination conditions are not available.

Controlled Atmospheric Conditions

Both temperature and humidity have been shown to be directly related to accident frequency.[5] In mining, minor accidents progressively increase as the temperature in different pits rises from 62 degrees to 85 degrees Fahrenheit. In pits having the highest temperature, the minor-accident frequency was over three times that of pits having the lowest temperature. Major accidents showed little relation to temperature, however. For machine work the optimum temperature for the English worker is 67.5 degrees. An increase of 35 per cent in accidents is obtained by a drop in temperature to 52 degrees or a rise to 75 degrees. Accidents of men and women are affected similarly by temperatures, except that high temperatures influence women somewhat less than they do men. It is probable that optimum temperatures vary with the way the worker dresses and the temperature to which the worker is accustomed at home. For these reasons the optimum temperature in this country may be somewhat higher than in England.

It is probable that conditions which are optimum for production will also favor the reduction of accidents. The problem of atmospheric conditions in relation to production will be considered in the next chapter.

Psychological Safety Devices

Safety Committees

One method of insuring employee participation is for each plant to have a safety committee, and several subcommittees as well, if the number of employees is large. The personnel for such committees should include workers, and a safety officer, who will serve with the committee. Such a group, if it meets regularly and obtains reports, complaints, and suggestions from workers, can keep alive an interest in safety. National safety organizations exist, and various plants could send representatives to their meetings. A committee of this sort can serve in an educational capacity as well as discover careless workers and potential hazards. Suggestions from workers have frequently led to constructive safety measures. With an active committee, social pressure will make unpopular the worker who declines to use safety measures and is generally careless.

Safety Campaigns and Posters

The use of posters and slogans is often effective in raising support for safety. However, as in all advertising, the appeal should be simple, reasonable, and constructive (see Chapter 13). A statement such as "Only fools are careless" is untrue and un-

---

[4] De Silva, H. R. *Why we have automobile accidents.* New York: Wiley, 1942, pp. 18–21.
[5] Vernon, *op. cit.,* pp. 75–85; also Viteles, M. S. *Industrial psychology.* New York: Norton, 1932, pp. 364–368.

reasonable. Emotional appeals may have temporary value, but if they arouse fear, they may do more harm than good.[6] A frightened worker is not a safe worker. Although a gruesome picture invariably attracts attention, it seldom creates a desirable effect.

Perhaps the most important requisite of an effective poster is that it contain a positive message. Telling children to leave a box closed is more effective than telling them not to open it. Advertising a remedy for cold feet has more appeal when the description is headlined "warm feet" than "cold feet." People with cold feet respond to the goal of warm feet and are not attracted by a discussion of cold feet. A poster that tells you not to have accidents neither describes what you do want to have nor tells you *how* not to have the accidents. The following statements illustrate helpful information that could appear on posters placed in appropriate locations:

> "Pedestrians Cross Here"
> "Smoking Permitted in the Next Aisle"
> "Wear Hard Hats Here"
> "Gasoline Fumes in This Area"

Specific forms of behavior conducive to safety can be advertised in appropriate departments and serve a constructive purpose. The important thing is to approach safety as an educational problem.

Safety Habits

The discussion of skill in Chapter 12 emphasized the desirability of stabilizing the efficient behavior pattern and building it into a strong habit. This notion should also include safety as another characteristic of the habit. There are certain ways of holding a tool, specific body postures, and a few methods of applying pressure which are relatively safe, even if slippage or inaccuracies occur. On the other hand, certain movements which are unrelated to the job expose the person to injury and should be eliminated. The proper methods of work should be studied and taught to new employees.

Safety methods that are added to a job are difficult to enforce. The use of safety goggles does not become part of the grinding operation, thus the operators must decide whether or not to use them each time they sharpen a tool. The probability of an unfavorable decision is increased (*a*) if the goggles were left behind and must be retrieved, (*b*) if the goggles are uncomfortable, or (*c*) if they interfere with vision. To the extent that safe methods can be incorporated into the job as a habit and not tacked on as a precaution to be taken, the problem of enforcement of safety will be reduced. Incorporation of safe behavior into the job is facilitated if the activity is pleasant or helpful, and is resisted to the extent that it is unpleasant.

Study of various industrial operations from the point of view of safety can lead to the building of habits which are highly dependable and natural. These habits

---

[6] Hovland, C. I. Changes in attitude through communication. *J. abnorm. soc. Psychol.*, 1951, *46*, 424–437; Vernon, *op. cit.*, pp. 259–264.

may be thought of as *psychological safety devices.* Like the design of mechanical safety devices, the design of safety habits requires ingenuity.

When safe work habits have been made a part of the work pattern, it is unnecessary to warn employees to attend to the danger in their work. They can relax with the assurance that their habits will automatically make their actions safe. An illustration of the importance of stabilizing safe work habits is the method used by many electricians. A building can be wired with the current either off or on, but the procedure is different under the two conditions. It might be supposed that the current should be turned off whenever possible to avoid unnecessary injury. However, if the electrician is not allowed to turn off the current and is forced to work with live wires on all occasions, one procedure is habituated. With a single procedure, one does not constantly have to be conscious of whether working with live or dead wires. Accidents caused by the worker's absent-minded handling of a live wire are largely prevented by this method. Eliminating absent-minded behavior is difficult; telling people not to be absent-minded is little more effective than telling them not to be the kind of human beings they are.

In many cases, the chosen pattern of work may not be superior to others, but safety demands that one method be used exclusively. Suppose five different things have to be done to cut the current in a line. As long as they are all done, the job is satisfactory. If they are always performed in the order, A-B-C-D-E, accidents arising from various sources may be avoided. First, one worker can take over where another left off without the possibility of any misunderstanding as to what things remain to be done. Second, the worker can be interrupted after finishing Item C, and, upon returning can orient himself by discovering that C has been done and go on from that point. Finally, there is a routine to follow without having to remember the five acts.

Habits are strong and dependable. These properties become apparent if we try to oppose them. Thus, habits are forces which may make us do foolish things, but they can also be made into forces which make us do safe things.

Motivating Safety

Because of the flagrant way people sometimes appear to disregard safety, some writers have been led to believe that accidents are a goal, that persons sometimes unconsciously wish to punish themselves in order to remove guilt feelings.[7] This view may fit psychoanalytic theory, but few facts support it.

Another hypothesis is that workers have accidents to get time off the job. This assumption has been tested statistically.[8] Employees who had been with the company for four years were divided into two groups; those having no accidents (200 persons) and those having one or more accidents (89 persons). It was postulated that if persons had accidents to get time off, then those having accidents should absent themselves more from the job for other reasons also. Analysis of the data

[7] Fenichel, O. *The psychoanalytic theory of neurosis.* New York: Norton, 1945.

[8] Hill, J. M. M., and Trist, E. L. A consideration of industrial accidents as a means of withdrawal from the work situation. *Hum. Relat.,* 1953, *6,* 357–380.

showed that the accident-free group averaged 15.0 noninjury absences and the accident group averaged 24.4 noninjury absences. This difference was not removed when job hazard was considered, and therefore it was not an artifact. A more reasonable interpretation of the results may be that poor emotional adjustment is the cause. Emotional maladjustment induces absenteeism and, as will be seen later, also causes accidents. According to the present writer's interpretation, an accident may occur because a person is preoccupied with other things and other behaviors, not because an accident is a means to escape guilt or work.

Another aspect of accidents that makes them appear as a positive choice is the presence of countermotivation. Two conflicting aspects of a job may be emphasized: safety and production. Furthermore, the emphasis for each may come from different sources: the safety department promotes safety and the supervisor presses for production. Although some may claim that the two goals are not in conflict, close inspection will reveal instances in which they are. No job is so completely analyzed and controlled that hurrying and shortcuts are not possible. Hurrying introduces new hazards, and shortcuts circumvent safety practices.

The influence of hurrying on accidents was clearly demonstrated in a survey of home injuries.[9] Table 17.1 shows that ordinary hurrying was responsible for more than one-third of the accidents that occurred in or around the home. Dispensing with activities designed to make work safe makes a person appear to disregard safety, but the motivation for these behaviors can be found by further exploration. Not wearing goggles saves the machinist the trouble of getting them and putting them on; carrying a line up a pole by fastening it to his person saves a trip up the pole for the lineman (he is supposed to put a pulley in place at the top and then pull the line up); not wearing a hard hat when passing through certain structures makes it unnecessary for the worker to look after his hat; and not shutting off the motor to remove something from the machinery eliminates two acts. When a foreman criticizes a person for doing less work than the others, he introduces motivation

Table 17.1 / Percentage of Home Injuries Due to Various Behaviors

Cause	Per Cent
Hurry	35
Not paying attention; absorbed, distracted	22
Excitement (except hurry or anger)	11
Doing wrong thing, but knew better	11
Doing wrong thing, but did not know better	7
Just wanted to do it; don't know why	8
Anger	4
Attention getting, "showing off"	2

Based on data from the University of Michigan School of Public Health (see footnote 9).

[9] University of Michigan School of Public Health. *Investigation and application of home injury survey data in development of preventive procedures*, 1953.

to cut corners.[10] The conflicting reinforcement between fast and safe performance is a frequent cause of accidents.

Safety measures may not only interfere with production but also cause the worker some distress. This unpleasantness may stem from several sources ranging from discomfort to attitudes. Safety belts, goggles, gloves, and other devices to be worn are often resisted because they are uncomfortable. Electrical workers avoided using hard hats because these caused them to be mistaken for construction workers; drill press operators used matches instead of fingers to depress electric switch safety buttons, placed shoulder height, because holding the arms in this position was most uncomfortable. To conclude that employees are not interested in safety because they violate rules is to overlook important details in motivation.

Accident Proneness

Speculation Concerning the Distribution of Accidents

When considering the question of how accidents are distributed in the population, four distinctly different possibilities come to mind. It may be assumed that accidents happen on a chance basis so that everyone is equally subject to them, and that having accidents is a matter of bad luck. It may be assumed that having an accident will make a person more careful, hence less subject to future accidents. It is also reasonable to assume that having an accident so upsets individuals that they will tend to have future accidents because of a loss in confidence. Finally, the possibility exists that some individuals are so constituted that they are destined to have accidents because of their biological and psychological makeup.

Results of Investigations

One of the earliest studies bearing on these problems dealt with an analysis of the distribution of accidents among 648 women employees in a shell factory.[11] The distribution of accidents obtained is shown in Table 17.2. This distribution does not conform to chance expectancy. On the basis of chance, only 8 per cent of the women should have between three and five accidents. That 96 per cent of the women should have only 72 per cent of the accidents, while 4 per cent of them have 28 per cent of the accidents suggests that accidents tend to happen to certain people. The fact that such a large number had no accidents does not create a problem since it merely means that the period of observation was too brief to allow members of this group enough time to differentiate themselves from one another.

Another approach, cited in the same investigation, involved comparison of the accident frequency of 198 women during two successive periods. This analysis revealed that 136 women had no accidents during the month of February, whereas 62 women had one or more accidents (an average of 1.3 accidents) during the same

---

[10] Altman, J. W. Behavior and accidents. *J. Safety Res.*, 1970, *2*, 109–122.

[11] Greenwood, M., and Woods, H. M. *The incidence of industrial accidents with special reference to multiple accidents.* Industr. Fat. Res. Bd., 1919, Rep. No. 4.

Number of Accidents	Number of Women	
0	448 ⎫	622 women had a total of 216 accidents, or 96 per cent of the women had 72 per cent of the accidents.
1	132 ⎬	
2	42 ⎭	
3	21 ⎫	26 women had a total of 85 accidents, or 4 per cent of the women had 28 per cent of the accidents.
4	3 ⎬	
5	2 ⎭	

From M. Greenwood and H. M. Woods, *The incidence of industrial accidents with special reference to multiple accidents.* Industr. Fat. Res. Bd., 1919, Rep. No. 4.

Table 17.2 / Distribution of Accidents

period. From March to July, the 136 women in the no-accident group had an average of .16 accidents per month, whereas the 62 women in the accident group had an average of .35 accidents per month, or more than twice as many. This finding reveals that accidents not only fail to follow a chance pattern, but that they tend repeatedly to involve the same individuals. There is, then, no external justice which evens out the "bad luck."

That the accident rates of the women during the second period did not exceed those during the first period indicates that there is no increase in the tendency to have accidents. This fact reveals that accidents are not associated with the same individuals because a previous accident has some kind of detrimental effect on people making them more susceptible. To explain the facts, there remains only the possibility that accidents are associated with certain people because they have behavior characteristics which make them accident susceptible.

The importance of the individual's characteristics in the incidence of accidents is also apparent when the relationship between two separate accident records of a group of individuals is measured. To indicate this relationship, accident scores of one observation period may be plotted against the scores of a second period. Correlation coefficients indicating the extent of relationship between two such periods commonly range from .37 to .72.

A comparison of accident scores of a group of persons in two different situations does not show as close a relationship as does a comparison of accident scores of the same persons over two periods in the same situation. This means that certain individual characteristics predispose greater accident proneness in one situation than in another. Nevertheless, some degree of relationship usually exists. Even the frequency of home accidents and factory accidents reveals a correlation of .2 to .3.[12] A correlation between such dissimilar situations demonstrates the contribution of the

[12] Newbold, E. M. *A contribution to the study of the human factor in the causation of accidents.* Industr. Fat. Res. Bd., 1926, Rep. No. 34.

individual in accident incidence; at the same time, the low correlation demonstrates that the human contribution and the causal factors vary from one situation to another.

Evidence showing that accidents were related to individuals gave rise to the concept of *accident proneness,* and the early investigators made it one of the important factors in the causes of accidents.

Accident Liability

Accidents depend upon the behavior of the person, upon the degree of hazard in the situation, and upon pure chance. For example, a person may be cut by plate glass while walking past a store window. Suppose he just happened to be going by when someone else broke the window. This is the kind of injury that, from the standpoint of the person injured, may be described as due to chance—an accidental combination of circumstances. However, if store windows were broken frequently, a person going down a street in the shopping district would be exposed to considerable danger, and although chance would still operate, the frequency of injuries would be increased. The probability of chance combinations leading to injury is the measure for the degree of hazard. If the person were cut by flying glass because his reflexes were slow, he would have made a personal contribution to the accident. The differences in the degree to which various people contribute to accidents is the measure of proneness. The term *accident liability* includes all these factors and represents a more inclusive concept for evaluating accident data.[13]

Although a person's accident *record* also depends upon all these factors, an individual's accident *liability* is not the same as an accident record. Liability refers to the expectation of a person having a given degree of proneness working under a constant degree of hazard and having an average amount of luck, whereas the record shows what actually happened. This is analogous to saying that a particular baseball team may be more likely to win than its opponent, but the actual score for a game may be very different from this likelihood. Like a team's standing, liability for accidents is a statistical concept.

Because of this approach to accident analysis it is apparent that the accident proneness of an individual should not be decided from limited evidence. To be accident-prone, a worker must have more than a fair share of accidents, not because of exposure to more dangers, exposure for a greater amount of the time, or a run of bad luck, but because some of the personal things done to contribute to accidents. A driver's liability for car accidents may be high because he drives a lot, drives at high speeds, is on the road during all weather conditions, has a car with poor brakes and faulty lights, has poor vision in one eye, is too small for the truck he drives, drives for long stretches, is worried, has poor coordination, or has a constant companion who engages in horseplay. Only those factors that are characteristic of the person and would not necessarily apply to another driver placed in the same situation can be classified as aspects of accident proneness. Actually a person with

[13] Mintz, A., and Blum, M. L. A re-examination of the accident proneness concept. *J. appl. Psychol.*, 1949, *33*, 195–211; Mintz, A. The inference of accident liability from the accident record. *J. appl. Psychol.*, 1954, *38*, 41–46.

high liability may be accident-free for a considerable period because of good fortune or because others look after him.

Accident Proneness Reexamined

If the term accident proneness is confined to the permanent characteristics of an individual that contribute to accidents, one must exclude inexperience, age, fatigue, and temporary worry or frustration from the concept. It is doubtful that accident proneness so defined will reveal a single set of traits that accident repeaters have in common. The traits that contribute to accidents may differ from one situation to another since there are a great variety of ways in which to have accidents.

The more recent studies, therefore, have tended to deemphasize the concept of accident proneness as a major cause of accidents.[14] A survey of 27,000 industrial and 8000 nonindustrial accidents indicated that the accident-repeater contributed only .5 per cent of them, whereas 74 per cent were due to relatively infrequent experiences of a large number of persons.[15] Is this decline in evidence for accident proneness due to changing causes of accidents because of modern safety development, or to better statistical analyses? Probably both factors are involved.

The comparison of job groups shown in Table 17.3 reveals that accident frequency for the utility workers is associated more with the job than with the individual. The average rates for the various job groups range from .12 to .65 per worker, with an average of .30. Evidence of accident proneness was uncovered only after

Table 17.3 / Accident Frequency Rates for Job Groups Matched in Terms of Hazard Exposure

Job Group	Number of Employees	Number of Accidents	Accident Frequency Rate
Lineman 1/C	160	72	.45
Lineman 2/C	112	35	.31
Lineman 3/C	34	22	.65*
Groundman	189	47	.25
Maintenance 1/C	43	9	.21
Maintenance 2/C	34	4	.12
Maintenance 3/C	28	5	.18
Meterman 1/C	36	7	.19
Meterman 2/C	79	11	.14
Meterman 3/C	22	8	.36
Total	737	220	.30

*Significant at .01 level of confidence.

From P. L. Crawford, Hazard exposure differentiation necessary for the identification of the accident-prone employee. *J. appl. Psychol.,* 1960, *44,* 192–194. Copyright 1960 by the American Psychological Association, and reproduced by permission.

[14] de Reamer, R. Accident proneness: Fact or fiction. *Supervisory Mgmt.,* 1956, *3,* 1–14; Kirchner, W. K. The fallacy of accident proneness. *Personnel,* 1961, *38* (6), 34–37.

[15] Schulzinger, M. S. Accident proneness. *Industr. Med. and Surgery,* 1954, *23,* 151–152.

close scrutiny of individuals with multiple accidents, and only six clear-cut instances were found. This small number of accident-prone individuals suggests that accident proneness as an individual trait may be relatively insignificant today. However, one must also take into account the fact that the utility workers studied were a select and relatively stable group of employees so that accident-prone workers on the hazardous jobs may have been screened out.

Comparison of the accident rate of the same individuals while in the same jobs over two comparable periods of time is a better test of accident proneness than accident frequencies alone, and this method still reveals sound evidence of accident-proneness.[16] In a modern chemical company the correlation of accident scorces of individuals for odd and even one-year periods was found to be .349 (significant at the 5 per cent level of confidence). The correlation for scores of unsafe behaviors (recorded by foremen trained to make these observations) for odd and even one-week periods was .875.

Comparison of accident rates of the same persons over two periods are distorted because the worst offenders in the first period tend to be eliminated. However, data based upon South African bus drivers where this selective factor was minimal show correlations of accident frequencies over two four-year periods as follows:[17]

| Difficult traffic conditions | (N = 43) | .66 |
| Easy traffic conditions | (N = 46) | .36 |

When discipline for accidents was introduced some improvement was evidenced in individual records, and as high offenders were removed, improvements of 21 to 41 per cent were recorded between 1952 and 1960.

Kerr[18] believes that accident proneness must be supplemented by two additional concepts, both of which involve the work climate. One is the *goals freedom-alertness* theory that treats the accident as defective behavior caused by restrictions on the individual's freedom of action. The work climate should be such as to upgrade pride and initiative. The other is the *adjustment-stress* theory, which deals with accidents caused by the individual's stresses. These are caused by one's internal environment (disease, toxic factors, and so on) or by the external environment (excessive temperatures, noise, pressure). Both lack of freedom and stress in the work climate may cause individuals to be accident repeaters on certain jobs or under certain conditions. Insofar as the work climate causes individuals to do things that lead to accidents, accident proneness is not their basic cause, but insofar as the persons react differently to situational factors, human traits are involved. If individual differences in these traits make for variability in accident scores, accident proneness is indicated. It is not necessary to demonstrate that the same pattern of traits is related to accidents in all situations.

---

16 Whitlock, G. H., Clouse, R. J., and Spencer, W. F. Predicting accident proneness. *Personnel Psychol.*, 1963, *16*, 35–44.

17 Shaw, L., and Sichel, H. *Accident proneness: Research in the occurrence, causation, and prevention of road accidents.* Oxford: Pergamon Press, 1971.

18 Kerr, W. Complementary theories of safety psychology. *J. soc. Psychol.*, 1957, *45*, 3–9.

Psychological Tests and Accident Frequency

Introduction

It is helpful to differentiate between accidents caused by a person's tendency to get into accident situations and the inability to prevent an accident when in an accident situation. The fast driver or the driver who neglects to check the car brakes may get into accident situations but may show unusual skill in manipulating the car and thus avoid a collision. His skill and rapid perception saved him, but if he persists in getting into such situations, he will acquire an accident record. Another individual may carefully avoid accident situations, but when he is in one he may either lack sufficient skill to cope with it or go to pieces and lose whatever skill he possesses. Such a person also acquires an accident record, because accident situations cannot be entirely avoided.

It is sometimes puzzling to find that some highly skilled individuals have more accidents than less skilled persons. Actually, such individuals do not have the same accident exposure. The skilled person works on a narrower margin of safety and so is exposed to greater hazard. For example, young drivers may show greater skill than older drivers in handling a car, but at the same time have more accidents. Because of their superior skill, they may drive faster and allow less distance for passing other cars, so that, if something goes wrong, they have little leeway. The older person would have more accidents than the young driver if they drove under the same conditions. That the older person has fewer accidents is not evidence of greater skill, but of the tendency to maintain a larger margin of safety.

This situation suggests that accident proneness may depend on a rather complex set of traits and that these traits need not be the same for all accident-prone individuals. However, if accident proneness is to have any application to industry, it is necessary to determine the traits which are associated with accident susceptibility and develop tests for detecting their presence.

Sensorimotor Tests

Measures of muscular coordination are related to certain types of accident proneness. In one investigation this group of abilities was measured by a dotting test, by speed in reacting to a signal, and by adjustment of muscular performance in accordance with changing signals.[19] When over 600 employees were divided into two groups according to test scores, the poorer half of the test performers had 48 per cent more accidents than the better half. The poorer quarter had 51 per cent more accidents than the better three-quarters, indicating that elimination of 25 per cent of the poor performers on such tests would significantly decrease accidents. The relation between the test score and accident rate also existed when the data were analyzed according to the occupation of the employees. Other investigations have revealed similar relationships between motor coordination and accidents.[20] In one

[19] Farmer, E., and Chambers, E. G. *A psychological study of individual differences in accident rates.* Industr. Fat. Res. Bd., 1926, Rep. No. 38.
[20] Vernon, *op. cit.,* p. 40.

case the 25 per cent making the poor scores on a series of motor-coordination tests had twice as many accidents as the remaining 75 per cent. Correlations between test scores and accident frequency ranged from .10 to .44.

The relationship between test scores and accidents also increases with length of time on the job.[21] Apparently, the causes of accidents become more uniform with experience, and the sensorimotor tests reveal this persisting personal factor in accident causation.

Of great practical importance is the fact that there is a definite relationship between the above accident-proneness tests and proficiency on the job. By selecting employees who do well—that is, score low—on accident-proneness tests, managers can reduce accidents and improve the caliber of the employees at the same time.

Emotional Stability and Personality Tests

Instruments which measure the degree of emotional reactions (in terms of glandular changes) and tests which measure tremor have been found effective in showing a relationship between certain aspects of emotionality and accident frequency.[22] The accidents of taxicab drivers have been greatly reduced by the use of psychological tests, among which tests of emotional stability were found to be highly important.[23] Even closer relationships are found when an individual's responses are measured under disturbing and distracting conditions.[24] For example, taxicab drivers who made five or more errors on such tests averaged three accidents, whereas those who made less than five errors averaged only 1.3 accidents. Furthermore, considering only individuals who had no accidents, it was found that this accident record of no accidents was attained by 46.1 per cent of the drivers who made no errors on the test, by 18.8 per cent of those who made from one to three errors on the test, and by 12.5 per cent of those who made five or more errors. Thus, the probability of being accident-free is nearly four times as great in the high-scoring group as in the low-scoring group.

In the extensive research of South African bus drivers (mainly Bantu) applicants were screened for motor skills and then given projective personality tests. Despite adequate motor skills, poor risks could be detected from the personality tests. High accident producers were immature, impulsive, hostile, and inclined toward aggression. Disciplinary and accident records showed correlations of .45 and .57 with the personality test scores and were significantly correlated with each other (.42).

After refining the personality tests, prediction of accident risks became strikingly accurate. These results are shown below.

Driver success rate of test passers	(N = 433)	80%
Driver success rate of test borderlines	(N = 175)	48%
Driver success rate of test failures	(N = 531)	14%

---

[21] Farmer, E., and Chambers, E. G. *A study of personal qualities in accident-proneness and proficiency.* Industr. Fat. Res. Bd., 1929, Rep. No. 55.

[22] Farmer and Chambers, *op. cit.*

[23] Snow, A. J. Tests for chauffeurs. *Industr. Psychol.,* 1926, *1,* 30–45.

[24] Wechsler, D. Test for taxicab drivers. *J. Personnel Res.,* 1926, *5,* 24–30.

In another study[25] a high accident group was compared with a low accident group matched for age, education, intelligence, sex, socioeconomic background, and exposure to hazard. The responses of the high accident group to a sentence completion test indicated that they were significantly different from the matched group with regard to self-centeredness and the presence of a negative attitude toward employment. The matched group was higher on responses indicating optimism, trust, and concern for others.

Moods also seem to be highly important. In one study it was found that half of 400 minor accidents occurred while the employees were emotionally "low," although this emotional condition existed only 20 per cent of the time.[26] Production was 8 per cent higher during the happy moods, showing that emotional conditions favorable to accident prevention are also favorable to production.[27]

Intelligence Tests

The investigations which revealed that accidents were related both to sensorimotor coordination and emotionality showed no relationship between accidents and intelligence.[28] One study in a vocational school demonstrated a relationship between intelligence and accidents, but in this case it is difficult to know to what extent the intelligent students acquired skill more rapidly and so avoided accidents, and to what extent they were permanently less accident-prone.[29]

In data on automobile accidents it is frequently found that high accident records are associated with low mentality. Intelligence, when inadequate for the situation, is probably an important trait in accident proneness. For example, it has been found that one-third of the cases referred for mental-hygiene study by the Traffic Court of Detroit were feeble-minded (I.Q. 43–72).[30] When adequate intelligence is present, it may cease to operate as a factor. Since employees who are satisfactory in their work probably have the minimum intelligence requirement, their accident proneness is more likely to be attributable to sensorimotor and emotional factors than to low I.Q.'s. Certainly the importance of intelligence in avoiding accidents has been overrated in the popular mind.

Ratio between Muscular and Perceptual Speed

In examining the characteristics of accident-prone and accident-safe individuals, the relationship between motor and perceptual speed was quite different in the two groups.[31] Individuals who were quicker at recognizing differences in visual patterns than they were in making purely muscular manipulations tended to be accident-safe.

[25] Hersey, R. B. Emotional factors in accidents. *Personnel J.*, 1936, *15*, 59–65.
[26] Hersey, R. B. Rates of production and emotional state. *Personnel J.*, 1932, *10*, 355–364.
[27] Divids, A., and Mahoney, J. T. Personality dynamics and accident-proneness in an industrial setting. *J. appl. Psychol.*, 1957, *41*, 303–306.
[28] Farmer and Chambers, *op. cit.*
[29] Henig, M. S. Intelligence and safety. *J. educ. Res.*, 1926, *16*, 81–87.
[30] Selling, L. S. Feebleminded drivers. *Amer. J. ment. Def.*, 1943, *47*, 337–341.
[31] Drake, C. A. Accident-proneness: A hypothesis. *Character and Person.*, 1940, *8*, 335–341.

Individuals who were slower in recognizing visual patterns than they were in making muscular responses were inclined to be accident-prone. The relationship between the two tests can be expressed by subtracting the motor-test score from the perceptual-test score. Accordingly, 15 per cent of the workers with the poorest safety record all had negative scores. The striking effectiveness of this measure is also brought out by comparing scores on the test. Seven per cent made scores as low as −25 and 7 per cent made scores as high as +25. All of the former had accidents, whereas none of the latter had accidents. Of the 42 per cent who made scores of −10 or less, 82 per cent had accidents. When this test was used in the selection of 18 new employees, the accident index of the new group was 70 per cent below average. This reduction was obtained despite the fact that the plant had already achieved a low accident record by means of a safety program.

Tests of Visual Skills

Vision plays an important part in many occupations, and accidents often are associated with defective vision.[32] In a study made in a paper mill the vision of 52 accident-free employees was compared with that of 52 workmen who had one or more serious accidents.[33] It was found that 63 per cent of the no-accident group passed the test, whereas only 33 per cent of the accident group passed it. In another investigation 12 groups of jobs were studied to determine the visual skill requirements of each.[34] Workers were then tested to determine whether or not they met the visual skill requirements of their jobs. It was found that in eleven groups, the percentage of safe workers was higher for workers passing the test than for those failing it.

Two groups of employees were distinguishable after a 10-year study of a fertilizer plant—an accident-free group and an accident-repeating group.[35] A visual acuity test was administered to employees who were matched on age, education, experience, and pay. The accident-free workers scored significantly better both on monocular and binocular vision than the accident repeaters.

Setting up the visual requirements of a job and testing workers for them is more time-consuming and less objective than the general practice of using a single test, but it brings the examination closer to individuals and their work. This more specific approach to some extent simulates the clinical method and may be expected to yield some of the benefits of the personal approach. It should be extended to other sense capacities because it is probable that hearing, touch, smell, and other sensory requirements are essential to safety in specialized occupations.

[32] Stump, F. N. Spotting accident-prone workers by vision tests. *Factory Mgmt. and Maint.,* 1945, *103*, 109–112.
[33] Wirt, S. E., and Leedke, H. H. Skillful eyes prevent accidents. *Annual News Letter*, Natl. Safety Council (Industr. Nursing Section), November, 1945, 10–12.
[34] Kephart, N. C., and Tiffin, J. Vision and accident experience. *Natl. Safety News*, 1950, *62*, 90–91.
[35] Menon, A. S. Role of visual skill in safe operational behavior. *Psychol. Annual*, 1970, *4*, 18–21.

Physical Examinations

Preemployment physical examinations can serve as a protection against injury claims. One company reduced its back-injury claims by 93 per cent by introducing such examinations.[36]

Other Personal Factors Related to Accidents

Frustration and Accident Proneness

Since widely different tests were found to be related to accident records, it is apparent that accident proneness is not a specific trait, and the manner in which it reveals itself will vary with the job. Thus jobs involving avoidance of risks might be related to personality traits and those involving coordination might be related to the sensorimotor abilities. The study of South African bus drivers clearly revealed that the best drivers did not have lower accident rates.[37] Driving requires both skill and emotional stability, and since traffic situations are stressful, the latter ability becomes relatively more important in driving than in other occupations.

Insofar as accidents are related to such personality traits as hostility and emotional immaturity, one may question the use of some personality tests as measures of accident proneness since these behaviors may be temporary conditions. Thus the frustrated person shows aggression, regression, and fixations, all of which are in opposition to constructive and safe behavior. However, as pointed out by the studies of South African bus drivers, the hostile behavior is not always present but in many it lies near the surface. Thus we may describe individuals as differing in frustration thresholds, and the proneness aspect of the personality test would be the frustration threshold rather than the state of instability.

Experience

Van Zelst[38] plotted the monthly accident rates of 1237 workers in a newly opened copper plant against their length of experience. He found that the accident rate dropped from nearly six per 1000 hours to around 3.5 during the first five months. After the initial drop no further improvements occurred during the remainder of the five-year period studied. His investigation shows experience to be an important factor during the early stages only. A comparable group of employees who left the company before the end of the five-year period showed a similar learning trend, but leveled off at a higher rate (in the vicinity of four accidents per 1000 hours). Part of the continued decline with experience over extended periods of time, shown in some studies, may be due to the greater turnover rate of the accident repeaters.

The fact that experience and safety are related suggests the importance of proper training and guidance for new employees. If accidents are reduced by experience,

---

[36] Stewart, R. D. How to manage your injury problems. *Personnel J.*, 1970, *49*, 590–592.
[37] Shaw and Sichel, *op. cit.*
[38] Van Zelst, R. H. The effect of age and experience upon accident rate. *J. appl. Psychol.*, 1954, *38*, 313–317.

many of them can be eliminated by training. Practice on hazardless duplicates of machinery, such as are used in achievement tests, would develop basic skills.

Age

In a well-controlled study Van Zelst[39] compared a group of 639 young workers (mean age $= 28.7$, SD $= 1.4$), with approximately three years' experience, with 552 older workers (mean age $= 41.1$, SD $= 2.9$) having about the same amount of experience. The plot of the monthly accident rate over an 18-month period showed that the older group's rate fluctuated in the vicinity of 3.4 per 1000 hours as compared to 4.0 for the younger group. Not once during the period of the study did the younger group have as good a record as the older group. This study clearly indicates that the age factor in accidents is not entirely a function of experience.

In the transportation industry generally accidents decline with age, but data are usually contaminated with differing exposure times and experience. With exposure time matched the older age group still tends to be safer.[40]

The Clinical Approach to Accident Proneness

Viteles has emphasized the importance of carefully studying accident-prone individuals, diagnosing their difficulties, and recommending remedies.[41] By means of this approach, the accident rate of 44 accident-prone motormen dropped from 1.3 accidents per 1000 miles to .75 within one year.

That this procedure is valuable is shown by its reduction of accidents. However, such an analysis of accidents is largely subjective. To conclude, for example, that an accident is attributable to a faulty attitude is an interpretation of the facts rather than a statement of facts. The person who had the accident may actually lack the necessary coordination, a deficiency which may have caused the development of an inferiority attitude. Because being on the defensive causes one to be anti-social, the person's attitude is judged faulty.

A similar source of error is present in psychological analyses based on human judgments. When two people are engaged in an argument, one may ask how it started and be told that the cause was a disagreement over politics. Yet behind may lie the fact that the two thoroughly dislike each other; the political issue might be quite incidental. Analyzing the causes of arguments will not necessarily clarify such hidden factors. Similarly, the analysis of accidents by this procedure has limited value and is not a substitute for methods which relate individual traits with accident proneness. This is probably the reason why the testing method and the clinical method do not agree more closely on the nature of accident proneness. For the present, both approaches should be used. The testing method is particularly valuable in selecting employees, whereas the clinical approach is important in helping the accident-repeater.

[39] Van Zelst, *op. cit.*
[40] McFarland, R. A. *Human factors in air transportation*. New York: McGraw-Hill, 1953.
[41] Viteles, M. *Industrial psychology*. New York: Norton, 1932.

To the extent that accidents are influenced by emotional maladjustments, the clinical approach is of special value since it deals with the person as a whole rather than a cross-sectional analysis of many persons. Before a person can be helped, unsafe behavior must be considered against the background of the particular person's social attitudes and set of values. It also follows that two people who have accidents because of their aggressive behavior may have quite different sources of frustration. It is the source of the frustration rather than the symptoms that the clinical student must accept as the problem and through which make a unique contribution.

The Case-Study Approach

An accident may involve a complex series of events and a change in any one of them might alter the outcome. Thus far we have discussed the characteristics of the individual and his relation to the hazards. These varied factors can give us statistical relationships. What can be learned by careful analysis of specific accidents? The following is an example of the case approach used by the Harvard Medical School.[42]

"At 2:00 P.M. of a clear October afternoon, Miss Jane Smith and Miss Mabel Jones were returning to Boston from a trip to Gloucester. As they came over the crest of a hill on Route 128, they were in the left (high-speed) lane but were actually within the speed limit (50 mph). At this moment (Cause Number 1) the right-front tire of Miss Smith's car lost all its air. This was not a blowout; this was a *maintenance failure.* Some weeks earlier, Miss Smith's practically new tubeless tire had been cut by a rock and had gone slowly flat. The gas-station man 'fixed' it by pouring some rubberlike glop over the inside of the scar. But the cut 'sawed' back and forth on itself, and finally sawed through the repair compound. (The tire should have been thrown away. Did Miss Smith insist on repair instead of replacement? Did the garageman recommend repair as adequate? Or did he tell her he'd replaced her tire when he'd only 'fixed' it? No one knows.)

"At this point, Miss Smith was not in real trouble. At her speed and with the low density of traffic around her, she should have had no difficulty taking her car slowly off the road and gently braking to a stop. But Miss Smith (Cause Number 2) had *inadequate driving skills* for this situation. She promptly turned a minor problem into a major crisis. She vigorously grabbed the wheel to straighten the wobbly course of her car, and she slammed on the brakes. A straight-line 'panic stop' with a flat tire is virtually impossible. Miss Smith's car swerved way to the right and went up on the wide, grassy berm alongside the road. Happy day! Miss Smith was now safely out of traffic, pointed in the right direction, and had one-half mile of grass paralleling the road in which to roll gently to a stop with moderate periodic braking. But Miss Smith didn't know about stopping gently with a blowout. She kept her brakes on hard. And now she was on grass. Her car swung back left and headed across her side of the highway toward the dividing grass mall in the center.

[42] Schwartz, R. L. The case for fast drivers. *Harper's Mag.,* 1963, 227, 65–70. © 1963, by Minneapolis Star and Tribune Co., Inc. Reprinted from the September, 1963 issue of *Harper's Magazine* by permission of the author.

"At this point, no one still need have died. But Cause Number 3 was looming ahead. The mall was too narrow and had no guardrail to separate opposing traffic. If (Cause Number 3) *inadequate highway environment* had not been a factor, Miss Smith might have bounced along a retaining barrier and come to a noisy, fender-bending halt, hurt but still alive. (Divider barriers on roads with center malls drastically reduce fatalities by preventing head-on collisions.)

"But by now, (1) Bad Maintenance, (2) Inadequate Driving Skills, and (3) Inadequate Highway Environment had already gone a long way toward causing a fatal accident. At this point, one and possibly two persons were apparently doomed to death, but Cause Number 4 was still to take an additional life.

"Miss Smith went across the mall and into the path of a car being driven by David Brown, returning from the beach with his family of four. Brown was in the fast lane and was going approximately 50 mph. Miss Smith, her speed now down to, say, 40, smashed at an angle right into the middle of the front bumper of Brown's car.

"A head-on collision is always serious because of the combined speeds of the two cars, in this case, approximately 90 mph. What happened was predictable—though little understood and quite startling. Both cars hit each other four times. In an action much like the bouncing ping-g-g-g when a hammer strikes an anvil, the two cars impacted again and again and again, with such force that one bolt of the Smith car made four distinct, close-together dents in the bumper of the other car. (Passengers are also subject to this injury-producing series of impacts.) In the instant that this was happening, the rears of both cars rose high in the air. An impacting car, whether it hits a tree, a wall, or another car, always goes down in the front and way up in the rear. This action flipped Miss Smith and Miss Jones right through the windshield of their car and sent Miss Jones completely over the Browns' car and into the windshield of a third car, trailing behind Brown. This windshield did not break, but splintered, and the driver, braking hard but without success, smashed under the raised rear end of the Browns' car, still off the ground from impact. So quickly did all this occur that Miss Jones was dead against the windshield of the third car before Brown's car had even settled to the ground.

"When the noise and dust had settled, Miss Smith and Miss Jones were dead, Brown, the driver of the second car, was mortally injured (he would die twenty-nine days later while apparently recovering), and all six other passengers were injured.

"One safety device almost saved Brown; another saved the driver of the third car. Brown would have died instantly but for the deep-dish steering wheel (a product of Cornell research) which cushioned his impact against the steering column. The driver of the third car would have been killed by the arrival of Miss Jones through his windshield if it had not been safety glass of high-strength modern construction. As it was, no one—neither police nor survivors—would believe that Miss Jones had actually hit that windshield until the Harvard researchers showed lab tests proving the hair on it was hers. The police also (a) would not believe Miss Smith wasn't speeding, (b) would not accept the wobbly brake marks as indicating she had had a flat tire prior to impact, (c) were indifferent to the cut-and-repaired tire as additional evidence, and (d) preferred to ignore an autopsy report showing no alcohol in Miss Smith's blood. Instead, they accepted the 'direct evidence' of their observation that Miss Smith was found with beer cans all around her. No one was interested in the Harvard lab report showing that Miss Smith's body finally came to rest among some half-rusted beer cans that had been on the mall for at least one month.

"Miss Jones and Mr. Brown would be alive today if there had not been (Cause Number 4) lack of restraining devices. If all persons involved had been wearing seat belts, two of three deaths would have been prevented and more than half the injuries. This confirmed a typical Harvard finding: the group has never investigated a multiple-death accident without finding that at least *half* the deaths could have been prevented with seat belts. Yet only a small minority of Americans wear them."

It is difficult to determine the extent to which the tendency to blame speed, youth, and alcohol distorts automobile accident statistics, but this case study suggests it may be considerable. Certainly the dangers of speed are greatly overrated, and a person suspected of drinking has several strikes against him in a report. The above analysis represents a new and fresh approach to the study of accidents. It is interesting to observe that the garage man, who may be regarded as the initial cause, will never know how he contributed to the deaths of several persons.

Thus far the case approach to fatal accidents has failed to support three widely held causes, namely, speed, traffic violations, and lack of courtesy. Minor human, mechanical, and highway failures, which vary from one situation to another, loom as critical factors. The study of minor accidents may reveal a different kind of failure. Until they are studied in a similar manner it is necessary to recognize possible differences between minor and fatal accidents.

The Promotion of Safety

The Foreman's Dilemma

Disciplinary action is often associated with accidents or safety violations so that regardless of how a superior feels about punishment he may be involved in administering penalties. What does a supervisor do when an employee is found breaking a company regulation for which disciplinary action is specified?

Many foremen have reported to the author the dilemmas they face when a good worker commits a violation. They know that laying off a worker often creates hardships, destroys friendly relations, and lowers morale. Sometimes grievances are filed, and when this occurs, their decisions are frequently reversed. Foremen also know that they can get into trouble if they ignore violations because all guilty persons are supposed to receive the same penalty. It is not uncommon for higher supervisors to demand strict enforcement of company regulations. Some companies go so far as to have the safety department police the job because foremen are too lax. When they take this action they remove safety from the foreman's duties. Campaigns and training programs are then instituted to make foremen more safety conscious. Foremen disillusioned by such experiences resolve the dilemma by not "seeing" the violations.

The Influence of the Union Steward

When foremen fail to invoke penalties they give excuses such as: (1) the violation was in doubt; (2) the penalty is too strict; (3) the worker cannot afford the lay-off; or (4) the employees will resent the disciplinary action taken.[43] In a simulated experiment excuses of this sort were largely eliminated by creating a situation in which there was no doubt about the violation of a "no smoking" rule; the penalty was only a three-day lay-off; and the foreman had already laid the man off. What would he do when the union steward attempted to get him to change his decision?

The results are shown in Table 17.4. Only 34.9 per cent of the foremen failed to alter their decision, with another 13.4 per cent unable to settle the matter in the allotted time. Both outcomes resulted in a good percentage of grievances. Foremen who took a less rigid stand and did some problem-solving retained the union steward's good will and even gained his assistance in promoting safety. In these instances grievances were rare.

The legalistic stand of determining guilt and invoking punishment, even if accepted by the company philosophy, is not supported by foremen in general. They are inclined to recognize the feelings of the workers and to think in terms of future safety and the effects on morale.

The training of foremen should be in terms of positive motivation. Obviously workers do not want to have accidents, so attempts to make accidents less attractive by punishment misses the point. If people behave in unsafe ways it is due to the

Table 17.4 / Decision Regarding Punishment for Violations Challenged by the Union Steward

Decision	Frequency (Per Cent)	Result in Grievance (Per Cent)
Full three-day lay-off	34.9	45
Reduced lay-off	4.6	
Warning	22.7	
Forgiven	7.5	
Consult higher management	8.7	2
Consult workers	3.5	
Other	4.6	
No decision	13.4	43

From N. R. F. Maier, and L. E. Danielson, An evaluation of two approaches to discipline in industry. *J. appl. Psychol.,* 1956, *40,* 319–329. Copyright 1956 by the American Psychological Association, and reproduced by permission.

[43] Maier, N. R. F., and Danielson, L. E. An evaluation of two approaches to discipline in industry. *J. appl. Psychol.,* 1956, *40, 319–329.*

presence of conflicting goals. Punishment is frequently seen as the price for getting caught and therefore often motivates employees to find ways to avoid detection or to reduce the pain of the penalty. The Federal Aviation Agency, which can ground pilots for violating safety regulations, discovered that the pilots' union pays the salary of the grounded pilot during the lay-off, thus neutralizing the punishment.

One cannot conclude that all forms of punishment can or should be abolished. Instead, the need is to find better ways to accomplish objectives, by studying the motivational alternatives.

Group Decision and Safety

The foreman will find many uses for employee participation and group decision in dealing with safety. The group-decision approach is advantageous for the following reasons: (1) there are mutual interests in safety goals; (2) the problems can readily be stated in situational terms; (3) the workers have much information to contribute (which they withhold when punishment is part of the picture); (4) social pressure will keep more individuals in line with the group decision; and (5) sources of danger not noticed by safety engineers may be uncovered.

This approach deals with the safety of the crew in which there are varied reactions: many who accept safety regulations; some who object to working with others who are unsafe but who cannot expose them because of group loyalty; others who have violated regulations but have not been caught; and violators who have been reprimanded. Varied experiences and viewpoints can lead to new approaches to safety as well as to better understanding.

Counseling Skills

The modern supervisor must also deal with individual problems. Persons with emotional problems are temporarily accident-prone, regardless of whether the source of the disturbance is on the job. More frequently the supervisor is expected not only to be sensitive to a worker's emotional condition but also to acquire some elementary skills in dealing with such employees. In this capacity the supervisor acts as a helper or counselor rather than as a critic or judge. A presentation of the counseling skills that can safely be used by supervisors at all levels of management will be found in Chapter 20. These skills are an extension of the interpersonal relations skills discussed in Chapters 3 and 4.

Application of Causation Model to Accident Prevention

The study of accidents involves a consideration of the four variables discussed in Chapter 2: the accomplishment, the behavior, the individual or organism, and the situation. Figure 17.1 shows how each is involved.

The accomplishment (A) is largely a matter of probability. Whether or not a fall results in an injury is pretty much beyond the control of the individual involved. However, the situation in which the fall occurs can reduce the probability of injury.

Figure 17.1 / Summary of Various Approaches to Accident Prevention. There are many approaches to safety. These include the S, the O, the B, the A, and the relationships among them. Although causation is a function of the interaction of S and O, it is essential to analyze the whole causation model to explore completely the potentials for increasing safety. The items listed in each of the four divisions summarize the progress that has been made in isolating the types of factors involved.

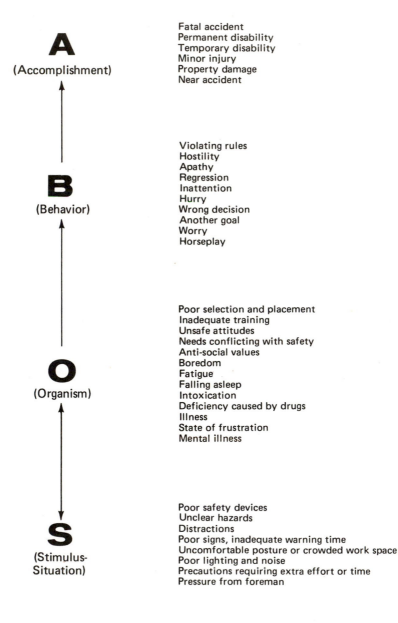

A
(Accomplishment)

Fatal accident
Permanent disability
Temporary disability
Minor injury
Property damage
Near accident

B
(Behavior)

Violating rules
Hostility
Apathy
Regression
Inattention
Hurry
Wrong decision
Another goal
Worry
Horseplay

O
(Organism)

Poor selection and placement
Inadequate training
Unsafe attitudes
Needs conflicting with safety
Anti-social values
Boredom
Fatigue
Falling asleep
Intoxication
Deficiency caused by drugs
Illness
State of frustration
Mental illness

S
(Stimulus-Situation)

Poor safety devices
Unclear hazards
Distractions
Poor signs, inadequate warning time
Uncomfortable posture or crowded work space
Poor lighting and noise
Precautions requiring extra effort or time
Pressure from foreman

Thus the various accomplishments should be studied to determine whether they relate to the other factors in the causation sequence.

The behaviors (*B*) of the persons involved also need to be evaluated to determine those most likely to lead to the various accomplishments. Although the behavior is caused by the interaction of the situation (*S*) and the organism (*O*), it is important to isolate and classify the behaviors that have the greatest probability of leading to accidents. Behaviors already known to be associated with accidents are shown in the figure.

Advances made in the prevention of accidents fall into two types: changes in the organism and changes in the situations in which the individuals behave. The varied factors in the *S* and *O* that are associated with accidents are also shown in Figure 17.1. Methods for removing these sources have been found effective.

Between 1926 and 1950 when careful records were kept, a great deal of progress was made in reducing both severity and frequency of industrial accidents. Since 1950 the curves for all types of accidents in manufacturing as well as nonmanufacturing industries have leveled off.[44] It appears that the traditional methods for promoting safety have made their contribution, but if further progress is to be achieved new approaches may be needed. Decisions regarding safety require a high degree of acceptance if they are to be effectively implemented. The group-decision method involves both workers and first line supervisors and this would increase their responsibility as well as focus attention on dangers in the work situation as seen by those closest to it. It is important that the discussion leader pose the issue in terms of removing hazards rather than as behavior problems.

Laboratory Exercise

Role Playing: The Case of the Safety Belt

(*Students are asked not to read the case materials before participating in the laboratory exercise.*)

A. Preparation for role playing.
1. This case requires two persons to role play and a third to act as an observer.
2. The class is to separate into units of three and distribute themselves by units as widely as possible in different parts of the room. (If the class is not divisible by three, one or two teams of two persons should be formed.)
3. Each group counts off: 1, 2, 3.
4. The instructor will assign to the *ones,* the role of Jim Welch, the foreman (E.1); to the *twos,* the role of Bill Smith (E.2); and to the *threes,* the task of the observer (E.3).
5. Each person should study his part only, and when finished he should lay it aside.

[44] *Accident Facts,* Chicago: National Safety Council, 1972.

B. The role-playing process.

1. When persons with roles have finished studying their parts, the instructor will give the following directions:
   a. The Bill Smiths are to stand on a chair next to a wall and pretend to be working on top of a telephone pole.
   b. The Jim Welches are to move some distance away and await the instructor's signal to begin.
   c. The observers are to stay close enough to hear the conversation of their pair but are to be as unobtrusive as possible.
2. An opportunity should be given for any questions.
3. On signal, the Jim Welches approach the Bill Smiths and begin the action.
4. The observers are to inform the instructor when their role players have finished.
5. When approximately two-thirds of the role players have finished, the instructor should ask the others to settle their problems in the next two minutes.

C. Collecting results.

1. On the chalkboard the instructor will prepare column headings under which to record results for each group of role players.
2. Each observer should report on the following:
   a. The solution reached.
   b. The method used by the foreman to influence the future behavior of the employee.
   c. His estimation of each participant's satisfaction with the interview.
   d. The key things done or said by the supervisor that caused the interview to take a turn for the better or for the worse.
3. Each foreman should report on whether or not:
   a. The employee has gone down in his estimation.
   b. He thinks the employee will be more safe.
   c. He thinks the employee's work will suffer.
4. Each employee should report on whether or not:
   a. The foreman has gone down in his estimation.
   b. He will work more safely in the future.
   c. His other work will suffer.

D. Discussion questions.

1. What conclusions can be drawn from the results obtained?
2. Why was the repairman not laid off by more of the foremen?
3. Can a foreman get into difficulty if he warns the repairman rather than lays him off?
4. What are the pros and cons of not discussing Smith's probable safety violation at all and holding a safety meeting with the whole crew instead?

E. Materials for the case.

1. ROLE FOR JIM WELCH, FOREMAN

You are the foreman of a repair crew of the telephone company. You have 12 men who go on jobs. The men usually work alone or in pairs. As foreman you spend your time visiting the work locations of your men, checking on progress, and giving such help, training, and instruction as may be needed. You are also responsible for the safety of your men, and the company judges you partly on the safety record of your crew. At the present time a company safety drive is on. The slogan is, "No job is so important that it cannot be done safely." The company has passed a ruling that anyone found violating a safety practice will be laid off for three weeks.

You have just driven up to the place where Bill Smith is working. You stop your car some distance away (you cannot drive directly to the work location) and see Bill working on top of the pole. As you stop the car you have a distinct impression that Smith just snapped his safety belt. Apparently he was working without using his belt and this is a safety practice violation.

Smith is an employee with 20 years of service. He has four children ranging in age from five to 12. He is a good workman but is quite independent in his thinking. You wish to do what you can to correct this man and give him a better attitude toward safety. You have been a supervisor of this crew for two years and don't know too much about Bill's past record. You have 10 years of service with the company.

2. ROLE FOR BILL SMITH, REPAIRMAN

You are a member of Jim Welch's repair crew in a utility company. You have been in the company for 20 years, and for the past two years Jim has been your supervisor. You feel you know the job and consider your technical knowledge perhaps somewhat greater than that of Welch, who has worked in the company for a total of 10 years. You believe Jim has done a fair job as foreman but feel that he supervises too closely.

You usually work alone on repair jobs except for several visits a week from your supervisor. You are now working on top of a pole and haven't bothered to snap your safety belt. You are a careful worker and use it when it is necessary, but you find it uncomfortable and in the way and so frequently you don't bother to snap it. By winding your leg over the cross bar and hooking your foot against the pole you can hold yourself firmly in place when working in a particular position. Actually there are a lot of hazards in your work that the company hasn't bothered about. Work pressures, poor tires on your truck, an uncomfortable belt, and supervisors who are more interested in catching a man at a violation than in helping him to do a job—all are factors that cause a man to have accidents, but the company ignores these things. The only time you ever had a scare was when a former foreman made you work on a wet pole after a rain.

Welch has just driven up, so you hasten to snap your belt. There is an annual safety drive on and the company has threatend to lay men off for safety violations. You can't afford having time off. You have four children, and living expenses use up

Working out a laboratory problem (see pp. 475–479) through role playing. Students gain insight into supervisory programs by imagining themselves in a given situation. Only the simplest "props" are needed—here standing on a chair represents a man working atop a telephone pole; the man standing is playing the role of foreman, and the woman seated is playing the role of observer.

all your earnings. You are quite sure Jim didn't see you snap your safety belt. He is walking toward your pole now.

3. Instructions for the Observer

You will witness an incident in which Jim Welch, the foreman of a telephone repair crew, either catches a man or thinks he has caught him in a safety violation. Note how the foreman opens the conversation, and observe whether he wants the repairman to come down off the pole. Does he use an approach that makes the man feel at home or does he put him on the defensive? Make notes of the things the foreman says that are key factors in determining whether the interview becomes pleasant or unpleasant and whether the workman confides, exaggerates, or lies.

You will be asked to report on the method used by the foreman to promote safety. He will be attempting to motivate the repairman by means of fear if he punishes, threatens to punish, discusses accidents, etc.; he will be using positive motivation if he praises the repairman for his record, requests his help in training others in safety, or tries to get him to participate in safety meetings. It is possible that the foreman will try to get the repairman to talk in order to learn about his attitude, or the foreman may do the talking and try to sell the man on the merits of safety. He may attempt to determine whether a safety violation occurred, or he may go so far as to avoid finding out the actual facts.

In reporting the solution, it is necessary to state whether the man is disciplined, warned, forgiven, or whether the violation is overlooked or ignored. The solution may include some follow-ups, such as training others, group meetings, and new duties, and these should also be reported.

When the role playing is finished, you will be asked how the participants feel toward each other. Do not ask the participants this, but form your own opinion. In this way you will learn how sensitive an observer you are.

Suggested Readings

Accident facts. Chicago: National Safety Council, 1972.

Haddon, W., Suchman E. A., and Klein, D. *Accident research.* New York: Harper & Row, 1964.

McFarland, R. H., and Moseley, A. L. *Human factors in highway transport safety.* Cambridge, Mass.: Harvard University Press, 1954.

Shaw, L., and Sichel, H. *Accident proneness: Research in the occurrence, causation, and prevention of road accidents.* Oxford: Pergamon Press, 1971.

Simonds, R. H., and Grimaldi, J. V. *Safety management* (rev. ed.). Homewood, Ill.: Richard D. Irwin, 1963.

18

Organizational Environment

Introduction

In this chapter we will consider the effect on the worker of such factors as the location of the plant, crowded and polluted cities, and various other off-the-job stresses as well as the effects of illumination, atmospheric conditions, noise, and other factors that influence job performance. The influence of music has already been discussed in connection with boredom in Chapter 16, whereas the problem created by work shifts has been treated in Chapter 15.

Demographic Considerations

The location of an industrial complex is influenced by: (1) the labor supply; (2) the source of raw materials which determines the location of mining, petroleum and lumber industries; and (3) closeness to major markets, which makes cities and sea-coasts important. Rivers and railroads once were influential factors in locating cities, and although still significant they are less critical.

The importance of the above considerations makes it clear that job locations and desirable places to live are likely to conflict. Except for research laboratories located near universities in smaller cities most persons will be required to live where the jobs are available, which means they will live near cities.

Cities once were desirable places to live because they offered excitement and entertainment in theaters, museums, libraries, parks, and music. Transportation was available by streetcars and trains. However, the modern city offers smog, congestion, noise, and crime as well. The suburb was a temporary escape from the deteriorating city, but overcrowding and traffic problems have greatly reduced their value. The romance of cities has disappeared and love songs about cities are old songs.

College graduates no longer prefer large cities as work locations when given a choice, and for married applicants the large city is even less attractive despite wage differentials. The migration from rural areas to cities is not motivated by their attractiveness but by the reduction in farm labor due to mechanization.

The need to restore some of the desirable features of city life is universally acknowledged, but industry cannot do it alone. Government action is necessary to find ways to make the city attractive and habitable. Moving plants to outlying districts did not solve the problem of the city, but merely promoted suburban living while the city deteriorated further. Freeways likewise are a temporary solution because they too have created a new kind of congestion by promoting individual transportation and pollution. The tendency to blame or to find individual solutions should be changed to one in which society's values move away from individual freedoms to group freedoms. How to make a virtue out of crowded conditions poses a challenging problem. The crowd at a football game is stimulating, but in a supermarket or on the expressway it is frustrating. The attitude of the people in the crowd changes with these situations so that individual attitudes and values contribute to the negative attitudes of fault finding instead of a constructive search for solutions. Creative solutions are needed to save cities which continue to grow while people develop negative attitudes.

Size of City and Job Satisfaction

Studies of job satisfaction and size of the city show a negative correlation.[1] However, the poorer the slum conditions as contrasted with overall prosperity, the greater was job satisfaction with pay received. In other words, wages perceived against a background of undesirable living conditions seem higher than the same wages perceived against a desirable background.[2] The community variables were not related to satisfaction with supervision and coworkers. Apparently the financial factor is the most important job-satisfier when community conditions are unfavorable.

Rural workers are most satisfied with highly involving jobs while city workers found satisfaction in lesser skilled work and fewer social contacts. Intrinsic job satisfaction seemed to be much lower in city workers.[3] It appears that many urban workers are alienated from middle-class societal norms because of living conditions, high urban growth and increasing living costs.[4] Since rural workers also have more roots in the community in which they work the values important to them may be attributed to their identification with the community.

A recent study of the mental health of city and small town workers (matched for age and sex) compared employees in two plants having similar jobs and patterns

[1] Bass, B. M. *Organizational psychology*. Boston: Allyn & Bacon, 1965; Katzell, R. A., Barrett, R. S., and Parker, T. C. Job satisfaction, job performance, and situational characteristics. *J. appl. Psychol.*, 1961, *45*, 65–72.

[2] Hulin, C. L. Effects of community characteristics on measures of job satisfaction. *J. appl. Psychol.*, 1966, *50*, 185–192.

[3] Turner, A. N., and Lawrence, P. R., *Industrial jobs and the worker: An investigation of response to task attributes*. Boston: Harvard University Press, 1965.

[4] Blood, M. R., and Hulin, C. L. Alienation, environmental characteristics, and worker response. *J. appl. Psychol.*, 1967, *51*, 284–290.

of management.[5] Results indicated that positive interpersonal family relationships favored the small town workers, whereas the development of mature responsibility regarding success and achievement favored large city workers. Political climate and the news media might also be regarded as factors influencing values existing in organizations. The UAW sitdown strike in the automobile industry (1936–1937) had the support of the news media,[6] whereas at about the same time, the strike in the shoe industry (Johnstown, Pa.) found the news media against the workers. The extent to which the outcomes, favorable to the workers in the first and unfavorable in the second, were due to the pressures exerted by the media is a matter of speculation, but their potential influences on industrial relations should not be overlooked. Public support plays an increasing part in shaping organizational behavior.

Off-the-Job Stresses

The stresses in urban living are not only attributable to the nature of the work, the hours, and supervision, but to factors beyond the control of the organization in which an individual works. The organization may furnish parking facilities, but stresses due to traffic, both husband and wife working, shopping problems, and inability to obtain household help, and to get small jobs done, are beyond the reach of the organization. To cut costs on home repairs "do it yourself projects" are increasing. Thus while working hours on the job become shorter, transportation time and home responsibilities increase. These developments which have changed economic and social values are most marked in city communities.

Pollution

Pollution of the air and water are a part of much city living, although disturbing to the health and comfort of its inhabitants. Legislation will determine gains made, but public opinion also will influence organizational decisions. Placing blame on the polluter does not solve the problem. Punishing the offending industries can destroy them and the jobs they create, as well as prevent pollution. Since industry produces for the consumer, he must also share the responsibility for solving the problem. The driver of the car, as well as the producers of gasoline and cars, creates the smog. The problem of pollution became acute because so many people live in cities. To solve the problem requires that values change enough so that the public is willing to give up some of its freedom and convenience.

Noise pollution likewise is associated with cities. This type of pollution is particularly apparent near airports and freeways. Intense noise in addition to causing deafness can disturb sleep and conversation. However, human beings readily adapt to such noises.[7] Interviews with persons living near sources of sound report that they

[5] Meltzer, H., and Ludwig, D. Community differences in positive mental health of younger workers. *J. Psychol.*, 1970, *75*, 217–223.

[6] Personal communication with H. Meltzer.

[7] Grant, G. Life beside freeway: Unbelievable noise. *Los Angeles Times*, Part II, October 5, 1971.

soon learn to sleep through the noise and adjust their communication by talking louder. However, they develop habits of talking too loud and friends visiting them are disturbed. Certain advantages are mentioned: houses are cheaper and one is free to make his own noise without criticism from neighbors. Obviously individual differences in the ability to adjust become a factor. But again blaming doesn't solve the problem because it asks others to make the correction without suggesting a way to influence them. Unfortunately, often the ability to invade another's privacy can be an individual free decision, but the ability to stop the invasion requires legislation and enforcement.

Illumination and Job Performance

Introduction

The lighting arrangements of the factory are the particular problem of the lighting engineer, but a number of psychological questions concern the plant manager. One cannot judge the adequacy of lighting merely by trying it out; careful tests of human performance must be made under different lighting conditions to determine optimal conditions.

Since the human eye has a remarkable ability to adjust to illumination, even relatively great differences in lighting may not be noticed. For instance, out-of-doors, on a clear midsummer day, from 8,000 to 10,000 foot-candles of light may fall on a given surface, making it about two thousand times as bright as it would be when viewed in an office which is well illuminated by artificial light, yet the difference may not be particularly noticeable. However, the difference between shaded and exposed areas out-of-doors is readily noticed, although the difference in brightness in this case may be only in the ratio of 1 to 10. One notices the difference between shaded and nonshaded areas relatively more than the difference between indoor and outdoor areas because the eye makes necessary adjustments when the individual is entirely in one illumination or another. A little experience with light meters and cameras will further demonstrate to the reader the deceptiveness of human judgment on differences in illumination.

A foot-candle of light (illumination of a surface by a standard candle at a distance of one foot) is approximately the amount of illumination a person would obtain on a completely dark night if a 100-watt lamp were placed 10 feet above his head. Indoors, the ceiling and walls return a good deal of light which is lost outdoors, the amount of this reflected light varying with the color of the surfaces. A 100-watt bulb in a bridge lamp (12-inch parchment shade) in a typical room would throw about 25 foot-candles of light on a surface 34-inches away, and about ten foot-candles of light on a surface 52 inches away.

White surfaces reflect 80 to 85 per cent of the light which falls upon them, while medium gray reflects 20 to 40 per cent. Such colors as light green and sky blue reflect approximately 40 per cent of the light they receive; and cardinal red, about 16 per cent. The lighting of a factory can be greatly improved by the use of pale-colored paints. The "Munsell System" of colors provides an admirable guide in selecting attractive colors which also have desired high or low reflective characteristics.*

In considering proper lighting, it is necessary to take into account the distribution of light, the intensity of the light, and its wave length (color). Although each of these aspects has its own specific advantages, they are somewhat interdependent. For instance, increase in intensity alone may be a disadvantage if glare effects are thereby increased.

Distribution of Light

The adjustment of the eye to illumination varies with the total amount of light the eye receives and not merely with the amount of light which strikes the eye from the working surface or from the object under observation. Even when one eye is closed, the other eye must adjust to the reduced visual stimulation. In considering the adequacy of illumination, it is necessary to take into account the lighting of the *total visual field* rather than the lighting of the *field of observation.* For instance, the light from the sky may be brighter than that at the worktable; thus, if a person is facing a window, his visual mechanism adjusts to the combined value of the light rather than to that of the work space alone. If one eye receives more light than the other, the adjustment is similarly disturbed, since neither eye is adjusted to its specific illumination. The practical implication is that the whole area should be uniformly illuminated, although the working surface may have some additional light supplied from a source directly overhead. Walls which have poor reflecting qualities reduce the illumination of the outer parts of the visual field, so that, even though a large amount of light is used in the room, the total field is not uniformly lighted.

A second reason for avoiding variations in the lighting of the total visual field is the tendency of the eyes to fixate high points of light. When these points do not coincide with the focus of the work, opposite muscles must overcome the tendency of the eyes to turn away from the work. It was pointed out in Chapter 15 that when a person is asked to look at a dark space between two high points of light placed some distance apart, he not only has difficulty in doing so but soon shows discomfort and fatigue.[8]

Another source of fatigue is changes in the illumination which are too rapid for the pupillary contractions and relaxations to follow. Flashes of light occurring in rapid succession quickly produce fatigue and eyestrain. In this case the strain develops from the tension of opposing pupillary responses. A similar condition arises when the eye passes over an area of varied illumination, as occurs when there are highly polished objects in the visual field. Such objects should be removed or painted.

Variation in the illumination of the visual field results in shadows, which interfere with the desired contrast between the different parts of an object which must be

---

* The *Munsell Book of Color* contains charts and tables of aesthetic color combinations. Baltimore: Munsell Color Co., 1929.

[8] Bartley, S. H. A factor is visual fatigue, *Psychosom. Med.,* 1942, *4,* 369–375; Bartley, S. H. Conflict, frustration, and fatigue. *Ibid.,* 1943, *5,* 160–163.

distinguished. It is also responsible for various forms of glare which may be caused by: (1) excessive stimulation (e.g., the direct light source); (2) an overlay of scattered light; and (3) reflections of light from the working surface out of the eyes' focus. Subjects given the task of keeping a pointer aligned with a moving target made significantly more errors when facing the glare of a 100-watt bulb for a period of only 20 minutes.[9] Both glare and lack of contrast reduce accuracy of perception and increase fatigue. The visual difficulty posed by an extreme condition of this type is similar to that experienced when driving toward a car with bright headlights.

Indirect lighting is the best method for producing uniform illumination. In this type, all the usable light is reflected light; high points of light, caused by light from the source striking the eye directly, are out of the visual field. Semi-indirect lighting reduces the high point of light by means of milk-glass or ground-glass shields and provides a good deal of indirect light because these shields reflect considerable light to the walls and ceiling. The condition is further improved if the sides of such globes are guarded by opaque screens, which prevent direct light from striking the worker's eyes, but permit it to pass to the ceiling or directly down on the work. With the source of light directly overhead, it cannot strike the worker's eyes unless he purposely looks up at it. In direct lighting, the source is concentrated at small points; thus, shadows, glare, and high points of light are at a maximum. Vapor lamps avoid these difficulties to a considerable degree because the source is less concentrated. Thus, lighting by vapor lamps is similar to semi-indirect lighting methods; moreover, it is less costly.[10]

A disadvantage of the vapor lamps is the flicker that occurs when alternating current (A.C.), rather than direct current (D.C.), is the source of energy. In one study fluorescent lights operated on D.C. (no flicker) and on A.C. (flicker) were compared at 20 foot-candles of brightness.[11] Although the flicker was noticed by only 25 per cent of the subjects, it resulted in a less efficient seeing performance in general. The simple remedy is to use more than one lamp and install them so that their flickers will be out of phase with one another.

The disadvantage of indirect lighting is its cost, since considerable light is lost through absorption. The benefits, however, seem to be more than worth the extra cost. In a three-hour reading test, little fatigue and practically no change in ability to sustain clear vision were found under conditions of indirect lighting. Direct lighting was the least favorable condition, while semi-indirect lighting produced effects more similar to direct than to indirect lighting.[12] These findings suggest that,

[9] Pepler, R. D. Warmth, glare and background of quiet speech: a comparison of their effects on performance, *Ergonomics*, 1960, *3*, 68–73.

[10] Gray, J. S., and Prevetta, P. Fluorescent light versus day light. *J. appl. Psychol.*, 1950, *34*, 235–236; Luckiesh, M., and Moss, F. K. Vision and seeing under light from fluorescent lamps. *Ill. Engng.*, 1942, *37*, 81–88; Luckiesh, M., and Taylor, A. H. Radiant energy from fluorescent lamps. *Ill. Engng.*, 1945, *40*, 77–88.

[11] Zaccaria, A., Jr., and Bitterman, M. E. The effect of fluorescent flicker on visual efficiency. *J. appl. Psychol.*, 1952, *36*, 413–416.

[12] Ferree, C. E., and Rand, G. Lighting in its relation to the eye. *Proc. Amer. Phil. Soc.*, 1918, *57*, 440–478.

in improving lighting, it is better to go all the way to indirect lighting than to stop at a midway position, particularly when the work requires sustained and detailed vision.

Further studies will undoubtedly suggest improved methods for obtaining uniform light distribution. The height and shape of the ceiling and the height of the light sources will alter the effects of both direct and indirect lighting methods. Enough is known, however, so that in most instances the lighting engineer can institute marked improvements.[13] A low ceiling, highly illuminated by indirect lighting, might bring the bright ceiling into the field of vision. Because conditions of this sort, as well as many others, influence the end result, broad generalizations cannot be made without taking into consideration the work situation, as well as the type of work.

Illumination Intensity

Visual acuity increases with light intensity and is about equal to daylight acuity as 100–foot-candle intensity is approached. However, this degree of acuity is seldom required, and it is apparent that the desired amount of lighting will vary with the amount of detail in the work. For instance, for very fine work, such as distinguishing black thread on black cloth, intensities of 400 foot-candles have been recommended.[14]

Table 18.1 shows the recommended intensities for five types of tasks. The given levels of light intensity roughly represent the steps in visual requirements into which industrial work might be divided or classified. These requirements are conservative and are considerably lower than those recommended by illuminating engineers.[15]

Table 18.1 / Recommended Lighting Intensities

Visual Condition	Light Intensity (Ft. Candles)
Most severe work requirements	40 to 50
Tasks comparable to discriminating 6-point type*	30 to 40
Situations requiring reading of handwriting, etc.	20 to 30
Reading newsprint and the like	15 to 20
Reading good sized print (10-point) on good paper†	10 to 15

*This line is set in 6-point type.

†This line is set in 10-point type.

From M. A. Tinker, Illumination standards for effective and easy seeing. *Psychol. Bull.,* 1947, *44*, 435–450. Copyright 1947 by the American Psychological Association, and reproduced by permission.

[13] Moon, P. H. *The scientific basis of illuminating engineering.* New York: McGraw-Hill, 1936.

[14] Luckiesh, M., and Moss, F. K. *The science of seeing.* Princeton, N.J.: Van Nostrand, 1937, pp. 308 and 345.

[15] Illuminating Engineering Society Committee. Report No. 1 Recommendations for quality and quantity of illumination. *Illuminating Engineering,* 1958, *53*, 422–432.

Industrial surveys indicate that production continues to rise as illumination is raised from six to 20 foot-candles, and that at 20 foot-candles the rise in production follows a sharper upward trend than does the increase in the cost of lighting.[16]

In general, industrial surveys show production increases ranging from 8 to 27 per cent with increased illumination, the actual increase depending upon the kind of work. That the type of work is a factor in the extent of the increase shows that the rises in production cannot be attributed entirely to an improved attitude, but that improved vision and reduced fatigue continue to increase production even when the lighting intensity greatly exceeds minimum requirements. Since the cost of these improvements in lighting, calculated in terms of production, is less than 5 per cent, a net gain in practically all types of work may be expected.

In concluding this discussion of the intensity factor in illumination, it should be stated that increased intensity must be accompanied by facilities for uniform distribution of light. Increases in intensity may be disturbing if the light is not properly distributed. High illumination with direct lighting may actually be very disturbing.[17]

Colored Lights

Vapor lamps produce light of different colors depending upon the chemical substance vaporized. For example, sodium lamps produce a yellow light (light of medium-long wave length), mercury lamps produce a blue light (light of short wave length), and fluorescent lamps produce a mixture of lights the resultant of which is a light approaching daylight.

The economical operation of vapor lamps makes it desirable to know the relative effectiveness of colored light for vision. Although some findings differ, the results of careful experiments seem quite conclusive. When acuity, speed of discrimination, power to sustain clear seeing, and loss in visual efficiency were tested under spectral lights of equal intensity, for all four functions the middle of the spectrum was superior.[18] In nearly all cases the order of superiority was found to be yellow, yellow-green, orange, green, red, blue-green, and blue. For acuity the best part of the spectrum was 2.2 times more effective than the poorest, while for speed of discrimination the best color was 9.7 times more effective than the poorest. However, since light from a Mazda lamp was superior to any of the colored lights, the authors of the investigation warn against extensive use of colored light.

In an experiment involving an actual industrial job—inspecting white flannel cloth for defects—results of work done under three sources of light were compared. The light sources were an ordinary Mazda lamp, a "daylight" Mazda lamp (blue glass to filter out excess yellow), and a mercury-vapor lamp (blue).[19] Acuity was greatest under the "daylight" lamp and least under the mercury-vapor lamp.

[16] Luckiesh, M. *Light and work*. Princeton, N.J.: Van Nostrand, 1924, p. 267.
[17] Ferree and Rand, *op. cit.*
[18] Ferree, C. E., and Rand, G. Visibility of objects as affected by color and composition of light. Part 1, *Personnel J.*, 1931, *9*, 475–492; Part 2. *Ibid.*, 1931, *10*, 108–124.
[19] Fernberger, S. W., Viteles, M. S., and Carlson, W. R. The effect of changes in quality of illumination upon visual perception. *J. appl. Psychol.*, 1934, *18*, 611–617.

Although colored illumination seems to be less deficient when the whole visual field, rather than just the work space, is lighted by a light of the same hue, the findings in general favor the use of mixed or white light. With fluorescent light available, there seems little reason for continuing the mercury-vapor (Cooper-Hewitt) lamp. More economical lighting may also be developed by the proper use of reflecting surfaces. Screens and walls arranged around the work space so that they diffuse the light and give uniform white illumination to the whole visual field may do much to reduce the cost of indirect lighting.

Visual Signals

When lights are used as signals they are most effective when they contrast with the visual field. A flashing signal light against a background of steady light is highly effective, but if the background is flashing it serves as a distractor regardless of the nature of the signal light.[20] Background lighting that serves as a distractor is called visual "noise." Neon signs, Christmas lights, and so on which line many of our highways and streets offer examples of such "noise" which interferes with our ability to locate traffic signals.

Effects of Good Lighting on Morale

Good lighting is cheerful and stimulating. Undoubtedly, some of the improvement in production which results from proper illumination is attributable to the favorable attitude created by pleasant surroundings. Although individuals differ in the amount of light they find most desirable, 65 per cent of the subjects of one study judged intensities between 10 and 30 foot-candles the most comfortable for reading.[21] This range in preference is not excessive. With 15 or 20 foot-candles, the majority of individuals could work under a lighting intensity close to that which they found most comfortable; at the same time they would have an illumination which has been found to be highly efficient and economical from the point of view of production.

Invariably, people prefer light of daylight color. Since this light is also superior to all others in visual efficiency, ideal lighting would demand the use of correcting filters on filament lamps in order to obtain daylight color, as well as the discontinuation of colored vapor lights. The use of white light also reduces differences in the appearance of objects and people in daylight and artificial light, thus eliminating the necessity for workers to accustom themselves to the strange appearance of their surroundings. Further advances in matching the physical properties of daylight and white artificial light will gradually reduce the changes which colored objects undergo when viewed under first one and then the other source of light.

In judging the heat given off by lights of various colors, subjects rank blue and green as "cool," yellow and amber as "warm," and white as intermediate. However,

[20] Crawford, A. The perception of light signals: the effect of the number of irrelevant lights. *Ergonomics*, 1962, *5*, 417–428.

[21] Ferree, C. E., and Rand, G. Good working conditions for eyes. *Personnel J.*, 1937, *15*, 333–340.

when subjects were asked to press a switch when they experienced discomfort while performing a tracking task, the temperature-humidity index was the same.[22] Thus the warmth of color seems to be psychological.

Atmospheric Conditions and Work

The Various Aspects of the Atmosphere

A number of properties of the air may be expected to influence the work of individuals, since they breathe the air and their bodies are immersed in it.[23] These include: (1) the chemical composition of the air, which in a pure condition consists of 20.93 per cent oxygen, 79.04 per cent nitrogen, and .03 per cent carbon dioxide; (2) the addition of substances given off by people through exhalation and perspiration; (3) temperature; (4) barometric pressure; (5) the movement of the air, and (6) humidity.

The *chemical composition* of the air is often a cause for concern because it is widely known that oxygen is inhaled and carbon dioxide is exhaled. It is commonly believed that, when a large number of people are in a room, or when one person remains in an enclosed space for a considerable length of time, the proportions of gases are so altered as to make breathing difficult. Because of this belief, people customarily open their windows at night to obtain fresh air.

That human beings give off poisons or that they deplete the oxygen supply are possibilities which must be checked by research. The presence of a large number of people in a room also raises the temperature and the moisture content.

The *temperature* of the air obviously influences body temperature. The body tends to maintain a constant temperature by reflex responses which lower or raise its temperature. In cool air, excessive heat is lost by convection and radiation; this heat must be resupplied relatively rapidly if the body is to maintain a constant temperature. In very warm air (warmer than the skin), on the other hand, the body absorbs heat from the surroundings; thus, it must be cooled by the evaporation of perspiration and exhalation of heat through breathing. Atmospheric temperature, therefore, is a factor which influences the way the body must function to maintain a constant temperature.

Barometric pressure changes somewhat from day to day, but marked constant differences are present in low and high altitudes. When the pressure is low—that is, at high altitudes—the air is thin, and a person must breathe more air to get the necessary oxygen supply. The effects of barometric pressure on psychological functions are particularly important in aviation and in mountainous regions,[24] but under usual conditions the barometric variations are not sufficiently great to influence activity.

---

[22] Berry, P. C. Effects of colored illumination upon perceived temperatures. *J. appl. Psychol.,* 1961, *45,* 248–250.

[23] Ford, A. *A scientific approach to labor problems.* New York: McGraw-Hill, 1931, pp. 134–144.

[24] Poffenberger, A. T. *Principles of applied psychology.* New York: Appleton, 1942, pp. 150–151.

The *movement* of air prevents stagnant air from accumulating about the body or around machinery. Any undesirable property of such air (for example, its temperature or moisture content) is removed by its mixture with other air in the room. Circulation prevents formation of pockets of warm and moist air. In factories which do not have forced circulation there may be a great deal of variation in the cooling properties of the air in various parts of the same room, although the temperature difference may be very small.

The *moisture* content of the air may function in two ways. The heat conductivity of the air increases with humidity, so that on a cool day humid air rapidly carries heat from the body (convection) and the air feels cooler than the temperature reading would indicate. On the other hand, humid air interferes with evaporation. Since evaporation of perspiration serves a cooling function, this process is inhibited by high humidity. Warm, humid air feels warmer than its temperature warrants because it interferes with evaporation to a greater degree than it conducts from the body surface. At between 68 degrees and 70 degrees Fahrenheit, humidity is negligible in its influence on the bodily function of maintaining a constant temperature.[25]

Effects of the Air Breathed

Investigations made by the New York State Ventilation Commission clearly showed that the air that is breathed does not cause the symptoms produced by "bad" air, such as headache, drowsiness, and lassitude.[26] A number of people confined in an airtight chamber for several hours showed the symptoms only when this so-called "bad" air surrounded the body. Persons in the room who breathed "fresh" air through tubes showed the symptoms, and persons outside the room who breathed "bad" air from the room failed to show the symptoms.

The air that is breathed is harmful only when the oxygen content is reduced to 14 per cent and the carbon dioxide is increased to 2.4 per cent. Oxygen content seldom falls below 19 per cent and carbon dioxide content rarely exceeds .3 per cent, even in poorly ventilated schools and factories, because enough air is exchanged through the walls and around windows to maintain fairly constant proportions.

The facts do not support the prevalent notion that symptoms of poor ventilation appear because "bad" air is inhaled. Body odor may influence some individuals who are highly sensitive to odors, and the suggestion or belief that air is "bad" may affect others, but a knowledge of the facts will decrease these effects. For example, employees working in a building which had no windows, but which had an excellent ventilation system, constantly complained about the air. Their complaints and symptoms disappeared when the modern ventilation system was shown and explained to them. This example indicates that suggestion is an important contributor to the ill effects caused by breathing "bad" air.

Dust and foreign matter in the air may produce harmful effects on health as well as on attitudes, and such foreign matter obviously should be removed, perhaps by

[25] Poffenberger, *op. cit.,* pp. 166–168.
[26] *Ventilation: Report of the New York State Commission on Ventilation.* New York: Dutton, 1923.

filters in the ventilating system. These filters also remove pollen from the air, thus reducing the incidence of allergic disturbances among the workers.

The effects of general air pollution and localized industrial wastes on workers are sometimes accepted as unavoidable, or minimum precautions are taken. A common effect of such pollution is eye irritation. Smog-induced irritations, although they may be uncomfortable, result mainly in reduced endurance and increased eyestrain and fatigue rather than serious loss of visual acuity.[27]

Atmospheric conditions that may not affect visibility can affect the pulmonary functions, causing such diseases as emphysema.[28] This is more serious and harder to detect since it may not immediately result in decreased performance. In many cases it is much easier to avoid concentrated areas of chemicals, fumes, or dusts than try to counteract them. Knowledge of tolerance levels of common pollutants and the ability to recognize overexposure symptoms are helpful to avoid industrial accidents and long term illnesses. When exposure is unavoidable such precautionary measures as goggles or masks are easy to initiate and may protect against all but the most dangerous industrial pollutants.

Effects of the Air Surrounding the Body

The New York State Ventilation Commission's findings showed that the symptoms caused by "bad" air disappeared when the interference of such air with the regulation of body temperature was removed. Cooling, drying, or moving the air with fans corrected the conditions in the airtight room. Statistical studies which relate weather conditions with behavior show that barometric pressure has little effect, whereas temperature and humidity have considerable effect on behavior. The production of factory workers, the errors of bank clerks, the work of college students, and even the level of civilization show variations with weather conditions.[29]

Weather affects employee behavior in still another way. One study demonstrated that punctuality was dependent upon the weather.[30] On fine days employees were more likely to be late than on bad days, despite the fact that bad weather interfered somewhat with transportation. It appears that on fine days employees are reluctant to go indoors and linger to enjoy the outdoor attractions.

Effects of Ventilation on Physical Work

The New York State Ventilation Commission's investigations showed that physical work was definitely impaired by high temperature and stagnant air. In one experiment men were required to lift a five-pound dumbbell through a distance of 2½ feet and were motivated by a bonus. They were tested under temperatures of 68 degrees

[27] Berkhout, J. Psychophysiological stress: Environmental factors leading to degraded performance. In K. DeGreene (Ed.), *Systems psychology*. New York: McGraw-Hill, 1970.

[28] Green, H. L., and W. R. Lane. *Particulate clouds, dusts, smokes, and mists*. London: Spon, Ltd., 1964.

[29] Huntington, E. *Civilization and climate*. New Haven, Conn.: Yale University Press, 1924; Dexter, E. G. *Weather influences*. New York: Macmillan, 1904.

[30] Mueser, R. E. The weather and other factors influencing employee punctuality. *J. appl. Psychol.*, 1953, 37, 329–337.

and 75 degrees Fahrenheit, with the air either fresh or stagnant. The findings are shown in Table 18.2

Production was at its highest level when the temperature was 68 degrees and the air was fresh. Using this as a base, it will be seen that stagnant air caused production to fall off approximately 9 per cent under each of the two temperature conditions. It was also shown that, with the 75 degree temperature, production fell off nearly 15 per cent both with fresh and with stagnant air. The production under the least favorable conditions (warm, stagnant air) was nearly 24 per cent below production under the most favorable conditions (cool, fresh air).

When the amount of work (lifting 50-pound loads) under two temperature conditions was equated, the effects of temperatures were revealed by an increased pulse rate and a higher bodily temperature.[31] With continued work in the hot climate, there was some adaptation in that the body temperature and pulse rate increments declined rapidly during the first few days in the heat. However, these bodily changes continued to remain above the cool-climate levels even after 12 days of acclimatization.

In a factory situation physiological measures of workers' energy expenditure were obtained.[32] The thermal load (measured by Wolf respirometer) was found to be greatest in the warmest parts of the plant and in locations where there was the least air movement. This effect held for light as well as for moderately heavy work. The physiologically unfavorable locations also were the areas in which employees registered the greatest number of complaints about discomfort from heat.

In an industrial study on ventilation, electric fans were operated on alternate days for a period of six weeks, in order to test the effects of air movement on production in a weaving shed during the summer months.[33] For every hour of the eight-hour day, production with the fans running exceeded production with the fans stopped. In general, the beneficial effect of the fans was greater in the afternoon than in the

Table 18.2 / Effects of Temperature and Air Movement on Physical Work

Temperature in Degrees	Air	Units of Work (100 Optimum)	Fall in Production Due to Stagnant Air	Fall in Production Due to Increase in Temperature
68	fresh	100.0		
68	stagnant	91.1	8.9	
75	fresh	85.2		14.8
75	stagnant	76.6	8.6	14.5

[31] Edholm, O. G., Adam, J. M., and Fox, R. H. The effects of work in cool and hot conditions. *Ergonomics,* 1962, *5,* 545–556.

[32] Grieve, J. I. Therman stress in a single story factory. *Ergonomics,* 1960, *3,* 289–306.

[33] Wyatt, S., Fraser, J. A., and Stock, F. G. L. *Fan ventilation in a humid weaving shed.* Indust. Fat. Res. Bd., 1926, Rep. No. 37.

morning, although the third hour of the morning and the second hour of the afternoon showed the greatest increases in production.

The trend of results shows that physical work is definitely influenced by atmospheric conditions which interfere with the maintenance of a constant body temperature. Radical differences between indoor and outdoor temperature may disturb body adjustment as well as complicate the manner of dressing.

When the limit of an individual's resistance to heat is reached, symptoms of heat stroke become apparent: increased heart rate, a change in rhythm or intensity of heart beat, and dilation of the blood vessels near the skin. Care should be taken to discover probable limits of safe exposure since once these symptoms begin to appear, little time elapses before total heat prostration.[34]

Tolerable limits of exposure to heat are a function of prior acclimatization and required work load. Although moderate heat has little effect on performance, extreme heat exposure can result in impairment of rhythmic sense and interval estimation.[35] An individual's performance is affected by cold long before potentially fatal exposure has been suffered. The body adjusts to cold by constricting blood vessels next to the skin and reducing the flow of blood, thus limiting loss of heat to the air. Strength and duration of effort is compromised by reduced circulation in the limbs, while shivering obviously interferes with fine motor coordination.[36]

The method of heating seems to be unimportant. Comparison of radiator with floor heating found them to be equally acceptable under most conditions.[37] With the latter, however, when the floor temperature exceeded 86 degrees Fahrenheit complaints of hot feet tripled, whereas, when it was 77 degrees Fahrenheit such complaints were no greater than for radiator heating.

Obviously dress is an important factor in comfort. Since women generally wear lighter clothing men adjust by wearing lighter weight suits. Where air conditioning is used women are likely to be the first to complain about the room being cold and about the presence of drafts. Of course, individual differences also are present, and are perhaps more pronounced for cooling than for heating problems.

Effects of Ventilation on Mental Work

The experiments of the New York State Ventilation Commission demonstrated that mental work may be performed as effectively under humid (80 per cent), hot (86 degrees Fahrenheit), and stagnant air conditions as under optimal conditions (circulating air at 68 degrees and 50 per cent humidity). Although the subjects showed some tendency to take rest pauses more frequently under the most unfavorable conditions, the surprising fact is that mental work, even under these conditions, was affected little, if at all.

[34] Berkhout, *op. cit.*

[35] Hendler, E. *Unusual environments and human behavior.* New York: Free Press of Glencoe, 1963.

[36] Fox, W. F. Human performance in the cold. *Human Factors,* 1967, 9, 203–207.

[37] Karvinen, E., Turmola, T., and Äikas, E. Effect of floor heating on human comfort. *Ergonomics,* 1962, 5, 289–290.

A more recent experiment requiring students to perform multiplication problems under hot and comfortable conditions (109 degrees, 40 per cent humidity and 77 degrees, 40 per cent humidity) also revealed no differences. The high motivation present in these experimental tests apparently removed any unfavorable effects of discomfort.[38] However, some increase in errors was found in a vigilance task that required the subject to keep a pointer aligned with a moving target when the temperature was 100 degrees as compared to 60 degrees.[39]

Since the statistical studies have shown some influence of weather conditions (temperature and humidity) on mental work performed outside experimental situations, the possibilities (1) that weather may affect moods, and so influence all forms of human activity, and (2) that extreme and continual unfavorable conditions may influence mental performance, must be entertained. The fact remains, however, that controlled ventilation is more essential for physical than for mental work.

The influence of controlled ventilation on attitudes and job satisfaction obviously affects all types of workers, and a favorable attitude of employees toward the management is an indirect benefit which should not be overlooked. Laboratory studies do not have to contend with this attitude factor because people performing under experimental conditions usually try to do their best. Since this degree of motivation is seldom present under usual working conditions, the possibility that the productivity of mental workers is influenced by conditions that do not disturb laboratory subjects must be entertained. The factor of body odor also must be considered.

Effect of Noise on Work

Introduction

The disturbing effects of noise probably have been exaggerated in the public mind. The worker apparently is not as disturbed by factory noises as is the visitor, who is likely to judge the disturbance by its effects on him, without realizing the ability of the organism to make adjustments to such stimulation when it is constant. Still, some discussion of the subject is required, since laboratory and factory studies are not in complete agreement, and some factors may operate in the factory which are absent in the laboratory. Obviously, work which requires hearing will be influenced by a background of noise, since noise, in such cases, would be equivalent to a certain amount of deafness. However, when verbal communication is involved, people compensate by adjusting their voices to the noise level.[40] In considering the effects of noise, it will be assumed that hearing and verbal communication are not the essential conditions being evaluated.

---

[38] Givoni, B., and Rim, Y. Effect of thermal environment and psychological factors upon subjects, responses and performance of mental work. *Ergonomics*, 1962, *5*, 99–114.

[39] Pepler, *op. cit.*

[40] Kidd, J. S. Line noise and man-machine system performance. *J. Engr. Psychol.*, 1962, *1*, 13–18.

Results of Laboratory Investigations

When loud noises are introduced in a laboratory situation, the first effect is a startle reaction that definitely interferes with work, particularly mental work. Soon the subject adjusts, and eventually he performs better during the noisy periods than during the quiet periods which precede and follow it. The improved performance is attributable to a form of adjustment and to the fact that, at first, greater effort is expended. The extra effort seems to be great enough so that the distraction is not only overcome, but work is actually improved.[41] Even the muscles show increased tensions during noise. With continued testing, these tensions diminish, indicating that the noise becomes less disturbing from day to day and that the person has less difficulty in adjusting to it.[42] Actually it is the change that is disturbing. Once subjects have become accustomed to the experiment, going from noise to quiet is about as distracting as the reverse.[43]

Although the general laboratory findings show performance during noise to exceed that during quiet, the nature of the various effects of noise must be separated. Noise can serve as a distractor, but concentrations on the task may counteract this influence. Noise as a distractor depends upon its ability to compete with the task for attention. Its disturbing effect therefore depends on the nature of the task as well as the nature of the noise. This effect involves the processes of perception and motivation. Noise that is an accompaniment to a task is less disturbing than a noise which is not essential to the task.[44] A worker is less disturbed by the noise of a machine he is operating than is a nonmachinist working in an adjoining room.

Certain skills also may be relevant because perceptual organization is necessarily selective, in that figure and ground must be separated. In this case, the task becomes the figure and the noise becomes the background. People differ in ability to separate relevant from irrelevant sounds, an aspect of hearing quite different from auditory acuity. The importance of this selection in auditory perception becomes apparent when one uses a hearing aid. Background noises then are difficult to separate from voices. Apparently the reduced ability to localize the various sounds makes it more difficult to separate figure from background.

Although intermittent noises might be expected to be highly distracting, one study showed that they decreased errors in target detection and that increasing the intensity of the noise up to 100 decibels showed further improvement.[45]

The ear adapts to loudness, but the ability to adapt is influenced by off-on se-

[41] Berrien, F. K. The effects of noise. *Psychol. Bull.,* 1946, *43,* 141–161; Ford, *op. cit.* pp. 154–155; Morgan, J. J. B. The overcoming of distraction and other resistances. *Arch. Psychol.,* 1916, *35,* 1–89.

[42] Poffenberger, *op. cit.,* pp. 133–317.

[43] Ford, A. Attention-automatization: An investigation of the transitional nature of mind. *Amer. J. Psychol.,* 1929, *41,* 1–32.

[44] Blum, M. L., and Naylor, J. C. *Industrial psychology: Its theoretical and social foundations.* New York: Harper & Row, 1968.

[45] Warner, H. D. Effects of intermittent noise on human target detection. *Human Factors,* 1969, *11,* 245–250.

quences. This is largely a physiological problem involving the auditory mechanisms. Both adaptation and overcoming distraction are influenced by the length of the work period so that the measured effects of noise may be quite different at various times.[46]

An interesting explanation for the improved performance under noise is that it has an arousal value which facilitates performance of the type of repetitious tasks (lacking adequate arousal) that require vigilance. McBain found that a task, such as printing seven pairs of block letters at a prescribed pace, was aided by a background of nonintelligible noise. He theorizes that performance is a function of an optimal arousal value, which includes the combined stimulation from the task and the background. Thus tasks lacking stimulation are aided by background noises, but too much noise may be disturbing. This is an interesting notion and needs further exploration. His finding suggests that the nature of the stimulation received from the total situation must be taken into account in studies of noise. However, intelligible noises lack arousal value and instead are interpreted as distractions that must be overcome.[47]

If overcoming disturbance caused by noise requires effort, to work in noisy surroundings would prove highly fatiguing and would eventually result in lowered ability to work. The failure to find evidence of fatigue in experiments may be explained by the subjects' increased motivation. In Chapter 16 evidence was presented to show that motivation can compensate for fatigue by making more energy available. The high motivation in a laboratory situation may cause the body to allocate an excessive amount of energy to the task, thus not only covering fatigue effects but also increasing performance. According to this view the way people react to a situation is important, since it determines the amount of energy that will be made available. For long jobs, they unconsciously hold back; for difficult jobs, they are able to summon extra energy. If workers overestimate the difficulty of a noisy environment, they may have excessive energy to expend on the job. However, since the reactions of workers to the job are an important determiner of motivation, the degree of motivation may vary considerably from the laboratory to the factory situation.

Effects of Noise on Job Performance

A comparison of the productivity of four typists when working in a quiet office and when working in a noisy office showed no significant difference when errors, amount typed, and the number of discarded letters were considered.[48] Reports on the feelings of fatigue, taken from time to time, also showed no clear difference between the two working environments.

In an intensive investigation of the effects of reducing noise, measurements of the production of eleven weavers (women) were made when they were working

---

[46] Teichner, W. H., Arees, E., and Reilly, R. Noise and human performance: A psychological approach. *Ergonomics*, 1963, *6*, 83–97.

[47] McBain, W. N. Noise, the "arousal hypothesis" and monotonous work. *J. appl. Psychol.*, 1961, *45*, 309–317.

[48] Kornhauser, A. W. The effects of noise on office output. *Indust. Psychol.*, 1927, *2*, 621–622.

with and without ear-defenders that reduced the noise of the machines about 10 per cent (from 96 to 87 decibels).[49] Comparison of the productivity of the group when ear-defenders were in use and when they were not (alternate weeks) showed an improvement of only 1 per cent in production with their use. However, the amount of production in weaving depends partly upon the efficiency of the machinery and partly upon the skill of the worker. The mechanical operation of the loom is a constant factor, and the operations controlled entirely by the weaver occupy only five minutes in every hour. If the results are interpreted in terms of the reduction in time of the weaver's personal operations, then the improvement in efficiency amounts to 12 per cent. Occupations which involve a greater proportion of personal performance, therefore, may be expected to show the greater increase in efficiency with noise reduction.

The increase in production was considerably greater for weavers who reported that they were disturbed by the noise than for those who reported indifference, yet every weaver showed some improvement when using the ear-defenders. Interesting also is the fact that the benefits of the reduced noise were more marked in the morning than in the afternoon, and that the general effect was to produce a more regular rate of output. As may be expected, noise is more disturbing for mental than for manual work,[50] with irregular, meaningful, and loud noises being the most distracting.

Although adequate details are lacking, one report on the effects of noise in industry shows a variety of striking improvements with noise reduction.[51] For example, the work of assembling temperature regulators increased more than 37 per cent, and errors fell to one-eighth of their former number when the work was moved from the proximity of a boiler shop to a quiet area. Office work increased 8.8 per cent and typists' errors fell 24 per cent with a noise reduction of 14.5 per cent. The noise reduction also decreased turnover by 47 per cent, and absenteeism by 37.5 per cent. Since this report so strongly emphasizes the highly detrimental effects of noise, there is reason for believing that extreme conditions were selected.

A carefully controlled study compared work (threading cinefilm on perforation machines) in rooms with acoustic treatment with that in rooms not so treated.[52] Seven criterion measures were used; one showed a difference and was significant only at the 5 per cent level. Rate of work, coordination, and other measures of performance seemed unaffected by ordinary noise levels, but there was some indication that noise increases the frequency of lapses (see Mental Blocks, Chapter 16).

In general, the industrial studies agree that a reduction in noise is associated with

[49] Weston, H. C., and Adams, S. *The effects of noise on the performance of weavers.* Indust. Hlth. Res. Bd., 1932, Rep. No. 65.

[50] Pollock, K. G., and Bartlett, F. C. *Two studies in the psychological effects of noise. I. Psychological experiments on the effects of noise.* Indust. Hlth. Res. Bd., 1932, Rep. No. 65.

[51] McCartney, J. L. Noise drives us crazy. Reprinted by the Natl. Noise Abatement Council, New York City, from the *Pa. Med. J.*, August, 1941.

[52] Broadbent, D. E., and Little E. A. J. Effects of noise reduction in a work situation. *Occup. Psychol.*, 1960, 34, 133–140.

some forms of improvement. Although an increase in production may be questionable in some cases, it is apparent that noise does not increase production. When the noise level is decreased, production does not necessarily increase (except for a general morale factor) but human error is less frequent.[53] One study[54] suggested that task complexity influenced results. Data indicate that people may have a reserve perceptual capacity which is usually unused. Should the perceptual demands of a task or of the situation increase, this reserve capacity may be drawn upon, maintaining task performance at a high level. This reserve may account for the results of studies showing that noise produces no decrement in task performance. By increasing task complexity and introducing a secondary task in this study, the reserve capacity was used, making it unavailable to draw upon when noise was introduced. Errors increased on the secondary task, although performance of the primary task was maintained.

The difference between the results of laboratory and practical investigations is probably attributable to differences in motivation. Men can do as well during noise as during quiet, but they must be highly motivated to do so. Differences between individuals, the degree and character of the noise, and the type of work are important.

Effects on Health

Harmful effects of noise are largely confined to the startle reactions produced by a sudden noise. Health may be impaired if noise interferes with sleep, and mental health must be considered when noise is a source of irritation. Unfotunately, acoustical engineers have had little influence on housing construction and home equipment.[55] Modern walls, heating systems, cheap piping for plumbing, ventilating fans, and air conditioners have increased home noises and undoubtedly are sources of irritation which may also interfere with sleep.

Although the human body has great adaptability to its environment this adjustment may be prevented when noise produces irritation. In an experiment using physiological measures of activity in the gastric and duodenal regions, it was found that the functional level was influenced by periods of intermittent noises.[56] Two conditions were tested. One group of subjects was able to prevent the noise, scheduled at 30-second intervals, if they pressed a button during the five-second period before the onset of the noise. The other group had no control over the noise. The group that could control the noise showed increased physiological activity. The other group apparently adjusted, since they exhibited no increase in either gastric or duodenal activity. Kryter points out that high-level noise causes vasoconstriction of the extremities, but there is no evidence to suggest that this is debilitating.[57]

[53] Broadbent, D. E., and Little, E. A. Effects of noise reduction in a work situation. *Occup. Psychol.*, 1960, *34*, 133–140.

[54] Boggs, D. H., and Simon, J. R. Differential effect of noise on tasks of varying complexity. *J. appl. Psychol.*, 1968, *52*, 148–153.

[55] Foote, F. D. Noise. *Science*, 1964, *143*, No. 3602, 101.

[56] Davis, R. C., and Berry, F. Gastrointestinal reactions during a noise avoidance task. *Psychol. Rep.*, 1963, *12*, 135–137.

[57] Kryter, K. *The effects of noise on man.* New York: Academic Press, 1970.

Undoubtedly, some individuals are hypersensitive to noise and cannot make effective adjustments. Industrial studies ordinarily would not include highly sensitive individuals, since these would have left for other positions. The facts that noises will bring on fits in some epileptics and that some strains of rats and mice can be induced to have violent convulsions by being exposed to such noises as the jingling of keys suggest that there are distinct hereditary factors which make noises irritating and intolerable to some individuals.[58] Sudden and loud noises produce fright reactions in all persons, and loud and persistent noises (particularly those of high pitch) may produce deafness to certain pitches.[59] Such noises should obviously be eliminated, if possible, or reduced with earplugs. Protection against loud noises can also be achieved by the use of a warning signal.[60] The acoustic reflex involves a contraction of the middle ear muscles and reduces the transmission of sounds. If a warning tone can be given automatically just prior to the loud noise, the acoustic reflex reduces its impact.

Effect on Morale

Insofar as factory or office noise is of such character that it is generally unpleasant, its correction will lead to better morale for the same reason that any consideration for the welfare of employees tends to produce a favorable reaction. Extreme quiet, however, also may be disturbing, and too much attention to noise reduction may be undesirable. In a quiet background, even the slightest noise may stand out and be more disturbing and disruptive than a constant background of noise.

The fact that noises are generally unpleasant may be a factor in social reactions and relations, even when they do not markedly influence individual performers.[61] Intermittent noises are certainly the most disturbing as far as emotional reactions are concerned, while noises which are meaningful (conversational) are the most distracting. In a highly motivated situation, these can be overcome by extra effort, but the necessity of overcoming them may create a source of irritation between individuals, particularly if an individual is the source of the noise.

Vibration

Helicopter pilots and air hammer operators are among the workers who cannot escape exposure to vibration. Vibration and sound are closely related since vibrations reaching the body by air are acoustic. Mechanical oscillations between 20 and

---

[58] Maier, N. R. F. Studies of abnormal behavior in the rat: XIV. Strain differences in the inheritance of susceptibility to convulsions. *J. comp. Psychol.*, 1943, *35*, 327–335; Maier, N. R. F., and Parker, W. Studies of abnormal behavior in the rat: XVIII. Analysis of stomachs of rats repeatedly exposed to auditory stimulation. *J. comp. Psychol.*, 1945, *38*, 335–341; Maier, N. R. F., and Longhurst, J. U. Studies of abnormal behavior in the rat: XXI. Conflict and "audiogenic" seizures. *J. comp. Psychol.*, 1947, *40*, 397–412; Morgan, C., and Waldman, H. "Conflict" and audiogenic seizures. *J. comp. Psychol.*, 1941, *31*, 1–11.

[59] *The relations of hearing loss to noise exposure.* New York: Amer. Standards Assn., Inc., 1954.

[60] Chisman, J. A., and Simon, J. R. Protection against impulse-type industrial noise by utilizing the acoustic reflex. *J. appl. Psychol.*, 1961, *45*, 402–407.

[61] Pollock and Bartlett, *op. cit.*

20,000 frequencies per second (Hz) will be heard as sound, whereas airborne vibrations below 16 Hz will be perceived as vibration, not noise. Intense vibrations and noise produce stresses which are distracting and can produce an alarm reaction, autonomic arousal, anxiety, and irritation.[62] They can produce a temporary hearing loss and a decrease in fine motor coordination. If exposure to loud sound continues over long periods of time, the regaining of hearing acuity is delayed.

The eyeball has a critical resonance frequency which when approached, causes decreased visual acuity and impaired performance. At critical frequencies, vibration of the body produces greater perceptual impairment than vibration of the stimulus object.[63]

Although prolonged exposure to intense vibration is detrimental, vibratory stimulation can be used to advantage. Gilmer[64] lists 14 situations where vibration is useful; among these are: (1) to alert or warn quickly; (2) where unusual stimulation is desirable; (3) as an aid to vigilance through both warnings and redundance; (4) where conditions handicap both the eye and ear. Hahn[65] demonstrates that while vibrotactile discrimination has advantages in certain situations, it is far less sensitive than visual discrimination.

Other Environmental Factors

Most companies are sensitive to attractive building designs and to creating comfortable lounges and making working conditions as attractive as the work permits.[66] Office space arrangements influence the extent to which employees will form social groups. Some offices are designed so that hundreds of desks occupy one section. Certain designers argue that such a situation offers more privacy than a room limited to four to six desks. A large open area offers one kind of privacy—that of not being an obvious member of a group. Such situations are cold and impersonal and appear to be designed to prevent the formation of groups.

Common sense seems to have persuaded some modern architects and managers to think of friendships as making for too much sociability. When office workers belong to the same clubs or bowling teams they talk about their off-job interests on the job. This is nonwork activity. In order to use these natural groups it is necessary to find ways to organize them around the job so the friendship will lead to cooperation, good communication, and job interest. A unified group has little value to an organization unless it results in improved job satisfaction and productivity. This unity can lead to increased participation and involvement in job activities. Job contacts can improve interpersonal relations and job satisfaction, but also can detract

---

[62] Berkhout, *op. cit.*

[63] Dennis, J. P. Some effects of vibration on visual performance. *J. appl. Psychol.,* 1965, *49,* 245–252.

[64] In Hawkes, G. R. (Ed.), *Symposium on cutaneous sensitivity.* Fort Knox, Ky.: U. S. Army Medical Research Laboratory Report 424, 1960.

[65] Hahn, J. F. Unidimensional compensatory tracking with a vibrotactile display. *Perceptual and Motor Skills,* 1965, *21,* 699–702.

[66] For a discussion of the architectural aspects of the organizational environment see E. Pauley, Esthetics, architecture, and city and regional designs. In K. B. DeGreene, *Systems psychology.* New York: McGraw-Hill, 1970, Ch. 17.

from productivity. Field research is needed to explore the effects of various space arrangements.

Clean and adequate toilets and washroom facilities (showers when the workers feel the need) characterize work conditions of progressive companies, and management complaints that employees do not keep these clean is an admission of poor employee morale. Good food should be available when possible and if prices are reasonable employees will be motivated to eat well and enjoy the period. Employees' pride in their jobs is related to the consideration that management demonstrates in the overall environment it creates for them. Employees identifiy with their company if they can take pride in it.

Laboratory Exercise

Role Playing: The Promotion Interview

(Students are asked not to read the case materials before participating in the laboratory exercise.)

A. Preparation for role playing.
1. The instructor will select two players and give them their assignments at least a day ahead of time.
2. One person is to play the role of Trudy Pearce and should study carefully "Background Information" (E.1) and become thoroughly acquainted with "Special Instructions for Trudy Pearce" (E.2).
3. The other is to play the role of Jim Smith and should study carefully the "Background Information" (E.1) and become thoroughly acquainted with "Special Instructions for Jim Smith" (E.3).
4. The rest of the class should refrain from reading any of the materials in Section E.

B. Role-playing procedure.
1. The instructor will read the "Background Information" aloud to the whole class, and copy the schedule of jobs held by Smith on the chalkboard.
2. All persons not assigned a role are to act as observers.
3. The instructor will introduce Trudy Pearce to the class and seat her at desk in front of class, indicate that Pearce has an appointment with Jim Smith, and signal Smith to arrive for his appointment with Pearce.
4. The interview is then to be allowed to proceed to a solution or conclusion as in a real-life situation.

C. Discussion analysis with observers. (Pearce and Smith may enter discussion to evaluate correctness of conclusions reached but they should not divulge the nature of their "Special Instructions.")

1. Determine degree to which Pearce established a mutual interest.
2. What use did Pearce make of various types of questions?
3. List feelings expressed by Smith.
4. Which feeling areas were thoroughly explored? Which not?
5. Obtain opinions on degree to which Pearce understood Smith and vice versa.
6. List cues which indicate there was failure to communicate.
7. Did Pearce change as a result of the interview or was she justified in maintaining her original estimation? List reasons.
8. How was Smith's attitude changed by the interview?

D. Repeat role playing of interview if time permits.
1. The class is to divide into groups of three.
2. The instructor will assign the role of Pearce to one member of each group, the role of Smith to a second member, and ask the third member to act as group leader and supervise the role playing.
3. Role playing should be terminated 10 minutes before end of the class period.
4. Group leaders will hold discussion with role players and evaluate progress made.

E. Materials for "Promotion Interview."

1. Background Information

The American Consolidated Chemical Company has chemical plants located in various sections of the country. The main plant is in Detroit. Important branches are at Houston; St. Louis; St. Paul; and Cleveland. All the products are manufactured in Detroit, but each of the branches specializes in making chemicals that either utilize local raw material available in the locality or have a concentration of outlets. Thus the Cleveland plant manufactures products needed in the Cleveland area, and the Houston plant manufactures products which utilize petroleum derivatives.

Since the Detroit plant makes all the products, an experienced person can be moved from Detroit to any of the other plants. When a vacancy opens up in a particular department in Detroit, it is possible to fill the vacancy by choosing someone local or by bringing in an employee from a branch that produces the product corresponding to the one made by a particular department in Detroit. Thus there has been a great deal of movement within the organization, and since the company has been expanding, opportunities for promotion have been good. Generally speaking, morale has been quite satisfactory.

Trudy Pearce is the assistant to the Works Manager of the Detroit plant. One of her duties is to keep track of the college recruits and plan their development. The company hires several college recruits each year and from these selects the employees for promotion and development in higher management positions. Pearce is about to have an interview with James Smith, a college graduate who was brought into the company 10 years ago. The following schedule shows the positions which Smith has held during his 10 years with the company.

Detroit	Dept. A	1 year	Regular employee
St. Paul	Depts. A, B, C	2 years	Regular employee
Detroit	Dept. A	1 year	Foreman
St. Louis	Depts. B, F	2 years	Foreman
Cleveland	Depts. D, E	1½ years	Foreman
Houston	Dept. G	1½ years	Foreman
Detroit	Dept. H	1 year	Foreman

2. ROLE INSTRUCTIONS FOR TRUDY PEARCE

Ever since *Jim Smith* graduated from college and joined the company as a college recruit ten years ago you have kept an eye on him. During his first year in the company you were impressed by his technical ability and even more by his leadership. After he'd had one year in Department A you sent him to St. Paul where they needed an employee with his training. He made a good showing and worked in Departments A, B, and C. After two years you brought him back to Detroit and made him a foreman in Department A. He did very well on this job, so you considered making some long-range plans for him. Here was a man you thought you could groom for an executive position. This meant giving him experience with all operations in all plants. To do this with the greatest ease you decided to make him a foreman in each of the eight departments for a short period of time and to get him assignments in each of the branches.

During the past two years you have had some disturbing reports. Jim didn't impress *Bill Jones,* the department head at Houston, who reported that he had ideas but was always on the defensive. Since his return to Detroit he has shown a lack of job interest, and the employees who work for him don't back him up the way they used to. You feel you have made quite a mistake in this man and that he has let you down after you've given him good build-ups with various department heads. Maybe the confidence you have shown in him and the praise you have given him during the several progress interviews have gone to his head. If so, he hasn't the stature it takes to make the top grade. Therefore, you have abandoned your plans of moving him up to superintendent at St. Paul (a two-step promotion) and think it may be best to send him to Houston where there is a job as general foreman in Department C. (Note that this is not the department in which Jones is the head.) This won't mean much of a promotion because you have moved his pay up as high as you could while he was a sort of roving foreman. However, you feel that he has earned some promotion even if he hasn't lived up to your expectations. This St. Paul position is still open, but unless you are convinced to the contrary he doesn't seem up to it.

Of course, it's possible that Jim is having marital trouble. At a recent company party you found his wife to be quite dissatisfied and unhappy. Maybe she is giving Jim a rough time.

While you are waiting for Jim to arrive you have his folder in front of you showing the positions he has held.

3. ROLE INSTRUCTIONS FOR JIM SMITH

You have been with the American Consolidated Chemical Company for ten years now. You joined the company on graduating from college with a major in chemistry. At the time you joined the company you were interviewed by *Trudy Pearce,* and were told that a good employee could get ahead in the company. On the strength of the position you married your college sweetheart and moved to Detroit. You preferred the Houston and St. Paul branches but Pearce thought Detroit was the place to start. So you took your chance along with other college recruits. Because you were a good student in college and were active in college affairs, you had reason to believe you possessed leadership ability.

During your first few years you thought you were getting some place. You got moved to Minnesota and felt Pearce was doing you a favor by sending you there. After the first year you bought a home and got started on a family. During two years in Minnesota you gained considerable experience in Departments A, B, and C. Then you were offered a foremanship in Detroit, and since this meant a promotion and you had a second child on the way, you decided to return to Detroit. When you came to Detroit Pearce again saw you and told you how pleased she was with your progress.

Since this time however, you have been given a royal run-around. They tell you they like your work, but all you get are a lot of lateral transfers. You have been foreman in practically every department and have been moved from one branch to another. Other people that came to the company, even after you joined, have been made general foremen. They stick in a given department and are working up while you get moved from place to place. Although the company pays for your moves, both you and your wife want to settle down and have a permanent home for your children. Why can't people be honest with you? First they tell you what a good job you are doing and then the next thing they do is get rid of you. Take for example *Bill Jones,* the department head at Houston. He acted as if you had done him a favor to go there, but you can tell he isn't sincere. Since you've gotten to know him you can see through him. From little remarks he has dropped you know he's been saying some nasty things about you to the home office. It's obvious that the Houston man is incompetent, and you feel he got rid of you because he considered you a threat to his job.

Your wife realizes that you are unhappy. She has told you she is willing to live on less just to get you out of the company. You know you could hold a superintendent's job, such as *George Wilson* got, who joined the company when you did, and he was just an average student in college. As a matter of fact, if the company were on the ball they should realize that you have the ability to be a department head if George is superintendent material.

Pearce has asked you to come up and see her. You are a bit nervous about this interview because the news may not be good. You've felt her to be less friendly lately and have no desire to listen to any smooth manipulations. Last night you and your wife had a good talk about things, and she's willing that you should look around for another job. Certainly you've reached the end of your patience, and you're fed up with any more of her attempts to move you around just because someone is jealous of your ideas.

Suggested Readings

Borow, H. *Man in a world at work.* Boston: Houghton Mifflin, 1964.

Burns, N. M. (Ed.). *Unusual environments and human behavior.* New York: Free Press of Glencoe, 1963.

Cotton, H. *Principles of illumination.* New York: Wiley, 1961.

Davis, K., and Blomstrom, R. L. *Business and its environment.* New York: McGraw-Hill, 1966.

Harris, C. M. (Ed.). *Handbook of noise control.* New York: McGraw-Hill, 1957.

Leithead, C. S., and Lind, A. R. *Heat stress and heat disorders.* London: Cassel, 1964.

Reed, R., Jr. *Plant layout: Factors, principles, and techniques.* Homewood, Ill.: Richard D. Irwin, 1961.

Selye, H. *The physiology and pathology of exposure to stress.* Montreal: Acta, 1950.

Winslow, C. E. A., and Herrington, L. P. *Temperature and human life.* Princeton, N.J.: Princeton University Press, 1949.

Yaffe, C. D., and Jones, H. H. *Noise and hearing.* Washington, D.C.: U. S. Government Printing Office, 1961.

19

Psychological Factors in Labor Turnover

Basic Considerations

Cost of Labor Turnover

Separations of employer and employee come about for many reasons. Some are inevitable; others may be avoided. A knowledge of the basic factors in avoidable labor turnover may lead to a reduction in the rate of turnover and create a saving in hiring and training costs. These savings may be considerably more than they first appear. Replacing an employee who has been in service for many years may require hiring and training several persons before a relatively permanent employee is again found. In addition, new employees are more subject to accidents, cause more breakage, and make more errors than experienced workers, so that costs of replacing a worker may greatly exceed the hiring estimate of 482 dollars for the average company.[1] The average cost for hiring college graduates now exceeds 1300 dollars, with the turnover rate for recruits sometimes reaching 75 per cent during the first five years.[2]

Another important aspect of turnover is the fact that it reflects conditions in the plant.[3] A company which has high labor turnover is regarded unfavorably by employees and by society. By analyzing the reasons for turnover, we can determine some of the faulty practices that are more prevalent in one company than in another. Before judging a company, however, we must take into account the nature of the causes of separation.

Types of Causes of Labor Turnover

Unavoidable forms of turnover are constant factors and influence all forms of work, as well as all organizations. Death, permanent disability, retirement, and change of residence cause separations that fall into this category.

---

[1] Stessin, L. Figures that management doesn't see: High cost of labor turnover. *Dun's Rev. & Mod. Indust.,* 1961, 77 (2), 75–77.

[2] Odiorne, G. S. How to get the men you want. *Nation's Business,* 1964, 52 (1), 70–72, 74.

[3] Scheer, W. E. Reduce turnover: Increase profits. *Personnel J.,* 1962, 41, 559–561.

Turnover caused by layoffs and seasonal conditions may depend upon factors beyond employers' control, but they can influence these to a considerable degree. By careful planning of work, it is possible to approach a uniform production schedule so that a permanent staff is employed throughout the year. If employers were required to hire on an annual basis, much of this planning would become a necessity. The problem of seasonal fluctuations in the demands for a product can in many cases be solved (1) by storing nonperishable products (coal, for example), (2) by combining the manufacture or distribution of two types of seasonal products (air conditioning and heating units, candy and ice cream, summer and winter sports equipment), and (3) by introducing incentives that influence the demand (time of change in car models, reduced prices, and so on). In other cases, part-time employment of married women, college students, and the like may be arranged to handle extra employment demands. Such individuals may be semipermanently employed during rush periods without disturbing the balance of the labor market. In handling unexpected demands overtime is frequently the solution. Successful maintenance of a permanent staff promotes the formation of a faithful and conscientious working force.

The number of discharges required because the employee is incompetent can be reduced by more careful selection and by shifting employees into work for which they may be better fitted. A low rate of discharge does not mean that the employment methods are satisfactory, however. A company that lacks competition and does not measure individual productivity may have a low discharge rate because of low production standards.

Resignations that occur because employees prefer to work elsewhere are the most revealing. To what extent was the job accurately described when the employee was hired? Often the employment interviewer is only concerned with determining whether the employee is satisfactory and forgets that the job and company must also be satisfactory to the employee if he is to remain. The job may even be misrepresented during the interview in order to induce a desirable candidate to take the job. Seldom does the candidate meet the supervisor for whom he will work. This one-sided interviewing condition may account for a large proportion of employee departures during the first three months of employment.[4]

Quitting a job may also be an individual employee's method of retaliation—a form of aggression arising from frustration. The same conditions that cause this type of turnover also cause grievances.[5] When employees have no opportunity for reemployment elsewhere, they express their frustration by interfering with production (being wasteful of materials, rough with equipment, and disrespectful of rules) and by looking for injustices in supervisory behavior so that grievance procedures may be undertaken.

Although job dissatisfaction of some sort or other is a major factor in resignations, there are other reasons for quitting. Misfits wander from job to job, until by

---

[4] Kilwein, J. H. Turnover as a function of communication during employment procedure. *Personnel J.,* 1962, *41,* 458.

[5] Fleishman, E. A., and Harris, E. F. Patterns of leadership behavior related to employee grievances and turnover. *Personnel Psychol.,* 1962, *15,* 43–56.

trial and error they eventually may find satisfactory employment. In these cases vocational selection seems to be the ultimate solution. Other individuals are chronic quitters, and it would be desirable if selection methods could detect them. Their previous record of instability would be one index of this tendency. It is for this reason that employment interviewers should seek information about the number of previous jobs, the length of time employed, and the reasons for quitting.

In determining the kind of individuals who voluntarily leave their employment, it is important to distinguish between the resignation of satisfactory and unsatisfactory employees. If those who quit are inferior in workmanship, the separation may be desirable; but if the resignations are predominantly among the more satisfactory employees, then the condition is serious. When employees leave their jobs, a selective factor may be operating that can either raise or lower the quality of the permanent working force.

Specific Factors Related to Labor Turnover

Length of Service

An analysis of turnover in terms of length of service is very revealing, since it shows that, even when turnover is high, a large proportion of the employees are stable, whereas a minority is moving from one job to another.[6] This means that the same positions must be filled repeatedly. Turnover is highest for persons who have been with a company less than a month and drops rapidly during the first year. In one company it was found that 80 per cent of the employees leaving the job had served less than three months.

The relation between turnover and length of service constitutes a strong argument for seniority rewards. In order to replace an employee who has been in service for a year, there is a strong probability that as many as ten will have to be hired and trained to obtain another year's service. Data of this sort show also that there is a moving labor supply which is responsible for most of the expense of hiring and training.

Age

If part of the unstable labor supply is due to trial-and-error job-seeking, one would expect young employees to show higher labor turnover than older employees. This point is supported by an analysis of labor turnover in relation to age.[7]

The importance of responsibility in preventing turnover is shown by the fact that labor turnover again increases among workers who are more than 35 years of age and reaches another high point at about 45 years. This new high point in turnover comes at an age when family responsibilities begin to decline because the children

[6] Scott, W. D., and Clothier, R. C. *Personnel Management.* New York: A. W. Shaw, 1923, pp. 469–472; Scott, W. D., Clothier, R. C., and Spriegel, W. R. *Personnel management* (6th ed.). New York: McGraw-Hill, 1961, p. 466.

[7] Scott, W. D., Clothier, R. C., Mathewson, S. B., and Spriegel, W. R. *Personnel management* (3rd ed.). New York: McGraw-Hill, 1941, p. 504.

have reached working age. Dissatisfied laborers seem to take this opportunity of reduced responsibility to better their conditions.

After workers reach the age of 45 years, the length of service increases rapidly; beyond this age it is difficult for persons to obtain new employment, so they must remain with the old job, whether they like it or not.

Marital Status

Although the proportion of married people increases with age, a separate analysis of the data in terms of marital status shows that it is one of the factors which influence the age trend in turnover rate. Among common laborers the average length of service for married men was found to be about three times as great as that for single men. It is probable that marriages make for both stability and responsibility, factors which reduce turnover rate under normal conditions of employment. But the possibility that job instability and avoidance of marriage may be caused by the same personality traits should not be overlooked.

Turnover among Men and Women

Among office employees the turnover rate for females was found to be three times as high as for males, largely because of the high rate of female resignations.[8] It is apparent that the roles of males and females in our society influences their employment behavior. The extent to which family responsibility, temporary needs, marital status, and discrimination account for the differences is difficult to determine. The success of the women's liberation movement will undoubtedly change some of these relationships by equalizing wages and promotions, but how it will influence turnover rates remains to be determined.

In general, there is a tendency to promote intelligent individuals more rapidly than less intelligent ones, but this relationship has been more marked for men than for women. In one company the correlation between intelligence and rate of promotion was .58 for men and only .39 for women. In another company 18 per cent of the men who were below average in intelligence were promoted, whereas only 2 per cent of the women who were below average were promoted. Among employees of superior intelligence, 39 per cent of the men were promoted to responsible positions, as compared with 17 per cent of the women.[9] Although intelligence influenced the promotions of both men and women, men below average in intelligence had as good a chance for being promoted as women of superior intelligence. As discriminatory practices of this type are removed there should be a general decline in the turnover of the more intelligent women. If, however, the turnover of female employees continues to be high because of family responsibilities, then turnover in higher jobs would increase.

[8] The American Society of Personnel Administration. *Employee turnover: A graphic analysis of the separation rates in the offices of 99 business establishments and 2 educational institutions*, Berea, Ohio, 1963.

[9] Pond, M., and Bills, M. A. Intelligence and clerical jobs: Two studies of the relation of test score to job held. *Personnel J.*, 1933, *12*, 41–56.

Turnover and Race

The past practice of discrimination on the basis of race would also tend to cause the more intelligent members of minority groups to resign because of lack of promotion. However, cultural norms, educational differences, and family history complicate the picture so that a comparison of turnover rates by race has little meaning under the changing conditions of our society. When proper comparisons can be made and discrimination is removed, racial differences in turnover can be expected to disappear.

Relation between Turnover and Job Complexity

Since the relationship between intelligence and turnover varies for different jobs, one may expect job complexity to be the important factor in causing people of low and high intelligence to show different degrees of dissatisfaction for the same job. This point has been clearly verified by a study made on clerical workers.[10] Tests of mental alertness were given to employees at the time of hiring. The jobs were classified into five categories (*A, B, C, D,* and *E*) according to their level of difficulty, *A* jobs being the least difficult, and *E* jobs the most difficult. In analyzing the data, the average-scoring individuals were eliminated so that comparisons between the two extreme groups could be made. The extreme groups used were those with mental alertness scores below 80 and those with mental alertness scores above 100.

The first part of Table 19.1 shows the results for the individuals who scored above 100. In originally placing the individuals, the tendency was to assign a greater proportion of them to the more complex jobs. Nevertheless, 30 months later the proportion of these individuals in complex jobs increased (because of the high turnover of low-scoring individuals), whereas the proportion of these individuals in simple jobs decreased (because of their own high turnover).

The second part of the table shows the results for the individuals who scored below 80. An opposite trend in personnel shift occurred in this group. After 30 months, the complex jobs had a lower proportion of low-scoring individuals, whereas simple jobs showed no such losses.

The last column shows that turnover among individuals with high scores declines as job complexity increases, demonstrating that a basic cause in turnover among these individuals is dissatisfaction with work that is too easy for them. Among individuals who are below 80 in mental alertness, turnover, in general, increases with job complexity, showing that these individuals are dissatisfied with work that is too difficult for them. Thus, individuals with high and low intelligence are dissatisfied with their jobs for quite different reasons, and a determining factor in this difference in behavior is the complexity of the job. This study demonstrates also that turnover functions as a selective process by which the individuals who remain are more suited to their work.

[10] Bills, M. A. Relation of mental alertness test score to positions and permanency in company. *J. appl. Psychol.*, 1923, 7, 154–156.

Grade of Work	Percentage Scoring 100 or Better		
	Original Group	30 Months Later	Percentage of Turnover
A (most simple)	26	0	100
B	20	0	100
C	45	27	72
D	46	51	53
E (most difficult)	50	57	41
	Percentage Scoring Under 80		
A	50	57	37
B	53	50	62
C	53	36	50
D	30	23	58
E	13	7	66

From M. A. Bills, Relation of mental alertness test score to positions and permanency in company. *J. appl. Psychol.,* 1923, *7,* 154–156. Copyright 1923 by the American Psychological Association, and reproduced by permission.

Table 19.1 / Relation between Intelligence and Job Complexity

That scores on motor and personality tests would show similar relationships with turnover is indicated by the fact that there are occupational differences in some of the traits measured by these tests. Apparently, turnover also operates in these cases to achieve select groups of individuals. Analysis of turnover with reference to other human traits might reveal significant tests that could be used to place employees in jobs suited to their mentality, personality, and motor equipment. Reduced labor turnover may therefore be considered a by-product of scientific selection methods.

Turnover and Job Satisfaction

An organization's concern for promoting job satisfaction not only influences motivation but turnover resulting from dissatisfaction with the job or the company. This voluntary turnover depends in part on the ease of finding another job that is perceived as more desirable (the pull), as well as on the degree of dissatisfaction with the present job situation (the push). Using a model to predict turnover (based upon prior studies of job satisfaction) it was possible to do better than chance to predict turnover among scientists and engineers.[11] Measures of job satisfaction were made while the participants were employed and comparisons were made between those who quit within five years and those who stayed. The same questionnaires also indicate that the best performers tend to give responses similar to the turnover groups.[12]

[11] Farris, G. F. A predictive study of turnover. *Personnel Psychol.,* 1971, *24,* 311–328.
[12] Pelz, D. C., and Andrews, F. M. *Scientists in organizations.* New York: Wiley, 1966.

In a longitudinal study of voluntary turnover in a manufacturing firm it was found that the rate fluctuated with the labor-management relationship. During periods of harmony the rate was low and during periods of unrest it was high.[13] Thus the attitude toward the company was related to turnover.

Using a female clerk population, five aspects of job satisfaction were explored: work done, pay, supervision, promotional opportunities, and coworkers.[14] On the basis of the results the company made a number of changes which included intra-company transfers, altered wage policies, merit raise procedures, and certain job changes. At the time of the survey turnover was 30 per cent. In one year it fell to 18 per cent and a year later it was 12 per cent. During the two-year period significant improvements in job satisfaction were obtained in four of the five job satisfaction indices.

Since factors influencing job satisfaction have been discussed at length in Chapter 16, it need only be pointed out that turnover can be reduced by the same methods that produce job interest. Reducing turnover by higher pay, however, introduces a conflict since job interest is not increased. Thus a person may be induced to stay on a job that offers little job interest.

Turnover and Absenteeism

Lack of job satisfaction may be expected to influence absenteeism as well as turnover, but differing motivations are also present. Quitting a job implies the availability of an alternative, whereas absenteeism is largely an avoidance response, and if excessive can lead to discharge. It has been generally found that both absenteeism and turnover are related to dissatisfaction with the job, but the overall relationship is usually significant for absenteeism only.[15] The attitude toward the firm, the degree of repetitiousness of the job, and sex of worker seem to influence both absenteeism and turnover, but the relationships differed even when two similar manufacturing firms in the same geographical area were compared.[16] Broad generalizations regarding the relationship between absenteeism and turnover therefore cannot be justified.

Both absenteeism and turnover have been reported higher in large than in small organizations because of the impersonal nature of large firms.[17] However, the size-absentee relationship seems to be more general than the size-turnover relationship. The reason why the turnover relationship does not hold up seems to be due to motivational differences.[18] Persons with strong economic motivation tend to seek

[13] Knowles, M. C. A longitudinal study of labour turnover. *Personnel Pract. Bull.,* 1965, *21,* 6–17.

[14] Hulin, C. L. Effects of changes in job satisfaction levels on employee turnover. *J. appl. Psychol.,* 1968, *52,* 122–126.

[15] Talacci, S. Organizational size, individual attitudes and behavior: an empirical study. Doctoral dissertation, University of Chicago, 1959.

[16] Kilbridge, M. D. Turnover, absence, and transfer rate as indicators of employee dissatisfaction. *Indust. Labor Relat. Rev.,* 1961, *15,* 21–32.

[17] Porter, L. W., and Lawler, E. E. III. *Managerial attitudes and performance.* Homewood, Ill.: Dorsey-Irwin, 1968.

[18] Ingham, G. K. *Size of industrial organization and worker behavior.* London: Cambridge University Press, 1970.

employment where the pay is high and thus find themselves working in large organizations where the relationships are impersonal. Thus, the economic choice
causes them to sacrifice job satisfaction, which reflects itself in absenteeism but not
turnover. In contrast, persons who are motivated by interpersonal relationships seek
employment in small companies where relationships are more informal. They sacrifice wages for greater job satisfaction and hence have lower absenteeism.

Insofar as employees have a choice in the job they hold or the company they
work for, the reason for the choice made may differ from one individual to another.
Studies of turnover must therefore be regarded as trends based on average differences. Since no individual fits the average, too much reliance on statistical differences
can lead to misunderstanding the individual.

Discovering Employee Needs

Various Purposes a Job May Serve

Although it is desirable to relate certain general factors such as intelligence and
wages to turnover, the importance of making a job fit the personal needs of the
individual should not be overlooked. A job may serve any one of a number of purposes, depending upon the individual. Four general classifications of these purposes
are discussed briefly.

1. *Temporary arrangement during period of transition.* Women awaiting marriage, young men expecting a draft call, young married women supplementing their
husbands' incomes, students on vacation, and people waiting for a better job provide
examples of this kind of job interest. Although many of these temporary employees
(and they usually do not say they are temporary when they seek regular jobs) may
be exploring vocational possibilities while employed, most have a major interest in
wages.

2. *Trial-and-error exploration of jobs.* One way of learning about jobs and companies is to hold a variety of jobs. Young men perhaps make up most of this exploratory group of employees. Usually they are not dependent upon the job for a
livelihood but can fall back on the family for help, and as a consequence their major
interest is not wages. Some expect to try out several jobs before deciding; others
become interested and remain with a company to become part of the group of stable
employees.

3. *Security and permanent occupation.* Many men and women of all ages enter
occupations as seriously as they enter marriage. They have given the matter a good
deal of thought and have taken a job they believe they can endure if not enjoy. They
are a stable group of employees who will undergo a good deal of dissatisfaction
before quitting. Most of their need-satisfactions are outside the company and the
job is a means to these ends.

4. *Stepping-stone to career.* College graduates and others with high levels of
aspiration accept positions with the understanding that they must start at lower
positions and work up to the top ones. They have their sights on the higher positions
and experience progress as they move up the ladder. For such employees the job is a
central part of their lives and they depend upon job success for happiness.

Clearly, the purposes that a job may serve will influence turnover in different ways. To expect all employees to respond to the same incentives and working conditions is unrealistic. There are many conditions that reduce turnover, but they are not cumulative: any one may be adequate if applied to the right person.

Transient Employees

Employees who take a job as a temporary condition will select jobs primarily for their pay rates, and there is little the company can do to prevent these employees from quitting. If this type of turnover is to be reduced, the place to do it is in the employment office. In one study the expression of interest in going to college was associated with clerical workers who stayed on the job three months or less.[19] Skilled interviews and the previous employment record can do much to detect the transient worker. In a pharmaceutical firm, a study of applications showed turnover-prone women to have a higher number of previous jobs than stable employees. By properly weighting the items in an application form, turnover can be significantly reduced.[20]

The short-term employee need not, however, be an undesirable one. Frequently such employees offer a high degree of skill or training in a specialized field of knowledge. Spouses of college students are a source of such employees in a university community because they have a temporary economic need or have time on their hands. High school students often help reduce the extra load created by summer vacations, some married women work as part-time employees or as substitute teachers, and retired men sometimes are called back for special assignments. The problem of transients is created primarily because the company does not know which employees are temporary. Employment interviews must not make permanence a condition of employment if deception in this matter is to be avoided.

Fitting Employees to Jobs

If employees are told what to expect on the job and if supervisors and employment interviewers know the job requirements, much of the shopping around for jobs can be eliminated. In an investigation in which a clerical aptitude test and an interest questionnaire were given along with an intelligence test, prediction of turnover was greatly improved.[21] The inclusion of an interview in which biographical background factors and job interests were explored added further relevant data.

Failure to have the essential qualifications to do the job is readily recognized by employees and they are likely to quit even before they give themselves a fair chance. Such employees can easily be mistaken for transients. In lens inspection, for example, certain visual skills are essential to good job performance. To explore the relationship between turnover and visual requirements, employees were given tests to

[19] Kriedt, P. H., and Gadel, M. S. Prediction of turnover among clerical workers. *J. appl. Psychol.*, 1953, *37*, 338–340.

[20] Scholl, C. E., Jr., and Bellows, R. M. A method for reducing employee turnover. *Personnel*, 1952, *29*, 234–236; Green, F. W. Use of the application blank can help reduce turnover. *Hospitals*, 1969, *43*, 62–67.

[21] Kriedt and Gadel, *op. cit.*

determine whether or not they had the adequate visual skills for the job.[22] It was found that of those having adequate skills, 43 per cent belonged to the employee group that had been on the job eight months or more, but of those lacking the adequate skills only 4 per cent had as much as eight months service. As a matter of fact, most of the employees lacking visual skills left the company in less than four months.

Employees who failed to make the production standard also were found to quit their jobs more readily than successful ones.[23] Those making just below standard experienced failure more acutely and showed a higher rate of quitting than those making well below standard. The experience of failure, rather than failure as such, seemed to be the determining influence.

Reducing Experiences of Failure

Proper selection and placement are obvious answers to turnover caused by job failure, but it must also be recognized that incompetence is not the only cause of an experience of failure. Below-average performance and fear of being a failure are common experiences in any new undertaking. Beginners cannot compete with experienced operators, and although the supervisor does not expect top performance from them and often makes adequate allowances, the new employees usually are not aware of the degree of understanding extended to them.

One approach to dealing with experiences of failure among beginners is to have a job training program. It is the general experience of the telephone industry that the use of training classes reduces the anxiety of new employees. This benefit occurs because (*a*) the standards for learners are obviously different from those of experienced workers and apply equally to all members of the class, and (*b*) a coach is constantly present to give the badly needed attention and encouragement a learner requires.

Some research in Sweden with telephone operators demonstrates the value of training supervisors to take responsibility in getting new employees adjusted to their jobs.[24] When supervisors took the initiative for following the progress and development of new employees, and saw to it that they were kept informed of the reasons behind rules and regulations, an improved relationship between employees and supervisors developed. Employees so treated saw their supervisors as helpers rather than as critics; consequently they went to them with their problems, accepted service monitoring, increased their production, and accepted responsibility on the job more quickly than others. In one company employees were given training away from the job before being placed in the actual situation. As a result of this preliminary training, terminations during the first 30 days dropped to 6 per cent as compared to 13 per cent terminating when the employees were "broken in on the floor."[25]

[22] Kephart, N. C. Visual skills and labor turnover. *J. appl. Psychol.*, 1948, *32*, 51–55.
[23] Coch, L., and French, J. R. P., Jr. Overcoming resistance to change. *Hum. Relat.*, 1948, *1*, 512–532.
[24] Westerlund, G. *Group leadership: A field experiment.* Stockholm: Nordisk Rotogravyer, 1952.
[25] Lawshe, C. H., Jr. Eight ways to check the value of a training program. *Factory Mgt. and Maintenance*, 1945, *105*, 117–120.

Poor job aptitude is only one source of a failure experience on a new job. Employees who are new to a unit, be they beginners or transfers from another group, must make a social adjustment and become accepted by their new associates. Since job satisfaction is influenced by the satisfaction of needs, acceptance by one's peers becomes vital. Having an older employee assigned to help new employees get acquainted during the first week or two can reduce some of the experience of social failure. Supervisors should be aware of problems new employees face in making social adjustments.

Problems of Stable Employees

A large proportion of employees remain with one company, and this group is often forgotten in studies of labor turnover. Although high turnover is related to dissatisfaction, employees who remain with a job are not necessarily satisfied. As already pointed out family responsibility decreases turnover. However, this type of influence does not make for job satisfaction. Company retirement plans and even wage inducements similarly reduce turnover without increasing job satisfaction. How many of the stable employees stay with their companies because they are really satisfied, and how many are afraid to make the break? Security may be an undesirable influence if it causes employees to remain on jobs that give them no satisfaction. Both employee and employer lose by such an arrangement. Since there is a good group of stable employees, it is important to find ways to motivate and interest them. Chapters 6, 13, and 14 contain much that is relevant.

Long-term employees also should be studied from the point of view of their interests. Interests change over a period of years, and job transfers as well as opportunities to help employees develop along new lines should be explored. A study of the changes in interests after employees had been on the job a number of years revealed that many were showing an interest in other kinds of jobs.[26] This shift in interest is a first sign of dissatisfaction, which eventually leads to turnover in the less timid employees. Most companies have a diversity of jobs and are able to satisfy a variety of interests if they are aware of them in their employees.

Ambitious Employees and Delegation

Higher-level employees often view working for a company as the process of progressing from one job to a higher one. Such employees see the company rather than a specific job as the source of satisfaction, and they tend to be permanent employees because previous achievement in the company is usually a prerequisite to higher positions.

Under such conditions people are motivated to find ways of speeding up the progression schedule. This frequently leads to behaviors such as discrediting associates who are seen as competitors, trying to make good impressions on superiors, and joining the "right" clubs. Although competence and job performance should be

[26] Herzberg, F., and Russell, D. The effects of experience and change of job interest on the Kuder Preference Record. *J. appl. Psychol.*, 1953, *37*, 478–481.

the determining factors in promotions, one often finds ambitious employees completely overlooking these as the means for getting ahead. The fact that methods of questionable relevance and ethics continue to be practiced by persons who want to be promoted suggests that these methods may be successful and that managements can be effectively deceived.[27] If this practice is to be discouraged, management must find better ways of recognizing merit. The problem of measuring merit was discussed in Chapter 8, and other aspects will be discussed in Chapter 20. At the present time a good deal of attention is being given to the problem of executive training and development, indicating that top management too is aware of deficiencies in the present methods of promoting through the ranks.

Employees who successfully use false values to obtain advancement, discourage conscientious accomplishment and job interest in others. In order to derive true job satisfaction, an employee must experience accomplishment within the job itself. This means that the objectives of the job, not what the job will do for the person, must become the central interest of the employee. Frequently the promise of promotion is used as an inducement to employees, but this too detracts from an interest in the intrinsic nature of the present job.

Stimulating job interest not only requires that the known principles of motivation be more effectively applied, but also demands that supervisors make it a practice to discuss with each of their subordinates what they hope to get from their jobs. Supervisors will better understand the behavior of employees if they know how the employees see their jobs. These job discussions should cover (*a*) ways for improving the job, (*b*) methods for making work more satisfying, (*c*) opportunities for growing on the job, (*d*) suggestions for overcoming difficulties of communication, and (*e*) better delegation of responsibility. Within certain limitations, each job can be modified to some extent to suit the needs of the persons holding it. There is no reason why a predecessor should determine the complete job description, but it is natural for this to occur because a person often supervises an employee holding his old job. People differ greatly in the amount of responsibility they like and the amount of pressure they can stand. Frequently it is easier to change assignments somewhat (always with the participation of those involved) than to try to find the person who completely suits the job.

Engineers and Scientists

The number of engineers and scientists employed in industry has shown a marked increase in recent years and this trend is likely to continue. Many of these specialists eventually move into top management positions where they have little opportunity for scientific achievement. Questionnaires designed to measure various interests show engineers to be positively oriented toward the concrete and to thinking along scientific lines, while being negatively oriented toward dealing with people or expressing ideas. However, engineers who have progressed to higher management

[27] Odiorne, G. S. Maverickism—a new business value? *Michigan Bus. Rev.*, 1960, *12*, 2, 15–19.

positions have broader interests, including those of literary and artistic natures. A study of engineers who left a company within two years after employment shows that some had interest patterns similar to those of the engineers in higher management.[28] Thus a portion of the engineers who leave a company may be the very ones who would derive satisfaction if they had greater opportunities to perform management functions. If such people are needed, adequate procedures for selecting them are not enough; ways to keep them should be found.

Studies of engineers and scientists working in industry have found them unique in the extent to which they derive satisfaction from solving problems, creating, and innovating.[29] They also resist regimentation, resent close supervision, and expect more freedom of movement. If they are promoted to supervisory positions they lose their former opportunity for individual scientific achievement and must find satisfaction in interpersonal accomplishments since they now must work *through* people. This means they must undergo a change in their expectancies as they advance in an organization. They find themselves in a conflict situation because, in most organizations, advancement lies along managerial lines.

Management training programs, which develop executive skills in dealing with people, may solve the problem in part by whetting the engineer's appetite for management problems and by opening doors for other forms of innovation. Additional possibilities lie in creating promotional opportunities of a nonsupervisory nature. Job complexity is not merely a measure of how many people report to a given organizational level. The need for invention, new products, and new ideas may be more acute than the need for supervisory talent. If technical creativity is an asset for an organization it would be unfortunate to remove scientists from the work they love in order to show them recognition. There is a need to change the concept of job grades so that engineers and scientists can be promoted through ranks and, in this manner, recognize their contribution.

Since persons with specialized training have different expectancies and interests, they often are isolated and limited in their friendships. A study of college recruits entering a three-year program of training revealed that when peer groups of three or more had opportunities to interact by being placed in the same department, their turnover rate was significantly below that of dyads and isolates.[30] When three or more trainees were assigned to the same department, 90 per cent of 70 such persons were still with the company three years later, as compared to 45 per cent out of 84 for dyads and 51 per cent out of 126 for isolates. The effect of this opportunity for peer-group interaction on turnover exceeded that of scholastic performance, although more trainees receiving low grades left the firm than did those whose scores fell above the median.

[28] Boyd, J. B. Interests of engineers related to turnover, selection and management. *J. appl. Psychol.*, 1961, *45*, 143–149.

[29] Herzberg, F., Mausner, B., and Snyderman, B. B. *The motivation to work.* New York: Wiley, 1959; Danielson, L. E. *Characteristics of engineers and scientists.* Ann Arbor, Mich.: University of Michigan, Bureau of Industrial Relations, 1960; Dunnette, M. D. A note on the criterion. *J. appl. Psychol.*, 1963, *47*, 251–254; Pelz, *op. cit.*

[30] Evan, W. M. Peer group interaction and organizational socialization: a study of employee turnover. *Amer. Sociol. Rev.*, 1963, *28*, 436–448.

Working Women

A survey of work experience made by the U.S. Bureau of the Census shows that females have been most often employed in positions which involve (1) performance of tasks usually included in traditional housewifery, (2) little hazard and light physical labor, (3) skillful use of hands and fingers, (4) routine and patience, (5) social or cultural orientations, (6) care or training of young children, and (7) sex appeal.[31]

Historically, the approach to working women has been one which emphasized the temporary nature of their employment, and the high rate of turnover among young women employees has frequently been cited as reason for not promoting women to more responsible positions (positions of authority). Young women have been recruited in large numbers to perform highly necessary tasks in which they play an auxiliary or decision-implementing rather than a decision-making role. For many of these young women, the fact that their diplomacy, patience, and alertness would do little to assure future advancement has been made tolerable by the fact that their jobs provided a pleasant interlude between school and marriage, were a means of enabling their husbands to complete college degrees, or resulted in immediate savings. Despite the boring nature of their jobs and the limited opportunities for advancement, women tended to remain keen and unembittered because they viewed their positions as temporary.[32]

However, the role of the woman is undergoing a change. Table 19.2 shows the percentage of women in various age groups who were employed in 1970. The number exceeds 40 per cent for all age groups, up to 65 years. Furthermore, 38 per cent of the labor force were women, 41 per cent of these being married (husband present).[33]

Table 19.2 / Women Workers by Age Group (1970)

Age	Percentage of Women in Labor Force
16–19	44
20–24	58
25–34	45
35–44	51
45–54	54
55–64	43
65–	10

From U.S. Dept. of Labor, Employment Standards Administration, Washington, D.C.: Women's Bureau, 1971.

[31] Bogue, D. J. *The population of the United States.* New York: Free Press, 1959, p. 453.
[32] Gellerman, S. W. *Motivation and productivity.* New York: American Management Assn., 1963, pp. 206–208.
[33] *Handbook on Women Workers, 1971.* U.S. Dept. of Labor, Employment Standards Administration, Washington, D.C.: Women's Bureau, 1971.

Among the working women who are married,[34] turnover may be closely related to changes in the location of the husband's job. The fact that working wives often have excessively long workweeks, sometimes extending to 84 hours in the case of women with one or more children,[35] may also account for some absenteeism and job terminations. Certainly the home responsibilities of the working woman (married or unmarried) traditionally exceed those of the working man.

Men's jobs are ordinarily believed to be of greater importance to a family than are those held by women so that their job locations are given priority. However, among highly educated couples, the choice of firm and of geographical location may be determined on the basis of the career opportunities afforded both husband and wife. Knowledge about the needs of female as compared to male employees, and of married as compared to unmarried males and females, would also help employers. Such information would give firm basis for similar treatment where it would be most effective, and for differential treatment where needed or desired.[36]

If the trend for married women to work is to continue, some basic social and organizational changes in policy are required. Child care centers will be needed to deal with families with children, maternity leaves will have to become company policy, and ways of relieving women of a large share of the housework and family responsibilities will have to be found. The development of child care centers seems not to pose serious obstacles although some may question its effect on the mental health of the children and who should bear the cost of the facilities.

Leaves of absence create no serious problems in some occupations such as teaching, but can the job of an executive be turned over to a substitute? Many mothers would like to have several years away from the job while the children are young. Can a business guarantee an employee that her job will be available when she is ready to return? If not, she may have difficulty in locating a job that is as good as the one she left.

The problem of relieving the woman of home responsibilities can be solved in a number of ways. Husbands can share these responsibilities, which will require the changing of some male attitudes. Shorter work days and work weeks for women or for both sexes may supply some relief, and this trend is encouraging. The ideal solution is increased, inexpensive, and competent domestic help, but this solution is most improbable. The supply of such help is declining and the immigration of help is not likely to be encouraged. Some relief is evidenced by companies supplying cleaning services that have work crews do the job, but this is expensive and most impersonal. Home designs that permit easy cleaning and efficient kitchens will help some, while packaged foods may supply some further relief.

34 Fleming, T. J. The world of women at work. *This Week,* Feb. 9, 1964, 2, 4–5.

35 Girard, A. Le budget-temps de la femme marieé dans les agglomerations urbaines. *Population,* 1958, *13,* 591–618.

36 Bardwick, J. M. *Psychology of women.* New York: Harper & Row, 1971; Maier, N. R. F. Male versus female discussion leaders. *Personnel Psychol.,* 1970, *23,* 455–461; Maier, N. R. F., and Sashkin, M. The contribution of a union steward vs. a time-study man in introducing change: Role and sex effects. *Personnel Psychol.,* 1971, *24,* 221–238; Sashkin, M., and Maier, N. R. F., Sex effects in delegation. *Personnel Psychol.,* 1971, *24,* 471–476.

Scheduling family life also becomes complicated because work schedules of husband and wife may differ. This becomes acute on days off and vacations. How much consideration can companies be expected to extend employees so that families can vacation together?

It appears we are on the brink of some revolutionary changes in family living if, and when, male and female employees are given equal treatment. Basic changes in company policies as well as in the attitudes of males, females, and children will accompany this revolution.

Dealing with Personalized Needs

Although employees may be classified according to their view of a job, these classifications are for convenience only and each employee must be viewed in terms of his own set of needs and values. Satisfaction with one's lot in life does not require that all needs be satisfied, but the satisfactions must approach each individual's expectations.

In order to learn about employee needs, the supervisor must be a good listener and he must be willing to discuss ways for dealing with individual situations and individual problems. Running an office with general rules and practices may prevent grievances but it also excludes the proper consideration of important individual needs. The possibilities of group decision, discussed in Chapter 6, and of counseling, which will be discussed in Chapter 20, should be examined in this connection.

In Chapter 5 the influence of supervisors' behavior on morale was discussed in detail. The leader behavior called "consideration" was mentioned as one of the indices used to measure supervisory traits. Fleishman and Harris classified 57 foremen into low, medium, and high "consideration" categories and compared the turnover in their work groups.[37] The turnover rate of groups whose foremen were classified as showing low consideration was about three times as high as for the other two classes of foremen. Groups that had high turnover also had high grievance rates.

Discharging Employees

Its Limitations for Upgrading the Work Force

Although many employees can readily leave one company for another, it has become difficult for companies to discharge unsatisfactory employees. To support a case for discharge it is often essential to have (1) a permanent merit rating record of the employee (to rule out a charge of discrimination), (2) memoranda indicating attempts to correct the employee's faults, (3) a copy of a final warning, and (4) a letter of discharge stating the reason for the action. Although criticisms and warnings are frequently ineffective procedures for correcting a poor performer, they are prerequisites instituted to safeguard against arbitrary action. Many compa-

[37] Fleishman, E. A., and Harris, E. F. Patterns of leadership behavior related to employee grievances and turnover. *Personnel Psychol.*, 1962, *15*, 43–56.

nies do not permit a discharge to be made by the immediate superior, but require that it be handled by a department head or the personnel director. In actual practice today, discharges of rank-and-file employees are rare and the reasons given are more likely to be character and personality traits (such as dishonesty, lack of cooperation, excessive absences) than incompetence.[38] Because of these complications, the risk of grievances, and desire for improved labor relations, discharge ceases to be a practical method for upgrading personnel. This means that the initial selection of employees, and other methods to improve the working staff, grow in importance as methods for upgrading the quality of employees.

Lateral Transfer as Alternative to Discharge

Supervisors usually still have the authority to transfer employees out of their units. Although this procedure involves the cooperation of other persons it remains a method for dealing with employees who are unsatisfactory because of poor job placement. One supervisor is rarely willing to accept another's unsatisfactory employee, but mutual interests can be established as supervisors find ways to exchange their misfits. The author has found this a practical approach in several departments of companies willing to experiment.

Capitalizing on the Probationary Period

Another opportunity for screening employees lies in the effective use of a probationary period. Most companies have a six-month probationary period and, even though union pressure usually attempts to reduce this period, the opportunity to be selective during this time is ample. Regardless of the length of the probationary period, it should be used to appraise the employee's potential competence. Supervisors often tend to be overly generous in their appraisals of new employees because they are reluctant to give an evaluation that leads to discharge. Biases in the direction of generosity must be carefully explored and the considered judgment of several persons should be utilized so that none feels he is the hatchet man. Observation of performance on the job over a period of a few months can serve as a good indication of an employee's aptitude for learning the job and of social and personal adjustment. These are traits the person brings to the job. Inadequacies of aptitude and personality are difficult to correct. Some of the undesirable traits are developed after the employee is hired or are acquired in the work climate. They cannot be detected beforehand and should be corrected by improving the work environment and the supervision.

Deficiencies acquired after employment due to off-the-job problems, aging, and altered job demands are responsibilities that companies may be expected to assume, as they have assumed responsibility for hospitalization and retirement.

Some rare employees put on their best behavior during the probationary period and, once secure, revert to their true selves. The appearance of such behavior indicates that the employee is capable of both forms of behavior; thus satisfactory

---

[38] Scott, W. D., Clothier, R. C., and Spriegel, W. R. *Personnel management* (6th ed.), New York: McGraw-Hill, 1961.

behavior is within his control. This being the case, the problem for management is one of finding the motivation that induces the satisfactory behavior.

Is Discharge Cruel?

Discharge of an employee, even when considered judgment indicates it the best solution, is often postponed. Executives do not like to dismiss a long-term employee even if he is unable to cover the job. It is important to face this reality rather than continue to delay action and live in a state of indecision and frustration.[39] If the employee cannot perform the job and if the supervisor who has the responsibility of discharging him is unable to accept and execute this decision, other alternatives must be generated. Postponing a decision may appear generous but the subordinate may actually be as unhappy with the situation as the supervisor.

Assuming that lateral transfers are out of the question, what alternatives remain? We assume that a lesser job with reduced pay would be unacceptable and are concerned about the employee's reaction. Demotion without reduction in pay is sometimes used, but it creates problems with other employees doing the same work. Paying the employee at a lower rate and, at the same time paying an additional benefit payment from a personnel or retirement fund, set aside for this purpose, might be more acceptable to the department heads who must pass on exceptional pay rates.[40] Another alternative is liberal severance pay.[41]

Often an employee's inability to perform a job does not reflect a deficiency in the person but arises and becomes apparent because the job has increased in complexity. When an employee cannot grow as fast as the job, a problem is created by growth or technical advances in the company. To blame a person for not growing as fast as the company amounts to holding the employee responsible for changes in the company. It has become a fairly common practice (resulting from union pressure) to assure rank-and-file employees that improvements in production methods will not jeopardize their jobs. This guarantee is essential to gain cooperation from labor. Employees whose jobs have grown too fast for them are entitled to similar assurance, and when the situation is viewed in this manner they are not incompetent, rather it is the company's problem to relocate them or be ready to compensate them for their loss.

Problem-Solving Interviews

Each discharge situation tends to have its unique aspects so that specific rules do not apply. The supervisor knows his own situation, but does he know the situation from the employee's point of view? The employee may know the job has grown beyond him and may welcome a lesser job. He may have the problem of saving face with other employees or at home. He may have ideas about things he can do and he may

---

[39] Randall, C. When to fire him. *Atlantic Mon.,* 1963, *211* (1), 58–60.
[40] Maier, N. R. F. How to get rid of an unwanted employee. *Personnel Admin.,* 1965, *28,* 25–27.
[41] Big steel strives to thin its ranks. *Business Week,* Aug. 25, 1962, *1721,* 106, 108.

welcome a recommendation for a less demanding job elsewhere. To some, severance pay would be welcome; to others, it would be degrading. What are a person's opportunities when discharged? The answers to these and many other questions are relevant to solving the problem, and the needs of both company and individual must be explored before a solution acceptable to both can be found. Problem-solving, as a method for resolving differences, has already been touched upon in Chapter 6 and will be again approached from the point of view of the interview situation in Chapters 20 and 22.

The Exit Interview

When managers discharge employees they seldom give the whole or even the true reason. The objective is to give a reason that sounds plausible or one that they can defend. This is also true when an employee leaves the company. The reasons given are not always dependable facts.

On the one hand, some employees may not wish to appear critical of a supervisor, so they fabricate a plausible reason for quitting, such as a better offer, when actually they have accepted the same position in another company. Others may blame the job or the supervisor for their leaving when the real dissatisfaction is inability to cope with the responsibilities. On the other hand, the interviewer should not assume that just because an employee wishes to leave the company he is dissatisfied. An attractive offer or a desire to live elsewhere may have motivated the decision. Continued probing can become a source of irritation, while failure to explore feelings can be interpreted as disinterest. In addition to good public relations the objective of the exit interview is to use it as an opportunity to communicate and learn, to explore alternatives, and to solve any problems of mutual interest. Skills in permissive listening, understanding, and sensitivity to feelings are needed. These contrast with the more common practice of trying to persuade others to change their minds or attempting to get them to understand our position.

A skilled interviewer can learn a great deal about the company and about employees from the exit interview. In many instances employees will change their minds and decide to remain with the company. In other instances, job changes, supervisory adjustments, or corrections of misunderstanding may make it possible to retain a good employee. The role-playing exercises at the end of this chapter and that of Chapter 18 furnish opportunities to practice and develop the interviewer's ability to handle situations arising in the exit interview. The outcome in these cases is largely dependent on the interviewer's skill. If the cases are not role played they should be read in this connection to reveal how different the situation looks from the employee's and the interviewer's points of view.

If an undesirable employee is leaving, listening skills also are relevant. Retaining the employee may no longer be an objective, but the public relations objective can be the same. The exit interview can be of real assistance to the employee by helping him analyze his job difficulties and to seek a job more suitable to his interests and ability. Giving advice is likely to be a waste of time, but listening to a person helps him face reality.

Laboratory Exercise _____

Role Playing: The Personnel Interview[42]

(Students are asked not to read the case materials before participating in the laboratory exercise.)

A. General preparation.
  1. The instructor will select three persons to participate in this case.
  2. One person will play the part of Robert Welch, personnel director of the company. He leaves the room to study his role (G.4).
     CAUTION: He is to read *only* his own role.
  3. The instructor will read aloud the "Setting of the Case (G.1) to the class as a whole, including the two participants who will play the parts of Ken Hardy and Walt Henderson.
  4. The person who is to be Walt Henderson takes a seat at a table placed in front of the room. He is to assume that he is working at a drafting board. A copy of the dialogue (G.2) should be placed in front of him.
  5. Ken Hardy is also supplied with a copy of the dialogue.

B. Reading the dialogue.
  1. Ken Hardy approaches Walt from behind and begins reading the dialogue.
  2. Proceed through the complete dialogue.
  3. When the scene is completed, Ken Hardy resumes his place in the class.
  4. Walt leaves the room to study the material "Additional Information for Walt Henderson" (G.3).

C. Preparing for role-playing.
  1. The instructor asks the person who was given the role of Robert Welch to return and take a seat at the table.
  2. The instructor places another chair at the table and informs the class that Robert Welch is in his office and will shortly conduct an interview with an employee of the company who has asked to see him on an "urgent matter."

D. Role playing the scene between Mr. Welch and Walt.
  1. The instructor asks Walt to return and indicates that Mr. Welch is in his office and can see him now.
  2. Role playing proceeds to a natural termination point.
  3. Role players might agree to have another interview later on, or an interview between Hardy and Welch; or the single interview might end the incident, with Walt deciding either to quit or to forget his problem.

[42] Case taken from N. R. F. Maier, Dramatized case material as a springboard for role playing. *Group Psychother.*, 1953, 6, 30–42. Materials reproduced with permission of Beacon House Inc., publisher, and J. L. Moreno, editor.

E. Subsequent role-playing scenes.

1. Interviews or problems growing out of the first interview should be role played by assuming the time set for them has arrived.

2. If Ken Hardy becomes a participant in role playing, he should be instructed to assume he has not witnessed the first role-playing interview.

F. Discussion questions.

1. Did the interview between Welch and Walt influence Walt's final decision? Discuss.

2. Did Welch learn anything that was relevant in the initial interview? Discuss in detail.

3. Did Walt really have another offer or was he bluffing? Did Welch learn the facts?

4. What did Walt need as a concession to make him remain with the company? Was this concession unreasonable?

5. Should Welch consult Hardy about any commitments he makes to Walt? If he did consult Hardy, did he antagonize him by assuming more authority than he had? Discuss.

6. What are the face-saving problems in the case?

7. If time permits, other class members may try out some of their ideas by taking any of the parts and role playing a brief scene with the appropriate person.

G. Materials for the case.

1. SETTING OF THE CASE

The work place is a drawing table in a large drafting room of the Wilson Construction Company. There are 30 draftsmen in the office and two supervisors. Walt Henderson, a draftsman, is working busily as his supervisor, Ken Hardy, comes by. It is 10 o'clock Tuesday morning.

2. DIALOGUE

KEN: How's the work going, Walt?

WALT: Fine. All caught up.

KEN: Even that set of specifications of Joe's that I gave you to check yesterday?

WALT: Yep. Took it home and worked on it there so I wouldn't be too rushed today.

KEN: Well, now, I don't want you to have to be taking work home, Walt. I didn't know you were going to do that or I'd have asked Fred to help Joe out on it instead.

WALT: Oh! That's O.K. I didn't mind doing it. I knew Joe was going to have a rough time getting it all done by noon today, anyway.

KEN: What are you working on now?

WALT: Some plans for that little boat I told you I was going to build.

KEN: I see. Think you should be doing that on company time, Walt?

WALT: Well, I don't know. I've done all my own work and put in three hours of my own time last night to help Joe out. And besides I don't have my own equipment at home to do this drafting. What's the harm in it?

KEN: It just looks bad to be doing something like that on company time. You know that as well as I do.

WALT: Well, when I have all my work done and more, what does the company expect me to do—twiddle my thumbs?

KEN: Now let's not get hasty. We went through all this last year when you got both of us on the hot seat with Johnson over that garage of yours that you drew up here. Remember?

WALT: Sure, I remember. And I still don't think it's anybody's business what I work on here so long as my own work is done and I don't bother anybody else.

KEN: That's what you think. Now let's get this straight. Nobody's telling you what to do before or after office hours, but when you're here drawing pay you're supposed to be earning it. And I don't want another mess like the one we had on that garage of yours. Understand?

WALT: Yes, but I don't see why we have to set up such rigid rules. Just because Johnson doesn't know how much work I turn out is no reason why you should take your cue from him.

KEN: Look, Walt, I'm not taking my cue from him. I didn't like the idea of you doing your own work here either, but I decided to let it pass. Then when the chief caught you at it and you didn't have the good judgment to be a bit more careful—well, you've just got the wrong attitude.

WALT: How can you say that? You know perfectly well I turn out more work for the company than anyone else. Is it my fault if you can't keep me busy?

KEN: Walt, I know you're a top-notch draftsman, but a good employee is something more than that.

WALT: Yeh—a good employee is a yes-man.

KEN: Not at all. A good employee works well with others. He's got to follow rules so that he doesn't set a bad precedent. Suppose the others brought their own work down here?

WALT: Well, make them do their job first.

KEN: How can I if they say I let you work on your personal things?

WALT: But I do company work at home and more than make up the time.

KEN: Walt, am I supposed to let you choose when and where you do company work? What a mess that would make if I had to keep track of everyone's homework. Anyway we've never asked you to do work at home. When we have more to do than you can handle during working hours we'll pay you overtime.

WALT: Ken, I'm not asking for overtime. All I want is to be treated as an honest person. I've never gypped the company out of anything and whenever the company is behind schedule I've worked like the devil to help out. Now I've got a personal problem and all I'm asking is to borrow some of the facilities. Is that unreasonable?

KEN: I can see your side, Walt, but we can't give favors to some and not to others.

I've just got to make a rule, and remember you've forced me into it. There will be no more personal work done during company hours. I'll let you finish this job, but that will have to be the end. I am not going to have the others say I play favorites. Sorry, but that's it.

3. Additional Information for Walt Henderson

Walt was disturbed by this conversation. At noon he called his friend Bill Alden, who told him they had an opening in the drafting department in his company (Jones Bros., Inc.). Walt asked him to check up on details. That afternoon Bill's boss, Mr. Hansen, called Walt and told him he was very anxious to have Walt come to work for Jones Bros. He told Walt that he would take him on Bill's recommendation and the salary he quoted was five dollars a week more than Walt was getting. From his description, the work seemed about the same as Walt was now doing. When Walt expressed interest Hansen asked him if he could start next week. That would be next Monday. Since Jones Bros. had another applicant for the job, he asked Walt if he could let him know right away. Walt asked if he could have until Wednesday morning so as to have time to talk it over with his wife. Hansen said that would be O.K. He suggested that Walt give the Wilson Company a good excuse for quitting so suddenly because he wanted to stay on good terms with the Wilson Company.

After this talk Walt thought a bit and decided it would be nice to work in Bill's office. They had often compared companies, and although Walt had sometimes thought of making a change he could find little difference between the companies. Since he had eight years with the Wilson Company he had some seniority and retirement benefits. Now he had a reason for quitting. He knew his wife would go along with any decision. The important thing to do now was to go to the personnel office and let the company know about his decision. Walt therefore called Robert Welch of the Personnel Department and asked to see him on an urgent matter. Welch asked him to come right down.

4. Role for Robert Welch

You are head of the Personnel Department of the Wilson Construction Company. Your department does all the hiring, and must O.K. all recommendations for changes in pay rates. You have the authority to turn down recommended increases and to make changes in job classifications and are in a position to influence personnel policy. Your door is open to employees who want to discuss company matters or even their own personal problems. You or your staff interview all employees who leave the company.

Walt Henderson of the drafting department has just called you and wants to see you on "an urgent matter." You've asked him to come right down. Just to prepare yourself on factual matters you have looked up his record. He works for Ken Hardy, a drafting department supervisor, whom you regard highly, and Ken has given him a very good rating. The record shows Walt Henderson to be a top-notch draftsman who turns out a lot of work. He has eight years with the company, which is about average for the drafting room. Walt Henderson is married and has a four-year-old daughter. As his hobbies he has listed fishing and sailing. The door opens and Walt Henderson walks in.

Suggested Readings

Calhoon, R. P. *Managing personnel.* New York: Harper, 1963.

Gaudet, F. J. *The literature on labor turnover: A classified bibliography.* New York: Industrial Relations News, 1960.

Gaudet, F. J. *Labor turnover: Calculation and cost.* New York: American Management Assn., 1960, AMA Res. Study No. 39.

Longgood, B., and Wallace, E. *The pink slip.* New York: McGraw-Hill, 1959.

Palmer, G., *et al. The reluctant job changer.* Philadelphia: University of Pennsylvania Press, 1962.

Turnover and Job Satisfaction, Washington, D. C.: Bureau of National Affairs, Inc., 1970.

20

Counseling, Interviewing, and Job Contacts

Counseling and Interpersonal Relations

Problems in Misunderstanding

We have already considered many of the principles and skills essential to success in dealing with people. Chapter 3 discussed misunderstandings arising between employees and supervisors because of differences in attitudes, emphasizing the importance of discovering the attitude of the other person in order to communicate effectively. The importance of helping the frustrated person release feeling was emphasized in Chapter 4. There we saw that constructive and cooperative behavior could result only from removal of interference of frustration-produced behaviors. But even with frustrating conditions corrected, effective motivation was not assured. To understand how to deal with differences in employees it is necessary to understand their needs—particularly their acquired needs. The importance of discovering needs and of finding positive rather than negative incentives was described in Chapters 13 and 14. It seems that regardless of whether we are faced with attitude problems, frustrated employees, or motivation difficulties—and any of these would introduce communication problems—the remedy lies in the same direction. A supervisor who sees difficulties with people as problems to solve and who wants to understand the employee's situation will utilize the employee as a source of information. This means the supervisor must become adept at drawing the other person out. In any conversation the person who talks the most is the one who learns the least about the other person. The good supervisor therefore must become a good listener.

Although most dealings with people do not involve unpleasantnesses or misunderstandings, instances that do occur are sufficiently disturbing to cause management personnel to become interested in some of the basic counseling skills. Among groups of supervisors there is general acceptance of the statement that about 10 per

530

cent of the employees are problems. Meltzer[1] reports that the adjustment problems found in industry include almost the whole array of behaviors found in the clinic.

Many so-called "problem employees" are known to higher management, which means that a single problem employee is discussed at several levels of management. This inclusion of higher management in discussions about employees involves the use of expensive time. One president of a large company spent over half an hour describing a problem his company had with an elevator operator. To know all the details, he must have been in close touch with the matter over a period of months.

Certain valuable byproducts of counseling skills brighten the picture by helping to compensate supervisors for time spent in counseling activities. Ordinarily, misunderstandings come to one's attention when they become acute. However, a supervisor who has counseling skills may use them to prevent subsequent problems or minor disturbances that merely depress morale. Anything that can be done to make good conditions better or to reduce the number of temporary dissatisfactions and disappointments represents a gain. In interviewing a cross section of over 100 male and female employees, this writer found that more than 85 per cent indicated there were times when they would welcome an opportunity to speak their minds and complain about something. However, only a scattered few individuals said they ever discussed personal problems with anyone who was their superior, and an even smaller number felt free to speak up and criticize at all.

The Selection of Safe Skills

Some of the important skills for dealing with emotionally disturbed people have been developed in clinics and counseling centers. Many of these skills may be carried out of the original settings and practiced in industry. The most extensive application to industry of a clinically sound method was described in the classic Hawthorne study.[2] However, any clinical or therapeutic procedures which are to be practiced or used by laymen must be foolproof. Sometimes a little knowledge is dangerous; sometimes a little knowledge is better than no knowledge. The principles that are to be practiced by supervisors must be above criticism. Fortunately the researches of Carl Rogers[3] and his students[4] have supplied procedures, which, if practiced by skilled persons, seem to be as good as any known alternatives, and if practiced with minimum skill, at least permit supervisors to do no worse than they would have done before training.

---

[1] Meltzer, H. Frustration, expectation and production in industry. *Amer. J. Orthopsychiat.*, 1945, *15*, 329–343; Meltzer, H. Mental health realities in work situations. *Amer. J. Orthopsychiat.*, 1963, *33*, 562–565.

[2] Roethlisberger, F. J., and Dickson, W. J. *Management and the worker.* Cambridge, Mass.: Harvard University Press, 1939; Roethlisberger, F. J. *Management and morale.* Cambridge, Mass.: Harvard University Press, 1941.

[3] Rogers, C. R. *Counseling and psychotherapy.* Boston: Houghton Mifflin, 1942; and *Client-centered therapy.* Boston: Houghton Mifflin, 1951.

[4] Snyder, W. U. *Casebook of non-directive counseling.* Boston: Houghton Mifflin, 1947; Axline, Virginia M. *Play therapy.* Boston: Houghton Mifflin, 1947.

The Nature of Nondirective Counseling

This counseling approach which lends itself to human relations practices in industry is known as nondirective counseling and also as client-centered counseling. The method differs from the common sense view of counseling, as well as from some other counseling practices, in that no diagnosis is made, no solution to a problem is supplied, and no advice is given. Rather, the counselor stimulates the client to discover his problem himself and to decide his own course of action. A person is more likely to act upon a solution he works out himself because it is acceptable to him. This approach to counseling is called *nondirective* because the counselor does not direct the client with counsel or advice at any stage. It is called *client-centered* because the client, not the counselor, determines what will be discussed, and interest centers on the client's feelings rather than on a diagnosis. Giving advice, asking questions, making a diagnosis, and supplying the solution characterize the directive approach.

In actual practice many of the skills used by directive and nondirective counselors are much alike, and a counselor can subscribe to a point of view part way between purely directive and purely nondirective counseling. Nevertheless, it is important to differentiate between the two approaches and objectives in order to be able best to see the applications to industry. A counselor may stimulate a client to talk about himself either because he wishes to make a diagnosis or because he wants the client to discover and understand himself. The nondirective approach avoids the need for making a diagnosis and also avoids all the possible dangers associated with either making wrong diagnoses or suggesting action considered suitable to solving the client's problem.[5]

Nondirective Skills

Active Listening

Philosophers in the past have spoken of the wisdom of listening, but the development and refinement of listening as a clinical tool is relatively recent. Listening means more than refraining from speaking. A listener must show by his behavior that he is trying to understand, that he accepts the person as well as what he says. For a counselor or a listener to indicate doubt, surprise, disagreement, or criticism places him in the role of a judge or critic; for him to express agreement, pity, or even sympathy, places him in the role of a supporter. As a judge he stimulates defensive behavior; as a supporter he stimulates dependent behavior.

[5] Hunt, W. A. Diagnosis and non-directive therapy. *J. clin. Psychol,* 1948, *4*, 232–236; Patterson, C. H. Is psychotherapy dependent on diagnosis? *Amer. Psychologist,* 1948, *3*, 155–159; Rogers, C. R. Significant aspects of client-centered therapy. *Amer. Psychologist,* 1946, *1*, 415–422; Hart, J. T., and Tomlinson, T. M. (Eds.). *New directions in client-centered therapy.* Boston: Houghton Mifflin, 1970; Rogers, C. R. A theory of therapy, personality, and interpersonal relationships as developed in the client-centered framework. In S. Koch (Ed.), *Psychology: A study of a science* (Vol. 3). New York: McGraw-Hill, 1959.

The active listener's behavior includes a posture indicative of attention, a friendly facial expression, patience, and acceptance of pauses. Certain vocal expressions may rightly be included under listening. These include expressions such as "Uh-huh," "I see," "I understand," and "Do you want to tell me about that?" Even if the counselor is directly asked to express an opinion, he can avoid entering into a discussion by saying, "Would you like to tell me how you feel about it?" or "I think it is best for you to tell me about it."

Accepting Feelings

When a person expresses hostile feelings he may be told by a supervisor that he is reacting unjustly. He may feel that he is being judged and rejected so that he becomes defensive and attempts to justify himself. If a supervisor gives advice he is likely to give it before he understands the person's true problem, and hence the advice may be inappropriate and unacceptable. Hostile and childish feelings may require more than permissive listening and can be accepted and verbalized by the counseling supervisor without either agreeing or disagreeing with them. Examples of such verbal acceptance of feelings are given below:

"You must have been very upset to have walked out of his office like that."
"I can see that your feelings were hurt badly by that incident."
"I can see you were badly upset by my criticism of the job you did."

Such statements indicate sensitivity to feelings and avoid evaluation of them. If expressed in time they may prevent defensive behavior or, in many instances, confrontation. When the listener feels he is being attacked it is difficult to avoid retaliation, but a verbal acceptance of the feeling can prevent the situation from deteriorating. Ginott[6] gives many examples of how arguments between parents and children can be avoided by accepting feelings.

Acceptance should not be confused with agreement or approval. Ginott[7] points out "a physician does not reject a patient because he bleeds. Though unpleasant such behavior is tolerated; it is neither encouraged nor welcomed. It is merely accepted."

Reflecting Feelings

Although listening and accepting feelings are easy to describe, they are difficult to execute. Ordinarily, communication is a give-and-take interaction in which persons exchange views. Evaluation by agreeing or disagreeing characterizes such exchanges. Counselors are asked to inhibit these natural tendencies by listening and being sensitive to feelings and carefully avoiding an act of judgment.

In Chapter 12 it was shown that it was easier to give up a habit if a new one was substituted for the old than if the old one was just broken off. This principle of learning suggests that counseling skills should permit the replacement of advice-

[6] Ginott, H. G. *Between parent and child.* New York: Macmillan, 1965.
[7] Ginott, H. G. *Between parent and teenagers.* New York: Macmillan, 1969, p. 32.

giving responses with some *useful* kind of verbal response. The method of responding to feelings by restating or *reflecting* them effectively satisfies this requirement. Since substituting one response for another is easier than withholding a response, training in reflecting another person's feelings should be introduced at an early stage.

Reflecting feelings seems awkward at first but supplements the benefits of listening and at the same time makes it necessary for the counselor to speak. However, in order to reflect feelings properly a counselor must listen carefully and selectively. Selective listening means paying attention to certain things in a speech. In a debate or argument one listens selectively to his opponent and pays strict attention to see if he violates facts or expresses inconsistencies. An opponent attacks what is said, not what is meant. A counselor, however, pays attention to feelings while factual material is allowed to fall into the background. Inconsistencies indicate to the counselor the need for clarification through further expression. Because of this rationale, the technique of reflecting feelings is also known as "empathically understanding the client."

The method of reflecting feelings is analogous to the counselor or interviewer serving as a *selective* mirror. The counselor mirrors or restates some parts of the conversation and allows other parts to pass (Figure 20.1). Facts, incidents, justifications, details of arguments and reasons, the chronology and geography of events are relatively unimportant; but how the person feels about any of these things *is* important. These feelings must be reflected so they can be seen and viewed in a different setting. Seeing oneself in a home movie gives one an objective look at one's body, and what is seen sometimes comes as a surprise. The counselor helps a person get a more objective view of his feelings by restating them in different words.

Figure 20.1 / The Counselor Serves as a Selective Mirror. A disturbed person may say many things (solid-line arrow) to a counselor. The counselor responds by allowing factual content to pass (broken-line arrow on right) but reacts to feelings by summarizing and restating them (broken-line arrow on left).

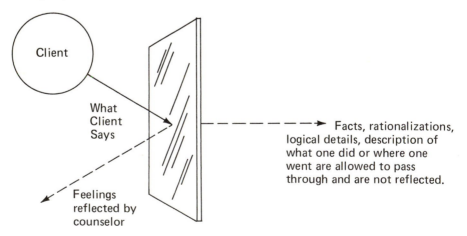

An angry employee may say, "There is no reason why this promotion should not have been given to me. I've been with this company a long time, I've never taken advantage of sickness benefits, I work hard, and I certainly could use the extra money more than the fellow who got the job." An appropriate reflecting remark of a supervisor would be, "You feel that you were not treated fairly considering all you've done for the company." Any disputing or recounting of points in the argument given by the employee would violate the method of reflecting feelings since these are factual items or refer to things outside the person. An individual who tells his life's story on a bus is not receiving nondirective counseling from a listener because events rather than feelings are being expressed. But if the listener responds to feelings rather than to events, such an encounter can become a counseling interview.

In learning to reflect feelings the following points should be observed:

1. Restate the other person's expressed feelings in your own words rather than mimic or parrot.

2. Preface reflected remarks, at first, with "You feel . . . ," "You think . . . ," "It seems to you that . . . ," "It sometimes appears to you that . . . ," and so on. Later in the interview you can dispense with such prefatory phrases.

3. Formulate reflected remarks as statements, not as questions. Speak quietly, slowly, and without emotional tone.

4. Wait out pauses. Long pauses often enable a person to say things that are hard to say. Inexperienced interviewers often are embarrassed by pauses and make distracting remarks to fill them.

5. When many feelings are expressed, as in a long speech, only the last feeling area expressed should be reflected. (Confusion about many things is one feeling area, but feeling immature and hating one's mother are two feeling areas, and only the last should be reflected.)

6. Only feelings actually expressed should be reflected. It may be apparent that a person distrusts another, but distrust should not be reflected unless and until it is explicitly stated. A couselor who diagnoses or anticipates may injure the counseling relationship. Skilled counselors sometimes *lead*, in that they reflect feelings just a little ahead of those expressed, but unless this leading is accurately and skillfully done it hinders the relationship and may frighten the client.

7. When a person contradicts himself, saying on one occasion that he can't understand why someone did something, and on another, that he knows why the person acted as he did, one should reflect each opinion when it is expressed and proceed as if no inconsistency were stated. Such changes in expression indicate progress and a clarification of feeling.

8. If a person cries during an interview, references to the act may be made in reflecting remarks, provided the person is not attempting to hide the tears.

9. Watch for mixed feelings involving a conflict between (1) what the person wants to do and feels he should do; (2) what others think and what he thinks; and (3) his values and those of society. These ambivalent feelings should be reflected.

10. Decisions, solutions, and constructive ideas may be reflected when they predominate over feelings of confusion, hostility, fear, insecurity, rejection, and the like. The unskilled counselor is likely to overevaluate these and reflect them before a person is ready to act upon his own suggested possibilities. Searching behavior reveals many possible actions, and a counselor must not try to hasten the decision process.

11. In reflecting another's state of mind, any indication of approval or disapproval should be avoided. It is important to refrain from questioning, probing, blaming, interpreting, giving advice, persuading, reassuring, and giving sympathy.

12. Diagnoses should be avoided. A diagnosis is a counselor's interpretation of why the disturbed person feels as he does and leads to biased listening.

13. It is almost safe to assume that what initially appears to be the problem is not the real one.

14. Avoid being solution-minded. Remember that the solution must come as a result of the person's own insight.

The method of reflecting feelings helps and supplements listening, but it introduces two additional values. First, it gives the counselor a way to pass the conversation back to the client when expected to give some kind of reaction or judgment. Even a direct question, such as "What would you do if you were in my place?" can be reflected by "You feel you would like me to tell you what to do?" Second, the method stimulates further expression in the general feeling area reflected. Many of the everyday benefits of listening are never realized because the expression stops short of the important and more complete release of feeling.

Table 20.1 contains statements taken from case material, with four responses by a counselor or supervisor given in the right-hand column. The reader can test his skill by attempting to select the best reflecting response before checking against the answers.[8]

The Use of Questions

The unskilled counselor should avoid using questions as much as possible. Questions tend to direct the conversation, and put a disturbed individual at a disadvantage because usually he either doesn't know answers or he doesn't feel free to give them. The district attorney, in questioning a suspect, directs the discussion, disregards feelings and instead attempts to catch him in factual inconsistencies. This procedure, therefore, has a different objective than counseling.

Questions that are in the spirit of nondirective counseling may serve a convenient and helpful function, however. Questions such as "Would you like to tell me about it?" "Did that bother you a lot?" and "How did that make you feel?" stimulate further expression in a feeling area under examination. Such questions neither pry nor direct the course of the discussion. Care must be taken to avoid questions that can be answered by "Yes" or "No."[9]

[8] Matarazzo, R. G., Phillips, J. S., Wiens, A. N., and Saslow, G. Learning the art of interviewing: A study of what beginning students do and their pattern of change. *Psychotherapy: Theory, Research, and Practice,* 1965, *2,* 49–60.

[9] Erickson, C. E. *The counseling interview.* Englewood Cliffs, N.J.: Prentice-Hall, 1950.

Table 20.1 / Examples of Good and Poor Reflected Responses

Remark	Select Best Response to Reflect
1. The client has been on a new crew for three months. During a counseling interview he said: "I don't know why it is, but I just don't feel as though I'm one of the gang. They are all nice enough fellows, but somehow they seem to have a closed circle and make me feel like an outsider. Maybe it's me; I don't know."	(a) Why don't you use the first chance you get to do the boys a favor? (b) It seems to you that the group doesn't accept you. (c) It seems that the others dislike you for some reason. (d) You don't think they will accept you if you give them some more time to learn that you are a nice fellow.
2. Client is a twenty-year-old male. He states, "God, I hate my ma. She tries to run my life for me. I feel almost as strongly about my dad. He just sits back and lets her run everything, and never protests."	(a) You feel the father should be stronger than the mother. (b) You resent your mother for being too strong, and your father for being too weak. (c) You feel guilty because you can't accept the idea that you hate your parents. (d) Getting away from home for a while would relieve the immediate tension and give you a chance to work out this problem.
3. A clerical employee with ten years' experience told his supervisor: "I've been doing this job for years now and nobody had ever complained and now you send my work back and tell me to do it over. It isn't fair and it doesn't make sense. Maybe I do make mistakes now and then, but nobody is perfect and I don't know why I should get all the blame for what goes on around here."	(a) It isn't fair to ask you to correct your own mistakes. (b) Suppose you check your work before you bring it to me. (c) You think you are being blamed for not being perfect. (d) You feel that I am too strict.
4. The following statement was made by a patient during a counseling session: "There is nothing wrong with me. I only came to see you because my doctor insisted upon it."	(a) That may be true, but shall we wait and see? (b) You are resentful about coming here. (c) You really don't want to be here. (d) What do you think was his reason for sending you here?
5. During an interview with his supervisor, a member of a crew states: "I don't want to work with Jake any more. He's lazy and is always taking a superior attitude and complains about the rest of us not helping him as much as we should. He thinks he is too good for this kind of work and too good to work with the rest of us and I'm sick of being around him."	(a) You feel that Jake ought to be disciplined in some way. (b) Jake doesn't want to cooperate, is that it? (c) Jake's attitude makes the work unpleasant. (d) You think Jake might fit in better somewhere else.
6. A young man whose work showed a sudden drop in quality was sent to the employment manager for an interview. One of the things he said on arriving was: "I don't know why I should be asked to talk to you about my work. I haven't complained and I haven't time for	(a) You came to see me because you were sent and not because you feel any need for help. (b) Don't you feel that with my experience in the company I might be of some help?

(continued on the next page)

Remark	Select Best Response to Reflect
this kind of chit-chat. So give me what help you have in mind and I'll be on my way."	(c) You feel irritated for coming here because you don't think I can help you. (d) You mustn't jump to conclusions. Often people need help when they are unaware of this need.
7. Man — age fifty-nine: "I couldn't let my son help me now that I'm down and out. I've got that shred of pride left — because you see I remember when he was a kid and I didn't turn my hand to help him. I traipsed around the country — his mother died when the kid was born — and I let the relatives push him around and stuck him in foster homes — and now — it certainly was like a knife stuck in me when we met the other day and he said, 'We can make a go of it together, Dad — I've got a little money saved up.' No — No — I won't let him do it. I will clear out of here. It'll be hard — but — I haven't done one thing for him — or anyone else for that matter."	(a) What was your married life like? Had you and your wife planned for a child? (b) Have you thought what it will mean to your son if you don't let him do this thing which he wants to do for you? (c) I see what you mean. You feel that you don't deserve the help he wants to give because in the past you did nothing to earn it. And your statement that you never have done anything for anyone else makes it look as if it might be a real problem for you to accept responsibility for helping others, and to accept help from others. (d) Your behavior in the past makes you unworthy of the help your son wants to give you now, is that what you mean?
8. In the middle of a counseling interview with her boss, a fifty-eight-year-old woman said, "You don't want me here, you just want young women. I'm getting old so I guess I should get out."	(a) It's not true that I favor the young women employees. (b) You believe I'd like to have you leave because of your age. (c) You feel you have reason to believe that I prefer young girls. (d) I can see that I must have done something to hurt your feelings.
9. A supervisor was discussing the work of a young man about a year out of high school. The supervisor was trying to determine why important details on procedure were often overlooked or clearly violated. Suddenly the young man shouted "You're the worst supervisor I've ever had. If a person shows initiative you work him over. I refuse to follow silly rules."	(a) Why don't you check with me before you make a change in procedure. (b) You resent me for criticizing your work. (c) Perhaps it's my fault that I didn't train you on the correct procedures. (d) You feel I should have someone else go over your work.
10. In a counseling interview a young woman talked at length about her husband's lack of consideration, going into considerable detail to justify why she should divorce him. After a pause she remarked that she never had long term relationships with anyone. "Other people seem to have old friends, but I get tired of them after I get to know them. Maybe I expect too much of people."	(a) You feel a divorce may be the solution to your problem. (b) You think perhaps you should reconsider your divorce. (c) After you get to know people they cease to be interesting. (d) It seems now that expecting too much of friends may interfere with long term relationships.

11. Man — age forty-one: "I've been married four times and each time I've thought, 'Boy, this is the real thing!' None of them has ever been like this girl. She's the most beautiful girl you ever saw — and dance! And she dresses like a million dollars. She's out of this world!"

   (a) You're really enthusiastic about her.
   (b) How does she compare with your other wives? How did you feel about them before you married?
   (c) If she's anything like you seem to feel she is, she must be quite a catch. Maybe this time you'll stick.
   (d) Doesn't it strike you as odd that every time you've felt the same way?

12. Man — age thirty-five: "I'm determined to get ahead. I'm not afraid of hard work. I am not afraid to take a few hard knocks — if I can see my goal out there in front. And I'm not adverse to climbing over a few people — who get in my way — because this means a lot to me. I can't be satisfied with just a mediocre job. No, I want to be somebody."

   (a) You feel that you just have to be out on top no matter what you may do to others.
   (b) You see yourself as a deeply ambitious person, is that it?
   (c) What do you suppose is behind this strong determination of yours to get ahead?
   (d) Strong ambition can be a real asset to any man. Are you really sure, though, that you mean it when you say you're not adverse to climbing over those who get in your way? Couldn't that turn out to do you more harm than good?

13. Man — age twenty-nine: "I keep remembering how I walked out on Mary and the two kids. Five years ago — the law never caught up with me — I thought I was pretty smart — but now — God, but I was a heel. I don't see how I could do it. And I'm so ashamed I can't look people in the eye. Now I can't find her — not a trace. Her relatives won't tell me where she is. I don't blame them — but how could I have done it? Just because it was tough going. I tell you, I'll never have any self-respect. Never! And I — I don't know what to do — or how I can try to rectify my big mistake. I don't know —!"

   (a) There are a number of things you might do to try to find her. You could list her as a missing person and get police help. You could get a private detective agency to handle it for you. You might even be able to get a court order that would force the relatives to give her address.
   (b) When did you decide that you wanted her back? Tell me the circumstances.
   (c) The hopelessness there seems pretty clearly connected with the feelings of guilt.
   (d) As you see it then, your past behavior is just plain unforgivable.

14. A secretary began to cry when asked whether or not she had finished typing a first draft of a speech the personnel director was preparing and said: "Everything I do is wrong. I just can't do anything to please you. I don't mind when you criticize me to my face but when you start writing me up as if I were a case — a good joke — well, I just can't take it." (Assume that the speech included a humorous anecdote about a secretary.)

   (a) There is no reference to you as a person in that speech.
   (b) You feel I criticize you too publicly.
   (c) I'll be glad to take that out, but aren't you being a bit sensitive?
   (d) You feel I'm making fun of you in that story.

Correct responses: 1-b, 2-b, 3-c, 4-c, 5-c, 6-a, 7-d, 8-b, 9-b, 10-d, 11-a, 12-a, 13-d, 14-d.

When the counseling process has reached the stage of exploring various behavior possibilities, questions may be used to explore consequences. Such questions as "What do you think would happen if you did that?" "How would that affect the others?" and "Do you feel you could eventually adjust to that?" cause the person not only to evaluate actions but also the consequences of actions. Note, however, that none of the questions indicate approval or disapproval; they merely explore whether or not the consequences of various actions have been considered.

Essential Attitudes

The counselor's attitude toward a client will influence the skill with which he practices his methods. If he likes and respects another person he can do a better job of listening and reflecting feelings than if he dislikes or feels superior to this person. In nondirective counseling certain attitudes, beliefs, and values are consistent with and supportive of the methods. Fortunately these same attitudes also are consistent with the leadership skills discussed in Chapter 6. This means that training in counseling will improve a person's conference leadership and vice versa.

The following values, beliefs, and attitudes toward people are consistent with the development of skill in nondirective counseling.

1. A belief that the individual is basically responsible for himself and a willingness to let him keep that responsibility.

2. A belief that a person is capable of solving his problems once interfering obstacles are removed and that every person basically wants to do the right thing.

3. An appreciation of the fact that every solution to life's problems must conform with a person's values and beliefs, and that each individual knows his own feelings and aspirations better than an outsider.

4. The development of an acceptant attitude because a person will bring out his true feelings only when he feels confident that he will be understood and not judged. A permissive atmosphere is necessary if a person is to express absurd, unconventional, contradictory, and hateful feelings.

5. Two kinds of acceptance are involved: (*a*) acceptance of the disturbed person as a worthy individual whose problems merit attention; and (*b*) acceptance of what is said as important and of interest. Because a disturbed individual often feels that he doesn't belong, is outside the pale, or is different, it is especially important that the counselor be able to show an attitude of acceptance. Thoughts and feelings expressed must also be accepted if they are to stimulate the expression of even more guarded and deep-seated feelings.

6. A profound respect for the importance of feelings in learning to live a full life. In most of life's situations people are asked to justify or give reasons for their opinions. Innocent remarks such as "I don't like that person," "I don't feel comfortable there," or even "I don't like olives" are met with the question "Why?" and unless a person can supply good reasons he is judged as biased or not too bright. Since feelings are so often misunderstood, they frequently are withheld. The counselor must respect the dignity of feelings, no matter how unreasonable they at first appear, if he is to help another person express them.

Experience in listening and in reflecting feelings will assist in the development of the attitudes and beliefs described above, and these states of mind will assist in refining the skills. Training in listening, in reflecting feelings, and in the essential attitudes should be carried on simultaneously, and is perhaps best accomplished by role-playing procedures. If training results in an attitude change there is sound reason to expect a basic change in behavior. Castle[10] has shown that the human relations training of supervisors that produced a change in attitude resulted in an improvement in their behavior.

Accomplishments of Counseling

Attitudes and Needs Are Discovered

The importance of preventing misunderstandings as well as correcting them has been emphasized throughout this book. One can have more satisfactory dealings with employees if one knows why an employee turned down a particular promotion; why another showed resentment when an unwanted job was not offered; what is behind the lack of cooperation between two otherwise good employees; why certain employees violate company rules; or why a change in work procedure is resisted by a certain individual. One's moral judgment of a person who takes advantage of another person changes when one discovers that the person injured was perceived as an enemy. Nondirective counseling skills provide a way for recognizing and dealing with misunderstandings caused by differences in attitudes and needs even when the question of therapy is not raised. Not only does the nondirective interviewer better understand an employee but the employee better understands himself. A person's own attitudes and needs may be vague and confusing until they are expressed. The mere telling of a complex experience clarifies it by showing up hitherto unperceived defects, inconsistencies, and gaps in continuity.

Because the nondirective approach to people respects attitudes and needs as well as clarifies them, sincerity and skill in its use become important assets for many interview and face-to-face situations. Furthermore, the basic skills are essential to conference leadership where permissive climates are prerequisites to constructive participation.

Frustrated Condition Is Reduced

Any procedure which permits expression of hostile and regressive behavior without introducing unfavorable experiences reduces tensions and relieves frustration. The process of obtaining relief from emotional tension through the mere expression of feeling (such as talking out loud about a deeply felt problem) is known as *catharsis*. Supervisors who understand the process of frustration, and who can furnish a climate in which employees can gain relief from frustration, will be able to deal with many types of emotional behavior problems. Some of the situations may be passing affairs

[10] Castle, P. F. C. The evaluation of human relations training for supervisors. *Occup. Psychol.*, London, 1952, *26*, 191–205.

and relief is all that is needed;[11] others may continue and so the relief will be merely temporary. However, even temporary relief may be sufficient to introduce some problem-solving behavior and create opportunities for readjustment.

Many frustrations go back to childhood experiences. Memories of unjust punishment or parental rejection may be vague and seemingly forgotten, but their emotional effects remain strong and color adult reactions to marriage, reprimand, men of superior rank, or failure. If these pockets of feeling are located and the childish hostilities are expressed, marked changes in meanings may occur and behaviors can become more mature. A state of frustration common to a whole group may be released through "gripe sessions." In this instance the discussion leader uses his permissive skills and his ability to reflect feelings in a way that will stimulate further expression in a group discussion.

True Problem is Located and Accepted

Whatever a disturbed person describes as the problem can usually be assumed to be incorrect. The cause of an emotional maladjustment must be distinguished from the alleged reason, which is likely to be a justification.

In a state of frustration people are inclined to blame others, insist that there is nothing they can do, doubt the worthwhileness of life, and generally bemoan their misfortune. But regardless of how unfortunate persons may be, they must come face-to-face with the present. If they are to achieve an adjustment each must ask "What can *I* do about it?" Suppose a young man, through no fault of his own, has lost an arm. Quite naturally he feels that his problem is the loss of an arm and that there is nothing to do about it. An artificial arm is a poor solution. As he sees it, his problem is insoluble. Before problem-solving behavior can occur, one must be confronted with a soluble problem. Strictly speaking, the loss of an arm is an obstacle rather than a problem. Problem solving is the search for a way to circumvent, remove, or overcome an obstacle that is blocking progress toward some goal. This goal must be a part of any description of a true problem. If our young man's goal is to live a happy life, then his problem becomes, "How can I get the most out of life with what limbs and abilities I have?"

Accepting reality—including one's deficiencies, injuries, and bad luck—is the first prerequisite to solving life's problems. As long as people blame others, hide weaknesses (e.g., poor hearing), or faults, they have not located the difficulty in a way that permits them to solve the problem. Looking backward, thinking of what might have been, and wishing are important feelings; and they must be expressed so that they do not stand in the way of discovering the soluble problem.

Only as persons obtain relief from frustration are they able to focus on their true problems. Until then they are too preoccupied with feelings to be able to see a problem. If anyone points out how they should constructively view their situations,

---

[11] Roethlisberger and Dickson, *op. cit.;* Maier, N. R. F. *Frustration.* New York: McGraw-Hill, 1949. Reissued Ann Arbor, Mich.: University of Michigan Press, 1961. Maier, N. R. F. Frustration theory: Restatement and extension. *Psychol. Rev.,* 1956, 63, 370–388.

they are unable to accept the counsel and instead may feel more than ever that they are in an unsympathetic world. Until persons are ready to *accept* their problems they are unable to see them, and from the good advice given to them they merely learn that no one understands.

When an individual seeks consolation or pity he is not accepting his true problem; rather, he wants others to join him in his misery. Because pity comforts rather than stimulates problem-solving behavior, it is as important for the counselor to avoid giving pity as it is to avoid criticizing.

Problem Solving Is Stimulated

Problem solving behavior is characterized by exploratory or searching activity and a ready recognition of existing realities. Various routes or approaches to goals must be examined and evaluated before the best decision is reached. Listening and reflecting ideas helps this process because it stimulates the flow of ideas. A person will persist in an idea if it is challenged, but when the idea is accepted and reflected he has to go beyond it. Furthermore, the restatement of an idea in other words enriches it, encourages new meanings, and stimulates examination of different approaches.

Once a difficulty is recognized as a problem, questions may serve a useful purpose. One can increase the range of a person's or a group's thinking by asking good questions. A question can take a person out of a rut in thinking, cause exploration of various ideas, stimulate evaluation of good and bad features of various alternatives, and generate an interest in or a search for facts without imposing, evaluating, or suggesting.

Responsibility Is Developed

People who have difficulty coping wih life's problems often are dependent persons. They look to someone to get them out of one difficulty after another. Frequently, the background reveals parents who have always made all the decisions. Such individuals have been denied the opportunity to become emotionally mature; even if a counselor or friend gave them good advice and even if they took it, the basic problem—that of immaturity—would not have been solved. Nondirective counseling, from the outset, makes no pretense of solving clients' problems. Instead, they are told that they must decide and do what they think best. The role of the counselor is that of helping persons to help themselves.

Nothing creates a sense of responsibility as quickly as having responsibility. This principle is basic to group decision and basic to the success of nondirective counseling. The couselor gives individuals responsibility for solving their own problems, even for returning for other visits. If a client asks, "Do you want me to come again?" the counselor may reply, "That is up to you. If you feel that you would like to come again the time is yours." Clients who have been requested to visit a counselor and show resentment on their first visit usually return voluntarily.[12]

[12] Rogers, C. R. *Counseling and psychotherapy, op. cit.*

Solutions Fit Personal Value System

When persons can be induced to solve their own problems, the solutions conform with their personal sets of value. Solutions supplied by other persons overlook individual differences in values. If persons act on decisions that are contrary to their value systems they often develop guilt feelings and these may become more serious than the original problem. Examples of decisions which may conflict with some systems of values and not with others are given below.

1. A pregnant woman who doesn't want a child has an abortion.
2. A boy participates in vandalism under social pressure.
3. A superior discharges a long-term employee because he can't adequately cover the job.
4. An employee dishonestly collects sickness benefits when he knows other employees get away with it.
5. Parents place their feeble-minded child in a state institution.

Whether or not decisions of this type create future problems cannot be judged by the facts alone. Only persons whose value systems do not conflict with the actions can avoid subsequent feelings of guilt.

The Counselor as an Expert[13]

Once persons have rid themselves of feelings that interfere with solving problems, they often are in a position to solve them. However, the counselor or supervisor often has useful knowledge. The very information or relevant facts that may be avoided because they are threatening to a disturbed person become realities that must be faced in the problem-solving stage. The counselor should be willing to assist a client in obtaining information that can help in solving problems and making decisions.

In supplying information the following precautions should be observed by a counselor.

1. Do not try to change a disturbed person's feelings by supplying information to prove him wrong. Understanding is needed instead.

2. Do not supply information to sell your point of view. Remember that attitudes select facts.

3. Do not avoid giving facts when the person *really* wants them. People often desire knowledge and information to solve problems or even out of curiosity. The nondirective approach can irritate a problem solver. (Distinguish between requests for information that are based on curiosity and those that are wishes for assurance.)

---

[13] Bordin, E. S. *Psychological counseling* (rev. ed.) New York: Appleton. 1968: Fenlason, A. F., Ferguson, G. B. and Abrahamson, A. C. *Essentials in interviewing.* New York: Harper, 1962; Patterson, C. H. Counseling: Self-clarification and the helping relationship. In H. Borow, *Man in a world at work,* Boston: Houghton Mifflin, 1964; Barrett-Lennard, G. T. Dimensions of therapist response as causal factors in therapeutic change. *Psychol. Monogr.,* 1962, *76,* 562, 7; Moos, R. H., and Clemes, S. R. Multi-variate study of the patient-therapist system. *J. consult. Psychol.,* 1967, *31,* 295–303.

4. Do not supply overwhelming amounts of information as a lecturer or teacher. Get feedback on how it is received and whether or not it is welcome. The feeding-in of information should be a two-way process.

Counselors play dual roles: on the one hand, they facilitate the client's expression of feeling (to deal with frustration); on the other hand, they aid in the problem-solving process (to develop constructive action). Students who don't know what courses to take often are advised by the counselor. The skilled counselor will explore whether the indecision is due to fears, conflicts, and pressures from home, or whether they need knowledge about professional alternatives. Information on courses should be supplied only when the student is ready to explore alternative choices realistically.

Some Practical Considerations in Counseling

Number and Length of Interviews

If the purpose of the counseling interview is to assist a disturbed or confused person to improve his emotional adjustment, a number of interviews may be required. Such interviews should have a time limit—for example, half or three-quarters of an hour. A prearranged time for terminating an interview makes it unnecessary for the interviewer to find an excuse for breaking off a long and sometimes unprofitable session. Then, too, the spacing of interviews allows a person time to consolidate gains and grow between visits.

The actual number of visits needed varies with the problem. Surprising improvements have occurred after one interview. However, for personal off-the-job problems involving personality difficulties, a skilled counselor regards ten to 20 visits as typical. Problems not extending into a person's past require fewer visits because in these it is relatively easy to locate the disturbing factor or condition. An interviewer must not, however, assume that just because a problem points to a difficulty on a job, its true character has been located. Incidents that set off an emotional reaction must not be mistaken for causes.

Single interviews of the counseling type can and do solve some complex job problems, prevent others, and clarify still others. Some typical examples are briefly described below to illustrate the opportunities for counseling that present themselves in industry.

1. A repairman appeared unusually stubborn when he was asked to cooperate by giving up his truck and accepting a ride to his work location with another driver. He began by giving all kinds of excuses and defending his rights. Finally, he revealed that he was an epileptic—having very mild attacks or blackouts. He felt that as long as the company allowed him to drive he was normal and just as good as anyone else.

His condition had eluded detection for 20 years because he had learned to cover up. He was able to anticipate an attack, and as soon as he felt one coming on he would drive to the curb, put his head on the steering wheel, black out for a minute or less, rest a moment, and then drive on again. When someone was with him he would explain that he was taking a quick nap to get over a sleepy spell. In the interview he decided to visit the medical department. The doctor prescribed dilantin, which was a satisfactory remedy for his condition.

2. An employee had been repeatedly interviewed regarding a job change from lineman to office work. Over a period of 25 years he had received training on three different jobs but was found unable to handle them. He now insisted that he be given another opportunity because of his health. His medical report did not substantiate his claims. The supervisor responded to certain references he made to off-the-job experiences, and before long he talked freely about them. His background revealed marital difficulties and adjustment problems going back to his childhood. Although these personal problems were not solved by the interview, it became apparent to the employee as well as to the supervisor that a job change would not help him. In this instance counseling prevented further waste of interview time.

3. A young woman was in the process of leaving the company because she would not work the night shift as she had agreed to do. The personnel exit interview revealed that she could not work nights because that would leave her husband at home with her friend, whose husband worked nights. The two couples shared an apartment, and certain changes in the relationships between the couples had occurred since the time this woman had promised to work nights. The personnel office was able to arrange a different assignment for her.

4. A senior employee caused considerable trouble and talked about filing a grievance when he was bypassed in a promotion to a supervisory position. In an interview with his supervisor he revealed that he did not want the job; rather, he objected to the man who got the promotion, imagining that the young man had told the supervisor some things about the senior employee's poor hearing. Without refuting any of these charges the supervisor helped the senior employee discover that his imagination had played tricks on him—also that he ought to get the hearing aid his wife had been trying to induce him to buy for the past two years.

Time and Place

Time and place arrangements should take into account the employee's feelings. An interview should be of interest to both parties, and the employee should be invited and given a choice of times available to the interviewer. The setting for the interview should be one in which the employee can feel at home. Elegant surroundings, being seated in an open area while the interviewer is protected by a desk, distractions, interruptions—any of these make for a strained atmosphere. When suitable surroundings are not available at the plant, it is sometimes best to adjourn to the coffee shop. The president of one company wondered why he learned so much more from his division heads when he visited them in the field than when they came to his office. He failed to realize that a president's office furnishings often reflect his high position and introduce a barrier to communication. Most supervisors, however, are close enough to the men who report to them so that their offices are familiar places. If not, things should be done to make them more familiar.

Keeping Confidences

Confidences should be strictly kept. To use nondirective methods to gain information that will be used to the detriment of the employee will cost more in the long run than the immediate gain or saving warrants. Even so, the method, no matter how skillfully used, will not cause employees to give a supervisor the incriminating evidence that they give to a professional counselor or a priest. The fact that a supervisor is an authority-figure is one of the important limitations of counseling as practiced by supervisors. However, not all problems involve this limitation, and it is not necessary to confine counseling to supervisors. Rather, counseling skills make people better supervisors.

If employees do say things to supervisors that they may later regret the supervisors should show by their manners that they have not been angered. And with experience in listening they will learn not to be angry when employees tell them frankly how they feel.

On some occasions a counseling interview may disclose a problem that can be solved by making changes or by involving other people. The implementation should always be worked out in discussions with the employee to avoid any feeling that confidences have been betrayed, even when the change is to the employee's advantage.

Location of Counseling Services

The management of a company might recognize the value of counseling and wish to make the services available to its employees. How should this be done? The company could hire professional counselors and make them a part of either the medical or the personnel department, or it could train its supervisors and thereby expand the scope of their responsibility. The arguments in favor of each alternative are shown in Table 20.2.

Table 20.2 / Location of Counseling Service

Advantages to Training Supervisors	Advantages to Using Experts in Medical or Personnel Departments
1. more available to employees	1. more skillful service
2. more natural part of job relationship	2. more confidential
3. no stigma involved	3. less conflict due to other duties
4. job performance known to counselor	4. no bias due to knowledge of person's work history
5. no induction of program needed	5. no emotional involvement in the case.
6. skill acquired for counseling useful in other supervisory functions.	

Inspection of the table reveals that each approach has distinct advantages. Perhaps the greatest disadvantage in the use of expert counselors is that the service is not readily used. Only a limited number of employees seek help when the service is available in medical and personnel departments. The experience of Western Electric and the Ohio Bell Telephone Company, who pioneered in counseling programs, showed that it was rather difficult to get employees and supervisors to accept counselors. Supervisors felt threatened by the program because they felt employees could unjustly criticize them. The general experience was that acceptance of the counseling program required from one to two years. Both the pioneering companies abandoned their programs, not because they failed, but because top-management support was lacking after the initial supporters had retired.

The strongest arguments against training supervisors for counseling are limitations of skill and time. However, a limited amount of skill will assist the supervisors in dealing with superficial disturbances and it can do a great deal in helping them prevent problems. Furthermore, the basic counseling skills are prerequisites to interviewing and to handling many communication problems. Psychopaths, of course, require professional treatment.

Perhaps the ideal method is a combination of the two approaches. Training supervisors permits them to deal with some emotionally disturbed employees and at the same time gives them an understanding of the role an expert might play. If counselors and psychiatrists are available in either the medical or the personnel department, they pose no threat to supervisors, but instead become sources to which difficult cases can be referred.[14] An understanding supervisor can do a great deal to motivate an employee to visit the counselor.

Today, the trend in management training is toward increasing the amount of time and emphasis devoted to listening and to rudimentary counseling skills. Supervisors welcome this training and see it not as an increase in their work loads but as an aid in the performance of their jobs. There is also an increase in placement of psychologically trained persons in personnel departments, and a trained counselor in the department is not uncommon. The number of psychiatrists in industrial medical departments is small, and there is no indication that it is increasing.

Meltzer[15] describes opportunities for the skilled personnel man to improve the mental health of employees. These occur in various interviews he conducts (induction, appraisal, follow-up, and exit); his daily rounds; his attendance at monthly departmental meetings; safety committee meetings; his contributions to foremen's

[14] Himler, L. E. Psychiatric treatment: brief psychotherapy procedures for the industrial physician. *Intern. Med. and Surgery*, 1956, 25 (51), 232–236; Occupational rehabilitation following mental illness. *Intern. Med. and Surgery*, 1960, 29 (10), 480–483; Psychiatry in industry. *Intern. Med. and Surgery*, 1962, 31 (10), 450–452. Employment of the worker with emotional problems. *Arch. of Environmental Hlth.*, 1962. The application of psychiatry to industry. *Report of Committee on Psychiatry in Industry*. No. 20. Topeka, Kansas: Group for the Advancement of Psychiatry, 1951; Van der Veen, F. Basic elements in the process of psychotherapy: A research study. *J. consult. Psychol.*, 1967, 31, 295–303.

[15] Meltzer, H. Mental health realities in work situations. *Amer. J. Orthopsychiat.*, 1963, 33, 562–565.

meetings; his role in supervisory training problems; and his services as a counselor. Dr. Meltzer advocates a *projective* type of interviewing, in which the specific purpose of the interview is considered, and opportunity to learn about the employee is created. Details of his background, attitudes, feelings, history of frustration, and sources of pleasure and tension serve a useful purpose in providing understanding of some of his reactions that appear to be more irrational than the situation warrants. Skilled personnel in key positions can accomplish a great deal to make supervisory personnel aware of mental health problems and to create an appreciation for the types of counseling skills.

Interview Objectives

Unlike the usual face-to-face relationships between supervisors and subordinates, interviews are held off the job. Ordinarily arrangements for a time and a place are made, which makes them somewhat more formal than routine job contacts. Each interview has a purpose of its own, be it an employment interview, an appraisal interview, an exit interview, or a change of assignment. A casual visit between subordinate and superior is not called an interview, because it lacks this purpose. Job interviews differ from counseling interviews in that they are not client-centered but have an objective of their own. This does not mean, however, that the two objectives cannot be combined. Each kind of interview can be concerned with how the employee feels about a job, a transfer, development, or reasons for leaving.

Interviews have been used as fact-gathering devices and as ways to learn about another's potentialities. Their value for accomplishing these objectives is extremely limited, and frequently more confusion than clarification is accomplished by them. When objective methods (work records, birth certificates, school grades, tests, and so on) for obtaining facts are available, they should be used in preference to an interview. Memories may play tricks, the motivation of the person interviewed may be to withhold information, and the interviewer may change questions and style, thereby making comparisons between interview results unreliable. With proper precautions accuracy can be increased. In order to permit comparisons between responses of interviewees, the "standardized" interview has been developed.[16] (see pp. 226–227).

However, the interview can have a unique value and perform a useful service to all management personnel (interviewers and interviewees alike) if it is used to discover the interviewee's attitude toward some particular thing. It is this aspect of the interview that is directly related to all interpersonal relations problems and that makes use of nondirective counseling skills. When interviews conducted by psychologists were used to assess management potential, they obtained useful judgments of career motivation, dependency needs, and interpersonal skills which were correlated with management's overall assessment of the individual (which included the inter-

[16] Hovland, C. I., and Wonderlic, E. F. Prediction of industrial success from a standardized interview. *J. appl. Psychol.*, 1939, 23, 537–546; McMurry, R. N. Validating the patterned interview. *Personnel*, 1947, 23, 2–11.

view data).[17] Various judgments also were related to salary progress (period between assessment and the end of experiment). Of the 36 correlations, half were found to be statistically significant. The extent to which progress was predicted by the interview and influenced by it is not known.

Simulated situations (see Laboratory Exercise, Chapter 8) indicated that group judgments of deception in the interviewee were only slightly better than chance, but the percentage significantly increased when the group listened to the interview on a tape recorder or when they read a transcript of it.[18] Thus the presence of the interviewee reduces the accuracy of judgments. The judgments of deception seemed not to be based upon rational judgments of the interviewee's responses but were more intuitive in nature in that the responses were used to support the interviewer's judgment rather than to cause it.[19] Thus a defensive response was cited as evidence of honesty by some, and of dishonesty by others.

Basic Interviewing Principles

Establishing a Mutual Interest

People speak frankly and freely only when the situation is permissive and the interviewer is accepting and understanding. In such a situation two people can cooperate to achieve a common objective—that of solving the interviewee's problem. This working relationship makes the interviewer a helper rather than a judge.

But the fact that interviews have a purpose or objective of their own introduces some conflict. For example, in an employment interview the employment manager's objective is to screen the applicants and hire the person best suited for the job, but the applicant's objective is to be hired and to defeat the function of the screen. When people want to be judged favorably they are motivated to distort facts, cover up faults, fail to mention troubles, and even lie about age. They hide true feelings and say they don't mind working nights if this may be a job condition.

Cooperative behavior occurs when there is a *mutual interest.* In the case of job placement it is not difficult to find an interest that both parties share. Employees want jobs that will make use of their special aptitudes and training, and this is what a company may reasonably want. If this mutual or common interest is established (which it can be, providing the employee already has been hired), an employee will honestly express preferences and disclose true feelings and aspirations.

In any interview requiring cooperation, a mutual interest becomes the meeting ground for discussion. The Kinsey interviewers[20] capitalized on a general curiosity

[17] Grant, D. L., and Bray, D. W. Contributions of the interview to assessment of management potential. *J. appl. Psychol.,* 1969, *53,* 24–34.

[18] Maier, N. R. F., and Thurber, J. A. Accuracy of judgments of deception when an interview is watched, heard, and read. *Personnel Psychol.,* 1968, *21,* 23–30.

[19] Maier, N. R. F. Sensitivity to attempts at deception in an interview situation. *Personnel Psychol.,* 1966, *19,* 55–66; Maier, N. R. F., and Janzen, J. C. The reliability of reasons used in making judgments of honesty and dishonesty. *Perceptive and Motor Skills,* 1967, *25* 141–151.

[20] Kinsey, A. C., Pomeroy, W. B., and Martin, C. E. *Sexual behavior in the human male.* Philadelphia: Saunders, 1948. See also Maccoby and Maccoby, *op. cit.*

and interest in science to obtain cooperation. Some interviewers attempt to find a person's interest on matters not relevant to the interview. They talk about golf, fishing, or family in order to warm up to the task. Artificial warming-up has questionable value; not only may it be seen as a trick, but it may also keep the employee in an anxious state. The purpose of an interview should be established as soon as possible, and this purpose should be of interest to both parties. It is unwise to distort the truth in order to find a common interest. To tell employees that the company has their interests at heart is not likely to be believed, but to say that the company thinks that satisfied employees are good employees will make sense to them. Employees will feel more free to speak their minds about conditions if they can see why their opinions are of interest to the company.

Let us examine some interview problems in the light of the principle of mutual interest. Suppose a company is making extensive studies of each accident in order to improve its record of safety. If penalties for negligence are imposed, a mutual interest with employees who have been involved in accidents will be rare. In such a case the company behaves as if it wants to find someone to punish, and the employees know they want to escape punishment. If, however, the company does not desire to punish but merely to discover the causes of an accident in order to guard against future accidents, a common interest can readily be established. It then becomes possible for an employee to point out that he had been out late the night before and fell asleep on the job. Together interviewer and employee can discuss the problem of how to prevent such conditions in the future. Perhaps in hazardous work the workers should report when they haven't had enough sleep and be given a different assignment on such days. Regardless of how one wishes to view the practicality of such an approach to accidents, cooperation will improve if and when an acceptable common interest is found.

In conducting interviews concerning transfers, promotions, and demotions, one can easily locate mutual interests, and in the process of listening and reflecting feelings one can learn the nature of the problems such changes will create. Frequently reasonable adjustments, compromises, and new ideas emerge if an employee's development, utilization of his abilities, and a consideration of his aspirations are part of the interview.

An exit interview contains an obvious common interest in that a company is able to learn from people who are leaving, and interviewers can ask for suggestions on how the company can improve as a good place to work. Employees leaving the company often appreciate an opportunity to talk on this subject. As a matter of fact, between 30 to 40 per cent of the employees resigning from a certain company changed their minds and decided to remain when properly interviewed.[21] This suggests the desirability of holding exit interviews before an employee has made other commitments. Even better is to hold interviews when an employee has a complaint.

Interviews designed to inform employees (at all levels in the organization) of their evaluation or appraisal have a mutual interest if they are approached from the point of view of employee development. However, in order to accomplish growth

---

[21] McMurry, R. N. *Handling personality adjustment in industry.* New York: Harper, 1944.

and development the best approach is not the "telling" kind of interview. Rather, the employees may be asked to evaluate themselves; this can be done with a high degree of insight (often approaching a counseling-type interview) if the interviewer has received training in the nondirective approach.

When the interviewer's objective is to let the employees know where they stand, or to warn them of demotions unless radical changes in behavior are made, the supervisor is clearly functioning as a judge. With this relationship established it is more difficult to find a common interest. As a result, communication is faulty, acceptance frequently is low, and in some instances more problems are created than solved. This point will be discussed in detail later in the chapter.

The Use of Questions

Questions can direct or channel the topic of discussion. In client-centered counseling one does not wish to channel the discussion. However, since each interview has a specific purpose, questions should control the topic of discussion. A question can direct the discussion and still be open-ended as far as the exploration of feelings is concerned. Examples of such questions are:

1. "How do you feel about transferring to another district?"
2. "What are some of the problems you see in taking over this new work?"
3. "Do you see any disadvantages to this new method of operation?"
4. "What are the aspects of your job that you feel allow most opportunity for improvement?"

Open-ended questions specify the general topic, yet allow the interviewees a great deal of freedom. To the extent that the employee interviewed can select from a great range of possible reactions to a question, the interview is employee-centered and indicates an interest in him and his feelings. If the initial expressions of feelings are accepted and effectively reflected, such an interview approaches the counseling interview.

As confidence and trust grow during an interview, questions may move from the general to the specific. Examples of specific questions which will be honestly answered in a well-conducted interview are:

1. "Do you sometimes work without your safety belt?" "Under what conditions?"
2. "How many days do you think you would be absent on account of sickness if the company didn't pay for sickness?"
3. "Which employees do you feel are more qualified for supervisory positions than you are?"
4. "How many times would you say that your immediate supervisor criticized you unfairly during the past year?"
5. "Do you think that your spouse will object to the change in location more than you do?"

When mutual interests and a respect for differences in attitudes are present, a problem is frequently brought into focus. Suppose an employee feels that a transfer to another division may reduce chances for promotion because the change is into a job classification where opportunities for further progress are few. If interference with an employee's progress was not the superior's intent, the problem of how to prevent this condition is worth consideration. In this instance questions such as "Do you see any disadvantages in this transfer?" "How do the various divisions compare with respect to promotional opportunities?" would lead to more detailed analysis and perhaps an interest in fact finding. Pointing out that opportunities for progress are equally present on all jobs will carry little conviction.

Stimulating Problem Solving with Questions

Good questions direct attention to other areas and broaden the scope of thinking. Routine solutions to problems tend to appear first and discourage further searching. Problem solving can be facilitated by questions such as "Are there some other approaches?" and "Can you think of some additional possibilities?" An interviewer can play a constructive role encouraging the continuation of the problem-solving process.

Sometimes the ideas submitted by subordinates for approval are of questionable value, yet by rejecting them the superior discourages future suggestions. Instead of rejecting an idea because it has a fault, the superior might question, "How could we do that without being accused of favoritism?" or "How would that machine work in a cold climate?" Such questions pose problems for which the subordinate may have answers or they may point up the obstacles that have been overlooked. Either alternative leads to a constructive exchange rather than a rejection.

Many interviews can be upgraded by joint problem solving regarding the work situation or work relationships. Each party has information, and questions serve a useful purpose in stimulating exploratory behavior. However, the questions should not put a person on guard.

The Interview as a Whole

Problem Solving versus Tell-and-Sell and Counseling Styles

Thus far the interview has been treated in general terms with emphasis on listening and problem solving. The similarity between this *problem-solving* type of interview and the *group-decision* method is evident, and development of skills in either area will help in the other. The basic difference between the two approaches is that in the interview the supervisor deals with a person rather than a group.

The style of interview that corresponds to the autocratic style of leadership may be called the *tell-and-sell method*. In this kind of interview the supervisor has the information and the solution, which he *tells* to the interviewee. In order to get his ideas accepted he must convince the interviewee of the merits of his ideas—this constitutes the *sell* aspect of the interview. Like the autocratic style of leadership, the *tell-and-sell* interview fits traditional notions and causes no difficult training problems.

There is a place for the *tell-and-sell* style of interview. Sometimes it is the interviewer's objective to transmit information, and high acceptance of the objective is relatively unimportant. However, when acceptance, subordinate development, upward communication, or the utilization of the interviewee's ideas and initiative are desired, the problem-solving approach is recommended.

The counseling type of interview, discussed in the previous section, also has a counterpart in group processes. Group therapy methods and the T-group process (see pp. 323–324) require leaders who have nondirective counseling skills.

The interview styles also may be combined. For example, the *tell-and-listen* style of interview combines the "telling" aspect of the *tell-and-sell* method with the counseling type of interview. In practice this method has objectives similar to those of consultative management, in which the superior encourages feedback and participation but retains control of the decisions made. Thus it stops short of gaining the major benefits of participation in that it limits influence to that of making suggestions. However, it permits release of expression and some upward communication when practiced sincerely.

The *tell-and-listen* interview would be most useful in situations where the decision is beyond the interviewer's control. If an employee is discharged he must be told, but this does not preclude the desirability of listening to his feelings. Likewise a person must be told if he is doing the job poorly, but an interviewer can still listen to his reasons. Bad news of any kind requires telling, but the pain can sometimes be reduced by permitting feelings to be expressed.

Interview Situations

Space does not permit a discussion of all types of interview situations. Each has its own purposes or objectives and its pitfalls, but the various skills discussed and the relevance of the subject matter of attitudes applies to them all. In Table 20.3 the more common interview situations of interest to the manager are outlined with the specific objectives to strive for and pitfalls to guard against indicated. This table is a convenient guide for the reader in the application of the various skills to specific interview situations.

The Appraisal Interview

Conflicting Objectives

The appraisal interview has been selected for detailed treatment because it is widely used: many companies require all managers and supervisors to conduct such interviews annually.[22] Since the conduct of this interview can do harm as well as good its undesirable features should be reduced as much as possible.

A superior must assist subordinates and evaluate their performance, and thus is both a helper and a judge. The first function is acceptable to subordinates and brings

[22] Planty, E. G., and Efferson, C. A. Counseling executives after merit rating or evaluation. *Personnel,* 1951, *27,* 384–396; Rowland, V. K. *Evaluating and improving managerial performance.* New York: McGraw-Hill, 1970.

Table 20.3 / Specific Objectives and Pitfalls in Common Interview Situations

Type of Interview Situation	Specific Objectives to Strive for	Pitfalls to Guard Against
Employment	Screen applicant. Discover work attitudes. Discover interests.	Applicant is motivated to make a favorable impression. "Factual" information has limited accuracy. Personal bias and premature judgment lead to poor decisions.
Lateral Transfer	Make best use of employee's ability. Capitalize on employee's strong interests. Discover aspirations for advancement.	Employee may feel forced to accept change. (Permit choice without penalty.) Interviewee may be reluctant to mention hardship and lack of interest in new job. Employee may be afraid of failing.
Promotions	Inform employee of new opportunity. Discover aspirations. Discover attitude toward added responsibility.	Joy of good news often hides anxiety. Anxiety should be released and verbalized. Anxiety does not indicate incompetence.
Appraisal	Evaluate past job performance, not the person. Improve future job performance. Opportunity to use problem-solving approach.	Criticism produces defensive behavior. Perception of job duties and requirements may differ for employee and superior. Degree of delegation should be clarified. Employee's job problems may not be known to superior.
Problem Solving	Discover problems faced by employee. Share problems involving employee's interests. Encourage employee to be critical of old methods. Stimulate employee to reveal ideas.	Subordinates are reluctant to admit having problems. Subordinates are reluctant to disagree with superiors.
Exit	Find real cause for leaving. Determine whether decision should or can be reversed.	Employees are inclined to give reasons that are convincing or acceptable to the superior rather than the real reason. If anger is expressed and accepted, employee may feel better.

the superior in close touch with them; the second function builds a wall between them and causes subordinates to withhold information that will reflect unfavorably on themselves. As a helper the superior needs to know the weaknesses of subordinates, but the role as a judge stands in the way.

The major objectives of appraisal are wage determination, job placement, and promotion, but when the superior is required to tell the subordinate about his strengths and weaknesses, these objectives are sacrificed to a considerable degree. Telling employees how they stand often leads to unpleasant relations, and, to avoid unpleasantness, the superior becomes overly generous in appraisals, thereby destroying the accuracy of the judgments.

The objectives of the appraisal interviews differ from those of the appraisal itself. The major purposes of the interview aspect of an appraisal program are to develop subordinate performance and to let employees know where they stand. The first objective could be achieved through problem-solving interviews, but the latter requires communication of an appraisal. In the process of discussing an employee's evaluation, he may be developed, but there is also the danger that he may lose job interest and work only to avoid criticism. Thus conformity rather than initiative may be developed.

Guidelines for Appraisal Interviews

1. The superior's personal needs will influence the interview with any subordinate. For example, the treatment and appraisal of a highly satisfactory employee will differ with the following three conditions: (*a*) being one of three persons fully qualified to fill a position opening up in the department; (*b*) being the only person fully qualified to fill a position opening up; and (*c*) being fully qualified to fill higher positions but there are no prospects of any.

2. Employees are more likely to feel reprimanded than praised as a result of reports on their evaluations. Even if an employee has five strong points and only two weaknesses, more interview time will be spent on the weaknesses. This is because the favorable characteristics are not challenged. Praising a person first does not take the sting out of criticism which follows.

3. Criticism is most likely to be accepted when (a) it is constructive, (that is, indicates what to do rather than what is wrong); (b) the subordinate feels the superior is more competent than he is; (c) the subordinate is still learning the job; and (d) superior and subordinate like each other.

4. If petty faults and unpleasant mannerisms are made part of an appraisal they give the impression that the appraisal of performance hinges on minor matters. Such problems should be handled on more appropriate occasions and should not await the annual appraisal.

5. There are many kinds of deficiencies. Some can be corrected easily, others require training, and in the case of still others the process of correction may do more harm than good. Mannerisms may be forms of adjustment, bad habits, or neurotic manifestations. Deficiencies in job performance may be due to poor job aptitude, inadequate training, poor supervision, incomplete communication, or low motivation.

6. Effective job performance is often a matter of opinion. A superior and subordinate may have differing views on how best to carry out assignments, how to budget time, and which activities have priority or are the most important. In Table 8.2 research evidence was cited indicating that superiors and their subordinates generally do not agree on the requirements and even many of the duties of a subordinate's job. They differ regarding the amount of initiative expected and the degree of delegation. It is inevitable, therefore, that when a superior evaluates performance in terms of his frame of reference the evaluation will appear unfair and unreasonable to a subordinate with a different frame of reference (see Chapter 3).

7. A subordinate is most highly motivated in work when free to participate in setting goals, determining priorities, planning, and deciding on the best way to accomplish objectives. There are usually several approaches to a job and superiors should not expect their ideas to be understood or accepted by all subordinates. These differences are good subjects for discussion and problem solving.

8. Performance can be viewed in the light of strengths and weaknesses. Usually one attempts to improve a person's performance by correcting weaknesses. When weaknesses in performance are a matter of deficiencies in aptitude they are difficult to improve. For this reason performance can be upgraded by further improvements in strengths. Superior performance can be made even more superior, and this opportunity should not be overlooked.

9. Deficiencies in performance should be put in situational terms if they are to be discussed. When a person's behavior is criticized he feels degraded and rejected, hence comes to his own defense.[23] When the *job* is examined, any deficiencies can be posed as problems to solve.

10. An employee's job performance can be improved in any of four ways: (1) change the employee; (2) change the duties or routines to capitalize on stronger abilities and interests; (3) transfer the employee to a more suitable job; and (4) change the superior's manner of supervision. The appraisal interview tends to concentrate on changing the subordinate, which is the most difficult way to accomplish improvement. The problem-solving interview permits improvement in performance by means of any of the four avenues.

Attempts to reduce the harmful effects of appraisal have led to a number of modifications of the procedure. One approach is based upon an attempt to remove supervisory bias by a committee approach to the evaluation. In this method each subordinate is rated by a committee in which a superior acts as chairman.[24]

Another approach uses the interview to get employees to evaluate themselves.[25] Still another is to make the evaluation less subjective by relating it to objective job standards.[26]

The extreme approach is to abandon the objective of letting the employees know

[23] Meyer, H. H., Kay, E., and French, J. R. P., Jr. Split roles in performance appraisal. *Harvard Bus. Rev.* 1965, *43,* 123–129.

[24] Rowland, V. K. *Improving managerial performance.* New York: Harper, 1958.

[25] McGregor, D. An uneasy look at performance appraisal. *Harvard Bus. Rev.,* 1957, *35* (3), 89–94.

[26] Likert, R. *New patterns of management.* New York: McGraw-Hill, 1961.

where they stand and to concentrate on developing their performance through improved motivation and communication. In the process, employees get a good notion of how they stand without being told directly.[27]

Effect of Interview Style

In order to give the reader a picture of the way different interview styles can be applied in an appraisal program, the cause and effect relations of three methods are shown in Table 20.4.

The *problem-solving* interview may be used in an appraisal program, although it may not completely conform to the viewpoint of the program. Nevertheless, it is a plan for improving performance by increasing job interests, developing a subordinate's problem-solving ability, and solving job problems. It has its greatest merit when used with superior employees or with employees who are reluctant to conform to bureaucratic procedures.

Superiors and subordinates frequently do not have the same picture of the subordinate's job (Table 8.2). The problem-solving interview offers an opportunity to prevent problems arising from these communication failures and permits the subordinate to participate in solving problems that require a resolution of differences. The duties of a supervisor vary in priority, the degree of freedom, and in the methods by which they can be performed. Delegation is a matter of degree. When do subordinates require approval of decisions? How much freedom and how much responsibility do they want? How much initiative is expected of them? These questions are seldom resolved. Furthermore, the answers do not depend on the job alone, but upon the superior's point of view and the subordinate's ability.

Once these matters are clarified, problem-solving interviews can be used to solve current problems raised by either subordinate or superior. New goals, ideas, obstacles, plans, and preferences constantly arise and are good topics for discussion in the problem-solving interview. (The discussion of problem solving in Chapter 6 and the case at the end of Chapter 21 should be reviewed in this connection.)

The *tell-and-listen* type of interview conforms with the spirit of most appraisal programs and permits upward communication because the subordinate is encouraged to respond. It also reduces some of the possible frustrations the subordinate might experience because the superior is expected to permit the employee to express any unpleasant feelings generated by the appraisal and by the recommendations made. A degree of problem solving also can be incorporated into this interview plan.

The *tell-and-sell* approach is perhaps most representative of the styles used in appraisal interviews. It has the same major objectives as the *"tell-and-listen"* plan; but in place of an emphasis on listening to gain acceptance, the superior tries to persuade (sell) the employee to change his ways. This approach can lead to arguments with subsequent face-saving problems; further, it tends to encourage conformity. These are two possible undesirable by-products which reduce the chances for true improvement. Although this plan is perhaps the most widely used, this writer recommends that the other two plans be given more widespread application.

[27] Maier, N. R. F. *The appraisal interview.* New York: Wiley, 1959.

Table 20.4 / Cause and Effect Relations in Three Types of Appraisal Interviews

Method	Tell and Sell	Tell and Listen	Problem Solving
Role of Interviewer	Judge	Judge	Helper
Objective	To communicate evaluation To persuade employee to improve	To communicate evaluation To release defensive feelings	To stimulate growth and development in employee performance
Assumptions	Employee desires to correct known weaknesses Any person who chooses can improve A superior is qualified to evaluate a subordinate	People will change if defensive feelings are removed	Growth can occur without correcting faults Discussing job problems leads to improved performance
Reactions	Defensive behavior suppressed Attempts to cover hostility	Defensive behavior expressed Employee feels accepted	Problem-solving behavior
Skills	Salesmanship Patience	Listening and reflecting feelings Summarizing	Listening and reflecting feelings Reflecting ideas Using exploratory questions Summarizing
Attitude	People profit from criticism and appreciate help	One can respect the feelings of others if one understands them	Discussion develops new ideas and mutual interests
Motivation	Use of positive or negative incentives or both (Extrinsic in that motivation is added to the job itself)	Resistance to change reduced Positive incentive (Extrinsic and some intrinsic motivation)	Increased freedom Increased responsibility (Intrinsic motivation in that interest is inherent in the task)
Gains	Success most probable when employee respects interviewer	Develops favorable attitude toward superior which increases probability of success	Almost assured of improvement in some respect
Risks	Loss of loyalty Inhibition of independent judgment Face-saving problems created	Need for change may not be developed	Employee may lack ideas Change may be other than what superior had in mind
Values	Perpetuates existing practices and values	Permits interviewer to change own views in the light of employee's responses Some upward communication	Both learn since experience and views are pooled Change is facilitated

From *The appraisal interview* by N. R. F. Maier. Copyright 1958, Norman R. F. Maier. By permission of John Wiley and Sons, Inc.

Improving Job Contacts

Nature of Job Contacts

Job contacts, like counseling and interviewing situations, involve the superior and a single subordinate rather than a group of subordinates. However, the job contacts are job related and take place in the normal operation of the job. It is in job contacts that personal motivations, job interests, and job satisfactions are likely to be developed. The psychological principles most appropriate for application in job contacts are found in the two chapters on motivation. A knowledge of widespread differences in abilities and needs among individuals is also valuable because it permits the supervisor to adapt expectations of performance to the person's capabilities and motivations. The chapter on attitudes is relevant in that communication failure and the need for sensitivity to differing viewpoints is essential to prevent misunderstandings. Finally, the chapter on frustration should help the supervisor locate persons with emotional problems and discover which aspects of the job cause resentment.

The chapters on morale and leadership emphasize the group as a whole and the need for avoiding favoritism. Despite the fact that supervisors are expected to be fair and impartial, they are also expected to treat each person as an individual. How is this to be done?

To take an extreme illustration, an amputee does not want to be helped to do things he can do for himself, but he would feel mistreated if he were expected to compete in activities in which his handicap would show him up as inferior.[28] Finding just what special treatment is needed requires considerable insight. Individual differences between workers follow a similar pattern. The employee with a child expects certain privileges; the superior worker may expect extra considerations and recognitions; the low-aptitude individual is degraded if compared to others; the person who does not desire to advance resents being criticized for lacking ambition. Thus people differ in many ways, and the supervisor who responds to these differences without showing favoritism will have warmer interpersonal relationships.

How can supervisors be expected to know all about their subordinates? There are many opportunities on the job for learning these things without taking up job time. Unofficial contacts occur when employees report for work, are met in the elevator, happen to be seen during the lunch hour, and so on. These meetings call for "small talk," and during such conversations a supervisor can learn of individual interests, family ties, important events in their lives (new baby, engagement, and the like). Later conversations can pick up from earlier fragments and soon supervisors not only learn to know the subordinates as individuals, but find each more interesting in certain respects. During job contacts they learn about each employee's job attitudes and interests. These added bits of information permit supervisors to work with people as individuals, without showing the kind of consideration regarded as unfair by others. If questionable special treatment is requested they can always resort to group-decision procedures to resolve conflicts.

[28] Dembo, T., Leviton, G. L., and Wright, B. A. Adjustment to misfortune—a problem of social-psychological rehabilitation. *Artificial Limbs,* 1956, *3,* 4–62.

Unique Opportunities in Various Job Contacts

Although most contacts have a job-related purpose, each can serve as a unique opportunity for improving interpersonal relations and for avoiding problems and misunderstandings. We have divided the job contacts into (1) unofficial or chance meetings; (2) those involved in giving job assignments; (3) inspecting, examining, or evaluating a job that has been done or is being done; (4) giving an individual employee some job training; and (5) introducing a new employee to other employees in the immediate situation. These five types of contacts have the common feature of informality and should remain unstructured in that developing good interpersonal relations is a common objective. However, each also has a special purpose.

Table 20.5 shows how each type of contact can achieve objectives of an interpersonal nature. The last column deals with points to which the supervisor may wish to become especially sensitive. Inspection of this table reveals how the various principles discussed in the preceding parts of the book can be applied in the daily routines of a job. Counseling and interviewing skills also have a place in that sensitivity becomes an important aid in interpreting the feedback in any communication, especially when rank differences exist.

Evaluation as a Barrier to Communication

Students and teachers may have observed how the relationship between teacher and class members chills after the first examination is returned. Appraisal interviews also tend to strain relations between superiors and subordinates. Job contacts can be used to reverse this trend and facilitate the supervisor's image as a helper rather than a judge. Simple devices, such as the boss or teacher asking subordinates or students to call them by their first names, or asking to be regarded as companions will not solve the problem. Parents cannot successfully be friends of their children because children want and need parents. Likewise employees and students need an official figure to be in charge of the activity.

If the act of holding a superior position and being inaccessible when needed are seen as threatening, the employee contacts can reduce the threatening perceptions of the boss and encourage his being viewed as a coach; a source of information about the job and the company; and a person busy with many responsibilities. This new perception may require some changes in the behavior of superiors, and the benefits may not be immediate because many employees have gained unfavorable perceptions from prior experiences.

Relations with new employees are not only strained by having a stranger as a boss, but by having work associates who are strangers. Peers also pass judgment and determine the social status of a new member. The group-decision method aids the acquaintance process because it permits group interaction, and extra attention by the supervisor is recommended for new employees. In addition, older employees could be given assignments of getting the new employees acquainted. Some further innovations in improving interpersonal relations through job contacts would make a good subject for class discussion.

Table 20.5 / Job Contacts and their Unique Opportunities

Type of Contact	Examples	Interpersonal Relations Objectives	Critical Points to Observe
Unofficial	Morning greeting. Meeting on elevator. Coffee break	Treat as individual. Increase job satisfaction.	Changes in attitude. Personal problems. Needs and outside interests.
Job Assignment	Work on new project Special job.	Permit participation. Generate ideas.	Feelings of unfair treatment. Possible misunderstanding. (Have employee summarize given assignment.)
Job Inspection	Checking workmanship. Analyzing results. Measuring output.	Help employee to improve. Constructive suggestions Generate ideas. Give feeling of progress. Be helper rather than critic.	Defensive behavior. Individual differences. Communication failure in assignment. Face-saving responses.
On-the-job Training	Teaching a new job. Teaching a new employee.	Improve skill and knowledge. Create job interest. Give feeling of progress. Demonstrate your role as helper.	Discouragement. Individual differences. Lack of interest. Lack of aptitude.
Inducting New Employees	New employee in company Transferred employee. New employee in special group.	Make employee feel free to come to you for help. Make employee feel welcome and important. Get employee to be group member not member of subgroup. Reduce high turnover of new employees.	Induction process requires a week or more. Need for companions for lunch. Discouragement. How group members react. Insecurity.

Laboratory Exercise ———————————————————

Skill Practice: Marjory Winkler

A. Preparation

1. The instructor will appoint one class member to read the part of Marjory Winkler, and another to read the part of the counselor. Assigning parts a day early will permit them to become familiar with the script (D.2).
2. Arrange two chairs at the sides of a table so that Marjory and the counselor will be able to face the class as well as each other.
3. The readers will bring a copy of the script with them (D.2). Other class members should not refer to the script before or during the exercise.

B. Reading the Script.

1. The instructor will read aloud the preliminary material, labeled "Situation" (D.1).
2. Marjory and the counselor are asked to take their positions at the table.
3. The class members are instructed to listen to each of Marjory's statements, think of an appropriate response, utilizing the reflecting feelings method described in this chapter, and write this response down.
4. Marjory will then be cued to read S.1.
5. The instructor will ask several volunteers to read the response they would give to Marjory's line. Care should be taken to insure that participation is distributed around the class so that a few members do not provide most of the answers.
6. After some interaction the instructor will nod to the counselor who will read the response C.1. This will serve to let participants learn how closely their own responses approximated that of the counselor.
7. Marjory will be asked to respond to the counselor by reading S.2. When she has finished, the class members should again try their skill at reflecting the feelings expressed. The instructor should remind the counselor to withhold his response until cued.
8. This same procedure will be followed after each of Marjory's speeches. If class members desire Marjory to repeat certain speeches, the instructor should permit this.
9. At the end of the reading the instructor will read the follow-up information (D.3) to let the class know that the case was taken from life.

C. Discussion

1. Use class discussion to evaluate the counseling session. What would have happened if the counselor had tried to advise, direct the course of the interview by asking Marjory questions, or had made value judgments about Marjory's behavior and feelings? What would the result have been if the

counselor had tried to diagnose Marjory's problem at the beginning of the interview?

2. Analyze what was typical of this case, and what was probably atypical. Apparent problem vs. real problem, length of counseling session, and value of catharsis may be discussed.

3. Discuss the difficulty the class members might have had in reflecting feelings. Did they find that they had to listen more closely in order to reflect feelings than they ordinarily might have? Discuss the merits of the reflecting feelings method of counseling.

D. Materials for the case[29]

1. Situation.

Miss Marjory Winkler was referred to the counselor by a physician, who reported the following symptoms: loss of weight, nervousness, crying spells, and fainting attacks. The physician stated that there were no apparent physical causes for the symptoms.

The client, an 18-year-old girl, had undergone plastic surgery, and it had changed her appearance completely. She was now a very attractive girl. The physician had insisted that she accept the counseling before he would continue with any further treatment of her physical condition. The case was phonographically recorded and transcribed as follows:

2. Script.

S1. Well, here I am. This is all perfectly silly, but the doctor *insisted* that I come in and see you. I promised the doctor that I would come for *one hour* and here I am.

C1. You're here because of the doctor's insistence and not because you feel any need for it.

S2. Yes, that's exactly it. The doctor says there isn't anything wrong with me physically—that all my symptoms are because I am emotionally disturbed about things. Well, that's a lie. I'm not emotionally disturbed about anything. (Spoken rapidly and with considerable heat.)

C2. You feel that the doctor is wrong when he says that you are emotionally upset to the extent that—

S3. (Interrupting) I have *nothing* to worry about. I have all the money I want. I live at the sorority house and have lots of friends. I'm getting good grades. What *could* be bothering me?

C3. You feel that you have lots of advantages and there is apparently nothing that could be bothering you.

S4. Yes. That sums it up. (Begins to cry) This is one of the things he said indicated that I was upset about something. (Sniffs, blows nose, wipes eyes, cries.)

C4. The doctor felt that the tears were caused by some emotional disturbance.

[29] From W. U. Snyder. *Casebook of Non-directive Counseling.* Interview conducted by Dr. Virginia M. Axline. Boston: Houghton Mifflin, 1947, pp. 312–322. Reproduced by permission of author and publisher.

S5. (Blubbering) For no reason at all I cry. I just feel like crying and never stop crying. I don't know why.

C5. You don't know why you get those feelings that you never can stop crying.

S6. Oh, I know why.

C6. You think you know why you do it.

S7. I had an operation. It's just a very natural aftermath of my operation. It was my face. I was terribly ugly as a child. My nose and chin. One day this summer Mother said to me, "I've made all the arrangements for you to go to New York and have some plastic surgery done. You will stay at the New Yorker and should be able to come home by August." That's all. Not asking *me* how *I* felt. Not giving a damn. And I had to go. It was such a shock and when it was all over and I looked in the mirror, there was another person. I even had to have my hair done over—a rinse. The ugly duckling was gone. Pretty swell job, don't you think? (The tone of her voice implied extreme sarcasm, bitterness, and resentment.)

C8. A swell job, but you're not very happy about it.

S9. (Voice drops very low.) How would you feel? I look entirely different. No one recognizes me. (Voice rises suddenly.) I feel like a cheat and a crook. I'm a masquerader. I'm not *me*. I'm artificial. And I *had* to come back here. And no one knew me. Not the sorority girls, or the professors. And when they found out what had happened—I told them right away—(voice drops very low) they said, "How wonderful! Why, you're beautiful. You're lucky you could afford it!" And I thanked them and pretended that I was tickled—but deep down inside of me my very soul cried out, "Fraud! Fraud!"

C9. Even though the girls you knew admired the change in your appearance, you couldn't feel that it was fair. You felt like a fraud.

S10. I cried myself to sleep many a night. Then one of my profs talked to me and he said, among other things, that a person who lost an eye wore a glass eye, and a person who lost an arm or a leg wore an artificial limb and it was considered a Godsend. "You're no more of a fraud than they are," he said. "No more of a fraud than all the girls who wear rouge and lipstick. You had the advantage of correcting a flaw of nature. There isn't any reason for you to feel like you do about it." And so—(Begins to cry again.) And so, I got over it.

C10. After he talked it over with you, you were able to accept it and you got over your feelings.

S11. Yes. (Long, long pause.) Yes. (Resigned tone of voice.) It doesn't bother me now. It is an improvement, God knows it is. The doctor thought that that was what was troubling me. I know he did. He said, "Sometimes when people have radical changes occur in their physical make-up it's difficult to adjust to it." (This is said very slowly and softly.) I know he would bet his year's income that it's because of the plastic surgery that I'm so upset. But he's wrong.

C11. You feel sure that the doctor has your case diagnosed incorrectly.

S12. (Emphatically.) I know he has. (Pause of several minutes. She wipes her eyes. The counselor watched the snow fall on the window sill. Then the client continued in a low, flat voice.)

A person can't spend a lifetime hating someone as badly and completely as I hate my mother (voice rises and speeds up) and not have it tear their nerves to pieces. As long as I can remember I have hated her and wished she would *die*. She was so dominating, she killed my father. She drove him to suicide. I —I found him. She killed my sister. She committed suicide, too. Just to get away from her. She is like a vampire—sucking the life's blood out of her children. The plastic surgery was incidental. I have been used since I was a child as a convenient housemaid. Mother was starting a business of her own. She was a dynamic power. Every energy she had was poured into making a success. And she did. She has a chain of stores now. And all of us remaining children have money in our own names. She wants us to help in the business. One of my sisters is a partner now. Another sister got married and when Tom didn't "fit in," Mother caused a separation and now Louise is home—brooding, but docile. Now she wants me to take over another branch. And won't she be surprised when she discovers that the minute I'm twenty-one out comes my money and away I go, never to return again. (Pause.)

C12. Your life has been made most unbearable by your mother's domination, and those feelings are—

S13. (Interrupts in a very calm, matter-of-fact voice.) This is the first time in my life that I have ever told anyone that I hated my mother and wished she would *die*. I *should* feel so ashamed of myself. It is a crime, I suppose. But I *don't* feel ashamed.

C13. You suppose that perhaps you should feel guilty about the feelings you have expressed, but somehow you can't.

S14. (Smiles bitterly.) I'm probably hard—like she has been toward me.

C14. You think you might have acquired some of the hardness your mother extended toward you.

S15. Yes. (Pause. Then in a very calm, pleasant tone of voice she adds:) I don't really think it is necessary *now* that I even waste my time wishing she would die. I don't believe that is exactly fair. Surely, I can stand on my own two feet even though she is alive.

C15. You think perhaps the wish that your mother might die is no longer necessary.

S16. I've made up my mind. I know now what I'm going to do. You see, my life has been really intense hell. You can't imagine how I had to live as a child. I was a little kitchen slave. I did all the housework—the cooking and scrubbing and washing. I was ugly and she never got me anything nice to wear. I went to school and I didn't have one friend in the school. I buried myself in my books. I crept to school and I crept home and the only words I said were the few I said to the teachers. They pitied me. I know now that they did. I didn't know it then. I felt so miserable and unhappy. I worked so hard. I just *had* to get the best grades in the school—it was the only thing I could do. But I never got any praise for it from my mother. And my father never said anything. My mother was the ruling force in the house. I hated her. She never said a kind word to me. It was always orders. "Get supper ready early tonight." "Do the washing after you get home from school." "Scrub down the bathroom. Do you want to live in a hog-pen?" And never any recreation. She didn't care how I looked then. My hands—I used to hide them! They were so rough and ugly and red. Always! And she didn't care about my face then. Or my clothes. I wore the drabbest clothes—the castoffs—but it was cheaper that way. She treated me like a dog—worse than a dog. She would have stopped and patted a dog once in a while. She was cold. She never showed me a bit of affection. I didn't her, either. And she and my father would go for days without speaking. She would snarl at him—call him a lazy, no-good bum, and say that he couldn't earn a living for his family. He, poor soul (Sighs deeply) I used to wish that she would die. I would stand in the door sometimes when she went out to work, and hope that she would get killed. Then I would feel terrible and afraid, and watch and watch for her to come home, and then when she did it was the same thing all over again. Then one day (Pause) I never went to any of the school affairs. I didn't have time. Besides, I never wanted to. At least, I didn't think I wanted to. And, besides, I didn't have any friends and I was miserable around the school. All I did was to go to school and come home and work like a slave and then, (Pause) then I would stay up most of the night studying because I had to get good grades. It was the only thing I ever had—the best grades, and the other kids hated me for it because the teachers would point out how I always had the best grades and the best papers. And *then* one day (Pause) well, he took all he could, I suppose. I found him. I went down in the basement to get some potatoes for the supper, and he was there. And I shall never forget how I felt. I just wished that she would die. I wished she would never get home again. I wished that so strongly that I got sick. For years I have carried that wish in my heart. I couldn't get rid of it. It came between me and everything. No, don't say anything yet. It has been with me so long. For years. But you see—it's just occurred to me, really right now, that I'm big enough to live and let live. I was really putting off facing a decision by hoping that something would happen to her. But it's up to me. I really pity her. She must be in hell herself. She hasn't any friends. No one wants to be a friend of a person like her. She is lonely and despised.

C16. You feel that your mother is really an object of pity—that she's probably unhappy, and miserable, and lonely.

S17. Yes. But she's able to live her life, and I shall live mine and avoid her as much as possible. Perhaps some day we can even become reconciled to one another on a fifty-fifty basis.

C17. You hope that some day you may be able to get along in a cooperative and congenial manner, with both respecting the other's rights.

S18. Yes. So you see I really didn't need to come here. I know the doctor had good intentions. He meant all right. Oh, well,—have I been here an hour?

C18. The time seemed to pass quickly.

S19. Well! I'll not be back. Thanks so much for your time.

C19. You don't feel that it will be necessary to make another appointment.

S20. No. Well, good-bye.

C20. Good-bye.

(The client leaves, but a few minutes later returns)

S21. Would you mind giving me your telephone number in case something else should come up, and I should want to see you again?

(The client did not contact the counselor again. A report from the physician stated that the girl showed considerable improvement.)

3. Follow-up Information.

Three months after this contact Marjory eloped with a young man whom she had known since entering the college. The physician reported that she seemed quite happy in her marriage.

A report two years later added this information to the case. Marjory's mother had suffered a stroke which had left her a helpless invalid. When Marjory learned of her mother's illness she went home and volunteered to care for her mother. In a very short time Marjory and her husband had met this situation in an interesting manner. The husband had taken over the business for his mother-in-law and Marjory was assuming the responsibility for her mother's care and also for the home. Voluntary reports from several sources indicated that things were moving along smoothly, that everyone seemed to be making the best of the situation, and that Marjory seemed to be disclosing an understanding, kindly, and friendly attitude toward her mother. How much, if any, of this was due to the counseling contact is purely a matter of speculation. The follow-up report is included as an interesting bit of information.

Suggested Readings

Black, J. M. *How to get results from interviewing: A practical guide for operating management.* New York: McGraw-Hill, 1970.

Bordin, E. S. *Psychological counseling* (rev. ed.). New York: Appleton, 1968.

Cook, P. E. (Ed.). *Community psychology and community mental health: Introductory readings.* San Francisco: Holden-Day, 1970.

Ginott, H. G. *Between parent and teenager.* New York: Macmillan, 1969.

Hart, J. T., and Tomlinson, T. M. (Eds.). *New directions in client-centered therapy.* Boston: Houghton Mifflin, 1970.

Interviewer's Manual, Survey Research Center, Ann Arbor, Mich.: Institute of Social Research, University of Michigan, 1969.

Kahn, R. L., and Cannell, C. F. *The dynamics of interviewing.* New York: Wiley, 1958.

Maier, N. R. F. *The appraisal interview: Objectives, method, and skills.* New York: Wiley, 1958.

Snyder, W. U. (Ed.). *Casebook of non-directive counseling.* Boston: Houghton Mifflin, 1947.

Sugarman, D. A., and Freeman, L. *The search for serenity: Understanding and overcoming anxiety.* New York: Macmillan, 1970.

21 Organizational Psychology

Introduction

Organizational Psychology, like Industrial Psychology, deals with leadership, group dynamics, morale, communication, motivation, job satisfaction, and effectiveness in work situations; in addition, it takes into account the influence of the organization as a whole on employee behavior. Whyte[1] in *The Organization Man* dramatizes the effect of the organization on one's way of life, detailing how big business can determine value systems, encourage conformity, and destroy individuality.

The chain of command, the location of power, and the hierarchical structure inherent in organizations makes essential the expansion of our treatment of social behavior to include the influence of people not physically present. Thus the organization becomes an environment in which people live and interact not only with each other, but also with influences exerted by company policies and goals. This more global perspective of behavior in industry suggests comparisons of large vs. small organizations, centralized vs. decentralized companies, and family-owned vs. incorporated businesses. Since organizations involve a number of levels of management, a variety of problem situations are created which involve effective delegation, span of control, the limitations of the chain of command, conflicts in the roles of supervisors, ambiguity in the supervisors' roles, perceptions of power vs. responsibility, advantages and disadvantages of bypassing, clarification of the area of freedom, leadership climate, upward communication between levels, the influence of the informal organization (grapevine), and lateral communication between line and staff and between work groups.

Derived from this change from traditional industrial psychology to organizational psychology is the potential generalization of solutions from business organizations

[1] Whyte, W. H., Jr. *The organization man.* New York: Simon & Schuster, 1956.

to other organizations. Government agencies, city departments, labor unions, hospitals, public schools, and colleges have psychological problems similar to those of business and industry, and the advances made in business are being examined to determine the extent to which the findings can be generalized. Public school principals are seeking to learn from business how to conduct appraisal interviews, how to deal with unions, and how to discipline. This chapter, however, will be confined primarily to business organizations.

Some Distinctions between Organizations

Some industries produce products, others produce services. The automobile is a product produced by General Motors, whereas person-to-person communication is a service offered by the American Telephone and Telegraph Company. Generally speaking, service-type organizations have been the more sensitive to interpersonal relations problems, probably because they have had to deal with the public, the direct recipient of their services. Many service organizations (utilities) are monopolies and hence governmental regulations control their profits and losses. Favorable public images can influence legislation, which generates a practical reason for being people-minded. Governmental agencies, hospitals, and schools are service organizations that need not make a profit. However, banks deal in services and at the same time must make a profit. Survey studies are needed to determine which, if any, of the above distinctions are factors in job satisfaction, and organizational studies are needed to test these points.

Recent Developments in Protests Against Organizations

Employees have struck industrial organizations, and teachers have struck the school system, indicating that both product and service organizations are subject to labor unrest. An interesting phenomenon in recent years has been student strikes. In this case, students are the consumers of service (the teachers are the producers); this relationship would correspond to patients striking hospitals or the consumers of products closing down the manufacturers. This dimension of influence does not come from within the organization, but from the ability of the striking group to exert power through joint effort.

Ordinarily consumers can influence producers by selective buying, but if consumers are organized and become a power group, their influence can be more direct. Whether they can go so far as to shut down a plant with picket lines or with other organized effort remains to be seen. In any case, student strikes represent a kind of influence that should be differentiated from strikes of employees, since organizationally they arise from different sources. They also represent a demand to participate. The values of participation described in Chapters 5 and 6 represent a change in management originating from within the organization where accountability was retained. When participation is demanded from outside the organization the question of accountability must be given serious consideration.

The student movement is like the union movement in its power relationship. Whether it will serve to influence universities in a manner similar to the way unions have influenced industry remains to be seen.[2] Also to be determined is the extent to which the movement is frustration instigated or goal oriented (see Chapter 4).

Structural Differences in Organizations

Organizations may differ in a number of ways, but the types of differences are so varied that it is difficult to isolate the influence of any one of them. In working with family-owned businesses a consultant often runs into problems that are unique in that they involve family relations. A personnel officer was discharged because the son of a part owner had graduated from business school and was given his position. A man who started a business which became a national corporation wished to retire; his three sons and his daughter's husband were vice presidents; problems arose because all of them were vying for the presidency. Family problems can play a unique role in organizational behavior not only in small companies but also in large corporations. These family influences are so varied and changeable that it would be difficult to generalize about their effects.

The literature lacks adequate comparisons between different types of companies. Although blue- and white-collar workers are explored in surveys, comparisons between service vs. manufacturing lead to no general conclusions. Likewise comparisons of unionized vs. nonunionized organizations are questionable because influence varies with the times, the type of union, the level of job skill, and the type of leadership.

Size of Work Groups

As groups increase in size, each member of the group becomes less important. This inverse relationship both reduces self-centered behavior and the individual's sense of importance. The skill of the leader becomes a factor in such cases. As groups become larger, the demands on the leader become more numerous and complex.[3] Clique formation also increases with group size.[4]

The influence of group size on productivity has not been established. Too much congeniality as well as too little could interfere with production, so that the skill of the leader becomes a determining variable. When group bonuses and group piece rates are incentives, effectiveness declines as group size increases from less than 10 to 50.[5]

Although the nature of the task must be considered in determining the size of a work group, the general conclusion is that smaller groups perform better than larger

[2] Harberson, F. H. The campus revolt from an industrial relations perspective. In G. G. Somers (Ed.), *Proceedings of the twenty-second annual winter meeting. Industrial Relations Research Association,* 1970, pp. 2–14.

[3] Hemphill, L. Relations between the size of the group and the behavior of "superior" leaders. *J. soc. Psychol.,* 1950, *32,* 11–22; Mass, H. S. Personal and group factors in leader's social perception. *J. abnorm. soc. Psychol.,* 1950, *45,* 54–63.

[4] Homans, G. C. *The human group.* New York: Harcourt, Brace, 1950.

[5] Marriott, R. Size of working group and output. *Occup. Psychol.,* 1949, *23,* 47–57; Campbell, H. Group incentive payment schemes: The effect of lack of understanding and group size. *Occup. Psychol.,* 1952, *26,* 15–21.

The purposes of organizations differ. Some produce products, others services. Some depend on profits, others on subsidies. Labor unions, schools, hospitals, government agencies, and local governments are examples of organizations that require financial support. All organizations have organizational problems because all involve the process of working through people to achieve the organizational goals.

Courtesy of General Motors

Frank Siteman

Courtesy of NBC

Courtesy of Massachusetts Department of Commerce and Development

Arthur Lavine, courtesy of Chase Manhattan Bank

Courtesy of New England Deaconess Hospital

groups because they interact more effectively and require less guidance from higher authority.[6] Most organizations are structured into hierarchies so that leaders seldom have more than 15 subordinates. A foreman who has as many as 50 subordinates usually has strawbosses or group leaders who may be considered at an intermediate level in management. Even when the intermediate level is not formally established, the leader finds himself dealing with subgroups.[7]

Organizational Size

As organizations increase in size, the individual finds it more difficult to identify with them. School spirit has declined as universities have increased in enrollment, and blind loyalty has often been replaced by fault finding. If people are to have feelings of loyalty, they must have a sense of identification. In industry it has been generally found that both the size of the organization and of the department have an influence on absenteeism, tardiness, accidents, and strikes, and small plants (under 500 persons) have the best record.[8] A comparison of units in an airline, ranging from 172 to 3,205 employees, showed a decrease in absenteeism in the small units where identification with the organization was more evident.[9]

Since there are many advantages in the growth and development of large organizations, the problem is to find ways to facilitate identification and involvement. Chapter 6 emphasized the potential uses of group decision making. Other methods involve the development of teams or smaller work groups. One of the tasks of organizational psychologists is to invent additional ways to develop identity and a feeling of belonging not only in a person's work group, but also in the community.

Organizational Hierarchy

Organizational hierarchies vary in the number of levels of management (as many as eight or more); and for a given size, the hierarchy might be described as "tall" (having many levels) or "flat" (having few levels). Large organizations would require more levels than small, but control might be centralized (tall) or decentralized (flat). What are the relative merits of this structuring of control?

First, job satisfaction within a given organization is greater for persons occupying higher levels than for those in lower levels.[10] This is understandable considering the increased influence and challenge higher positions allow. However, a selectivity factor operates in that job interest leads to promotion.

With regard to flat vs. tall structures, the confusing factor is that size and type of work lend themselves to either tall or flat hierarchies. Companies may be subdivided

[6] McGrath, J. E. *A summary of small group research studies.* Arlington, Va.: Human Sciences Research, Inc., 1962.

[7] Forehand, G. A., and Gilmer, B. Environmental variation in studies of organizational behavior. *Psychol. Bull.,* 1965, *62,* 361–382.

[8] Cleland, S. *The influence of plant size on industrial relations.* Princeton, N.J.: Princeton University Press, 1955.

[9] Baumgartel, H., and Sobel, R. Background and organizational factors in absenteeism. *Personnel Psychol.,* 1959, *12,* 431–443.

[10] Herzberg, F., Mausner, B., Peterson, R. O., and Campbell, D. F. *Job attitudes: Review of research and opinion.* Pittsburgh: Psychological Services of Pittsburgh, 1957.

either according to geographical dispersion or to functional specialization. A chain of stores would lend itself readily to decentralization so that each store manager would be in charge of all functions. His advancement would be one of moving from smaller stores to larger ones. In contrast, a utility would be divided on a functional basis, so that sales, services, accounting, overhead lines, and maintenance would become divisions. Generally speaking, industries involving technology have taller structures than mass production industries. For a given type of industry, companies that had the average number of echelons were the most successful.[11] Since a number of factors[12] influence the type of hierarchy established, it is desirable to determine if the type of structuring, as such, makes a difference. A disadvantage to centralization is that executives become specialized and cannot readily be moved from one department to another. With decentralization, all unit managers have more freedom for independent action. However, the freedom delegated to them might stop at their levels, unless they in turn share some decision-making functions within their divisions.

One of the earlier studies, using an attitude survey approach, reported that flat structures were associated with higher morale than tall.[13] Since then it has been found that the relationship is more complex. In a study in which large and small organizations were analyzed, job satisfaction in large and small organizations was related to structure in opposite ways.[14] Managers, whose job satisfaction had been measured by a questionnaire, were classified as belonging to tall, intermediate, and flat structures. In organizations of less than 5000, job satisfaction was greater for the flat structures, but for large organizations, the reverse was true. Failure to distinguish between organizational size may explain why the relationship with structure was not more apparent.[15] The solution to organizational effectiveness apparently does not lie in the direction of finding the one most effective organizational structure. How the structure already in existence functions may be more crucial. Are the failures due more to the people or to the structure of the organization? Companies that attempt to solve their problems by repeated structural reorganizations may create dysfunctions in behavior by upsetting communication channels.

Differentiation and Integration

Organizations must be integrated in order to function as a unit. However, the problem of integration is more complex when function is highly differentiated. Specialization not only involves functional differences in work, but the persons who

[11] Woodward, J. Management and technology. London: Her Majesty's Stationery office, 1958; Bass, B. M. *Organizational psychology.* Boston: Allyn & Bacon, 1965.

[12] Stieglitz, H. Optimizing span of control. *Mgt. Record,* 1962, *24,* 25–29. Lawrence, P. R., and Lorsch, J. W. *Organization and environment.* Homewood, Ill.: Irwin, 1969.

[13] Worthy, J. Organization structures and employee morale. *Amer. Sociol. Rev.,* 1950, *15,* 169–179.

[14] Porter, L. W. and Lawler, E. E. The effect of tall versus flat organization structures on managerial job satisfaction. *Personnel Psychol.,* 1964, *17,* 135–148.

[15] Weiss, E. C. Relation of personnel statistics to organizational structure. *Personnel Psychol.,* 1957, *10,* 27–42.

perform the functions differ in interests, attitudes, training, and job objectives. Thus, the problem of finding mutual interests between different units so that cooperation is possible increases with specialization. A manager who has several specialized activities under his supervision must integrate these functions. His problem is quite different from that of a manager who has to integrate functions in different geographical areas rather than in different areas of specialization. The specialized industries in general require greater effort in order to achieve the same level of integration as less differentiated industries.

Taking specialization of function into consideration because of the different environments, variations in goal orientation and the degree of stability in the industry, Lawrence and Lorsch[16] postulated that organizations having a relatively slow rate of technological change and low diversity in environment (e.g., the container industries) should have less difficulty achieving integration than organizations having rapidly changing technologies and high diversity in job functions (e.g., the plastics industries). Their findings indicate that the most successful organizations were those that came closest to dealing with differentiation in a manner that was consistent with the type of industry and environment. Industries having a relatively slow rate of technological change were able to achieve integration between functions with little effort. The attitudes and goals of people in research and those in production, for example, were similar enough so that they could resolve conflicts involving their mutual areas through problem-solving conversations with one another. In the more differentiated industries, the outlook and job objectives of a research scientist and a production manager were so different that integration of function was achieved only with the help of a middleman, "the integrator," who understood both viewpoints and whose function was to help these specialists to communicate with one another.

When the problem of integration involves diverse functions, group problem solving could be highly beneficial. Both the specialists and the integrator would profit by training in group problem-solving skills.

Traditionally, a foreman supervised the jobs of several workers, and communication about the job was relatively simple; but in modern technical industries, an operator may have not only a foreman, but a safety advisor, an engineering advisor, and a quality control advisor as well. Obviously, the worker must deal with all of these influences, and conflicts are inevitable. The same problems in communication also arise at higher levels. Thus the importance of the integrative function is directly related to the amount of technological change and diversity in an industry.

Leavitt[17] has worked extensively with communication problems in organizations, finding that control, satisfaction, cooperation, and competition often conflict. Some suggested remedies are: (1) decentralization to shorten communication channels and transfer more decision making to lower levels; (2) separation of staff from

[16] Lawrence and Lorsch, *op. cit.*

[17] Leavitt, H. J. *Managerial psychology.* Chicago: University of Chicago Press, 1964; Leavitt, H. J. Task ordering and organizational performance in the common target game. *Behav. Sci.,* 1960, 5, 233–239.

line to distribute responsibility of function; (3) use of committees to open up channels of communication; (4) increase in amount of horizontal communication to coordinate goals that might be in conflict; and (5) development of methods for sensing organizational conflicts to permit problem solving before they become acute. It seems that the need for these remedies would vary with the degree of differentiation and the amount of required integration. Some organizational structures and communication channels might serve one purpose, others a different purpose. All seem to suffer from a deficiency in upward communication.

The persons occupying the positions should not be restricted by structured channels that impede informal communication. Successful communication depends more on the skill of the people involved than on the formal structure of the organization.

The Chain of Command

The Classical Concept

The classical organization chart shows the hierarchy of levels of management as well as the lines of accountability. Figure 21.1 is a simplified example of such a chart. In this figure the Works Manager would be in charge of a plant, and this manager and others in similar jobs might be accountable to the operating vice president, who would be accountable to the president. The president in turn would be accountable to the board of directors. Top management ordinarily would include persons involved with the overall operation of the company such as setting policy, finance, public relations, etc. Middle management begins at the level when functions become specific (manufacturing, marketing, quality control, research and development, etc.) and may include many levels. In Figure 21.1 only three levels are indicated (the Works Manager, department heads, and first-line supervisors or foremen), but in larger organizations departments may have section heads, superintendents, and general foreman levels between department heads and first-line supervisors. The first-line supervisor (foreman for blue-collar workers) is the lowest level of management. He is the person who has nonmanagement people (rank-and-file employees) reporting to him. He often is described as the man in the middle because he is under pressure from middle management above him and the union representing the workers reporting to him.

The chain-of-command concept implies that each person is accountable to an immediate superior and will receive assignments from one superior only. This concept is intended to provide top management with effective control and coordination and to provide satisfaction to the subordinates because they know what is expected of them and the criteria by which their performance will be judged. However, in actual practice, the chain of command does not function in the manner its structure suggests. Some members have more influence than others, and many find it more expedient to take short cuts to avoid red tape. Furthermore, pressures can come from varied sources to influence a person. A foreman's superior may expect him to produce, the safety department might impose safety procedures that slow down production, and morale surveys may supply higher management with evidence of

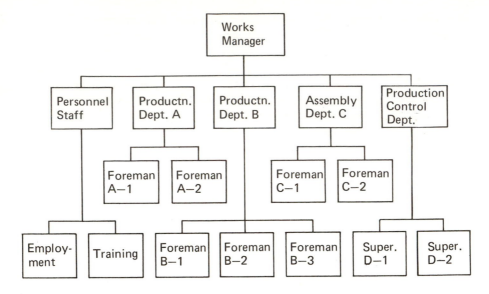

Figure 21.1 / Part of an Organization Chart. Three levels of management are indicated in the chart. The lines connecting the boxes show the superior-subordinate relationships.

poor worker attitudes. These varied expectations produce role conflict. Some organizations and some functions of an organization more readily lend themselves to the chain of command than others. In hospital settings, the nurse has a supervisor, but she must also take orders from the doctors. Who is her real boss? Lack of clarity in supervisory roles makes for role conflict and role ambiguity.

In large organizations the chain of command creates problems and is often slow and cumbersome. If the president followed the chain of command in getting a training program set up, he would have to go through the vice president of personnel, who would go to the training department head, who would go to the training specialist to get a program prepared. The sources of misunderstanding in conveying this assignment would be great. Why not let the president discuss the problem with the specialist?

It is generally claimed that violations of the chain of command reduce employee satisfaction, as well as performance, and increase stress because they create role conflict and role ambiguity. Some research bears this out.[18] However, Woodward[19] presents evidence that multiple-command relationships can be beneficial and satisfying. In one organization 30 supervisors received direction from five executives and 28 reported that close association with five superiors made them feel they knew what

[18] Kaplan, N. The role of the research administrator. *Administrative Sci. Quart.*, 1959, *4*, 20–41; Balu, P. M., and Scott, W. R. *Formal organizations.* San Francisco: Chandler, 1962; La Port, T. R. Conditions of strain and accommodation in industrial research organizations. *Administrative Sci. Quart.*, 1965, *10*, 21–28.

[19] Woodward, J. *Industrial organizations: Theory and practice.* London: Oxford University Press, 1965.

was going on. The nature of the activity and the type of interpersonal relations involved appear to play a deciding role.

The Role Concept

In organizational psychology studies, a person in a given position is described as having a role. Certain behaviors are expected of an individual in that position, so he has a role to play. The roles are not adequately defined so that what is expected from the person who occupies a position is not always the same as what the occupier of the role thinks is expected. In most organizations, job descriptions are prepared to reduce such discrepancies but, if followed, these make for formal and legalistic relationships. Only when there is a great deal of distrust do disputes arise regarding whether an assignment falls within the job description. In labor-management disputes this question may be raised, but in middle management, such disagreements are seldom aired.

Although violations of the chain-of-command principle may create role ambiguity and role conflict, these conditions can arise from other sources, such as failures to communicate, different interpretations of the area of freedom, conflicts in goals or values, and personality clashes. The questionnaire method was used to show that role conflict and ambiguity can be identified as separate factors.[20] Questions regarding how behavior is evaluated and the clarity of the job requirements were used to measure ambiguity. Questions relating to differences in values, the best way to do a job, reasonableness of assignments, the several roles involved, and incompatible requests were used to measure conflict. Both role conflict and ambiguity were negatively related to measures of need fulfillment and other job satisfaction variables.

Role Ambiguity

According to Kahn *et al.*[21] role ambiguity tends to increase with organizational size and complexity, rapid growth, frequent reorganizations, frequent changes in technology, and personnel changes accompanied by changes in management philosophies.

As expected, individual differences exist in ability to adapt to changes. Nevertheless, the study showed that 35 per cent of a national sample was disturbed by not having a clear idea of responsibilities. Ambiguity was associated with increased tension, anxiety, fear, hostility, lowered job satisfaction, and loss of self-confidence. In many instances, lower production could be associated with these stresses.

Role ambiguity also is influenced by the superior. In general, studies show[22] that ability to give clear instructions and clear information is an important managerial skill.

[20] Rizzo, J. R., House, R. J., and Lirtzman, S. I. Role conflict and ambiguity in complex organizations. *Administrative Sci. Quart.*, 1970, *15*, 150–163.

[21] Kahn, R. L. Wolf, D. M. Quinn, R. P. Snoek, J. P., and Rosenthal, R. A. *Organizational stress.* New York: Wiley, 1964.

[22] Mandell, M. M. Supervisory characteristics and ratings: A summary of recent research. *Personnel,* 1956, *32*, 435–440.

Role Conflict

Although the chain of command theoretically was to guard against a manager or supervisor having more than one boss, there still are other sources of role conflict. Kahn *et al.*[23] cite a number of sources of conflict including conflict between superior and subordinate's values or attitudes; gaps between role expectations and realistic ones; and conflict between expectations coming from different sources (e.g., quantity and quality of output). Whenever the person's job involves incompatible requirements, role conflict is a possible outcome. Surveys reporting the influence of role conflict are in general agreement that it "is associated with decreased satisfaction, coping behavior that would be dysfunctional for the organization, and experiences of stress and anxiety."[24]

How people handle conflict varies. Many undoubtedly ignore it. *The Change of Work Procedure* simulation exercise (Chapter 11) demonstrated that when foremen were instructed by their superiors to solve the problem of how to use time-study data to improve the job procedure, they behaved in the same ways as others given instructions to make the change suggested by the time study.[25] Under each set of conditions some behaved autocratically, some were permissive, most tried to sell the change, and some became threatening, but the proportion of each type was the same under the two conditions. Obviously, the instructions given to the foremen on how to handle a situation must have introduced conflict because half of them were requested to follow the group-decision approach, the other half to be autocratic. Since the foremen had various personal opinions on how to handle the situation, many must have been in conflict with the instructions. Because the two conditions produced similar distributions in the methods followed, the foremen resolved the conflict by following their own opinions. Furthermore, they were ready to defend their reasons for violating their superior's instructions. If subordinates are to behave differently, training rather than mere instructions are needed (see pp. 141–144). It is interesting to add that females in the role of the foreman are more likely than males to follow a superior's orders.[26]

Bypassing

Bypassing is a term used when one intermediate level (or more) is skipped in communicating upward or downward in the chain of command. The dotted line *a* in Figure 21.2 shows a subordinate going to his boss's superior regarding some matter. Most superiors would frown on this tactic, but suppose the subordinate wanted to get out of the boss' unit or questioned his competence? Should the subordinate quit the company or should "doors" higher up be open? Some companies

[23] Kahn *et al., op. cit.*

[24] Woodward, *op. cit.*

[25] Maier, N. R. F. The subordinate's role in the delegation process. *Personnel Psychol.* 1968, *21,* 179–191; Maier, N. R. F., and Thurber, J. A. Problems in delegation. *Personnel Psychol.,* 1969, *22,* 131–139.

[26] Maier, N. R. F. Male vs. female discussion leaders. *Personnel Psychol.,* 1970, *23,* 455–461.

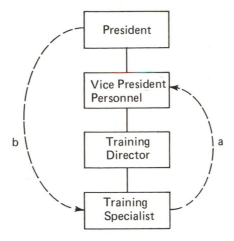

Figure 21.2 / Bypassing—Frowned upon in Traditional Management Theory.
A training specialist had an idea that required extra money for the Training
Department which needed the approval of the vice president. The idea would be
most likely to get approval if the training specialist could talk directly with the
vice president (dotted line a). However, this would compel a subordinate to
bypass his immediate superior. Bypassing in the opposite direction (dotted line b)
would occur if the president wanted to explore a problem in management training with the training specialist. It would be more fruitful to talk to the company
expert in the field than with generalists, but this would involve bypassing two
levels of supervision.

pride themselves on having an "open door" policy because it permits upward communication. The exercise at the end of Chapter 4 is relevant to this issue.

In other instances, a subordinate wants clarification. His boss's superior has requested a report which was passed on to the subordinate because he is an expert on
the matter in question. If he asks questions of his boss, who in turn must talk to his
superior, time is not efficiently used and many opportunities for misunderstanding
are introduced. Certainly such a matter could be best handled if the person who was
to do the job could talk it over with the man who requested it. How to do this without making the boss feel he was bypassed is really the issue and would be a good
problem to solve.

Bypassing also occurs when a higher-level manager gives an assignment to a
subordinate's subordinate (dotted line *b* in Figure 21.2) or to a specialist even
lower in rank. In small businesses this is a common problem because a top executive
(often the owner) might change a production schedule when getting a big order is
contingent on early delivery. In such instances it is most efficient to deal directly
with the person in charge of the production of the needed product. Shifting priorities and schedules may be good business in certain respects, but it may upset
carefully made plans regarding work units that are dependent on one another. Such

bypassing creates role conflict for the recipient and role ambiguity for the person bypassed.

Superiors also bypass when they have lost trust in their immediate subordinate and go around him because his subordinates are more competent. This practice creates new problems while avoiding others.

Instead of viewing bypassing as either desirable or undesirable it seems best to pose situations that generate bypassing as problems to be solved. How can a manager get priority changes made, when the need arises, with a minimal disruption of on-going plans? What should a superior do when an intermediate level of management complicates communication downward? When several levels of management and managers of different but concerned work groups are involved, group problem solving seems to be the way to resolve the various conflicts created. There is no simple rule; the chain of command relationship creates red tape and inefficiency, while ignoring formal relationships creates many forms of ambiguity and leads to loss of accountability. How to achieve the advantages and avoid the disadvantages of a practice generates a problem, and each problem needs to be solved separately because there is no general answer.

The Influence of Hierarchy on Function

Power as a Communication Barrier

Superiors tend to view their jobs in terms of their responsibilities. They must keep their subordinates busy, satisfied, and productive. Subordinates tend to view their superiors' jobs as positions of power. These differences in perception are sources of misunderstandings so that differences in rank become communication barriers. For example, if an employee meets a fellow employee in the washroom he may say, "Having a nice smoke, Joe?" Joe might respond by offering a cigarette, saying, "Yup, have one." If the foreman had entered and said the same thing in the same tone of voice, Joe's response might have been, "Yup, just finishing up, boss." If we take it a step higher and have the superintendent making the statement, Joe might have acted as if caught in the act and make a hasty exit. Thus the meaning of the same words spoken in the same tone of voice with the same friendly intent changes, depending on the number of levels between persons. The difference in level between rank-and-file workers and company officials is so great that workers do not see officials as human, often referring to them as "the brass." The president of a company may, while on the golf course, merely express a wish that the weather were like that in California, and it might give rise to an ugly rumor that the plant was to be moved.

All environmental factors that suggest status (rugs, desks, secretaries in an outer office, special parking, etc.) strengthen the barriers imposed by rank so that upward communication becomes an increasing problem. Subordinates keep bad news from their superiors, cover up problems, avoid taking chances, protect one another, and in general, "play it safe." Even though the superior does nothing to discourage free expression, his position alone is enough to inhibit it. The solution to this problem in an organization is not to abolish rank, but to make the barriers more permeable and eliminate needless status symbols. One need merely recall how much better communication proceeds when a discussion is held in the subordinate's office than in the superior's. Many top-management personnel follow this practice.

Awareness of the difference in perception is the first step in dealing with this communication barrier because misunderstandings create defensive behavior which in turn increases the barrier. The development of discussion leadership skills is a second, but this requires management training,[27] and will be discussed in the following chapter.

The influence of rank was demonstrated by a study which showed a correlation of .88 between an impartial observer's ratings of influence and rank in leaderless discussion groups.[28] When the discussion dealt with company matters, the correlation was higher than when it dealt with other topics.[29]

Subordinates also view their superiors in terms of the extent of their influence on higher management. Managers who are viewed as having high influence are more able to induce change in their subordinates than those who are seen as lacking in influence.[30] Whether perceived influence is desirable may be questioned. It may indicate that the supervisors are able to instill fear and as such, they violate the leadership principles discussed in Chapter 6 and the motivational principles discussed in Chapter 13. Or it might indicate that they are willing and able to remedy conditions when subordinates complain. Power and influence represent two types of control and are the bases for different leadership styles. Persons concerned with change, such as staff specialists, often feel that they could accomplish more if they had more power to impose the change with the backing of higher management. Such changes lack the acceptance of the line organization and communication barriers between staff and line (or different subsystems within the organization) become more firmly established.

Area of Freedom and Organizational Level

Every management position has an area of freedom which determines the kinds of decisions the manager can make (see Chapter 6). Even though the superior and subordinate do not always agree on the exact boundaries, each manager's behavior is restricted by the job, company policy, union contracts, and legislation. Within these boundaries a manager can make the needed decisions or share the function with subordinates. Regardless of how much decision making is shared, the manager is still accountable for the results the decision produces. As one examines the area of freedom at different levels in the organization the scope of the decisions' implications changes. Top management's area of freedom relates to such matters as

[27] Bass, B. M. *Organizational psychology.* Boston: Allyn & Bacon, 1965.

[28] Bass, B. M., and Wurster, C. R. Effects of company rank on LGD performance of oil refinery supervisors. *J. appl. Psychol.,* 1953, *37,* 100–104.

[29] Bass, B. M., and Wurster, C. R. Effects of the nature of the problem on LGD performance. *J. appl. Psychol.,* 1953, *37,* 96–99.

[30] Pelz, D. C. Leadership within a hierarchical organization. *J. soc. Issues,* 1951, *7,* 49–55.

financing, setting production goals, and establishing policies, all of which involve the company as a whole. Department heads are responsible for decisions that relate to their departments as a subsystem and involve the setting of department goals, integration of dependent functions, allocating departmental funds, implementing overall company policy, etc. A superintendent's function would involve how to integrate foreman groups, how to distribute overtime permitted by policy, and how to keep company practices uniform. If one supervisor allowed wash-up privileges and others did not, the practice would be nonuniform.

The supervisors' areas of freedom would be less concerned with what to do and more with such decisions as how the job should be done and who should do it. They would also be responsible for scheduling the work, maintaining discipline, etc. Thus a top-management decision of an airline to purchase a new type of plane would take the problem out of the planning committee and put it into operations. The implementation of the decision would affect sales, ground service, flight crews, reservations, accounting, personnel and flight scheduling departments in different ways, and each would have problems to solve. Within each department the problem would change from middle management to the first-line level. How the problems change from higher to lower levels is partly a matter of delegation. At each level certain functions are passed to the level below and in this way the successive boundaries for the areas of freedom are established.

Upward Communication

The fact that presidents of large organizations do not have the control that they are led to believe they have is illustrated by the following true incident. The company in question had a policy of giving its employees the day before Christmas off. Each year this gift was announced by the president. On one particular occasion, as was the custom, the vice president of personnel brought the official proclamation form to the president for his signature. The president noticed that the day to be announced as a holiday was December 23. He indicated that this was not in line with the company policy. The vice president pointed out that December 24 fell on a Saturday and since that was not a work day, he had assumed the day to be given as a gift would be December 23. The president's response was that since employees already had December 24 off, it would not be necessary to give it to them. He refused to sign the proclamation. When December 23 arrived no one except top management appeared for work. All others merely assumed they had the day off. No one ever told the president that his decision had been violated. Some time later the president indicated that the vice president's fears of a drop in morale had never materialized. Communication depends upon trust and when fear is involved, bad news is suppressed. In this respect subordinates show considerable cooperation.

An organization's hierarchy is designed to coordinate the functions of the various work groups. Middle management represents a link between top management and the primary work groups. How to facilitate communication through this hierarchy of middle management is one of the major problems in organizations. Traditionally, the direction of communication is downward. Yet it is well known that effective communication is a two-way street—both the receiver and the sender must be able to interact.[31] As a result of failure experienced while following the established channels, the lines of communication often are bypassed, unofficial channels (e.g., the grapevine) are created, and even channels of communication outside the line organization arise. These represent detours which have been developed because the official channels are inadequate.

Several types of communication channels outside the organizational chain of command exist. In recent years opinion surveys have been found useful. Workers' opinions are surveyed, and the results are communicated directly to top management. Thus they represent one form of upward communication initiated by management.

Other examples are the suggestion box and the personnel department. The suggestion box gives the individual employee an opportunity to present an idea up the line without depending upon a superior's approval. The personnel office can serve a communication function by interviewing disgruntled employees and persons who are quitting the company. The information gained can be shared with higher management.

The formation of the union by workers is an example of upward communication initiated by workers. The union serves as the voice of the workers and its representatives deal directly with representatives of top management. In the absence of adequate upward communication via middle management, the union office becomes an influential communication channel.

We have already seen how communication is facilitated in primary discussion groups. The discussion permits direct two-way communication. If first-line supervisors held problem-solving discussions, they would become aware of the attitudes and ideas of their subordinates. Suppose that the second-line supervisors also held discussions with the first-line supervisors reporting to them. They would not only learn their opinions but would also get some idea of the problems experienced by the first-line supervisors. In this way each first-line supervisor would be a potential source of information. Likewise the third level of supervision could have meetings with second-line supervisors who would become sources of information regarding not only their own problems but of the problems that had been communicated up to them.

If this type of process were practiced at each level, two-way communication inside the organizational structure, from bottom to top, would become a natural function. Even if some subordinates were not dependable or were reluctant to speak up, communication would not be blocked. Managers in the hierarchy would have as many sources of information as they had subordinates. They need only the desire and the skill to use the available sources.

---

[31] Dubin, R. Stability in human organizations. In M. Haire (Ed.), *Modern organization theory.* New York: Wiley, 1959; Guetzkow, H., and Simon, H. A. The impact of certain communication nets upon organization in task-oriented groups. *Mgt. Sci.,* 1955, *1,* 233–250; Leavitt, H. J. Some effects of certain communication patterns on group performance. *J. abnorm. soc. Psychol.,* 1951, *46,* 38–50.

Figure 21.3 / Upward Communication Channels. This simplified drawing is intended to show how each member of management is both the central figure for one circle and a peripheral figure on the next. It is this dual function of the supervisor that can promote better communication in the organization, providing there actually is a two-way process, as in group discussion. The small arrows in each circle indicate communication from the several subordinates to the leader, while the solid vertical line shows a communication chain from bottom to top. Right diagram shows detours developed because of inadequate upward communication. (After N. R. F. Maier, *Principles of human relations.* New York: Wiley, 1952.)

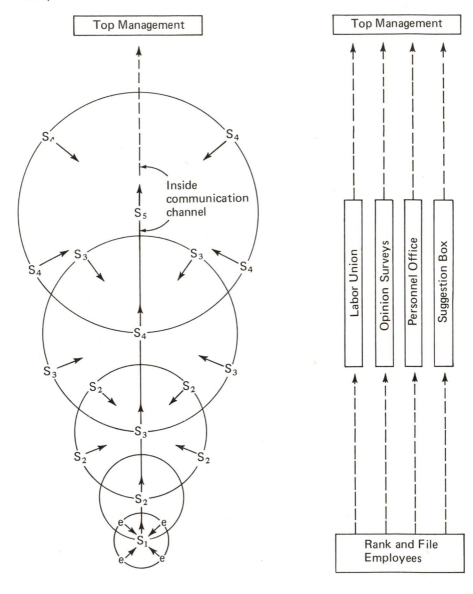

Figure 21.3 diagrammatically describes how the supervisor is both the leader (center of a circle) of the group reporting to him and a member of the group (point on circumference of another circle) reporting to his superior. Thus each member of management becomes a link between his subordinates and his superior. In these two roles, each member of management becomes a key figure in the communication channel inside the line organization.[32] The channel for one such chain is shown in Figure 21.3 as the heavy vertical line starting with S_1 and reaching to top management.

The left part of the figure shows how improved communication can occur inside the organization if all levels of management hold problem-solving discussions. The small circle shows a ring of employees (e) who have opportunities to participate in solving problems when discussions are led by the first-line supervisor (S_1). The next circle shows how the first-line supervisors participate in solving problems with their superior (S_2). To complete the figure these interlocking circles would have to be continued (to represent every hierarchical level) until the president was shown as the center of a group of vice presidents. Furthermore, if the total picture were to be represented, each supervisor should be surrounded by a circle of subordinates.

The right half of the figure shows the possible detours by which the workers may communicate upward in the absence of an adequate channel inside the organizational structure. The need to improve the two-way communication inside the organizational structure increases as companies become larger and the gap between top and bottom widens because of an increase in intermediate levels.

Because of inadequate upward communication, higher management must rely on surveys and the union to reveal worker attitudes and values. Upward communication within the organization would supply more constructive and accurate information.

The Process of Delegation

Introduction

One of the most effective keys to an organization's effectiveness resides in the process of delegation. A manager gets things done through other people, but there is more to running an organization than getting the work done. Problems must be solved, plans must be made, and priorities must be appraised. These activities as well as production work must be shared. Perhaps the most important reason why the traditional concept of management is unrealistic is that accountability can become a threat and hence restrict freedom to solve problems. The head man may excuse his own mistakes, but how generous is he with the mistakes of others? In an effort to retain control at the top, the organization tends to be governed by rules and regulations which allow no ways to adapt to unusual or changing situations. Employees

---

[32] Likert describes the supervisor who is a subordinate member in his superior's group and a superior in his own group of subordinates as a linking-pin which can serve a valuable coordinating function, not only within the line, but between line and staff functions. Likert, R. *The human organization.* New York: McGraw-Hill, 1967.

who for personal reasons cannot get to work on time may be discharged even if they were willing to work after hours and if this extra coverage were beneficial to the company. Without delegation, there is little opportunity to deal with problems that are exceptions to the rules. The manager then merely serves to administer the regulations.

As organizations have become larger and technologically complex more activities have been delegated so that even the lowest level supervisor has a freedom to solve certain problems and to make some decisions. In Chapter 6 the area-of-freedom concept was used to describe supervisors' decision-making opportunities. The use of this freedom is part of their jobs, and whether or not they share this freedom with subordinates or make all decisions themselves is beside the point. How effectively they use this freedom is a matter of accountability. In order to give each level of management opportunities to solve problems and permit adaptation to changing conditions, it is in the interest of an organization to pass down as much decision making as possible. Thus supervisors cannot be permitted to set working hours because uniformity of hours may be essential, but they should be able to make decisions about work assignments. In this matter they might make the decision themselves or be influenced by their workers. Department heads might make decisions regarding space priorities in their sections, but they could delegate to their subordinates the best way to use the space. In each case, the decision could be participative or unilateral, but the decision made indicates the area of freedom for the level below. As needs for problem-solving opportunities increase, the delegated areas of freedom might be expanded. However, it also follows that the larger the area of freedom, the more able the manager must be in utilizing it. The recent emphasis on management training indicates that recognition of the skill requirement of managers is increasing.

Boundaries of the Area of Freedom

Table 8.2 (p. 197) indicates that superiors and subordinates have quite different perceptions of the duties, responsibilities, and problems of the subordinate. There was more disagreement than agreement between them on these matters. The resolution to this discrepancy requires that a clear understanding between them be reached. This requires a discussion in which the perceptions of each are explored freely.

The effects of vague vs. clear and large vs. small areas of freedom were experimentally tested.[33] When the area of freedom is vague, subordinates behave as if they had less freedom than they actually have because they do not want to risk criticism. If the area of freedom is small, they are more inclined to do a poor job of problem solving because they think routinely. Merely telling managers how much freedom they have to carry out an assignment is not an effective way to delegate.

[33] Epstein, S. *An experimental study of some of the effects of variations in the clarity and extent of a supervisor's area of freedom upon his supervisory behavior.* Doctoral dissertation, University of Michigan, 1956.

In the experiment on delegation discussed on page 580, the foremen responded more to the demands of the situation than to their degrees of freedom. Delegation requires not only communication, but a solution that respects the needs of the superior and the subordinate.

Stages of Delegation

As previously pointed out, the job description does not successfully determine or communicate the tasks a manager should perform. With the same job description two managers do not permit the same freedoms of their subordinates and two subordinates of the same superior do not perceive their freedoms alike. Subordinates differ in personality and ability, and see their assignments in different perspectives. Generally speaking, superiors want their subordinates to be less dependent and to take more initiative, while subordinates, in general, feel they could do a better job if they had more freedom. Both supervisor and subordinate favor the subordinates having more freedom, yet subordinates do not take as much as is expected of them. The reason is largely fear. It is assumed that one can get into more trouble for what he *does* than for what he *fails to do.* Good decisions may not be noticed, but mistakes usually are. Such sources of inhibition, if real or imagined, can best be removed through clarification of delegation. Inconsistencies in a superior's behavior might be discovered as part of the problem.

Subordinates differ in experience, ability, and personality, and they should not be given the same amount of freedom. Likewise superiors differ in that they are not equally ready to grant the same degrees of freedom to others that their positions permit. Because of these differences, delegation should be tailored to fit the persons involved. In order to accomplish this, delegation should not be regarded as an all-or-nothing process, but one that involves stages so that different degrees of delegation may be given for the different activities a manager supervises. Table 21.1 shows four stages of delegation. In Stage 1 the subordinates work without supervision. They are given the responsibility of performing their duties, but they have no

Table 21.1 / Stages of Delegation

Stage	Area of Freedom
1	Carrying out assignments, enforcing rules, giving assignments. No decision making other than who does what.
2	Stage 1 plus the expectation to make suggestions for improvement. Changes must be approved by superior.
3	Stage 2 plus participation in problem solving and decision making. Assume superior practices group decision.
4	Full delegation. Subordinates run things as they see fit. They are accountable for results but not how results are obtained.

authority to alter the job procedures or introduce changes. They have freedom to plan their work and make assignments.

In Stage 2, the subordinates are expected to think and make suggestions to improve their operations, but they must obtain approval from higher management before making changes. Superiors should be aware that vetoing too many suggestions will cause subordinates to revert to Stage 1.

In Stage 3 a superior shares problem solving with individual subordinates, and with subordinates as groups when solutions involve the group as a whole. Training in group decision and group problem solving would tend to develop this type of delegation.

Stage 4 represents full delegation. The managers run their units as if they were the owners. As owners, they are accountable and suffer if the operation is not successful. Like the head football coach, who is not told by higher management how to run his team, having a poor season could cause termination of his contract.

These four stages of delegation do not apply to all subordinates and to all duties in the same way. For example, the regional head of overhead lines might have decisions to make regarding (1) transferring crews, (2) permitting overtime, (3) setting production goals, (4) enforcing safety, and (5) making changes in work priorities. How much freedom should the department head give the regional heads since they differ in experience and ability? Table 21.2 shows how the stages of delegation in each of these decision areas may be tailored to fit the subordinates involved. Subordinates B and E are trusted and experienced, Subordinate D is new and developing. Stage 3 can be used for training; and with respect to priorities, the group as a whole is consulted. As subordinates acquire more experience and as the superior develops more and more confidence in the judgments of certain individuals, the degree of delegation for various decision areas would change from year to year. These patterns of delegation should be reached through discussion, during which the needs of both superior and subordinate are frankly communicated. If one subordinate felt unfairly treated, the discussion in which priorities were set may not have been frank and open. Formal organization charts and job descriptions cannot be adapted to fit the personalities involved and hence lead to reduced effectiveness, informal organizations, and job ambiguity.

Table 21.2 / Delegation According to Ability and Decision Areas

Decision Areas	Crews	Overtime	Production	Safety	Priorities
Subordinate A	Stage 2	Stage 2	Stage 3	Stage 4	Stage 3
Subordinate B	Stage 4	Stage 3	Stage 4	Stage 2	Stage 3
Subordinate C	Stage 1	Stage 3	Stage 2	Stage 1	Stage 3
Subordinate D	Stage 1	Stage 1	Stage 2	Stage 1	Stage 3
Subordinate E	Stage 4	Stage 4	Stage 4	Stage 4	Stage 3

Modern Organizational Theories

Introduction

A theory brings order to a mass of information. When a detective has a theory about a crime, the motives, the time of the crime, alibis of suspects, footprints, fingerprints, evidence of a struggle, all fit into a framework, and the meaning of the parts depends on the frame. If the theory is correct, it should accurately describe the way the crime was committed and by whom. If new facts are inconsistent with the theory, the two must be reconciled or the theory should be altered or replaced. A good theory should suggest places to look for supporting or conflicting evidence and in this way the theory suggests research. Because a theory serves as a frame of reference, it gives the facts specific meanings and determines the relative importance of functions. In examining various theories what is important in one theory may have another meaning in a different theory. Since serious theorizing in this field is relatively recent, the reader may find the theories incomplete and oversimplified. Nevertheless, they reflect the current thinking in the field.

Theories X and Y

Traditional organization concepts were primarily concerned with the problem of exercising centralized control over all operations. Finding ways to best achieve this control thus became a vital concern. The importance of the human side was neglected, and theory was frowned upon because practical common sense was regarded as a virtue. McGregor[34] countered this claim by pointing out that the practical person in business actually follows a theory of human behavior. He called it Theory X and showed how management practice assumes that (1) most people will avoid work if they can; (2) coercion and punishment must be used to get people to expend adequate energy to achieve organizational objectives; and (3) the average person prefers to be directed, wants to avoid responsibility, and needs security above all else. In contrast he pointed out how psychological theory, which he called Theory Y, revealed that (1) expending mental and physical energy is as natural in work as in play; (2) people will exercise self-control to achieve goals they accept; (3) people seek responsibility; (4) problem-solving ability is present in a large segment of the population; and (5) industry does not utilize the full potential of its people. Thus Theory Y emphasizes the need to practice psychology.

Psychological principles, however, often are based on averages. Most students would not cheat on an examination so that an honor system could be used. However, if 1 per cent of the students cheat when trusted, should these be deterred? Social pressure might be an effective force, but what if it is not? Most of the constraints in organizations were established because of a small percentage of people who seem to be described by Theory X. The major contribution of the discussion of Theories X and Y was that so-called common sense was actually the practice of a theory. Theories must be practical if they are to serve a purpose.

[34] McGregor, Douglas. *The human side of enterprise.* New York: McGraw-Hill, 1960.

The Organization as an Organism

Haire[35] draws an analogy between biological organisms and business organizations. A single-celled animal performs all basic functions (feeding, locomotion, reproduction, etc.), but as it becomes larger, specialized functions develop. The increased volume does not expose enough body surface to permit feeding through the membrane, so a circulatory system gradually evolves. Instead of one cell performing all functions, the complex organism develops a nervous system, a digestive system, "sensory system," etc. The physiologist may study the functions of individual systems, but the behavior of the organism as a whole is the province of the psychologist.

Likewise, when a job grows to require more than one person can do, a helper is hired, who now is a subordinate. Whyte[36] describes how a one-man diner flourishes. The owner is cook, counterman, cashier, purchasing agent, and greeter. When he expands, the functions become specialized so that he has waitresses, a cook, and a cashier. If he expands further and has a chain of restaurants, he needs managers. Soon he will need specialized personnel, financial, and promotional help. Specialized functions that serve to aid coordination, development, and support are described as *staff*. These increase with organizational size and are usually distinguished from line functions which have to do with the product or the service the company performs.

When does growth become self-destructive? An animal that is too large to be able to eat enough in one day to maintain itself cannot survive. Haire[37] points out that a shelf bracket must be strongest where it receives the heaviest load, i.e., where it is most likely to break. If growth of organization can lead to self-destruction, then it becomes essential that a theory must locate the points of greatest weakness. Organization theories therefore may be expected to differ in terms of where organizational weakness is stressed.

Haire,[38] using growth trends, seeks to find lawful processes in growth and the interdependence of size, shape, and function. He studied the growth patterns of four different companies and found sufficient similarities to encourage the belief that growth models can be developed.

Organizations as Dependent Subsystems

Katz and Kahn[39] see the organization as made up of groups of people, each being a subsystem. Thus production, maintenance, and personnel functions became subsystems. Each subsystem develops group goals and values which frequently conflict with those of other subsystems. To view the subsystems as interrelated only so far as production is concerned is to overlook the potential conflict in values developed

---

[35] Haire, M. Biological models and empirical histories of the growth of organizations. In M. Haire (Ed.), *Modern organization theory.* New York: Wiley, 1959.

[36] Whyte, W. F. *Human relations in the restaurant industry.* New York: McGraw-Hill, 1948.

[37] Haire, *op. cit.*

[38] *Ibid.*

[39] Katz, D., and Kahn, R. L. *The social psychology of organizations.* New York: Wiley, 1966.

within the subsystem. Communication between subsystems is complicated by the invisible boundaries that separate them. Organizational psychology thus must be sensitive to groups and the dependence of individual behavior on group norms and loyalties.

Katz and Kahn think of the human aspect of organizations as role systems and see behavior as fulfilling roles. Thus, persons in a given position behave according to their perceptions of what their jobs require. Persons behave differently as they assume different roles or as their positions change. When a union steward is promoted to a foreman his behavior changes in accordance with his role.[40]

Organizations as Determined by the Nature of Man

Argyris[41] begins with individual motivations to study how these lead to group membership, either formal or informal. However, organizations coerce them to be dependent and subordinate, which often is a source of frustration. In order to facilitate behavior within an organization Argyris promotes T-group training (see p. 323) designed to develop self-insights in executives and break down some of the communications barriers. Thus for him the basic problem in organizations is the need to develop warm interpersonal relationships and trust.

The influence of group membership on individual behavior is also emphasized by Whyte,[42] Bakke,[43] Dubin,[44] and Blake and Mouton[45] in their theories of organizational behavior.

Organizations as Determined by Leadership Styles

Likert's[46] system relies heavily on individual motivation achieved through the supportive behavior (see Chapter 5) of the superior. This is a form of paternalism which he attempts to integrate with group-decision concepts (see Chapter 6) and describes supportive leader-subordinate relations as participative. Like Marrow[47] and McGregor[48] he makes a key issue of leadership styles.

The influence of Lewin (see Chapter 6) in describing autocratic, democratic, and laissez-faire leadership styles has been reflected in most organizational theories that emphasize leadership as the key factor. How these styles are adapted to the organizational hierarchy may differ somewhat on questions such as: Is one style the best for all types of situations? Can acceptance be achieved in the same way as quality

[40] Lieberman, S. The effects of changes in roles on the attitudes of role occupants. *Hum. Relat.,* 1956, 9, 385–402.

[41] Argyris, C. *Interpersonal competence and organizational effectiveness.* Homewood, Ill.: Irwin-Dorsey, 1962.

[42] Whyte, W. F. An interaction approach to the theory of organization. In M. Haire (Ed.), *Modern organization theory.* New York: Wiley, 1959.

[43] Bakke, E. W. Concept of the social organization. In M. Haire, *op. cit.*

[44] Dubin, R. Stability of human organizations. In M. Haire, *op. cit.*

[45] Blake, R. R., and Mouton, J. S. *Corporate excellence through grid organization development.* Houston, Tex.: Gulf, 1968.

[46] Likert, R. *New patterns of management.* New York: McGraw-Hill, 1967.

[47] Marrow, A. J. *Making management human.* New York: McGraw-Hill, 1957.

[48] McGregor, D. *Leadership and motivation.* Cambridge, Mass.: MIT Press, 1966.

in decision making? How does participative leadership differ from group decision? How important are training and skill in participative management?

Within an organization, personalities, motivations, training, and conceptions of leadership differ so that one cannot describe an organization's leadership in specific terms. At best one can describe the prevalent or average style despite the fact that no one might fit the average.

The next section on leadership styles is concerned with leadership and the nature of man in creating organizational climates. This climate becomes the social environment that influences organizational behavior.

Decision-making Models

Another group of theories emphasizes the decision-making process as the essential factor in organizational effectiveness. They[49] approach decision making with a logical analysis and attempt to develop mathematical models that might aid the solving of problems. For example, a formula might be developed for the amount of overtime that is justified considering backlog of orders, production scheduled, availability of temporary transfers, etc. When the need arose the manager would merely fill in the appropriate figures and solve the equation to reach a decision. This approach places emphasis on the quality dimension of the decisions rather than the acceptance dimension (see Chapter 6). It is not uncommon for a whole section to develop poor morale because the manager will not, or is not allowed to, deviate from a decision reached by mathematics.

An organization may be ineffective because its decisions do not utilize knowledge and logic sufficiently or because its decisions fail to gain the acceptance of the persons who must implement them. According to the conclusions reached in Chapter 6, problems fall into four different types because they vary in the degree to which acceptance and quality play a crucial part. If the decision-making method depends upon the type of problem, the use of models should be restricted to appropriate problems and this requires human judgment. It is not surprising that theories will differ depending upon the problems selected as representative of those of the organization.

Organizational Climate

Introduction

Chapter 6 pointed out that the style of leadership establishes a climate that influences the behavior of the group. Although each leader determines the climate he estab-

[49] Cyert, R. M., and March, J. G. *Behavior theory of the firm.* Englewood Cliffs, N.J.: Prentice-Hall, 1963; Goldberg, W. (Ed.), *Behavioral approaches to modern management* (Vol. 1), *Information systems and decision making* (Vol. 2), *Applications of marketing, production, and finance.* Gothenberg, Sweden: Studies in Business Administration, 1970; Hedberg, B. *On man-computer interaction in organizational decision-making: A behavioral approach.* Gothenberg, Sweden: Studies in Business Administration, 1970; March, J. G., and Simon, H. *Organizations.* New York: Wiley, 1958; Marshak, J. Efficient and viable organizational forms. In M. Haire (Ed.), *op. cit.,* pp. 307–320.

lishes, there are overall styles in the organization that create a general climate. Some organizations are described as punitive—control is largely maintained by rules and penalties administered through punishment. In contrast, some university administrations may be described as permissive because they allow students a high degree of freedom. Some organizations tend to be paternalistic, a style that is usually determined by the head (or founder) of the organization. Climates of this kind are largely influenced by the personality of the president and in the not-too-distant past, managers were untrained and operated the units on a "common sense" basis. Of course, common sense was influenced by the experience of how superiors were managed when they were subordinates. Thus, to some extent, the climate perpetuates itself and changes along with the personal values of the person in control.

A further factor also must be considered. Hiring and promotion practices involve the selection of individuals who satisfy the norms of the established leaders. In one organization a man may be regarded as unfit for a promotion because he is too rigid and punitive, while in another, he might be passed by because he isn't firm enough and would be a poor disciplinarian. In working with companies one can sense climates differing in friendliness, seriousness, graciousness, orderliness, and criticalness, etc.—traits often used to characterize various groups within an organization. Actors characterize audiences in a similar manner. Fraternity brothers develop a homogeneity so that stereotypes might well describe various fraternities. This homogeneity stems partly from the fact that people tend to prefer associates who are alike in personality and attitudes[50] and partly from the fact that they become more alike by working and socializing with one another. In this way, certain organizational value systems develop. Some years ago the hiring practices of the companies within the Bell System were such that it was frequently compared to a fraternity. However, within any given organization a variety of managerial practices can exist.

If the attitudes of persons in an organization are measured, differences within companies may be obtained, and overall comparisons between companies would be possible. This is a common approach to the study of organizational climate and how it influences behavior. Questionnaires about management practices can determine the influence of participation on attitudes, job satisfaction, and organizational effectiveness.

Various forms of participative management are in actual practice. These include having the opportunity to vote and influence majority decisions; having a chance to offer suggestions; being invited to a meeting and hearing officials describe plans; and serving on committees which may or may not lead to action. However, they all fall short of group decision, which requires a face-to-face problem-solving discussion in which the decision comes from the group and not the leader. On pages 132–133 emphasis was placed upon different types of problems and how different methods seemed to be called for. Thus skill in using the proper method for the type of problem becomes crucial.

[50] Newcomb, T. *The acquaintance process.* New York: Holt, Rinehart & Winston, 1961.

Since most companies studied by organizational psychologists have had limited management training, participative practices will vary considerably, but in general, organizational effectiveness is associated with participative types of practices.

Management by Objectives

A procedure known as management by objectives has been introduced and a number of companies have been influenced by it.[51] The basic concept is that superior and subordinate managers of an organization should participate in reaching agreement on goals of mutual interest and define the major areas of responsibility in terms of the results expected of the subordinate. With specific measurable goals established, the contribution toward these goals can be assessed. Thus a subordinate can be judged by results. Theoretically this practice should lead to motivation to produce, and the manager would be appraised by results, not in terms of how they were produced.

In practice a number of types of violations occur. Too frequently the superior dominates the goal setting and the subordinate submits, so the motivational value of goal setting by participation is lost. Then too, the goals discussed often are not measurable or they are too vague. A goal to outperform last year's record should specify in what ways and by how much. When asked to set goals does the subordinate assume he must do better and hence is inclined to set unrealistic goals, or does he play it safe and suggest low ones? Does the superior permit the subordinate to indicate in what way the subordinate expects certain kinds of help and does the superior explore these needs? Joint goal setting involves problem-solving skills on the part of the superior, and such interactions not only could lead to motivated performance but could go beyond mere goal setting by introducing improvements initiated from below.

Since management by objectives is more philosophy than training program, what can be expected when it is adopted as an organization's climate? A study of the results in two companies revealed some positive gains.[52] There were some gains in satisfaction of higher-type needs (self-actualization) and in security needs when the program had good support of top management. Essential to improvement seemed to be the need for progress interviews with superiors. Complaints also resulted.[53] These included excessive time spent in counseling and overemphasis on quantitative goals, the first of which is related to need satisfaction and the second of which reflects the need to escape measurement. Management by objectives seems to raise problems similar to those generated in post-appraisal interviews (see Chapter 20). If problem solving occurs, performance can be improved by correcting the situation rather than the person, but when the superior stands in judgment and attempts to improve the person, defensiveness is likely to occur.

[51] Drucker, P. *The practice of management.* New York: Harper & Row, 1954; Odiorne, G *Management by objectives.* New York: Pitman, 1965.

[52] Ivancevich, J. M., Donnelly, J. H., and Lyon, H. L. A study of the impact of management by objectives on perceived need satisfaction. *Personnel Psychol.,* 1970, *23,* 139–151.

[53] Raia, A. P. A second look at management goals and controls. *Calif. Mgt. Rev.,* 1966, *8,* 49–58; Ivancevich, *et al., op. cit.*

Likert's Systems

Likert[54] developed a questionnaire instrument that classifies management practices into four systems. System I may be called the carrot-stick principle (in which rewards and punishment are used to control behavior). System II is more benevolent in that emphasis is placed upon rewards rather than on punishment. System III introduces considerable freedom and allows subordinates more initiative and increased responsibility. System IV involves the sharing of responsibility and authority throughout the organization, which assumes a degree of participation in group problem solving and decision making. Likert presents survey data to support the conclusion that, generally speaking, organizational effectiveness (cooperation, motivation, productivity) increases progressively as one goes from System I to IV, but the various measures used do not always show the same trends. Although managerial styles may differ, he found that the system used by top management tended to set the style for the organization.

Since questionnaire responses are influenced by the amount of consideration employees receive from their superiors, a supervisor who is "people" rather than "production" oriented will appear to allow more freedom than a "production" oriented supervisor. The Likert systems tend to differ more in degree than in kind, and System IV falls considerably short of the skillful practice of group problem solving. Even so, there is a favorable trend as one moves from autocratic to more permissive and considerate climates.

Initiation and Consideration

The concepts *consideration* and *initiating structure,* (see pp. 105–107) make a qualitative distinction between consideration for people and activities related to getting the job done. (Consideration should not be construed as permissiveness or laissez faire since it includes evaluation of performance.) These two dimensions of supervisory behavior are individually measured by questionnaires. Consideration tends to promote lower absenteeism, less turnover, and fewer grievances[55] while initiation, if well handled, leads to increased productivity. Generally speaking, supervisors scoring high in the initiation dimension are highly rated by superiors and higher producing groups, while leaders scoring high on consideration have more satisfied subordinates than those scoring low,[56] but again, the results cannot be freely generalized because size of group, the skill level of the manager, and the type of work performed influence the relationship. A good deal of the inconsistency in data has been clarified by studying the effects of consideration and initiating structure in a leader's behavior by distinguishing between jobs varying in interest and ambi-

---

[54] Likert, R. *The human organization: Its management and value.* New York: McGraw-Hill, 1967; Bowers, D. G., and Seashore, S. E. Predicting organizational effectiveness with a four-factor theory of leadership. *Administration Sci. Quart.,* 1966, *11,* 238–263.

[55] Fleishman, E. A., and Harris, E. F. Patterns of leadership behavior related to employee grievances and turnover. *Personnel Psychol.,* 1962, *15,* 43–56.

[56] Filley, A. C., and House, R. J. *Managerial process and organizational behavior.* Glenview, Ill.: Scott, Foresman, 1969.

guity.[57] When jobs are ambiguous, initiating structure is related to job satisfaction, whereas in routine jobs the correlation is negative. As jobs increase in scope and autonomy, consideration becomes less important because job satisfaction comes from the work and is less dependent upon consideration. It appears that both types of leader behavior have their place. The type of work is one factor to consider, but the needs of different individuals and the aspect of the work on which to use it also must be considered.

Judgment and sensitivity about when and how much help to give, and judgment in distinguishing between consideration and permissiveness are skill factors. These skills are difficult to measure with a questionnaire, yet they can be crucial determiners of the importance of these behaviors of the leader.

The Managerial Grid

If one plots a manager's concern for productivity on a nine-point scale on the horizontal axis and his concern for people on the vertical axis, each manager can be depicted as a point on the grid.[58] Each individual could then be given a "production, people" score. The organization could be described in terms of the quadrant into which most managers fell. A tendency toward a "1, 1" system would indicate low concern for both people and production; a "1, 9" tendency would indicate low concern for production and high concern for people; and a "9, 1" system would indicate high concern for production and low concern for people. The ideal system would be a trend toward "9, 9". Under many conditions these dual concerns or goals would be difficult to reconcile and this then becomes the objective of the management training promoted by Blake and Mouton.

Sensitivity Training

How well an organization functions depends greatly upon the effectiveness of its communications. Perhaps the greatest change in thinking about organization has been the awareness of the need to communicate in a climate of trust. Cooperation depends upon trust and the development of mutual interests, but the nature of organizations does not facilitate this type of climate. The Training Laboratories at Bethel, Maine, which developed T-group methods (see p. 323), also known as Sensitivity Training, have influenced the thinking of organizational psychologists (including McGregor, Argyris, Likert, and Blake) who try to improve organizational effectiveness by training the higher levels of management.[59] The type of

---

[57] House, R. J. *A path goal theory of leadership behavior*. In press; Fiedler, F. E. *A theory of leadership effectiveness*. New York: McGraw-Hill, 1967.

[58] Blake, R. R., and Mouton, J. S. *The managerial grid*. Houston, Tex.: Gulf, 1964.

[59] Bradford, L. P., Gibb, J. R., and Benne, K. D. (Eds.). *T-group theory and laboratory method*. New York: Wiley, 1964; Argyris, C. *Integrating the individual and the organization*. New York: Wiley, 1964; Bennis, W. G., and Schein, E. H. *Personal and organizational change through group methods*. New York: Wiley, 1965; Marrow, A. J., Bowers, D. G., and Seashore, S. E. *Management by participation*. New York: Harper & Row, 1967; McGregor, D. *The human side of enterprise*. New York: McGraw-Hill, 1960; Bass, B. M. The anarchist movement and the T-group: Some possible lessons for organizational development. *J. appl. behav. Sci.*, 1967, *3*, 211–227. Tannenbaum, R., Wechsler, I., and Massarik, F. *Leadership and organization*. New York: McGraw-Hill, 1961; Leavitt, H. J. *The social science of organizations*. Englewood Cliffs, N.J.: Prentice-Hall, 1963.

leadership described in Chapter 6 is generally a basic premise in this type of training. Attitudes and self-insights must be changed in order to achieve the type of leadership that makes for understanding, acceptance, and communication. Such training is usually of longer duration than other programs of management development, so that the participants have a chance to become well acquainted. Through the efforts to reduce rank barriers and holding frank discussions about interpersonal conflicts, the group gradually develops trust and self-insights. Furthermore, such training sessions permit the solving of existing problems in the group. Insofar as these improvements in communication occur for persons within the same organization, organizational effectiveness might be increased, but convincing proof of such changes is lacking.[60] Changes in organizational effectiveness are more difficult to measure than changes in situations in which only one leader and group are involved. How much training and how many individuals must be changed to make a clear-cut difference in the organizational climate remains an experimental question. Also unknown is the appraisal of the aspects of such training that were of value. There is general agreement that the programs accomplish certain gains, the most common of which is employee satisfaction.[61] Negative effect can result if group leaders lack essential skills.

Measuring Organizational Change

Perhaps the largest project undertaken to change an organization through training was carried out in the Harwood Manufacturing Corporation after merging with the Weldon Manufacturing Company, to form the Harwood-Weldon Corporation.[62] Weldon had been a competitor of about equal size but had a different market, because it produced a higher-quality product (pajamas). Harwood had been the site of many progressive experiments largely because Marrow, its president, was a social psychologist. The merger of this progressive company with one having an authoritarian style of management created the need to change the management style of the acquired organization. About 1000 people were involved in this change program.

The program included the utilization of outside experts (change agents) who introduced the following types of changes:

1. redesigns of jobs, with workers in semiautonomous groups;
2. employee training (new workers previously had been trained);
3. retraining and coaching of poor performers;
4. sensitivity training for executives;
5. training seminars in interpersonal relations for supervisors and staff;
6. group problem-solving meetings at work-group levels;
7. new production methods with a pay rate increase;
8. employment selection tests (tests had not previously been used);
9. discharge of chronic low performers.

---

[60] House, R. J. T-group education and leadership effectiveness: A review of the empirical literature and a critical evaluation. *Personnel Psychol.,* 1967, *20,* 1–32; Campbell, J. P., and Dunnette, M. D. Effectiveness of T-group experience in managerial training and development. *Psychol. Bull.,* 1968, *70,* 73–104.

[61] House, R. J., and Tosi, H. An experimental evaluation of a management training program. *J. Acad. Mgt.,* 1963, *6,* 303–315.

[62] Marrow, Bowers, and Seashore, *op. cit.*

At the end of two years, productivity rose 30 per cent and survey data revealed changes in managerial behavior and employee satisfaction.

The research design permitted the identification of the causes of some of the improvements. Retraining and coaching contributed 11 per cent; discharging poor workers, 5 per cent; improved interpersonal relations, 5 per cent; group problem solving, 3 per cent. Considering the extent of the changes made by group problem solving, these gains may seem small, particularly when compared with what an individual leader may accomplish (see Chapter 6). However, such changes represented improvement achieved when group decision was used by a select leader.

Measuring changes in an organization is complicated by the fact that many managers and several levels of management are involved. Training in interpersonal skills or in group decision methods does not necessarily cause all trainees to acquire such skills or to practice them if they are acquired. A two-week training program may change the managerial behavior of a few persons to a considerable degree while not changing others at all. More training might change them, but there is no assurance that a given training approach will affect all participants, regardless of how extensive the program.

However, a change in one person in a crucial position is sometimes sufficient to pay for a training program. The beneficial results attributed to some of the sensitivity programs are likely to be due to changes in certain key individuals. Often merely reducing the harm they can do can lead to an improvement.

Organization Development (O.D.)

Introducing Change

Changing an organization is a large undertaking. This chapter has described various approaches to increasing organizational effectiveness either through the selection or the training of management personnel. The illustrations of organizational changes described indicate the magnitude of the training problems in attempts to change an organizational climate. Changes in organizational structure, new methods of production, the uses of computers, and engineering design changes represent changes in jobs and physical environment which are made to keep up with modern technology. This approach to modern organizations is known as Operations Research (O.R.). In recent years new developments have been so rapid that keeping up with the times has been a great source of frustration. Chapter 2 described how behavior (B) is a function of the situation or stimulus (S) and the nature of the person or organism (O). Changes required in B to increase an organization's accomplishment (A) therefore may involve either S or O or both. Some changes are initiated by technical staffs or are recommended by outside consulting firms (experts in business and engineering technology (O.R.)), while changes in supervisory behavior or worker skills are initiated by the staff (specialists in the training department), or by consulting firms whose members are likely to be trained in psychology or sociology (O.D.). Regardless of the source of the change, the initiation is likely to come from persons other than those who have to change or to adapt themselves to the changes.

Since change initiated from outside the group introduces a threat, it is resisted. Each change situation has its own types of threat so that the emotional condition should be diagnosed beforehand (see example described in the Changing Work Procedure case, pp. 345–346). Changes initiated through group problem solving, however, are welcomed. Involving people in change thus becomes an important change method, but how to adapt it to each change situation raises problems in the application of group decision on an organizational basis. Changes required at one level (foreman and workers) are relatively simple procedures, although getting a leader to try it out requires training (changing the O). Alternatives other than full participation include the building of trust and ability to give assurance that there will be no penalties. In most instances the research on dealing with resistance to change has involved the use of outside leaders rather than actual supervisors.[63] However, the illustrations of group decision discussed in Chapter 6 were initiated by line supervisors and their immediate subordinates. Because the negative results of resistance become apparent after the changes have been made (e.g., a move to a new plant), they are discovered too late for correction. Thus high-quality decisions fail because acceptance is zero or negative. Effective introduction of change in an organization is a complex problem, and the potential sources of fear must be anticipated in order to cope with them.

Changes initiated from the outside are obviously beneficial to those who initiate them, but what effect will they have on the recipients? It is to the interest of organizations to develop trust between organizational levels and between staff and line functions because higher management and staff personnel usually are the initiators of change. Job satisfaction increases in accordance with the degree of trust subordinates feel their superiors have in them and the degree to which there is participation in management decisions.[64]

The Function of Change Agents

Because changes involve emotions of fear and hostility, rational approaches are insufficient. The obstacles are the feelings of people, not engineering know-how. Since companies have had bad experiences with changes, it is not uncommon for them to utilize *change agents* to aid them. These are outsiders who then work closely with the organization for a period of time.

The change agent has three advantages: being professionally trained; being an outsider; and being free of any of the organization's cultural biases. The change agent's function is to obtain information (through interviews and questionnaire data) and to make a diagnosis of the organization's weaknesses and strengths.[65] The first step is to make a *diagnosis* which points up obstacles and the problems that

[63] Coch, L., and French, J. R. P., Jr. Overcoming resistance to change. *Hum. Relat.*, 1948, *1*, 512–532.

[64] Ritchie, J. B., and Miles, R. E. An analysis of quantity and quality of participation as mediating variables in the participative decision-making process. *Personnel Psychol.*, 1970, *23*, 347–359.

[65] Lippitt, R., Watson, J., and Westley, B. *The dynamics of planned change*. New York: Harcourt, Brace, & World, 1958; Bennis, W. G., Benne, K. D., and Chin, R. (Eds.) *The planning of change (2nd ed.)*. New York: Holt, Rinehart & Winston, 1969.

need to be solved, the relative importance of acceptance, and whether members of the organization can be involved in problem solving. Through problem solving with clients certain actions or programs become apparent. A program of planned change is developed by making use of the outside agents' resources, knowledge, diagnostic skills, and group problem-solving leadership.

The implementation of a program requires that specific actions, or *interventions,* be made from time to time. An example of an intervention by a change agent might be the halting of a management meeting in order to analyze certain points in the discussion process.[66] Experts agree that changes in an organization cannot be imposed from without. The change agent needs to work with and through *Internal Resource Persons* who have developed the essential interpersonal skills and have an understanding of the importance of the acceptance dimension of decisions. Argyris[67] uses the term *interpersonal competence* to indicate an essential ability in resource persons. This competence is characterized by the counseling and human relations skills (such as those discussed in Chapters 3, 4, 6, and 20) and may be acquired through sensitivity training, role playing, or training in counseling. If in a planned change program the change agent recommended sensitivity training for some executives, it would be called an *intervention.*

Most large changes are initiated at the level of top management, which then becomes the *point of entry.* Lesser changes (such as modifying safety or supervisory training programs, altering employment practices, and altering production-line procedures) may have points of entry at the level of superintendent, training or personnel departments, or the head of a particular plant. However, any of these changes must have the support of top management if they are to succeed. But such support does not assure success. The general acceptance of a specific change depends upon the way the individuals who have to live with the change feel about it. Change problems are difficult because both high quality and high acceptance are needed. This makes it a Type IV problem (see Chapter 6), the only type that makes considerable demands on conference skills. The employment of change agents represents a method for obtaining the needed skills, but any skills developed inside the organization are important gains in management development. The final chapter is designed to aid managers to improve their skills so that they can make more complete use of group resources in solving problems that require both quality and acceptance.

The Risk Technique

People who fear change often do not understand the nature of their fears. Such fears cannot be guarded against and so become anxieties. The first step in dealing with anxiety is to locate its sources. Once the anxiety becomes resolved into specific fears, the goal of guarding against them becomes a soluble problem.

The Risk Technique is a group method for clarifying fears. The leader (or change

---

[66] Schein, E. H. *Process consultation: Its role in organizational development.* Reading, Mass.: Addison-Wesley, 1969.

[67] Argyris, C. *Interpersonal competence and organizational effectiveness.* Homewood, Ill.: Irwin-Dorsey, 1962.

agent) whose activity up to this point has promoted change tends to build up anxieties. Managers in groups of 15 or 25 are invited to discuss some of the dangers they see in the change program. This method was successfully used in a management program designed to remove resistance to and acceptance of group decision. The function of the leader is to post the risks on the chalkboard. Before each risk is posed, there should be sufficient discussion to make the danger specific.[68] Participants need not agree on the risk discussed, but they should try to understand it. Typical examples of risks developed in discussion are shown in Table 21.3 Some of the risks represent misconceptions, some are imagined fears, some represent hostilities, others raise problems of how to adapt the learned principles to their work situations. Participants differ in the number or nature of risks they endorse, but the mere act of posting them reduces the anxiety (catharsis).

Once the risks are posted, methods for avoiding them become topics of mutual interest for problem solving. Such considerations as: (1) the area of freedom; (2) the need to share data; (3) the realization that the participants in group decisions include only a manager and immediate subordinates; (4) the importance of sharing information; (5) and the skill requirements of the leader then become relevant to an objective evaluation of their roles in the new type of leadership.

The use of the Risk Technique lends itself to a variety of types of changes, especially those in which persuasion methods are inadequate. When a large airline was planning a merger with a smaller airline, employees of the smaller line were assured that the merger would not result in discrimination against them. They were even told some might expect pay raises because the wage scale of the larger organi-

Table 21.3 / Risks Posted for Practice of Group Decision

1. Poor quality solutions would result.
2. Supervisor would lose status.
3. Not enough time for such discussions.
4. Groups would not be able to agree.
5. Management would lose control of the company.
6. Higher management would reverse decisions.
7. Employees would want raises because of their contributions to decisions.
8. Unofficial leaders (union steward) would take over.
9. Requires too much skill.
10. Poor morale because of conflicts resulting from discussion.
11. Discussions would be used to avoid doing work.
12. Decisions often would violate company policy.
13. Stockholders would object.
14. Decisions might violate union contracts.
15. Higher management would not permit me to use it.
16. Subordinates lack the essential information.

[68] Maier, N. R. F. *Principles of human relations.* New York: Wiley, 1952; Maier, N. R. F. *Problem-solving discussions and conferences: Leadership methods and skills.* New York: Wiley, 1963.

zation was higher. Entirely overlooked, however, was the fact that the merger would be a threat to the employees of the larger company. At their annual management training program, held during the period when the merger was imminent, morale was extremely low, and there was more hostility than interest in the executive program. The trainer soon realized that the merger was of great emotional concern to all of the participants. The merger was therefore made the discussion topic and the negative features (risks) of the merger were posted. The first group of 16 managers supplied 23 risks; the next group of 15 supplied 19; and the third group of 18 posted 25. The exercise greatly reduced anxiety, and the cooperation in the training seminars was normal. Merely accepting and trying to understand the negative features of the merger reduced the anxiety.

When organizational changes arouse fears and hostility, the expression of these feelings in gripe sessions can have a great value in permitting the resumption of problem-solving behavior. The potential contributions of group problem solving to organizational development becomes a chapter in itself.

Laboratory Exercise

Role Playing: Problem Solving the Appraisal Interview

A. Preparation for role playing.
1. The instructor will read "General Instructions" (D.1) and place the organizational chart shown in Figure 21.4 on the easel.
2. The class should then be divided into groups of three, one member being assigned the role of Stanley (D.2), the other the role of Burke (D.3) and the third the role of observer.
3. When the Burkes have finished reading their parts they should stand and remain standing until further instructions are given.
4. When all of the Burkes are standing, the instructor should be sure that they know who their Stanleys are and that the observer is somewhat on the sidelines. The observer's presence is to be ignored by Stanley and Burke.

B. The role-playing process.
1. When the stage is set, the Burkes will be instructed to knock on Stanley's door (make-believe door) to present themselves for the scheduled interview.
2. Role playing should proceed for about half an hour. Regardless of whether all have finished, they should have reached a point where comparisons in outcome can be made.
3. When the interviews have been terminated by the instructor, he should ask each Stanley to assign two letter grades (A, B, C, D, or E) to Burke; one, for his estimate of Burke before the interview, the other, for his present estimate. These grades should be written down and not be visible to either the observer or Burke.

4. After Stanley has assigned his grades, the observer and Burke should individually write on slips of paper the two grades they think Stanley wrote on his paper and avoid being guided by what grades they think he should have assigned. The appraisal judgments should be set aside for use in later discussions.

C. Discussion.

1. Each observer should report on any changes that will result from the interview. The instructor should check with the role players to determine the accuracy of the observers' judgments. The instructor should briefly summarize points on the chalkboard.
2. After each observer has reported the changes expected, they should in turn report on Tom's job interest. These judgments also should be checked with Tom. The findings should be posted on the chalkboard.
3. The observers should report the before and after interview grades they think Stanley assigned. Tom's opinion and Stanley's estimate should then be posted to test the observer's sensitivity as well as Tom's.
4. The observers should next be asked to go into a huddle with the Burke and Stanley they observed, and point out opportunities they missed, where things went wrong, and why problem solving was not effectively used. The instructor should terminate these discussions after five minutes.
5. The instructor should summarize the discussion, evaluating the place of appraisal programs in organizations, the differences in job perception of the superiors and subordinates, and the potential use of problem solving in situations of this kind.

D. Materials for the case.

1. GENERAL INSTRUCTIONS

George Stanley is the electrical section head in the engineering department of the American Construction Company. The work in the department includes design, drafting, cost estimates, keeping maps up to date, checking standards and building codes, field inspection, follow-up, and so on. Eight first-line supervisors report to George Stanley. The duties of the supervisors are partly technical and partly supervisory (see Figure 21.4).

Company policy requires that all section heads interview each of their supervisors once a year, the purposes being: (*a*) to evaluate the supervisor's performance during the year; (*b*) to give recognition for jobs well done; and (*c*) to correct weaknesses. The company believes that employees should know how they stand and that everything should be done to develop management personnel. The appraisal interviews were introduced to serve these purposes.

Tom Burke is one of the supervisors reporting to Stanley, and today we will witness an appraisal interview conducted by Stanley with Tom Burke.

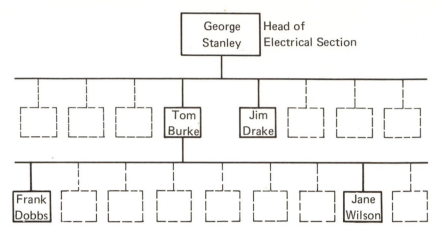

Figure 21.4 / Organizational Chart of Electrical Section of American Construction Company. The names of the persons that may be mentioned in this case are given, together with their positions in the organization. Only George Stanley and Tom Burke are involved in the role playing.

Tom Burke has a college degree in electrical engineering. In addition to his technical duties, which often take him to the field, he supervises the work of one junior designer, six draftsmen, and two women clerks. He is highly paid, as are all the supervisors in this department because of the high requirements in technical knowledge. Burke has been with the company for 12 years and has been a supervisor for two years. He is married and has two children. He owns his home and is active in the civic affairs of the community in which he lives.

2. ROLE FOR GEORGE STANLEY, SECTION HEAD

You have appraised all the supervisors who report to you and during the next two weeks will interview each of them. You hope to use these interviews constructively to develop each man. Today you have arranged to interview Tom Burke, one of the eight first-line supervisors who report to you. Here is the information and his appraisal as given in your files.

Thomas Burke: 12 years with company, two years as supervisor, college degree, married, two children. Evaluation: highly creative and original, and exceptionally competent technically. His unit is very productive, and during the two years he has supervised the group there has been a steady improvement. Within the past six months you have given him extra work and he has had it done on schedule. As far as productivity and dependability are concerned, he is your top man.

His cooperation with other supervisors in the section leaves much to be desired. Before you made him a supervisor his originality and technical knowledge were available to your whole section. Gradually he has withdrawn and now acts more as a lone wolf. You've asked other supervisors to talk over certain problems with him, but they tell you he offers no suggestions. He tells them he's busy or listens disinterestedly to their problems, kids them or makes sarcastic remarks, depending on his mood. On one occasion he allowed *Jim Drake,* one of the supervisors in another unit, to make a mistake he could have forestalled by letting him know the status of certain design changes which he knew about and had seen. It is to be expected that supervisors will cooperate on matters involving design changes that affect them.

Furthermore, during the past six months he has been unwilling to take two assignments. He said they were routine, that he preferred more interesting work, and he advised you to give the assignments to other supervisors. To prevent trouble, you followed his suggestion. However, you feel that you can't give him all the interesting work and that if he persists in this attitude there will be trouble. You cannot play favorites and keep up morale in your unit.

Burke's failure to cooperate has you worried for another reason. Although his group is highly productive, there is more turnover among his draftsmen than in other groups. You have heard no complaints as yet, but you suspect that he may be treating his men in an arbitrary manner. Certainly if he talks up to you and to other supervisors, he's likely to be even more that way with his men. Apparently the high productivity in his group is not due to high morale, but to his ability to use his men to do the things for which they are best suited. This method won't develop good draftsmen. You hope to discuss these matters with Burke in such a way as to recognize his good points and at the same time correct some of his weaknesses. Feel free to handle the interview in the manner you think best.

3. Role for Tom Burke, Supervisor

One junior designer, six draftsmen, and two women clerks report to you. You feel that you get along fine with your group. You have always been pretty much of an idea man and apparently have the knack of passing on your enthusiasm to others in your group. There is a lot of "we" feeling in your unit because it is obvious that your group is the most productive.

You believe in developing your subordinates and always give them strong recommendations. You feel you have gained the reputation of developing your employees because they frequently go out and get much better jobs. Since promotion is necessarily slow in a company such as yours, you feel that the best way to stimulate morale is to develop new people and demonstrate that a good worker can get somewhere. The two women in your unit are bright and efficient and there is a lot of good-natured kidding. Recently one of your clerks, *Jane Wilson,* turned down an outside offer that paid $35 a month more, for she preferred to stay in your group. You are going to get her a raise the first chance you have.

The other supervisors in Stanley's section do not have your enthusiasm. Some of them are dull and unimaginative. During your first year as supervisor you used to help them a lot, but you soon found that they leaned on you and before long you were doing their work. There is a lot of pressure to get out production. You got your promotion by producing and you don't intend to let other supervisors interfere. Since you no longer help the other supervisors your production has gone up, but a couple of them seem a bit sore at you. *Frank,* your junior designer, is better qualified than most of them and you'd like to see him made a supervisor. Since the company has some dead wood in it, Stanley ought to recognize this fact and assign such units the more routine jobs. Then they wouldn't need your help and you could concentrate your efforts on jobs that suit your unit. At present, George Stanley passes out work pretty much as he gets it. Because you are efficient you get more than your share of these jobs, and you see no reason why the extra work shouldn't be in the form of "plums." This would motivate units to turn out work. When you suggested to Stanley that he turn over some of the more routine jobs to other supervisors, he did it, but he was reluctant about it.

You did one thing recently that has bothered you. There was a design change in a set of plans and you should have told *Jim Drake* (a fellow supervisor) about it, but it slipped your mind. Drake was out when you had it on your mind and then you got involved in a hot idea that Frank, your junior designer, had and forgot all about the matter with Drake. As a result, Drake had to make a lot of unnecessary changes, and he was quite sore about it. You told him you were sorry and offered to make the changes, but he turned down the offer.

Today you have an interview with George Stanley. It's about this management development plan in the company. It shouldn't take very long, but it's nice to have the boss tell you about the job you're turning out. Maybe there is a raise in it, maybe he'll tell you something about what to expect in the future.

4. Instructions for Observers

Read the roles of Stanley and Burke for background, sensitizing you to the problem. Do not participate in the interview or offer suggestions. Your task is to observe and evaluate. Do not discuss observations or conclusions with Burke or Stanley since you will report to the class as a whole.

Although the *tell-and-sell* method is usually followed by supervisors in situations of this type, we are concerned with whether Stanley tries to involve Tom Burke in problem solving. Pay especial attention to the following points.

1. Does Stanley praise or criticise? How are these evaluations received by Tom?

2. Does Stanley raise problems to (a) invite participation in solving them or (b) to let Tom know about them?

3. Does Tom ask for certain things (e.g., special treatment of any kind)? If so, does Stanley explore with him how to do it without creating new problems, or does he turn Tom down?

4. What skills does Stanley display that have been discussed in the course? List them as they occur.

5. At the end of the interview, indicate how you think Stanley or Burke might behave differently in the future.

6. Has Tom's job interest gone up, down, or stayed the same?

Suggested Readings

Argyris, C. *Intervention theory and method: A behavioral science view.* Reading, Mass.: Addison-Wesley, 1970.

Berkhout, J. Psychophysiological stress: Environmental factors leading to degraded performance. In K. B. DeGreene, *Systems psychology.* New York: McGraw-Hill, 1970.

Campbell, J. P., Dunnette, M. D., Lawler, E. E., and Weick, K. E. *Managerial behavior, performance, and effectiveness.* New York: McGraw-Hill, 1970.

Filley, A. C., and House, R. J. *Managerial process and organizational behavior.* Glenview, Ill.: Scott, Foresman, 1969.

Hicks, H. G. *The management of organizations.* New York: McGraw-Hill, 1967.

Hornstein, H. A., Bunker, B. B., Burke, W. W., Gindes, M., and Lewicki, R. J. *Social intervention: A behavioral science approach.* New York: Free Press, 1971.

Lawler, E. E., III. *Pay and organizational effectiveness: A psychological view.* New York: McGraw-Hill, 1971.

22

Problem Solving for Organizations

Introduction

The previous chapter referred to group problem solving as a means for dealing with situations involving bypassing, job ambiguity, integration of diversified functions, area of freedom, organizational climate, and leadership. Group problem solving can resolve differences so as to gain acceptance and cooperation. It can also increase the quality of decisions when effectively used.

In this chapter group problem solving will be discussed as a unique *process*. The problem-solving *process* must be distinguished from *content* or subject matter of the discussion. The same process might be used with problems having such diverse contents as finance, engineering, production, and sales. Usually participants are so involved with content that they are unaware of the process. The problem-solving process differs from such processes as arguing, persuading, bargaining, visiting, and exchanging ideas or information. It is a searching process involving idea generation. If one diagrammed a problem-solving discussion, the conversation would zigzag among participants, while the leader would talk less than participants once the process got under way. The leader's function would be to pose the problem, share any information in his possession, restate ideas to facilitate understanding, and delay the evaluation process so that a solution is not prematurely selected for the decision. The leader would be expected not to use any authority or power to promote favored ideas, but his function is being in charge of the process. In Chapter 6 the leader was encouraged to share problems with subordinates to gain acceptance. In this chapter the training is being extended so that group problem solving can lead to higher quality decisions as well. A group has certain assets as well as certain liabilities. If the liabilities can be avoided and the assets utilized to their fullest advantage, the group effort can be made creative.[1]

[1] Crosby, A. *Creativity and performance in industrial organizations.* New York: Barnes & Noble, 1968; Hyman, R., and Anderson, B. Problem solving. In D. Allison (Ed.), *Technical*

Group Conditions Favoring Solution Quality

Greater Amount of Knowledge

A group has more knowledge and information than the most capable individual in the group. Since problem solving involves the processing of information, participants should feel free to share all information rather than feel the need to defend preferred solutions and to supply selected information. This willingness to share information depends on a problem-solving climate or attitude.

Greater Number of Approaches

Individuals get into ruts in their thinking and tend to persist in their initial approaches. Problem solving requires variety in thinking, and the group process generates more variety than the individual process. It also follows that the greater the differences in background of participants the greater the chances of innovation. In solving a technical problem this author has found that in groups of five or six, a nontechnical member often contributes the most to innovation. A problem that is difficult requires a new approach so that technical competence can be a handicap in that past thinking is repeated.

More and more management decisions are the product of group problem solving. There are assets as well as liabilities inherent in group vs. individual problem solving. Capitalizing on the assets and avoiding the liabilities depend largely on the skill of the leader.

Courtesy of E.I. du Pont de Nemours & Co., Inc.

men, technical managers, and research productivity. Cambridge, Mass.: MIT Press, 1969; Maier, N. R. F. Assets and liabilities in group problem solving: The need for an integrative function. *Psychol. Rev.,* 1967, 74, 239–249; Maier, N. R. F. *Problem-solving discussions and conferences: Leadership methods and skills.* New York: McGraw-Hill, 1963.

Better Comprehension and Acceptance of the Solution

When a group of persons solves a problem or makes a decision, all participants understand the solution. They also are aware of the way it was reached and the alternatives that were discarded. As a result, possible misunderstandings of the solution are avoided, the need to communicate the solution to others is eliminated, and persuasion is not required to gain the acceptance of the solution.

Group Conditions Detrimental to Solution Quality

Social Pressure

Social pressure is a major cause of conformity. The desire to be a good group member and to be accepted tends to inhibit disagreement and favors consensus. Majority opinions tend to be accepted regardless of whether or not their objective quality is logically and scientifically sound. In small groups members strive to reach full agreement and feel the problem is solved when agreement is reached. Unanimous agreement on the solution to an experimental problem was reached in over 75 per cent of three-person groups, even though the groups disagreed with one another regarding the best decision.[2] Since the decisions differed greatly, all of them could not have been of high quality. Thus social pressure favors acceptance of decisions at the expense of quality.

Individual Domination

In most leaderless groups a dominant individual emerges and captures more than an equal share of influence over the outcome. He can achieve this end through a greater degree of participation (valence), persuasive ability, or stubborn persistence (fatiguing the opposition). None of these factors is related to problem-solving ability, so that the best problem solver in the group may not have the influence to upgrade the quality of the group's solution. Hoffman and Maier[3] found that the mere act of appointing a leader causes that person to dominate a discussion. Thus, regardless of problem-solving ability, an untrained leader tends to exert an undue influence on the outcome of a discussion.

Preconditions to Problem Solving and Decision Making

Openmindedness

Participants frequently meet to discuss a problem, but often they have a solution in mind so that instead of solving a problem, they try to persuade one another. This prevents the group process of working together in search of a solution by replacing it with a conflict between members, all of whom may have committed themselves to

---

[2] Maier, N. R. F. Prior commitment as a deterrent to group problem solving. In press.
[3] Hoffman, R. L., and Maier, N. R. F. Valence in the adoption of solutions by problem-solving groups. *J. Person. soc. Psychol.*, 1967, 6, 175–182.

solutions beforehand. If group problem solving is to occur, it is necessary that the members remain openminded. This is best achieved if the problem is not known beforehand.

Agreement on Goal

An initial step in group problem solving is to determine whether there is agreement on the goal. Failure to reach agreement on solutions is often found to result from the fact that members have different objectives. If each participant favors a solution that gives him an advantage, little cooperation is possible, since members are in competition. One doesn't expect opponents in a card game to show their hands. Cooperation and trust are possible only when a goal of mutual interest is established. Finding this common goal therefore becomes a prerequisite to effective group problem solving.

Situational versus Behavioral Problems

Persons are more likely to cooperate in correcting or modifying situations than in changing themselves. When changes in themselves are suggested, they become defensive. It is essential that participants not be subjected to criticism if they are expected to cooperate in the problem-solving process. When the objective of participative problem solving is to improve work situations, it is most readily achieved. It is possible to restate all problems in situational terms, but this often is difficult (see skill No. 1, p. 141). When we find fault or blame someone we are concerned with a behavioral rather than a situational problem. Ability to restate the problem in situational terms is a skill.

Processes Involved in Decision Making

Differences between Solutions and Choices

Two processes usually are involved in decision making: problem solving (PS) and choice behavior (C). The first is the discovery of solutions which constitute ways of getting around or removing obstacles; the second is the evaluation process which leads to the selection of a solution from among available alternatives. The model for decision making (D) therefore may be stated as follows:

$$D = PS + C$$

Objectively, a problem situation, as illustrated in Figure 22.1, is similar to a frustrating situation. Various obstacles stand between the person and his goal. The difference between frustrated and problem-solving behavior is that in the first case the problem obstacle has become a source of irritation, whereas in the second it is a challenge. In order to solve a problem one must generate ideas or ways to remove or get around obstacles rather than fight or run away from them. Thus, problem solving is an *idea-getting process*.

Choices exist when one has two or more ways to get to a desired objective. In these instances behavior is also blocked because it cannot proceed until one of the

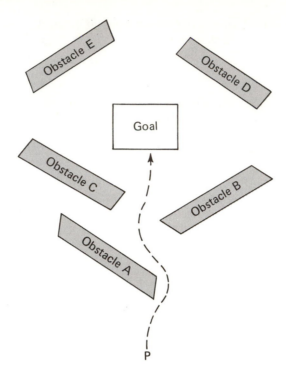

Figure 22.1 / Characteristics of a Problem Situation. Obstacles obstructing progress toward a goal present a problem. In this instance the person (P) is prevented from reaching his goal and must find some way around the obstacles. The dotted lines indicate possible solutions. Some obstacles are more readily circumvented than others. Thus, the search for surmountable obstacles and unusual ideas for getting around them are characteristics of good problem solvers.

alternatives is selected. The selection of an alternative involves an appraisal of their relative merits. In Figure 22.2, Alternative B usually would be selected because it is the shorter. Choice behavior thus is an *idea-evaluation process*.

Some investigators use the term decision making interchangeably with choice behavior.[4] In their studies the alternatives are supplied (e.g., choice of where to place bets in a gaming situation) and factors influencing the choice are investigated. Other investigators use the terms problem solving and decision making interchangeably so that the solution reached is regarded as the decision. Studies of group decision, in general, follow this terminology so that idea getting and idea evaluation are part of the discussion process. Since idea getting and idea evaluation are unique

[4] Thrall, R. M., Coombs, C. H., and Davis, R. L. *Decision procedures.* New York: Wiley, 1954; Luce, R. D., and Raiffa, H. *Games and decisions.* New York: Wiley, 1957; Wallach, M. A., Kogan, N., and Bem, D. J. Group influence on individual risk taking. *J. abnorm. soc. Psychol.,* 1962, 65, 75–86.

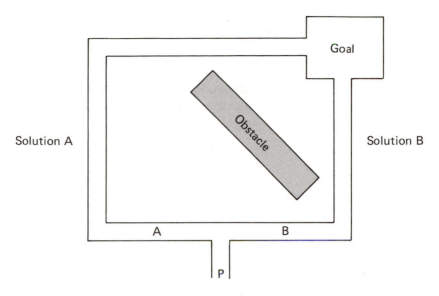

Figure 22.2 / Characteristics of a Choice Situation. When there are two given ways of getting around an obstacle, a person's (P) behavior is blocked until one is chosen. Making a good choice between alternative ideas (shown as pathways A and B) requires idea evaluation.

processes and depend upon different conditions to facilitate them and are subject to different sources of error, it seems desirable to treat them separately.

Causes of Low-Quality Decisions

Some decisions are of poor quality because a good alternative was not generated, others because the best alternative generated was not selected. The *brainstorming* discussion method (see p. 621) generates many alternatives, but the selection process is inadequate, whereas in unsupervised discussions the idea-generation process is terminated too soon.[5] Left to their own devices, untrained groups tend to: (1) confuse facts, opinions, and diagnoses, (2) substitute opinions for facts, (3) fail to differentiate obstacles and goals, and (4) pose solutions which bear no relationship to the diagnosis. Solutions are rationalized in that facts are invented to support them. It is evident that groups of college students do not engage in the problem-solving process by being placed in a problem situation, and that training

---

[5] Clark, C. H. *Brainstorming.* Garden City, N.Y.: Doubleday, 1958; Dunnette, M. D., Campbell, J., and Jaastad, K. The effect of group participation on brainstorming effectiveness for two industrial samples. *J. appl. Psychol.,* 1963, *47,* 30–37; Maier, N. R. F., and Thurber, J. A. Limitations of procedures for improving group problem solving. *Psychol. Reports,* 1969, *25,* 639–656; Collins, B. E., and Guetzkow, H. *A social psychology of group processes in decision-making.* New York: Wiley, 1964.

or guidance is needed.[6] Training in systematic methods, the use of experimentally proven principles for encouraging idea generation, and idea evaluation can improve a decision's quality as well as its acceptance.[7]

Principles of Group Problem Solving

Locating Surmountable Obstacles

Success in problem solving requires that effort be directed toward overcoming surmountable obstacles. It is a common error to persist in overcoming obstacles or trying to improve on ideas that lead to failure. There usually are a variety of ways to solve a problem. A disease might be conquered by immunization, sanitation, preventing germs from reaching people, preventing people from reaching the germs, or destroying the carriers of germs. Each approach has obstacles. Some approaches may have obstacles that can be overcome, others may have unsurmountable obstacles. There is no way of predicting the most practical approach, but this should not prevent careful exploration of a variety of approaches. Success in solving insight problems has been increased by instructing individuals to seek unusual obstacles and to avoid persisting in a given approach.[8]

The essential value of group thinking is that a greater number of possible approaches can be generated and individual persistence, which unfortunately comes naturally, is offset by the differences in viewpoint. The leader can do a great deal to reduce habitual ways of thinking by asking the group to think of unusual and different approaches. Difficult problems and creative solutions are most likely to require the uncommon and least obvious approaches.

A common source of insoluble problems is a tendency to blame or to talk about what should have been done. Such discussion cannot lead to solutions, since the past cannot be changed. Discussions of how to correct an error or to prevent its recurrence focus on the present and the future, which can be altered. Another common failing is to recommend solutions which cannot be implemented. Discussions of what *someone else* (e.g., the president) should do may be a solution for that "someone else," but a good solution that is not implemented is no better than a poor

---

[6] Kepner, C. H., and Tregoe, B. B. *The rational manager: A systematic approach to problem solving and decision making.* New York: McGraw-Hill, 1965; Maier, Assets and liabilities in group problem solving, *op. cit.,* Maier, N. R. F., and Thurber, J. A., *op. cit.;* Thurber, J. A. *Measurement of process-product relationship in group problem solving.* Doctoral dissertation, University of Michigan, 1970; D'Zurilla, T. J., and Goldfried, M. R. Problem solving and behavior modification. *J. abnorm. Psychol.,* 1971, *78,* 107–126.

[7] Maier, N. R. F. *Problem solving and creativity: In individuals and groups.* Belmont, Calif.: Brooks/Cole, 1970; Maier, N. R. F. The integrative function in group problem solving. In L. R. Aronson, E. Tobach, D. S. Lehrman, and J. S. Rosenblatt, *Development and evolution of behavior: Essays in memory of T. C. Schneirla.* San Francisco: W. H. Freeman, 1970.

[8] Colgrove, M. A. Stimulating creative problem solving: Innovative set. *Psychol. Reports,* 1968, *22,* 1205–1211; Maier, N. R. F. An aspect of human reasoning *Brit. J. Psychol.,* 1933, *24* 144–155; Raaheim, K., and Kaufmann, G. Level of activity and solving an unfamiliar task. *Psychol. Reports,* 1972, *30,* 271–274; Maier, N. R. F., and Casselman, G. G. Locating the difficulty in insight problems: Individual and sex differences. *Psychol. Reports,* 1970, *26,* 103–117.

solution that is not implemented. In such instances the problem is "how to influence that *someone* to adopt the favored solution."

Many problems posed by managers are insoluble because of the above two reasons: blaming and recommending solutions they cannot implement. If a group cannot locate surmountable obstacles the problem is insoluble for them. Under such circumstances the problem is one of accepting this reality and adjusting. Persistence in trying to solve insoluble problems leads only to frustration.

Importance of Problem Solver's Location with Reference to the Goal

The starting point of a problem is richest in solution possibilities.[9] The solution to a problem may be envisaged as a route from the starting point to the goal as shown in Figure 22.3. The process of thinking about a solution is like proceeding along a particular route. Once persons start in a particular direction, they move away from certain alternatives, and this reduces the number of possible directions that may be pursued.

Each route may present obstacles. As discussion of a problem proceeds, successive obstacles may appear. A group may have successfully bypassed two obstacles along the way and then find difficulty with others faced at their advanced stage of progress

Figure 22.3 / The Starting Point is Richest in Solution Possibilities. The first junction permits four alternatives; the second, three; the third, two; and the fourth, one. If routes D, C, and B are found to have insurmountable obstacles, but route A does not, it would be necessary to return to the first junction to solve the problem.

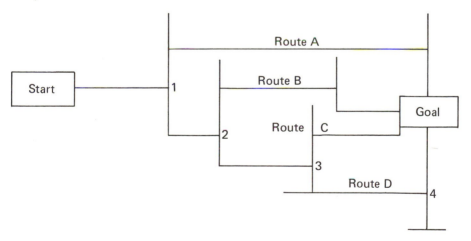

[9] Maier, N. R. F. *The appraisal interview: Objectives, methods, and skills.* New York: Wiley, 1958; Burke, R. J., Maier, N. R. F., and Hoffman, L. R. Function of hints in individual problem solving. *Amer. J. Psychol.,* 1966, *79,* 389–399; Maier, N. R. F., and Burke, R. J. Influence of timing of hints on their effectiveness in problem solving. *Psychol. Reports,* 1967, *20,* 3–8; Maier, N. R. F., and Hoffman, L. R. Quality of first and second solutions in group problem solving. *J. appl. Psychol.,* 1960, *44,* 278–283.

toward the goal. Because of this partial success in moving forward, it is difficult for them to turn back and start all over again, yet a new start is the only way to increase the variety of solution possibilities. For example, a great deal of progress was made with propeller-driven planes; however pilots were not able to fly above a certain height because of the lack of atmosphere. Increasing the power and design of the planes could raise the flying ceiling somewhat; nevertheless, the need for atmosphere limited the ceiling for propeller-driven craft. A plane with an entirely different power plant—the jet engine—represented a fresh start in aviation.

In the usual problem situation a group develops certain ideas about solutions. This means they move from the starting point in a particular direction toward the goal. A group that wishes to improve phone-answering services finds it difficult to think of approaches that do not limit personal calls. Hence they think of different ways to curb such calls and lose sight of the original goal: improving phone-answering service. The tentative solutions reached become confused with the problem. This is why statements of problems frequently contain suggestions of solutions (e.g. how to get employees to refrain from making personal calls). Obviously such statements of problems describe more the nature of the solution than the original goal and consequently prevent the search for other solution possibilities (e.g., making personal calls during slack periods).

In order to better appreciate the starting point of a problem, the group should ask why it wishes or favors a certain solution. What purpose does this solution serve? Such a question may suggest the nature of the starting point of the problem. Spending time to explore the prime objective, therefore, represents a procedure for finding the starting point.

All solutions represent methods for reaching a goal, but frequently sight of the starting point is lost. Practical consideration requires that we reach a goal from the point at which we find ourselves. It may be unrealistic to get to an ideal goal from certain points. If one could start from any point more problems could be solved or more ideal goals could be reached, but this is not realistic problem solving.

Exploring the Problem Areas[10]

Problem-mindedness should be increased while solution-mindedness is delayed. The solution to a problem is a goal and the motivational forces to reach it prevent a thorough exploration of the various factors in the problem. Conflicting perceptions of the problem tend to remain unexplored and so appear as conflicting preferences for certain solutions. Before members become committed to certain solutions, the perceptions of the problem should be explored and facts bearing on the situation should be discussed. People often begin to suggest solutions before they fully understand a problem and others often withhold essential information that they use later to reject solutions.

Experimental results show that the quality of a solution is upgraded if a discussion leader is instructed to explore the problem area with the group before begin-

[10] Kepner and Tregoe, *op. cit.*

ning with the problem-solving discussion.[11] In observing the group problem-solving process, this writer has found premature concern with reaching a solution to be an almost universal fault for members in general and leaders in particular.

Perception of Problem and Creativity

Non-obvious statements of a problem stimulate creative thinking. Even when emotional involvement does not curtail creative thinking, the statement of the problem is important. Some statements offer little challenge and cause thinking to be rather routine. A statement such as "How do we take care of an increase in enrollment of 20 per cent in this college" merely suggests 20 per cent more of what we are now doing. "How do we give a better education to 20 per cent more students with a reduced budget," however, requires original thinking.

Solem[12] used the Parasol Assembly problem (Laboratory Exercise, Chapter 16) with 154 three-person groups who were asked to discuss the problem as a team of consultants. The problem situation involves a bottleneck in a seven-person assembly team with the work piling up at the position of Joe who can't keep up. The team's low production has slowed down the factory production because their subassemblies are needed. The problem was posed to the groups in four different ways: how to (1) increase production of the assembly group; (2) capitalize on the fact that all other workers are faster than Joe; (3) reduce boredom of faster workers; and (4) permit each worker to adopt the pace he wishes.

The elegant solution to this problem is to have the group rotate positions periodically. This will permit the slower workers to move away from an accumulation of unfinished tasks, and faster workers to have extra work available to them. Each member thus contributes or takes from the accumulation according to ability, and production then is determined by the average ability rather than the lowest. This solution is elegant because it utilizes individual differences in ability, introduces variety to relieve boredom, allows for the substitution of another worker without disturbing the effectiveness of the procedure, and degrades no one for being slow. It assumes the work positions are simple and require no training, which is information supplied in the problem.

The frequencies with which this rotation solution was recommended by the groups assigned the problem in the four ways were as follows: (1) 6 per cent; (2) 8.6 per cent; (3) 14.7 per cent; and (4) 14.7 per cent. The last two statements of the problem caused the groups to think more creatively than the first two. "Getting rid of Joe" was mentioned about equally often for the four conditions (5.0 per cent, 4.3 per cent, 3.2 per cent and 4.3 per cent respectively).

The first two statements of the problem tend to make Joe the obstacle, which is rather obvious. They make the problem one of dealing with a bottleneck. The last two statements raise less obvious obstacles and channel thinking in new directions.

[11] Maier, N. R. F., and Solem, A. R. Improving solutions by turning choice situations into problems. *Personnel Psychol.*, 1962, *15*, 151–159.

[12] Solem, A. R. *Some effects of discussion orientation on the development of insightful solutions.* Unpublished manuscript.

The removal of these less obvious obstacles, however, does clear a path to the goal. The fact that groups under all conditions seldom suggest "getting rid of Joe" indicates that this rather obvious solution is seen by the consultants as one that the workers would not accept.

Disagreement and Creativity

Disagreement can lead either to hard feelings or to innovation, depending on the discussion leader. Persons who disagree often are troublesome to group members as well as to leaders. Disagreement indicates unwillingness to go along with others, yet it is essential for achieving change and improvement. The person who is a troublemaker in one group is hailed as an idea-man in another. Both conformity and deviant thinking have their place. Disagreeing for the sake of being different, as well as agreeing to obtain leader or group acceptance, hinders innovation. Conformity has merit in stabilizing relationships, but it is undesirable when it inhibits progress.[13]

Since life situations tend to foster conformity and produce "yes-men" in organizations, it becomes necessary to promote rather than stifle disagreement in group discussion.[14] Research studies have shown that heterogeneous groups are more innovative than homogeneous ones because personality differences lead to disagreement.[15] Groups in which disagreement with the leader is intense are more likely to develop innovative solutions than groups in which disagreement is mild. Table 22.1 shows that with strong opposition to the leaders' preferred solution, an innovative solution is developed in 45.8 per cent of the groups as compared to 18.8 per cent with weak opposition. Innovative decisions depend upon the generation of unusual

Table 22.1 / Frequency of Three Types of Solutions Under Weak Versus Strong Opposition

		Solution		
Type of Group	No. of Groups	Per Cent Group Wins	Per Cent Leader Wins	Per Cent Innovative
Weak Opposition	48	14.6	66.7	18.8
Strong Opposition	48	22.9	31.2	45.8

From L. R. Hoffman, E. Harburg, and N. R. F. Maier. Differences and disagreement as factors in creative group problem solving. *J. adnorm. soc. Psychol.,* 1962, *64*, 206–214. Copyright 1962 by the American Psychological Association, and reproduced by permission.

[13] Maier, N. R. F., and Hayes, J. J. *Creative management.* New York: Wiley, 1962; Walker, E. L., and Heyns, R. W. *An anatomy for conformity.* Englewood Cliffs, N.J.: Prentice-Hall, 1962.

[14] Hoffman, L. R. Group problem solving. In L. Berkowitz (Ed.), *Advances in experimental social psychology* (Vol. 2). New York: Academic Press, 1965, pp. 99–132.

[15] Hoffman, L. R. Homogeneity of member personality and its effect on group problem solving. *J. abnorm. soc. Psychol.,* 1959, *58*, 27–32; Hoffman, L. R., and Maier, N. R. F. Quality and acceptance of problem solutions by members of homogeneous and heterogeneous groups. *J. abnorm. soc. Psychol.,* 1961, *62*, 401–407.

alternatives, and when they are developed and adopted the satisfaction of all participants is enhanced and acceptance is highest.

The leaders' attitudes toward persons who disagree are also important. Groups in which the leaders perceive "disagreers" as *problem employees* reach innovative solutions less often than groups in which leaders perceive "disagreers" as *idea-men.* Disagreers prevent the obvious alternatives from being adopted, and this blocking may create frustration or it may lay the ground work for idea generation. When leaders try to persuade members to adopt their solution they either succeed or they fail, but if opportunities to generate alternatives arise, something new can happen.

Other evidence could be cited to show the value of disagreement. However, disagreement can also lead to argument (between nations, it leads to war) so that groups must learn to use disagreement constructively.[16] The leader is in the best position to do this, but a trained group would be the optimum condition.

Conflict between Idea Getting and Idea Evaluation

The idea-getting process should be separated from the idea-evaluation process because the latter inhibits the former. When an idea is suggested by one person others tend to pass judgment on it. As a consequence, there is a reduced tendency to generate additional alternatives because the *pros* and *cons* of the first idea are being explored. Further, the person who generates ideas tends to be placed on the defensive and consequently hesitates to reveal ideas likely to be criticized. Since innovative and original ideas are the most strange, hence the most questioned, evaluation stifles creativity.

The discussion method known as *brainstorming*[17] imposes certain ground rules to prevent evaluation. No one is permitted to criticize an idea and the group is asked to suggest anything that occurs to them. Silly and humorous ideas are encouraged because they remove inhibitions and often suggest practical but innovative variations.

Problem-solving discussions can be made more productive if ideas are collected before they are appraised.[18] The discussion of a particular idea should be limited to clarifying it. When clarified, it should be written out on a chalkboard or easel for later appraisal. Persons who wish to criticize an idea should be asked to make an alternative suggestion. After a number of ideas have been collected the process of appraisal can take place. This can lead to selection or interpretation of the ideas that seem to be most practical.

Studies of problem-solving discussions reveal that ideas or solutions to a problem become accepted when they receive a certain amount of support.[19] Thus solutions often are adopted before the less obvious alternatives are discovered. Because people are solution-minded there is too much haste in adopting solutions.

[16] Collins and Guetzkow, *op. cit.*

[17] Osborn, A. F. *Creative imagination: Principles and procedures of creative thinking.* New York: Scribner, 1953; Clark, C. H. *Brainstorming.* Garden City, N.Y.: Doubleday, 1958.

[18] Brilhart, J. K., and Jochem, L. M. Effects of different patterns on outcomes of problem-solving discussions. *J. appl. Psychol.,* 1964, *48,* 175–179.

[19] Hoffman, L. R., and Maier, N. R. F. Valence in the adoption of solutions by problem-solving groups: Concept, method, and results. *J. abnorm. soc. Psychol.,* 1964, *69, 264–271.*

Problem Situations Obscure Need for Choices

Problem situations should be turned into choice situations. Decision making involves both problem solving and choice behavior, but a situation in which the search for a solution is required (Fig. 22.1) tends to discourage further search once a workable solution is obtained. Task completion tends to be experienced (Zeigarnik effect, see p. 437) when the goal is reached so that the first solution becomes the decision. To fully utilize the decision-making processes, choice behavior should be included. In order to create a choice in a problem situation, two or more solutions need to be generated. Thus the idea-getting process should be continued until the group is unable to generate additional solutions. When a dominant individual is part of the group, the second solution to the problem is 2½ times as likely to be innovative because the dominant individual has spent his influence on the first solution.[20] Innovative solutions are not necessarily of better quality, but if they are not generated, it is impossible to break away from the confines of the past.

Choice Situations Obscure Need for Problem Solving

Choice situations should be turned into problem situations. A choice situation such as described in Fig. 22.2 supplies alternatives so that there is a tendency to overlook the need to generate them. Often alternatives are supplied through learning and past problem solving, and when two or more are available the need to make a choice tends to dominate the activity. Thus idea evaluation takes over. Whenever the need for making a change in a situation is suggested, two alternatives come to mind—the *new* vs. the *old*—so that idea generation is overlooked in change situations.

Every choice situation should be examined from the point of view of how to reach the goal in ways other than those already known. Just because there are two solutions to a problem does not preclude the possibility that others may exist.[21] In Figure 22.2 additional paths from *p* to the *goal* may be invented. Decisions can be improved by having good alternatives from which to choose, so the opportunities to generate ideas in choice situations should not be lost.

Principles for Evaluating Solutions

Introduction

Once a number of proposed solutions have been generated, a group must select from among them. Two overall approaches are possible: (1) eliminate the poorest ones; or (2) select the best. The first approach leads to defensive behavior. If member A finds fault with an idea suggested by member B, it is quite likely that B will attack A's solution when it is evaluated. It is not necessary to reject or devaluate any solu-

[20] Maier, N. R. F., and Hoffman, L. R. Quality of first and second solutions in group problem solving. *J. appl. Psychol.*, 1960, 44, 278–283; Maier, N. R. F., and Thurber, J. A. Innovative problem solving by outsiders: A study of individuals and groups. *Personnel Psychol.*, 1969, 22, 237–249.

[21] Maier, and Solem, *op. cit.*

tions; merely select the best. Reaching agreement on the best solution, therefore, is the preferred method because it reduces face-saving efforts and saves time.

If the number of ideas generated is large, a straw vote to reduce the list is suggested. Each participant can be asked to vote for three solutions considered most workable. Between two and four alternatives usually stand out and an equal number have little support. Several may receive no votes since even participants suggesting them have more preferred alternatives. Solutions that have no chance of gaining group acceptance can be set aside so that evaluation may be confined to the solutions receiving substantial support. These should be evaluated in terms of the criteria discussed below.[22] A group might agree to score each solution on each of the criteria.

Use of Facts

A solution should deal with an obstacle that blocks progress toward a goal. If a solution to a production problem recommends the introduction of music and no facts indicate the existence of boredom then the solution is not built upon facts. Why then was it developed? Usually because music has been used in other situations and produced favorable results. A common source of error in problem solving is overgeneralization. Generalization of solutions is successful only when the obstacles and facts are basically identical. The tendency to ignore available facts is greatest when information is limited, but having limited information is no excuse for ignoring the facts that are available. In many situations decisions have to be made on the information available and high-quality solutions require that the solutions be congruent with them. Good problem solvers require less information to solve problems than the lesser skilled. The scientists who first believed the earth was round had no additional information, they merely were influenced more by the facts and less by opinions available at the time.

New Problems Created

Sometimes the solution to one problem creates a new problem. Giving privileges to one employee to solve a problem may create a new problem in that several others will request the same consideration. Likewise, the introduction of a more efficient work method might create a walk-out. If the new problem is readily soluble, progress results, but if it is more difficult to solve than the original one, the opposite occurs. Each solution should be examined in terms of how its implementation will alter the situation by creating new problems.

Chances of Working

A person often argues that one solution might work or that another solution might fail. When such issues are raised, the solutions should be rated in terms of the risks that would be taken and the odds involved. To expect every solution to produce results is often unrealistic, but to take long chances may be reckless. Risk taking may be desirable or undesirable depending upon the relationship between potential re-

[22] Maier, N. R. F. *Problem-solving discussions and conferences.* New York: McGraw-Hill, 1963.

turn and chance of winning. Groups are more willing to take risks than individuals, but personality differences also are considerable.[23]

Cost of Implementing the Solution

Making choices always involves some value system. Beauty, speed, weight, size, and cost determine choices depending upon the dominant need. When several attributes have merit, choices become more complex. Business decisions often involve conflicts in value since the concept of a good solution may differ for sales, manufacturing, and research. In such instances the relative values should be considered in determining the goal. When several solutions achieve the same goal equally well, secondary values may be considered. Cost is assumed to be the determining value in business choice, but this value is perhaps overrated.

Respecting Personal Preferences

Some solutions are disliked and in order to reject them participants are expected to give logical reasons. Other solutions are liked for emotional reasons and participants are inclined to defend them with facts. Solutions can be liked or disliked for emotional or unknown reasons, but when participants are required to justify their positions, a great deal of unreal and untrue factors become part of the discussion.

For example, firing an incompetent manager might be a good solution to a problem but may be rejected because the group doesn't like to hurt someone. Reasons given might be that they are not absolutely sure he is incompetent, his replacement might be worse, or the fault lies in not having developed him. Such rationalizations merely confuse the issue. If the group does not like the solution, the feeling should be accepted so that alternatives or ways to make the solution more acceptable might be entertained. Paying him a termination bonus, training him, placing him in a position where he can do less harm, etc., might be practical alternatives. Every manager can locate individuals who would be worth more to the company if they were paid to stay home.

Liking or disliking solutions should not have to be justified or explained. Such reasons should be respected and accepted as emanating from legitimate values so that they can be dealt with for what they are. This does not mean that accepting feelings improves solution quality, but failure to respect them introduces interference and delays progress. When solutions are disliked, the evaluation should proceed to modifications or more attractive alternatives.

Improving Problem Solving in Organizations

Problem Solving by Insiders and Outsiders

If problem solvers are given someone else's problem they approach it as *outsiders*, with no emotional investment in the solution, other than having contributed to it. The major factor, therefore, becomes the quality of the solution recommended.

[23] Coombs, C. H., and Pruitt, D. G. Components of risk in decision making: Probability and variance preferences. *J. exper. Psychol.*, 1960, 60, 265–277; Kass, N. Risk in decision making as a function of age, sex, and probability preferences. *Child Develop.*, 1964, 35, 577–582;

Information tends to be freely shared and in many instances the same information is available to all participants. Examples of such problems are: finding the most efficient way to set up a job that other people will work at; building a bridge to carry a certain load in the cheapest way; and designing the safest possible car. Employees in staff and research units, as well as consultants, solve problems for others and therefore tend to approach the task as outsiders. Outsiders are prone to overlook the need to consider the acceptance that the solution must have by the persons who must implement the decision.

In contrast, when *insiders* solve problems, they deal with their own problems, and they must implement the solution. In such situations: (1) various alternatives represent gains for some and losses for others; (2) each participant may possess different areas of information, which are used to promote favored solutions and to reject others; (3) the information shared may be in conflict because it often is selective and exaggerated; and (4) there may be disagreement over the goals. The acceptance dimension thus becomes an important consideration and quality may be overlooked. It has been shown that the quality of solutions to an experimental problem is higher when solved by outsiders than by insiders.[24]

How Solutions Create Problems

It is common for policy makers or experts to have a problem because they have a solution in mind. Before they had the solution (e.g. standardizing use of computers) they were satisfied with operations. Once a person accepts a solution, the problem of gaining the support of others is created. In this sense solutions create problems, and if the needed support cannot be obtained, the implementation of the solution remains ineffective. Thus, many organizational objectives are sacrificed. However, if a solution has merit, it must be seen as accomplishing something (e.g., furnishing uniform data from various divisions). If the problem were posed in terms of how to achieve a certain goal without disturbing the goals of others (supply uniform data to the central office and at the same time permit each division to follow a system that suits its needs), the persons who are required to implement the solution could participate in searching and generating alternatives. The result might be the adoption of the solution the leader had in mind, or one not previously entertained. The new solution may be either superior or inferior in quality to the leader's, but it will have greater acceptance. Whether the effectiveness of the greater support will offset any decrease in quality depends on the degree of inferiority of the quality and the importance of acceptance needed.

Individual versus Group Problem Solving

Group problem solving increases in importance as problems increase in complexity. No single individual can be expected to process all the ramifications of facts and

---

Wallach, M. A., and Kogan, N. The roles of information, discussion and concensus in group risk taking. *J. exper. soc. Psychol.*, 1965, *1*, 1–19; Wallach, M. A., Kogan, N., and Bem, D. J. Group influence on individual risk taking. *J. abnorm. soc. Psychol.*, 1962, *65*, 75–86.

[24] Maier, N. R. F., and Thurber, J. A. Innovative problem solving by outsiders: A study of individuals and groups. *Personnel Psychol.*, 1969, *22*, 237–250.

ideas raised in many management decisions in a large company. Computers can handle part of the job but they cannot make judgments or generate alternatives. An increasing number of managers, specialists, and technical experts work in teams, not because they want to, but because single individuals cannot do the job. This trend will continue, and it is imperative that the efficiency of group effort be increased before too many persons have gained negative attitudes from their experiences in working with groups. The solution does not lie in returning to individual effort, but in improving group effort.

When an *individual* thinks, there is some organization built into his thoughts by the mere fact that he is an organism. A *group of people* is made up of separate entities, and no central nervous system integrates or organizes their separate functions. If a group is to function effectively some organization mechanism must be introduced and this can quite naturally become the function of the group leader.

An analogy is found in the behavior of a starfish. The five rays respond to stimuli and can influence one another through physical contact. But for them to function as a unified total response each ray must send messages to the central nerve ring, which in turn summates the varied data and permits the integrative responses essential to effective locomotion, pursuit of prey, or feeding behavior. The central nervous tissue thus uses the messages it receives to summate and integrate the data for the messages it returns to the rays, rather than serving as a source of data. If the central organization function is destroyed, the rays continue to respond, but as separate individuals responding and reacting on one another through physical contact and pressures.

The discussion leadership plays an important part in a group's performance. The controversy over whether persons working in groups are inferior or superior to the same number of persons working as individuals cannot be solved with a simple "yes" or "no."[25] The answer depends on a group's leadership, the nature of the problem, and whether superiority is measured in terms of the quality of the decisions, the acceptance of the decision, or the number of ideas generated.

Skill Requirements of the Leader

In Chapters 6 and 20 skills were discussed in connection with obtaining group decisions and successful interviews. In this chapter the discussion leader is viewed as being in charge of the group *process*. It is the leader's responsibility to see that (1) idea getting and idea evaluation do not interfere with one another; (2) neither idea getting nor idea evaluation is overlooked when certain situations seem to require only one process; (3) participants do not become solution minded; (4) disagreement is used constructively; (5) the starting point is reconsidered from time to time; and (6) a variety of obstacles is located. In addition, it is the leader's respon-

[25] Lorge, I., Fox, D., Davitz, J., and Brenner, M. A survey of studies contrasting the quality of group performance and individual performance. *Psychol. Bull.,* 1958, *55,* 337–372; Maier, N. R. F. Assets and liabilities in group problem solving. *Psychol. Rev.,* 1967, *74,* 239–249; Taylor, D. W., Berry, P. C., and Block, C. H. Does group participation when using brainstorming facilitate or inhibit creative thinking? *Administration Sci. Quart.,* 1958, *3,* 23–47.

sibility to indicate when idea evaluation is in order and to see that the problem-solving principles are utilized. Serving as the integrator of the group process, the leader's role is to elicit ideas from the group, not to supply them. A leader's ideas are improperly evaluated and tend to be either accepted or rejected. To prevent faulty evaluation, the leader should avoid expressing views unless the relationship in the group is such that his ideas receive the same treatment as those of others. The most common faults of discussion leaders are described below.

1. The tendency to take too much time in posing the problem, often restricting discussion by setting up ground rules. Clarification can come by way of member's questions. A short statement followed by a leader's willingness to wait out a pause is the surest way to get participation.

2. The tendency to suggest a solution by the way the problem is stated. A leader shows much more skill in stating a problem when at a loss in how to solve the problem. When the leader sincerely wants help, the group readily goes to the rescue. Often the leader poses an idea and thereby states the problem in terms of a choice: adopt or reject.

3. The tendency to respond to each participant's remark or question. True requests for information or clarification should be honored but often members pose questions to draw out the leader's opinions. Many such requests can be turned back to the group. Getting members to respond to one another soon takes the leader out of the central position and allows group problem solving to proceed.

4. The tendency to withhold vital information, often for fear of hurting someone's feelings or other considerate reasons. Facts are realities that cannot be avoided —only the way they are used makes them painful. An accident can be analyzed without blaming a person for an error.

It has been shown experimentally that two acts of the leader, how he poses the problem and the degree to which he shares information, significantly influence the quality of group solutions.[26] Leaders with some training performed these acts better than the untrained leaders, but even with such training the ratings were well below optimal.

Each of the above faults can be gradually reduced through training with simulated problems. A cognitive knowledge of them alters leader behavior insignificantly since the errors stem from habits based upon traditional conceptualizations of a leader's functions. This was clearly evident in a study in which leaders were given skill training in posing a problem and sharing data in a simulated problem situation.[27] They were trained to avoid suggesting solutions, to accept all ideas as possibilities, and to ask for other ideas. By keeping the searching process alive, avoiding persuasive situations, and not having a preference, the number of groups adopting innovative solutions rose to 68.0 per cent as compared to 10.3 per cent achieved under standard conditions. This was the highest innovative score ever achieved with

[26] Maier, N. R. F., and Sashkin, M. Specific leadership behaviors that promote problem solving. *Personnel Psychol.,* 1971, *24,* 35–44.

[27] Maier, N. R. F., and McRay, E. P. Increasing innovation in change situations through leadership skills. *Psychol. Reports,* 1972, *31,* 343–354.

this problem. Without the skill training, with only a knowledge of what to do, the leaders were unable to execute the training principles and could be trapped by arguments.

Management training at the cognitive level has greatly increased during the 10-year period 1952–1961. Most of the training programs utilized are in agreement regarding the values of participative management. Has this cognitive training influenced management skills in conducting problem solving discussions? During this period, this author has used the same problem (Laboratory Exercise, Chapter 11) for training management personnel in problem-solving skills. A comparison of comparable groups during this period reveals no significant change in results. High-quality solutions were no more likely to be achieved in 1961 than in 1952, but there is evidence to indicate an increase of more permissive and persuasive methods so that the leader tends to have his way at the expense of more inventive outcomes.[28] Considerate treatment, however, is not an adequate substitute for discussion leading skills, which greatly influence the quality of solutions to this problem.

The responsibilities described in this chapter, added to the interpersonal skills discussed in Chapters 6 and 20, give the leader's role a great deal of importance. In attempting to carry them out the leader must be careful to avoid the accusation of being a manipulator. Since untrained participants do not distinguish between the *process* and *content* of discussions, this unusual role of the leader may be misunderstood. In order to capture the full value of the discussion process, it is best that participants as well as the leader become aware of the importance of the problem-solving *process* in determining the quality of decisions. By training groups in problem-solving skills, a problem-solving attitude is developed so that the leadership function is greatly simplified by being shared (see pp. 633–635).

Bargaining versus Problem Solving

In bargaining situations conflicting parties meet to iron out differences. A simple example is the bargaining which may take place between a buyer and a seller. In such cases a conflict in goals precludes cooperation. Instead, executing strategies, second guessing the opposition's motives, and plotting to prevent one's motives from being detected characterize the process.[29] Each tries to outwit the other and winning becomes an important incentive. The seller asks a price much higher than he intends to get and the buyer offers much less than he expects to pay. Thus each offers a different solution. Settlement is somewhere between the two initial solutions (prices), and each may experience a victory. Persuasion and misrepresentation of intent characterize the bargaining process.

Studies of simulated bargaining situations indicate that potential mutual gains

[28] Maier, N. R. F. The integrative function in group problem-solving. In Aronson, *et al.,* *op. cit.*

[29] References to studies in bargaining may be found in C. Nemeth, Bargaining and reciprocity. *Psychol. Bull.,* 1970, *74,* 297–308; Siegel, S. and Fouraker, L. E. *Bargaining and group decision making.* New York: McGraw-Hill, 1960.

generate trust whereas potential ability to inflict injury creates suspicion.[30] Threatening points of view introduce new factors such as frustration and face saving. Pressures to reach agreement tend to evoke concessions but only when applied to both parties.[31] If one party thinks the other is under pressure he yields less, supporting the concept "It pays to bargain from a position of strength."

Labor-management bargaining introduces additional factors. Not only do the participants meet to present different solutions, but they represent the conflicting parties. Thus, even if discussion turned from bargaining to problem solving, the solution could not be adopted because the representatives would have to persuade the persons in authority. Since they have not been present, they would not be in a position to be fully influenced by the interaction between the bargainers.

Usually negotiation involves exchanging concessions so that each party keeps some things and gives up others. Thus, the usual solution to the bargaining process is an alternative that represents a compromise between the two initial solutions. As long as the discussion is confined to the merits of two conflicting solutions, nothing new can enter the discussion. As failure to reach a solution becomes more costly (painful), making concessions becomes relatively less painful. It is analogous to the case of two parties fighting over an orange: each wants it, and to fight might involve damaging the orange. A compromise would be to cut the orange in half, each receiving half of what he wanted. However, if the opponents could have communicated and discovered that one wanted orange juice while the other wanted the peel (for candy), each could have had all he wanted. This is characteristic of a solution as compared to a compromise.

The only problem solving that occurs in negotiation takes place during the period prior to the meeting. Each of the conflicting parties meets separately, and the bargaining representatives are made aware of guide lines and concession limits. Each side thus reaches a solution so that when the bargaining begins one party poses its solution and the other party rejects it or counters with a different solution. If the conflict between the parties were to be problem solved, it would be necessary for them to meet to discuss goals and see whether mutual interests could be located. Labor might demand an early retirement plan because the work was unpleasant. If unpleasantness of the work could be discussed there might be ways other than escape from the job to solve the problem. Increasing job satisfaction might be more important than waiting for retirement and then facing boredom. However, the true factors are not revealed in bargaining since the problem-solving stage was omitted because the parties separately reached solutions.

If mutual interests cannot be located, the solution does not lend itself to problem solving and becomes a matter of a choice between negotiating a settlement, a test of strength, or both. When solutions conflict, the problem-solving stage is passed over, and each side becomes committed to a solution. Can the situation be reversed?

---

[30] Deutsch, M., and Krauss, R. M. Studies of interpersonal bargaining. *J. Confl. Resol.*, 1962, *6*, 52–76; Deutsch, M. Trust and suspicion. *J. Confl. Resol.*, 1958, *2*, 265–279.

[31] Komorita, S. S., and Barnes, M. Effects of pressures to reach agreement in bargaining. *J. Personal. soc. Psychol.*, 1969, *13*, 245–252.

In conflicts between committed individuals, such as a union steward and a fore-man, confrontation can be avoided, and satisfaction for all parties concerned can be achieved if each participant tries to understand the other's position.[32] This was demonstrated in an experiment using a simulated situation. The foreman had laid off a worker for smoking in a restricted area while the steward had promised the worker he'd "go to bat" for him. Thus both parties were committed to solutions and were in face-saving situations. If each persisted, future cooperation would be lost. If each gave in a little, compromises (e.g., reduced layoff) could be achieved. Best results were obtained if each understood the other's problem. Thus, the steward might assume responsibility for controlling smoking and tell other workers that in the future regulations would be strictly enforced in exchange for rescinding this vio-lation. Since the purpose of the rule was to control smoking, the foreman gained (assuming the union steward kept his promise) and the union steward carried out his promise to the worker.

A good resolution of a conflict, however, is not always acceptable to others who are involved. In a simulated study, the union steward was present to protect the workers' interests in half the groups, and the time-study expert was present to aid the foreman's cause in the other half.[33] The presence of the union steward resulted in less satisfactory solutions for the workers than the presence of the time-study expert, but workers having the union steward present felt that he helped them, while workers having the time-study expert present felt he had not been helpful. It appears that a union steward who was belligerent toward the foreman made workers feel he was on their side, and hence they approved of him, even though his efforts did them more harm than good. These findings support the conclusion that when people are in a fighting mood they might not accept a rational approach even if it were productive.

When persons in conflict can and are willing to be brought together for group discussion, confrontation can often be prevented and the situation turned into a problem in which a mutual interest can be located. The two-column method of dis-cussion is useful for accomplishing this aim.

Problem-Solving Discussion Procedures

The Two-Column Method[34]

When people are in conflict, discussion tends to polarize the positions so that the group with which one identifies has all the virtues and the opposition has all the faults. It seems improbable that a point of view having only the faults should have any supporters, and yet this is the belief of each of the groups in conflict.

The procedure for reversing polarization is to designate two columns on the chalkboard, one in which to post the merits of position A, the other, those of posi-

[32] Maier, N. R. F., and Danielson, L. E. An evaluation of two approaches to discipline in industry. *J. appl. Psychol.*, 1956, *40*, 319–323.

[33] Maier, N. R. F., and Sashkin, M. The contributions of a union steward vs. a time-study man in introducing change: Role and sex effects. *Personnel Psychol.*, 1971, *24*, 268–278.

[34] Maier, Problem solving discussions and conferences. *Op. cit.*

tion B. Participants are invited to supply arguments for either position. The discussion leader's duty is to see that each argument is specific and understood by everyone. Clarification, not agreement, is the objective of any discussion. The point is then written in the appropriate column in abbreviated form.

Most likely, the next point will be contributed to the other column. As the columns increase in length, the same virtue might appear in both columns, and the points then neutralize each other. Soon emotionality is reduced, and some participants may begin contributing to both columns. This is a crucial development which could not occur while individuals are in conflict because this would be a sign of disloyalty. In place of having a conflict between individuals, the conflict is turned outward and becomes a conflict between the columns.

Once no further contributions can be made, the situation may be summarized as follows: "It seems both points of view have particular merits, so let us try to see if we can come up with a position that utilizes the merits of both positions." This can become a problem of mutual interest and generate problem solving.

Situations that do not lend themselves to two alternatives may be handled by posting the positive and negative aspects of a single point of view in two columns. Having the strengths in one column and weaknesses in the other stimulates the group to search and discover ways to capture the strengths and avoid the weaknesses of an idea, thereby leading to its improvement.

The two-column method is similar to the Risk Technique (pp. 602–604). However, in addition to catharsis, the two-column method lays a foundation for locating mutual interests in conflict situations.

The Developmental Discussion[35]

The product of a discussion is not only dependent upon the facts and the problem-solving skills of the people involved, but also on the procedure followed. When groups are left to their own devices, a number of inefficiencies tend to arise.

1. Members bring up different aspects of the problem so the discussion is not synchronized.
2. Some aspects of the problem may not be explored.
3. The topics usually are not covered in a systematic or logical order.

Generally, there is too much initiation and too little listening. The *developmental* discussion was designed to synchronize and systematize discussion so that participants would discuss the same aspects of the problem at the same time. The procedure is to divide a problem into meaningful parts and to discuss them in order. For example, a decision involving a promotion might be divided into the following five preliminary stages:

1. listing the duties performed on the present job;
2. evaluating the person's performance by agreeing on a grade to assign on each duty;

[35] Maier, N. R. F., and Maier, R. A. An experimental test of the effects of "developmental" vs. "free" discussion on the quality of group decisions. *J. appl. Psychol.*, 1957, *41*, 320–323.

3. listing the duties required on the new job;
4. assigning a grade to each (new duties raise questionable judgments);
5. reaching agreement on the three duties the new boss considers most important.

In experiments in which some groups reached decisions following a *free* (no procedure specified) discussion and others a *developmental* discussion, striking differences in outcome occurred. In the case used in these experiments (Exercise, Chapter 7), Viola Burns was offered a promotion to a job quite different from her present one, but she was disturbed because she couldn't decide whether or not to accept it. Groups of three persons acting as consultants were given the same information and asked to decide which of three alternatives would be the best: (1) encourage her (because she is well qualified); (2) discourage her (assuming she would be unhappy and should wait for a different opening); or (3) make no decision because the information is insufficient.

Table 22.2 presents the results. The first line shows the types of decisions reached when individuals were arbitrarily divided into groups (no discussion) and made the decision individually. *Encourage* decisions predominated and unanimous agreement appeared by chance in 23.0 per cent of these groups. The *free* discussion resulted in a predominance of *Insufficient Information* decisions. Disagreement over the other alternatives tended to cause a compromise on this intermediate decision (56.2 per cent) with unanimous decisions reached in 76.5 per cent of the groups. It will be seen that the *Encourage* decisions greatly outnumbered the *Discourage* decisions. The *developmental* discussion produced a predominance of *Discourage* decisions. Again, social pressure made for a high percentage of unanimous agreement (83.3 per cent), but very few intermediate decisions occurred. Thus these groups were more decisive.

Two sources of error are inherent in this type of problem. The first is the influence of liking Viola (her description encourages this); hardly a good criterion for promotion. The second is a desire to reward Viola for doing a good job by giving her a promotion, an unsound promotional procedure (see pp. 204–205) because superior ability on one job has little relation to ability on a different job. The devel-

Table 22.2 / Influence of Free Versus Developmental Discussions

Condition	N	Per Cent Encourage	Per Cent Insufficient Information	Per Cent Discourage	Per Cent Unanimous Groups
Individual	222	57.2	24.3	18.5[a,b]	23.0[d,e]
Free	153	35.9	56.2	7.8[a,c]	76.5[d]
Developmental	144	29.2	8.4	62.6[b,c]	83.3[e]

Note: Similarly superscripted figures are significantly different at the following levels: [a]$p < .01$, [b,c,d,e]$p < .001$.

From N. R. F. Maier, Prior commitment as a deterrent to group problem solving. *Personnel Psychol.*, 1973, *26* (in press).

opmental discussion tends to reduce these two sources of error, thus creating less indecision and the high-quality solution—*Discourage*. This solution is best for Viola and for the company.

This procedure can be used on all decisions involving promotion. In addition, many other problems lend themselves to logical breakdowns. Who gets the new equipment and which equipment should be discarded are separate problems arising whenever a new piece of equipment is introduced (see Laboratory Exercise for Chapter 6). Failure to separate these two parts of the problem leads to the assumption that the person with the worst equipment should get the new item. Budget problems may be broken down into categories such as maintenance of present operations, essential new developments, ideal operating conditions, etc. Thus, procedures as well as skills promote quality in decision making, but some skills are needed even in following procedures. If skills were unnecessary, the manager's job would be too simple to be challenging. It is the need for appropriate procedures, skills, and knowledge that make management a profession.

Conclusion

Chapter 21 presented evidence showing that managerial behavior was the critical factor in determining the organizational climate. Attempts to improve organizations through development of communication channels, altering organizational structure, or considerations of organizational size tended to include the behavior of people. Supervising large groups requires more skilled managers than supervising small groups; supervising technical workers requires different managerial styles than supervising routine jobs; supervising researchers requires different leaders than supervising salesmen; and one employee likes a different kind of boss than another. Finding a solution to each type of situation poses new problems because the solution that fits the average situation will be a poor fit for many others.

The solution to a problem is designed to fit a specific situation. Attempts to generalize a good solution to other situations can fail unless the situations are essentially alike, and this often cannot be determined from the outside. Insofar as solutions need to be tailored to fit specific situations and the make-up of particular groups there seems to be no alternative to the problem-solving approach.

However, the knowledge that problems can be solved as well as prevented by means of group discussion is not enough since group problem solving has liabilities as well as assets. There is no escape from the need for managers skilled in interpersonal relations and group interaction, and this requires training.

The Problem-Solving Attitude

The problem-solving approach is characterized not only by the skills and principles already discussed but by an attitude[36] represented by a willingness to back away

---

[36] Maier, N. R. F. The problem solving attitude (Study 39). In N. R. F. Maier, *Problem solving and creativity: In individuals and groups.* Belmont, Calif.: Brooks/Cole, 1970.

from an interest in the goal in order to explore the emotional investment one has in it. It represents a desire to share information, to share the belief that persons with different personalities and training are not only interested in, but can contribute to, the search for ideas.

Withholding judgments of agreement and disagreement until full understanding of ideas is reached is essential to the problem-solving attitude. Value judgments are barriers to communication because they tend to cause ideas to be classified into already-known categories. New ideas, if classified into old categories, are stripped of any unique character they may have initially possessed. The problem-solving attitude is characterized by a search for differences in situations and ideas, and a reluctance to generalize solutions. Once a solution is decided upon, there is adequate time to find other situations that may profit from a similar one.

The problem-solving attitude also focuses on the present and the future. What has happened cannot be changed but what can be done to prevent a recurrence or to correct damage already done represents a solvable problem.

The importance of adapting oneself to situations that cannot be corrected, rather than being distressed by them, is implied in the problem-solving attitude. Persons who have suffered a loss cannot adjust until they have accepted the loss and are ready to solve the problem of how to get the most out of life despite it. Often therapy is needed to aid a patient to change an attitude characterized by self-pity into a problem-solving state of mind. In like manner, groups must focus their thinking on things that can be done rather than concerning themselves with the past.

The problem-solving attitude requires the exclusion of fear so that participants can stimulate each other rather than feel they must screen their ideas in order to gain favorable evaluations. Trust seems to be an important ingredient, and trust requires the development of the attitude that more can be gained through cooperation than selfishness. The development of this trust is a group change since a dishonest person in a group can take advantage of naive trustfulness.

Groups that work together in problem-solving exercises and T-groups develop trust in a relatively short period of time. Trust is associated with a development of interpersonal respect. This type of respect is in contrast to the respect that stems from fear. Subordinates tend to regard superiors who have high influence more highly than those with low influence.[37] High influence means, in these instances, power, and power represents the ability to instill fear.

Students, blacks, and union groups have gained influence through their demonstrations of power, and in turn they have gained respect. This has been an historical method for gaining influence and hence respect. The type of respect and influence gained without the use of power emerges from contributions in group problem solving and represents a basic change in the attitude from that found when members use manipulative methods to gain their own goals.

[37] Pelz, D. C. Leadership within a hierarchical organization, *J. soc. Issues,* 1951, 7, 49–55.

Groups should be trained to distinguish between attempts to influence one another and problem-solving together. A knowledge of the difference serves as an aid to change from behavior that is leading to conflict and polarization to a discussion of goals, differing perceptions of obstacles, and the search for alternatives. After a group has been trained, merely a reminder is needed to cause the change in the discussion process from persuasion methods to problem solving.

Extending Uses of Problem Solving[38]

Problem solving is likely to be attempted only when there is awareness of the problem and it is most common when the content concerns things rather than people. Neglected areas of problem solving therefore are likely to be found in problems dealing with the management of people. The general problems of motivating individuals and groups, discipline, appraising and developing subordinates, dealing with job stress and ambiguity, delegation, upward communication, how and when to bypass, the introduction of change, dealing with frustration, making jobs more interesting, interpersonal relations and many others have been discussed in previous chapters. Problem solving each of these topics is aided by certain guiding principles, but exceptions need to be handled on an individual basis. Many of these problem situations arouse anger and, when this occurs, problem-solving behavior is inhibited.

If emotional involvement, common in dealings with people, is a deterrent to problem solving, it becomes desirable to work with situations in which things are going well rather than after a breakdown occurs. That no obvious obstacles block the existing goal does not preclude the possibility of improvement (setting higher goals). Often future breakdowns can be avoided if they are anticipated, or prevented, if minor adjustments are made. Preventive maintenance is possible with groups as well as with equipment. Locating problems that are not acute requires sensitivity, but can be aided by a type of group discussion known as *posting problems*.[39] Instead of searching for solutions, the leader asks the group to describe obstacles they encounter in the performance of the job. These problems should be briefly discussed, and clarified before being written on the blackboard. No attempt should be made to solve them at the time of posting. Thus attention is focused on problems rather than solutions. Since people are experts in the things they see as obstacles, participation is readily achieved if the items posted are accepted and not evaluated.

Groups that periodically work together can profit by becoming aware of one another's problems. Often the discussion becomes quite personal, but when located early, the emotional loading is less than if the problem surfaced later. The leader must be sensitive to face-saving situations and help members save face.

[38] Maier, N. R. F. Extending the uses of problem solving (Study 40). In N. R. F. Maier, Problem solving and creativity, *op. cit.*

[39] Maier, N. R. F. *Principles of human relations.* New York: Wiley, 1952; Maier, N. R. F. Problem-solving discussions and conferences, *op. cit.*

With a list of problems available, future discussion periods can be set aside for solving them. Some will disappear, the mere mentioning of them having improved communication and eliminated the problems. Others may be found to be reduced through the catharsis achieved in the discussion. For this reason the problems should be examined from time to time and the opportunities to add new ones encouraged. Although the common complaint that time pressures do not permit such luxuries is voiced, one must consider the fact that preventive maintenance pays off when it applies to machinery, and machines are more easily repaired than people.

Group problem-solving facilitates communication and can lead to the clarification of differences in goals. Since a great deal of the content of discussions associated with interpersonal conflict is based upon misunderstandings, face-to-face discussions are needed to correct them. Once misunderstandings are removed, the true facts and motives can be explored. This predisposition to *problem solve* issues involving real or potential interpersonal conflict creates a climate that can pervade the whole management structure so that the organization can function as a unified organism. Levinson[40] conceives of business as a problem-solving institution and with proper use, group problem solving can approach an organizational philosophy.

Summary

Participation in problem solving brings group members closer to agreement and tends to achieve acceptance of the solution as well as develop a sense of responsibility for its success. When this is the objective of a solution, the skill requirements are minimal. However, groups do not think systematically and a variety of sources of error are present which tend to downgrade the objective quality of decisions. When the success of decisions depends upon the selection of solutions of high quality as well as high acceptance, three sources of input play a crucial part: the problem situation, the behavior of the leader, and the training and background of the subordinates.[41] The specific factors that promote high quality solutions in each of these three sources are shown in Figure 22.4. All of these factors need not be essential to a high quality outcome but each contributes in its own way. When properly used, group thinking can be superior to the thinking of the best person in the group, but when improperly used, the group product tends to be that of the group's average thinking ability.

---

[40] Levinson, H. *The exceptional executive: A psychological conception.* Cambridge, Mass.: Harvard University Press, 1968.

[41] The relationship between leadership style and the characteristics of the situation are discussed in detail by Fiedler, who takes the position that different situations require different leadership styles. In F. E. Fiedler, *A theory of leadership effectiveness.* New York: McGraw-Hill, 1967; Sashkin, M. Supervisory leadership in problem solving groups: Experimental tests of Fred Fiedler's "Theory of leadership effectiveness" in the laboratory using role play methods. Doctoral dissertation, University of Michigan, 1970.

Figure 22.4 / Three Sources of Input Determine a Solution's Quality.

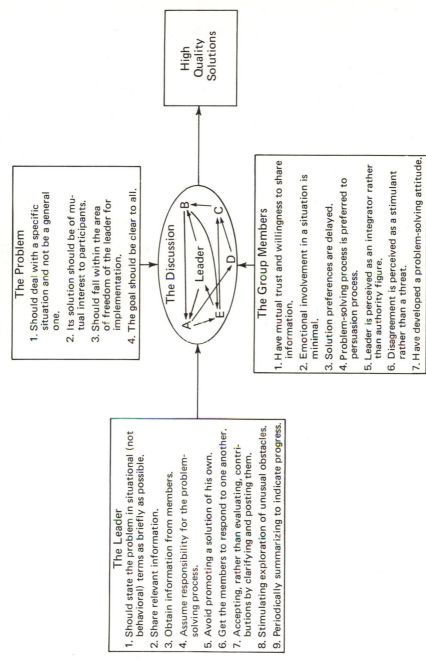

The Problem

1. Should deal with a specific situation and not be a general one.
2. Its solution should be of mutual interest to participants.
3. Should fall within the area of freedom of the leader for implementation.
4. The goal should be clear to all.

The Group Members

1. Have mutual trust and willingness to share information.
2. Emotional involvement in a situation is minimal.
3. Solution preferences are delayed.
4. Problem-solving process is preferred to persuasion process.
5. Leader is perceived as an integrator rather than authority figure.
6. Disagreement is perceived as a stimulant rather than a threat.
7. Have developed a problem-solving attitude.

The Leader

1. Should state the problem in situational (not behavioral) terms as briefly as possible.
2. Share relevant information.
3. Obtain information from members.
4. Assume responsibility for the problem-solving process.
5. Avoid promoting a solution of his own.
6. Get the members to respond to one another.
7. Accepting, rather than evaluating, contributions by clarifying and posting them.
8. Stimulating exploration of unusual obstacles.
9. Periodically summarizing to indicate progress.

The Discussion

Leader

High Quality Solutions

Suggested Readings

Crosby, A. *Creativity and performance in industrial organizations.* New York: Barnes & Noble, 1968.

Drefus, H. L. What computers can't do: A critique of artificial reason. New York: Harper & Row, 1972.

Duncan, C. P. (Ed.) *Thinking: Current experimental studies.* Philadelphia/New York: Lippincott, 1967.

Levinson, H. *The exceptional executive: A psychological conception.* Cambridge, Mass.: Harvard University Press, 1968.

Maier, N. R. F. *Problem-solving discussions and conferences: Leadership methods and skills.* New York: McGraw-Hill, 1963.

Maier, N. R. F. *Problem solving and creativity: In individuals and groups.* Belmont, California: Brooks/Cole, 1970.

Simon, H. A., and Newall, A. *Human problem solving.* Englewood Cliffs, N.J.: Prentice Hall, 1971.

Index of Names

Abelson, H. I., 54n
Abrahams, N. W., 261n
Abrahamson, A. C., 544n
Adam, J. M., 492n
Adams, D. K., 304n
Adams, J. S., 359n
Adams, S., 497n
Aikas, E., 493n
Albert, R. S., 97n
Albright, L. E., 224n, 225n, 242n, 253n
Alexander, L. T., 372n
Allport, G. W., 77n, 95, 95n
Alluisi, E. A., 425n
Altman, J. W., 458n
Alvares, K., 104n
Ammons, R. B., 310n, 371n
Anastasi, A., 160n, 212n, 222n

Anderson, B., 610n
Anderson, C. W., 228n
Andlinger, G. R., 321n
Andrew, D. M., 238
Andrews, F. M., 511n
Angles, A., 409n
Annett, J., 371n
Appel, V., 224n
Appley, M. H., 84n
Arees, E., 496n
Arendt, H., 435n
Argyris, C., 294n, 593, 593n, 598, 598n, 602, 602n
Armstrong, T. O., 178n
Arnold, P. A., 76n
Aromon, E., 49n
Arps, G. F., 371n

639

Index of Subjects

Ability (ies)
  areas of, 231–232
  creative, 243–246
  distribution of, 160–166
    practical implications of, 156–159
    sex and race differences in, 159–160
  in job profile, 198–199, 200
  measuring relationship between, 166–171
  mental, 236–240, *see also* Intelligence
  motor, 246–247
  nature of, 216–217
  performance and, 171–177
  primary, 237–238
  test scores in definition of, 210–212
Absenteeism, 336, 574
  turnover and, 512–513

Acceptance
  in counseling, 533
  of decisions, 130–135, 346
Accessibility, 274–275
Accident(s)
  case-study approach to, 469–471
  frequency of
    age and, 468
    experience and, 467–468
    fatigue and, 399
    psychological tests and, 463–467
  prevention of, 449
    application of causal model to, 473–475
Accident liability, 460–461
Accident proneness, 458–462
  clinical approach to, 468–469